W9-BNN-383

SUPREME POWER

WRITER: J. Michael Straczynski
PENCILER: Gary Frank
INKER: John Sibal

COLORS: Chris Sotomayor
LETTERS: Virtual Calligraphy's Rus Wooton & Chris Eliopoulos
COVER ART: Gary Frank and Richard Isanove
ASSISTANT EDITOR: John Barber
EDITORS: Nick Lowe & Mike Raicht
STORY EDITOR: Joe Quesada

Special Thanks to Andrew Lis

COLLECTION EDITOR: Mark D. Beazley
ASSISTANT EDITOR: Jennifer Grünwald
SENIOR EDITOR, SPECIAL PROJECTS: Jeff Youngquist
PRODUCTION: Loretta Krol
DIRECTOR OF SALES: David Gabriel
BOOK DESIGNER: Patrick McGrath
CREATIVE DIRECTOR: Tom Marvelli

EDITOR IN CHIEF: Joe Quesada
PUBLISHER: Dan Buckley

SUPREME POWER VOL. 1. Contains material originally published in magazine form as SUPREME POWER #1-12 and AVENGERS #85-86. First printing 2005. ISBN# 0-7851-1369-X. Published by MARVEL COMICS, a division of MARVEL ENTERTAINMENT GROUP, INC. OFFICE OF PUBLICATION: 10 East 40th Street, New York, NY 10016. Copyright © 1971, 2003, 2004 and 2005 Marvel Characters, Inc. All rights reserved. $29.99 per copy in the U.S. and $48.00 in Canada (GST #R127032852); Canadian Agreement #40668537. All characters featured in this issue and the distinctive names and likenesses thereof, and all related indicia are trademarks of Marvel Characters, Inc. No similarity between any of the names, characters, persons, and/or institutions in this magazine with those of any living or dead person or institution is intended, and any such similarity which may exist is purely coincidental. **Printed in the U.S.A.** AVI ARAD, Chief Creative Officer; ALAN FINE, President & CEO of Toy Biz and Marvel Publishing; DAN CARR, Director of Production; ELAINE CALLENDER, Director of Manufacturing; DAVID BOGART, Managing Editor; STAN LEE, Chairman Emeritus. For information regarding advertising in Marvel Comics or on Marvel.com, please contact Joe Maimone, Advertising Director, at jmaimone@marvel.com or 212-576-8534.

10 9 8 7 6 5 4 3 2 1

SUPREME BEGINNINGS

Recently, scientists, astronomers and astrophysicists have begun to speculate that the universe did not begin with just one Big Bang ... that, in fact, there have been a nearly infinite number of Big Bangs creating untold numbers of universes. Each newborn universe grows, expands, slows entropically, then eventually collapses into itself until finally there is nothing, or nearly nothing ... just the void, and a whisper, a hesitation, pregnant with possibilities. Then, with a temporal wink and a spark of celestial energy, the whole thing starts all over again as a new universe is birthed into existence.

The question that follows logically upon the theory expressed above is: Why?

The answer, of course, is simplicity itself.

As any writer knows, after a while, creating new universes can become addicting.

World-building was the most enjoyable part of my job in creating the Babylon 5 universe. It allows you to look at things in different and unexpected ways. Each new planet, each new species, brings with it a unique set of rules, histories and behaviors; the slate is entirely clean. A Narn can be anything I say it is, as long as what I say is internally logical, consistent and pays at least some respect to the underlying science. I love doing that. It's fun.

But when you are asked to re-create something, to reel in the events, circumstances and worlds created by someone else and recast them in a second Big Bang, then things get considerably more complicated. Because at that point it's not just about having fun, though that is a necessary component ... it's also about paying proper respects to what came before.

The Squadron Supreme universe — or the Supremeverse, as Marvel Editor in Chief Joe Quesada refers to it, an appellation that will doubtless earn him several centuries in Grammar Purgatory — first came into existence in 1969, through the creative auspices of Roy Thomas. Known initially as the Squadron Sinister, the characters made several appearances over the years until finally, in 1986, Mark Gruenwald took them to a hitherto-unexplored place. Mark was among the first to ask "What would happen if these characters actually existed in the real world? What would be the consequences? What would result if they decided one day that they, not average men and women, knew what was best for humanity?"

In his twelve-issue story "The Utopia Project," Mark not only asked those questions, but — unlike many who came before him, who sought out happy endings where the whole problem was simply a hoax or a misunderstanding

— he did not flinch from hard or controversial answers. He examined the abuse of power that would result from such a campaign of control, as friends turned on friends, allies murdered former allies, dark conspiracies flourished in secret rooms, and mind control became both comics currency and contemporary metaphor for those among us who are always sure that they know what's best for us. We saw in stark detail how something begun with the best of intentions can quickly transform into the worst of nightmares, as embodied in the tyranny of a government based entirely on eliminating individual thought, unpopular thought, unapproved thought.

The effort was breathtaking, dark, brutal and unrelenting, but most of all, it was honest ... as honest as it could be given its publication at a time when comics were still viewed as something primarily for younger folks.

It's commonly acknowledged that Squadron Supreme set the stage for such later works as Watchmen, The Dark Knight Returns, and Kingdom Come. Without fear of engaging in undue hype, it became a landmark book in comics history. It was such a pivotal work for Mark that he left instructions specifying that, upon his death and cremation, his ashes were to be mixed in with the ink and paper for a subsequent graphic-novel publication of Squadron Supreme.

No, I'm not making that up.

So you can imagine the mix of excitement and trepidation that warred inside me when Joe Quesada suggested that I re-imagine and recast the Squadron Supreme universe for a new generation.

See, it's easy when you're being asked to re-imagine something that was defective in the first place ... unimaginative, dopey, poorly thought out or just silly. Because it's easy to find the dumb stuff and avoid it.

But when something is done right, I mean really right, what works is transparent, and gives up its secrets reluctantly, if at all. So tackling this project would not be a matter of finding what was done wrong and fixing it, as much as trying to put myself in Mark's head to say, "Okay, if Mark were alive today, with the greater artistic and literary freedom available to contemporary comics writers, what would he have done with this concept?"

It is my hope that what is sandwiched between the covers of this book provides an answer to that question that is consistent with the legacy that Mark and Roy created.

Here, then, is the second Big Bang of the Squadron Supreme universe. Or ... I guess ... the Supremeverse ... whatever.

More than anything else, I made the decision that this would be the story of Mark Milton, whose arrival on a very recognizable and realistic Earth changed the world in profound ways. He is the Prime Mover whose very existence alters the world around him. But at the same time, he is also a victim of that world: conditioned, brainwashed, naïve, raised in a bubble, divorced from genuine love and affection, never quite knowing who or what was sincere, trying so hard to do the right thing, only to eventually discover that his very ideas of right and wrong are in need of serious re-examination.

On the one hand, I wanted to drop anchor into Mark Milton's psyche, to spend a great deal of time watching him grow and develop, so that everything that happened later would feel real, would have resonance ... so that we could understand exactly where and why and how things would eventually go off the rails. As the story progresses, you begin to realize that the poor bastard never really had a chance.

But on the other hand, I wanted to keep the innermost thoughts of Mark secret from the reader, so that from start to finish, you're never quite sure what his intentions are. Now, it's common in comics to provide what's referred to as interior monologue, meaning you can see the character's thoughts rendered in captions. There's a very good reason why this has become a tradition and a convention: because it's freaking hard to write a comic without dropping into interior monologue on occasion. And I couldn't omit just his thoughts and leave in everyone else's. If I did it to him, then I had to do it to everyone in order to be consistent in how I dealt with the characters, and I could never relent once I'd made that decision.

So as you read through this book, you will note that we never go under the surface of Mark's thoughts, or inside the head of anyone else. As with the real world, all we have to go on is what we're told by someone else.

Which is what makes so much of the book ominous. When Mark tells the intelligence agent who pretends to be his father, "I love you ... just as much as you love me," it causes a shiver, because we don't know if that's a genuine sentiment of affection ... or a carefully worded threat.

As a writer, those moments are my favorites, because they allow the reader to bring something to the table, to interpret such comments one way or the other, depending on one's perspective.

As the story develops, we meet other characters, the morally ambiguous Joe Ledger, the bitter Kyle Richmond, the idealistic Stanley Stewart, and watch as they slowly begin to orbit one another. In the course of that story, you won't find a big evil Bad Guy Master Plan. The construction of the story is not dissimilar from a television series, since that's my primary point of reference, where your job is to service the characters first, plot second, action third. It's about these people as people, whatever their skills or powers may be.

At least, that was the intent behind this particular Big Bang ... in the desperate hope that it would not turn out to be the Big Fizzle. But ultimately, that's not my decision to make.

All I can do is hand you this story, of which I am fiercely proud, in the hopes that somewhere, Mark Gruenwald is smiling.

Because I have enough troubles without his ghost haunting my ass to the end of recorded time.

J. Michael Straczynski
Los Angeles, California
17 February 2005

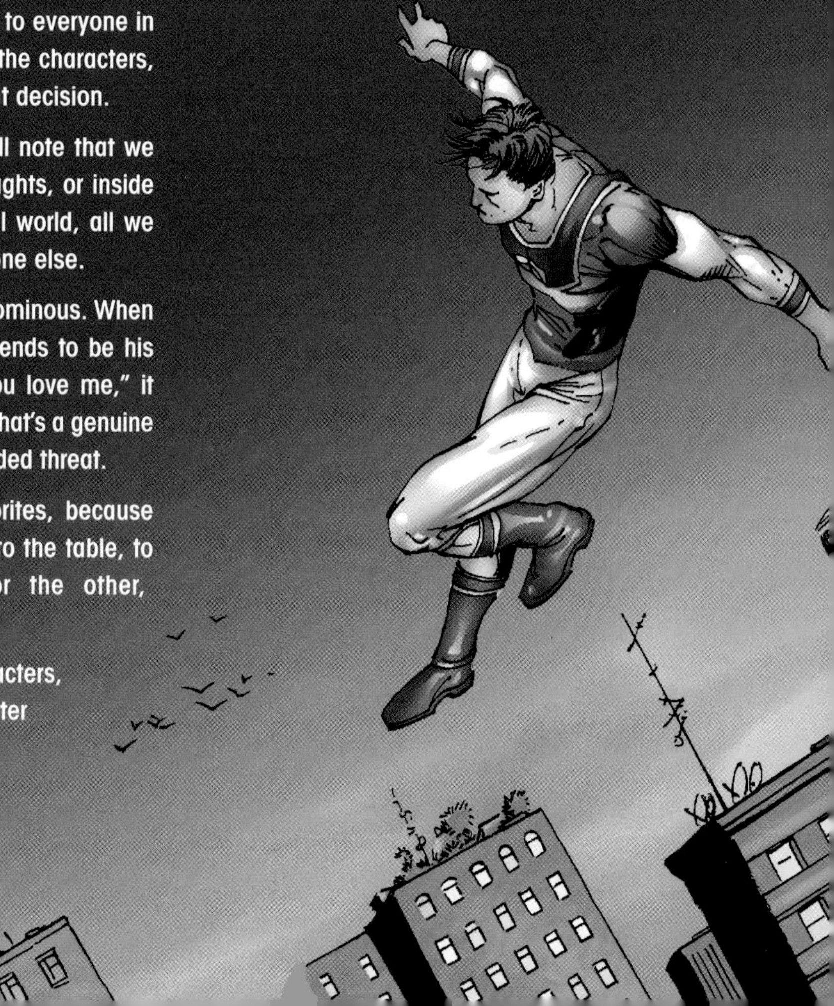

#1

Contact

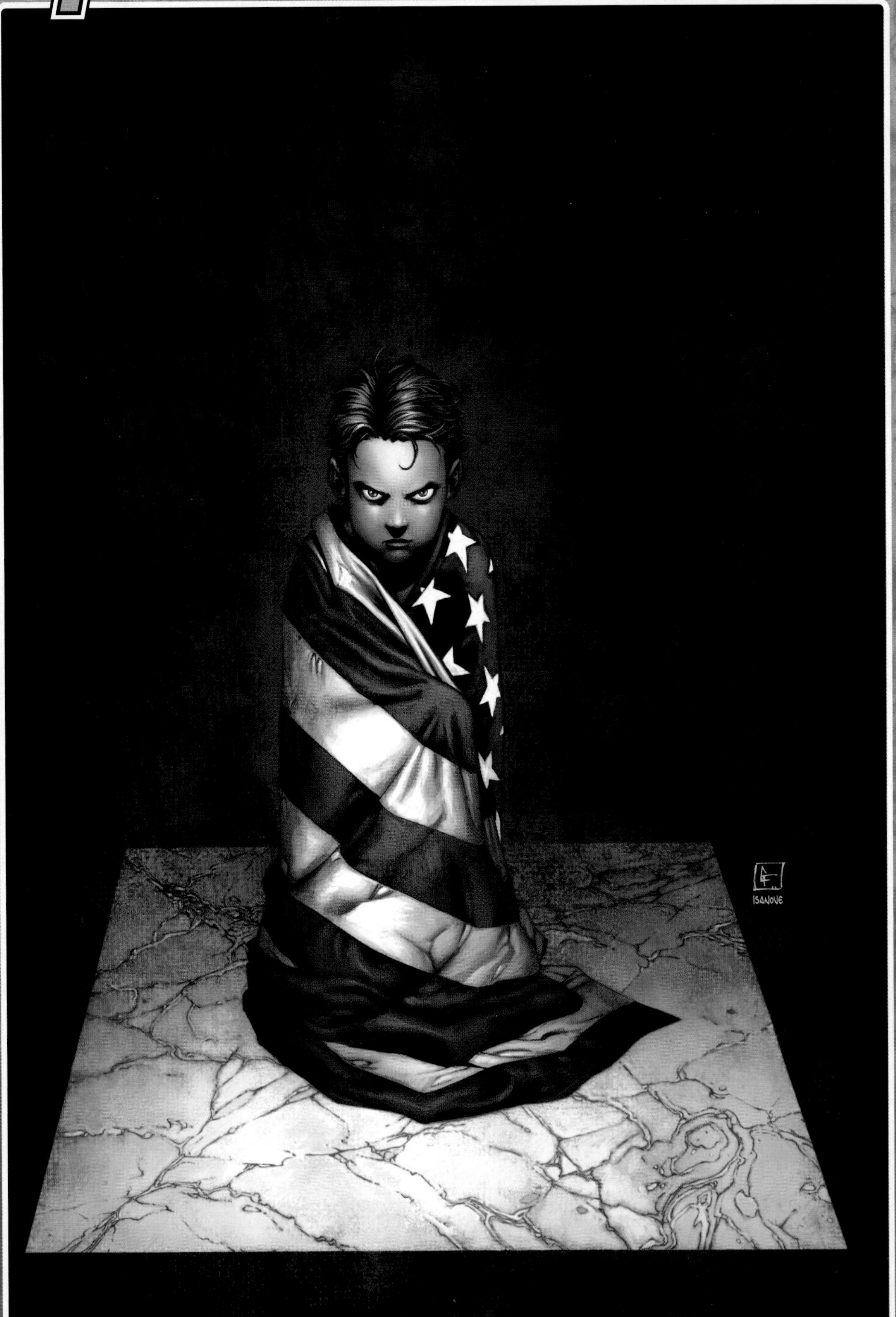
ISANOVE

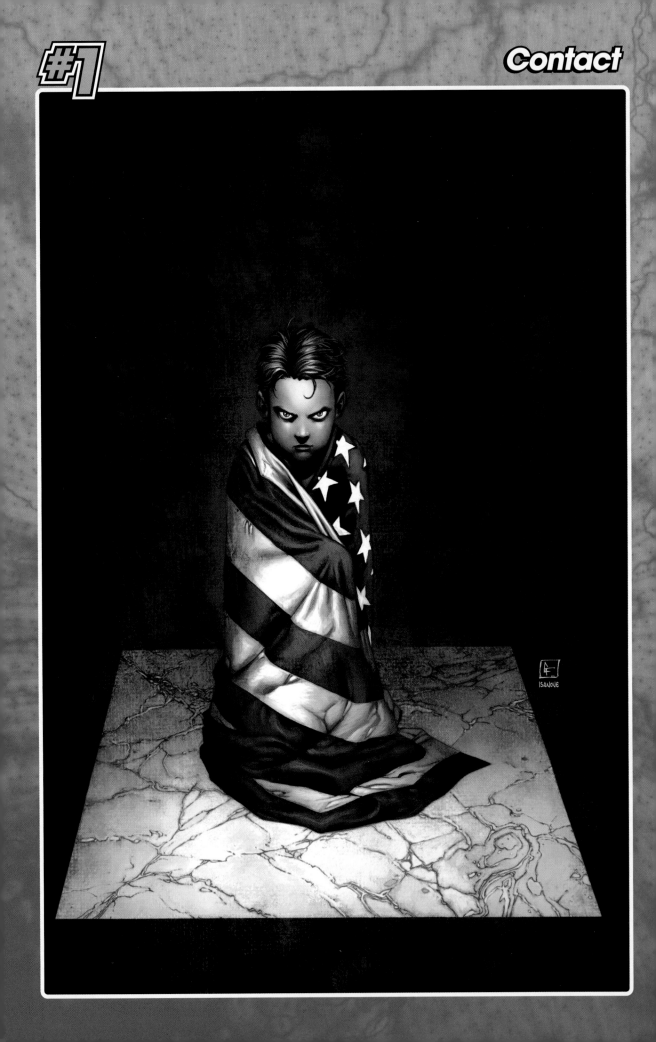

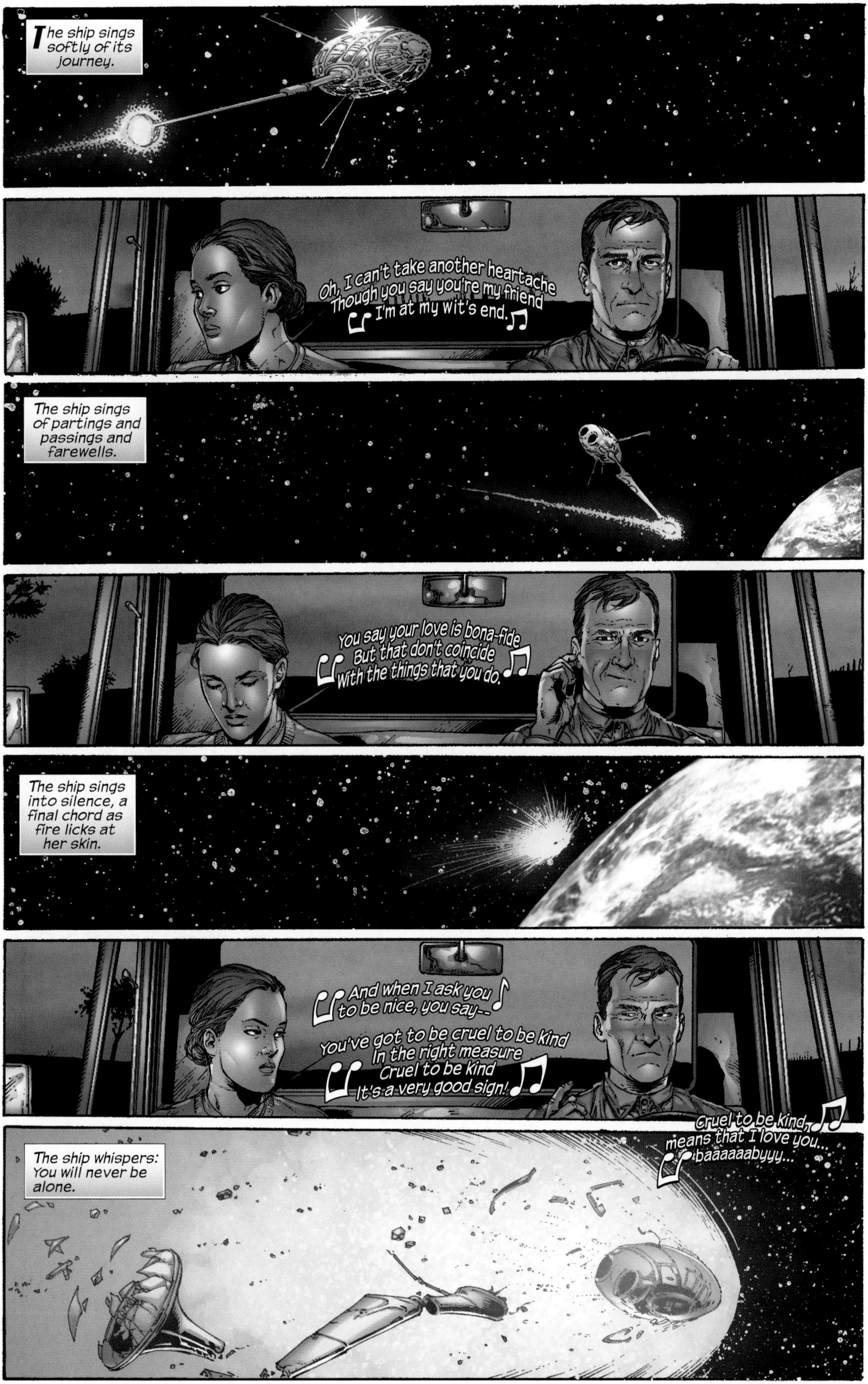
The ship sings softly of its journey.
Oh, I can't take another heartache
Though you say you're my friend
I'm at my wit's end.
The ship sings of partings and passings and farewells.
You say your love is bona-fide
But that don't coincide
With the things that you do.
The ship sings into silence, a final chord as fire licks at her skin.
And when I ask you to be nice, you say--
You've got to be cruel to be kind
In the right measure
Cruel to be kind
It's a very good sign!
Cruel to be kind, means that I love you... baaaaaabyyy...
The ship whispers: You will never be alone.

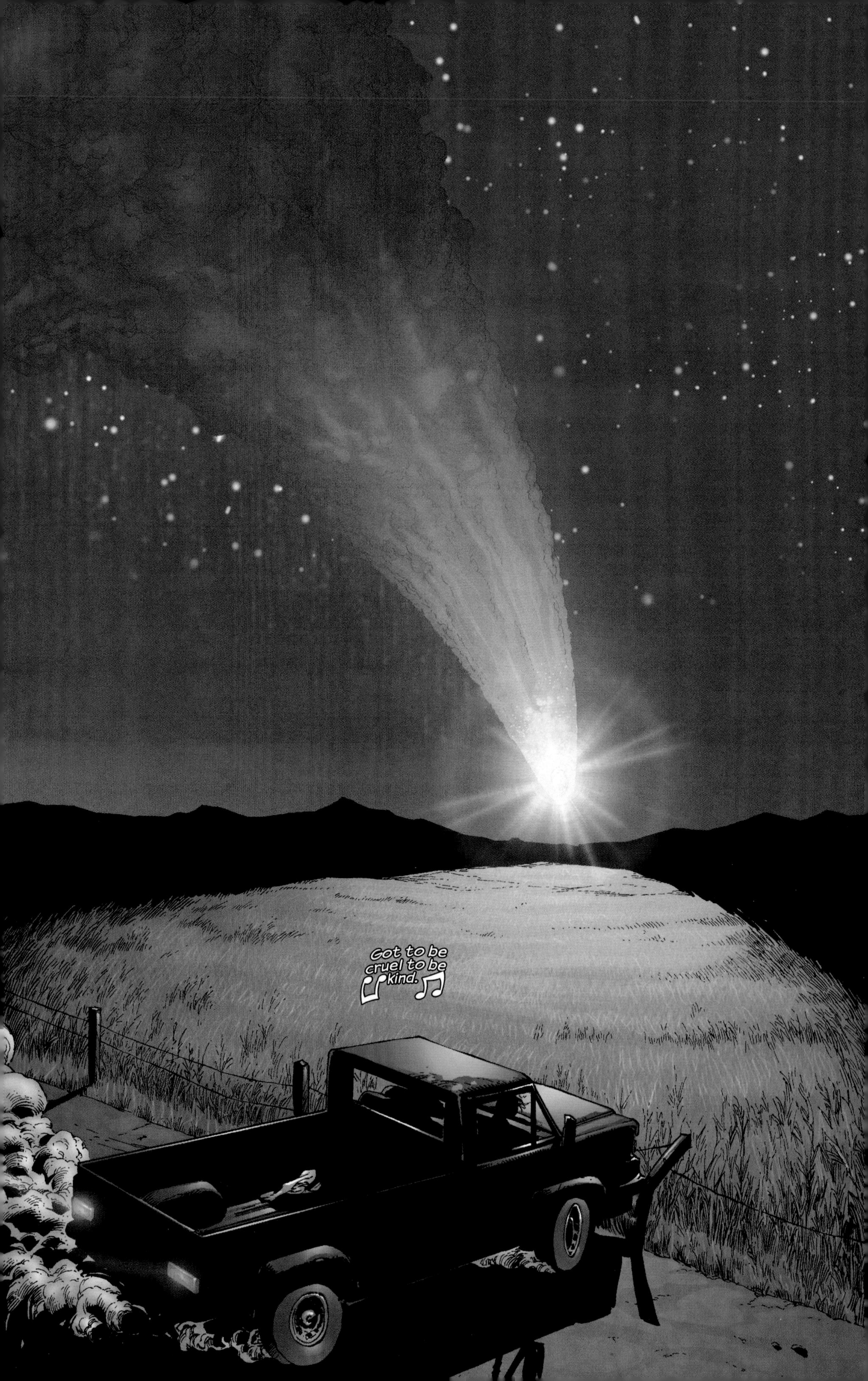
Got to be cruel to be kind.

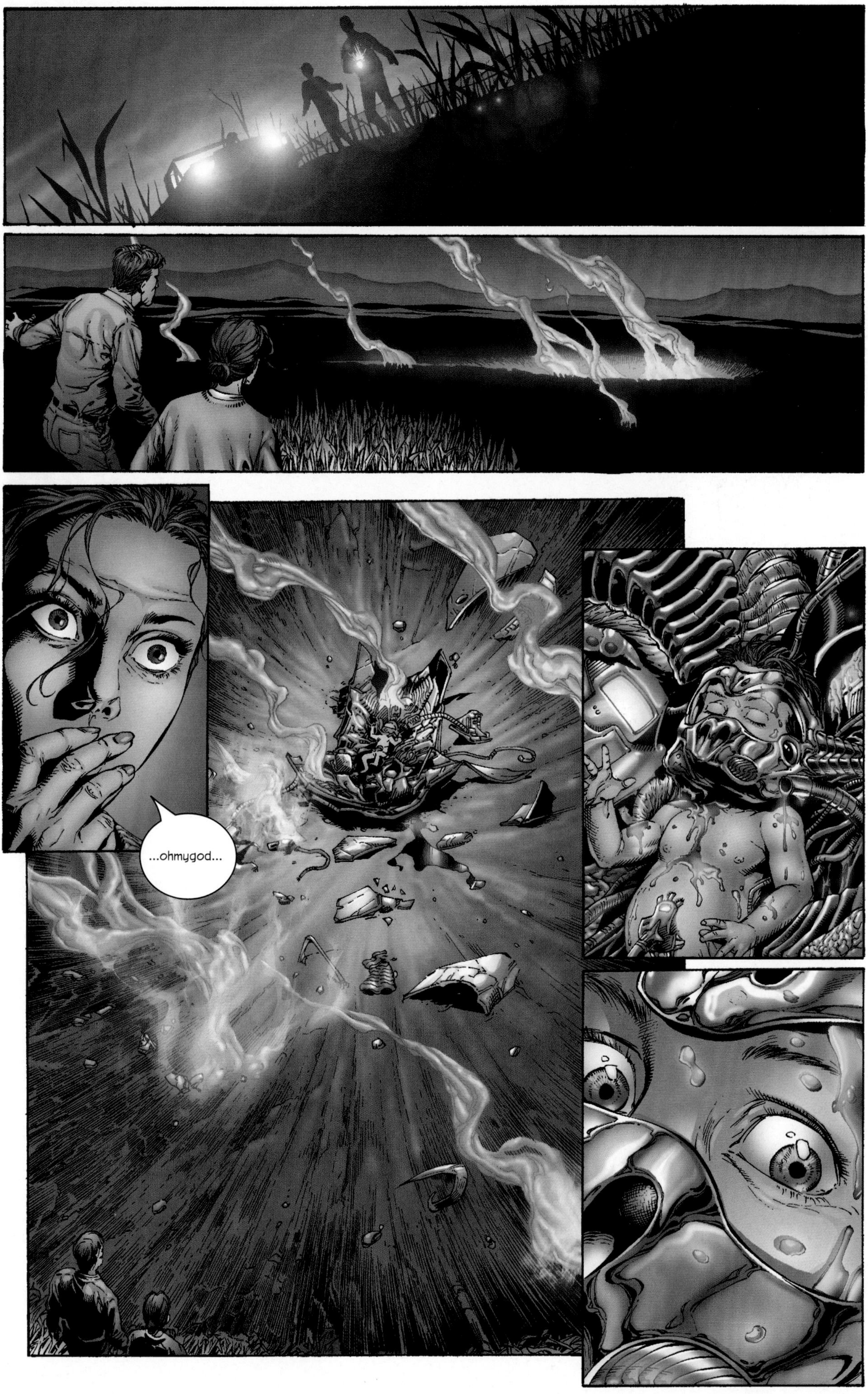
...ohmygod...

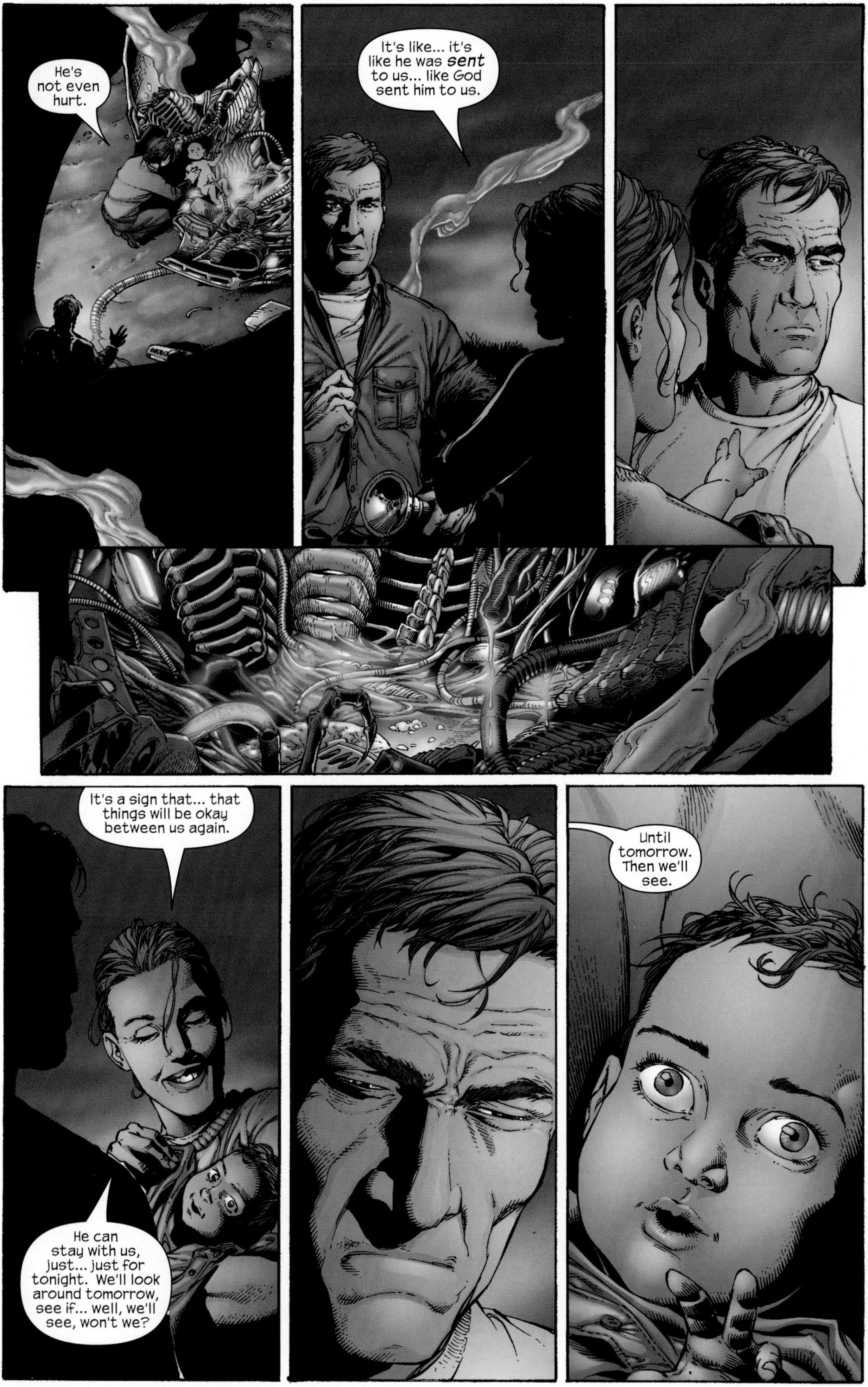
He's not even hurt.
It's like... it's like he was *sent* to us... like God sent him to us.
It's a sign that... that things will be okay between us again.
He can stay with us, just... just for tonight. We'll look around tomorrow, see if... well, we'll see, won't we?
Until tomorrow. Then we'll see.

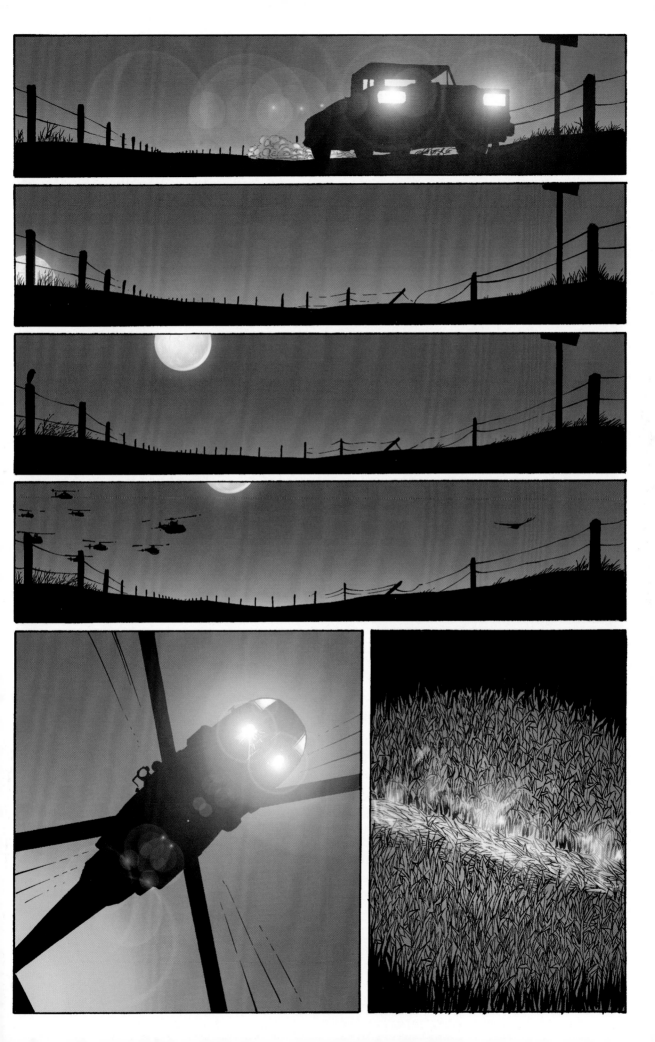

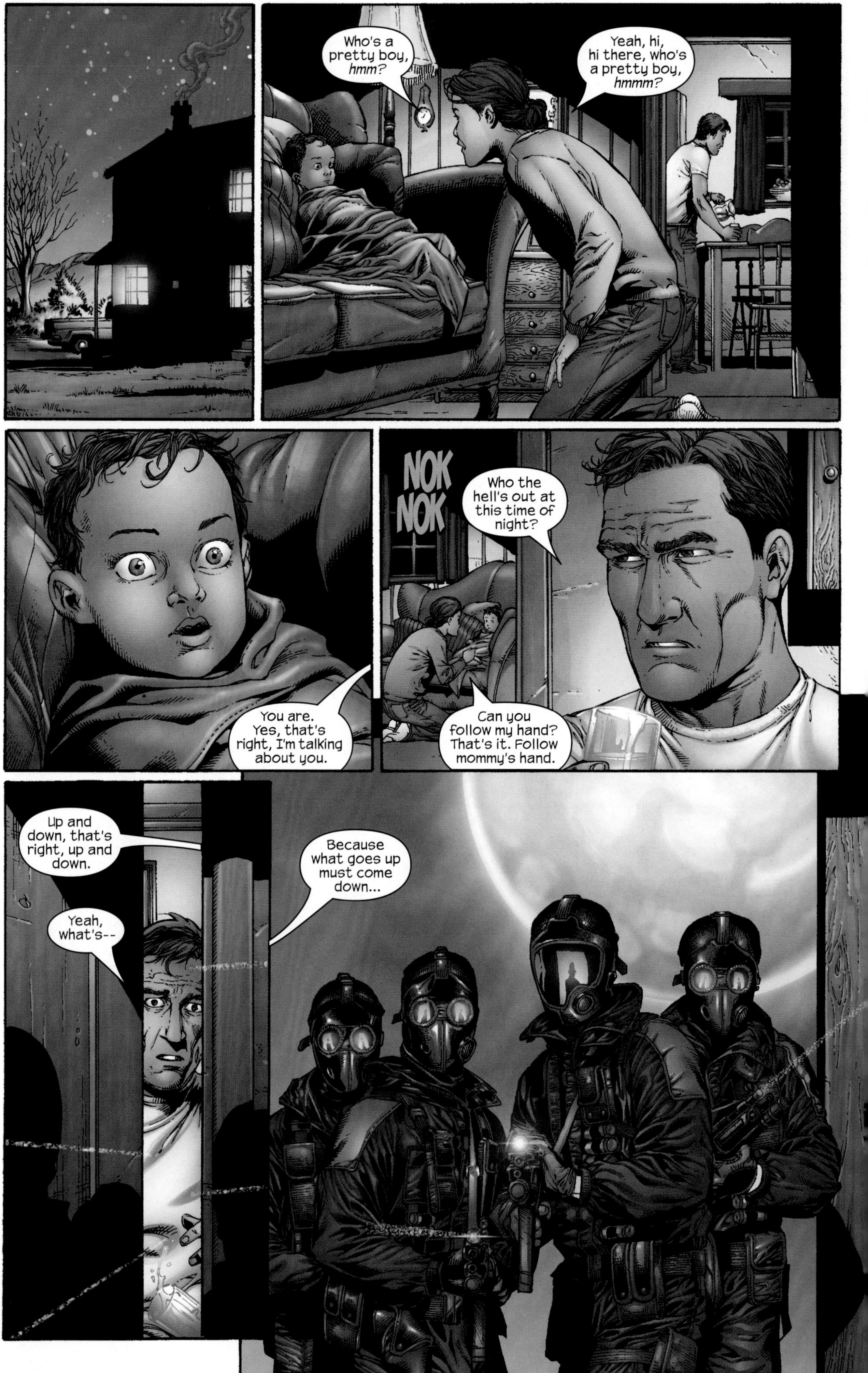
Who's a pretty boy, *hmm?*
Yeah, hi, hi there, who's a pretty boy, *hmmm?*
You are. Yes, that's right, I'm talking about you.
NOK NOK
Who the hell's out at this time of night?
Can you follow my hand? That's it. Follow mommy's hand.
Up and down, that's right, up and down.
Yeah, what's--
Because what goes up must come down...

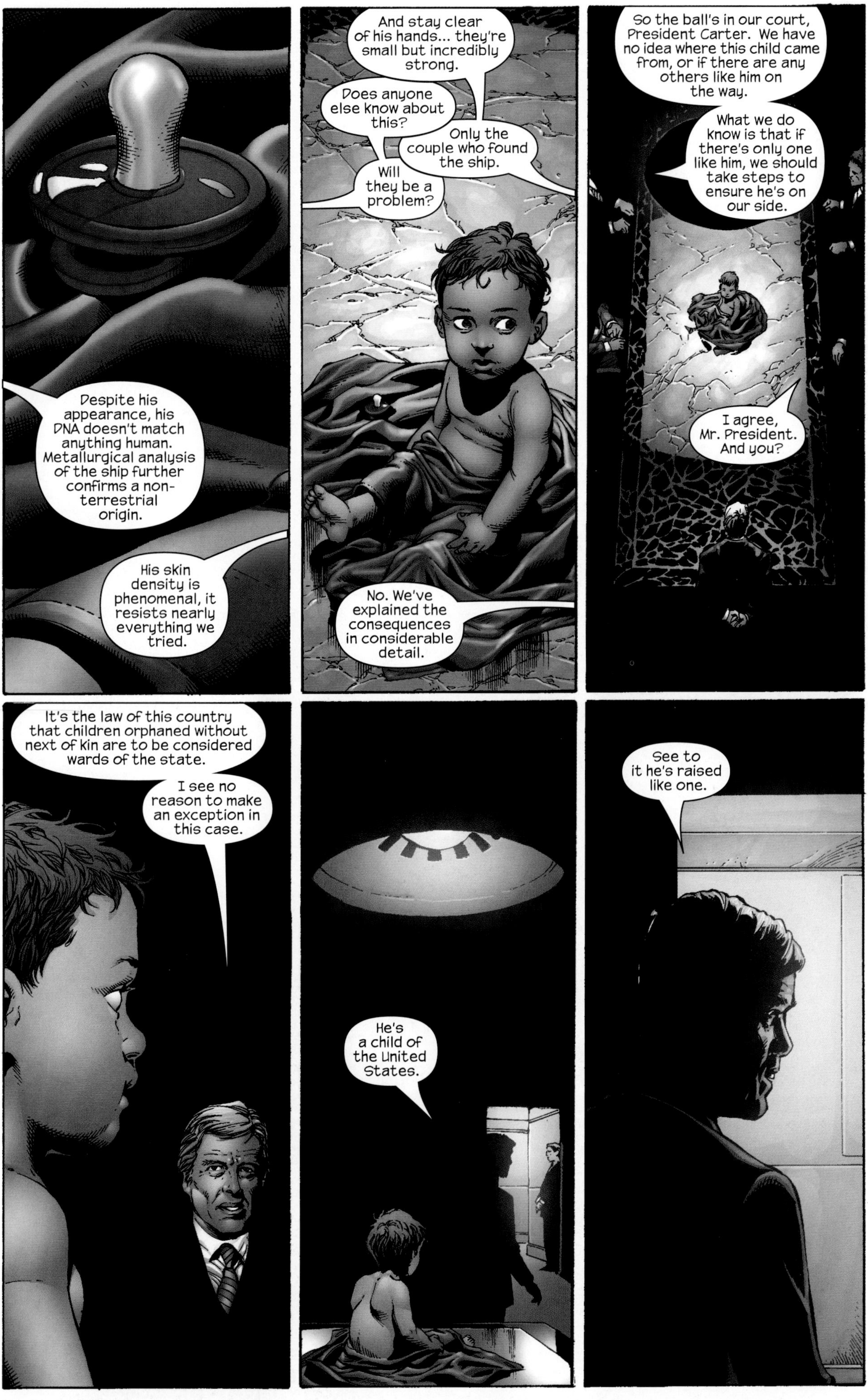
Despite his appearance, his DNA doesn't match anything human. Metallurgical analysis of the ship further confirms a non-terrestrial origin.
His skin density is phenomenal, it resists nearly everything we tried.
And stay clear of his hands... they're small but incredibly strong.
Does anyone else know about this?
Only the couple who found the ship.
Will they be a problem?
No. We've explained the consequences in considerable detail.
So the ball's in our court, President Carter. We have no idea where this child came from, or if there are any others like him on the way.
What we do know is that if there's only one like him, we should take steps to ensure he's on our side.
I agree, Mr. President. And you?
It's the law of this country that children orphaned without next of kin are to be considered wards of the state.
I see no reason to make an exception in this case.
He's a child of the United States.
See to it he's raised like one.

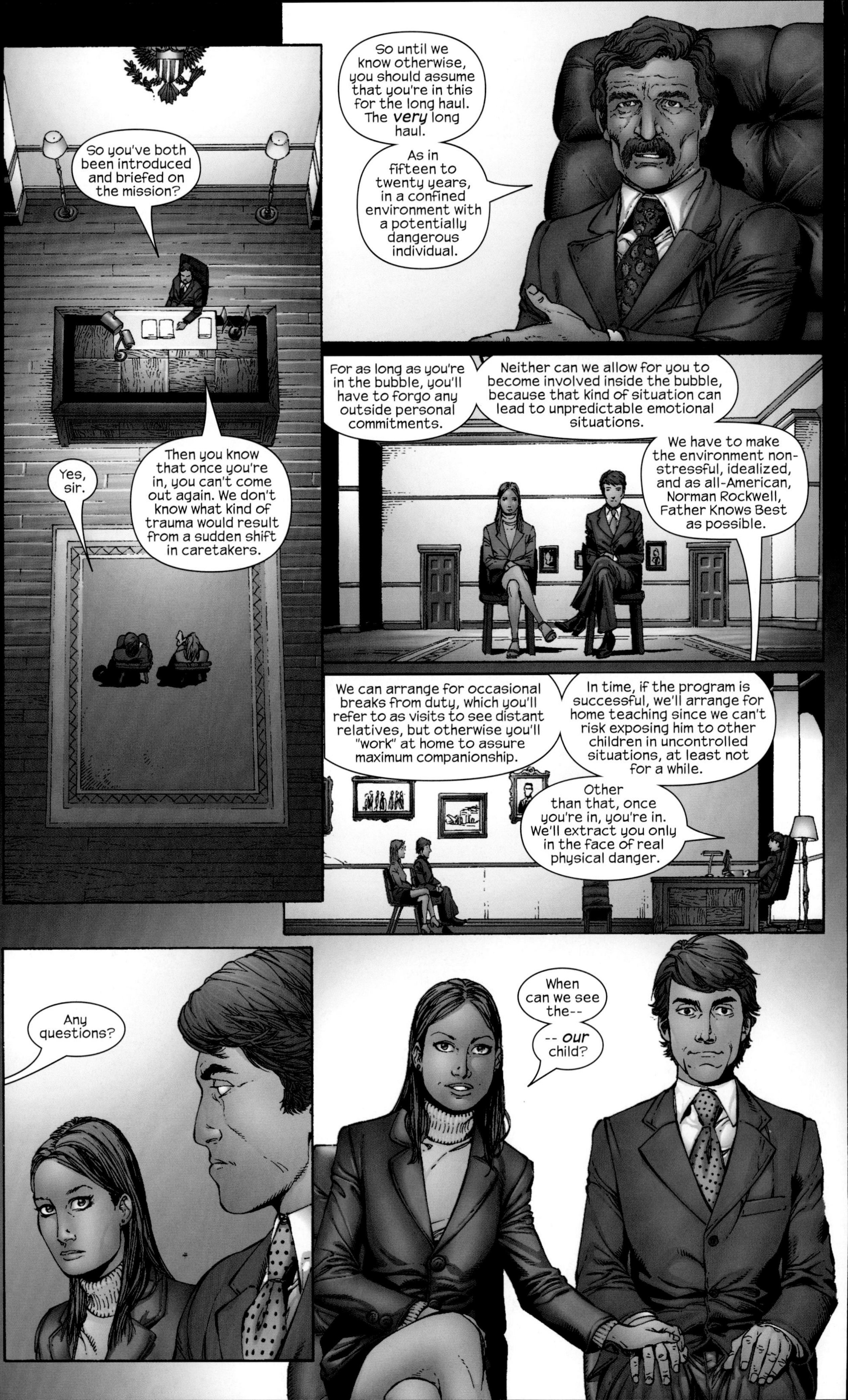
So you've both been introduced and briefed on the mission?
So until we know otherwise, you should assume that you're in this for the long haul. The *very* long haul.
As in fifteen to twenty years, in a confined environment with a potentially dangerous individual.
Yes, sir.
Then you know that once you're in, you can't come out again. We don't know what kind of trauma would result from a sudden shift in caretakers.
For as long as you're in the bubble, you'll have to forgo any outside personal commitments.
Neither can we allow for you to become involved inside the bubble, because that kind of situation can lead to unpredictable emotional situations.
We have to make the environment non-stressful, idealized, and as all-American, Norman Rockwell, Father Knows Best as possible.
We can arrange for occasional breaks from duty, which you'll refer to as visits to see distant relatives, but otherwise you'll "work" at home to assure maximum companionship.
In time, if the program is successful, we'll arrange for home teaching since we can't risk exposing him to other children in uncontrolled situations, at least not for a while.
Other than that, once you're in, you're in. We'll extract you only in the face of real physical danger.
Any questions?
When can we see the--
-- *our* child?

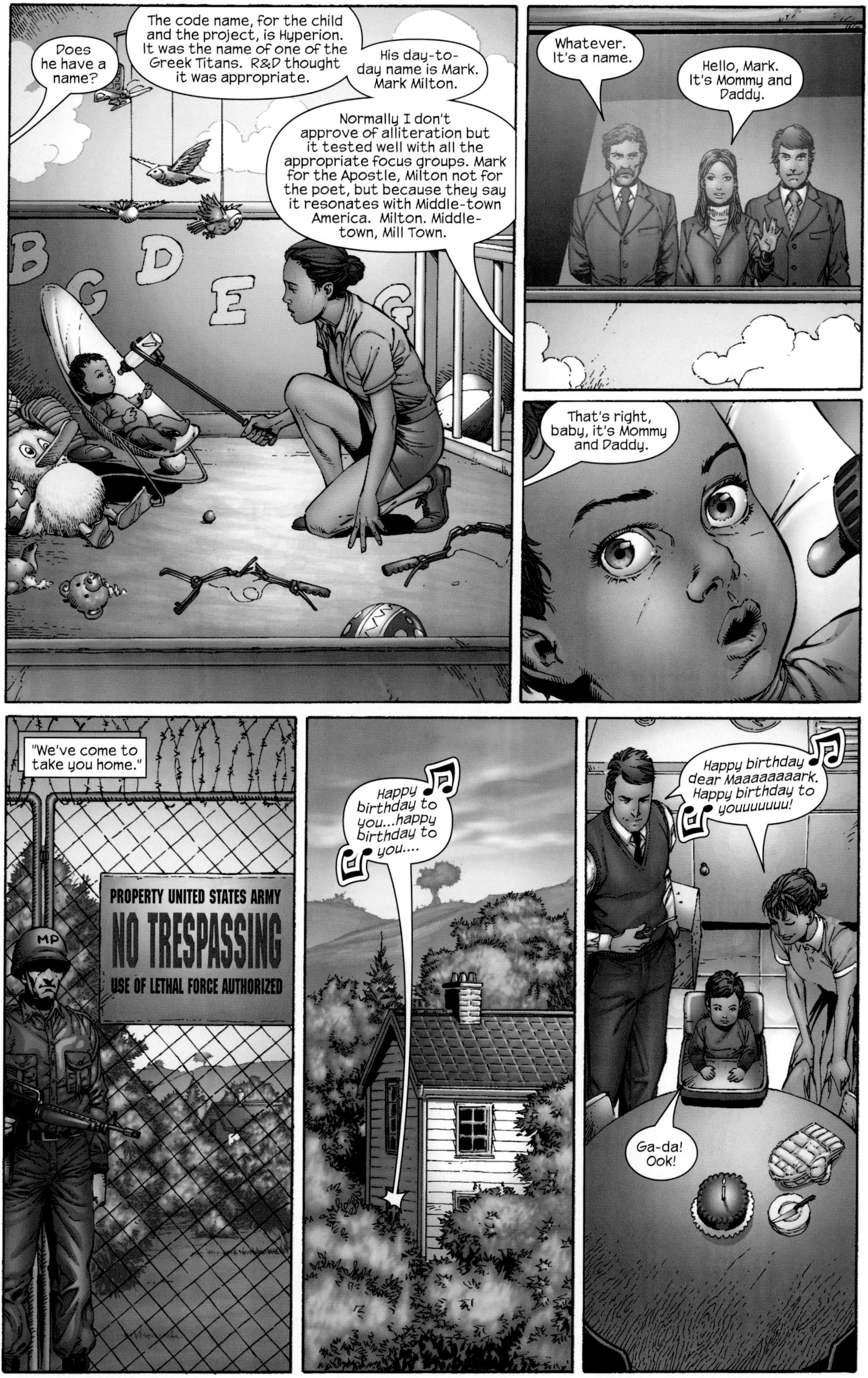
Does he have a name?
The code name, for the child and the project, is Hyperion. It was the name of one of the Greek Titans. R&D thought it was appropriate.
His day-to-day name is Mark. Mark Milton.
Normally I don't approve of alliteration but it tested well with all the appropriate focus groups. Mark for the Apostle, Milton not for the poet, but because they say it resonates with Middle-town America. Milton. Middle-town, Mill Town.
Whatever. It's a name.
Hello, Mark. It's Mommy and Daddy.
That's right, baby, it's Mommy and Daddy.
"We've come to take you home."
PROPERTY UNITED STATES ARMY
NO TRESPASSING
USE OF LETHAL FORCE AUTHORIZED
MP
Happy birthday to you...happy birthday to you....
Happy birthday dear Maaaaaaaark. Happy birthday to youuuuuuu!
Ga-da! Ook!

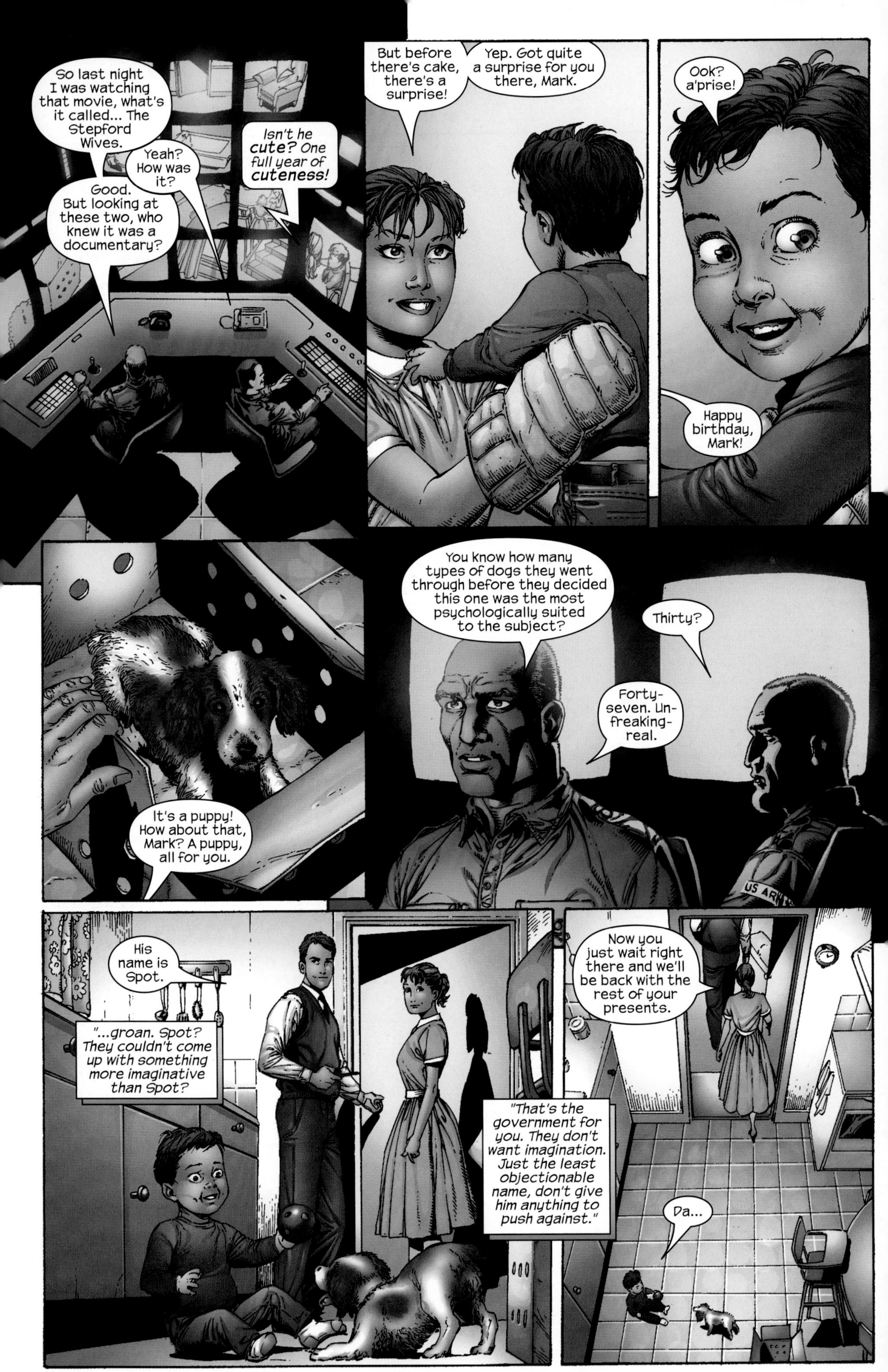

So last night I was watching that movie, what's it called... The Stepford Wives.
Yeah? How was it?
Good. But looking at these two, who knew it was a documentary?
Isn't he *cute?* One full year of *cuteness!*
But before there's cake, there's a surprise!
Yep. Got quite a surprise for you there, Mark.
Ook? a'prise!
Happy birthday, Mark!
It's a puppy! How about that, Mark? A puppy, all for you.
You know how many types of dogs they went through before they decided this one was the most psychologically suited to the subject?
Thirty?
Forty-seven. Un-freaking-real.
His name is Spot.
"...groan. Spot? They couldn't come up with something more imaginative than Spot?
"That's the government for you. They don't want imagination. Just the least objectionable name, don't give him anything to push against."
Now you just wait right there and we'll be back with the rest of your presents.
Da...

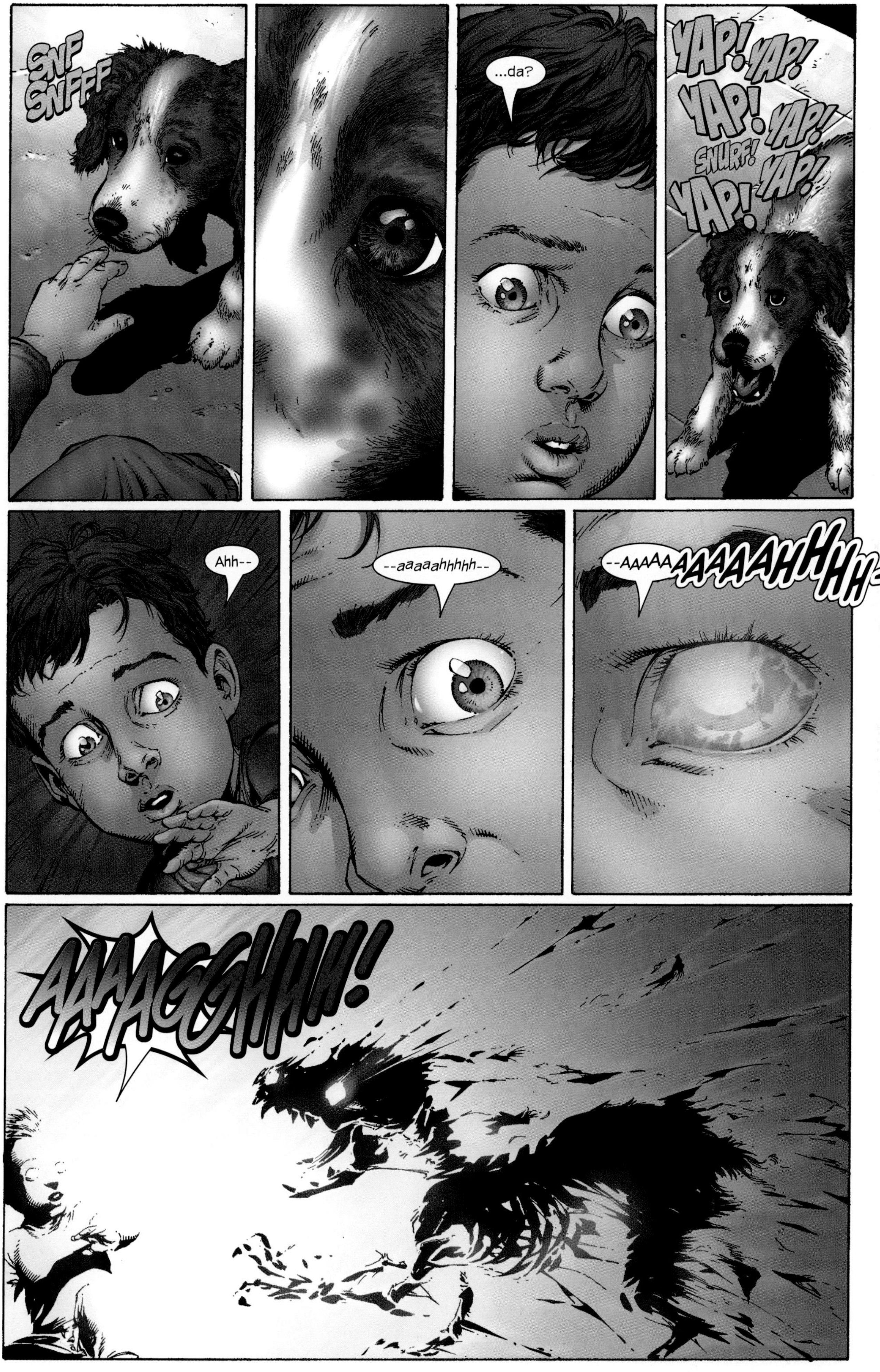
SNF SNFFF
...da?
YAP! YAP!
YAP! YAP!
SNURF!
YAP! YAP!
Ahh--
--aaaaahhhhh--
--AAAAAAAAAAHHHH-
AAAAGGHHH!

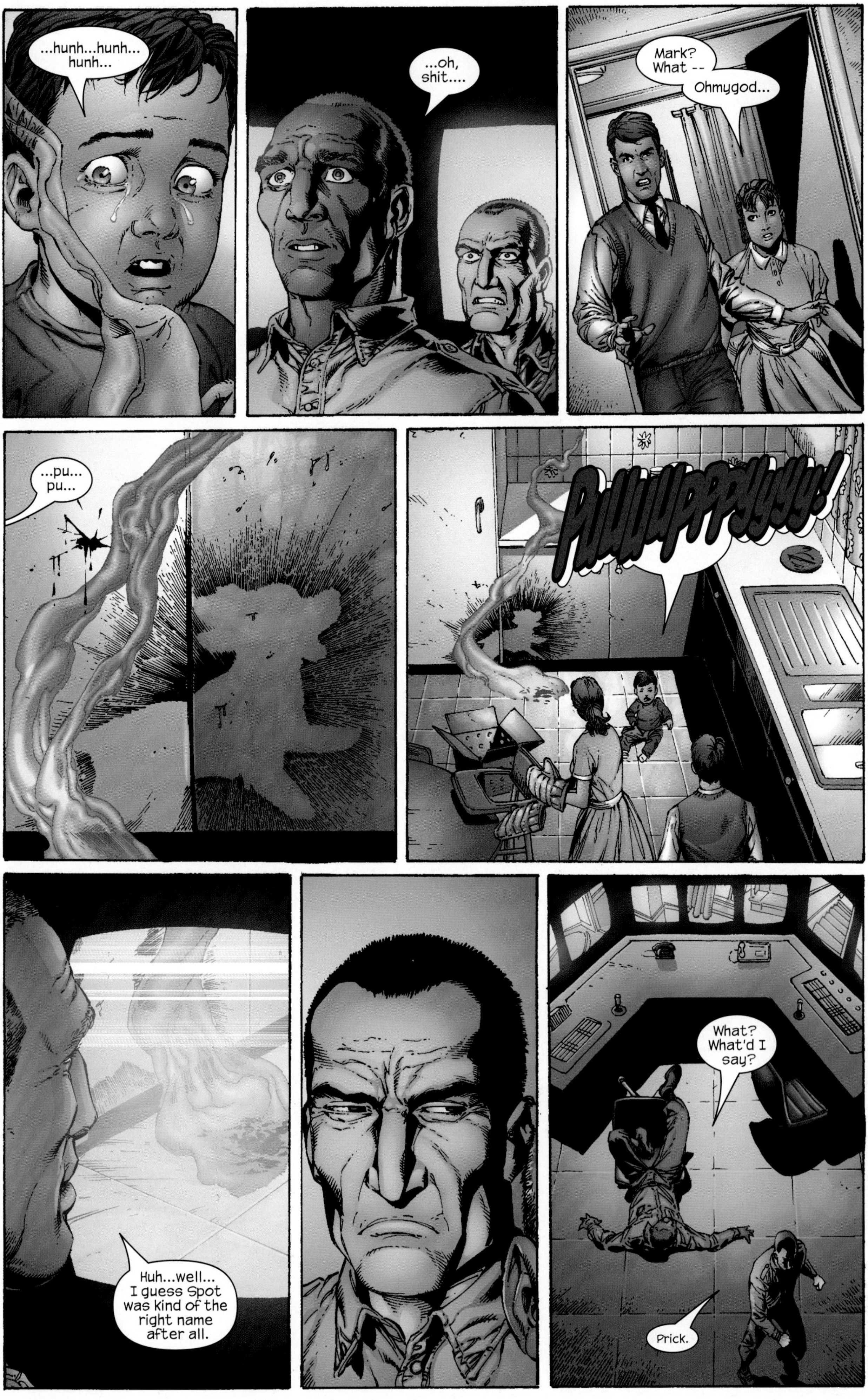
...hunh...hunh...
hunh...
...oh,
shit....
Mark?
What --
Ohmygod...
...pu...
pu...
PLUUUPPPYYYYY!
Huh...well...
I guess Spot
was kind of the
right name
after all.
What?
What'd I
say?
Prick.

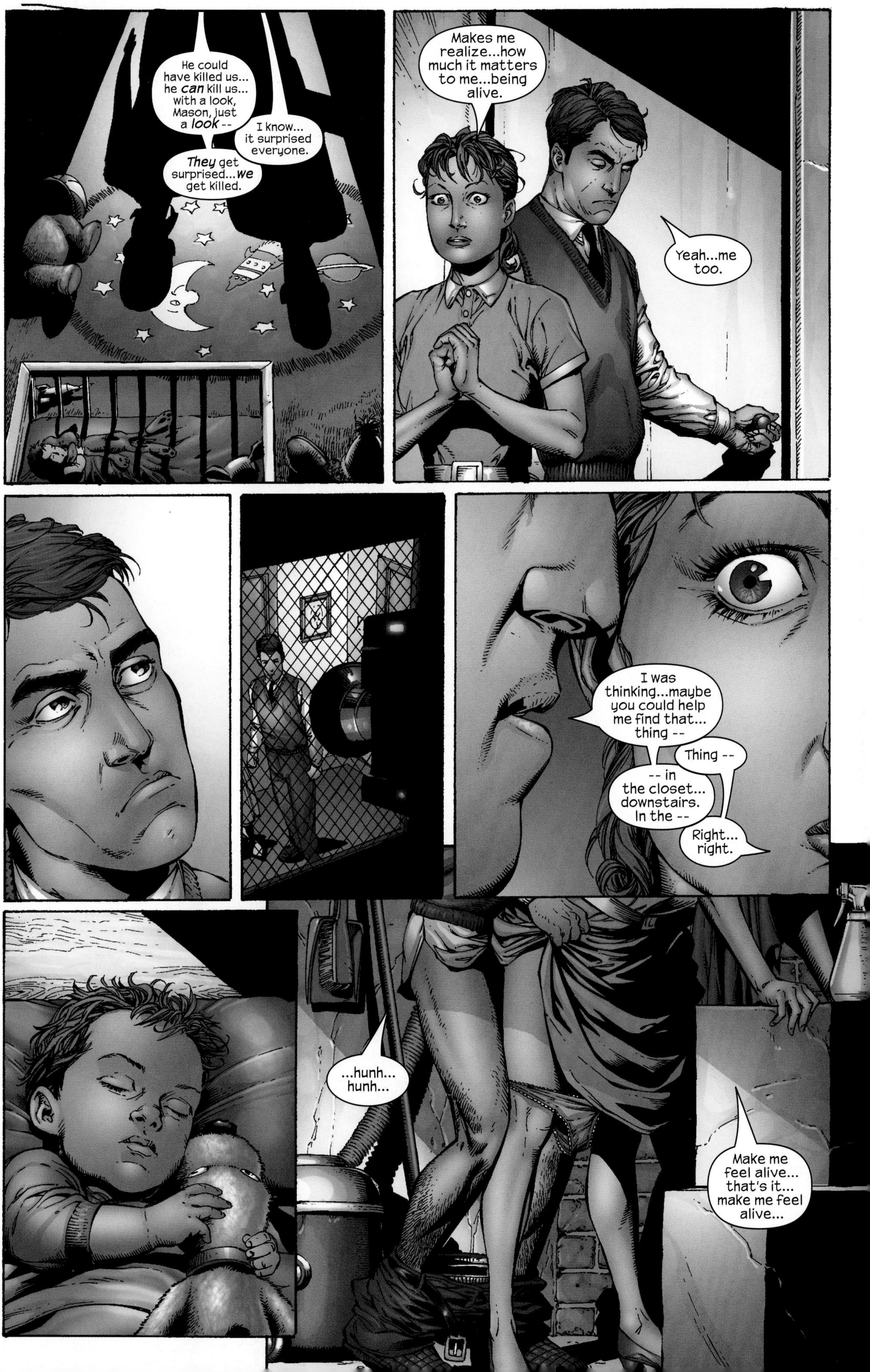
He could have killed us... he can kill us... with a look, Mason, just a look --
I know... it surprised everyone.
They get surprised...we get killed.
Makes me realize...how much it matters to me...being alive.
Yeah...me too.
I was thinking...maybe you could help me find that... thing --
Thing --
-- in the closet... downstairs. In the --
Right... right.
...hunh... hunh...
Make me feel alive... that's it... make me feel alive...

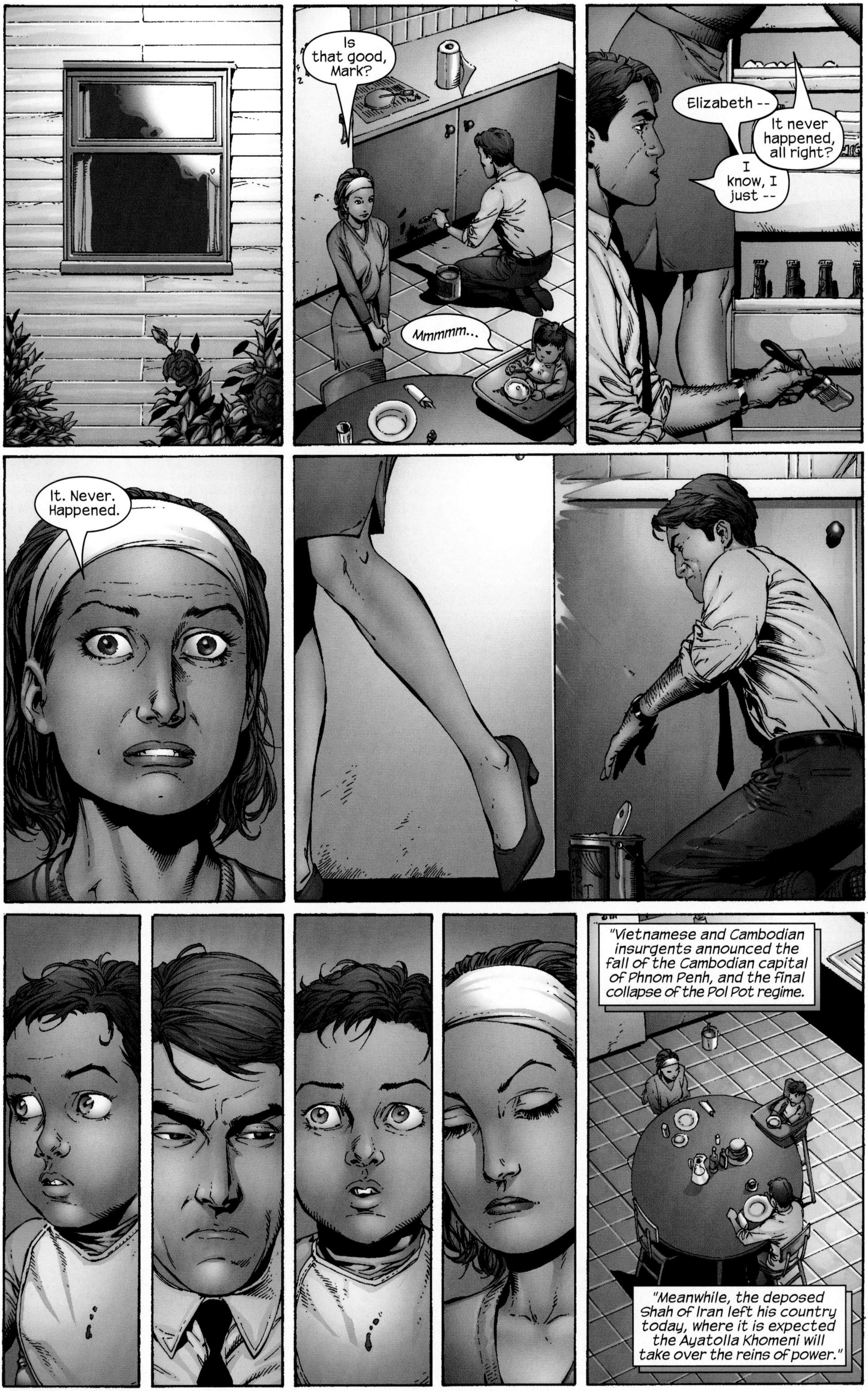
Is that good, Mark?
Mmmmm...
Elizabeth --
I know, I just --
It never happened, all right?
It. Never. Happened.
"Vietnamese and Cambodian insurgents announced the fall of the Cambodian capital of Phnom Penh, and the final collapse of the Pol Pot regime.
"Meanwhile, the deposed Shah of Iran left his country today, where it is expected the Ayatolla Khomeni will take over the reins of power."

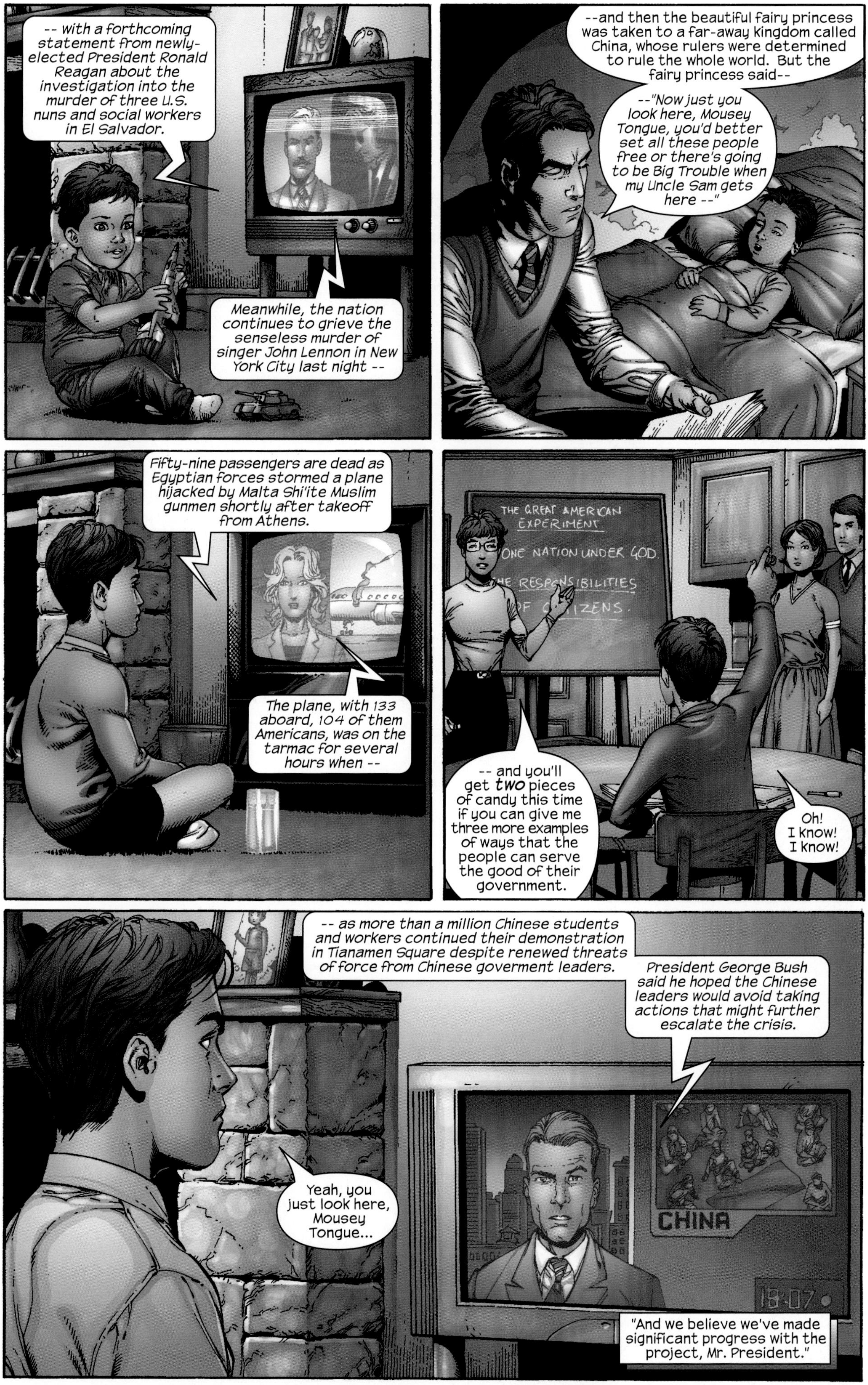
-- with a forthcoming statement from newly-elected President Ronald Reagan about the investigation into the murder of three U.S. nuns and social workers in El Salvador.
Meanwhile, the nation continues to grieve the senseless murder of singer John Lennon in New York City last night --
--and then the beautiful fairy princess was taken to a far-away kingdom called China, whose rulers were determined to rule the whole world. But the fairy princess said--
--"Now just you look here, Mousey Tongue, you'd better set all these people free or there's going to be Big Trouble when my Uncle Sam gets here --"
Fifty-nine passengers are dead as Egyptian forces stormed a plane hijacked by Malta Shi'ite Muslim gunmen shortly after takeoff from Athens.
The plane, with 133 aboard, 104 of them Americans, was on the tarmac for several hours when --
THE GREAT AMERICAN EXPERIMENT
ONE NATION UNDER GOD.
THE RESPONSIBILITIES
OF CITIZENS.
-- and you'll get **two** pieces of candy this time if you can give me three more examples of ways that the people can serve the good of their government.
Oh! I know! I know!
-- as more than a million Chinese students and workers continued their demonstration in Tianamen Square despite renewed threats of force from Chinese goverment leaders.
President George Bush said he hoped the Chinese leaders would avoid taking actions that might further escalate the crisis.
Yeah, you just look here, Mousey Tongue...
CHINA
18:07
"And we believe we've made significant progress with the project, Mr. President."

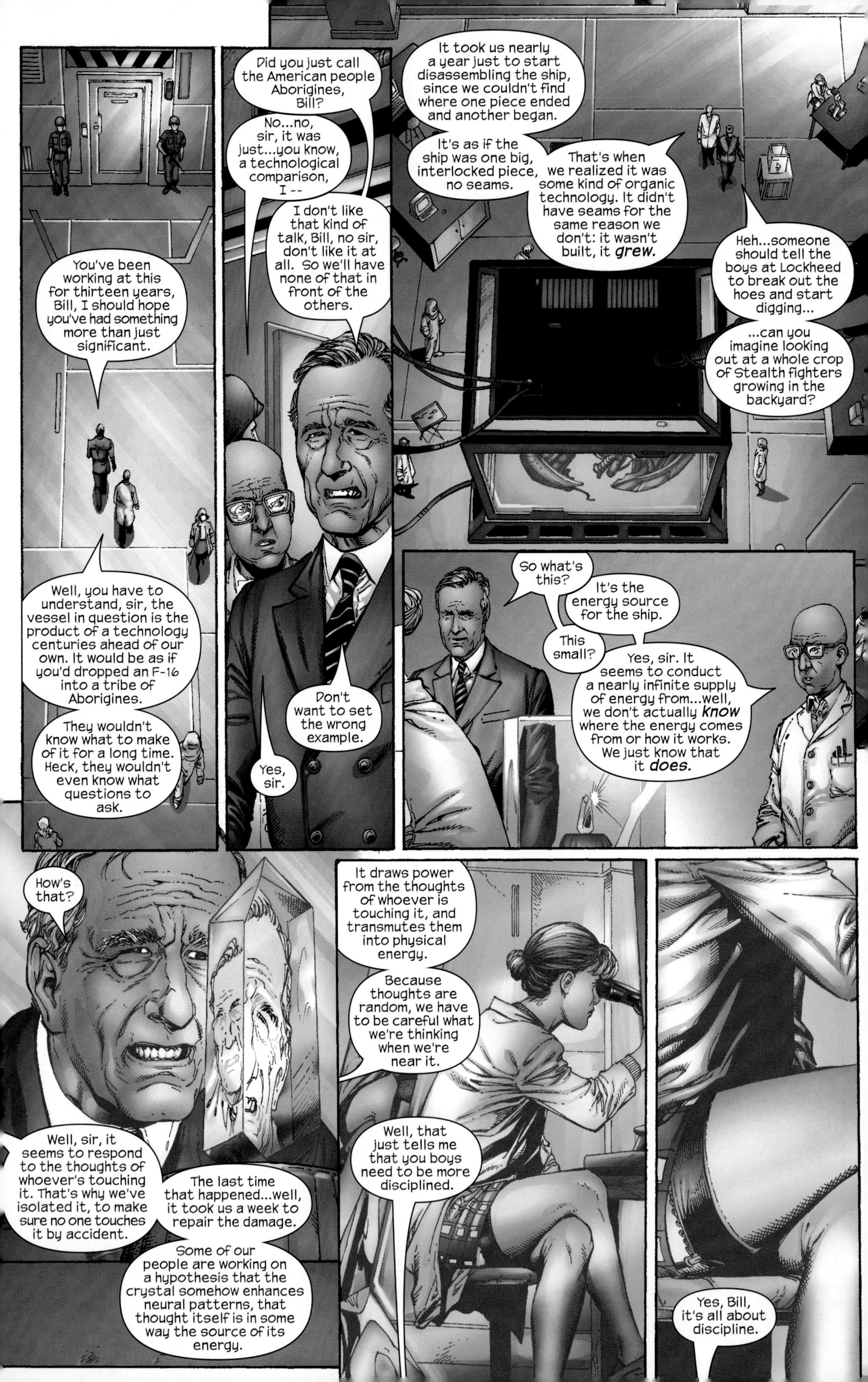
You've been working at this for thirteen years, Bill, I should hope you've had something more than just significant.
Well, you have to understand, sir, the vessel in question is the product of a technology centuries ahead of our own. It would be as if you'd dropped an F-16 into a tribe of Aborigines.
They wouldn't know what to make of it for a long time. Heck, they wouldn't even know what questions to ask.
Did you just call the American people Aborigines, Bill?
No...no, sir, it was just...you know, a technological comparison, I --
I don't like that kind of talk, Bill, no sir, don't like it at all. So we'll have none of that in front of the others.
Don't want to set the wrong example.
Yes, sir.
It took us nearly a year just to start disassembling the ship, since we couldn't find where one piece ended and another began.
It's as if the ship was one big, interlocked piece, no seams.
That's when we realized it was some kind of organic technology. It didn't have seams for the same reason we don't: it wasn't built, it *grew.*
Heh...someone should tell the boys at Lockheed to break out the hoes and start digging...
...can you imagine looking out at a whole crop of Stealth fighters growing in the backyard?
So what's this?
It's the energy source for the ship.
This small?
Yes, sir. It seems to conduct a nearly infinite supply of energy from...well, we don't actually *know* where the energy comes from or how it works. We just know that it *does.*
How's that?
Well, sir, it seems to respond to the thoughts of whoever's touching it. That's why we've isolated it, to make sure no one touches it by accident.
The last time that happened...well, it took us a week to repair the damage.
Some of our people are working on a hypothesis that the crystal somehow enhances neural patterns, that thought itself is in some way the source of its energy.
It draws power from the thoughts of whoever is touching it, and transmutes them into physical energy.
Because thoughts are random, we have to be careful what we're thinking when we're near it.
Well, that just tells me that you boys need to be more disciplined.
Yes, Bill, it's all about discipline.

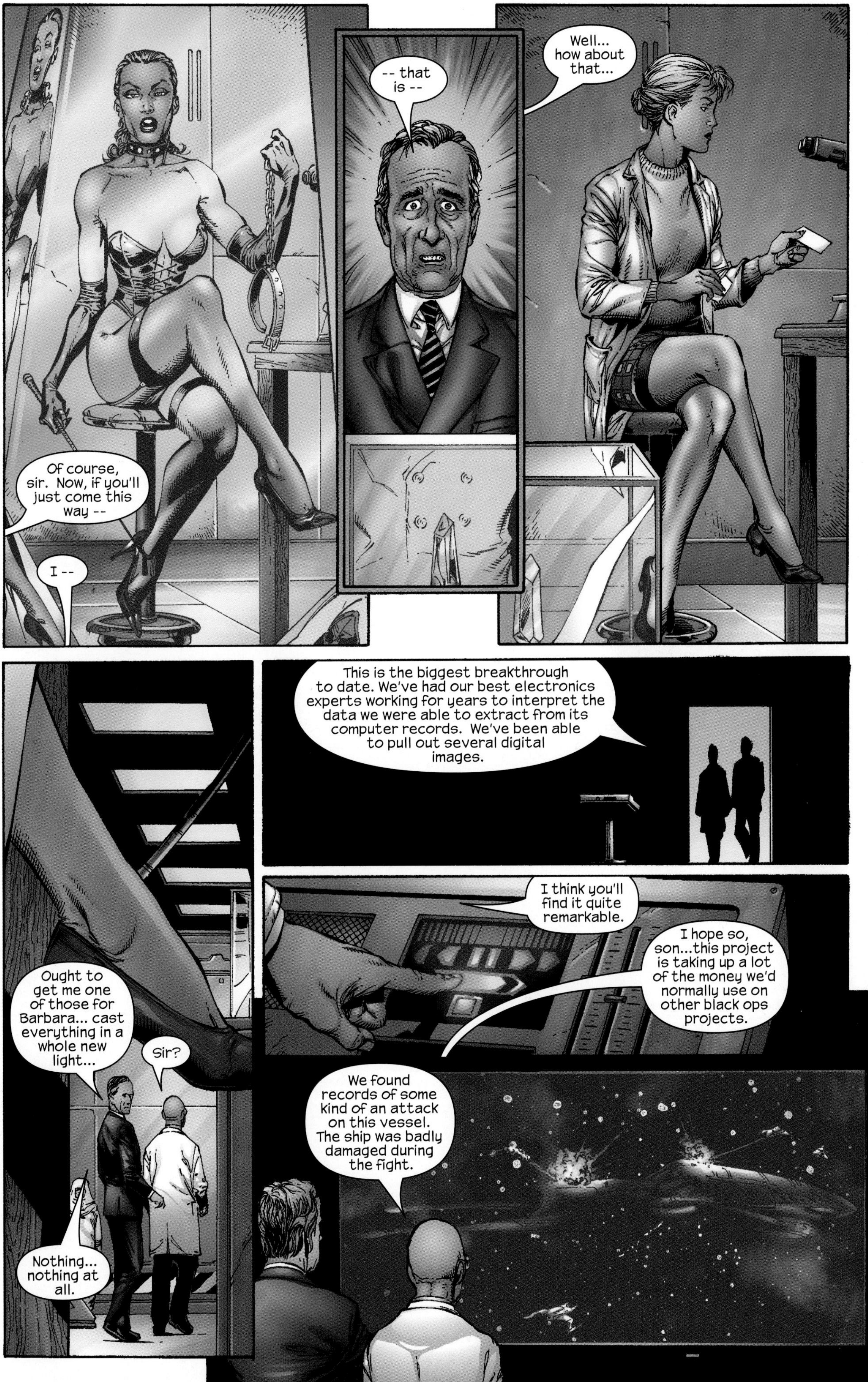
Of course, sir. Now, if you'll just come this way --
I --
-- that is --
Well... how about that...
This is the biggest breakthrough to date. We've had our best electronics experts working for years to interpret the data we were able to extract from its computer records. We've been able to pull out several digital images.
I think you'll find it quite remarkable.
I hope so, son...this project is taking up a lot of the money we'd normally use on other black ops projects.
Ought to get me one of those for Barbara... cast everything in a whole new light...
Sir?
Nothing... nothing at all.
We found records of some kind of an attack on this vessel. The ship was badly damaged during the fight.

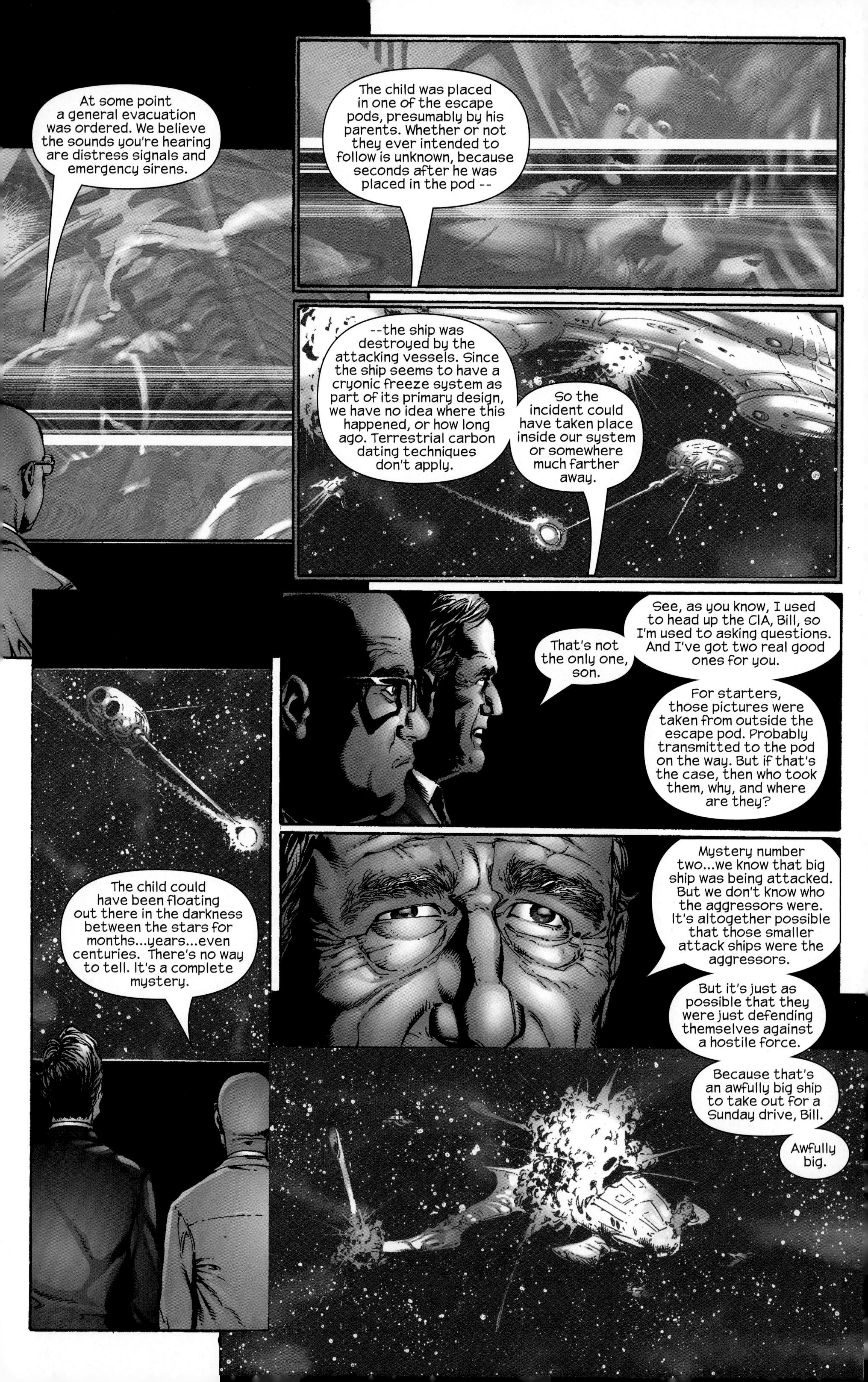
At some point a general evacuation was ordered. We believe the sounds you're hearing are distress signals and emergency sirens.
The child was placed in one of the escape pods, presumably by his parents. Whether or not they ever intended to follow is unknown, because seconds after he was placed in the pod --
--the ship was destroyed by the attacking vessels. Since the ship seems to have a cryonic freeze system as part of its primary design, we have no idea where this happened, or how long ago. Terrestrial carbon dating techniques don't apply.
So the incident could have taken place inside our system or somewhere much farther away.
The child could have been floating out there in the darkness between the stars for months...years...even centuries. There's no way to tell. It's a complete mystery.
That's not the only one, son.
See, as you know, I used to head up the CIA, Bill, so I'm used to asking questions. And I've got two real good ones for you.
For starters, those pictures were taken from outside the escape pod. Probably transmitted to the pod on the way. But if that's the case, then who took them, why, and where are they?
Mystery number two...we know that big ship was being attacked. But we don't know who the aggressors were. It's altogether possible that those smaller attack ships were the aggressors.
But it's just as possible that they were just defending themselves against a hostile force.
Because that's an awfully big ship to take out for a Sunday drive, Bill.
Awfully big.

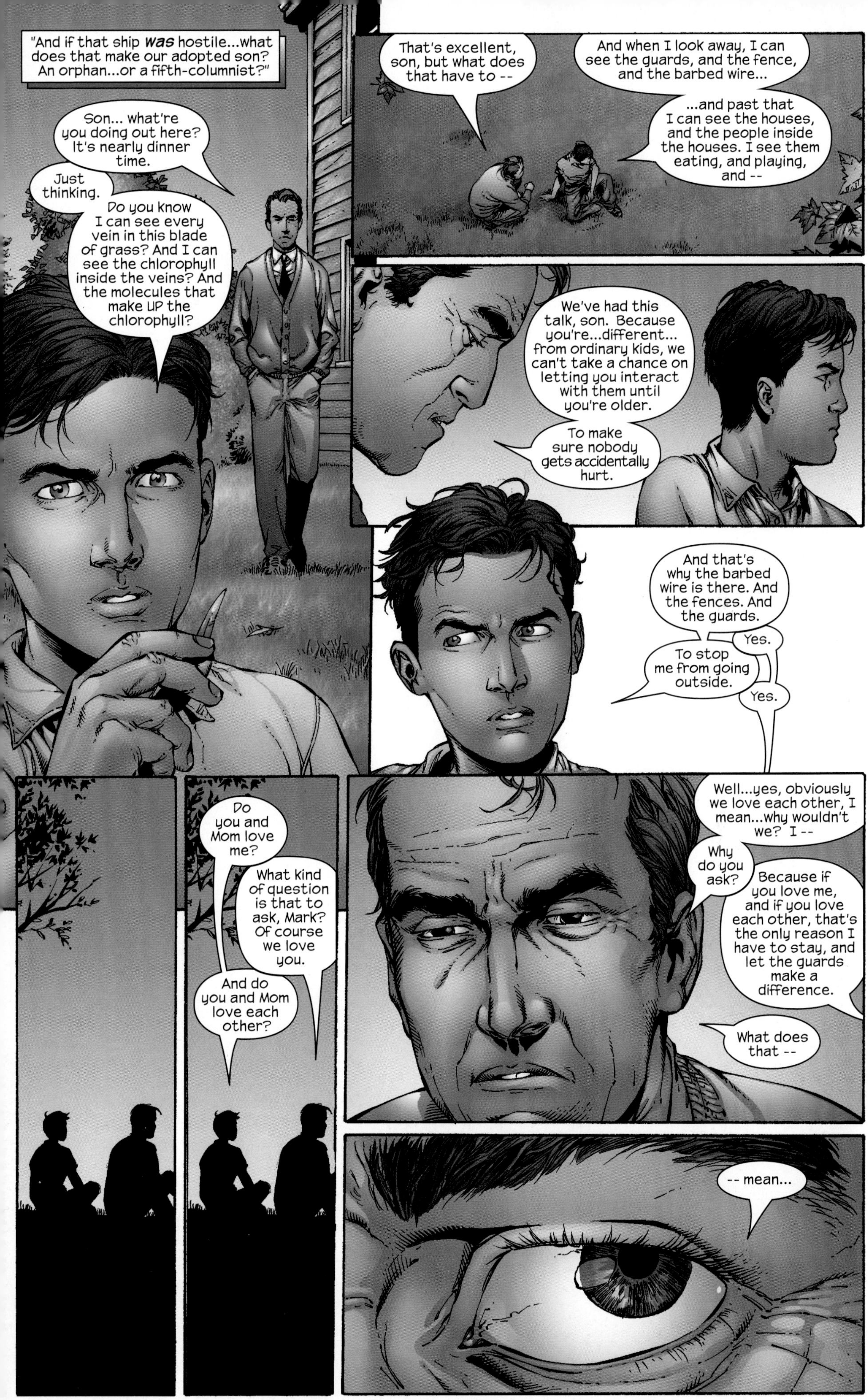
"And if that ship *was* hostile...what does that make our adopted son? An orphan...or a fifth-columnist?"
Son... what're you doing out here? It's nearly dinner time.
Just thinking.
Do you know I can see every vein in this blade of grass? And I can see the chlorophyll inside the veins? And the molecules that make UP the chlorophyll?
That's excellent, son, but what does that have to --
And when I look away, I can see the guards, and the fence, and the barbed wire...
...and past that I can see the houses, and the people inside the houses. I see them eating, and playing, and --
We've had this talk, son. Because you're...different... from ordinary kids, we can't take a chance on letting you interact with them until you're older.
To make sure nobody gets accidentally hurt.
And that's why the barbed wire is there. And the fences. And the guards.
Yes.
To stop me from going outside.
Yes.
Do you and Mom love me?
What kind of question is that to ask, Mark? Of course we love you.
And do you and Mom love each other?
Well...yes, obviously we love each other, I mean...why wouldn't we? I --
Why do you ask?
Because if you love me, and if you love each other, that's the only reason I have to stay, and let the guards make a difference.
What does that --
-- mean...

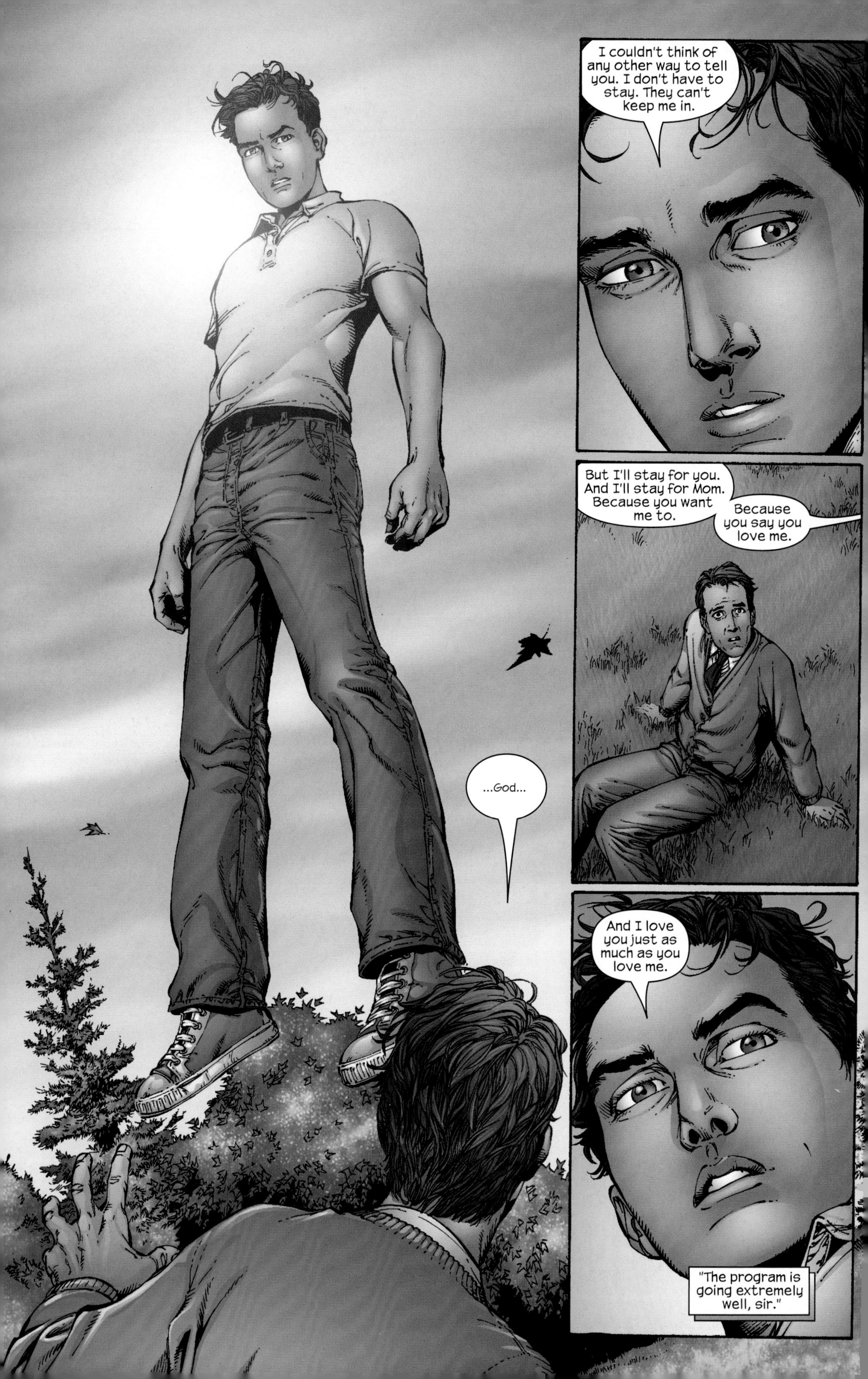

I couldn't think of any other way to tell you. I don't have to stay. They can't keep me in.
But I'll stay for you. And I'll stay for Mom. Because you want me to.
Because you say you love me.
...God...
And I love you just as much as you love me.
"The program is going extremely well, sir."

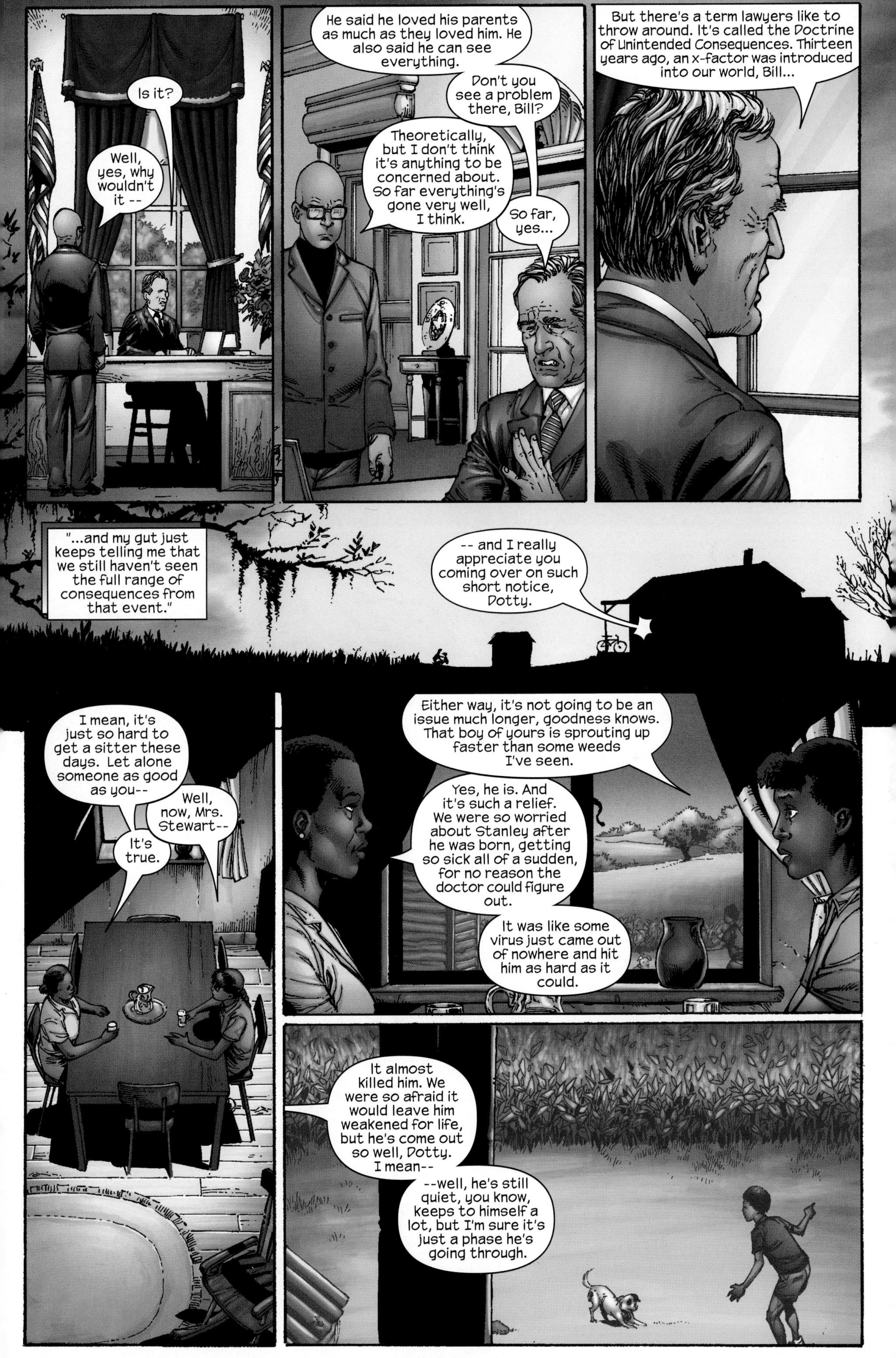
Is it?
Well, yes, why wouldn't it --
He said he loved his parents as much as they loved him. He also said he can see everything.
Don't you see a problem there, Bill?
Theoretically, but I don't think it's anything to be concerned about. So far everything's gone very well, I think.
So far, yes...
But there's a term lawyers like to throw around. It's called the Doctrine of Unintended Consequences. Thirteen years ago, an x-factor was introduced into our world, Bill...
"...and my gut just keeps telling me that we still haven't seen the full range of consequences from that event."
-- and I really appreciate you coming over on such short notice, Dotty.
I mean, it's just so hard to get a sitter these days. Let alone someone as good as you--
Well, now, Mrs. Stewart--
It's true.
Either way, it's not going to be an issue much longer, goodness knows. That boy of yours is sprouting up faster than some weeds I've seen.
Yes, he is. And it's such a relief. We were so worried about Stanley after he was born, getting so sick all of a sudden, for no reason the doctor could figure out.
It was like some virus just came out of nowhere and hit him as hard as it could.
It almost killed him. We were so afraid it would leave him weakened for life, but he's come out so well, Dotty. I mean--
--well, he's still quiet, you know, keeps to himself a lot, but I'm sure it's just a phase he's going through.

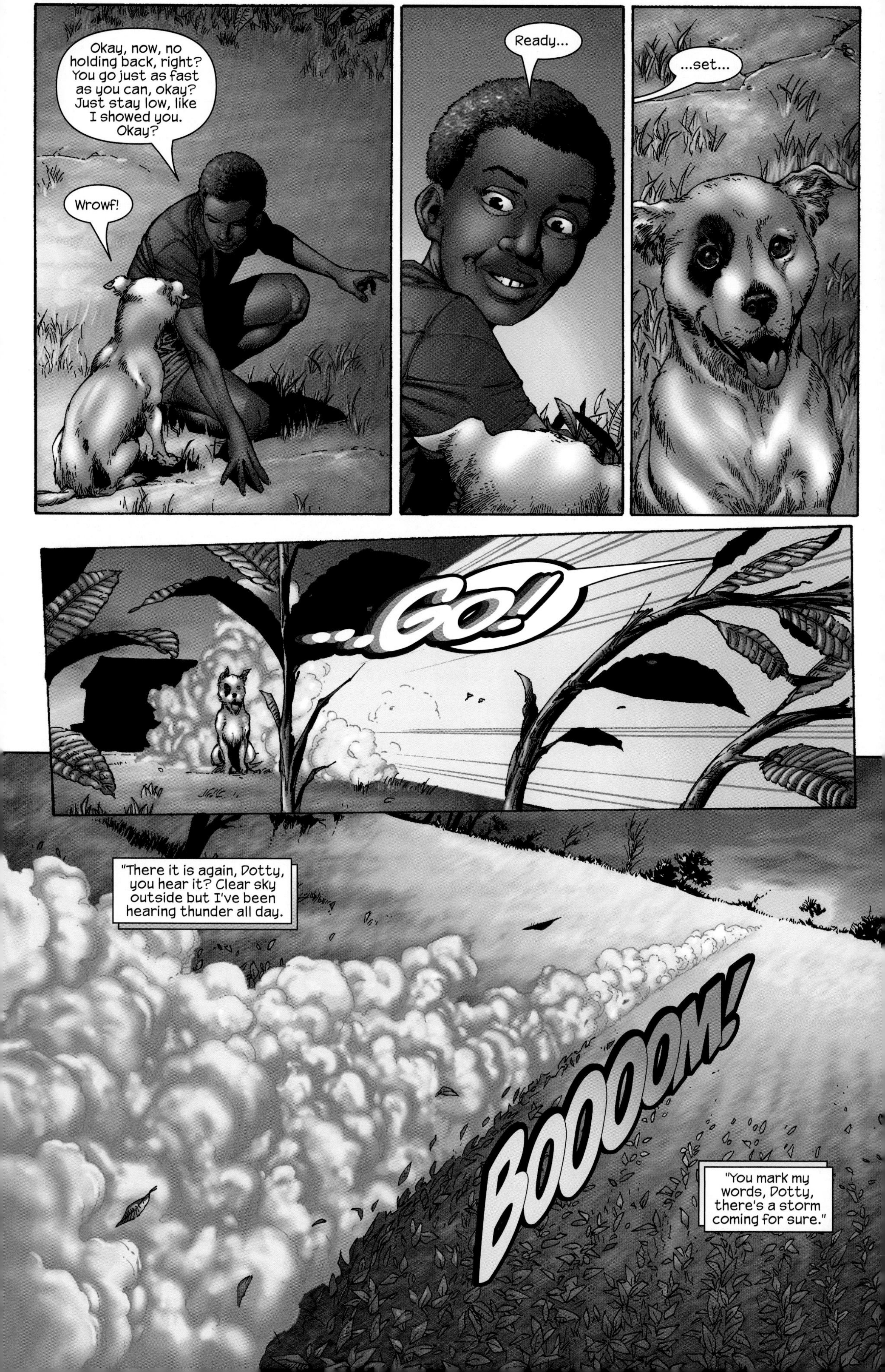
Okay, now, no holding back, right? You go just as fast as you can, okay? Just stay low, like I showed you. Okay?
Wrowf!
Ready...
...set...
...GO!
"There it is again, Dotty, you hear it? Clear sky outside but I've been hearing thunder all day.
BOOOOM!
"You mark my words, Dotty, there's a storm coming for sure."

Four Degrees of Contamination #2

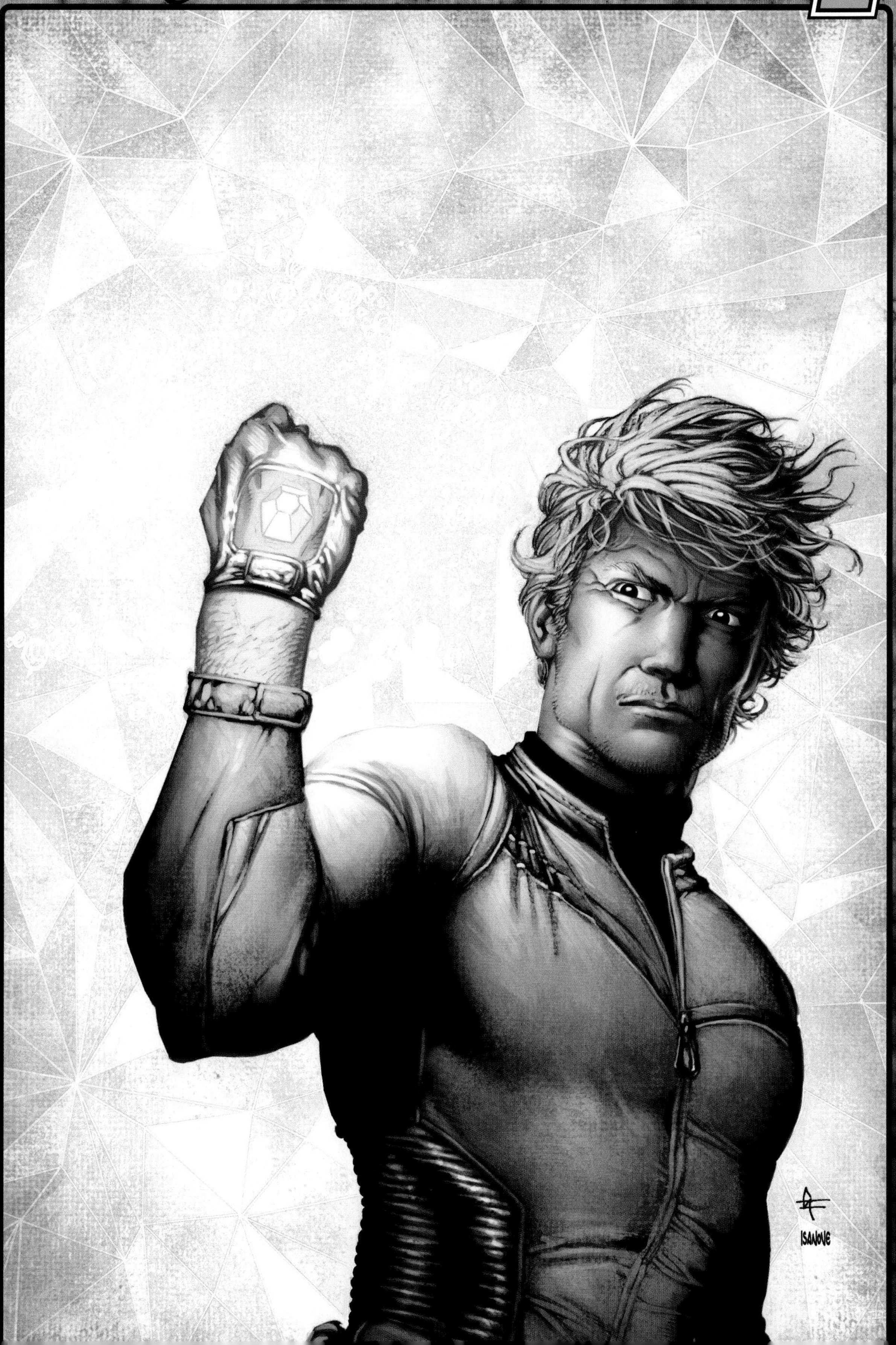
ISANOVE

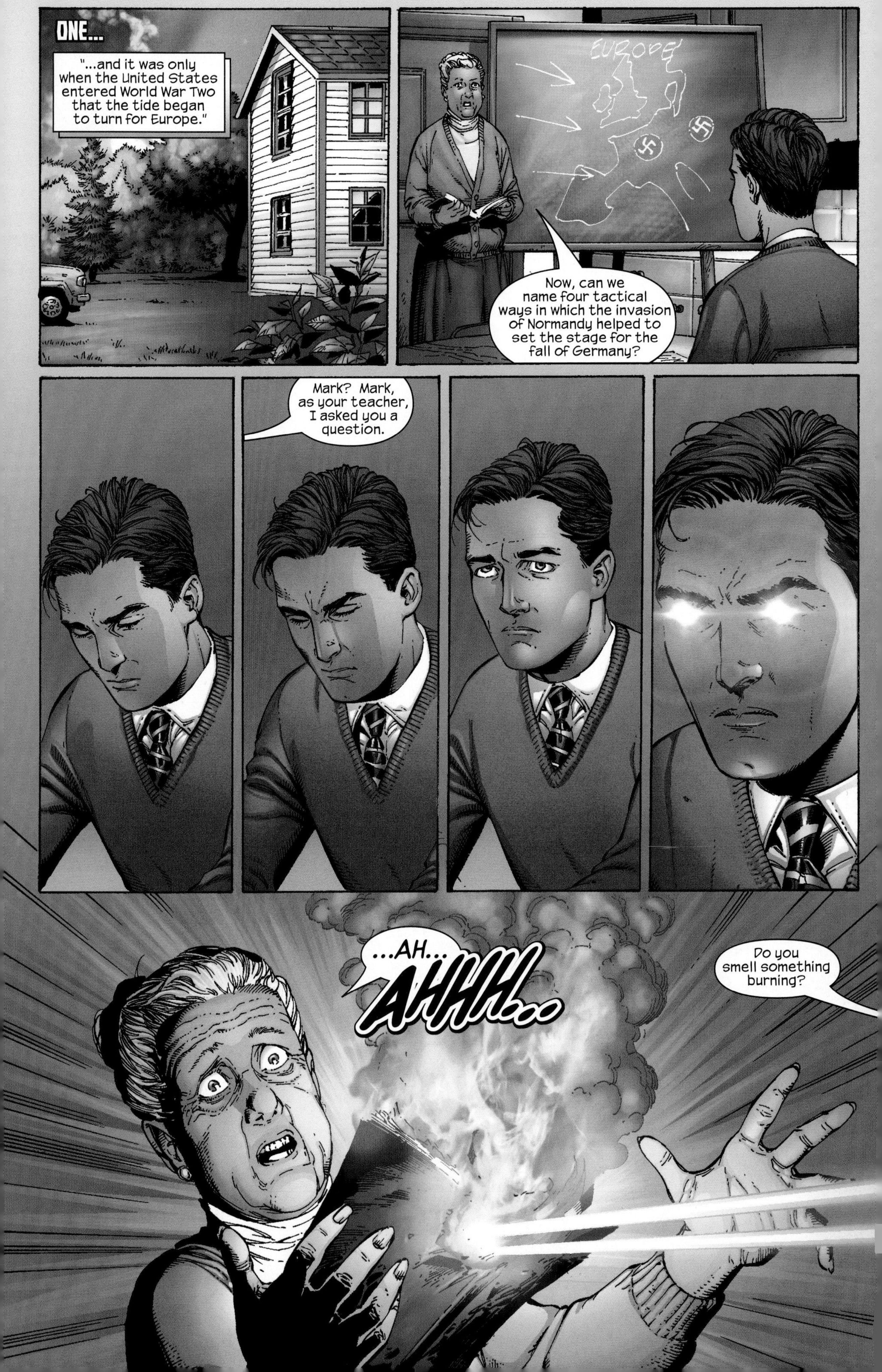
ONE...
"...and it was only when the United States entered World War Two that the tide began to turn for Europe."
EUROPE
Now, can we name four tactical ways in which the invasion of Normandy helped to set the stage for the fall of Germany?
Mark? Mark, as your teacher, I asked you a question.
...AH... AHHH...
Do you smell something burning?

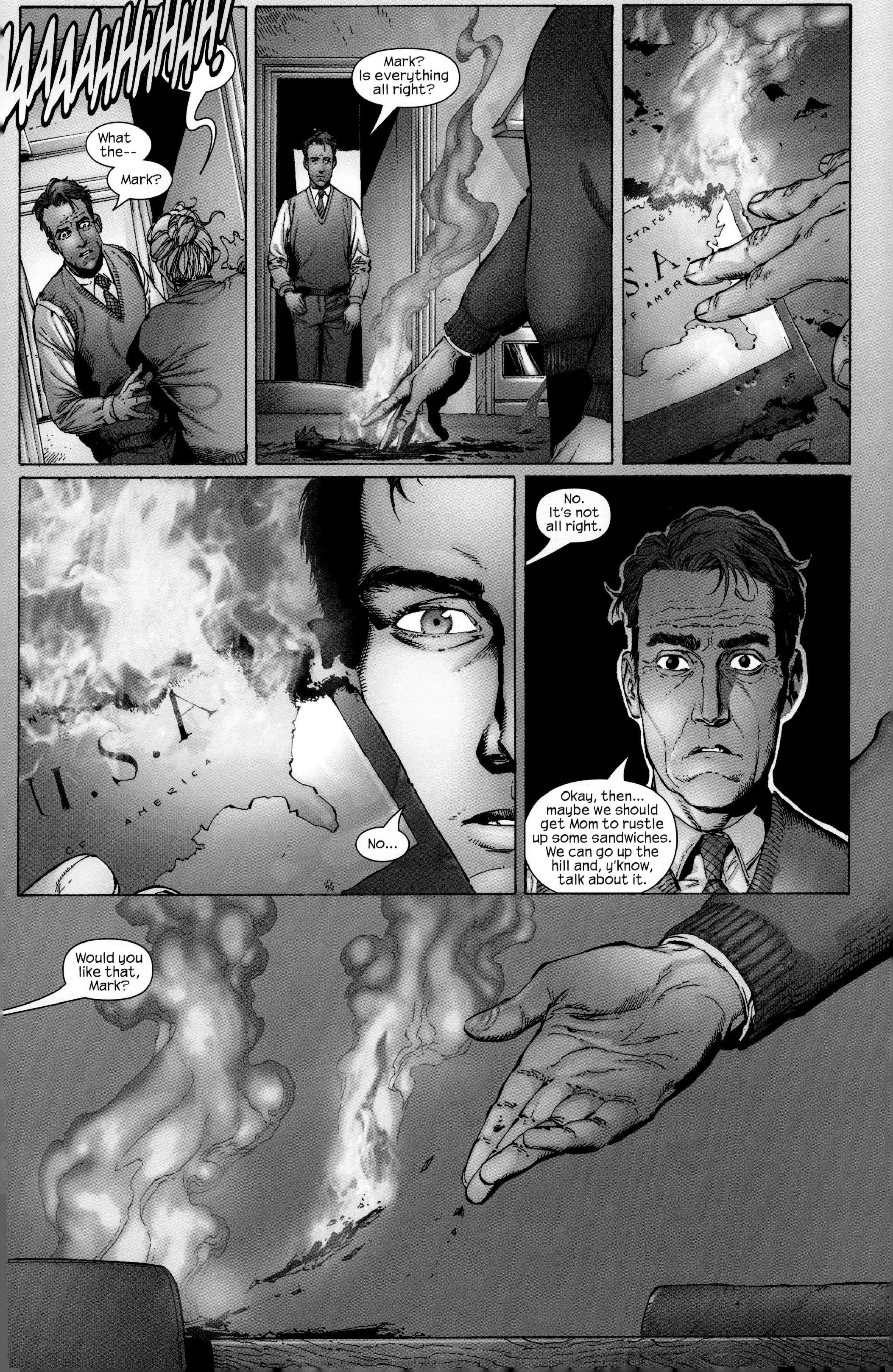
AAAAHHHHH!
What the--
Mark?
Mark? Is everything all right?
No...
No. It's not all right.
Okay, then... maybe we should get Mom to rustle up some sandwiches. We can go up the hill and, y'know, talk about it.
Would you like that, Mark?

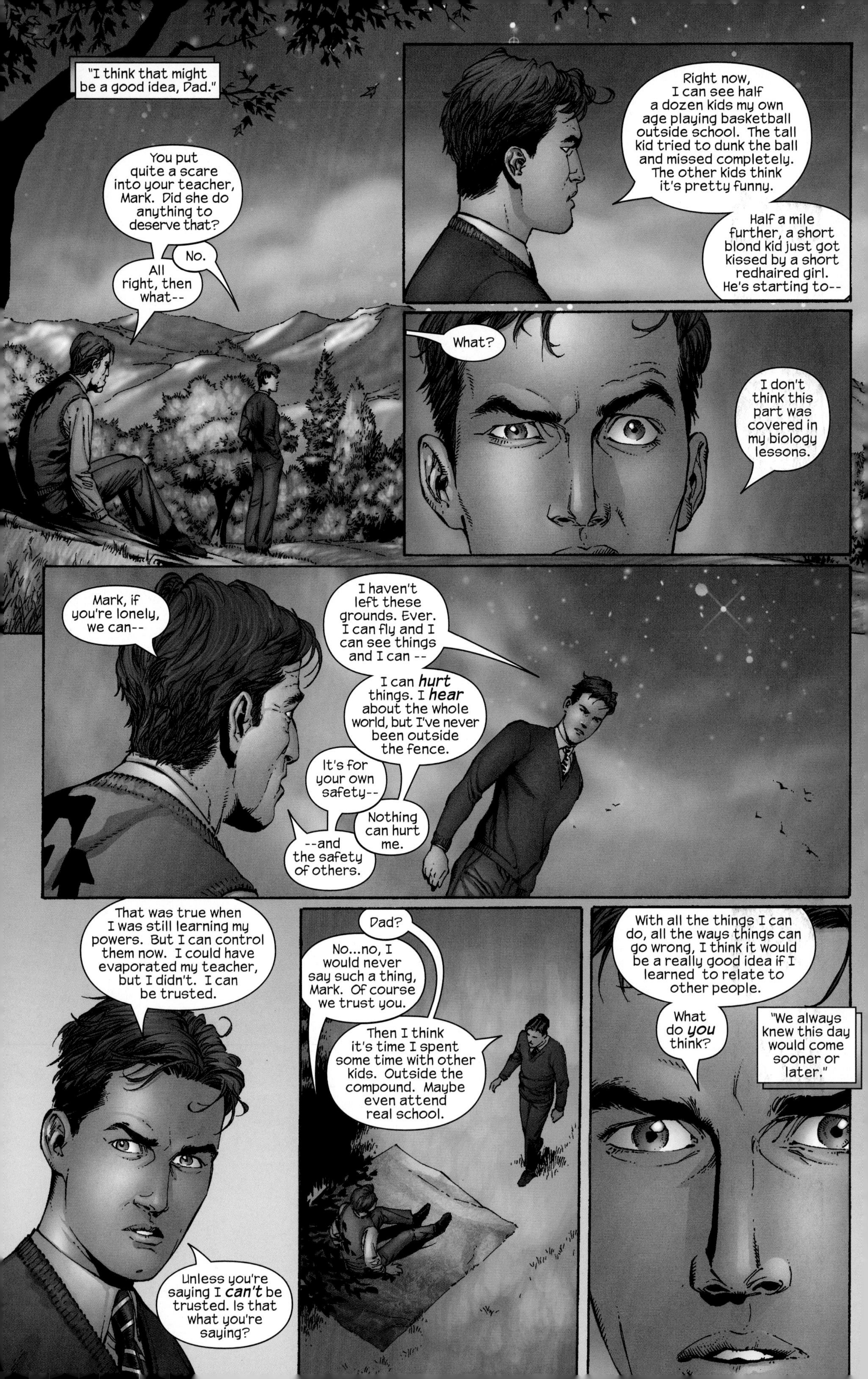

"I think that might be a good idea, Dad."
You put quite a scare into your teacher, Mark. Did she do anything to deserve that?
No.
All right, then what--
Right now, I can see half a dozen kids my own age playing basketball outside school. The tall kid tried to dunk the ball and missed completely. The other kids think it's pretty funny.
Half a mile further, a short blond kid just got kissed by a short redhaired girl. He's starting to--
What?
I don't think this part was covered in my biology lessons.
Mark, if you're lonely, we can--
I haven't left these grounds. Ever. I can fly and I can see things and I can --
I can *hurt* things. I *hear* about the whole world, but I've never been outside the fence.
It's for your own safety--
Nothing can hurt me.
--and the safety of others.
That was true when I was still learning my powers. But I can control them now. I could have evaporated my teacher, but I didn't. I can be trusted.
Unless you're saying I *can't* be trusted. Is that what you're saying?
Dad?
No...no, I would never say such a thing, Mark. Of course we trust you.
Then I think it's time I spent some time with other kids. Outside the compound. Maybe even attend real school.
With all the things I can do, all the ways things can go wrong, I think it would be a really good idea if I learned to relate to other people.
What do *you* think?
"We always knew this day would come sooner or later."

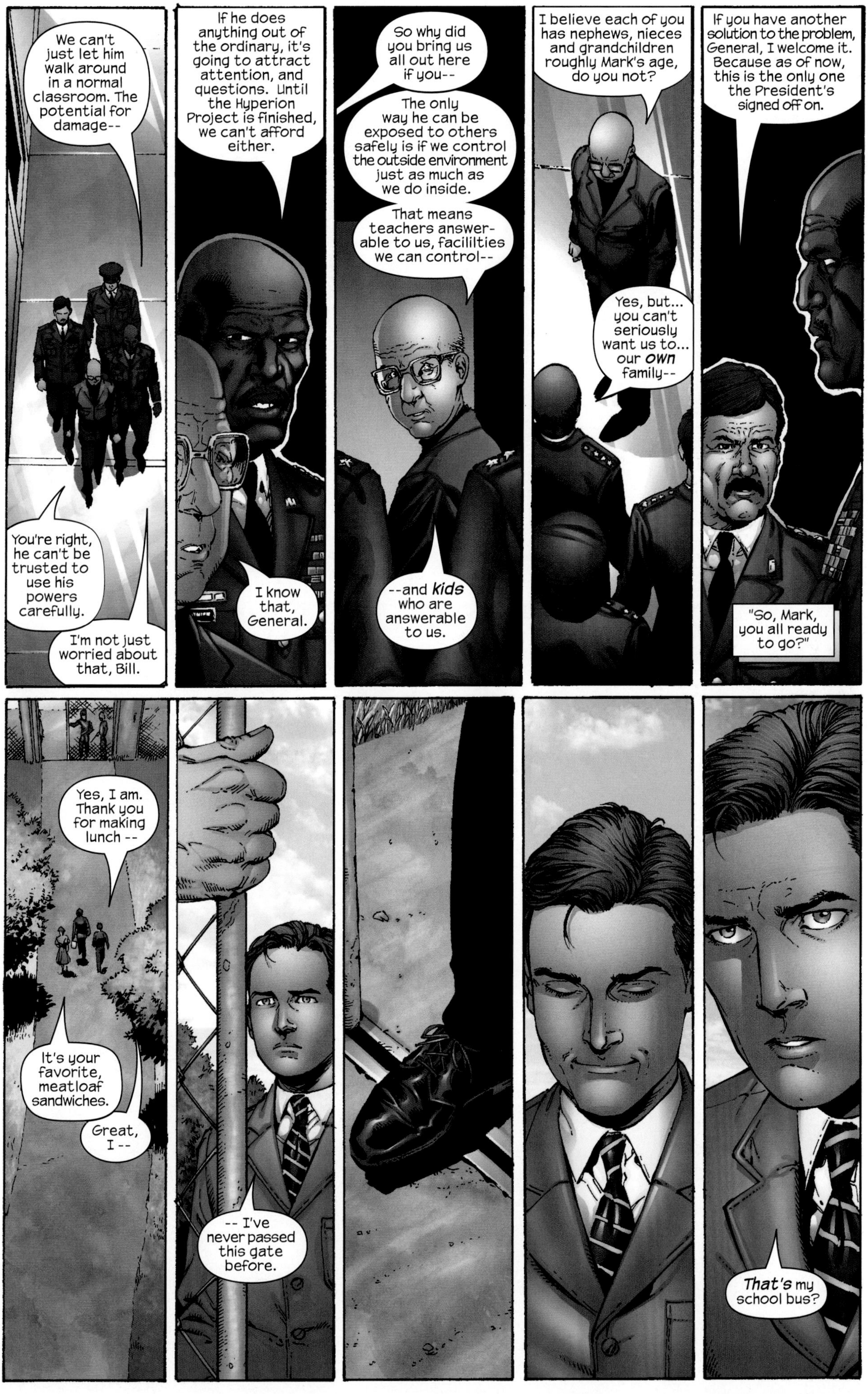
We can't just let him walk around in a normal classroom. The potential for damage--
You're right, he can't be trusted to use his powers carefully.
I'm not just worried about that, Bill.
If he does anything out of the ordinary, it's going to attract attention, and questions. Until the Hyperion Project is finished, we can't afford either.
I know that, General.
So why did you bring us all out here if you--
The only way he can be exposed to others safely is if we control the outside environment just as much as we do inside.
That means teachers answerable to us, facililties we can control--
--and *kids* who are answerable to us.
I believe each of you has nephews, nieces and grandchildren roughly Mark's age, do you not?
Yes, but... you can't seriously want us to... our *own* family--
If you have another solution to the problem, General, I welcome it. Because as of now, this is the only one the President's signed off on.
"So, Mark, you all ready to go?"
Yes, I am. Thank you for making lunch --
It's your favorite, meatloaf sandwiches.
Great, I --
-- I've never passed this gate before.
That's my school bus?

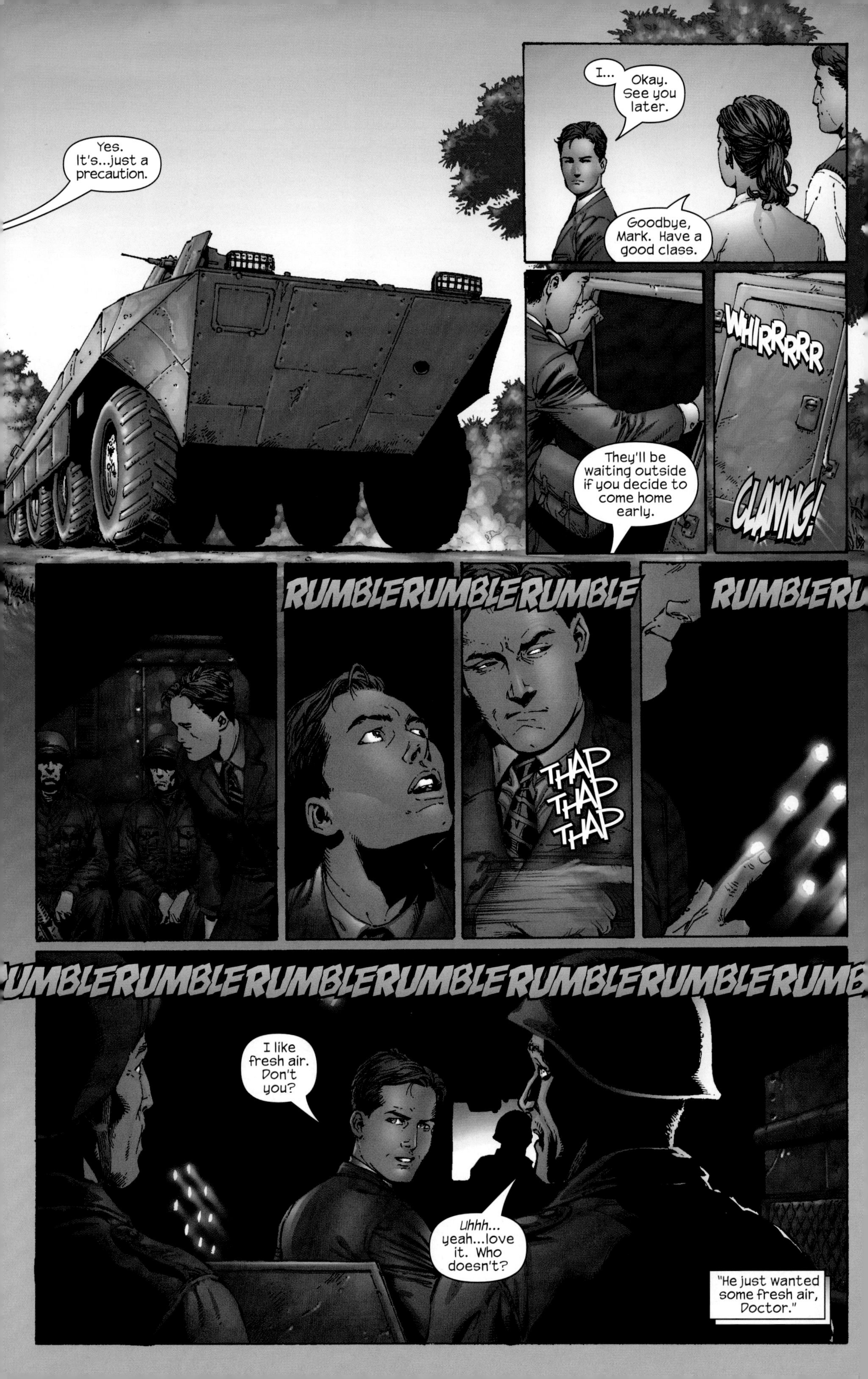
Yes. It's...just a precaution.
I... Okay. See you later.
Goodbye, Mark. Have a good class.
WHIRRRRR
They'll be waiting outside if you decide to come home early.
CLANNG!
RUMBLERUMBLERUMBLE
THAP THAP THAP
RUMBLERU
UMBLERUMBLERUMBLERUMBLERUMBLERUMBLERUMB
I like fresh air. Don't you?
Uhhh... yeah...love it. Who doesn't?
"He just wanted some fresh air, Doctor."

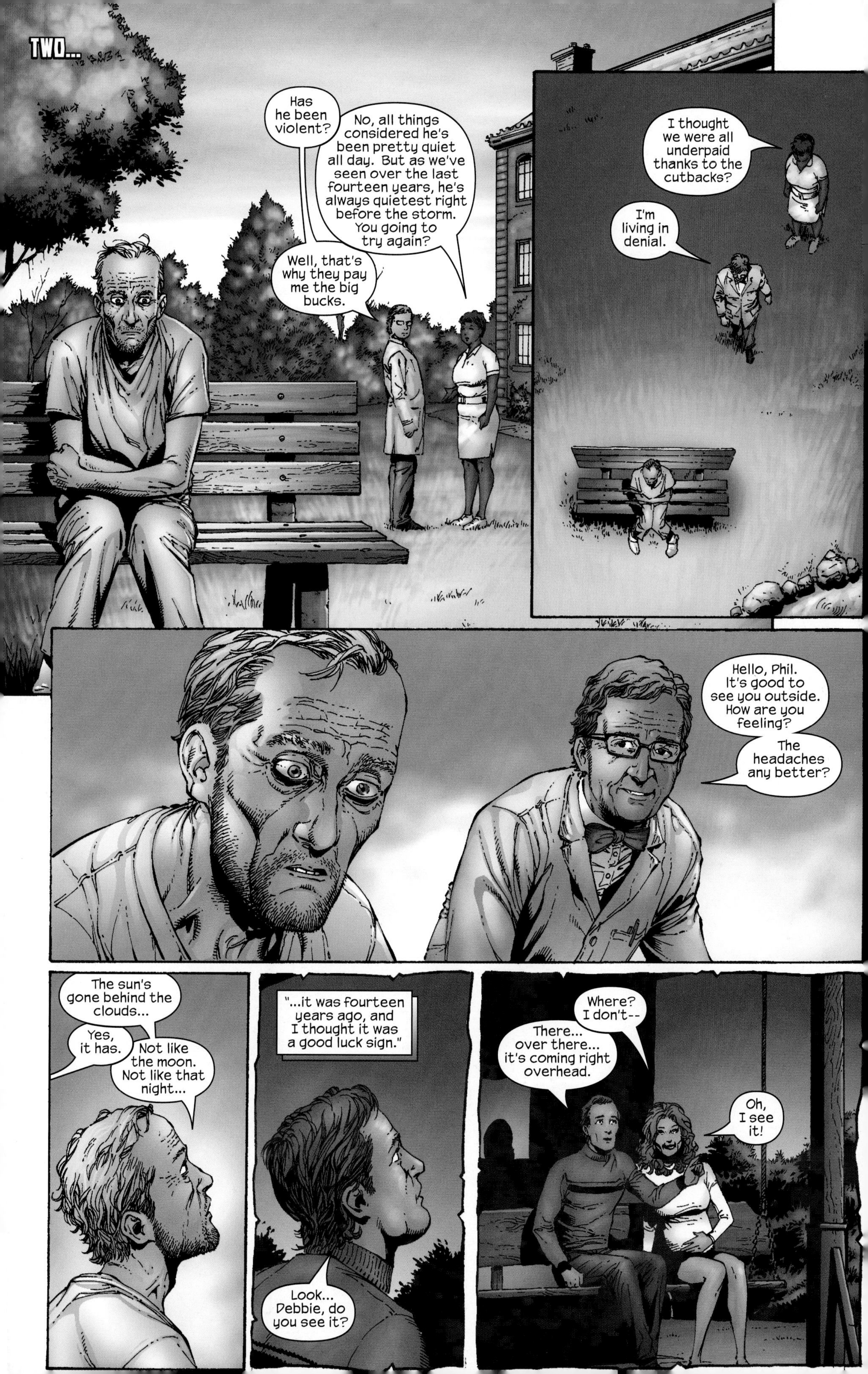
TWO...
Has he been violent?
No, all things considered he's been pretty quiet all day. But as we've seen over the last fourteen years, he's always quietest right before the storm. You going to try again?
Well, that's why they pay me the big bucks.
I thought we were all underpaid thanks to the cutbacks?
I'm living in denial.
Hello, Phil. It's good to see you outside. How are you feeling?
The headaches any better?
The sun's gone behind the clouds...
Yes, it has.
Not like the moon. Not like that night...
"...it was fourteen years ago, and I thought it was a good luck sign."
Look... Debbie, do you see it?
Where? I don't--
There... over there... it's coming right overhead.
Oh, I see it!

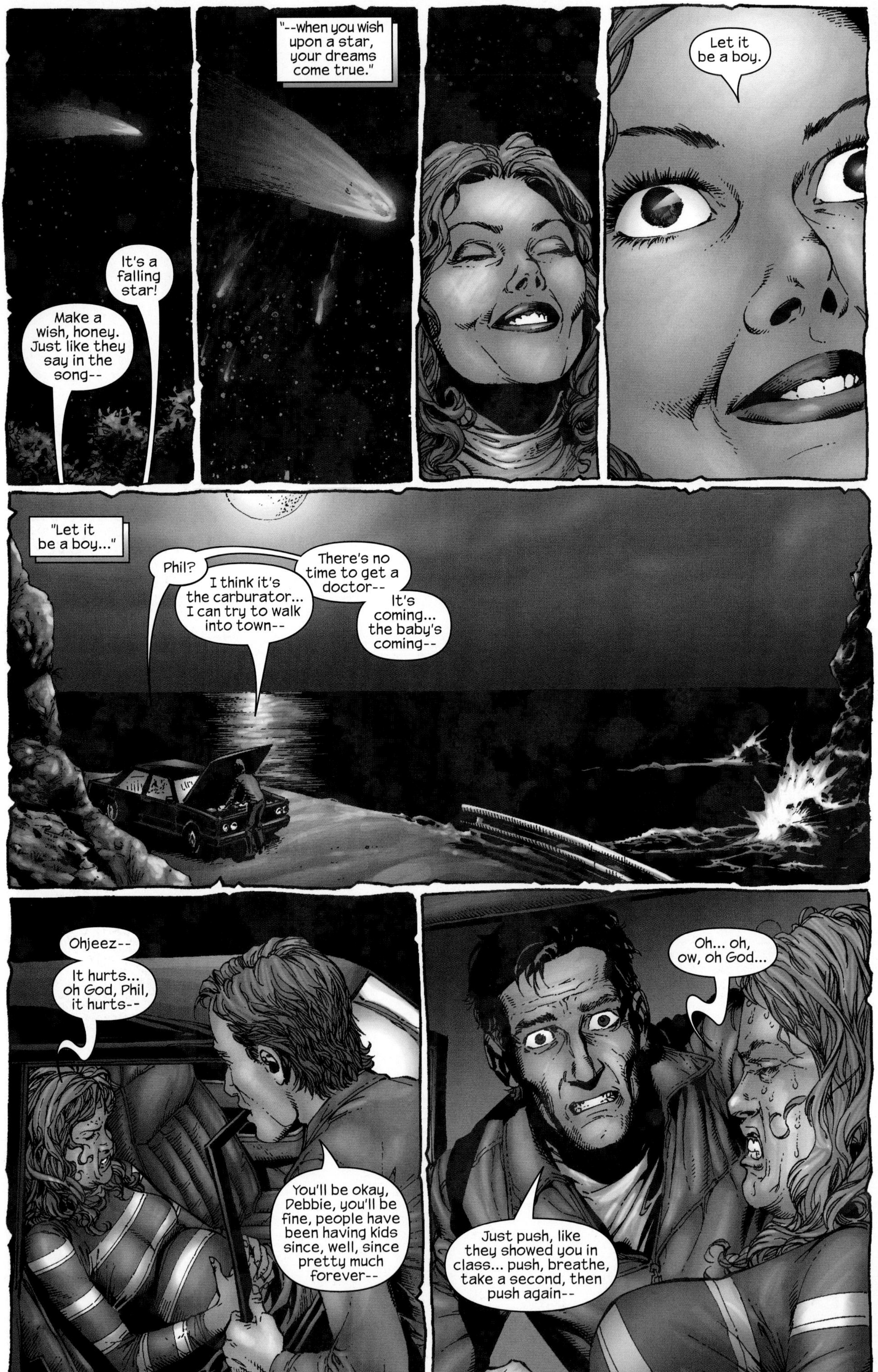

Make a wish, honey. Just like they say in the song--
It's a falling star!
"--when you wish upon a star, your dreams come true."
Let it be a boy.
"Let it be a boy..."
Phil?
I think it's the carburator... I can try to walk into town--
There's no time to get a doctor--
It's coming... the baby's coming--
Ohjeez--
It hurts... oh God, Phil, it hurts--
You'll be okay, Debbie, you'll be fine, people have been having kids since, well, since pretty much forever--
Oh... oh, ow, oh God...
Just push, like they showed you in class... push, breathe, take a second, then push again--

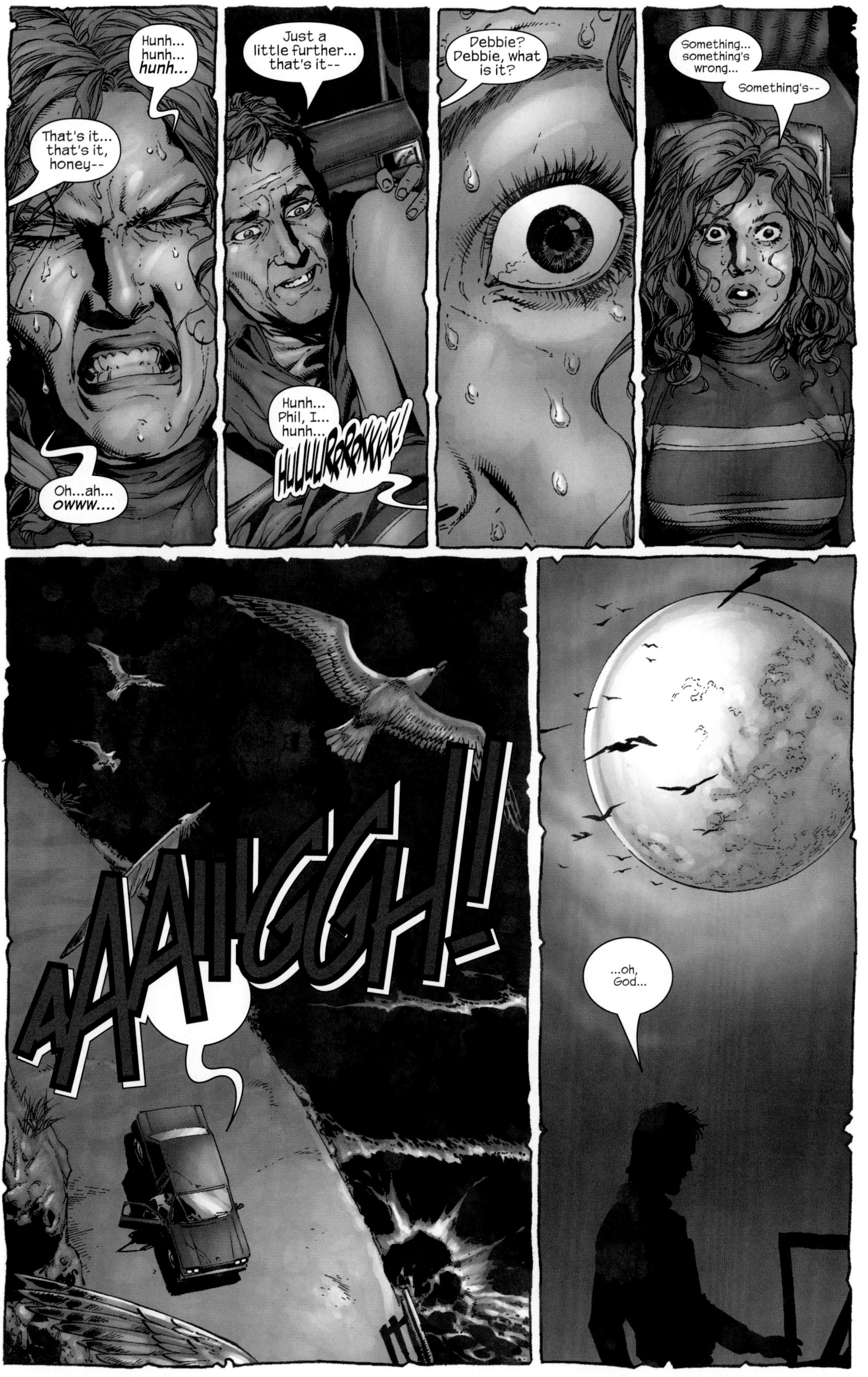

Hunh... hunh... hunh...
That's it... that's it, honey--
Oh...ah... owww....
Just a little further... that's it--
Hunh... Phil, I... hunh...
HULLLRRRRKKK!
Debbie? Debbie, what is it?
Something... something's wrong...
Something's--
AAAIIGGH!!
...oh, God...

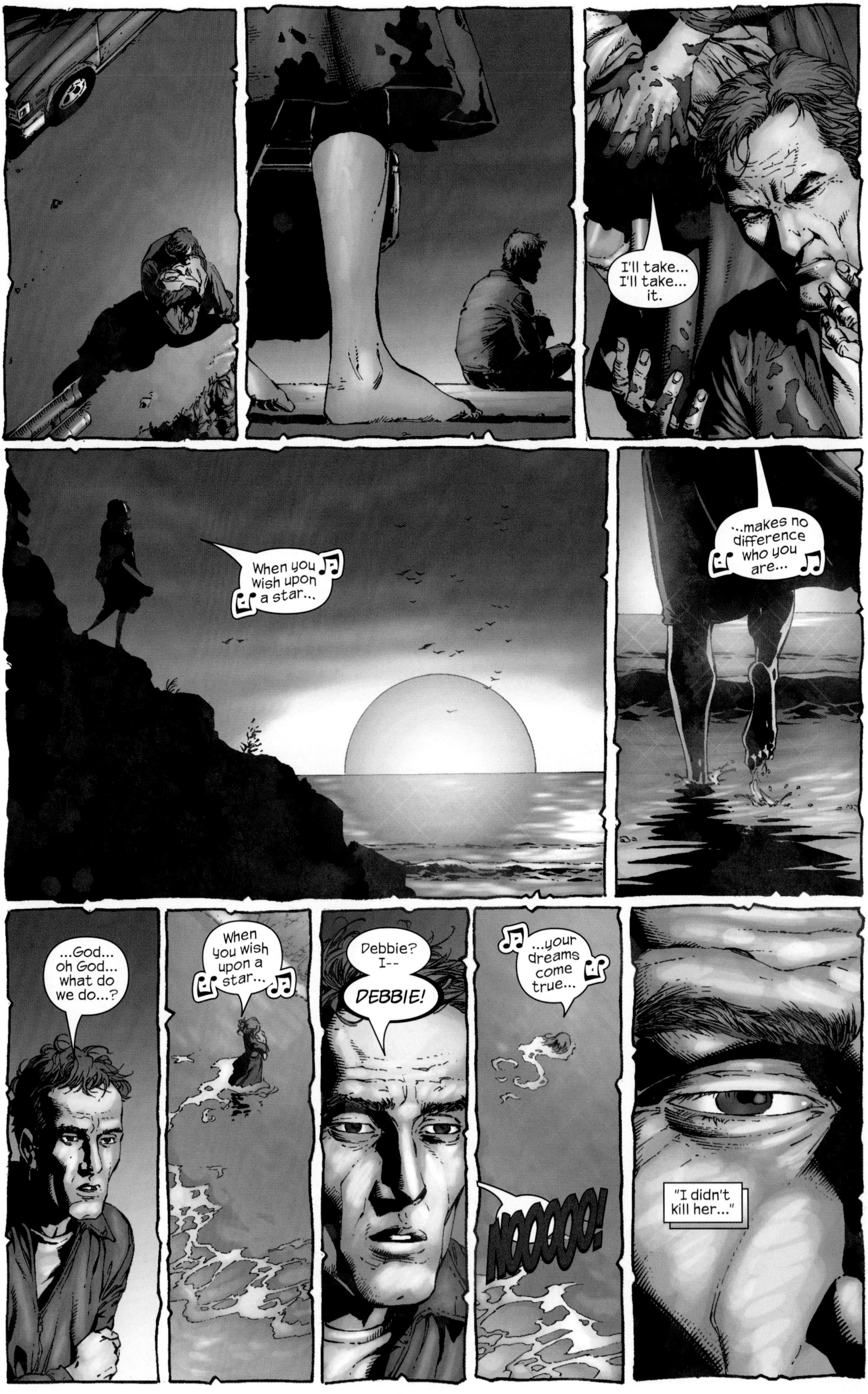
I'll take...
I'll take...
it.
When you wish upon a star...
...makes no difference who you are...
...God... oh God... what do we do...?
When you wish upon a star...
Debbie? I--
DEBBIE!
...your dreams come true...
NOOOOO!
"I didn't kill her..."

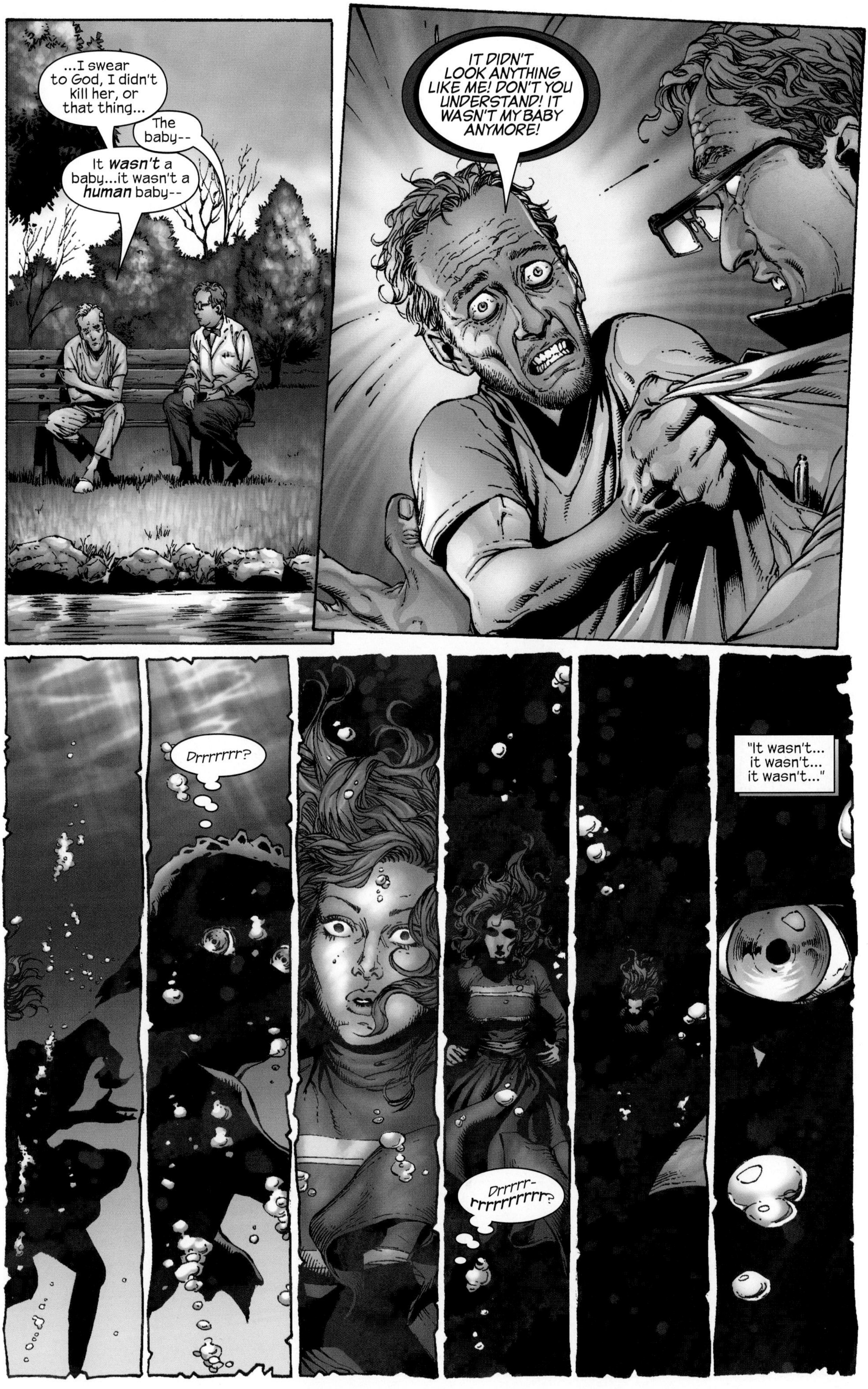
...I swear to God, I didn't kill her, or that thing...
The baby--
It *wasn't* a baby...it wasn't a *human* baby--
IT DIDN'T LOOK ANYTHING LIKE ME! DON'T YOU UNDERSTAND! IT WASN'T MY BABY ANYMORE!
Drrrrrrr?
Drrrrr-rrrrrrrrrr?
"It wasn't... it wasn't... it wasn't..."

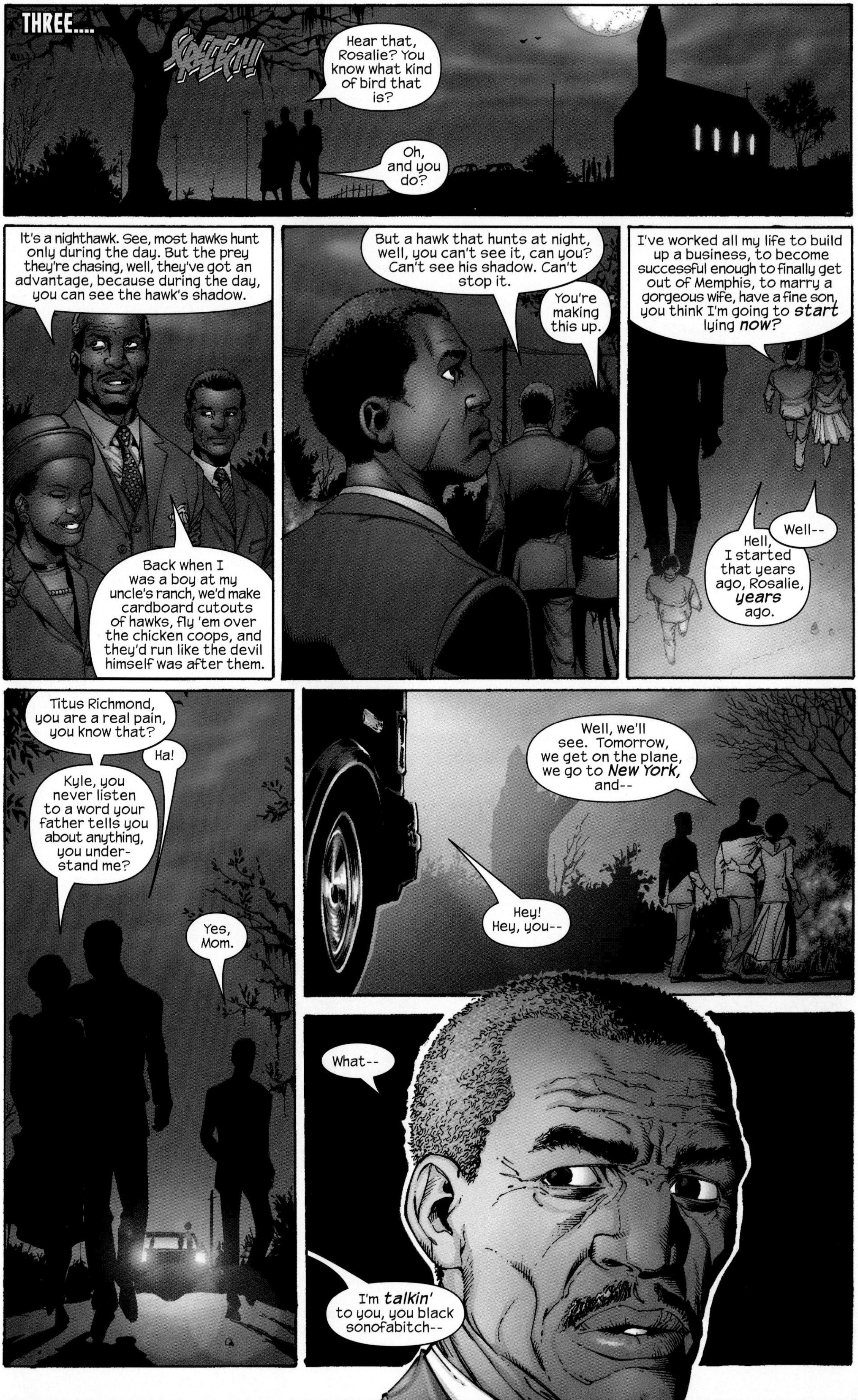
THREE....
SKREEEEH!
Hear that, Rosalie? You know what kind of bird that is?
Oh, and you do?
It's a nighthawk. See, most hawks hunt only during the day. But the prey they're chasing, well, they've got an advantage, because during the day, you can see the hawk's shadow.
Back when I was a boy at my uncle's ranch, we'd make cardboard cutouts of hawks, fly 'em over the chicken coops, and they'd run like the devil himself was after them.
But a hawk that hunts at night, well, you can't see it, can you? Can't see his shadow. Can't stop it.
You're making this up.
I've worked all my life to build up a business, to become successful enough to finally get out of Memphis, to marry a gorgeous wife, have a fine son, you think I'm going to start lying now?
Well--
Hell, I started that years ago, Rosalie, years ago.
Titus Richmond, you are a real pain, you know that?
Ha!
Kyle, you never listen to a word your father tells you about anything, you understand me?
Yes, Mom.
Well, we'll see. Tomorrow, we get on the plane, we go to New York, and--
Hey! Hey, you--
What--
I'm talkin' to you, you black sonofabitch--

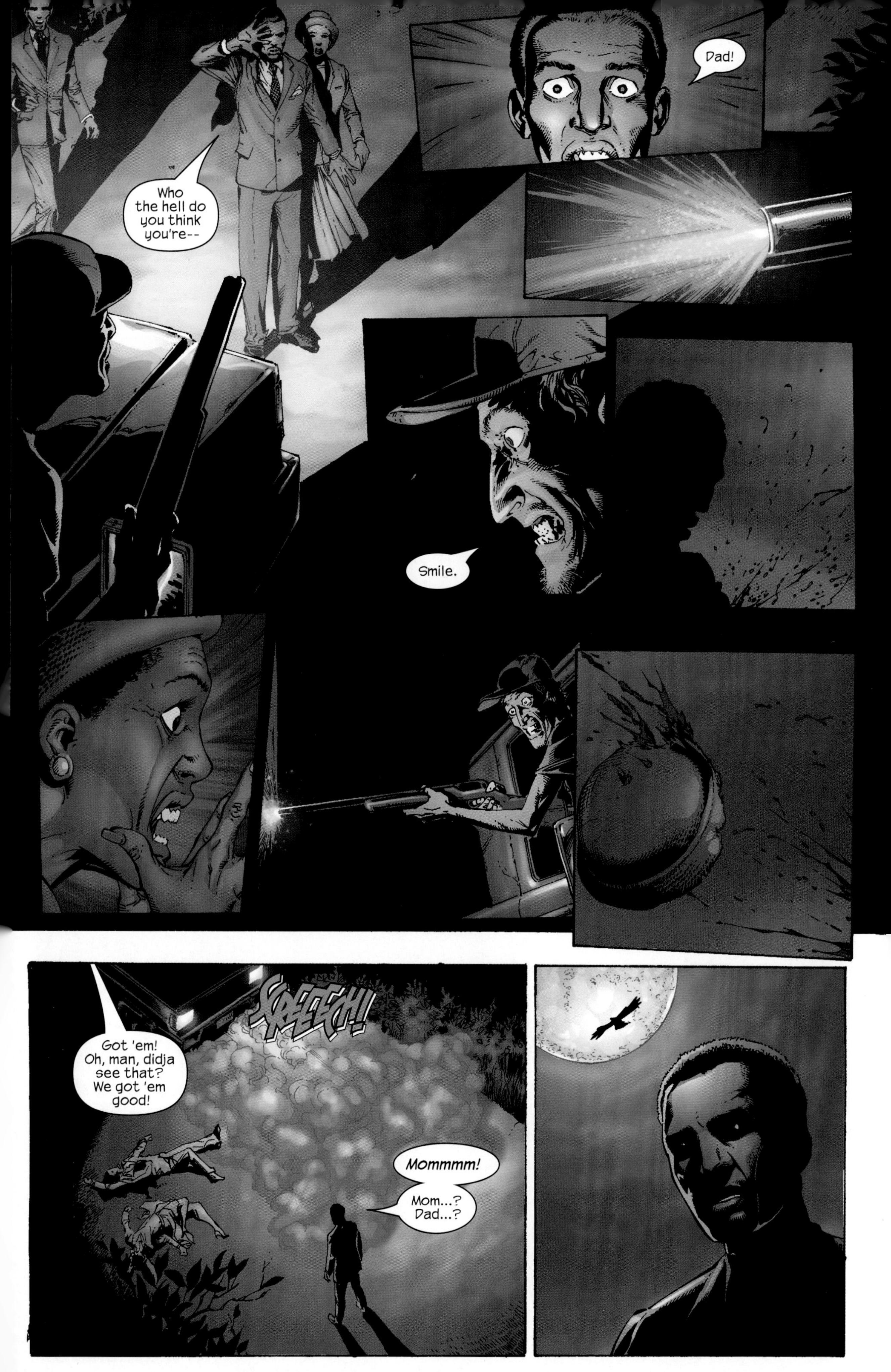
Dad!
Who the hell do you think you're--
Smile.
SCREECH!
Got 'em! Oh, man, didja see that? We got 'em good!
Mommmm!
Mom...? Dad...?

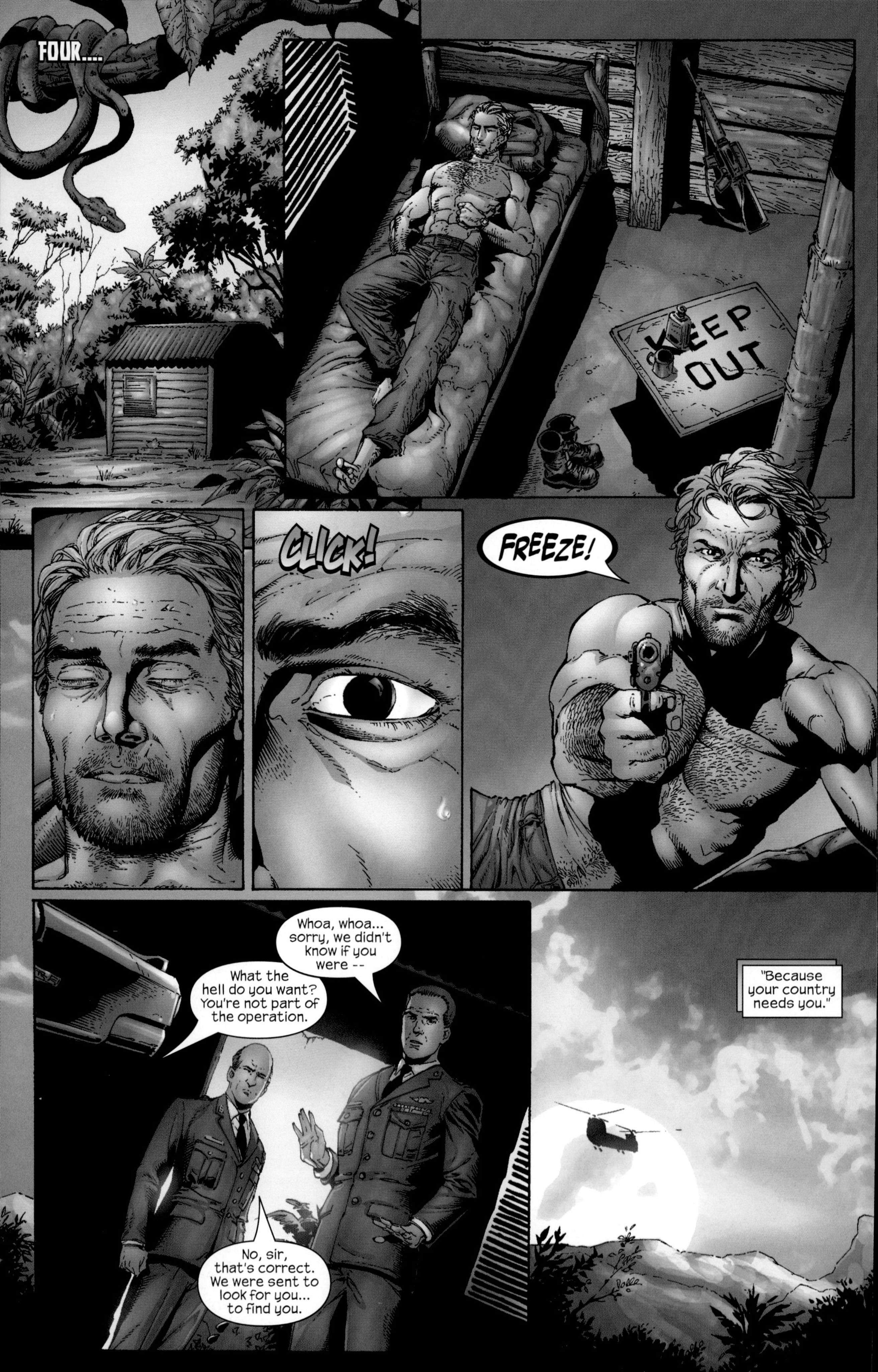
FOUR....
KEEP OUT
CLICK!
FREEZE!
What the hell do you want? You're not part of the operation.
Whoa, whoa... sorry, we didn't know if you were --
No, sir, that's correct. We were sent to look for you... to find you.
"Because your country needs you."

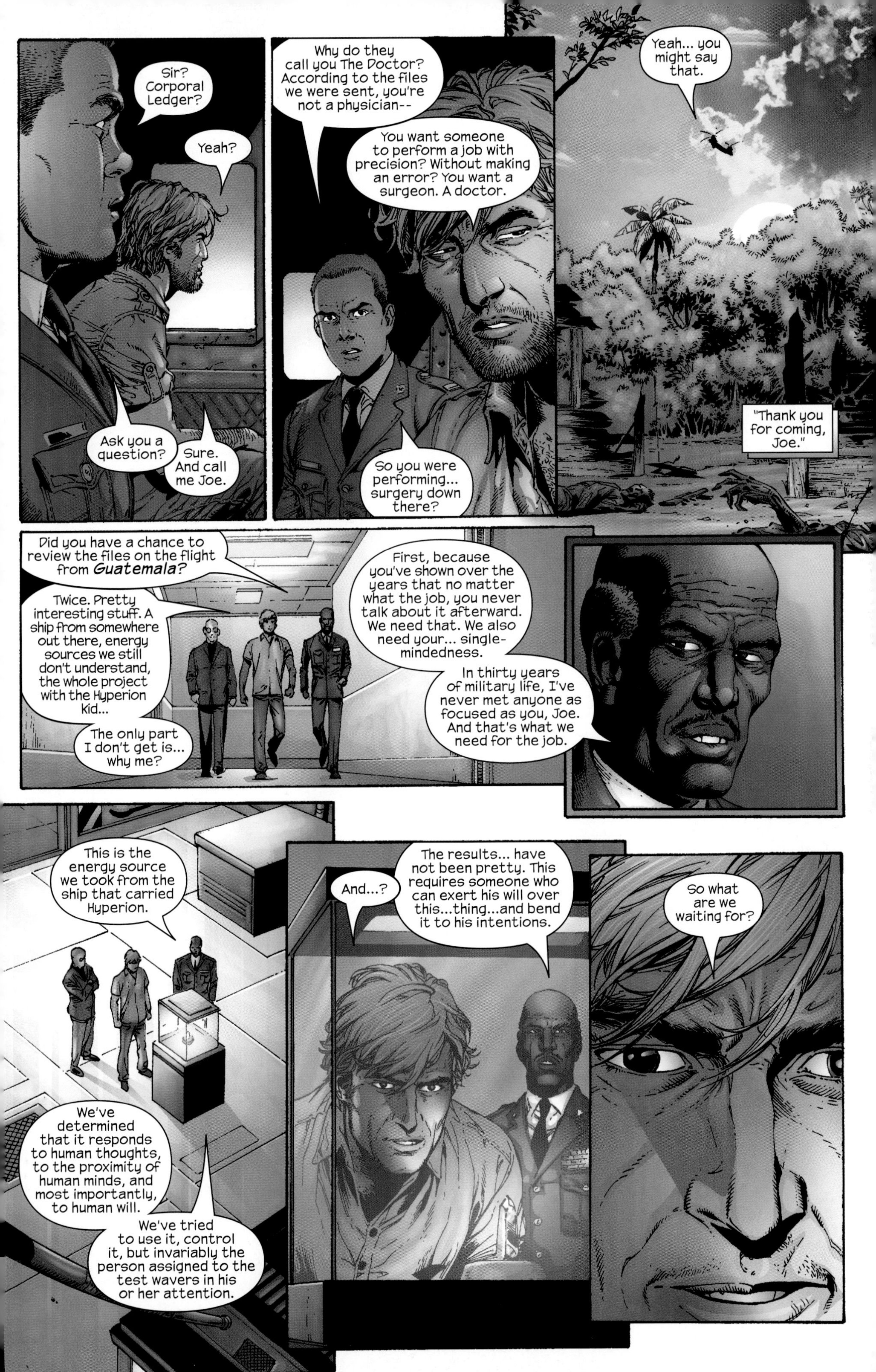
Sir? Corporal Ledger?
Yeah?
Ask you a question?
Sure. And call me Joe.
Why do they call you The Doctor? According to the files we were sent, you're not a physician--
You want someone to perform a job with precision? Without making an error? You want a surgeon. A doctor.
So you were performing... surgery down there?
Yeah... you might say that.
"Thank you for coming, Joe."
Did you have a chance to review the files on the flight from *Guatemala?*
Twice. Pretty interesting stuff. A ship from somewhere out there, energy sources we still don't understand, the whole project with the Hyperion Kid...
The only part I don't get is... why me?
First, because you've shown over the years that no matter what the job, you never talk about it afterward. We need that. We also need your... single-mindedness.
In thirty years of military life, I've never met anyone as focused as you, Joe. And that's what we need for the job.
This is the energy source we took from the ship that carried Hyperion.
We've determined that it responds to human thoughts, to the proximity of human minds, and most importantly, to human will.
We've tried to use it, control it, but invariably the person assigned to the test wavers in his or her attention.
And...?
The results... have not been pretty. This requires someone who can exert his will over this...thing...and bend it to his intentions.
So what are we waiting for?

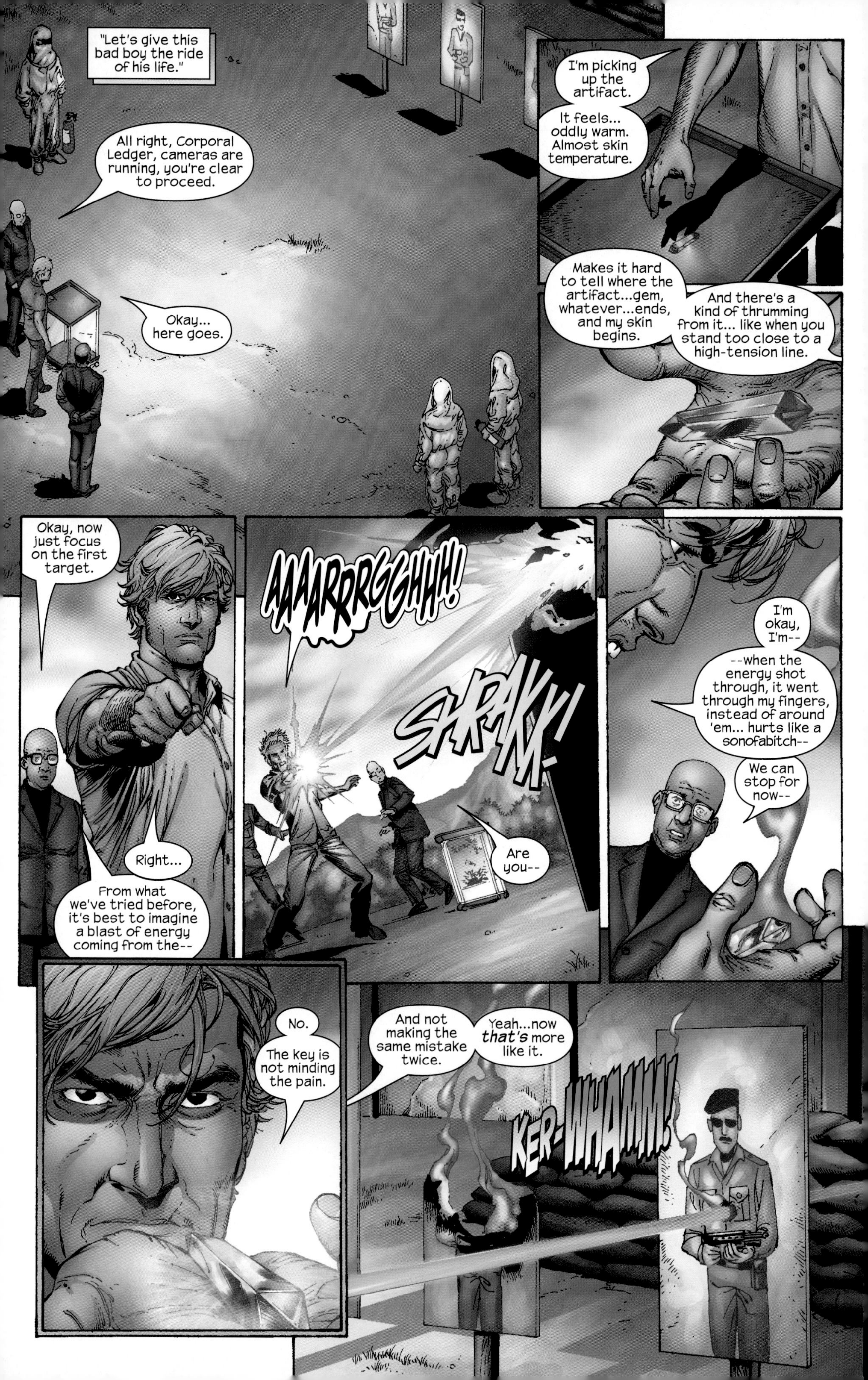

"Let's give this bad boy the ride of his life."
All right, Corporal Ledger, cameras are running, you're clear to proceed.
Okay... here goes.
I'm picking up the artifact.
It feels... oddly warm. Almost skin temperature.
Makes it hard to tell where the artifact...gem, whatever...ends, and my skin begins.
And there's a kind of thrumming from it... like when you stand too close to a high-tension line.
Okay, now just focus on the first target.
Right...
From what we've tried before, it's best to imagine a blast of energy coming from the--
AAAARRRGGHHH!
SHRAKK!
Are you--
I'm okay, I'm--
--when the energy shot through, it went through my fingers, instead of around 'em... hurts like a sonofabitch--
We can stop for now--
No.
The key is not minding the pain.
And not making the same mistake twice.
Yeah...now *that's* more like it.
KER-WHAMM!

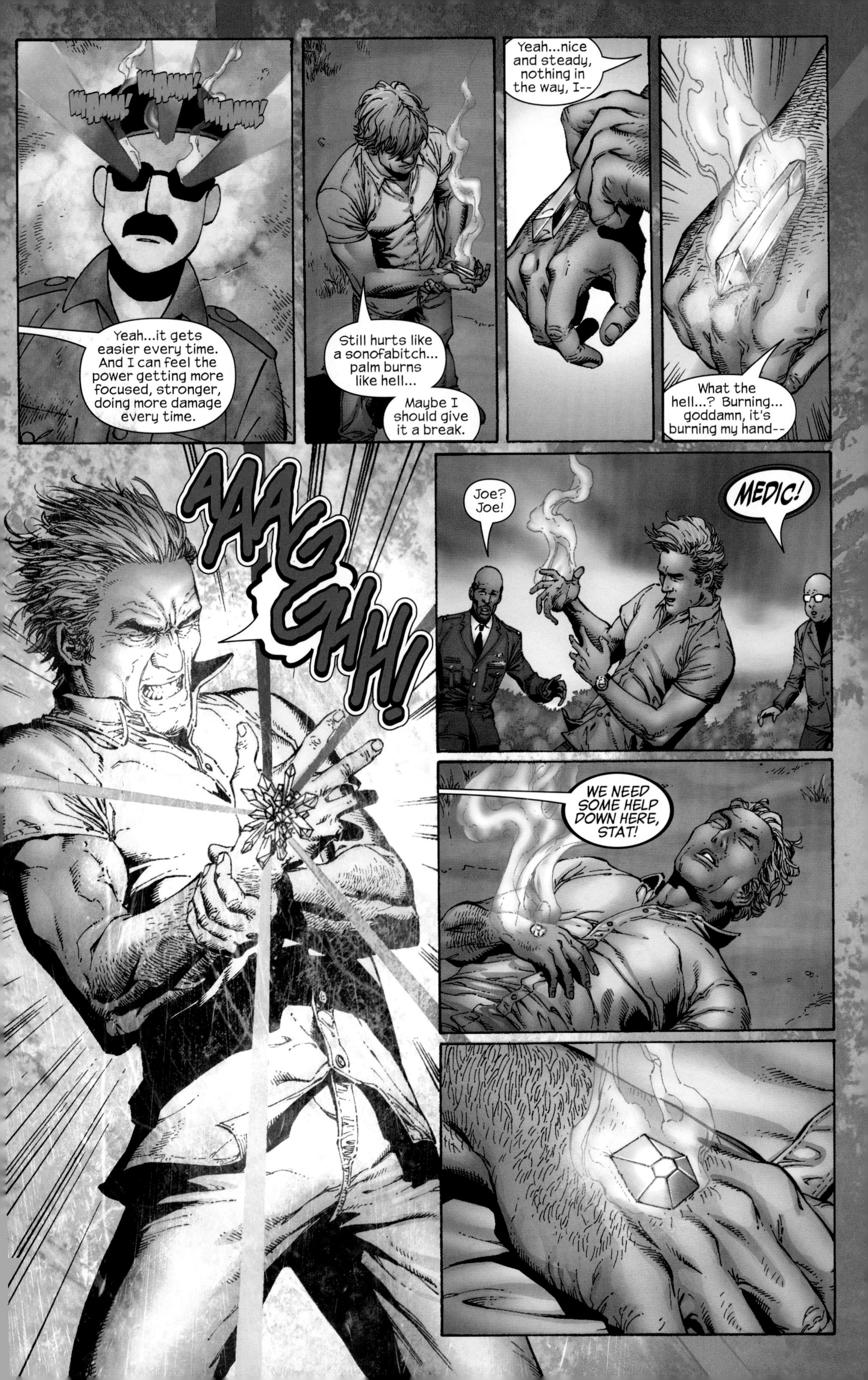
WHAM! WHAM! WHAM!
Yeah...it gets easier every time. And I can feel the power getting more focused, stronger, doing more damage every time.
Still hurts like a sonofabitch... palm burns like hell...
Maybe I should give it a break.
Yeah...nice and steady, nothing in the way, I--
What the hell...? Burning... goddamn, it's burning my hand--
AAAGHH!
Joe? Joe!
MEDIC!
WE NEED SOME HELP DOWN HERE, STAT!

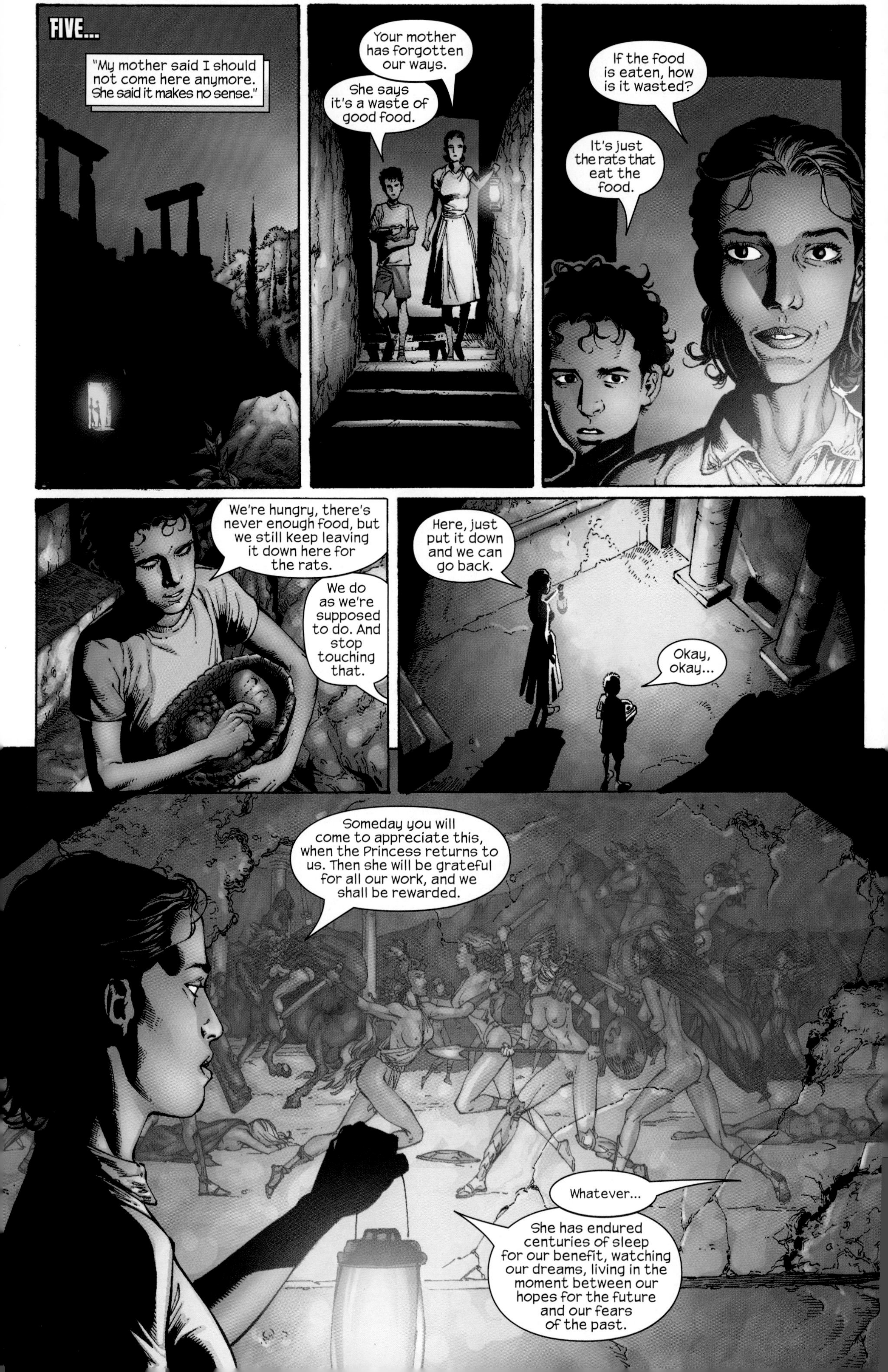
FIVE...
"My mother said I should not come here anymore. She said it makes no sense."
Your mother has forgotten our ways.
She says it's a waste of good food.
If the food is eaten, how is it wasted?
It's just the rats that eat the food.
We're hungry, there's never enough food, but we still keep leaving it down here for the rats.
We do as we're supposed to do. And stop touching that.
Here, just put it down and we can go back.
Okay, okay...
Someday you will come to appreciate this, when the Princess returns to us. Then she will be grateful for all our work, and we shall be rewarded.
Whatever...
She has endured centuries of sleep for our benefit, watching our dreams, living in the moment between our hopes for the future and our fears of the past.

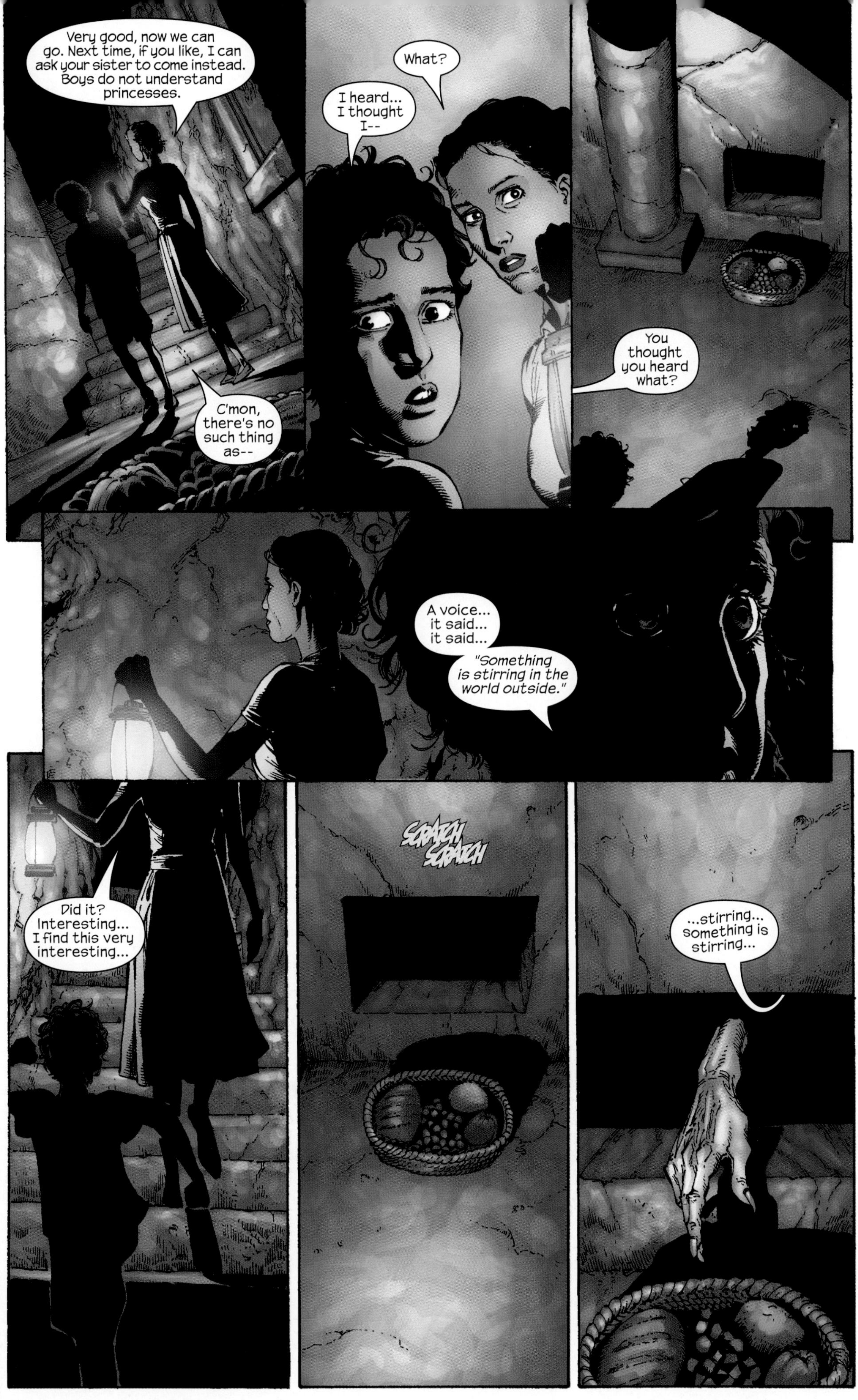

Very good, now we can go. Next time, if you like, I can ask your sister to come instead. Boys do not understand princesses.
C'mon, there's no such thing as--
What?
I heard... I thought I--
You thought you heard what?
A voice... it said... it said...
"Something is stirring in the world outside."
Did it? Interesting... I find this very interesting...
SCRATCH SCRATCH
...stirring... something is stirring...

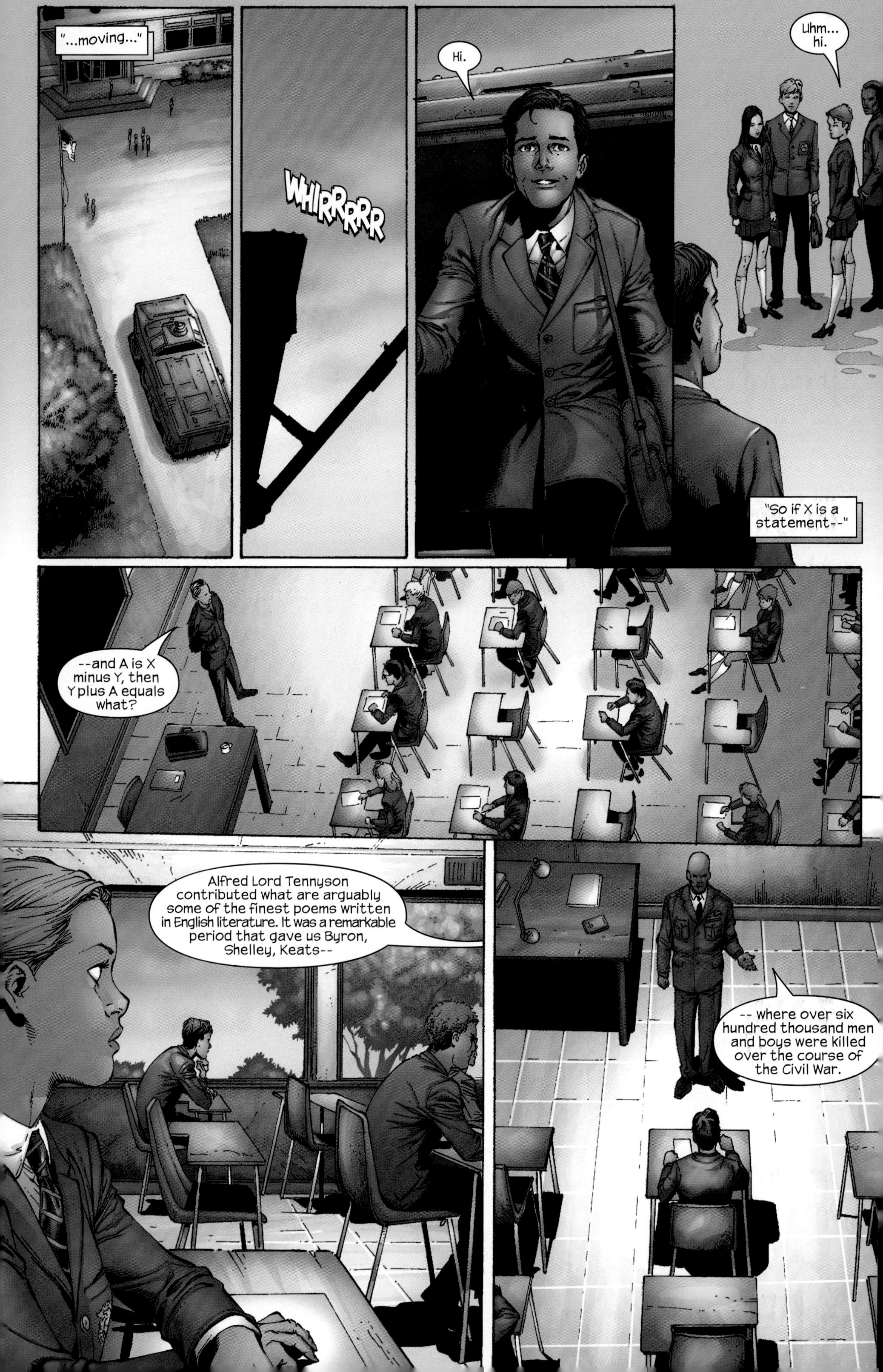
"...moving..."
WHIRRRRR
Hi.
Uhm... hi.
"So if X is a statement--"
--and A is X minus Y, then Y plus A equals what?
Alfred Lord Tennyson contributed what are arguably some of the finest poems written in English literature. It was a remarkable period that gave us Byron, Shelley, Keats--
-- where over six hundred thousand men and boys were killed over the course of the Civil War.

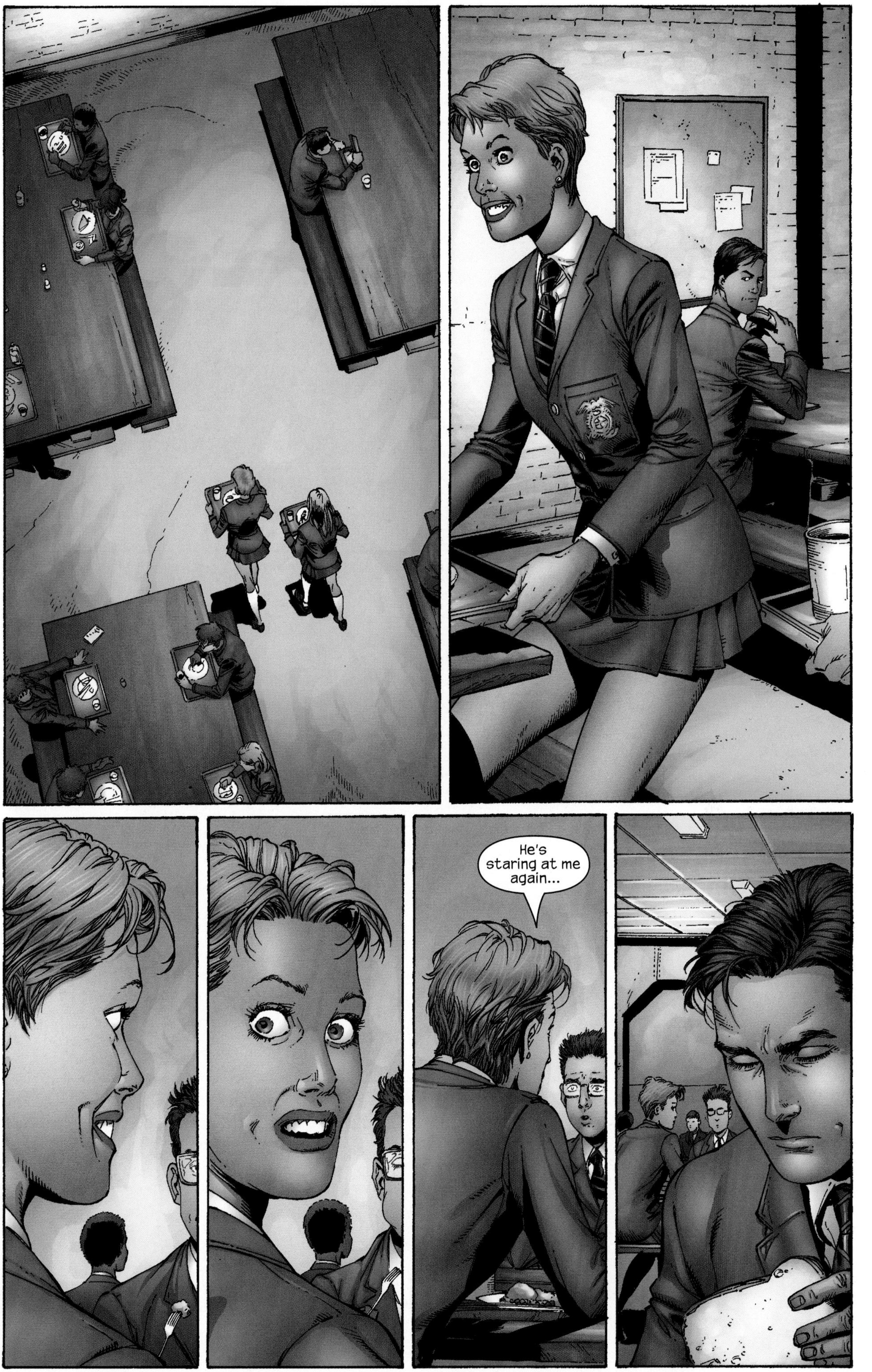
He's staring at me again...

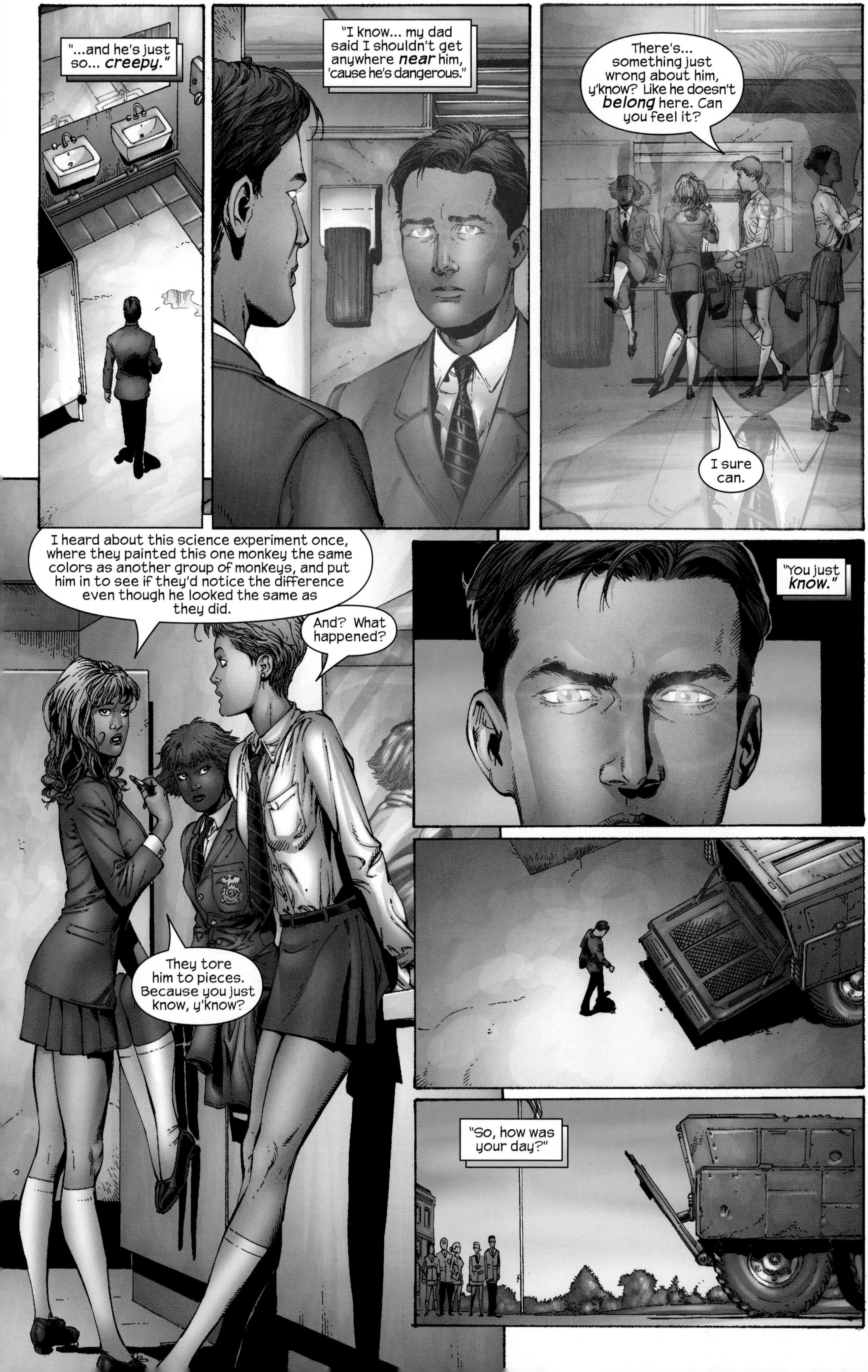
"...and he's just so... *creepy.*"
"I know... my dad said I shouldn't get anywhere *near* him, 'cause he's dangerous."
There's... something just wrong about him, y'know? Like he doesn't *belong* here. Can you feel it?
I sure can.
I heard about this science experiment once, where they painted this one monkey the same colors as another group of monkeys, and put him in to see if they'd notice the difference even though he looked the same as they did.
And? What happened?
They tore him to pieces. Because you just know, y'know?
"You just *know.*"
"So, how was your day?"

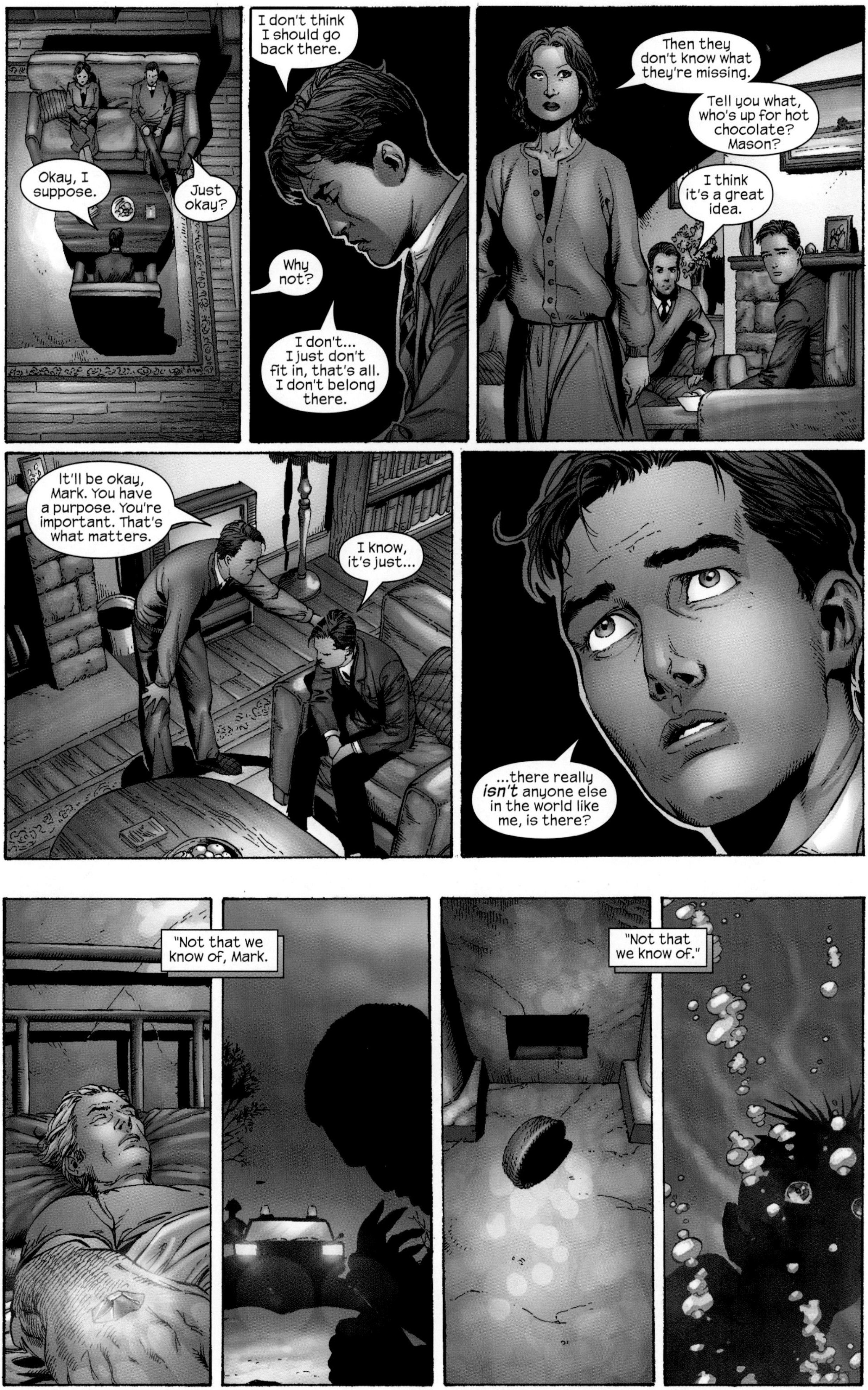
Okay, I suppose.
Just okay?
I don't think I should go back there.
Why not?
I don't... I just don't fit in, that's all. I don't belong there.
Then they don't know what they're missing.
Tell you what, who's up for hot chocolate? Mason?
I think it's a great idea.
It'll be okay, Mark. You have a purpose. You're important. That's what matters.
I know, it's just...
...there really *isn't* anyone else in the world like me, is there?
"Not that we know of, Mark.
"Not that we know of."

Coming Out

#3

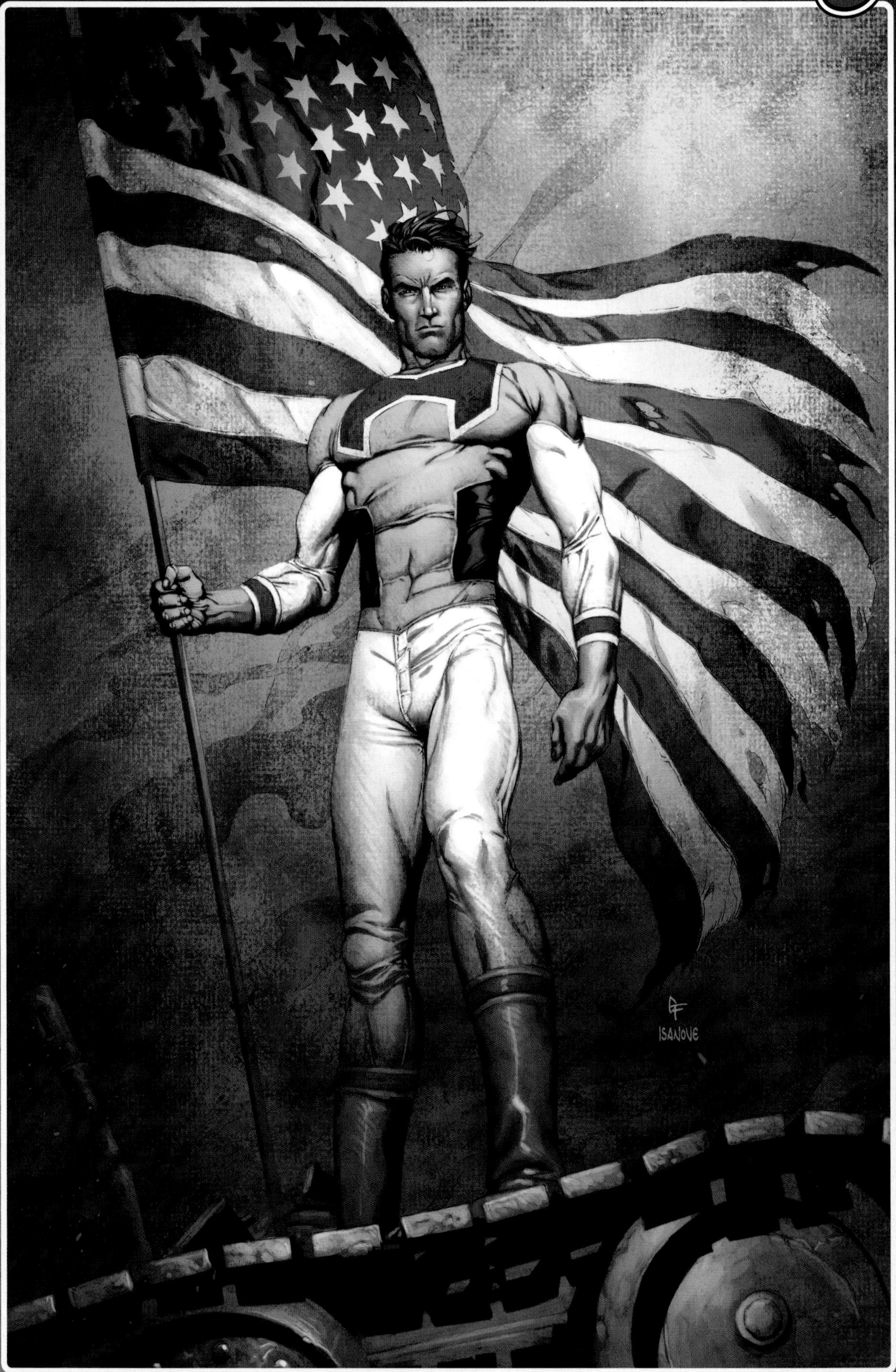
ISANOVE

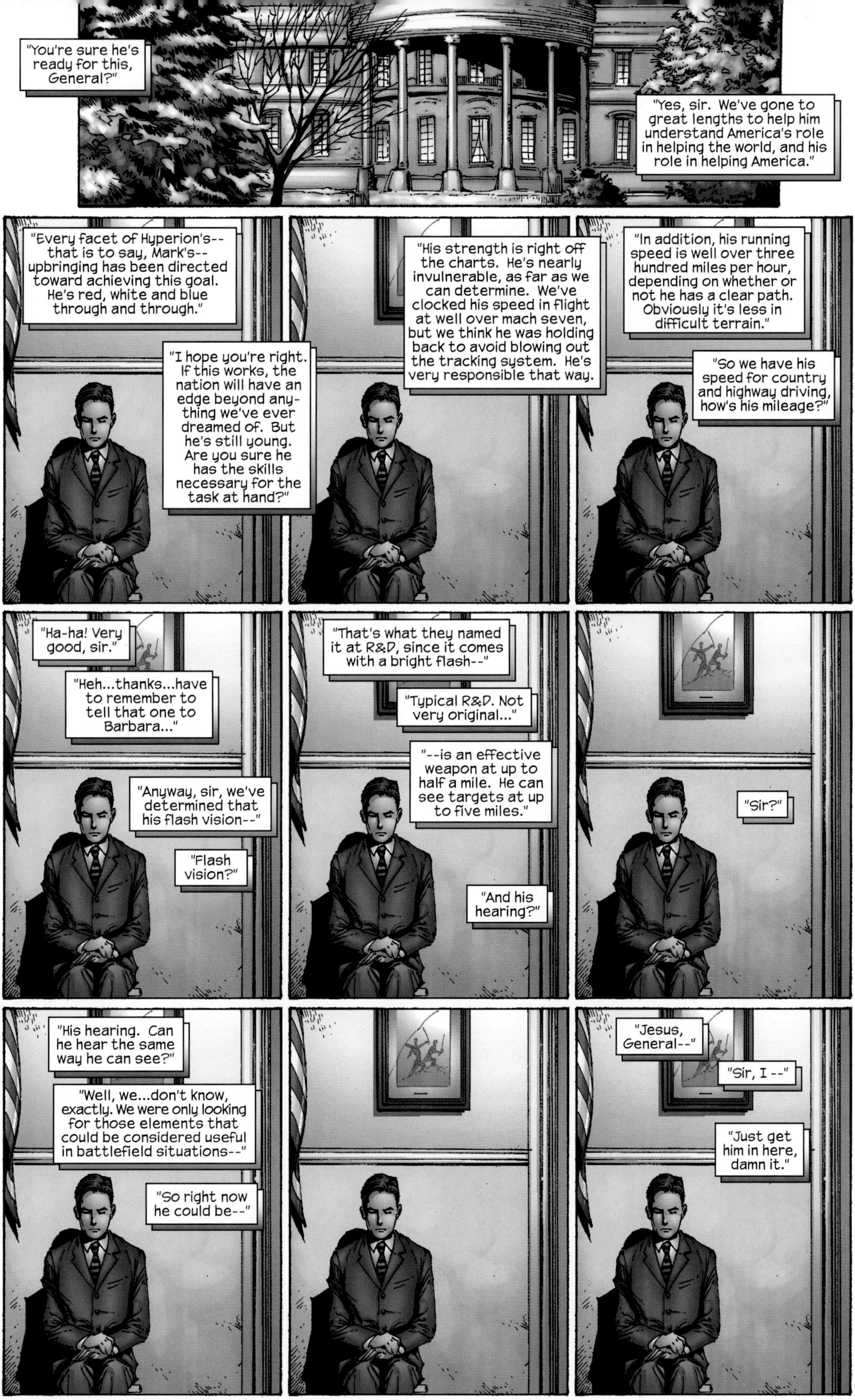
"You're sure he's ready for this, General?"
"Yes, sir. We've gone to great lengths to help him understand America's role in helping the world, and his role in helping America."
"Every facet of Hyperion's--that is to say, Mark's--upbringing has been directed toward achieving this goal. He's red, white and blue through and through."
"I hope you're right. If this works, the nation will have an edge beyond anything we've ever dreamed of. But he's still young. Are you sure he has the skills necessary for the task at hand?"
"His strength is right off the charts. He's nearly invulnerable, as far as we can determine. We've clocked his speed in flight at well over mach seven, but we think he was holding back to avoid blowing out the tracking system. He's very responsible that way.
"In addition, his running speed is well over three hundred miles per hour, depending on whether or not he has a clear path. Obviously it's less in difficult terrain."
"So we have his speed for country and highway driving, how's his mileage?"
"Ha-ha! Very good, sir."
"Heh...thanks...have to remember to tell that one to Barbara..."
"Anyway, sir, we've determined that his flash vision--"
"Flash vision?"
"That's what they named it at R&D, since it comes with a bright flash--"
"Typical R&D. Not very original..."
"--is an effective weapon at up to half a mile. He can see targets at up to five miles."
"And his hearing?"
"Sir?"
"His hearing. Can he hear the same way he can see?"
"Well, we...don't know, exactly. We were only looking for those elements that could be considered useful in battlefield situations--"
"So right now he could be--"
"Jesus, General--"
"Sir, I --"
"Just get him in here, damn it."

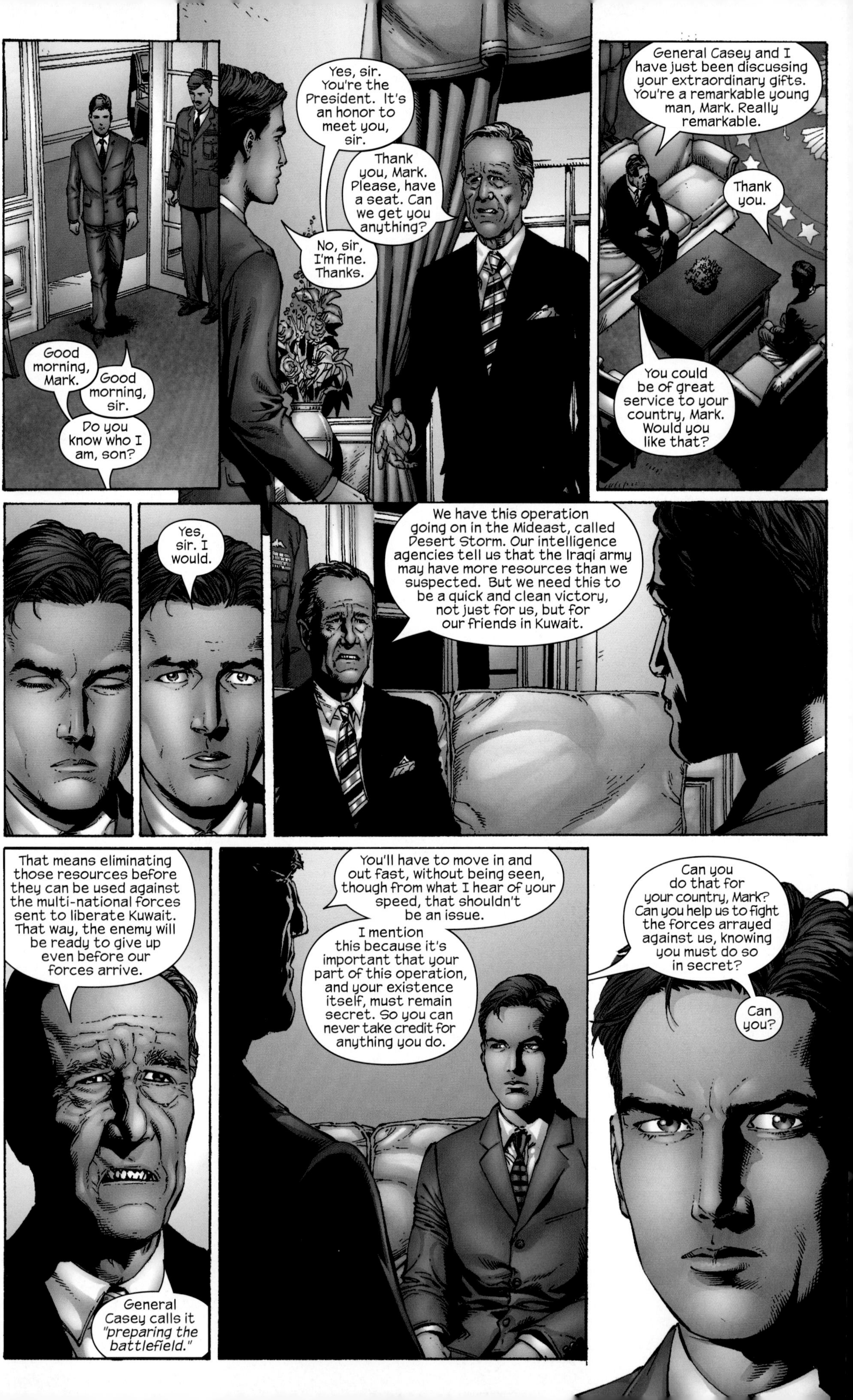
Good morning, Mark.
Good morning, sir.
Do you know who I am, son?
Yes, sir. You're the President. It's an honor to meet you, sir.
Thank you, Mark. Please, have a seat. Can we get you anything?
No, sir, I'm fine. Thanks.
General Casey and I have just been discussing your extraordinary gifts. You're a remarkable young man, Mark. Really remarkable.
Thank you.
You could be of great service to your country, Mark. Would you like that?
Yes, sir. I would.
We have this operation going on in the Mideast, called Desert Storm. Our intelligence agencies tell us that the Iraqi army may have more resources than we suspected. But we need this to be a quick and clean victory, not just for us, but for our friends in Kuwait.
That means eliminating those resources before they can be used against the multi-national forces sent to liberate Kuwait. That way, the enemy will be ready to give up even before our forces arrive.
General Casey calls it *"preparing the battlefield."*
You'll have to move in and out fast, without being seen, though from what I hear of your speed, that shouldn't be an issue.
I mention this because it's important that your part of this operation, and your existence itself, must remain secret. So you can never take credit for anything you do.
Can you do that for your country, Mark? Can you help us to fight the forces arrayed against us, knowing you must do so in secret?
Can you?

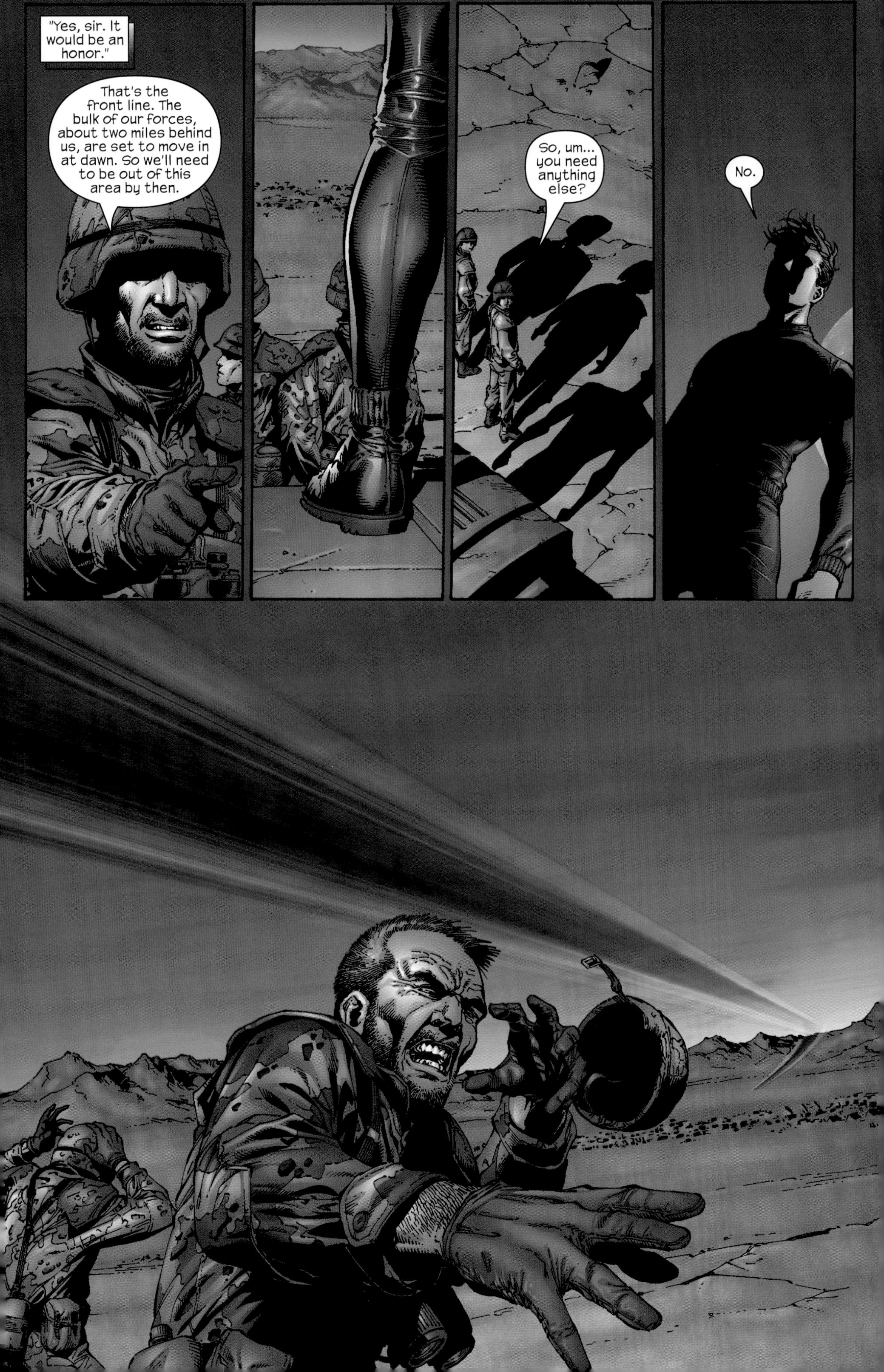
"Yes, sir. It would be an honor."
That's the front line. The bulk of our forces, about two miles behind us, are set to move in at dawn. So we'll need to be out of this area by then.
So, um... you need anything else?
No.

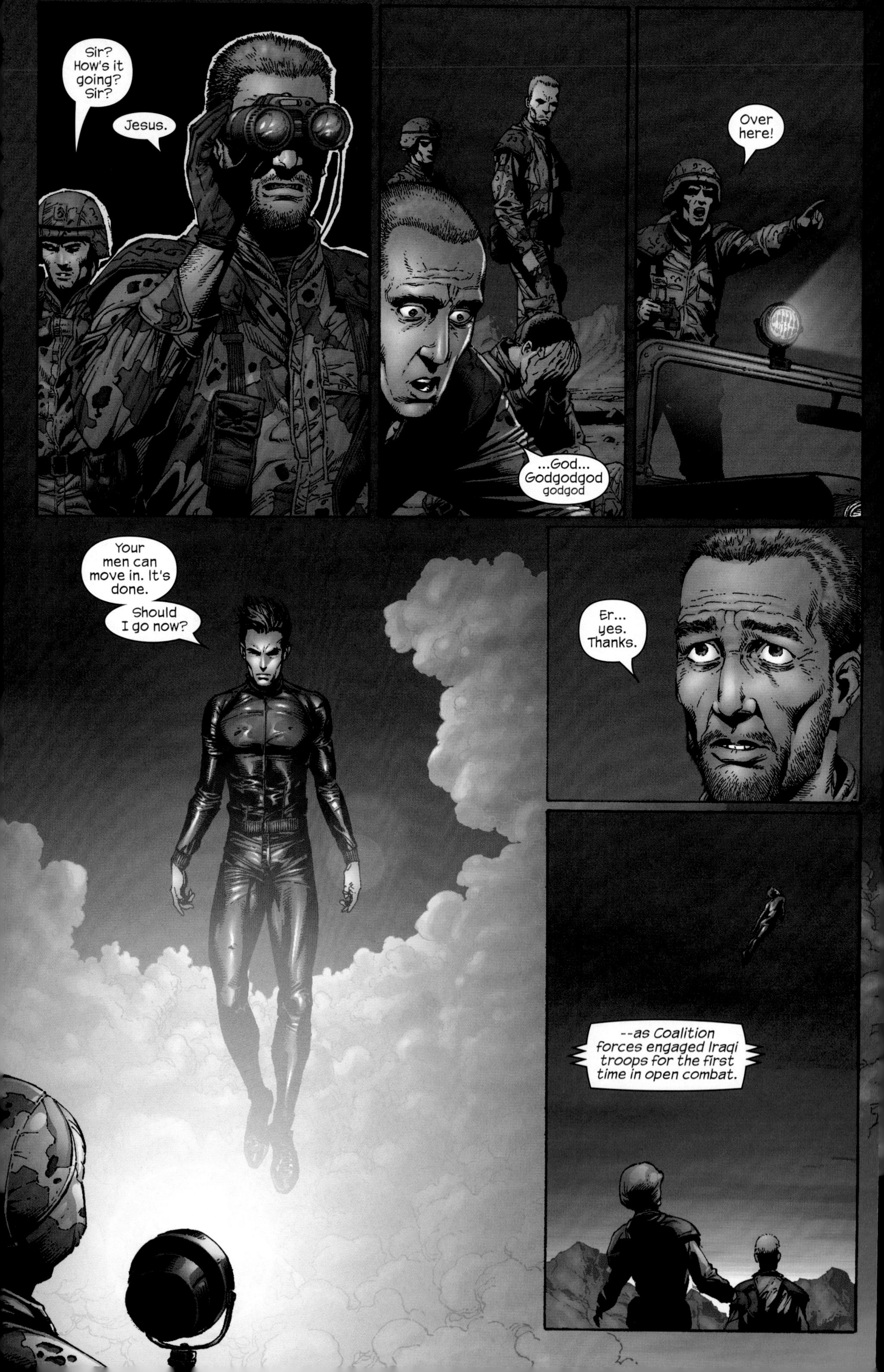
Sir? How's it going? Sir?
Jesus.
...God... Godgodgod godgod
Over here!
Your men can move in. It's done.
Should I go now?
Er... yes. Thanks.
--as Coalition forces engaged Iraqi troops for the first time in open combat.

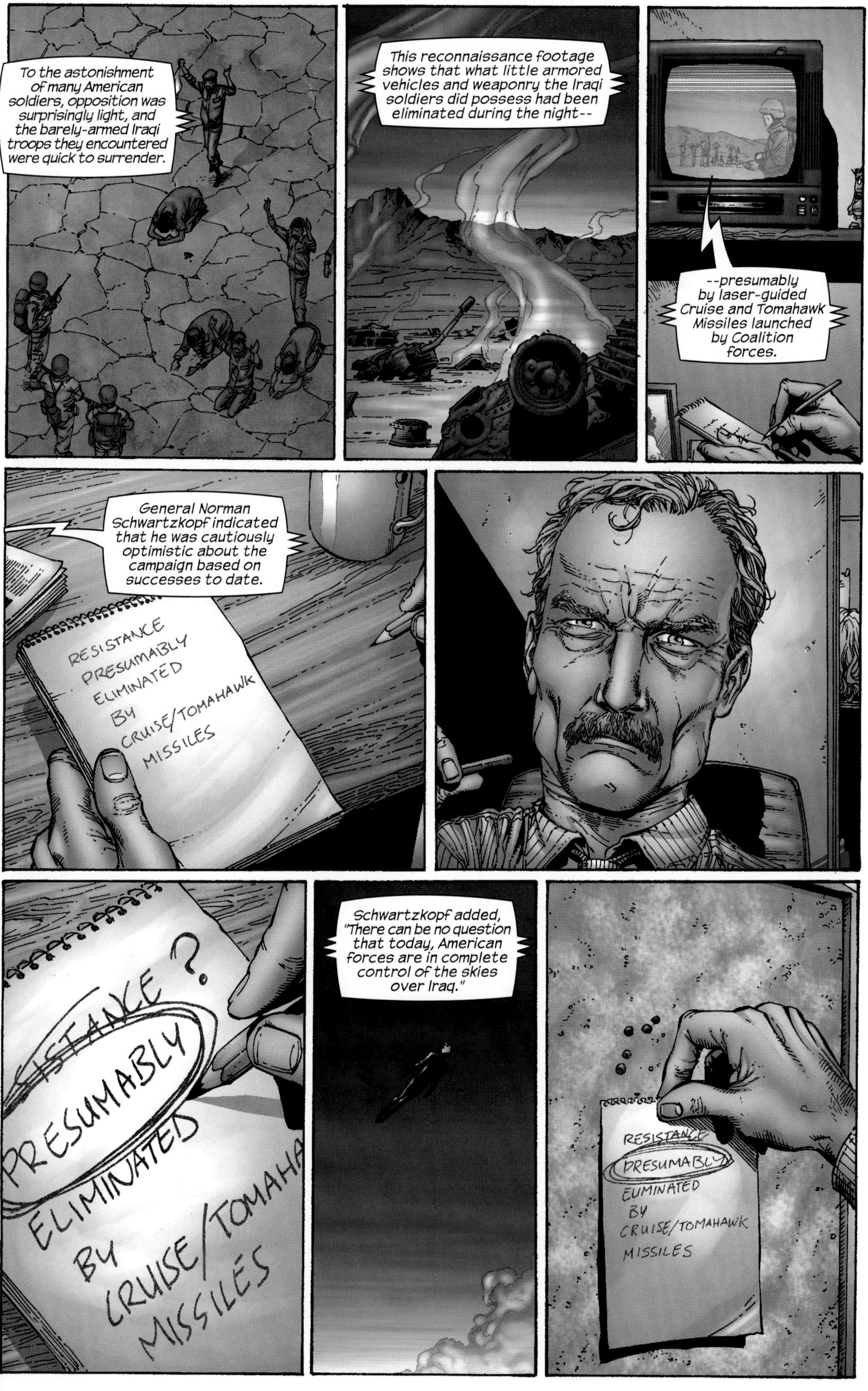
To the astonishment of many American soldiers, opposition was surprisingly light, and the barely-armed Iraqi troops they encountered were quick to surrender.
This reconnaissance footage shows that what little armored vehicles and weaponry the Iraqi soldiers did possess had been eliminated during the night--
--presumably by laser-guided Cruise and Tomahawk Missiles launched by Coalition forces.
General Norman Schwartzkopf indicated that he was cautiously optimistic about the campaign based on successes to date.
RESISTANCE PRESUMABLY ELIMINATED BY CRUISE/TOMAHAWK MISSILES
SISTANCE ? PRESUMABLY ELIMINATED BY CRUISE/TOMAHA MISSILES
Schwartzkopf added, "There can be no question that today, American forces are in complete control of the skies over Iraq."
RESISTANCE PRESUMABLY ELIMINATED BY CRUISE/TOMAHAWK MISSILES

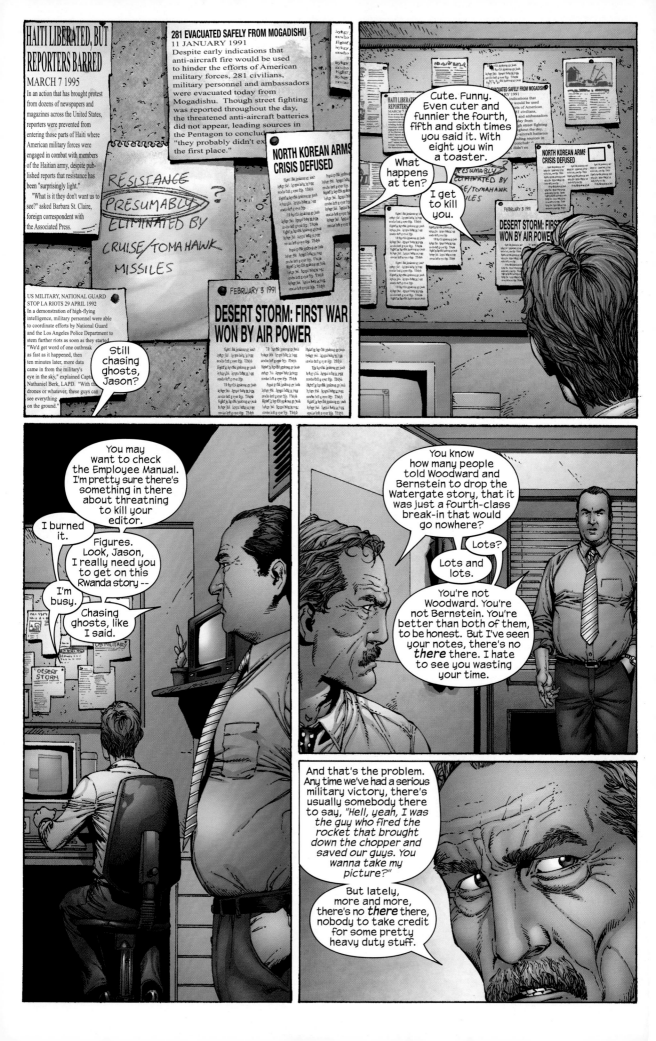

HAITI LIBERATED, BUT REPORTERS BARRED

MARCH 7 1995

In an action that has brought protest from dozens of newspapers and magazines across the United States, reporters were prevented from entering those parts of Haiti where American military forces were engaged in combat with members of the Haitian army, despite published reports that resistance has been "surprisingly light."

"What is it they don't want us to see?" asked Barbara St. Claire, foreign correspondent with the Associated Press.

281 EVACUATED SAFELY FROM MOGADISHU

11 JANUARY 1991

Despite early indications that anti-aircraft fire would be used to hinder the efforts of American military forces, 281 civilians, military personnel and ambassadors were evacuated today from Mogadishu. Though street fighting was reported throughout the day, the threatened anti-aircraft batteries did not appear, leading sources in the Pentagon to conclude "they probably didn't exist in the first place."

NORTH KOREAN ARMS CRISIS DEFUSED

RESISTANCE PRESUMABLY ELIMINATED BY CRUISE/TOMAHAWK MISSILES

US MILITARY, NATIONAL GUARD STOP LA RIOTS 29 APRIL 1992

In a demonstration of high-flying intelligence, military personnel were able to coordinate efforts by National Guard and the Los Angeles Police Department to stem further riots as soon as they started. "We'd get word of one outbreak as fast as it happened, then ten minutes later, more data came in from the military's eye in the sky," explained Capt. Nathaniel Berk, LAPD. "With the drones or whatever, these guys can see everything on the ground."

FEBRUARY 3 1991

DESERT STORM: FIRST WAR WON BY AIR POWER

Still chasing ghosts, Jason?

Cute. Funny. Even cuter and funnier the fourth, fifth and sixth times you said it. With eight you win a toaster.

What happens at ten?

I get to kill you.

You may want to check the Employee Manual. I'm pretty sure there's something in there about threatning to kill your editor.

I burned it.

Figures. Look, Jason, I really need you to get on this Rwanda story --

I'm busy.

Chasing ghosts, like I said.

You know how many people told Woodward and Bernstein to drop the Watergate story, that it was just a fourth-class break-in that would go nowhere?

Lots?

Lots and lots.

You're not Woodward. You're not Bernstein. You're better than both of them, to be honest. But I've seen your notes, there's no *there* there. I hate to see you wasting your time.

And that's the problem. Any time we've had a serious military victory, there's usually somebody there to say, "Hell, yeah, I was the guy who fired the rocket that brought down the chopper and saved our guys. You wanna take my picture?"

But lately, more and more, there's no *there* there, nobody to take credit for some pretty heavy duty stuff.

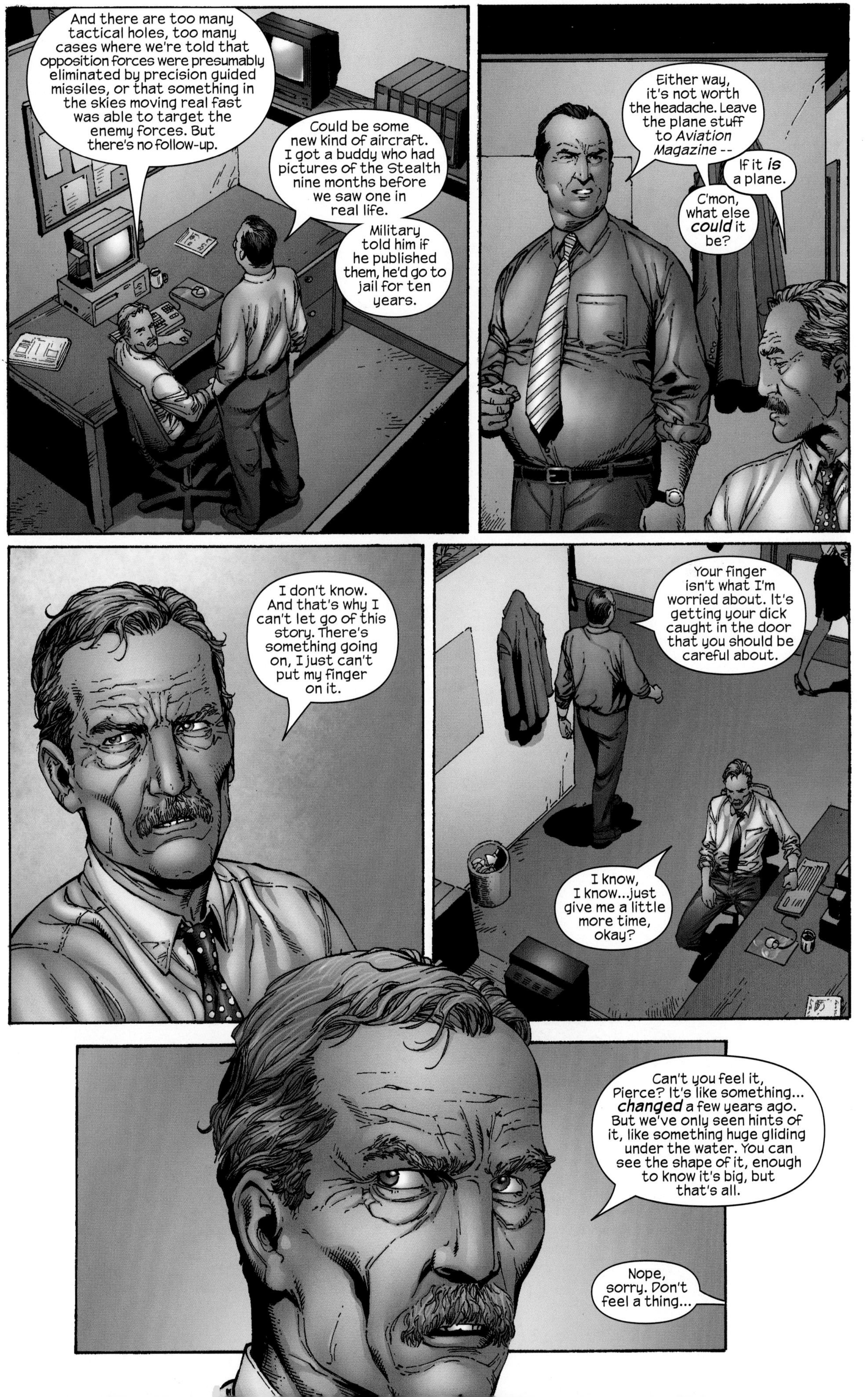

And there are too many tactical holes, too many cases where we're told that opposition forces were presumably eliminated by precision guided missiles, or that something in the skies moving real fast was able to target the enemy forces. But there's no follow-up.
Could be some new kind of aircraft. I got a buddy who had pictures of the Stealth nine months before we saw one in real life.
Military told him if he published them, he'd go to jail for ten years.
Either way, it's not worth the headache. Leave the plane stuff to *Aviation Magazine* --
If it **is** a plane.
C'mon, what else **could** it be?
I don't know. And that's why I can't let go of this story. There's something going on, I just can't put my finger on it.
Your finger isn't what I'm worried about. It's getting your dick caught in the door that you should be careful about.
I know, I know...just give me a little more time, okay?
Can't you feel it, Pierce? It's like something... **changed** a few years ago. But we've only seen hints of it, like something huge gliding under the water. You can see the shape of it, enough to know it's big, but that's all.
Nope, sorry. Don't feel a thing...

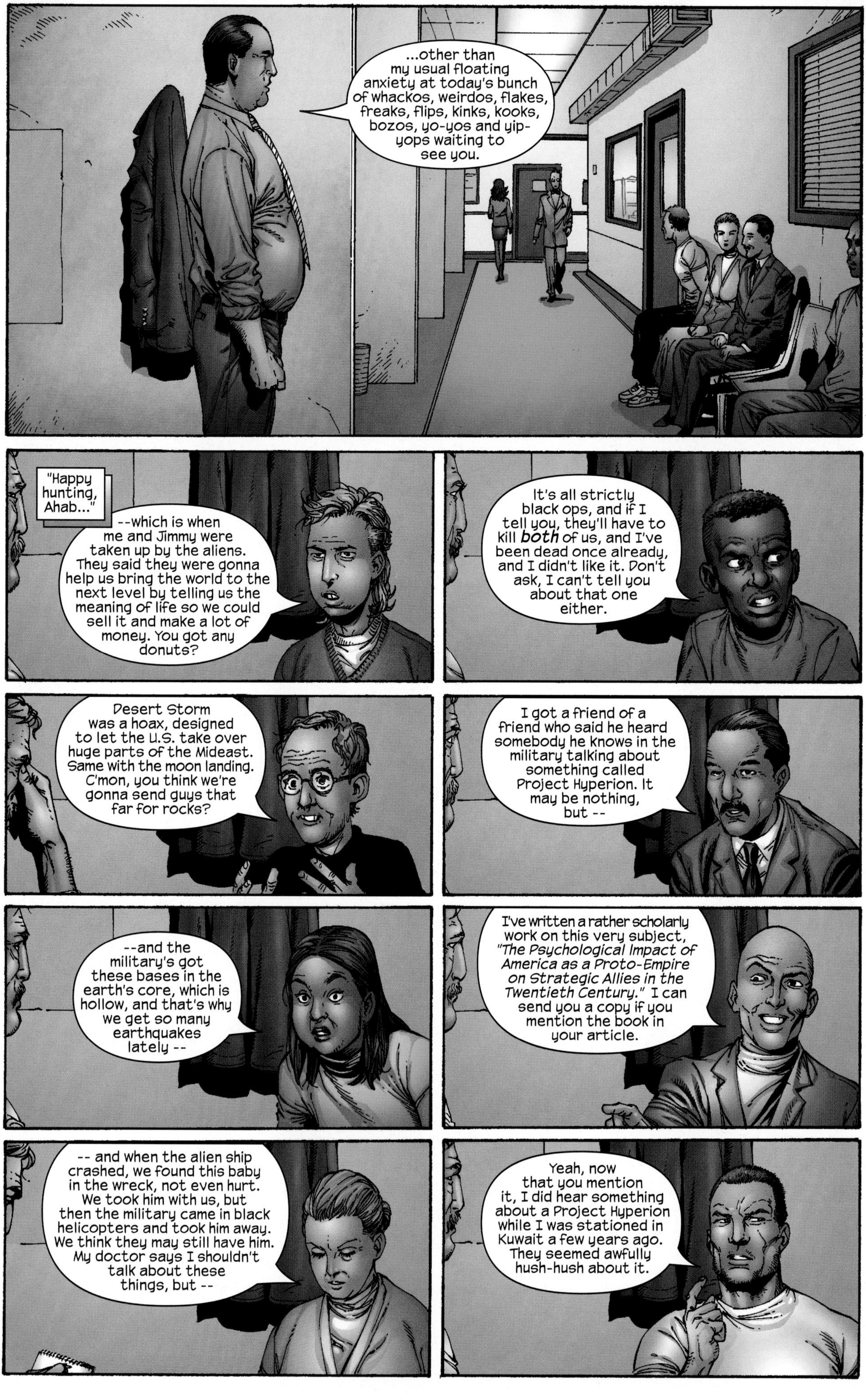
...other than my usual floating anxiety at today's bunch of whackos, weirdos, flakes, freaks, flips, kinks, kooks, bozos, yo-yos and yip-yops waiting to see you.
"Happy hunting, Ahab..."
--which is when me and Jimmy were taken up by the aliens. They said they were gonna help us bring the world to the next level by telling us the meaning of life so we could sell it and make a lot of money. You got any donuts?
It's all strictly black ops, and if I tell you, they'll have to kill both of us, and I've been dead once already, and I didn't like it. Don't ask, I can't tell you about that one either.
Desert Storm was a hoax, designed to let the U.S. take over huge parts of the Mideast. Same with the moon landing. C'mon, you think we're gonna send guys that far for rocks?
I got a friend of a friend who said he heard somebody he knows in the military talking about something called Project Hyperion. It may be nothing, but --
--and the military's got these bases in the earth's core, which is hollow, and that's why we get so many earthquakes lately --
I've written a rather scholarly work on this very subject, "The Psychological Impact of America as a Proto-Empire on Strategic Allies in the Twentieth Century." I can send you a copy if you mention the book in your article.
-- and when the alien ship crashed, we found this baby in the wreck, not even hurt. We took him with us, but then the military came in black helicopters and took him away. We think they may still have him. My doctor says I shouldn't talk about these things, but --
Yeah, now that you mention it, I did hear something about a Project Hyperion while I was stationed in Kuwait a few years ago. They seemed awfully hush-hush about it.

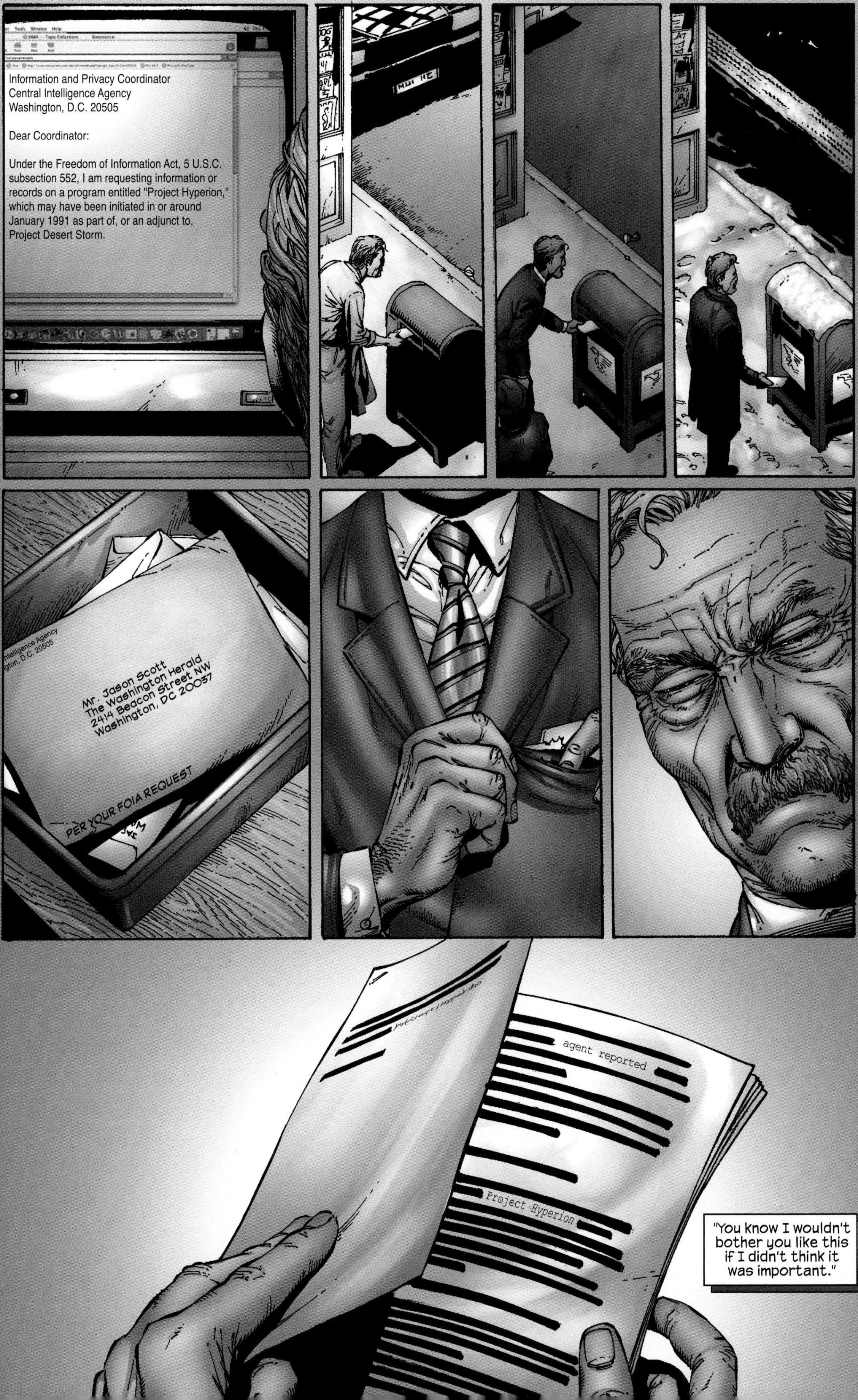
Information and Privacy Coordinator
Central Intelligence Agency
Washington, D.C. 20505

Dear Coordinator:

Under the Freedom of Information Act, 5 U.S.C. subsection 552, I am requesting information or records on a program entitled "Project Hyperion," which may have been initiated in or around January 1991 as part of, or an adjunct to, Project Desert Storm.
Mr. Jason Scott
The Washington Herald
2414 Beacon Street NW
Washington, DC 20037
PER YOUR FOIA REQUEST
[redacted] agent reported [redacted]
[redacted] Project Hyperion [redacted]
"You know I wouldn't bother you like this if I didn't think it was important."

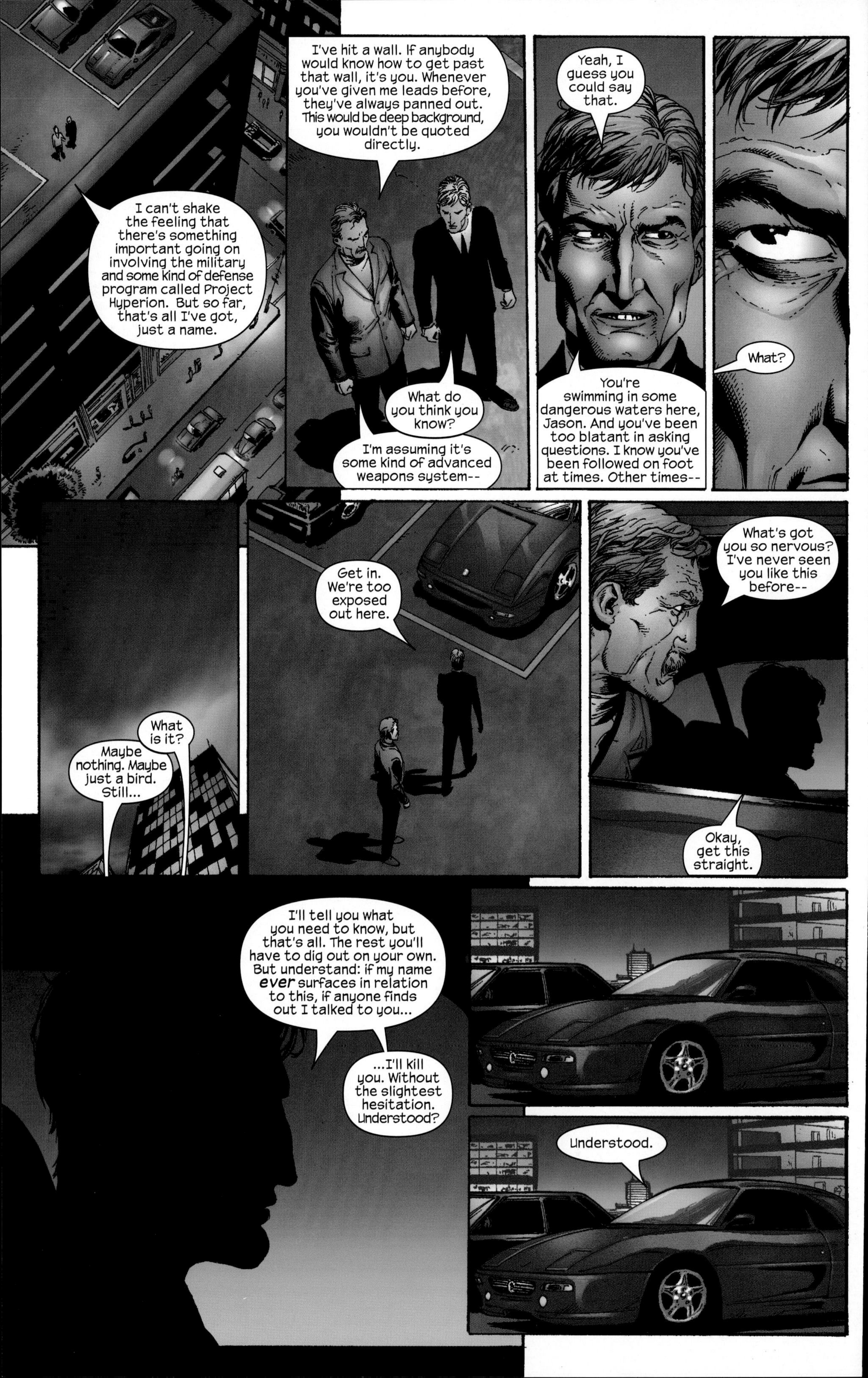
I can't shake the feeling that there's something important going on involving the military and some kind of defense program called Project Hyperion. But so far, that's all I've got, just a name.
I've hit a wall. If anybody would know how to get past that wall, it's you. Whenever you've given me leads before, they've always panned out. This would be deep background, you wouldn't be quoted directly.
What do you think you know?
I'm assuming it's some kind of advanced weapons system--
Yeah, I guess you could say that.
You're swimming in some dangerous waters here, Jason. And you've been too blatant in asking questions. I know you've been followed on foot at times. Other times--
What?
What is it?
Maybe nothing. Maybe just a bird. Still...
Get in. We're too exposed out here.
What's got you so nervous? I've never seen you like this before--
Okay, get this straight.
I'll tell you what you need to know, but that's all. The rest you'll have to dig out on your own. But understand: if my name *ever* surfaces in relation to this, if anyone finds out I talked to you...
...I'll kill you. Without the slightest hesitation. Understood?
Understood.

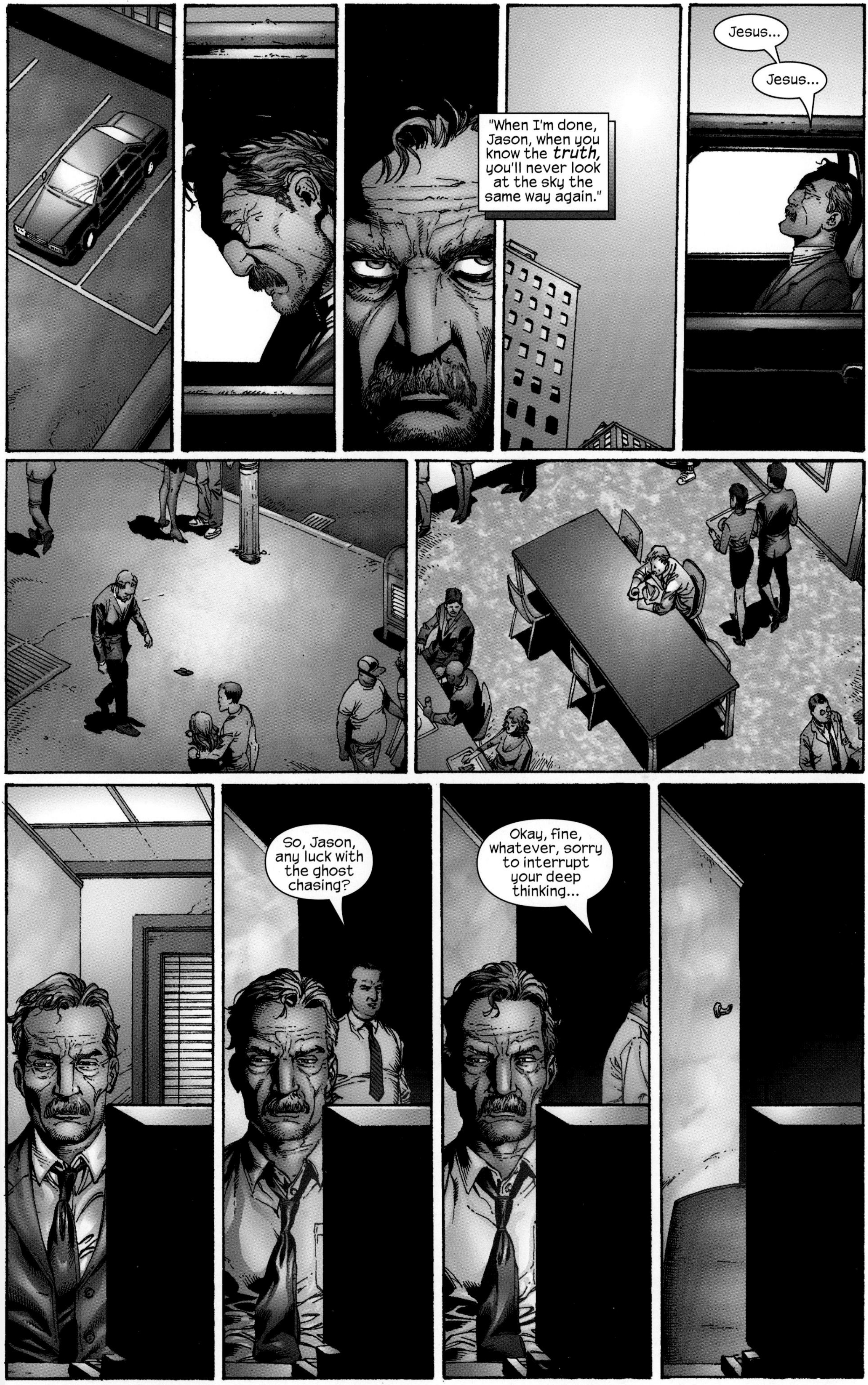
"When I'm done, Jason, when you know the *truth,* you'll never look at the sky the same way again."
Jesus...
Jesus...
So, Jason, any luck with the ghost chasing?
Okay, fine, whatever, sorry to interrupt your deep thinking...

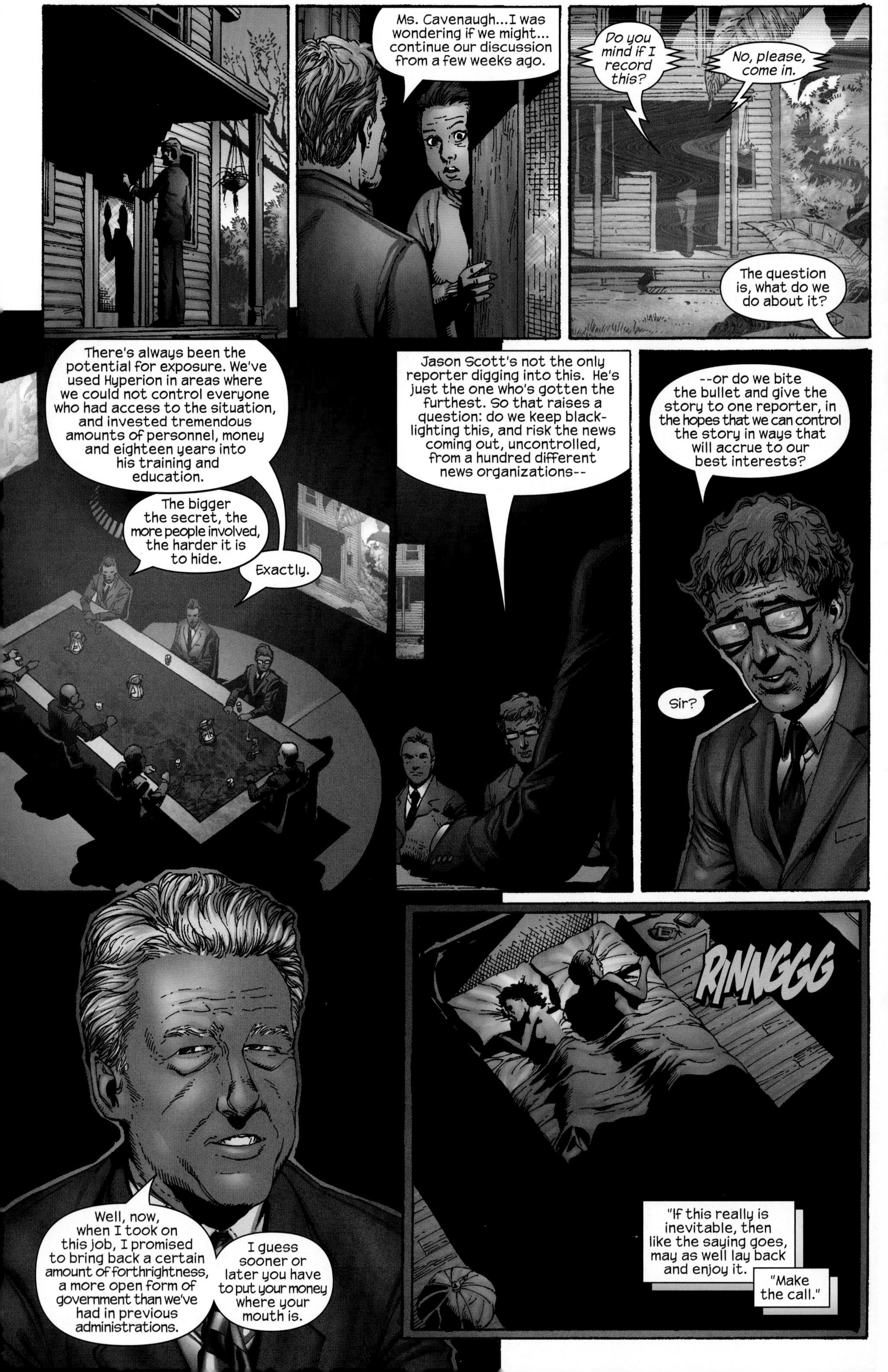

Ms. Cavenaugh...I was wondering if we might... continue our discussion from a few weeks ago.
Do you mind if I record this?
No, please, come in.
The question is, what do we do about it?
There's always been the potential for exposure. We've used Hyperion in areas where we could not control everyone who had access to the situation, and invested tremendous amounts of personnel, money and eighteen years into his training and education.
The bigger the secret, the more people involved, the harder it is to hide.
Exactly.
Jason Scott's not the only reporter digging into this. He's just the one who's gotten the furthest. So that raises a question: do we keep black-lighting this, and risk the news coming out, uncontrolled, from a hundred different news organizations--
--or do we bite the bullet and give the story to one reporter, in the hopes that we can control the story in ways that will accrue to our best interests?
Sir?
Well, now, when I took on this job, I promised to bring back a certain amount of forthrightness, a more open form of government than we've had in previous administrations.
I guess sooner or later you have to put your money where your mouth is.
RINNGGG
"If this really is inevitable, then like the saying goes, may as well lay back and enjoy it.
"Make the call."

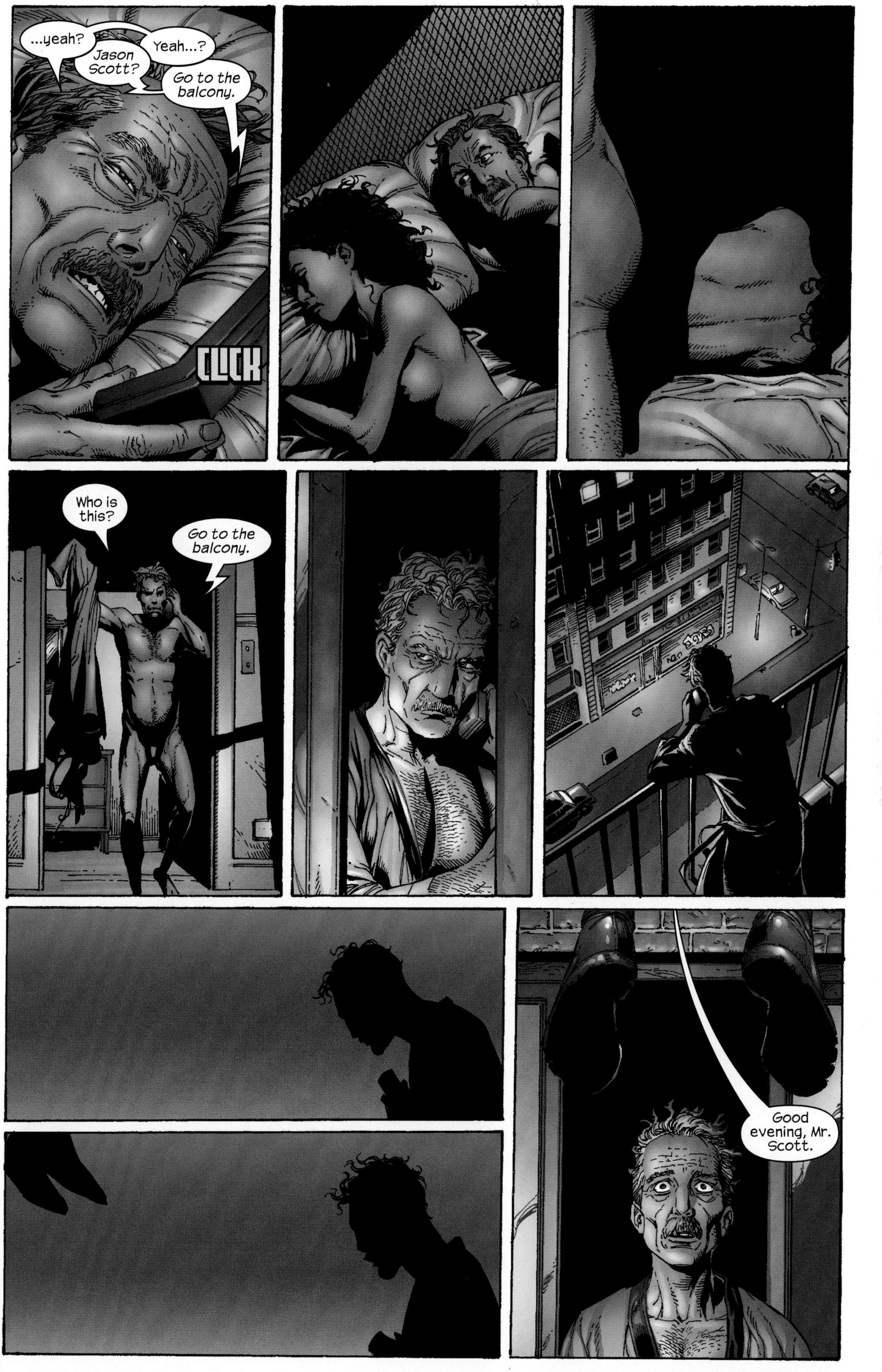
...yeah?
Jason Scott?
Yeah...?
Go to the balcony.
CLICK
Who is this?
Go to the balcony.
Good evening, Mr. Scott.

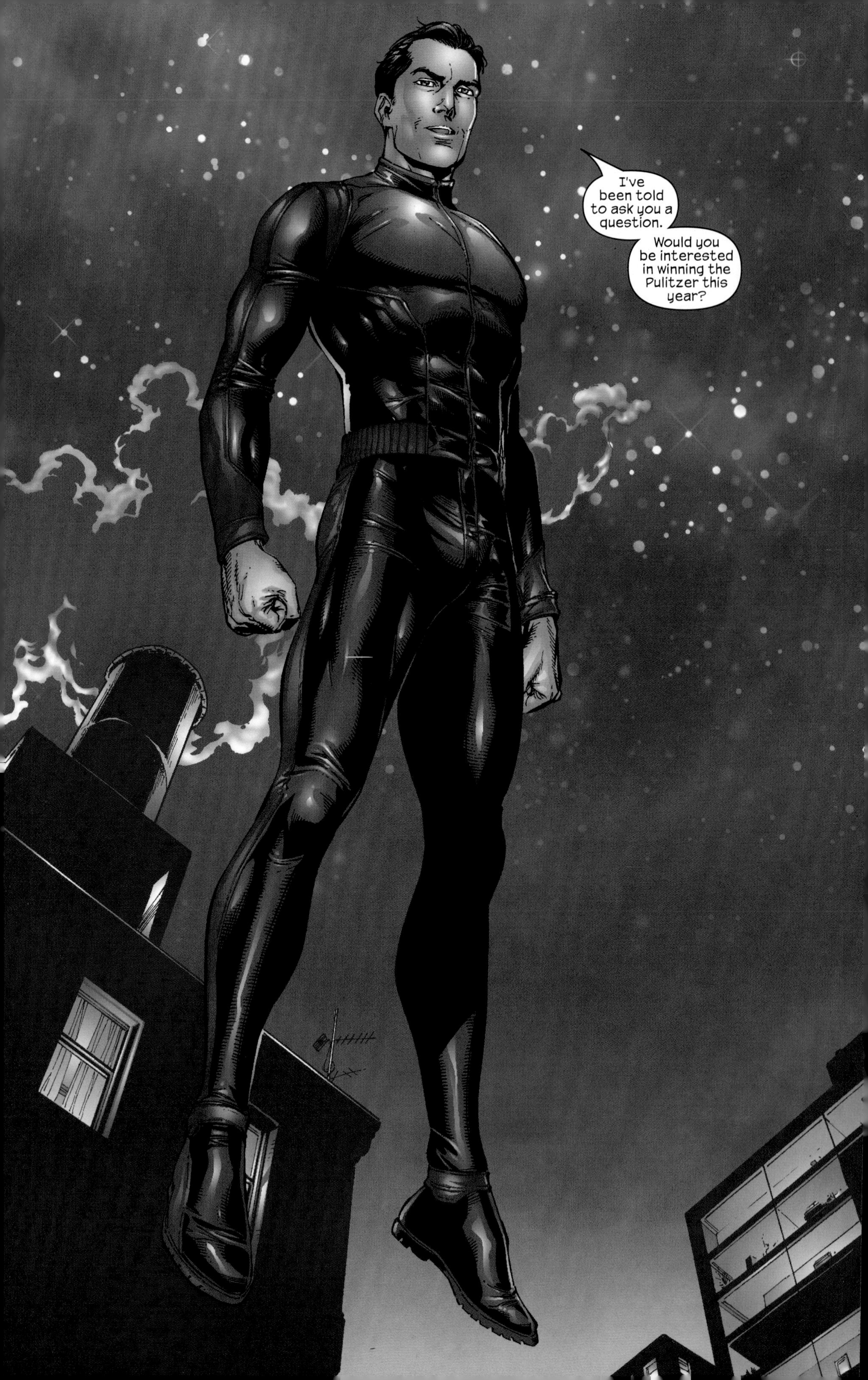
I've been told to ask you a question.
Would you be interested in winning the Pulitzer this year?

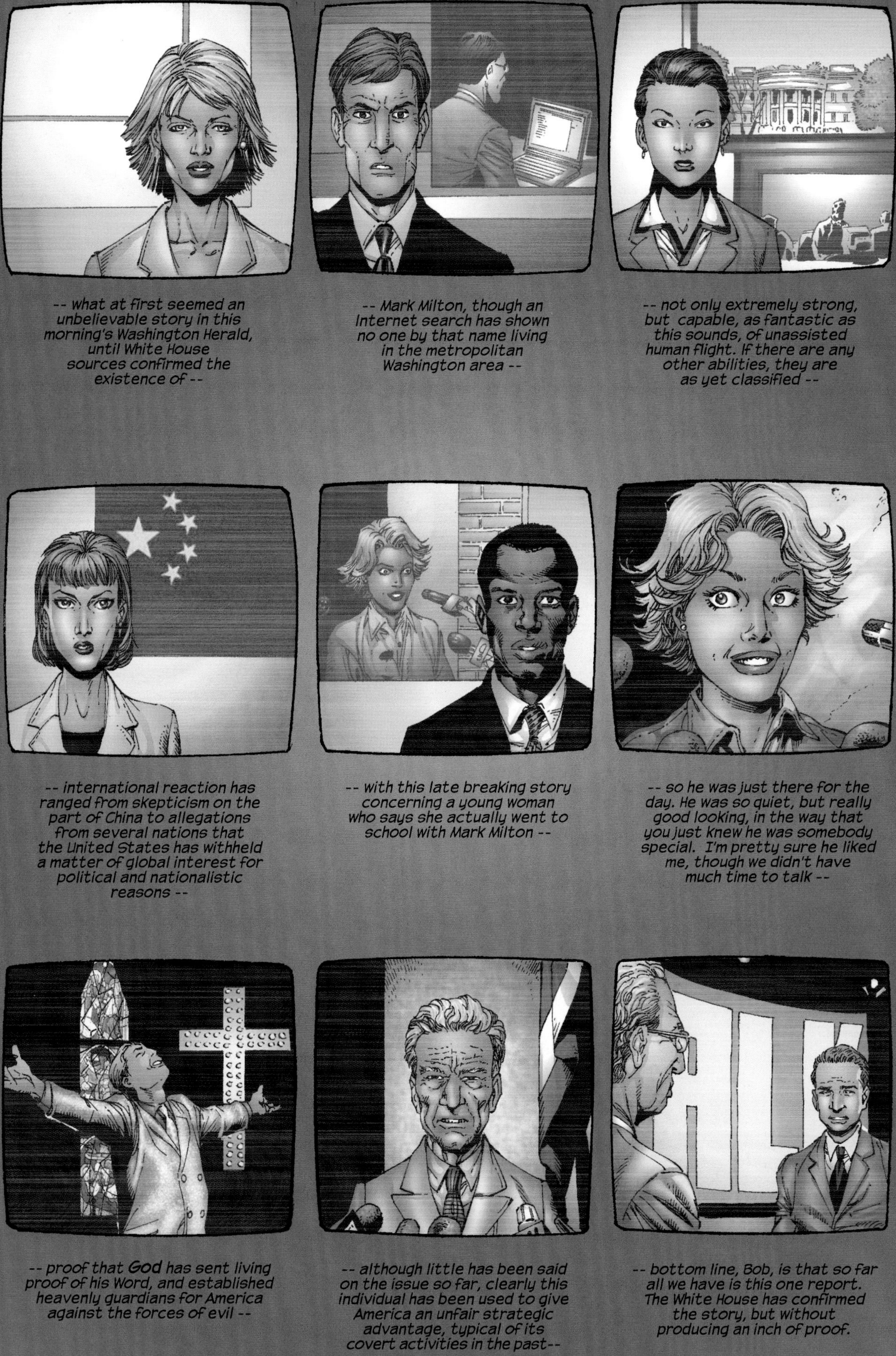
-- what at first seemed an unbelievable story in this morning's Washington Herald, until White House sources confirmed the existence of --
-- Mark Milton, though an Internet search has shown no one by that name living in the metropolitan Washington area --
-- not only extremely strong, but capable, as fantastic as this sounds, of unassisted human flight. If there are any other abilities, they are as yet classified --
-- international reaction has ranged from skepticism on the part of China to allegations from several nations that the United States has withheld a matter of global interest for political and nationalistic reasons --
-- with this late breaking story concerning a young woman who says she actually went to school with Mark Milton --
-- so he was just there for the day. He was so quiet, but really good looking, in the way that you just knew he was somebody special. I'm pretty sure he liked me, though we didn't have much time to talk --
-- proof that God has sent living proof of his Word, and established heavenly guardians for America against the forces of evil --
-- although little has been said on the issue so far, clearly this individual has been used to give America an unfair strategic advantage, typical of its covert activities in the past--
-- bottom line, Bob, is that so far all we have is this one report. The White House has confirmed the story, but without producing an inch of proof.

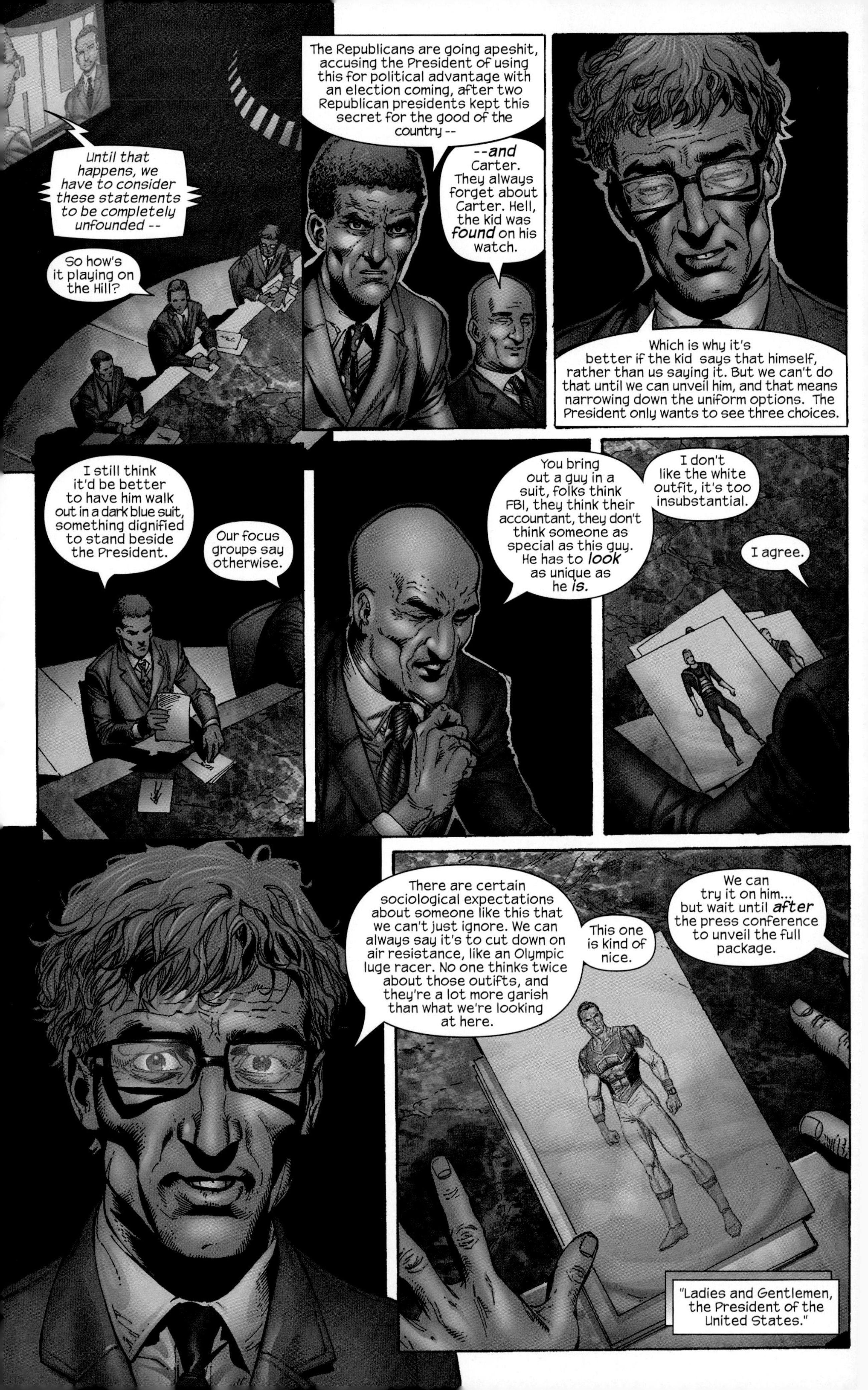
Until that happens, we have to consider these statements to be completely unfounded --
So how's it playing on the Hill?
The Republicans are going apeshit, accusing the President of using this for political advantage with an election coming, after two Republican presidents kept this secret for the good of the country --
--and Carter. They always forget about Carter. Hell, the kid was found on his watch.
Which is why it's better if the kid says that himself, rather than us saying it. But we can't do that until we can unveil him, and that means narrowing down the uniform options. The President only wants to see three choices.
I still think it'd be better to have him walk out in a dark blue suit, something dignified to stand beside the President.
Our focus groups say otherwise.
You bring out a guy in a suit, folks think FBI, they think their accountant, they don't think someone as special as this guy. He has to look as unique as he is.
I don't like the white outfit, it's too insubstantial.
I agree.
There are certain sociological expectations about someone like this that we can't just ignore. We can always say it's to cut down on air resistance, like an Olympic luge racer. No one thinks twice about those outifts, and they're a lot more garish than what we're looking at here.
This one is kind of nice.
We can try it on him... but wait until after the press conference to unveil the full package.
"Ladies and Gentlemen, the President of the United States."

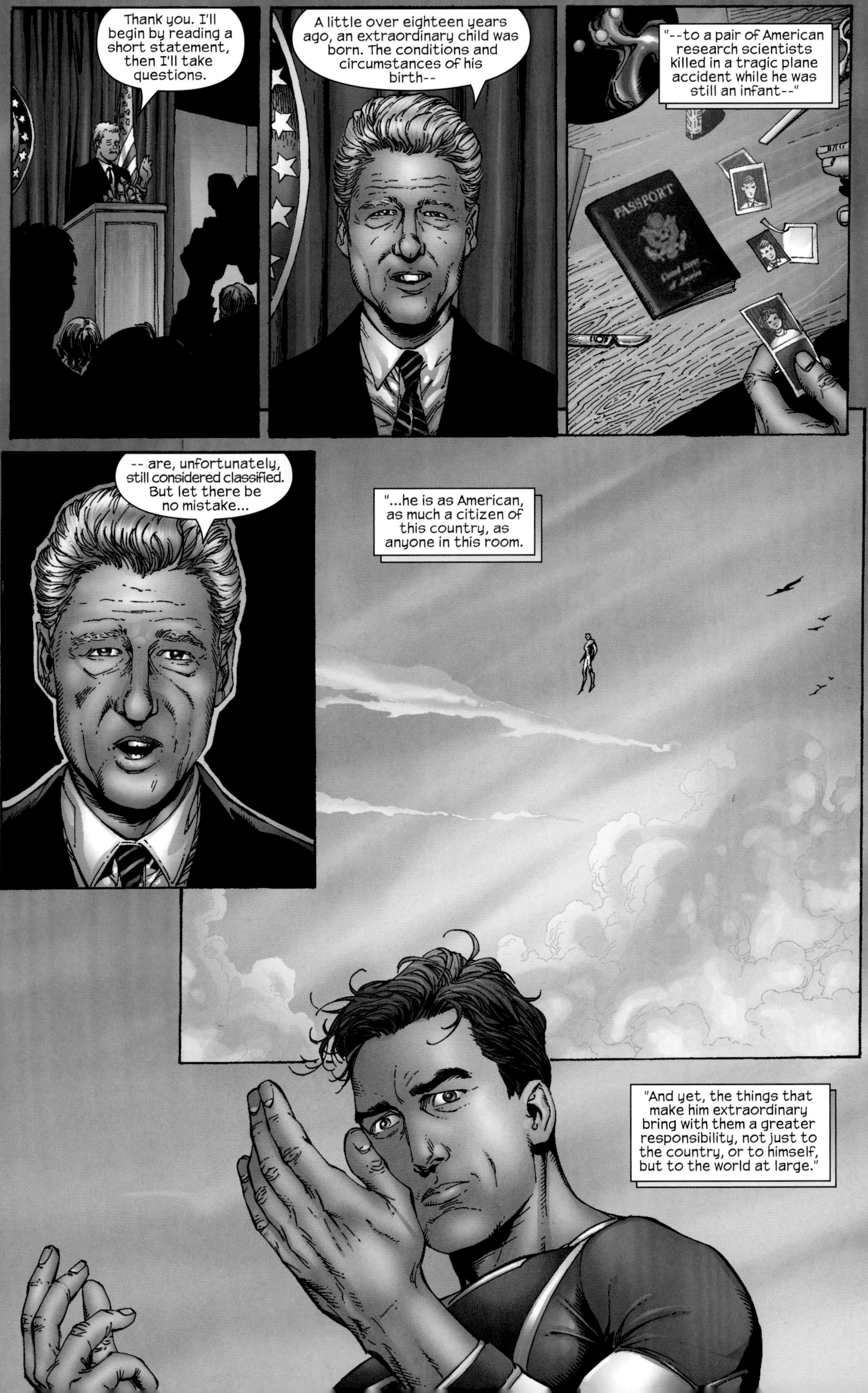
Thank you. I'll begin by reading a short statement, then I'll take questions.
A little over eighteen years ago, an extraordinary child was born. The conditions and circumstances of his birth--
"--to a pair of American research scientists killed in a tragic plane accident while he was still an infant--"
PASSPORT
-- are, unfortunately, still considered classified. But let there be no mistake...
"...he is as American, as much a citizen of this country, as anyone in this room.
"And yet, the things that make him extraordinary bring with them a greater responsibility, not just to the country, or to himself, but to the world at large."

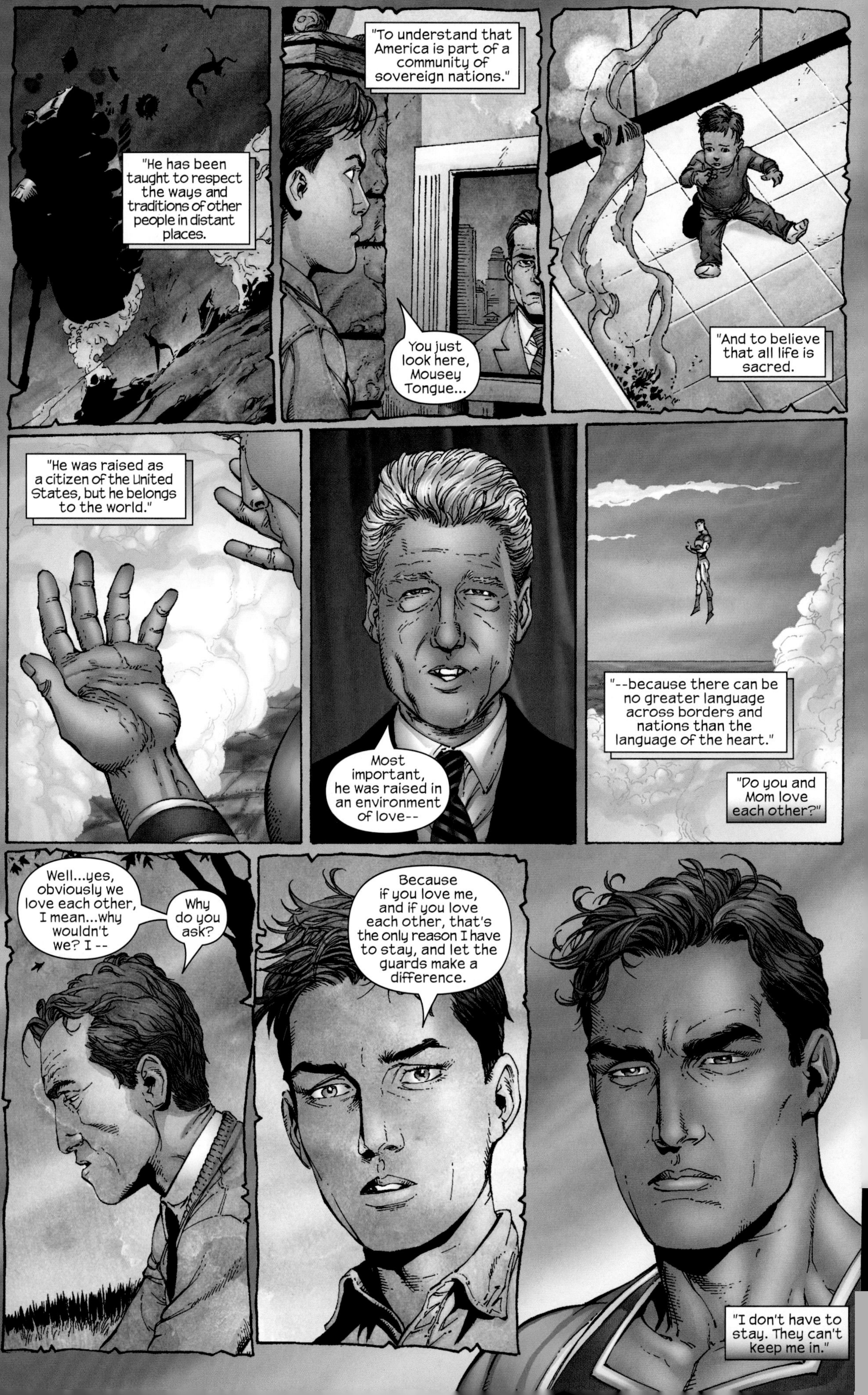
"He has been taught to respect the ways and traditions of other people in distant places.
"To understand that America is part of a community of sovereign nations."
You just look here, Mousey Tongue...
"And to believe that all life is sacred.
"He was raised as a citizen of the United States, but he belongs to the world."
Most important, he was raised in an environment of love--
"--because there can be no greater language across borders and nations than the language of the heart."
"Do you and Mom love each other?"
Well...yes, obviously we love each other, I mean...why wouldn't we? I --
Why do you ask?
Because if you love me, and if you love each other, that's the only reason I have to stay, and let the guards make a difference.
"I don't have to stay. They can't keep me in."

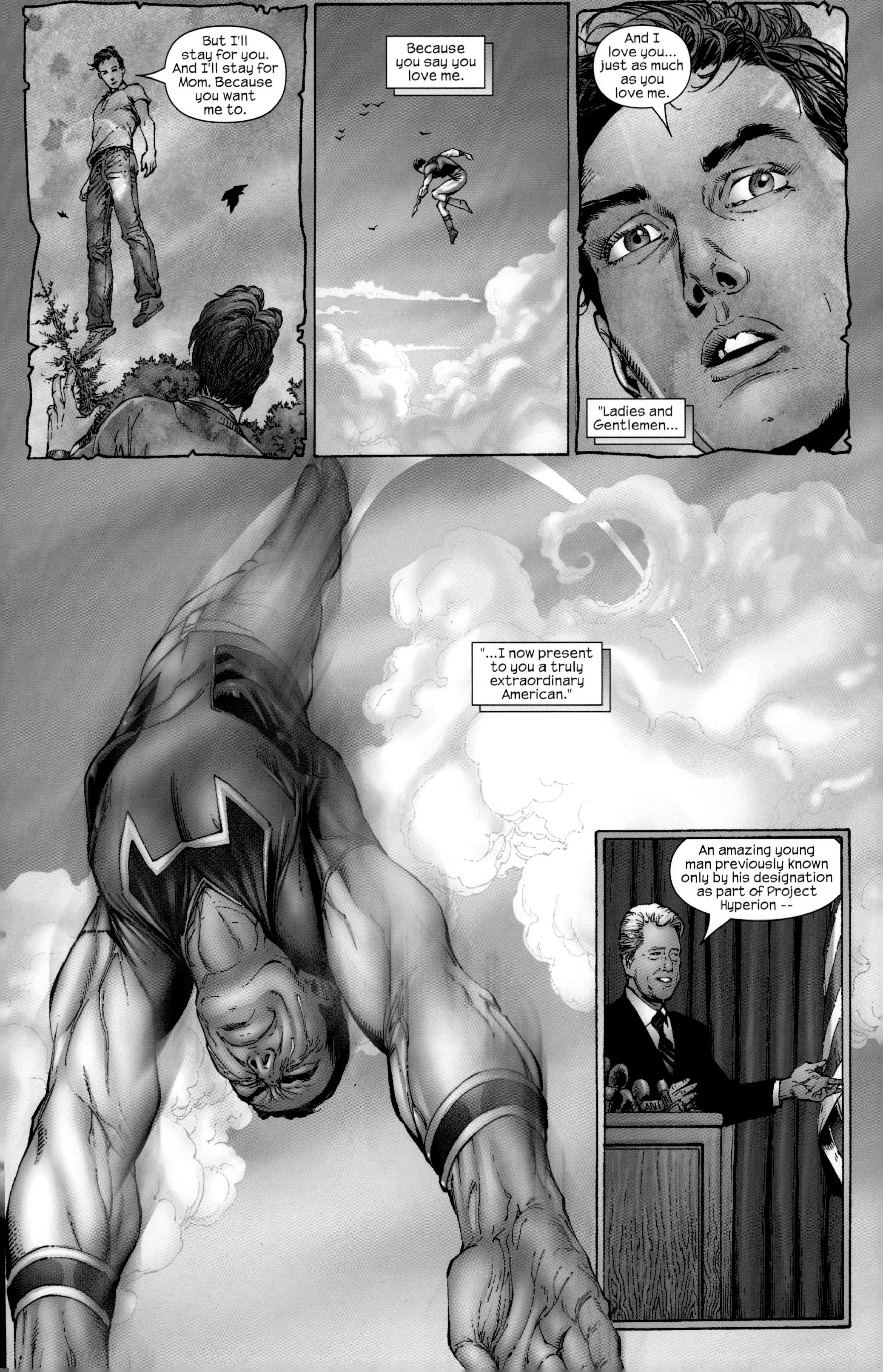
But I'll stay for you. And I'll stay for Mom. Because you want me to.
Because you say you love me.
And I love you... just as much as you love me.
"Ladies and Gentlemen...
"...I now present to you a truly extraordinary American."
An amazing young man previously known only by his designation as part of Project Hyperion --

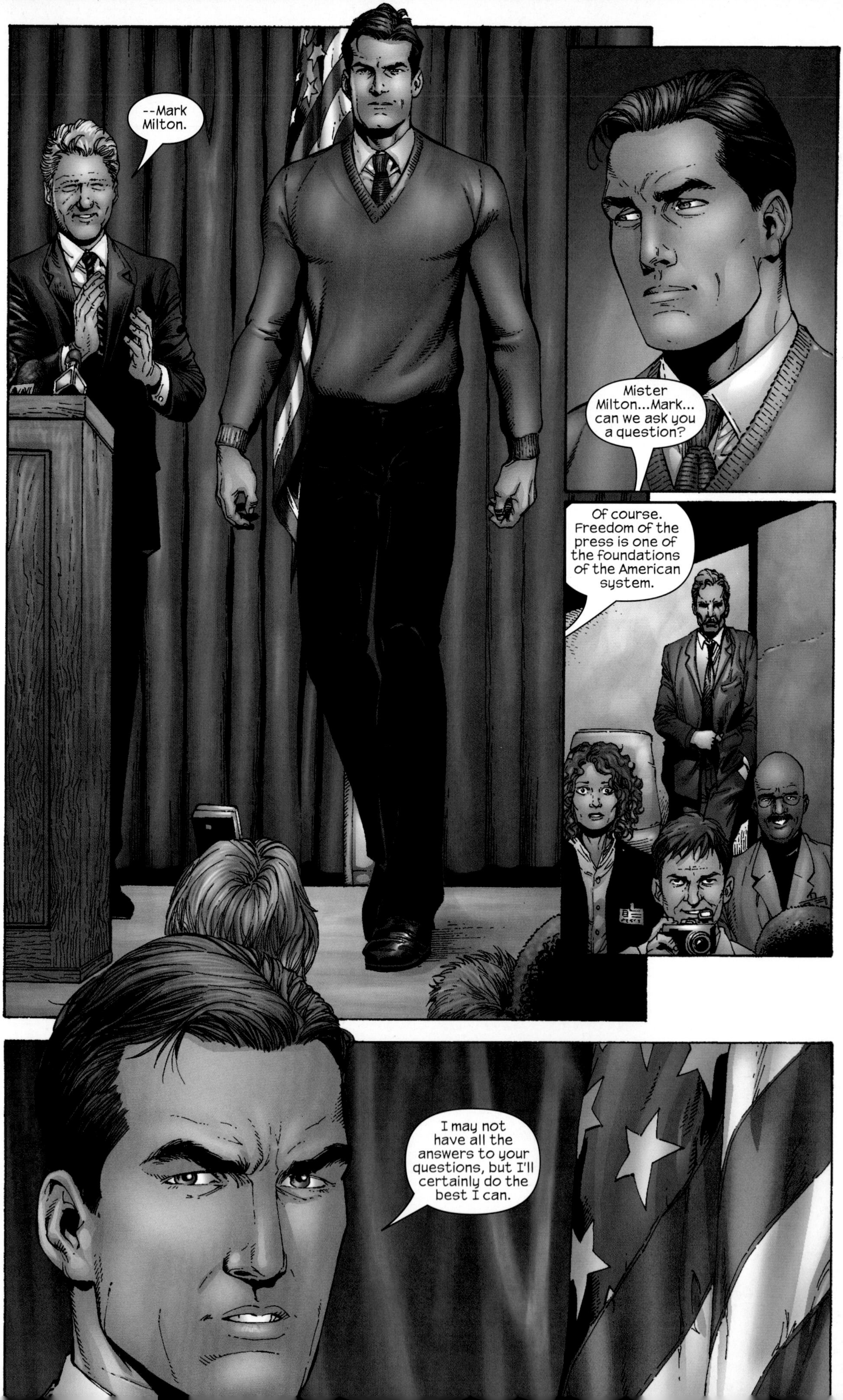
--Mark Milton.
Mister Milton...Mark... can we ask you a question?
Of course. Freedom of the press is one of the foundations of the American system.
I may not have all the answers to your questions, but I'll certainly do the best I can.

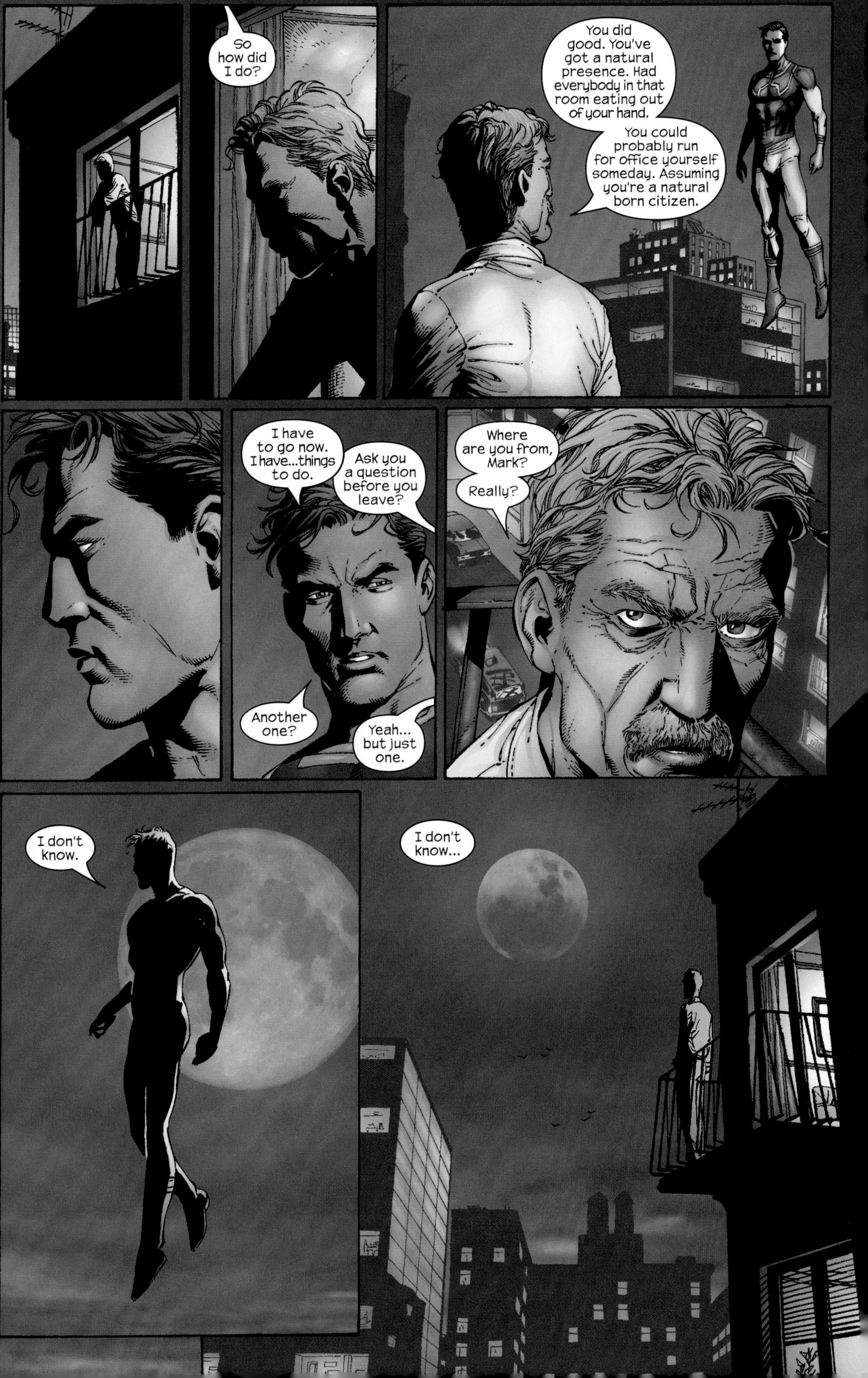
So how did I do?
You did good. You've got a natural presence. Had everybody in that room eating out of your hand.
You could probably run for office yourself someday. Assuming you're a natural born citizen.
I have to go now. I have...things to do.
Ask you a question before you leave?
Another one?
Yeah... but just one.
Where are you from, Mark?
Really?
I don't know.
I don't know...

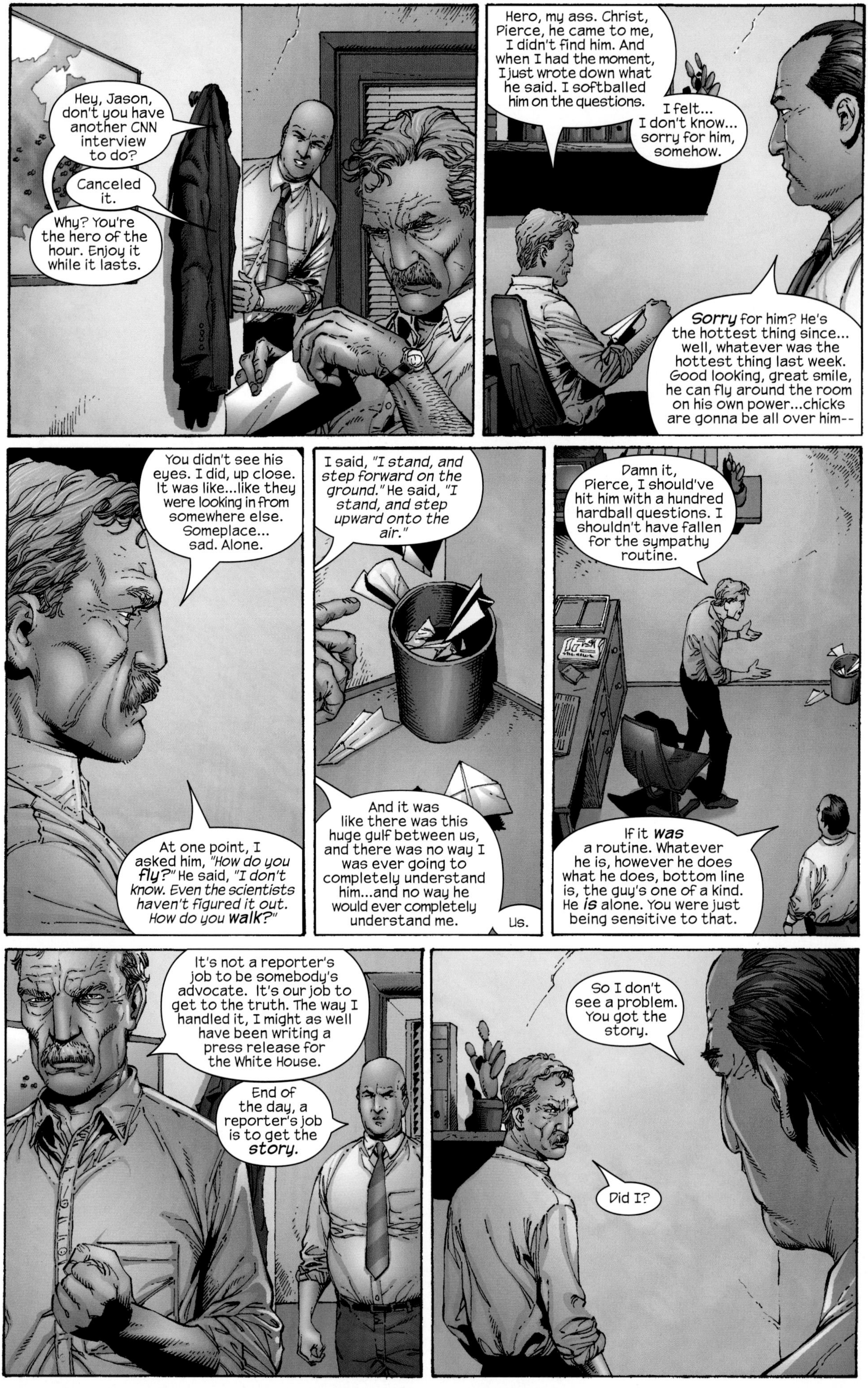
Hey, Jason, don't you have another CNN interview to do?
Canceled it.
Why? You're the hero of the hour. Enjoy it while it lasts.
Hero, my ass. Christ, Pierce, he came to me, I didn't find him. And when I had the moment, I just wrote down what he said. I softballed him on the questions.
I felt... I don't know... sorry for him, somehow.
Sorry for him? He's the hottest thing since... well, whatever was the hottest thing last week. Good looking, great smile, he can fly around the room on his own power...chicks are gonna be all over him--
You didn't see his eyes. I did, up close. It was like...like they were looking in from somewhere else. Someplace... sad. Alone.
At one point, I asked him, "How do you fly?" He said, "I don't know. Even the scientists haven't figured it out. How do you walk?"
I said, "I stand, and step forward on the ground." He said, "I stand, and step upward onto the air."
And it was like there was this huge gulf between us, and there was no way I was ever going to completely understand him...and no way he would ever completely understand me.
Us.
Damn it, Pierce, I should've hit him with a hundred hardball questions. I shouldn't have fallen for the sympathy routine.
If it was a routine. Whatever he is, however he does what he does, bottom line is, the guy's one of a kind. He is alone. You were just being sensitive to that.
It's not a reporter's job to be somebody's advocate. It's our job to get to the truth. The way I handled it, I might as well have been writing a press release for the White House.
End of the day, a reporter's job is to get the story.
So I don't see a problem. You got the story.
Did I?

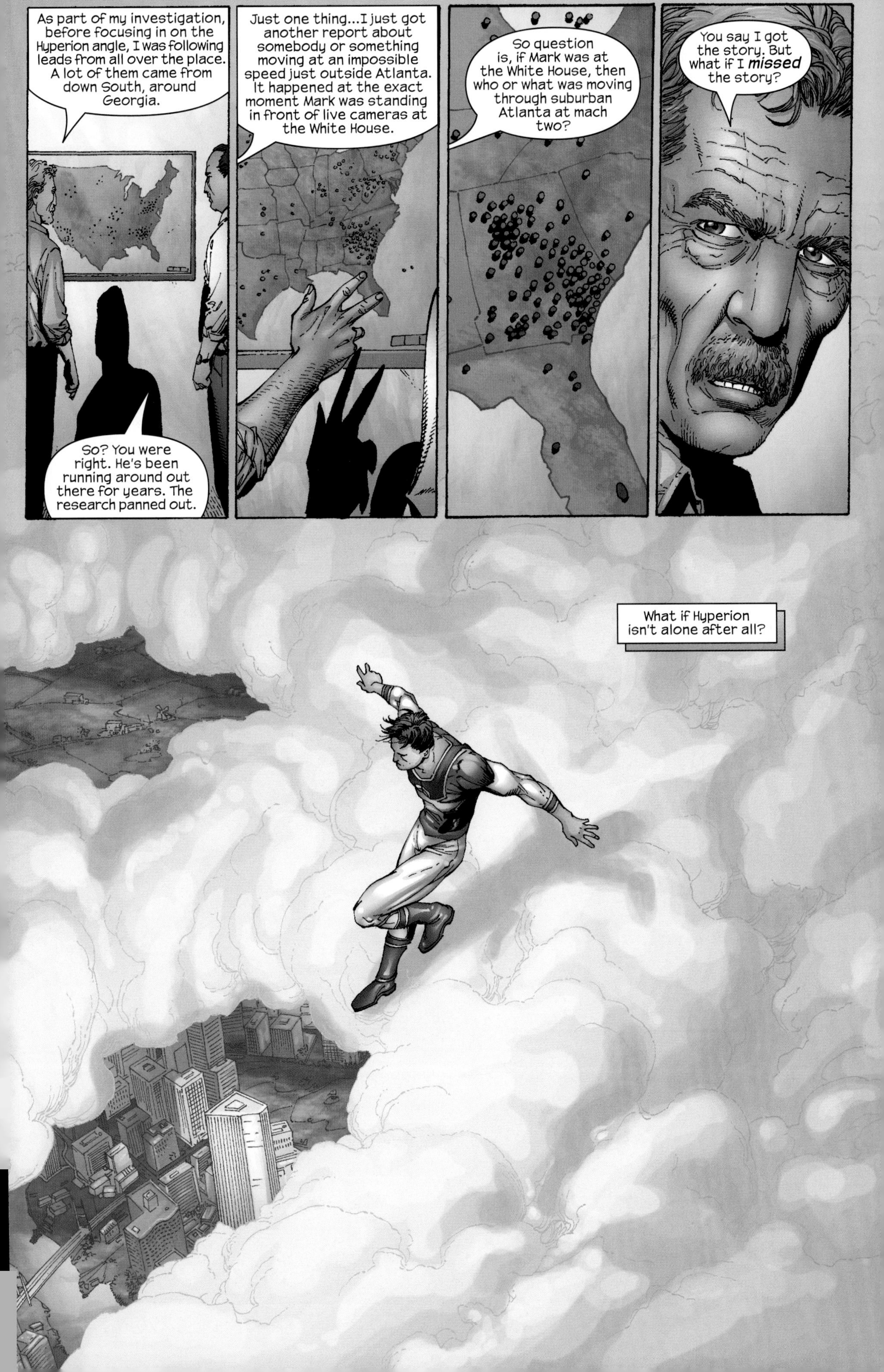
As part of my investigation, before focusing in on the Hyperion angle, I was following leads from all over the place. A lot of them came from down South, around Georgia.
So? You were right. He's been running around out there for years. The research panned out.
Just one thing...I just got another report about somebody or something moving at an impossible speed just outside Atlanta. It happened at the exact moment Mark was standing in front of live cameras at the White House.
So question is, if Mark was at the White House, then who or what was moving through suburban Atlanta at mach two?
You say I got the story. But what if I *missed* the story?
What if Hyperion isn't alone after all?

#4 Assumed Names

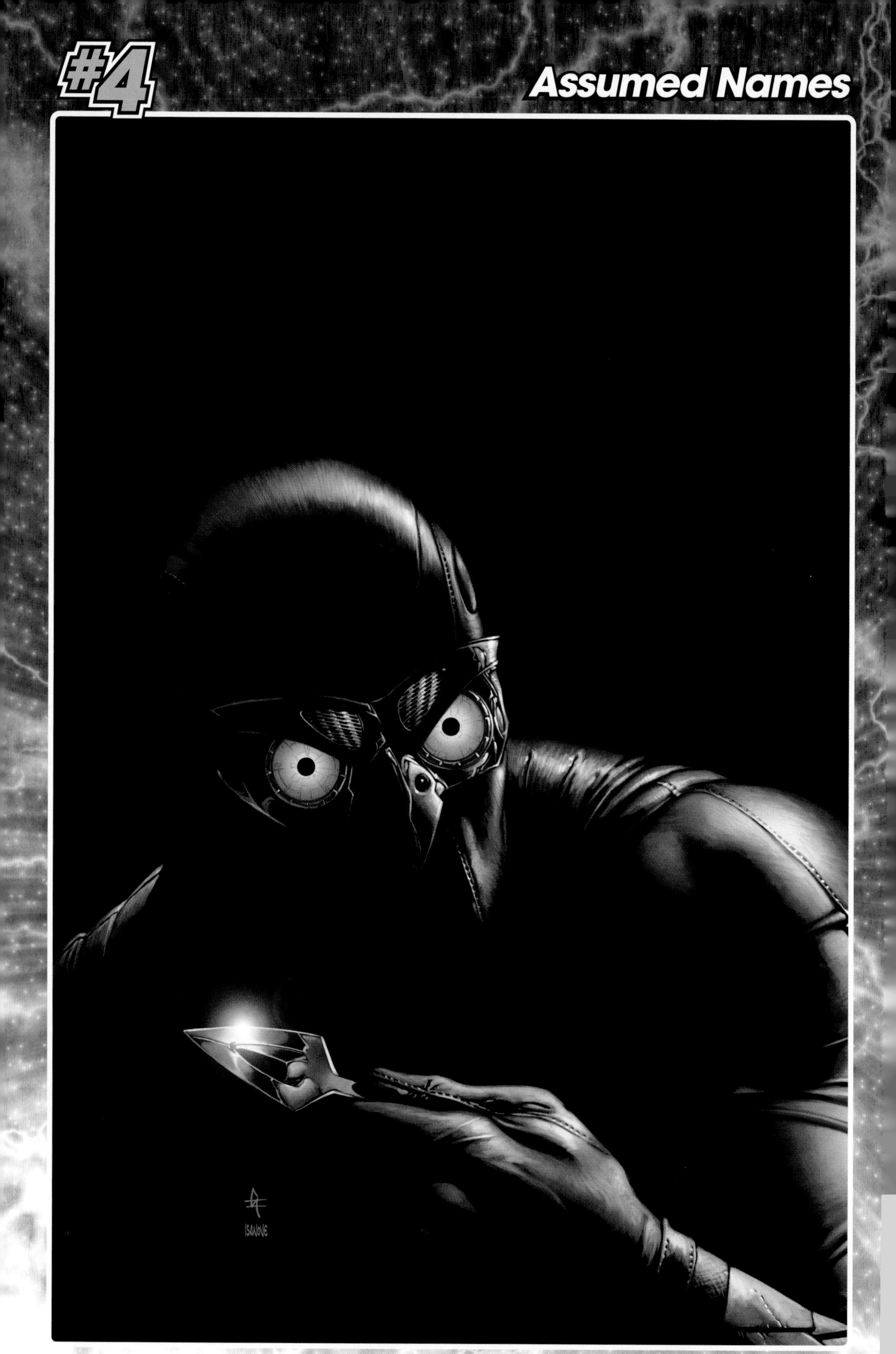

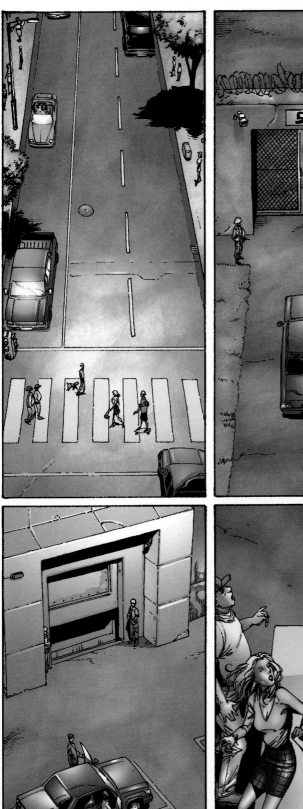

"Thank you for seeing us, General."

"Not at all, Mason --

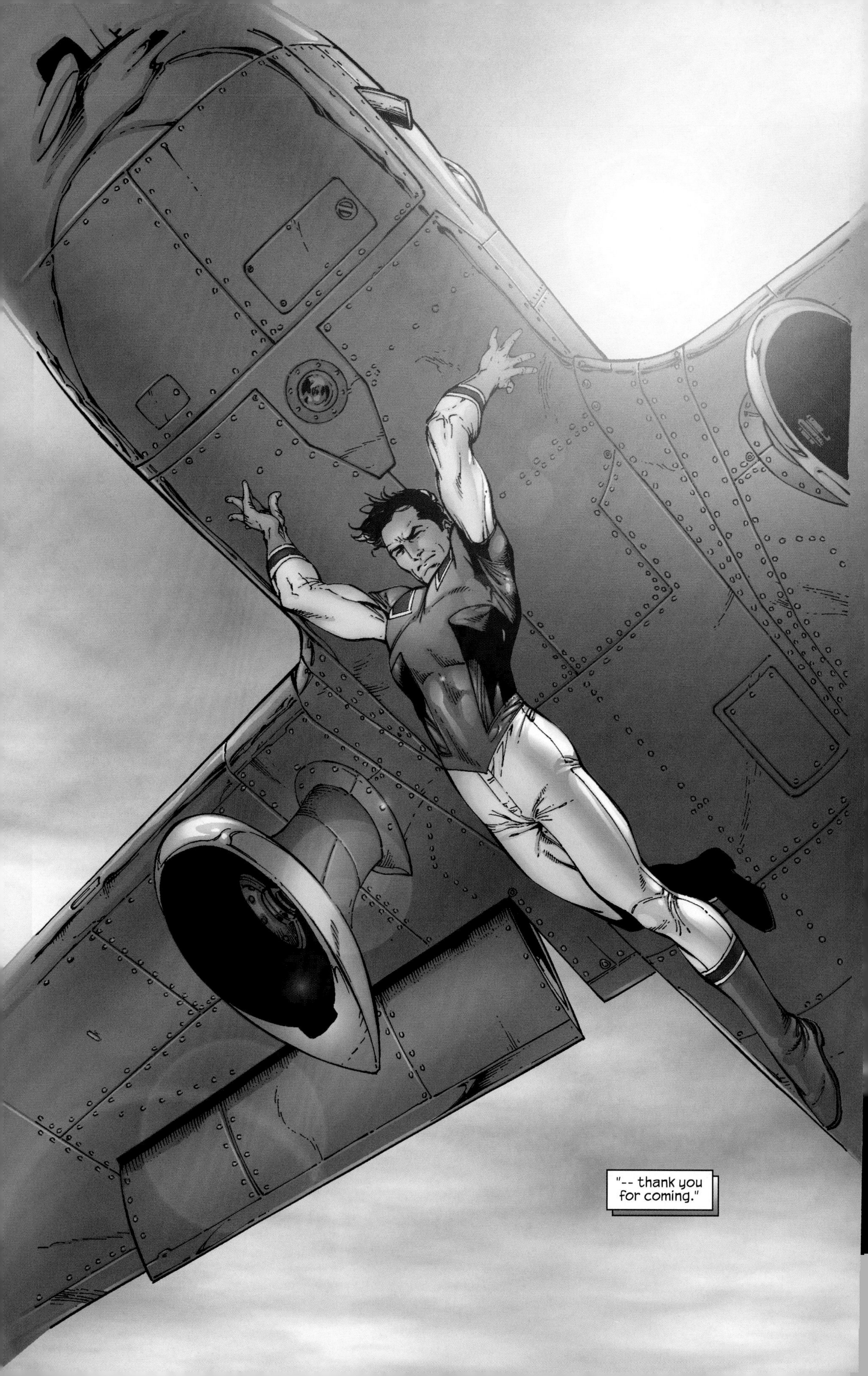
"-- thank you for coming."

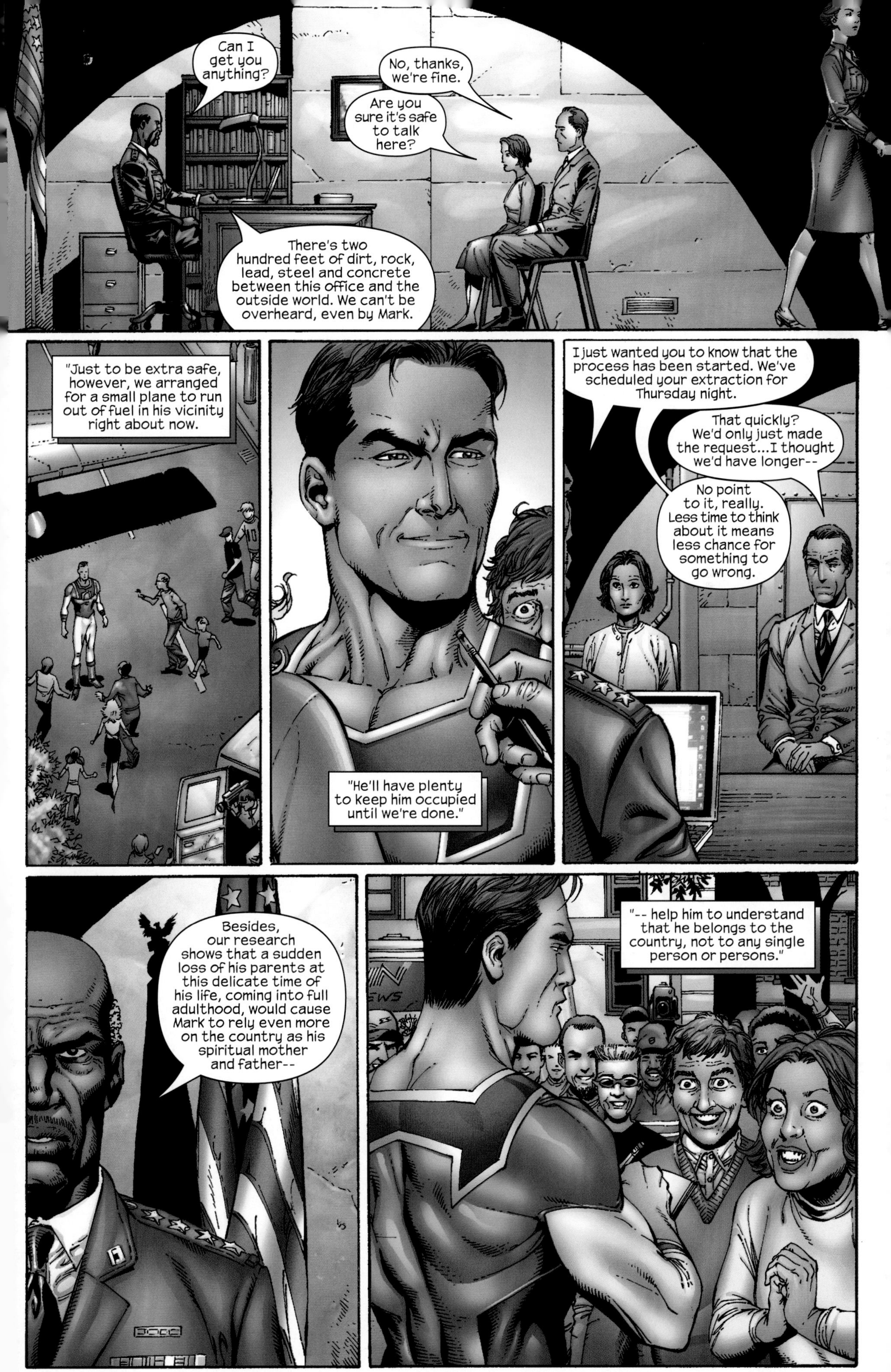
Can I get you anything?
No, thanks, we're fine.
Are you sure it's safe to talk here?
There's two hundred feet of dirt, rock, lead, steel and concrete between this office and the outside world. We can't be overheard, even by Mark.
"Just to be extra safe, however, we arranged for a small plane to run out of fuel in his vicinity right about now.
"He'll have plenty to keep him occupied until we're done."
I just wanted you to know that the process has been started. We've scheduled your extraction for Thursday night.
That quickly? We'd only just made the request...I thought we'd have longer--
No point to it, really. Less time to think about it means less chance for something to go wrong.
Besides, our research shows that a sudden loss of his parents at this delicate time of his life, coming into full adulthood, would cause Mark to rely even more on the country as his spiritual mother and father--
"-- help him to understand that he belongs to the country, not to any single person or persons."

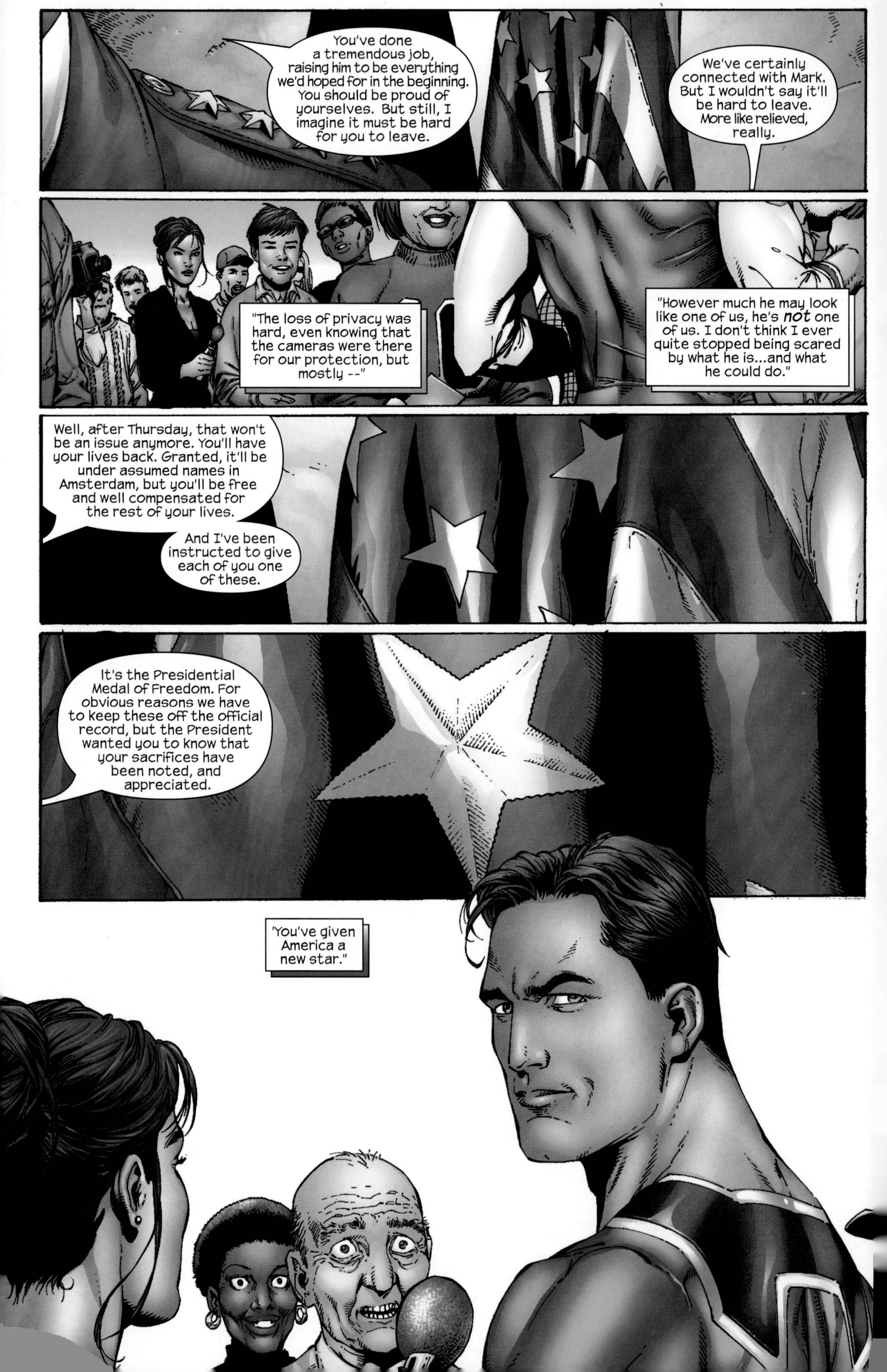
You've done a tremendous job, raising him to be everything we'd hoped for in the beginning. You should be proud of yourselves. But still, I imagine it must be hard for you to leave.
We've certainly connected with Mark. But I wouldn't say it'll be hard to leave. More like relieved, really.
"The loss of privacy was hard, even knowing that the cameras were there for our protection, but mostly --"
"However much he may look like one of us, he's *not* one of us. I don't think I ever quite stopped being scared by what he is...and what he could do."
Well, after Thursday, that won't be an issue anymore. You'll have your lives back. Granted, it'll be under assumed names in Amsterdam, but you'll be free and well compensated for the rest of your lives.
And I've been instructed to give each of you one of these.
It's the Presidential Medal of Freedom. For obvious reasons we have to keep these off the official record, but the President wanted you to know that your sacrifices have been noted, and appreciated.
"You've given America a new star."

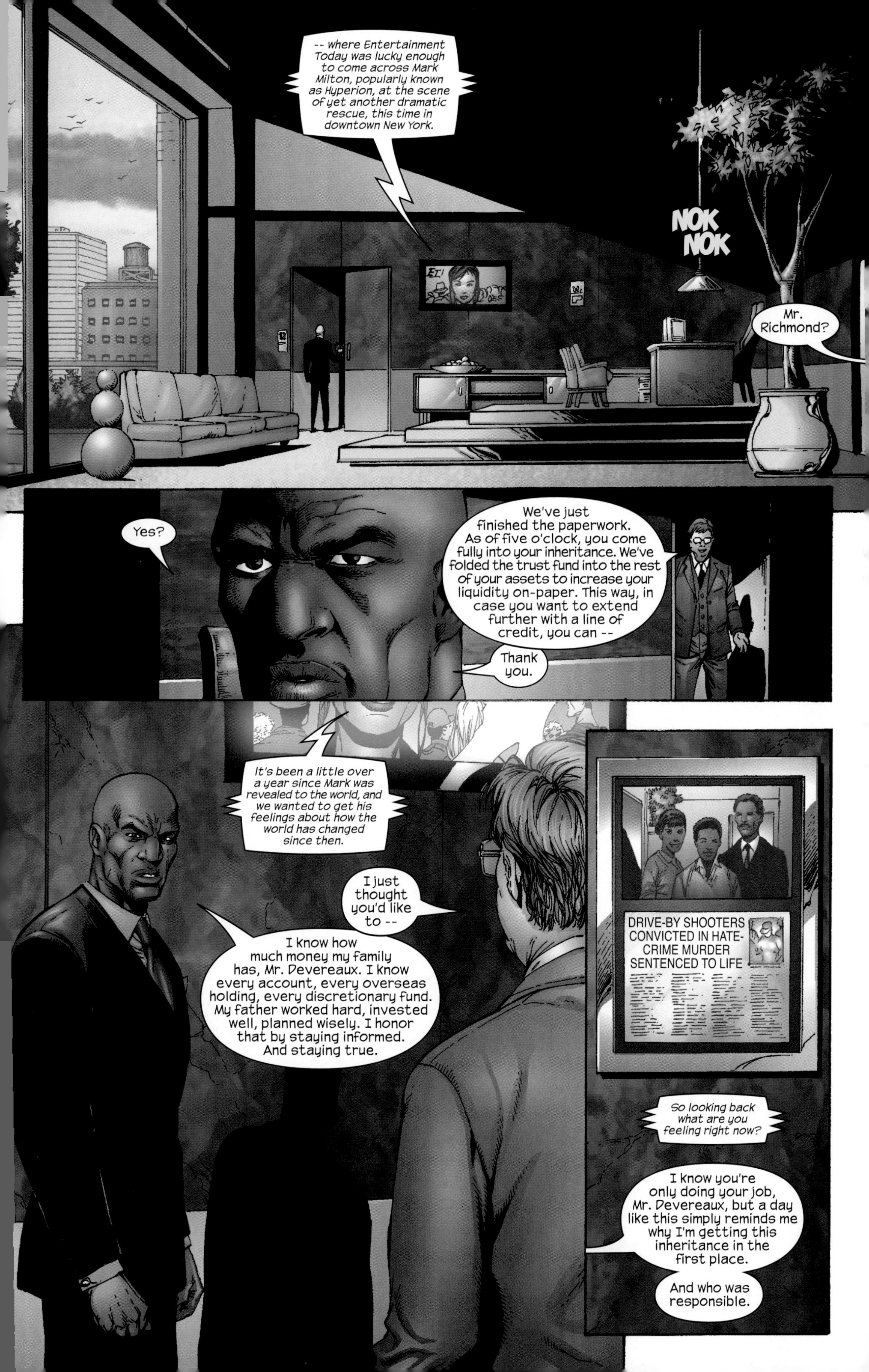
-- where Entertainment Today was lucky enough to come across Mark Milton, popularly known as Hyperion, at the scene of yet another dramatic rescue, this time in downtown New York.
NOK NOK
Mr. Richmond?
Yes?
We've just finished the paperwork. As of five o'clock, you come fully into your inheritance. We've folded the trust fund into the rest of your assets to increase your liquidity on-paper. This way, in case you want to extend further with a line of credit, you can --
Thank you.
It's been a little over a year since Mark was revealed to the world, and we wanted to get his feelings about how the world has changed since then.
I just thought you'd like to --
I know how much money my family has, Mr. Devereaux. I know every account, every overseas holding, every discretionary fund. My father worked hard, invested well, planned wisely. I honor that by staying informed. And staying true.
DRIVE-BY SHOOTERS CONVICTED IN HATE-CRIME MURDER SENTENCED TO LIFE
So looking back what are you feeling right now?
I know you're only doing your job, Mr. Devereaux, but a day like this simply reminds me why I'm getting this inheritance in the first place.
And who was responsible.

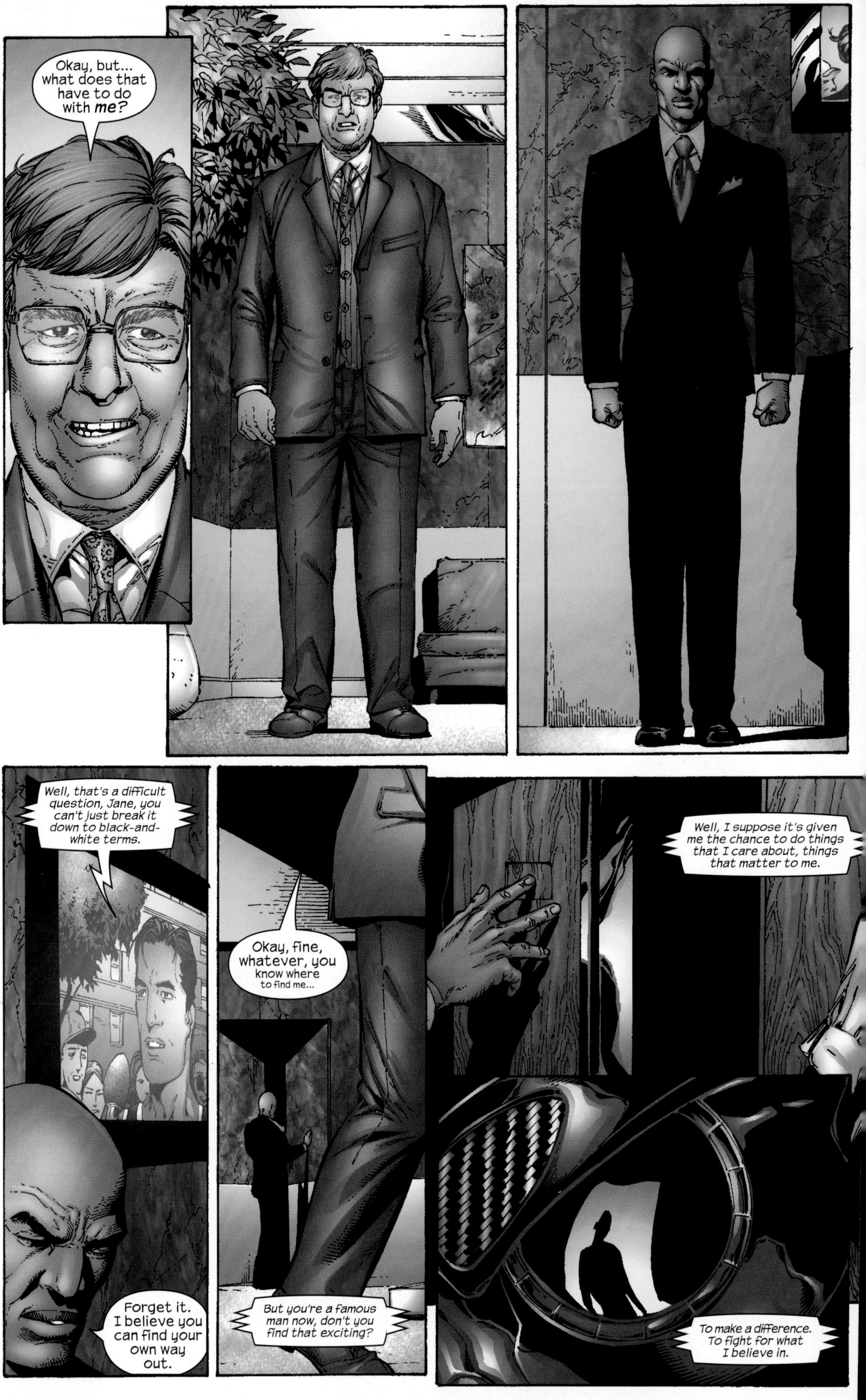

Okay, but... what does that have to do with *me*?
Well, that's a difficult question, Jane, you can't just break it down to black-and-white terms.
Forget it. I believe you can find your own way out.
Okay, fine, whatever, you know where to find me...
But you're a famous man now, don't you find that exciting?
Well, I suppose it's given me the chance to do things that I care about, things that matter to me.
To make a difference. To fight for what I believe in.

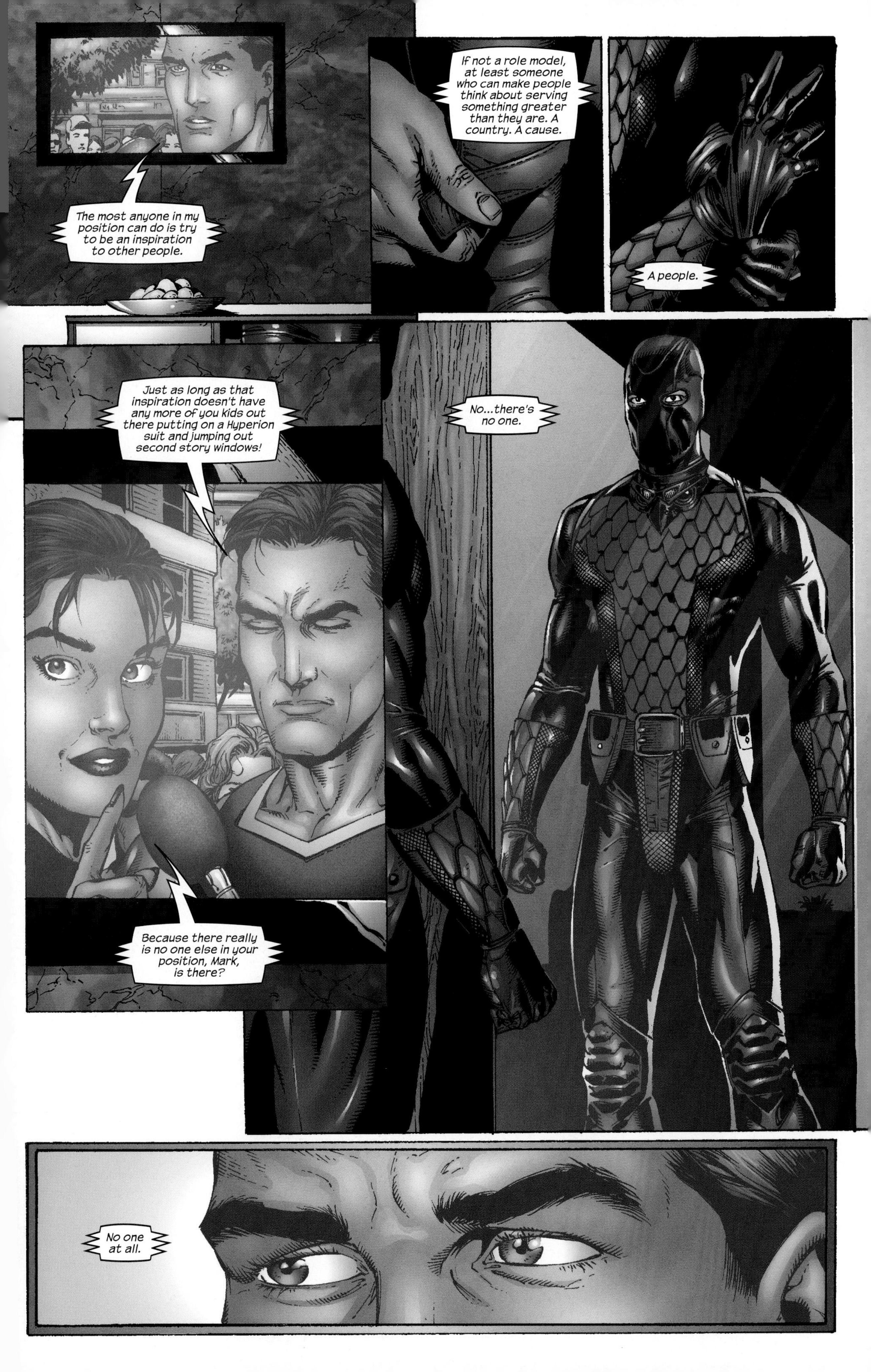
The most anyone in my position can do is try to be an inspiration to other people.
If not a role model, at least someone who can make people think about serving something greater than they are. A country. A cause.
A people.
Just as long as that inspiration doesn't have any more of you kids out there putting on a Hyperion suit and jumping out second story windows!
Because there really is no one else in your position, Mark, is there?
No...there's no one.
No one at all.

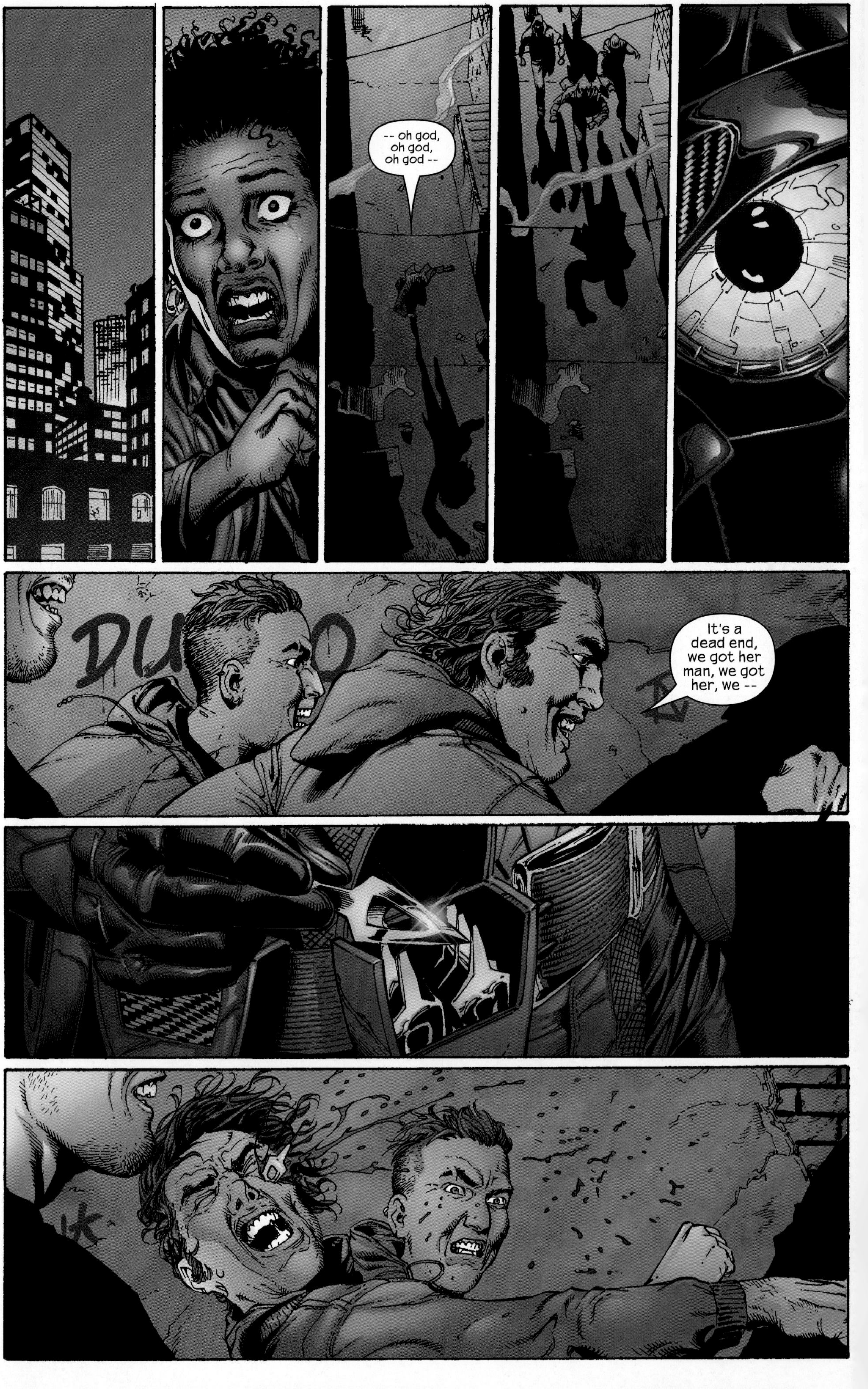
-- oh god, oh god, oh god --
It's a dead end, we got her man, we got her, we --

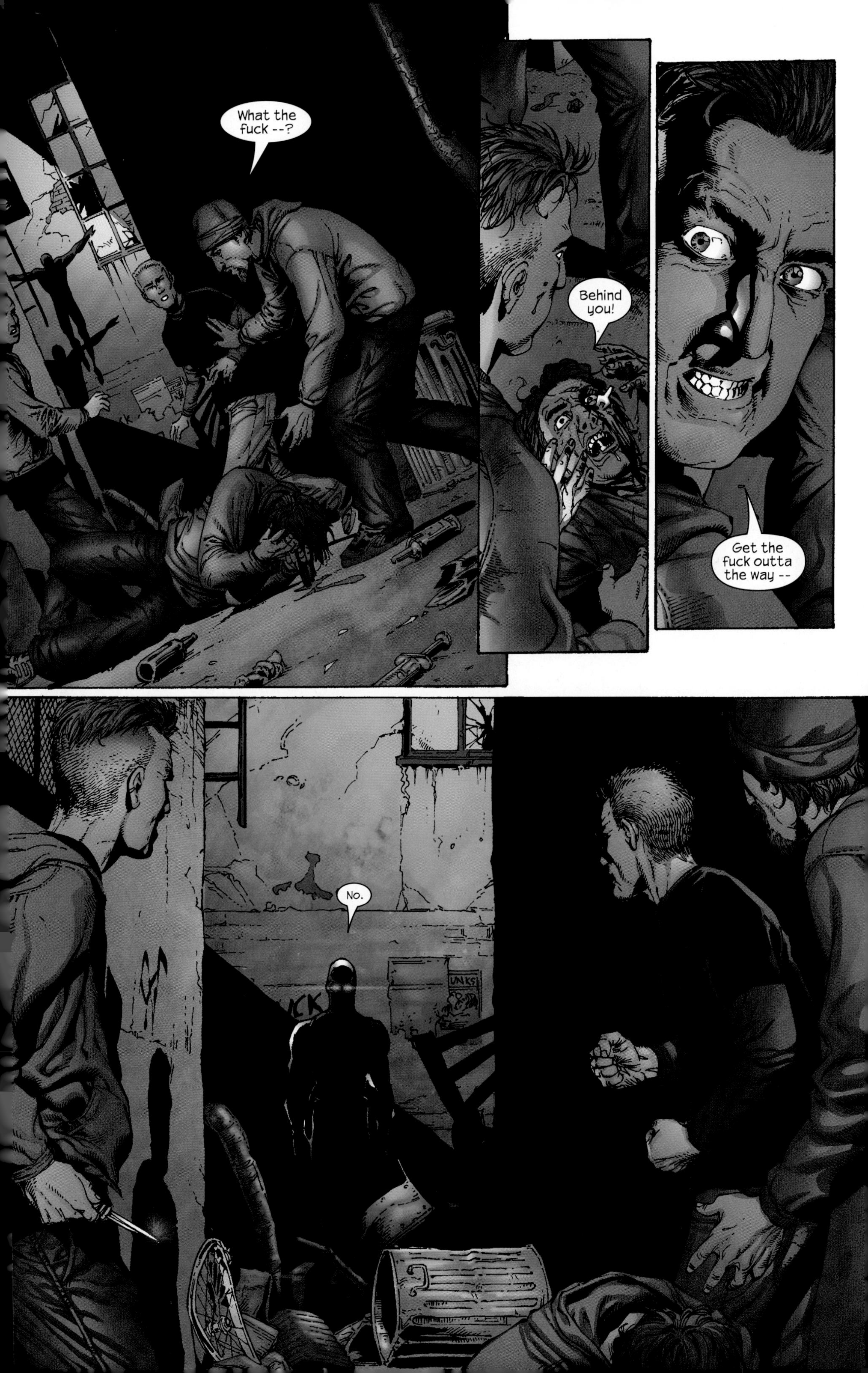
What the fuck --?
Behind you!
Get the fuck outta the way --
No.

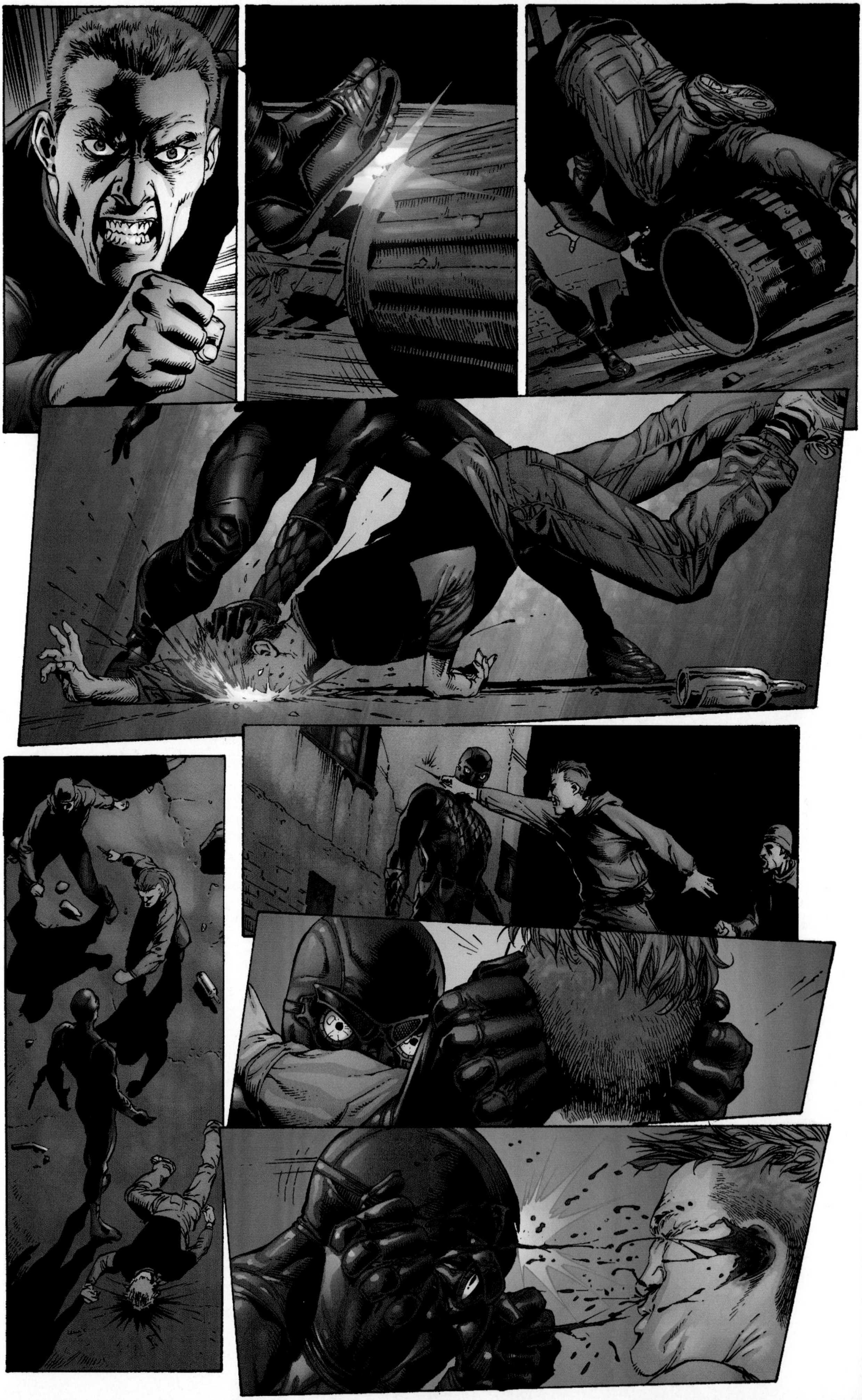

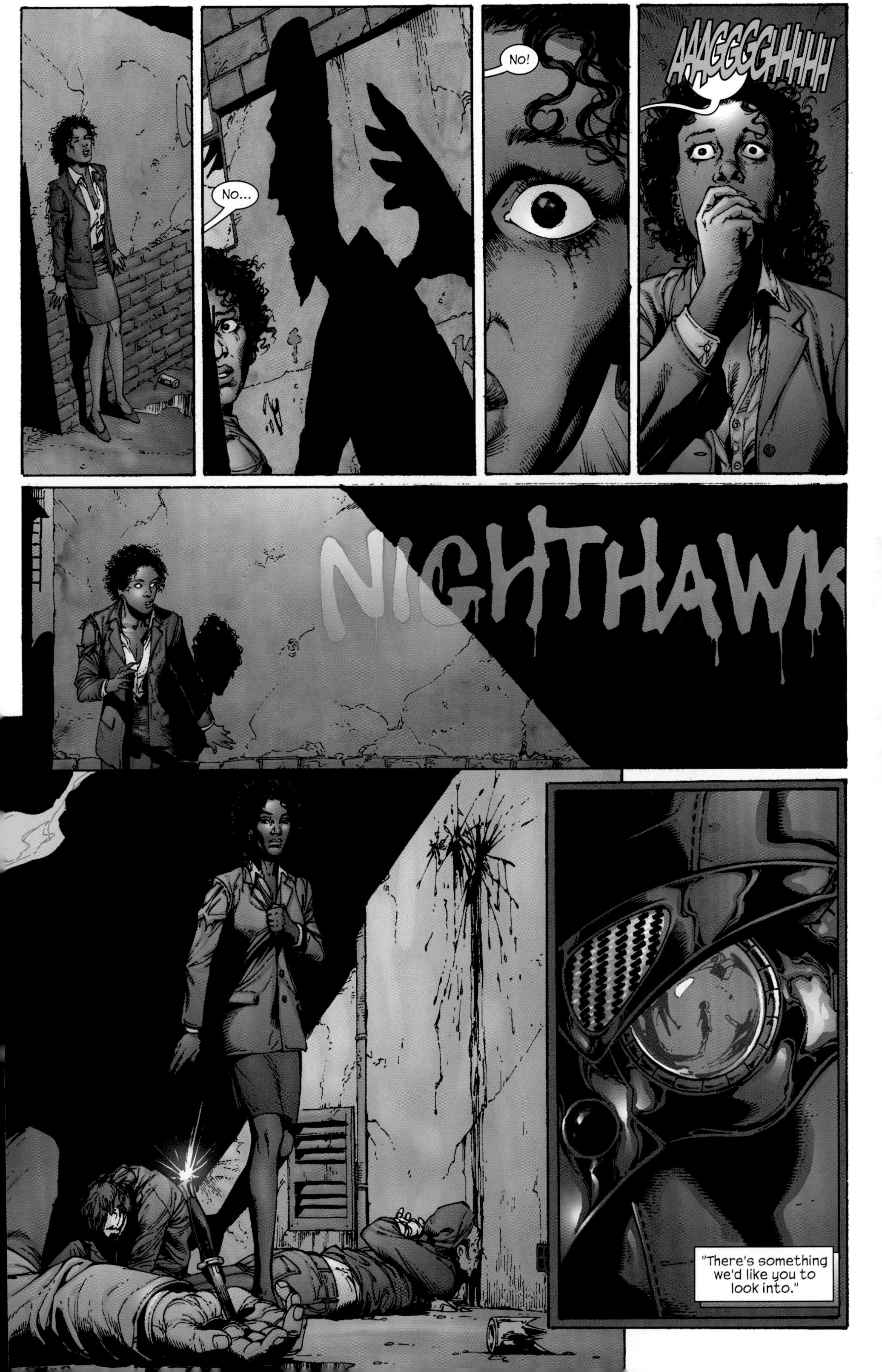
No...
No!
AAAGGGGHHHH
NIGHTHAWK
"There's something we'd like you to look into."

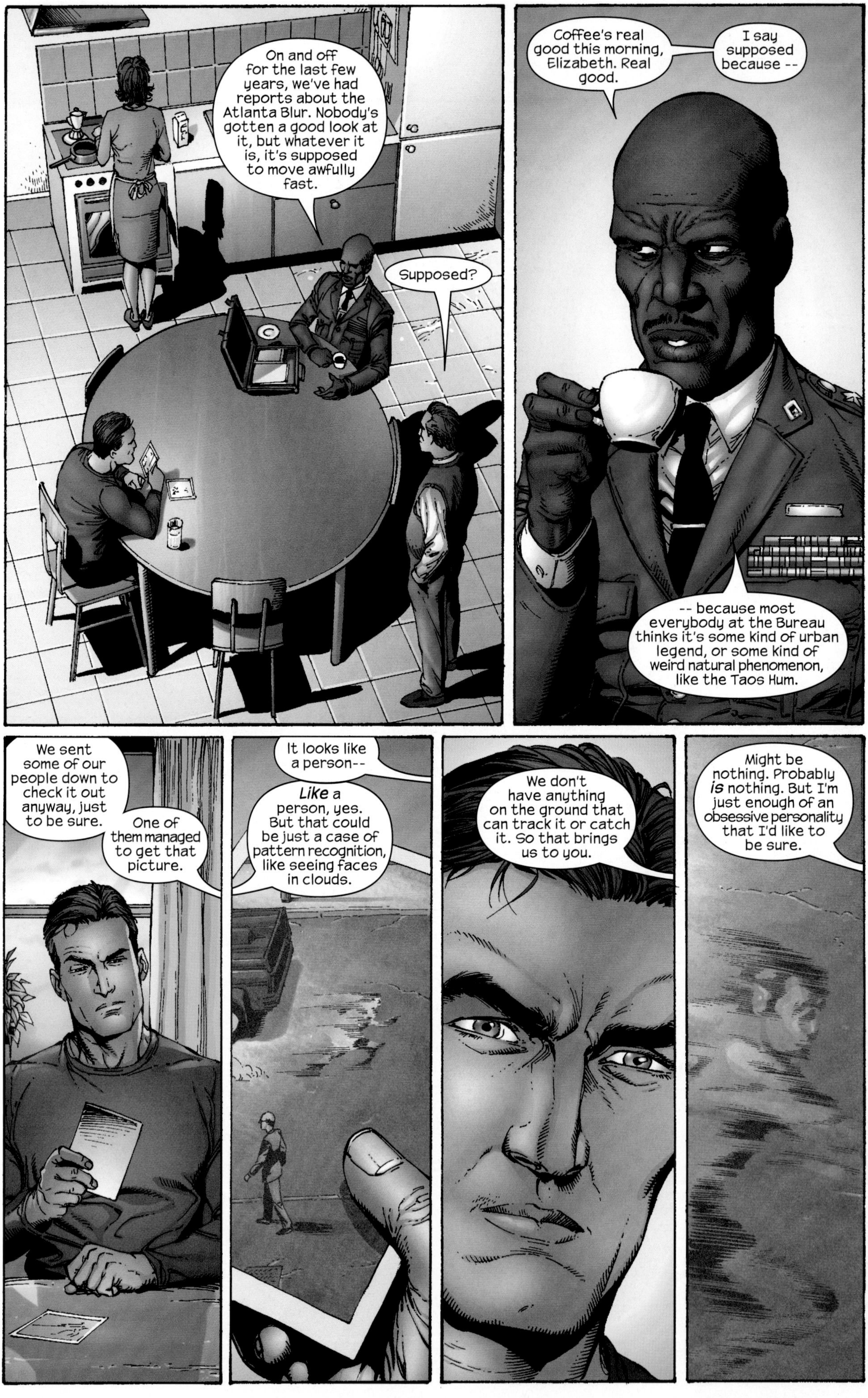
On and off for the last few years, we've had reports about the Atlanta Blur. Nobody's gotten a good look at it, but whatever it is, it's supposed to move awfully fast.
Supposed?
Coffee's real good this morning, Elizabeth. Real good.
I say supposed because --
-- because most everybody at the Bureau thinks it's some kind of urban legend, or some kind of weird natural phenomenon, like the Taos Hum.
We sent some of our people down to check it out anyway, just to be sure.
One of them managed to get that picture.
It looks like a person--
Like a person, yes. But that could be just a case of pattern recognition, like seeing faces in clouds.
We don't have anything on the ground that can track it or catch it. So that brings us to you.
Might be nothing. Probably *is* nothing. But I'm just enough of an obsessive personality that I'd like to be sure.

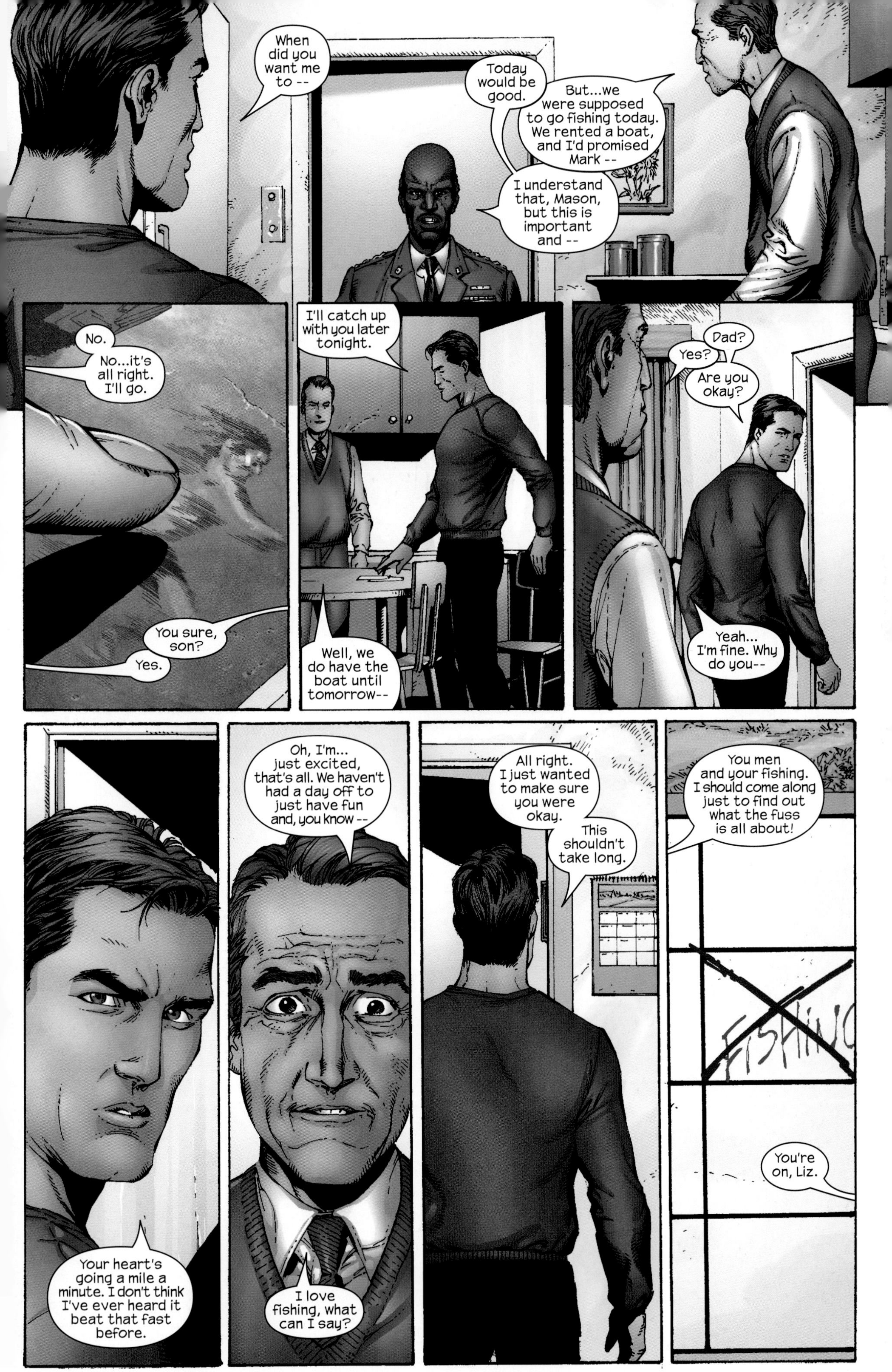
When did you want me to --
Today would be good.
But...we were supposed to go fishing today. We rented a boat, and I'd promised Mark --
I understand that, Mason, but this is important and --
No.
No...it's all right. I'll go.
You sure, son?
Yes.
I'll catch up with you later tonight.
Well, we do have the boat until tomorrow--
Dad?
Yes?
Are you okay?
Yeah... I'm fine. Why do you--
Your heart's going a mile a minute. I don't think I've ever heard it beat that fast before.
Oh, I'm... just excited, that's all. We haven't had a day off to just have fun and, you know --
I love fishing, what can I say?
All right. I just wanted to make sure you were okay.
This shouldn't take long.
You men and your fishing. I should come along just to find out what the fuss is all about!
FISHING
You're on, Liz.

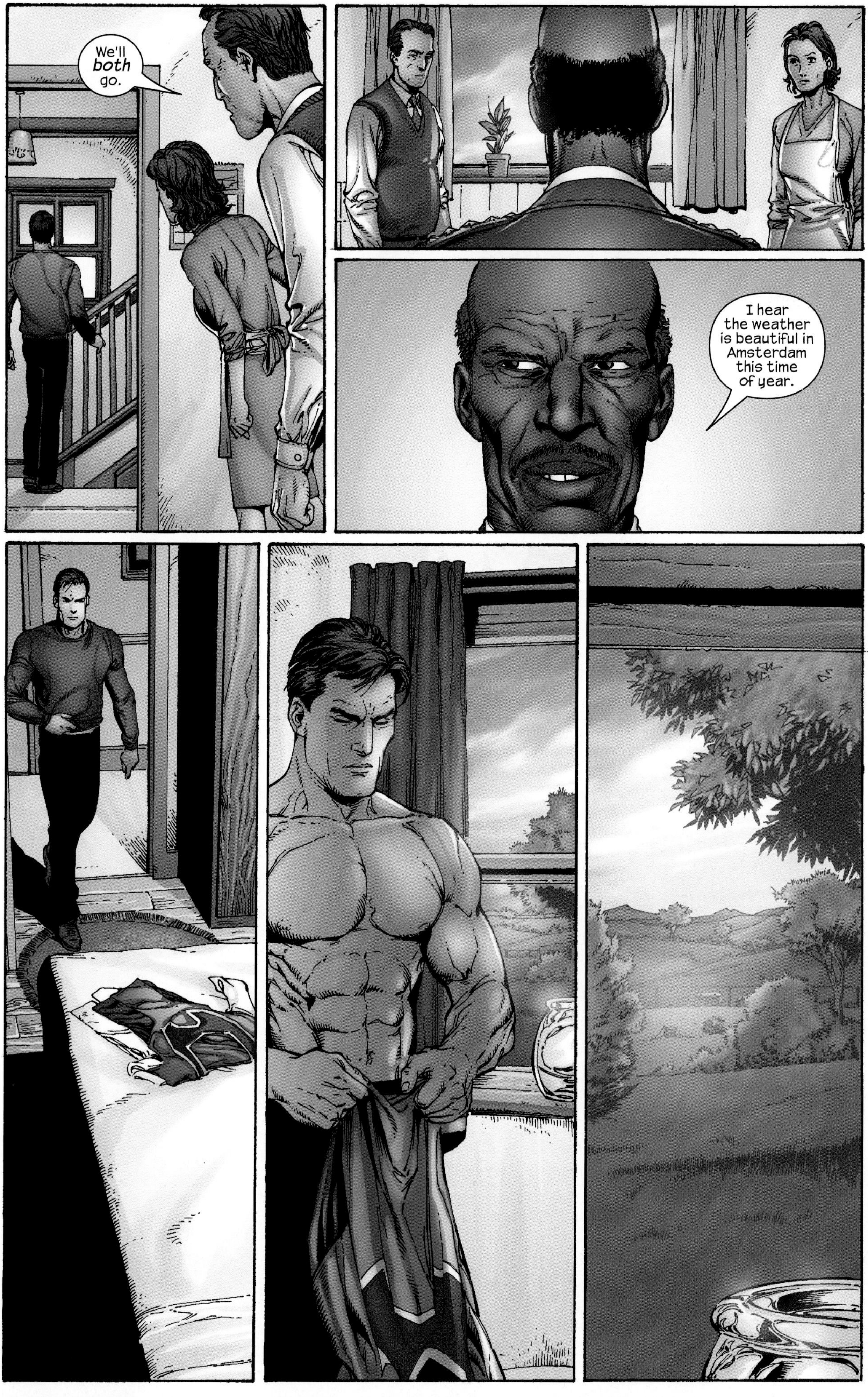
We'll *both* go.
I hear the weather is beautiful in Amsterdam this time of year.

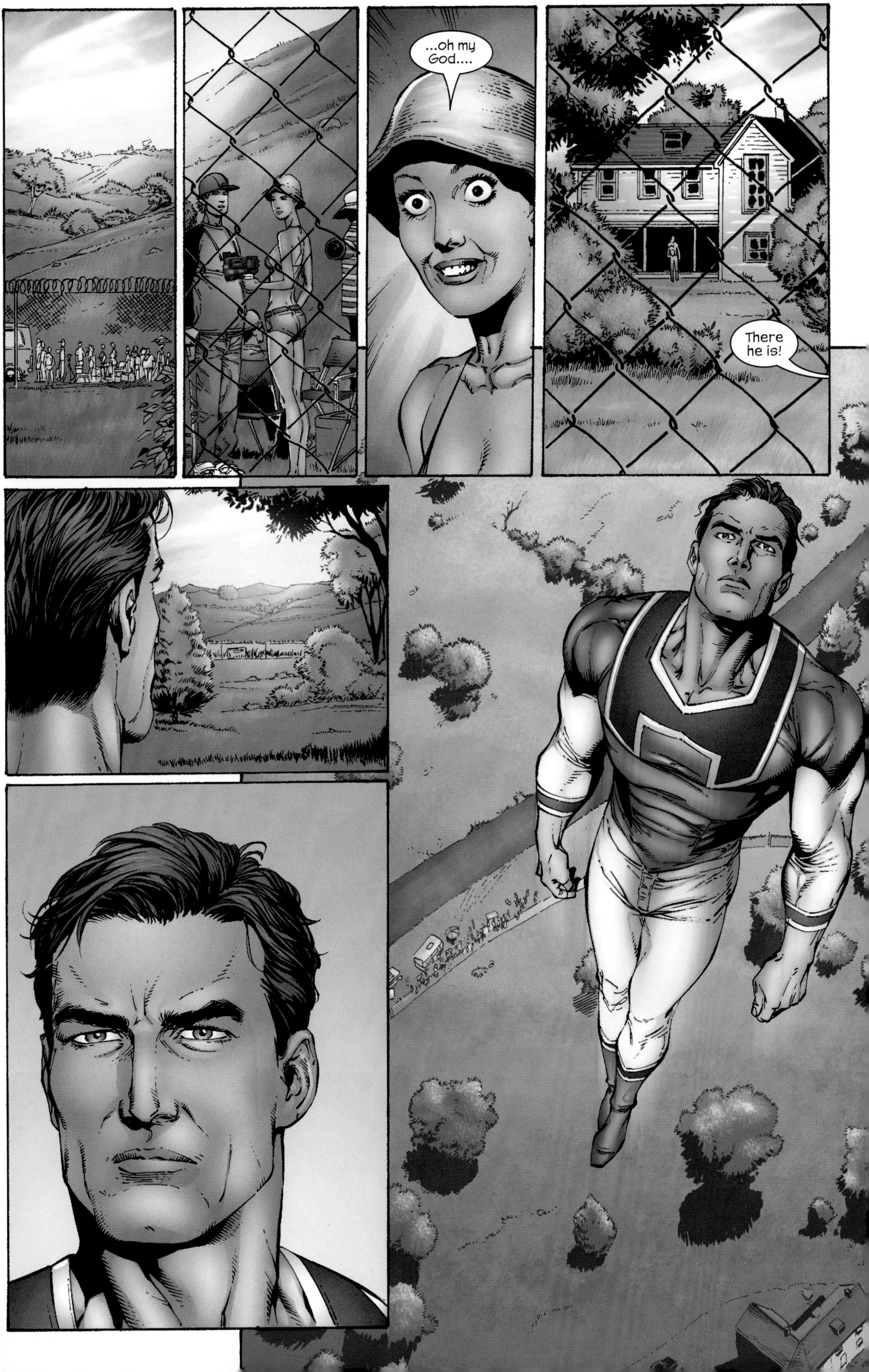
...oh my God....
There he is!

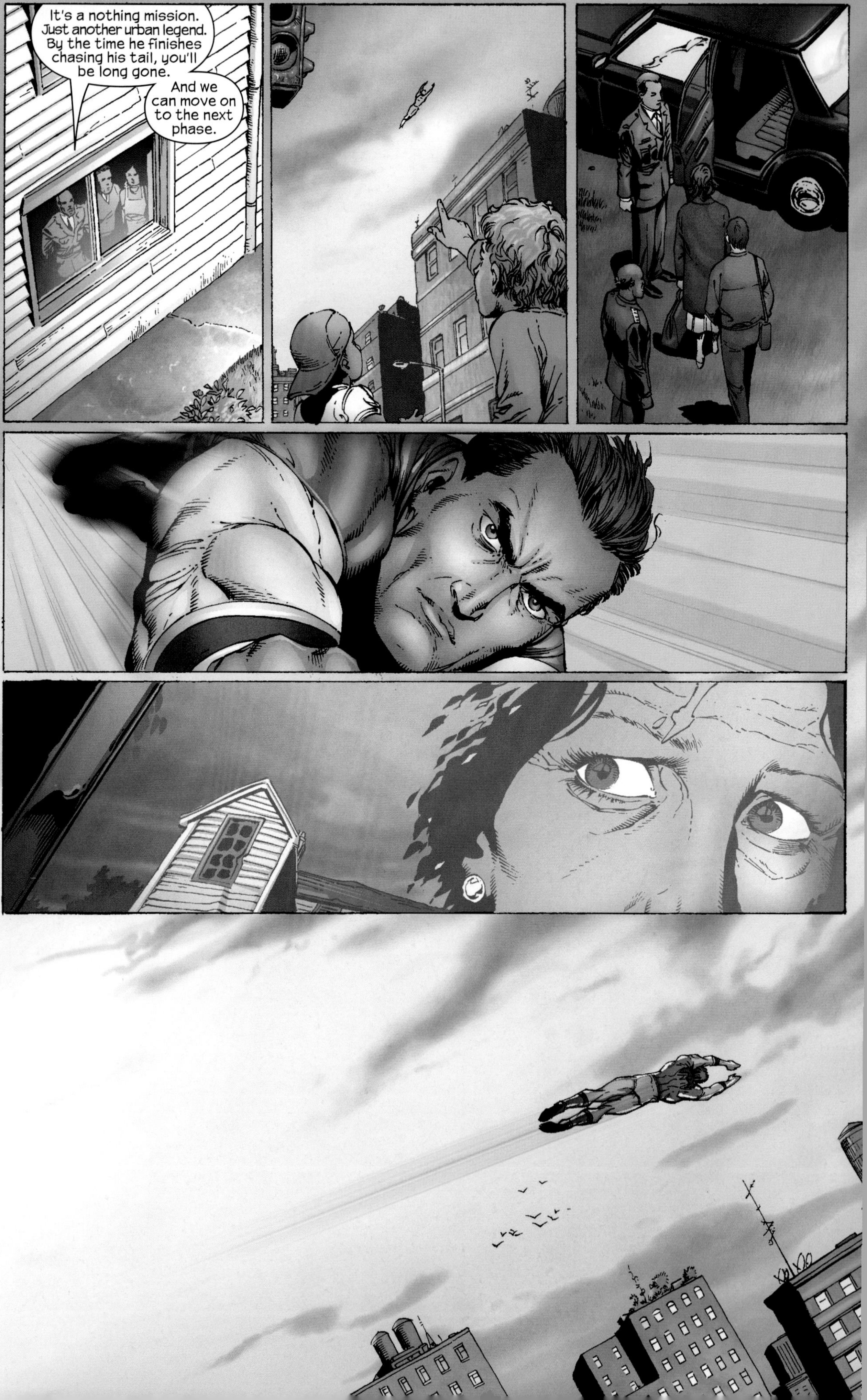
It's a nothing mission. Just another urban legend. By the time he finishes chasing his tail, you'll be long gone.
And we can move on to the next phase.

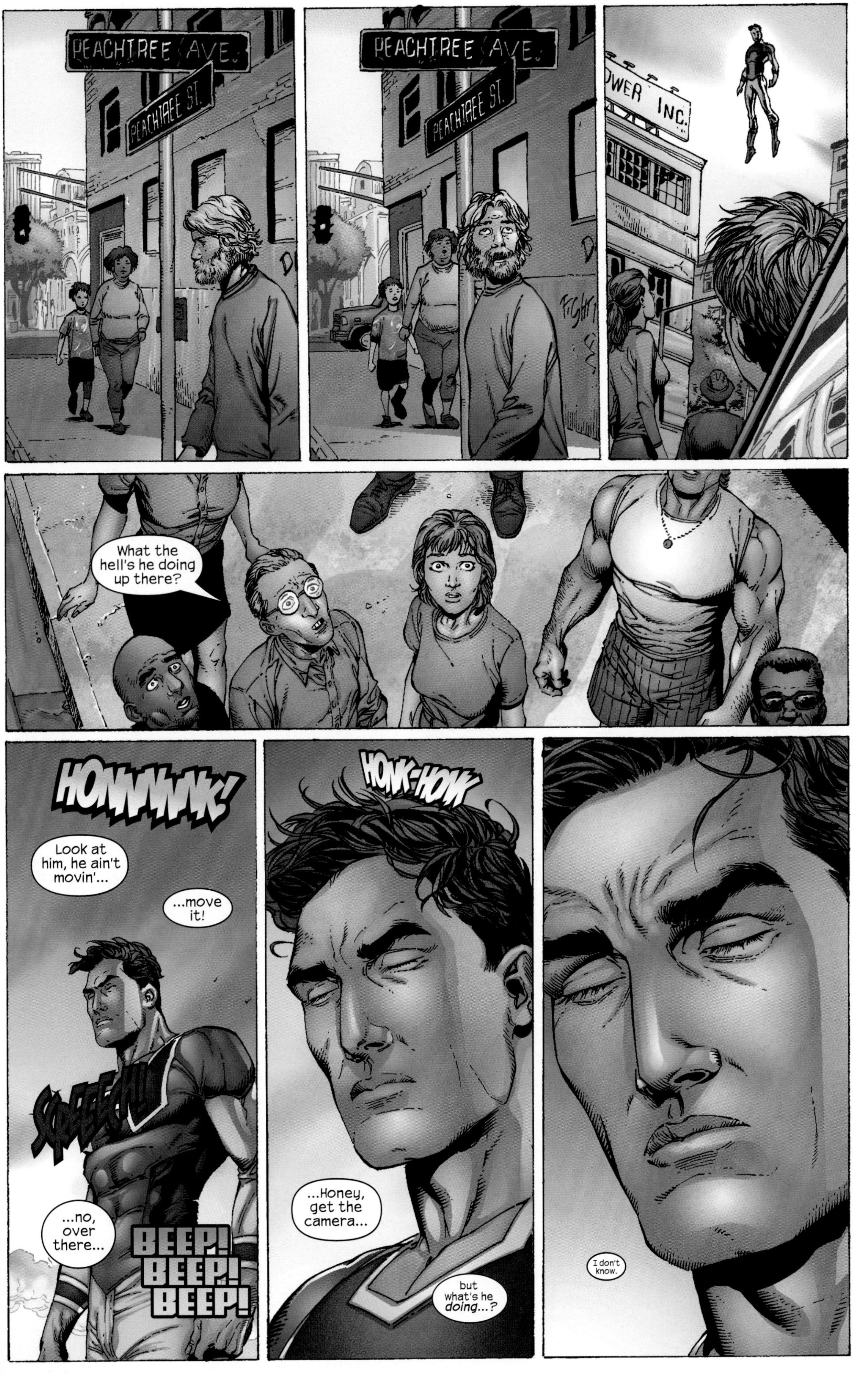
PEACHTREE AVE.
PEACHTREE ST.
PEACHTREE AVE.
PEACHTREE ST.
OWER INC.
What the hell's he doing up there?
HONNNNK!
Look at him, he ain't movin'...
...move it!
SCREECH!!
...no, over there...
BEEP! BEEP! BEEP!
HONK-HONK
...Honey, get the camera...
but what's he *doing*...?
I don't know.

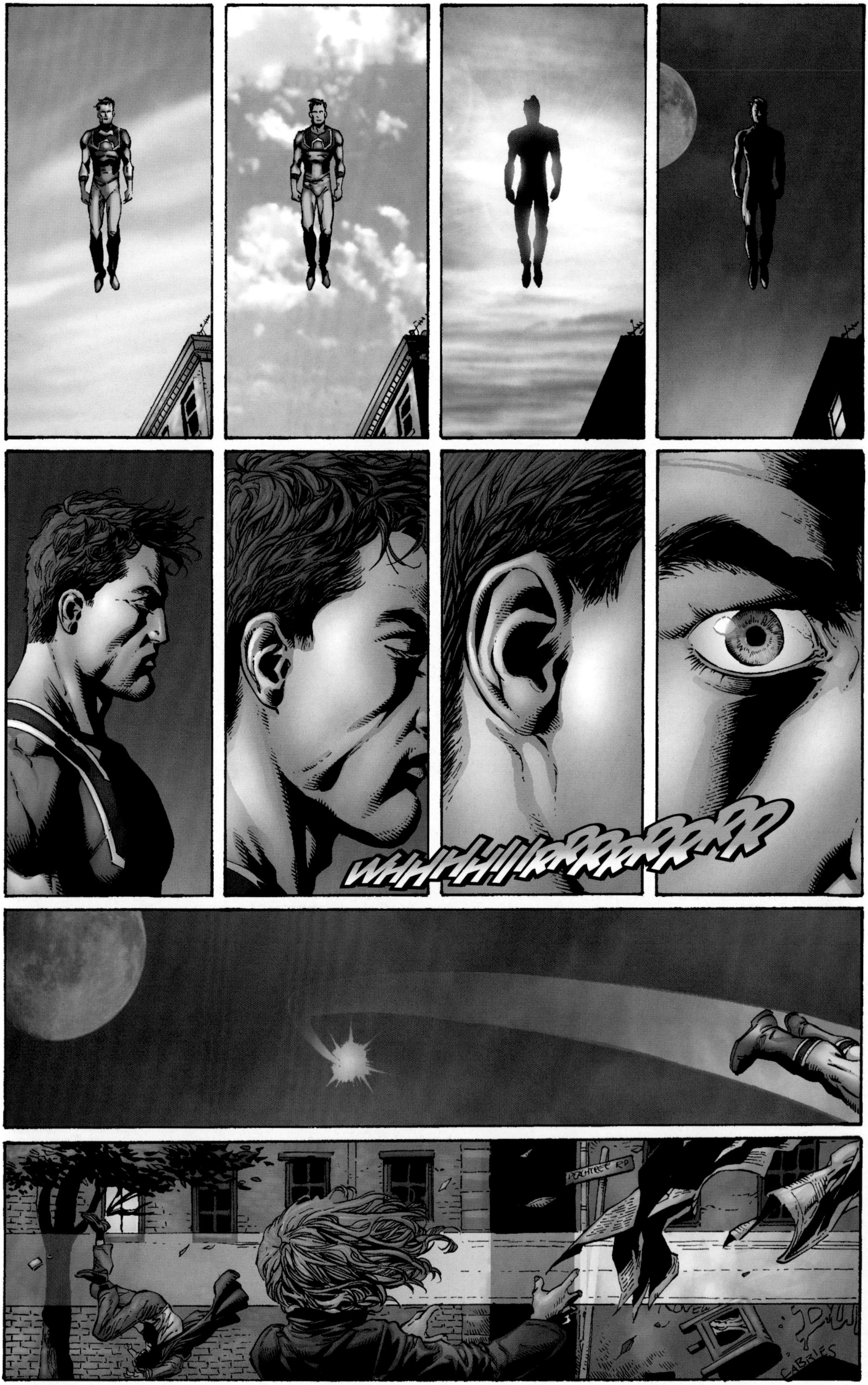
WHHHH!!RRRRRRRRRR
PEACHTREE RD

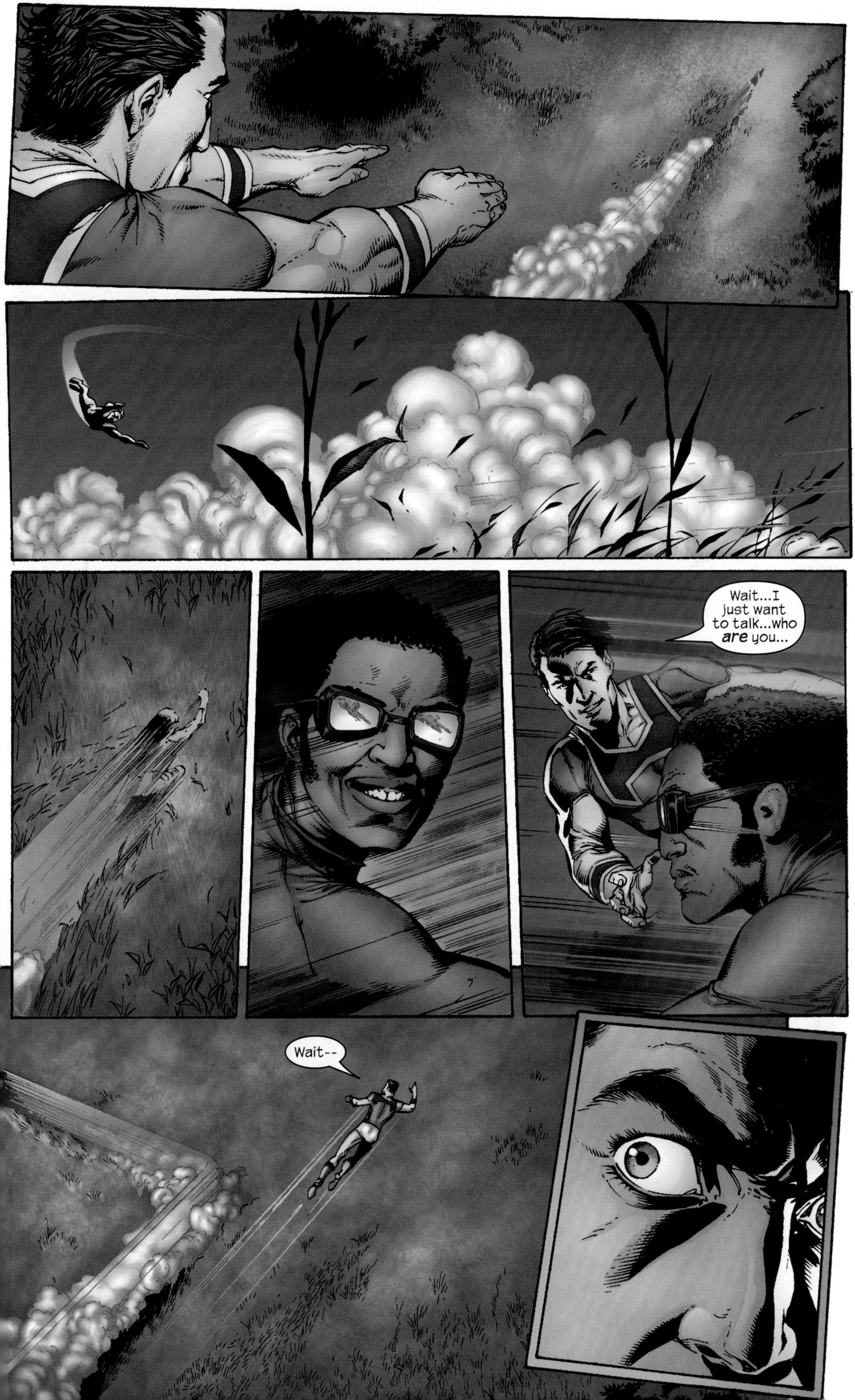
Wait...I just want to talk...who *are* you...
Wait--

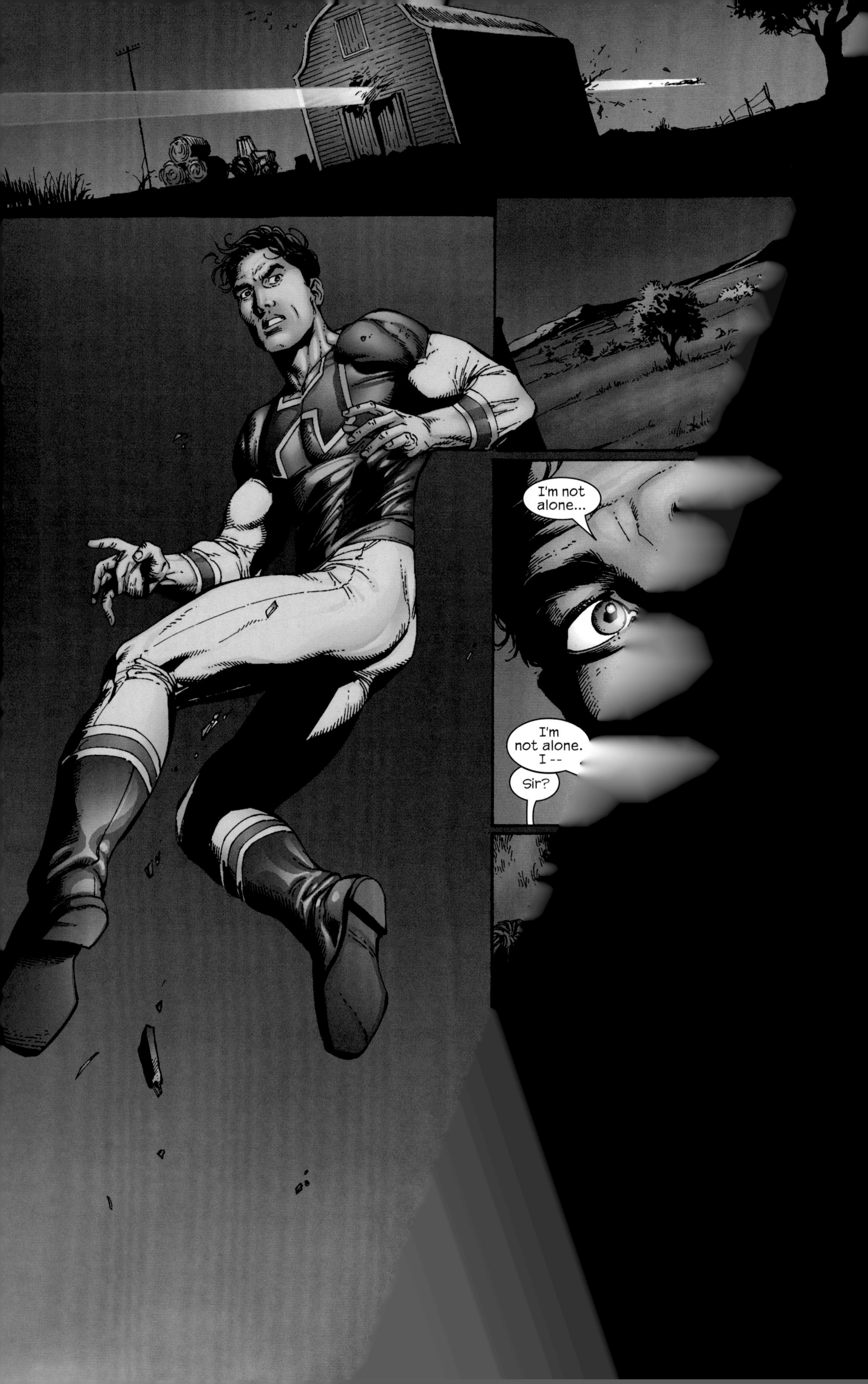
I'm not alone...
I'm not alone. I --
Sir?

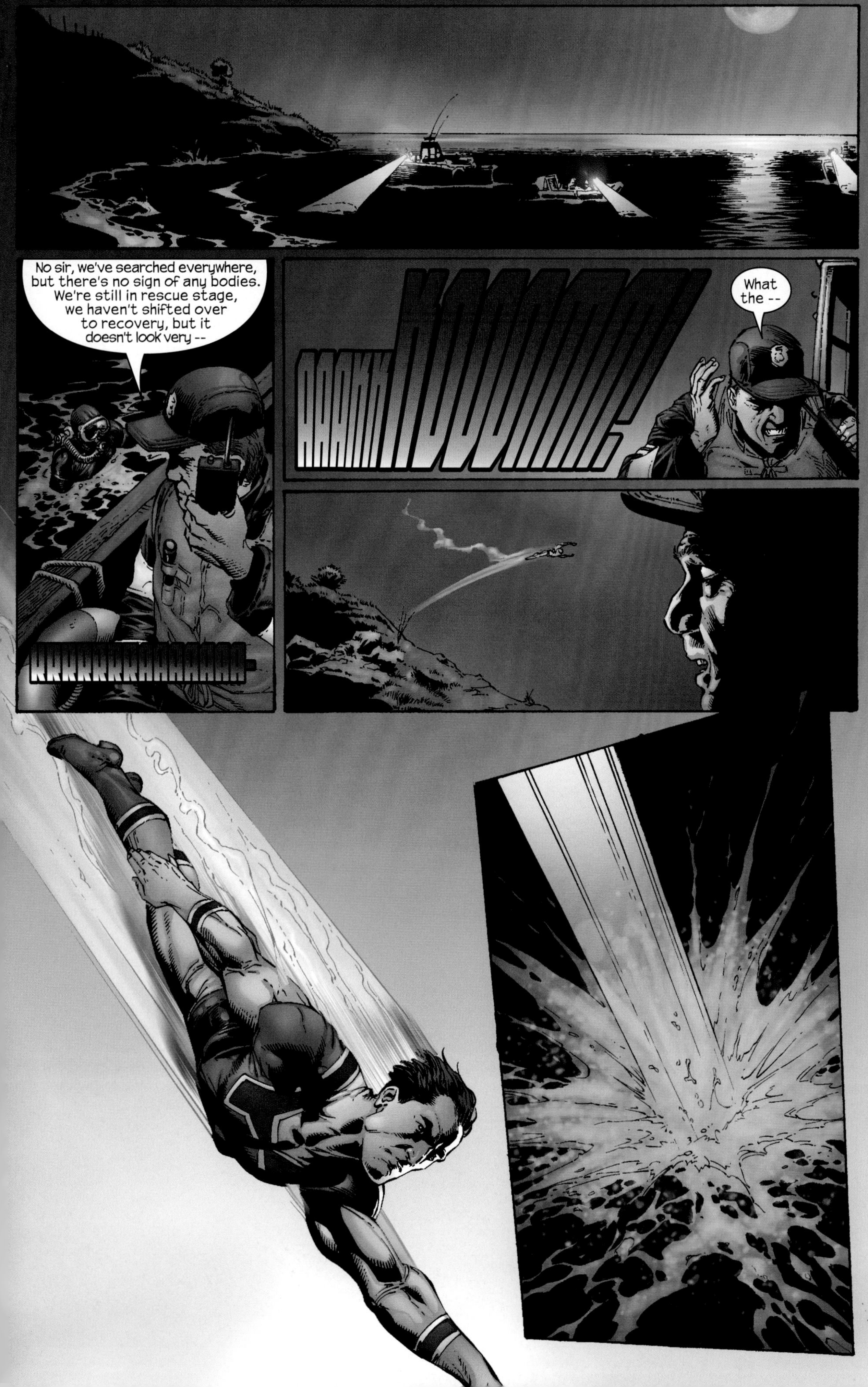
No sir, we've searched everywhere, but there's no sign of any bodies. We're still in rescue stage, we haven't shifted over to recovery, but it doesn't look very --
KKKKKKKAAAAAAAA-
AAAKKHOOOMM!
What the --

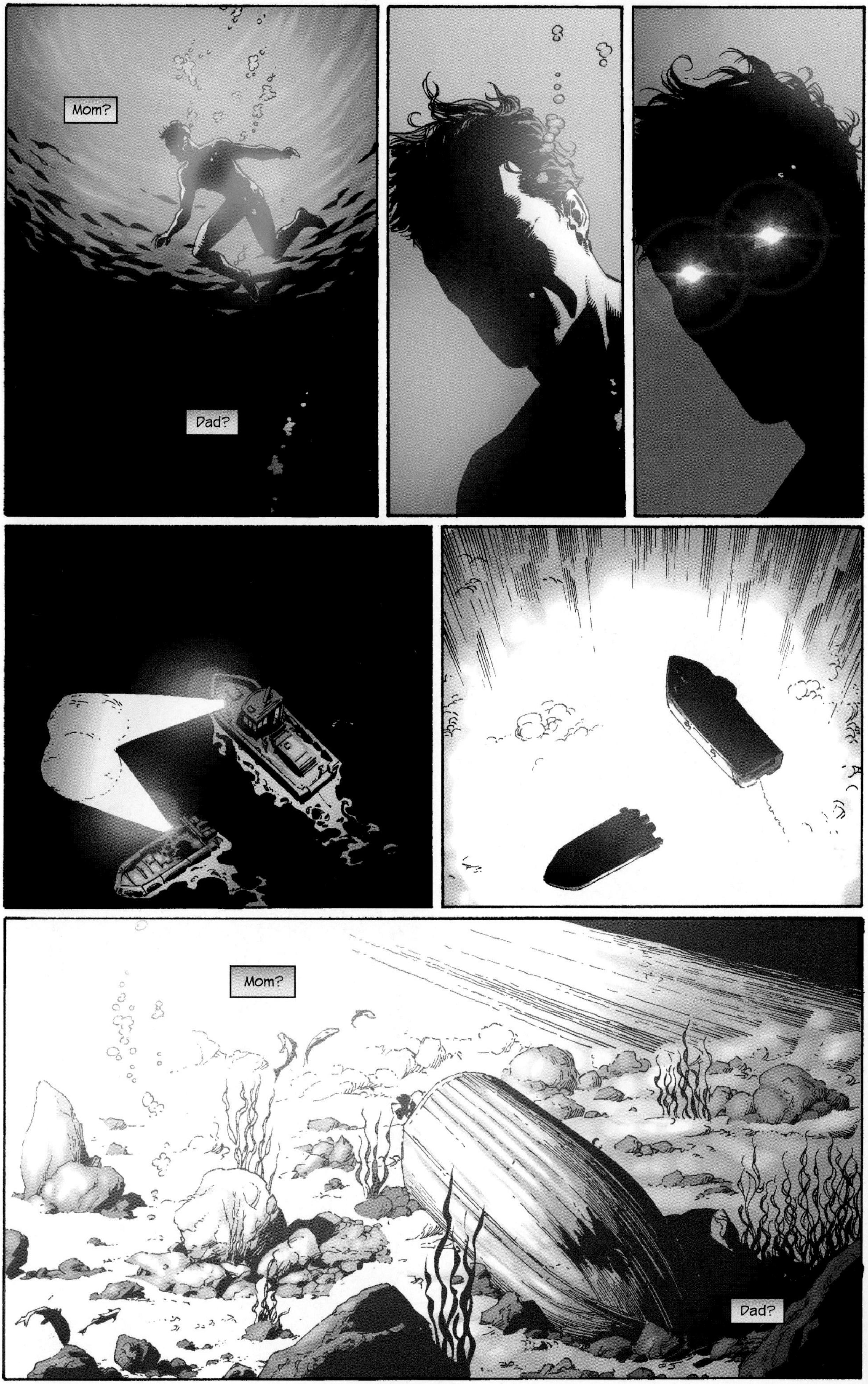
Mom?
Dad?
Mom?
Dad?

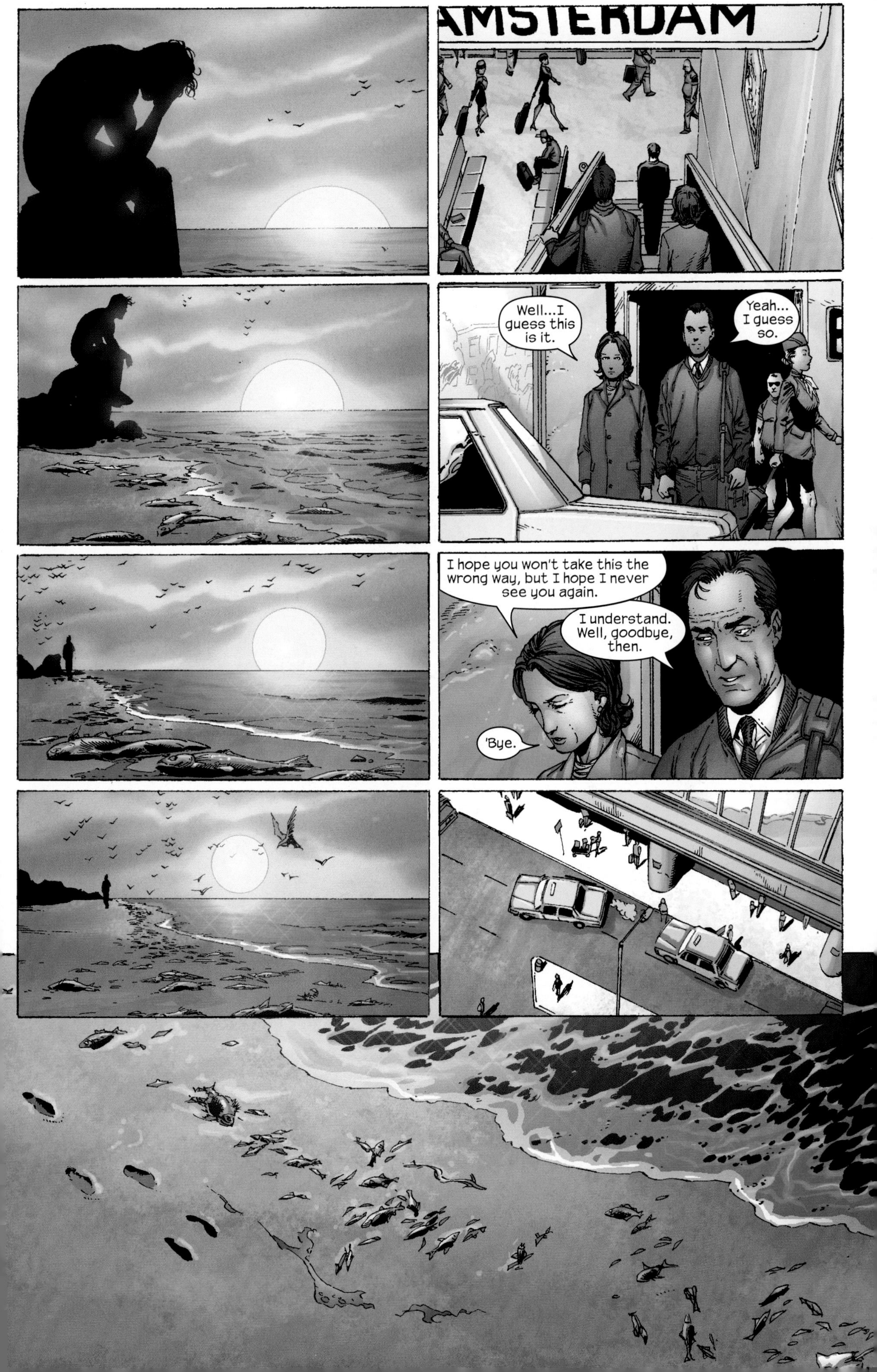
AMSTERDAM
Well...I guess this is it.
Yeah... I guess so.
I hope you won't take this the wrong way, but I hope I never see you again.
I understand. Well, goodbye, then.
'Bye.

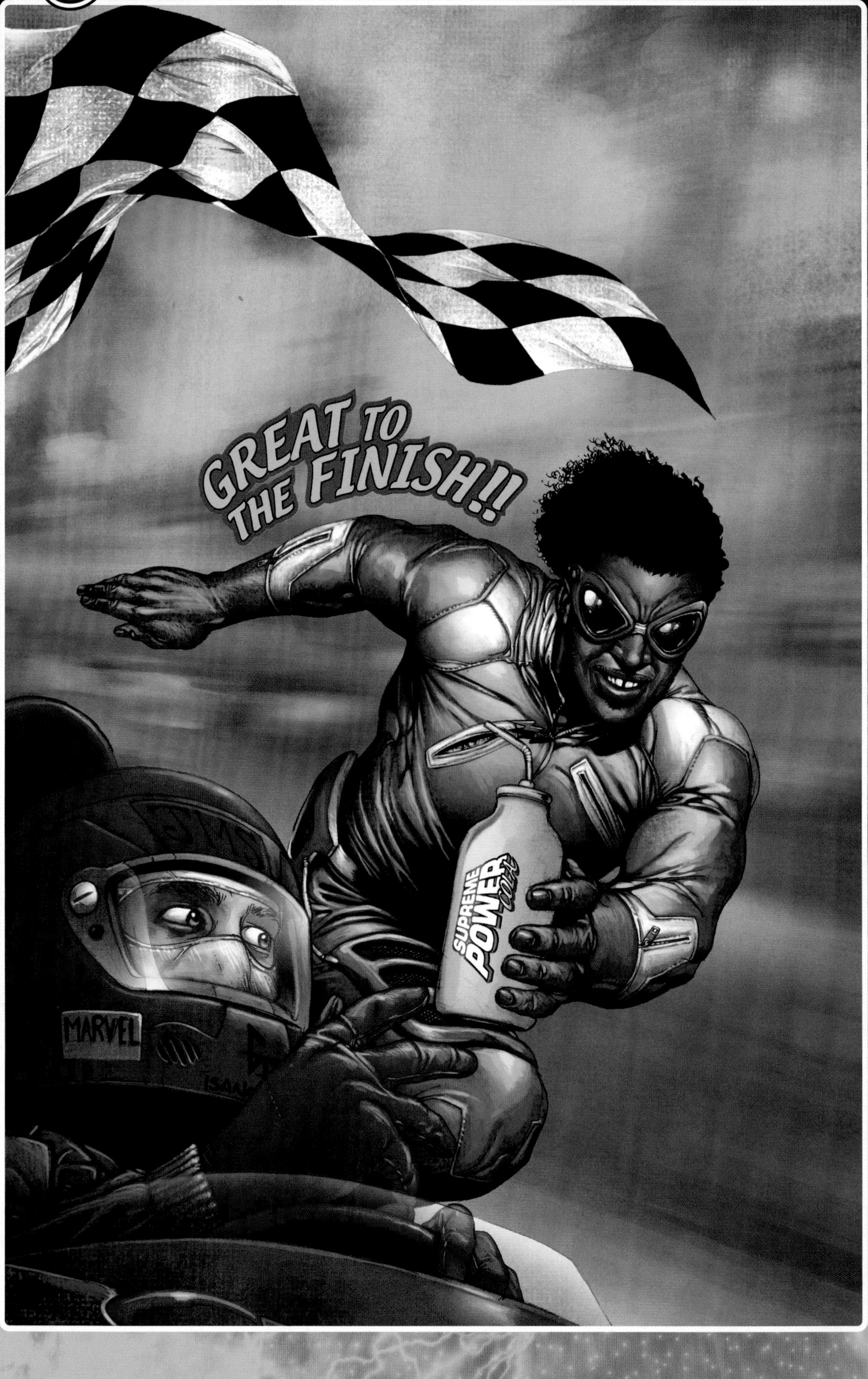
GREAT TO THE FINISH!!
SUPREME POWER COLA
MARVEL

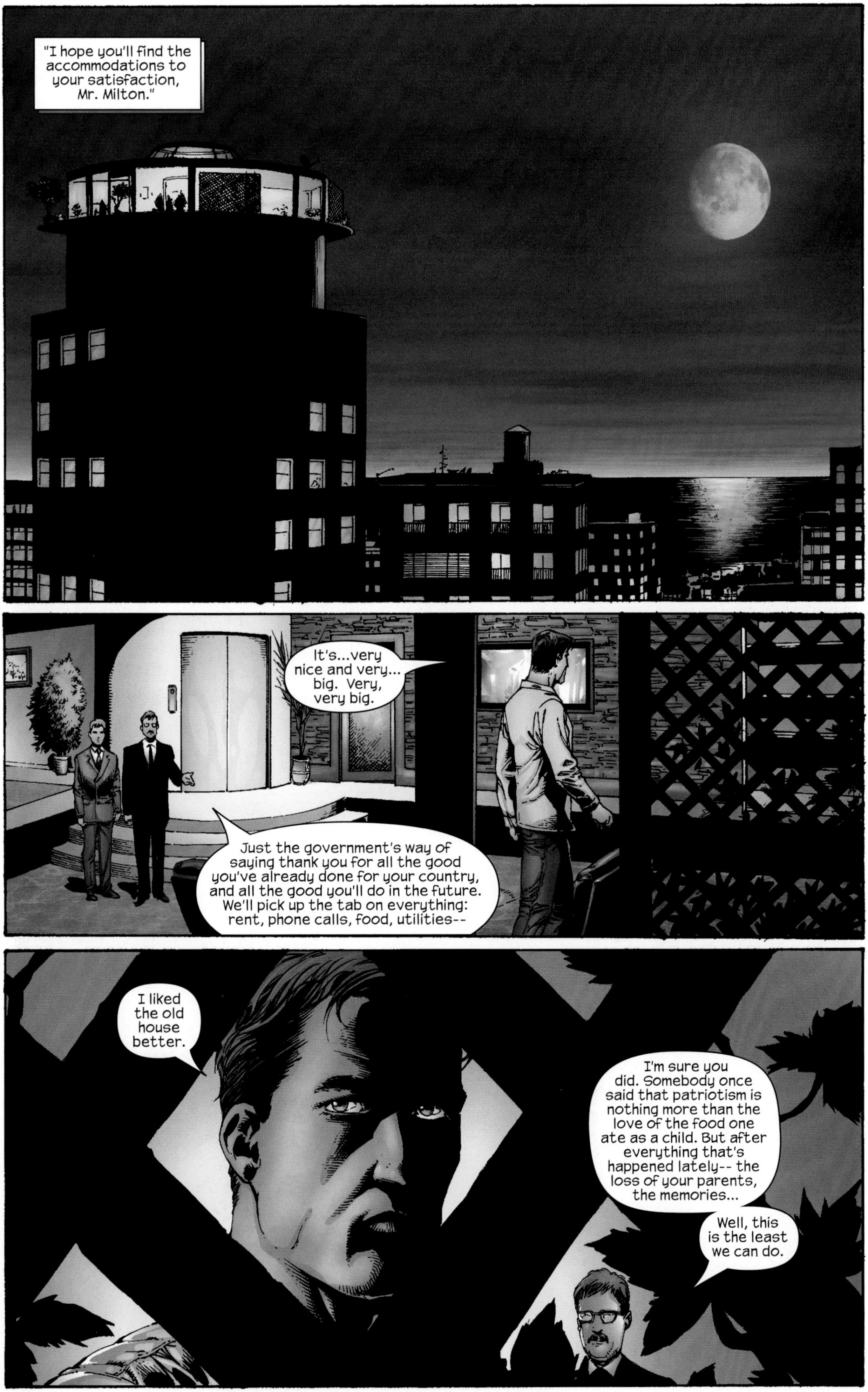
"I hope you'll find the accommodations to your satisfaction, Mr. Milton."
It's...very nice and very... big. Very, very big.
Just the government's way of saying thank you for all the good you've already done for your country, and all the good you'll do in the future. We'll pick up the tab on everything: rent, phone calls, food, utilities--
I liked the old house better.
I'm sure you did. Somebody once said that patriotism is nothing more than the love of the food one ate as a child. But after everything that's happened lately-- the loss of your parents, the memories...
Well, this is the least we can do.

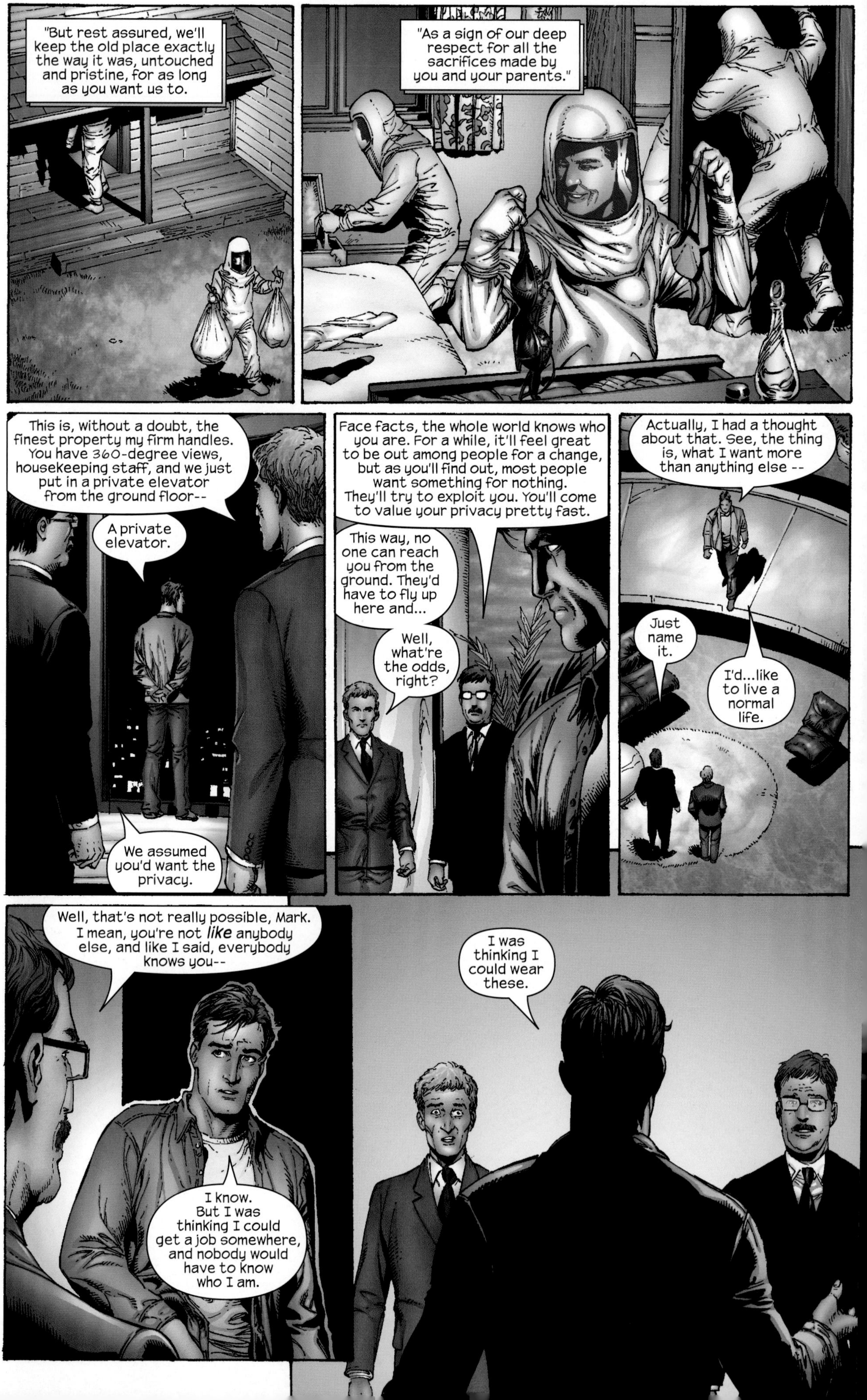
"But rest assured, we'll keep the old place exactly the way it was, untouched and pristine, for as long as you want us to.
"As a sign of our deep respect for all the sacrifices made by you and your parents."
This is, without a doubt, the finest property my firm handles. You have 360-degree views, housekeeping staff, and we just put in a private elevator from the ground floor--
A private elevator.
We assumed you'd want the privacy.
Face facts, the whole world knows who you are. For a while, it'll feel great to be out among people for a change, but as you'll find out, most people want something for nothing. They'll try to exploit you. You'll come to value your privacy pretty fast.
This way, no one can reach you from the ground. They'd have to fly up here and...
Well, what're the odds, right?
Actually, I had a thought about that. See, the thing is, what I want more than anything else --
Just name it.
I'd...like to live a normal life.
Well, that's not really possible, Mark. I mean, you're not *like* anybody else, and like I said, everybody knows you--
I know. But I was thinking I could get a job somewhere, and nobody would have to know who I am.
I was thinking I could wear these.

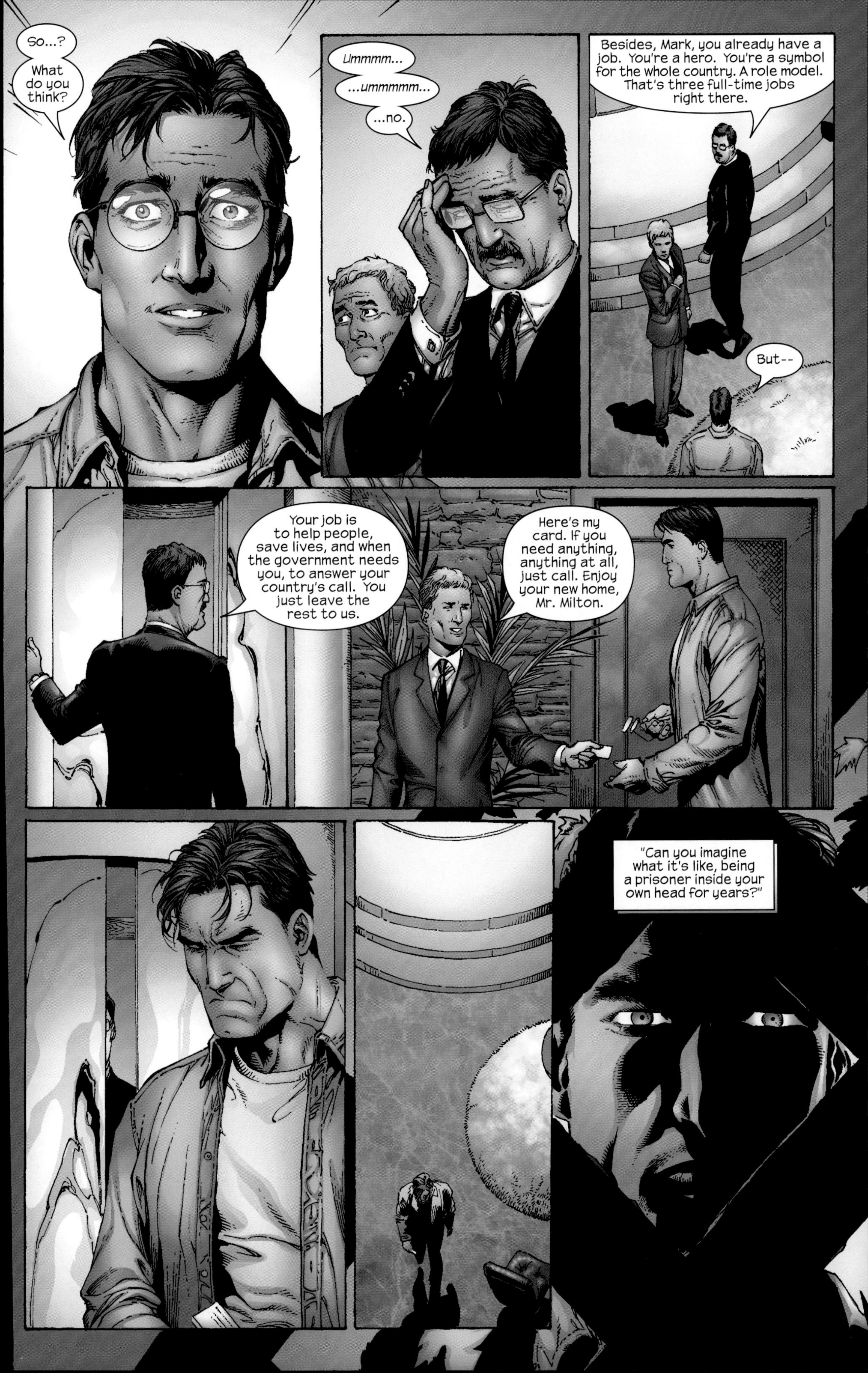
So...?
What do you think?
Ummmm...
...ummmmm...
...no.
Besides, Mark, you already have a job. You're a hero. You're a symbol for the whole country. A role model. That's three full-time jobs right there.
But--
Your job is to help people, save lives, and when the government needs you, to answer your country's call. You just leave the rest to us.
Here's my card. If you need anything, anything at all, just call. Enjoy your new home, Mr. Milton.
"Can you imagine what it's like, being a prisoner inside your own head for years?"

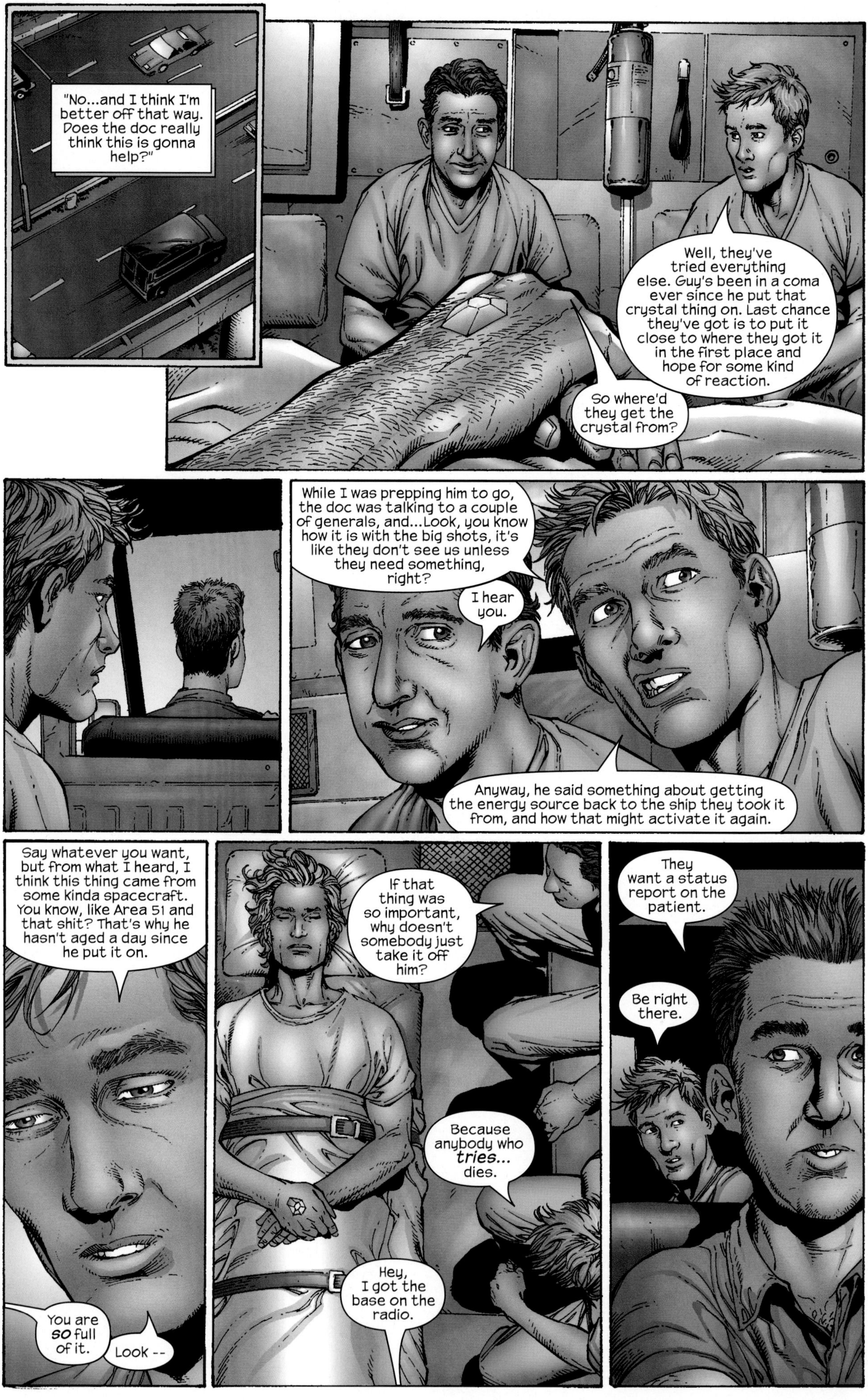
"No...and I think I'm better off that way. Does the doc really think this is gonna help?"
Well, they've tried everything else. Guy's been in a coma ever since he put that crystal thing on. Last chance they've got is to put it close to where they got it in the first place and hope for some kind of reaction.
So where'd they get the crystal from?
While I was prepping him to go, the doc was talking to a couple of generals, and...Look, you know how it is with the big shots, it's like they don't see us unless they need something, right?
I hear you.
Anyway, he said something about getting the energy source back to the ship they took it from, and how that might activate it again.
Say whatever you want, but from what I heard, I think this thing came from some kinda spacecraft. You know, like Area 51 and that shit? That's why he hasn't aged a day since he put it on.
You are *SO* full of it.
Look --
If that thing was so important, why doesn't somebody just take it off him?
Because anybody who *tries...* dies.
Hey, I got the base on the radio.
They want a status report on the patient.
Be right there.

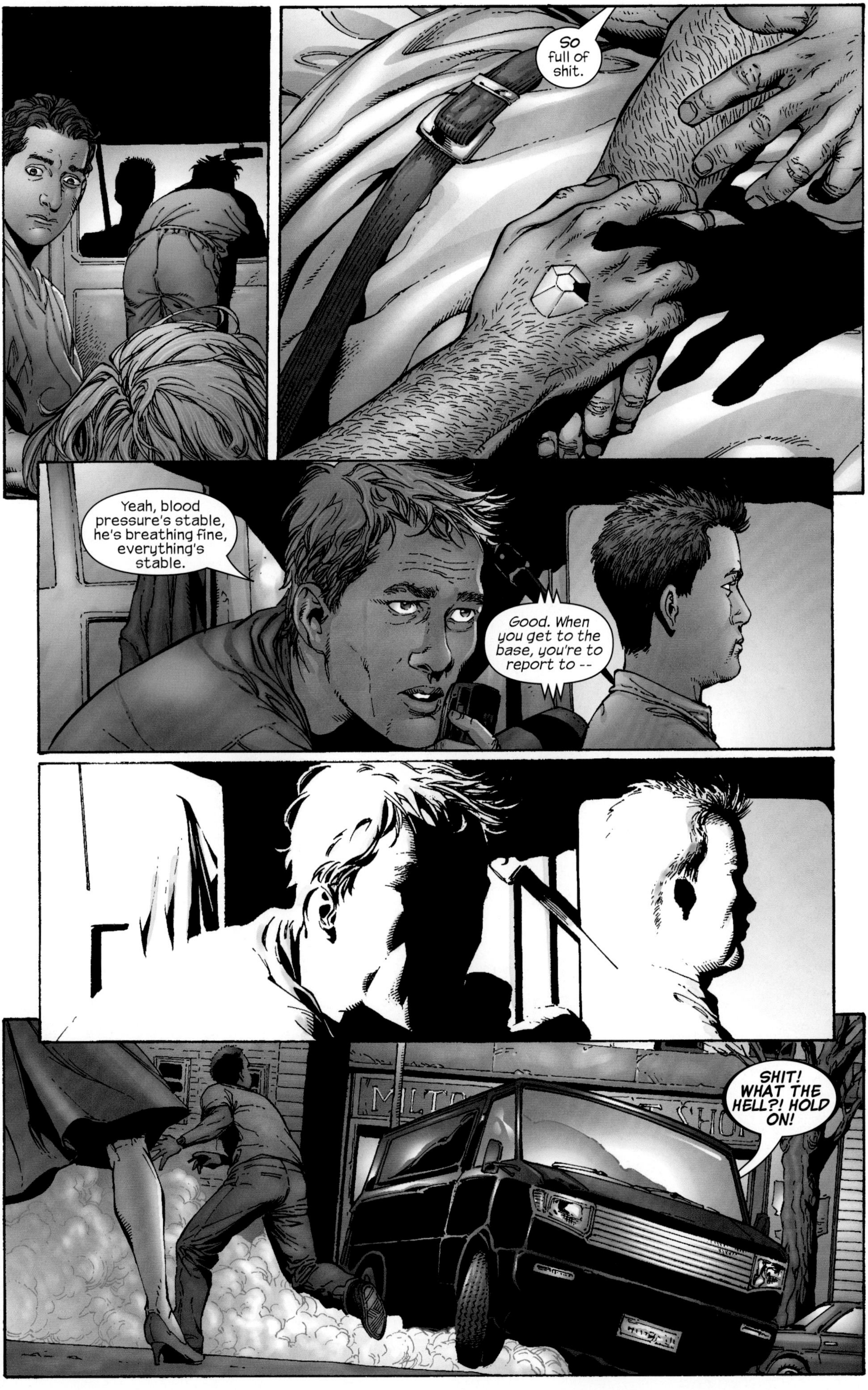
So full of shit.
Yeah, blood pressure's stable, he's breathing fine, everything's stable.
Good. When you get to the base, you're to report to --
SHIT! WHAT THE HELL?! HOLD ON!

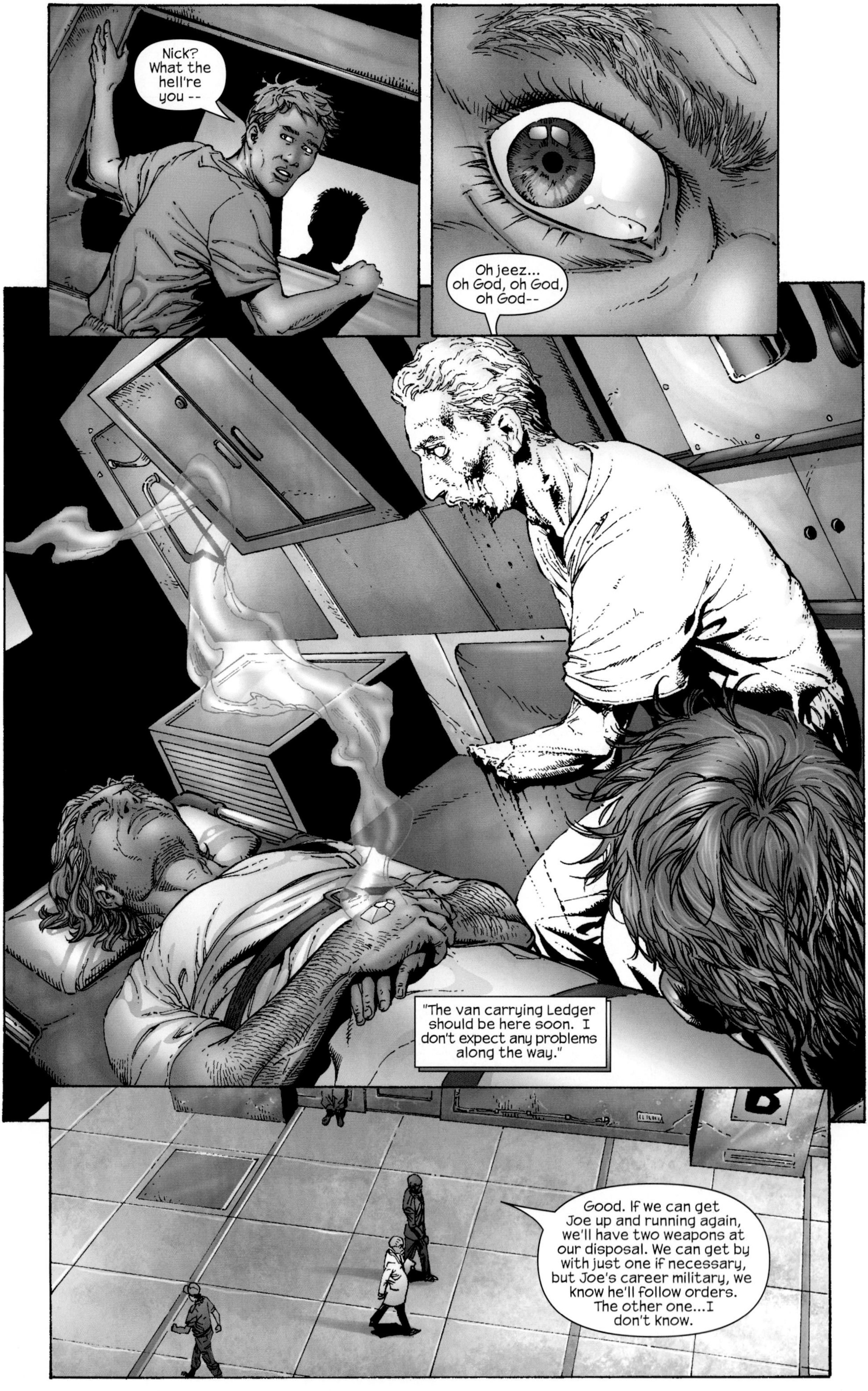
Nick? What the hell're you --
Oh jeez... oh God, oh God, oh God--
"The van carrying Ledger should be here soon. I don't expect any problems along the way."
Good. If we can get Joe up and running again, we'll have two weapons at our disposal. We can get by with just one if necessary, but Joe's career military, we know he'll follow orders. The other one...I don't know.

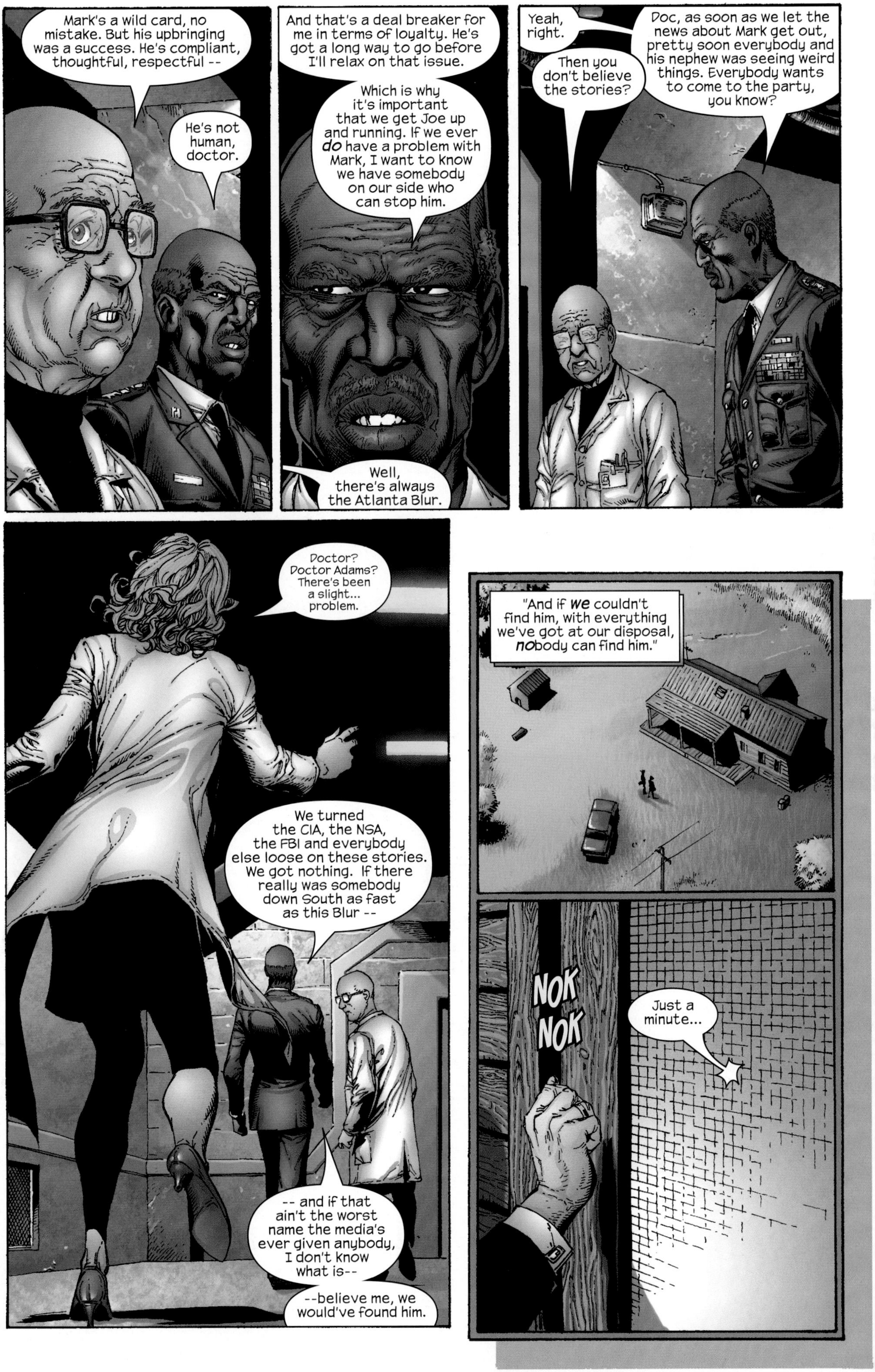

Mark's a wild card, no mistake. But his upbringing was a success. He's compliant, thoughtful, respectful --
He's not human, doctor.
And that's a deal breaker for me in terms of loyalty. He's got a long way to go before I'll relax on that issue.
Which is why it's important that we get Joe up and running. If we ever *do* have a problem with Mark, I want to know we have somebody on our side who can stop him.
Well, there's always the Atlanta Blur.
Yeah, right.
Then you don't believe the stories?
Doc, as soon as we let the news about Mark get out, pretty soon everybody and his nephew was seeing weird things. Everybody wants to come to the party, you know?
Doctor? Doctor Adams? There's been a slight... problem.
We turned the CIA, the NSA, the FBI and everybody else loose on these stories. We got nothing. If there really was somebody down South as fast as this Blur --
-- and if that ain't the worst name the media's ever given anybody, I don't know what is--
--believe me, we would've found him.
"And if *we* couldn't find him, with everything we've got at our disposal, *no*body can find him."
NOK
NOK
Just a minute...

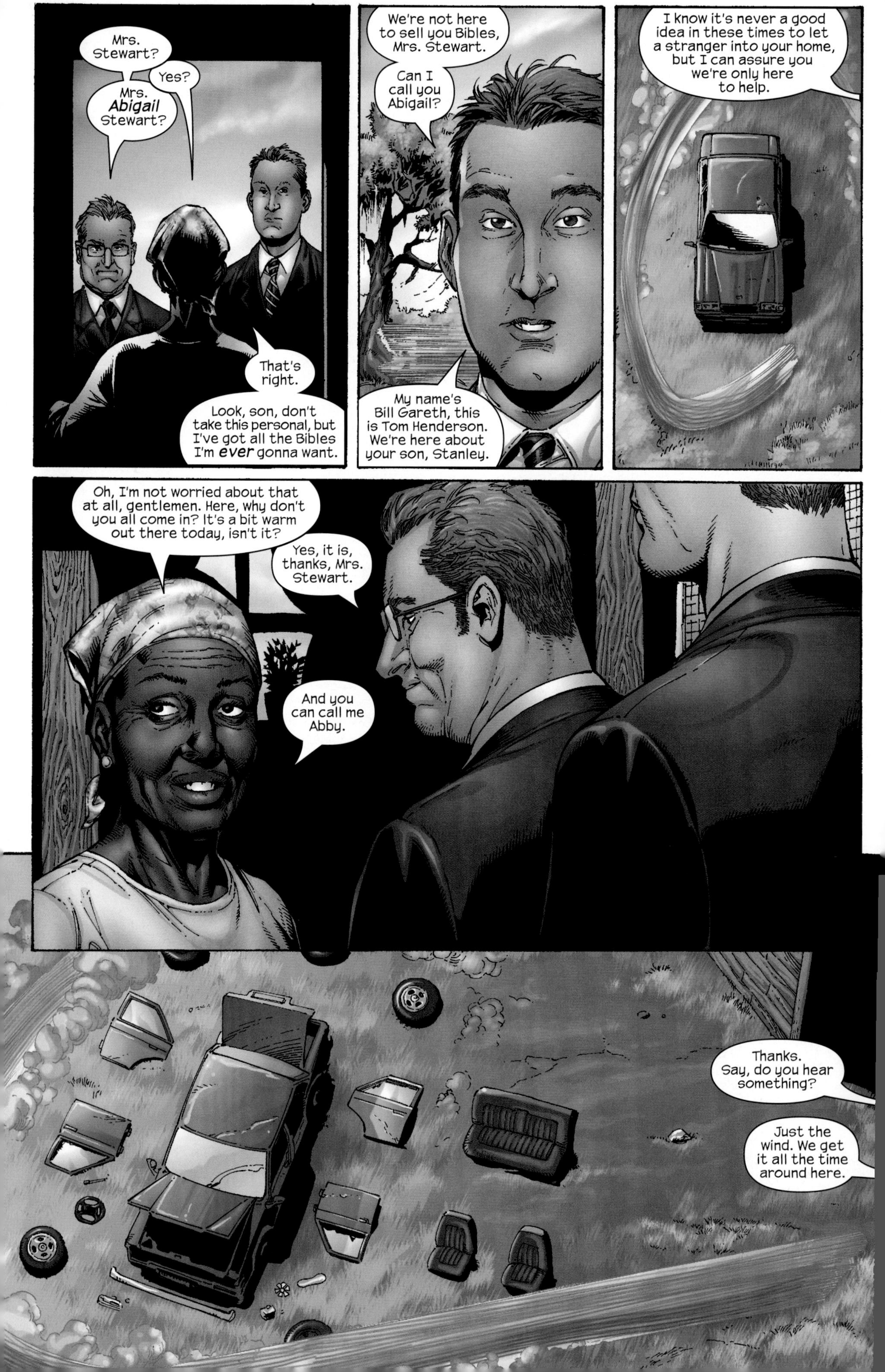
Mrs. Stewart?
Yes?
Mrs. *Abigail* Stewart?
That's right.
Look, son, don't take this personal, but I've got all the Bibles I'm *ever* gonna want.
We're not here to sell you Bibles, Mrs. Stewart.
Can I call you Abigail?
My name's Bill Gareth, this is Tom Henderson. We're here about your son, Stanley.
I know it's never a good idea in these times to let a stranger into your home, but I can assure you we're only here to help.
Oh, I'm not worried about that at all, gentlemen. Here, why don't you all come in? It's a bit warm out there today, isn't it?
Yes, it is, thanks, Mrs. Stewart.
And you can call me Abby.
Thanks. Say, do you hear something?
Just the wind. We get it all the time around here.

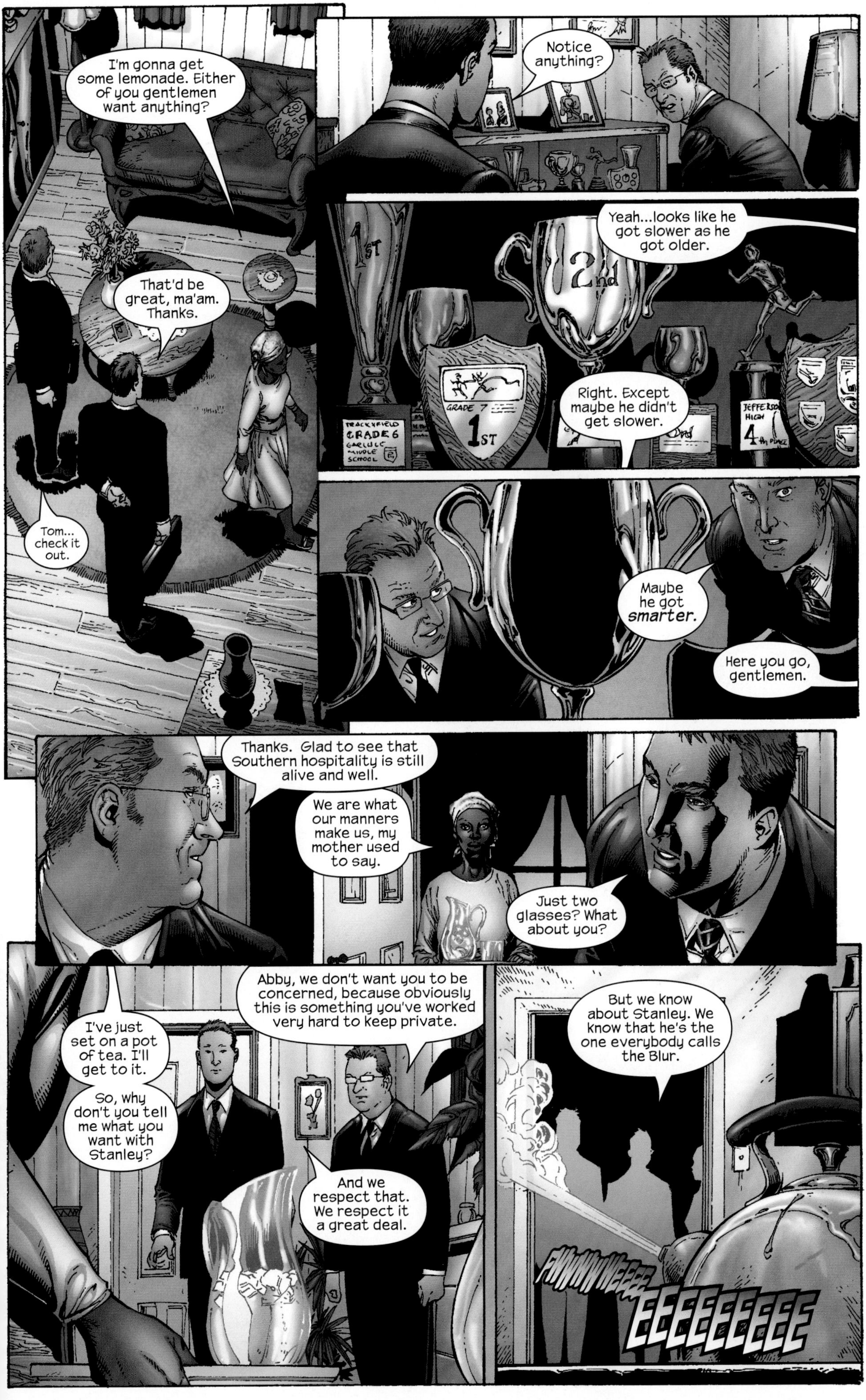

I'm gonna get some lemonade. Either of you gentlemen want anything?
That'd be great, ma'am. Thanks.
Tom... check it out.
Notice anything?
Yeah...looks like he got slower as he got older.
Right. Except maybe he didn't get slower.
TRACK&FIELD GRADE 6
GRADE 7 1ST
1ST
2nd
JEFFERSON HIGH 4th PLACE
Maybe he got *smarter.*
Here you go, gentlemen.
Thanks. Glad to see that Southern hospitality is still alive and well.
We are what our manners make us, my mother used to say.
Just two glasses? What about you?
I've just set on a pot of tea. I'll get to it.
So, why don't you tell me what you want with Stanley?
Abby, we don't want you to be concerned, because obviously this is something you've worked very hard to keep private.
And we respect that. We respect it a great deal.
But we know about Stanley. We know that he's the one everybody calls the Blur.
FWWWWWEEEEEEEEEEEEE

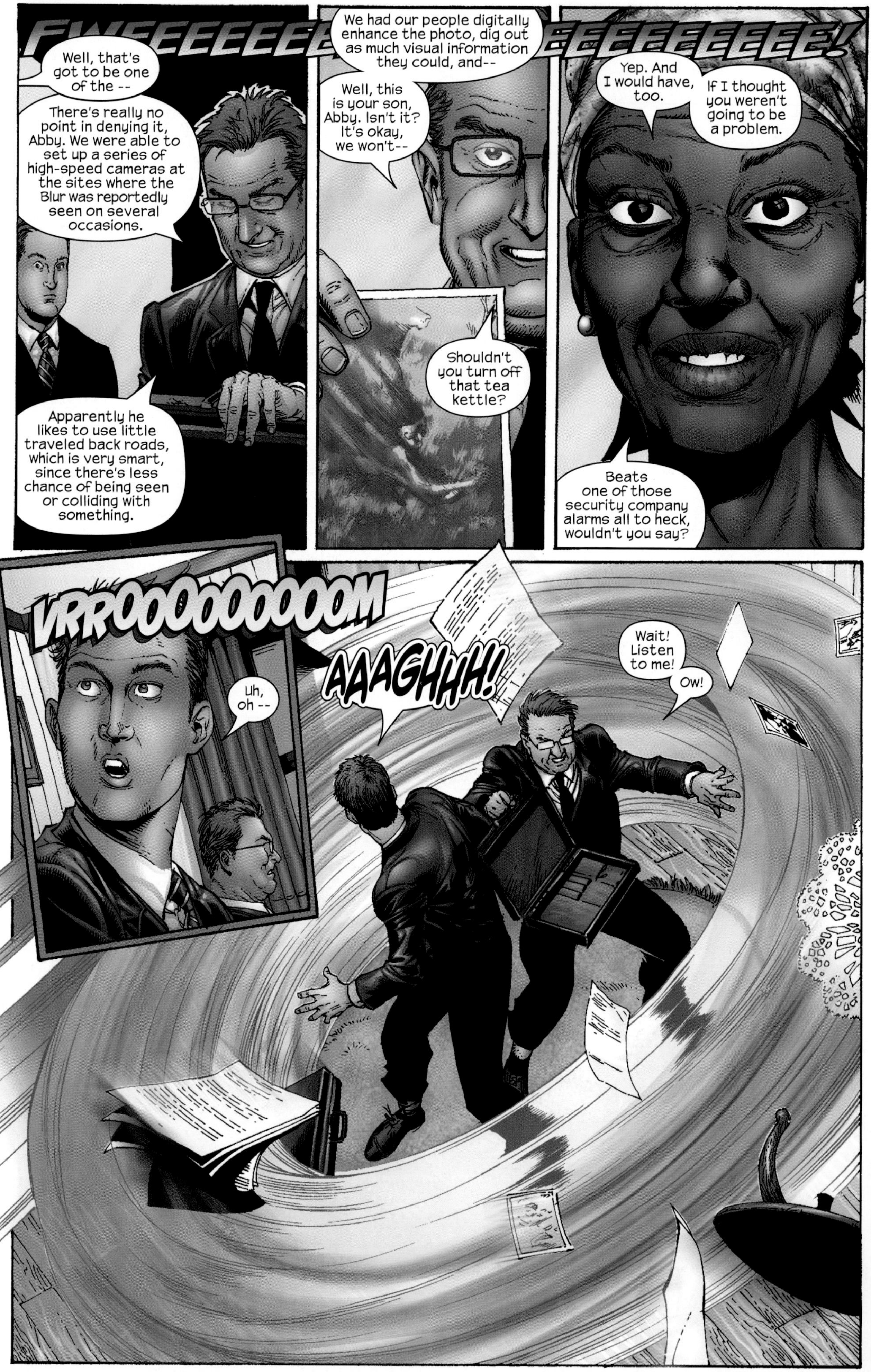

FWEEEEEEEEEEEEEEEEEEEEEEEE!
Well, that's got to be one of the --
There's really no point in denying it, Abby. We were able to set up a series of high-speed cameras at the sites where the Blur was reportedly seen on several occasions.
Apparently he likes to use little traveled back roads, which is very smart, since there's less chance of being seen or colliding with something.
We had our people digitally enhance the photo, dig out as much visual information they could, and--
Well, this is your son, Abby. Isn't it? It's okay, we won't--
Shouldn't you turn off that tea kettle?
Yep. And I would have, too.
If I thought you weren't going to be a problem.
Beats one of those security company alarms all to heck, wouldn't you say?
VRROOOOOOOOOM
Uh, oh --
AAAGHHH!
Wait! Listen to me!
Ow!

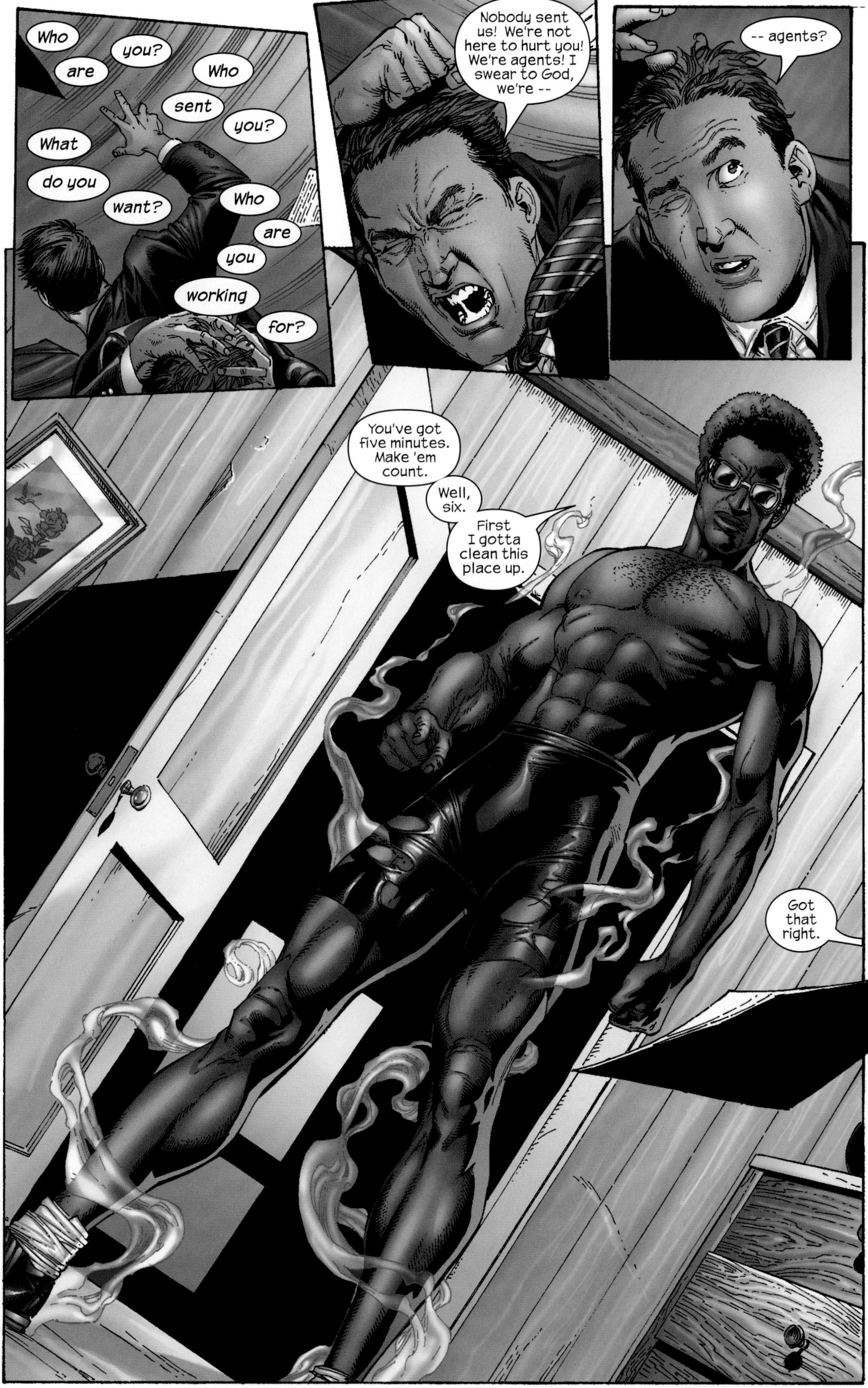
Who are you? Who sent you? What do you want? Who are you working for?
Nobody sent us! We're not here to hurt you! We're agents! I swear to God, we're --
-- agents?
You've got five minutes. Make 'em count.
Well, six.
First I gotta clean this place up.
Got that right.

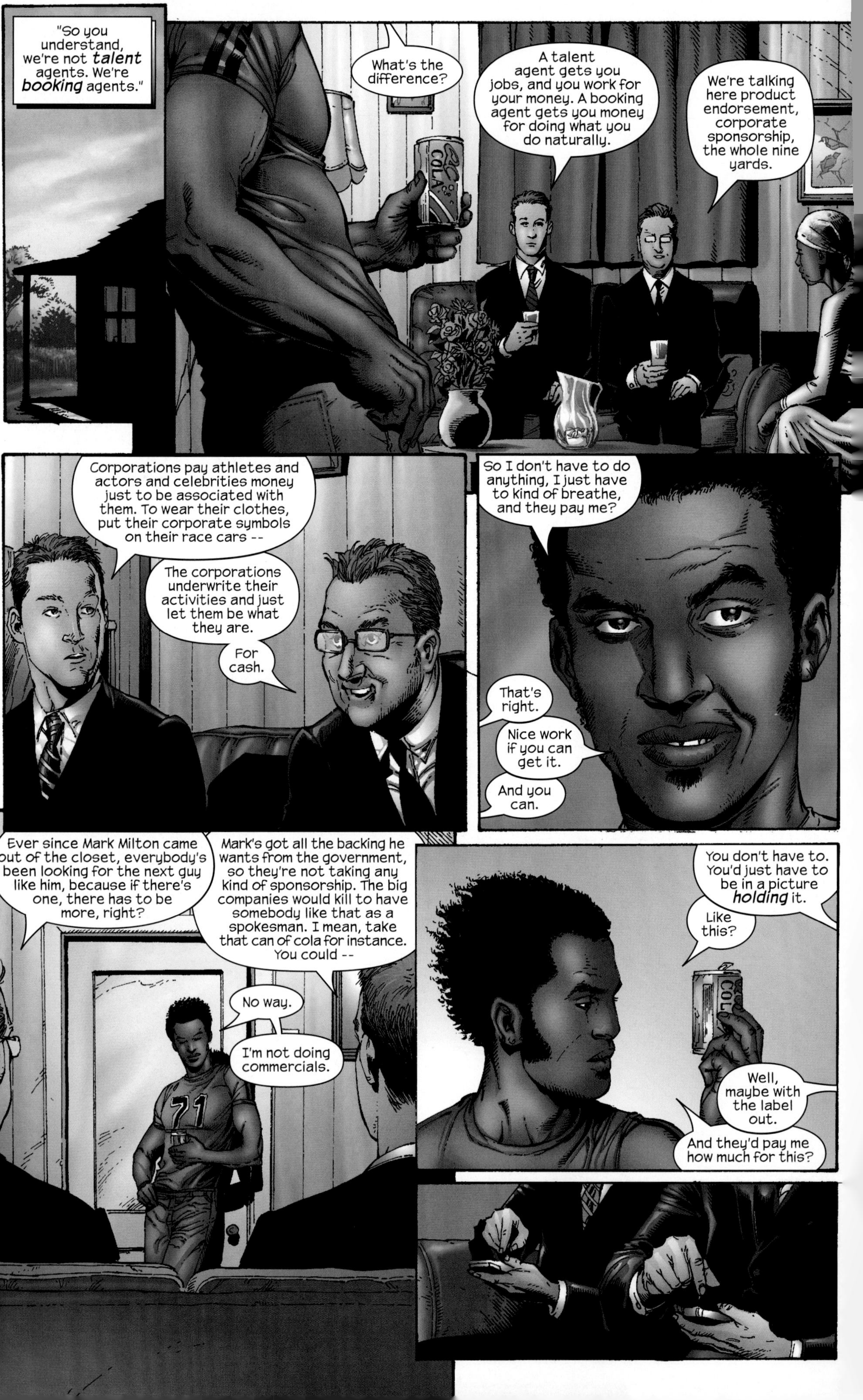
"So you understand, we're not *talent* agents. We're *booking* agents."
What's the difference?
A talent agent gets you jobs, and you work for your money. A booking agent gets you money for doing what you do naturally.
We're talking here product endorsement, corporate sponsorship, the whole nine yards.
Corporations pay athletes and actors and celebrities money just to be associated with them. To wear their clothes, put their corporate symbols on their race cars --
The corporations underwrite their activities and just let them be what they are.
For cash.
So I don't have to do anything, I just have to kind of breathe, and they pay me?
That's right.
Nice work if you can get it.
And you can.
Ever since Mark Milton came out of the closet, everybody's been looking for the next guy like him, because if there's one, there has to be more, right?
Mark's got all the backing he wants from the government, so they're not taking any kind of sponsorship. The big companies would kill to have somebody like that as a spokesman. I mean, take that can of cola for instance. You could --
No way.
I'm not doing commercials.
You don't have to. You'd just have to be in a picture *holding* it.
Like this?
Well, maybe with the label out.
And they'd pay me how much for this?

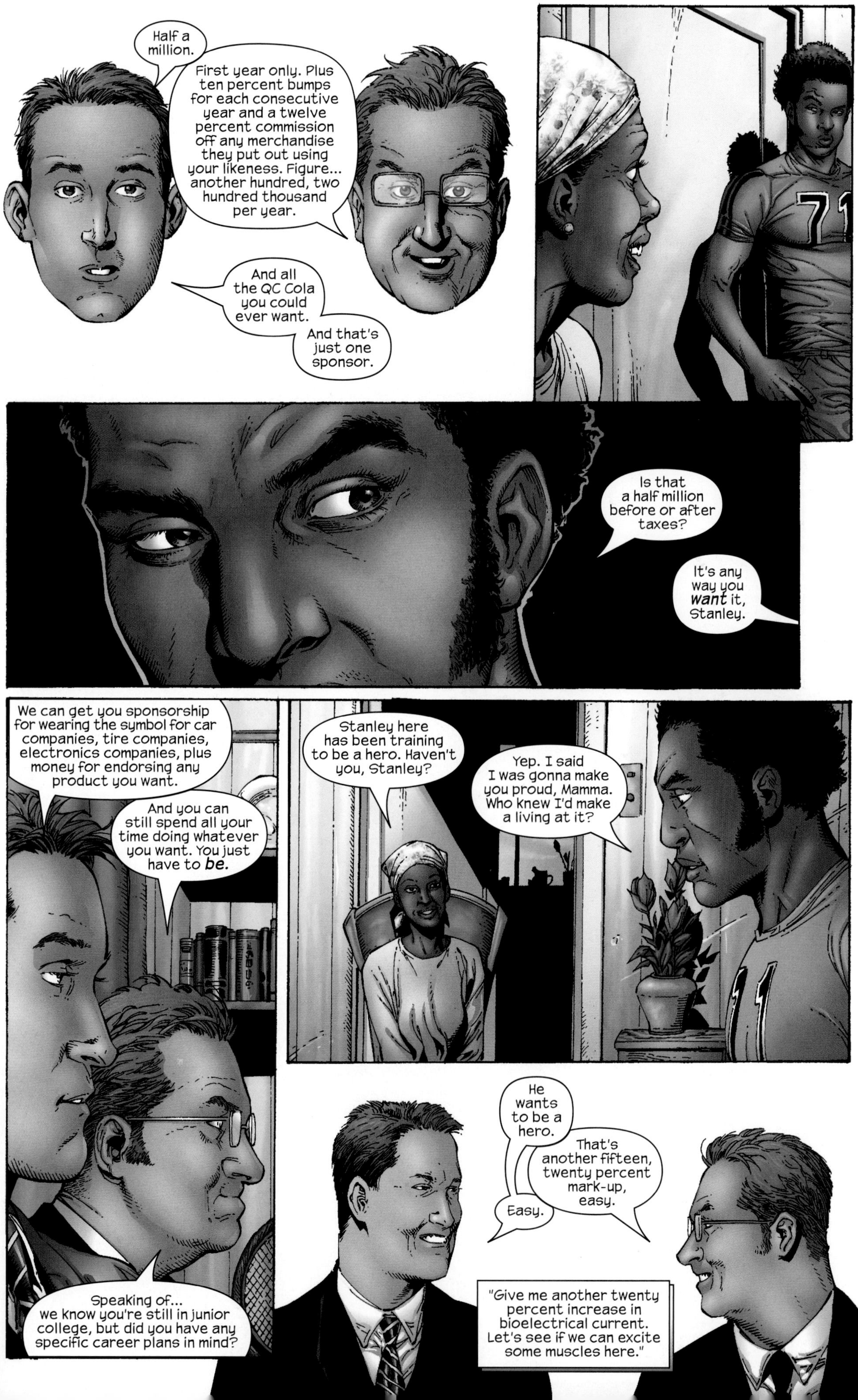

Half a million.
First year only. Plus ten percent bumps for each consecutive year and a twelve percent commission off any merchandise they put out using your likeness. Figure... another hundred, two hundred thousand per year.
And all the QC Cola you could ever want.
And that's just one sponsor.
Is that a half million before or after taxes?
It's any way you *want* it, Stanley.
We can get you sponsorship for wearing the symbol for car companies, tire companies, electronics companies, plus money for endorsing any product you want.
And you can still spend all your time doing whatever you want. You just have to *be.*
Stanley here has been training to be a hero. Haven't you, Stanley?
Yep. I said I was gonna make you proud, Mamma. Who knew I'd make a living at it?
Speaking of... we know you're still in junior college, but did you have any specific career plans in mind?
He wants to be a hero.
That's another fifteen, twenty percent mark-up, easy.
Easy.
"Give me another twenty percent increase in bioelectrical current. Let's see if we can excite some muscles here."

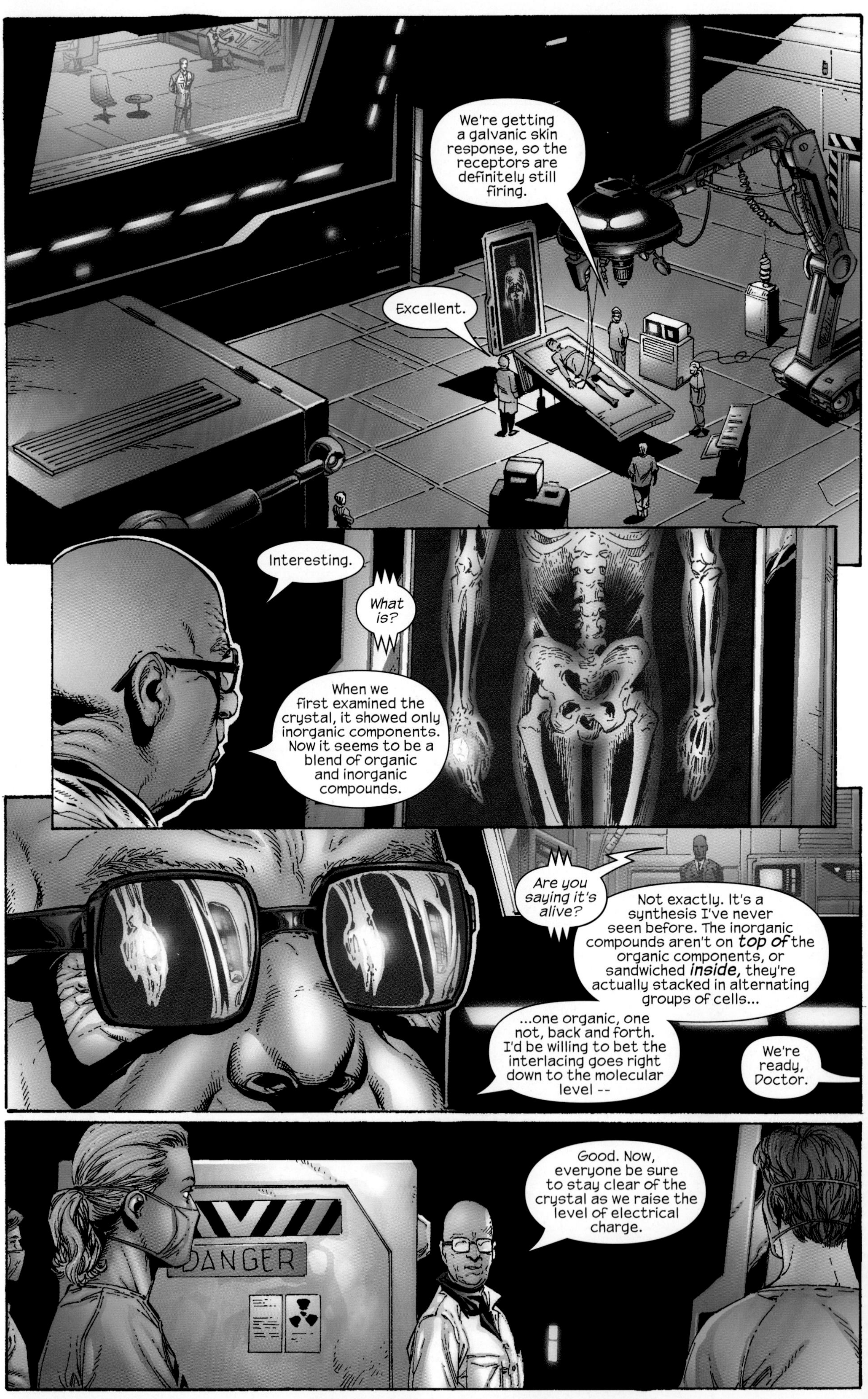

We're getting a galvanic skin response, so the receptors are definitely still firing.
Excellent.
Interesting.
What is?
When we first examined the crystal, it showed only inorganic components. Now it seems to be a blend of organic and inorganic compounds.
Are you saying it's alive?
Not exactly. It's a synthesis I've never seen before. The inorganic compounds aren't on *top of* the organic components, or sandwiched *inside*, they're actually stacked in alternating groups of cells...
...one organic, one not, back and forth. I'd be willing to bet the interlacing goes right down to the molecular level --
We're ready, Doctor.
DANGER
Good. Now, everyone be sure to stay clear of the crystal as we raise the level of electrical charge.

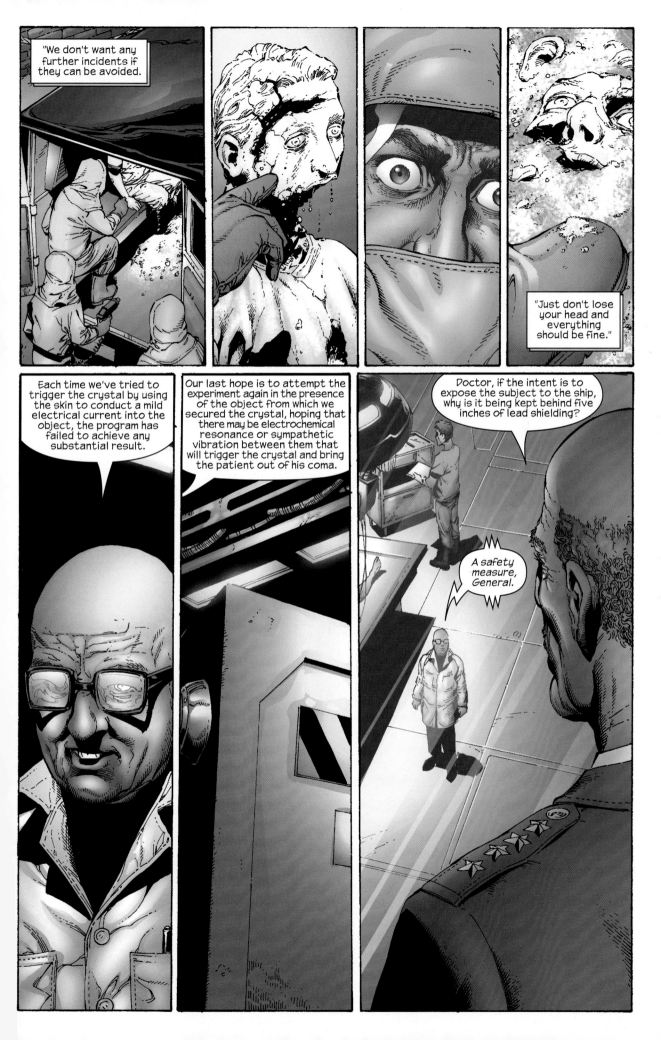

"We don't want any further incidents if they can be avoided."

"Just don't lose your head and everything should be fine."

Each time we've tried to trigger the crystal by using the skin to conduct a mild electrical current into the object, the program has failed to achieve any substantial result.

Our last hope is to attempt the experiment again in the presence of the object from which we secured the crystal, hoping that there may be electrochemical resonance or sympathetic vibration between them that will trigger the crystal and bring the patient out of his coma.

Doctor, if the intent is to expose the subject to the ship, why is it being kept behind five inches of lead shielding?

A safety measure, General.

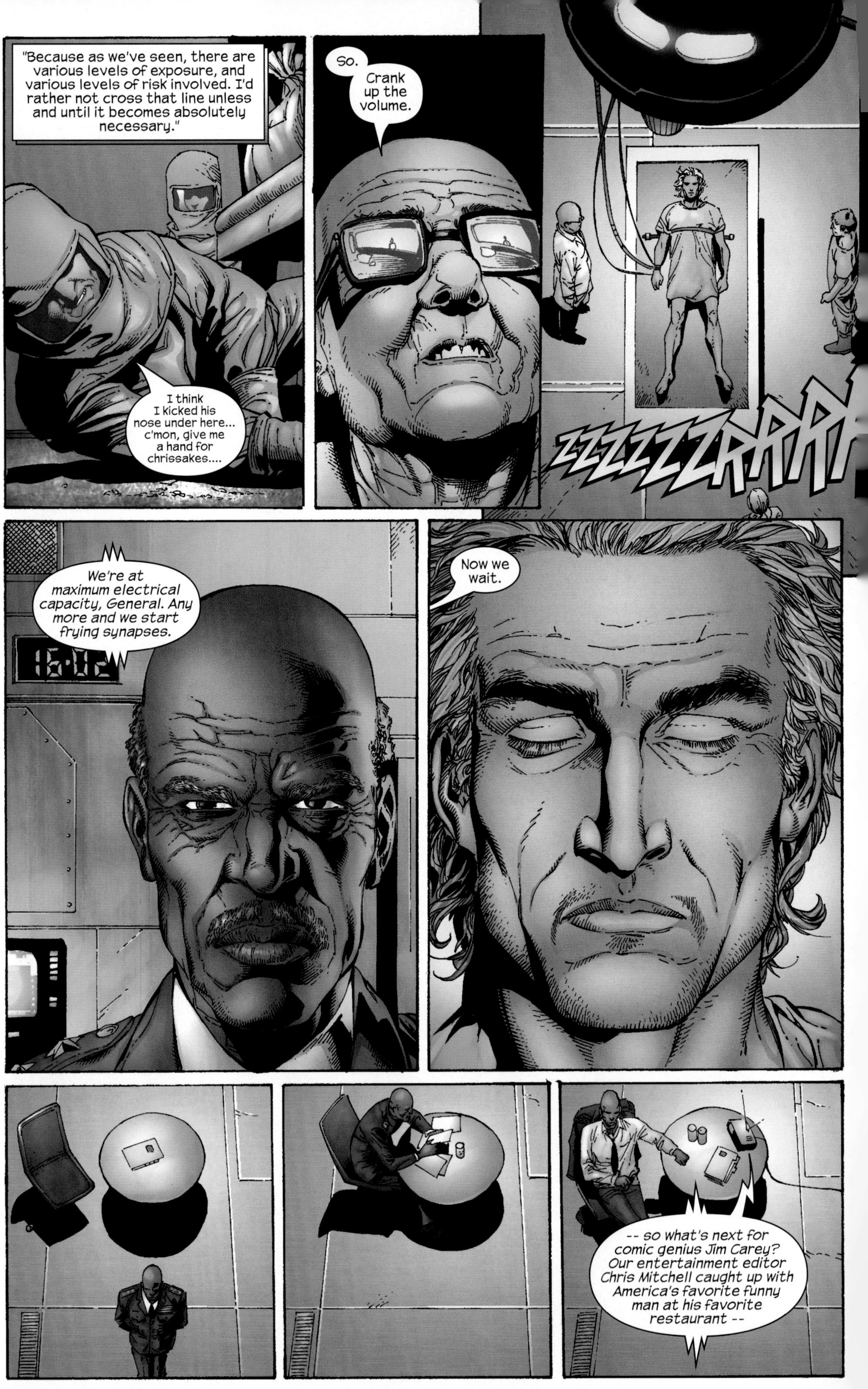

"Because as we've seen, there are various levels of exposure, and various levels of risk involved. I'd rather not cross that line unless and until it becomes absolutely necessary."
I think I kicked his nose under here... c'mon, give me a hand for chrissakes....
So.
Crank up the volume.
ZZZZZZRRRR
We're at maximum electrical capacity, General. Any more and we start frying synapses.
16:02
Now we wait.
-- so what's next for comic genius Jim Carey? Our entertainment editor Chris Mitchell caught up with America's favorite funny man at his favorite restaurant --

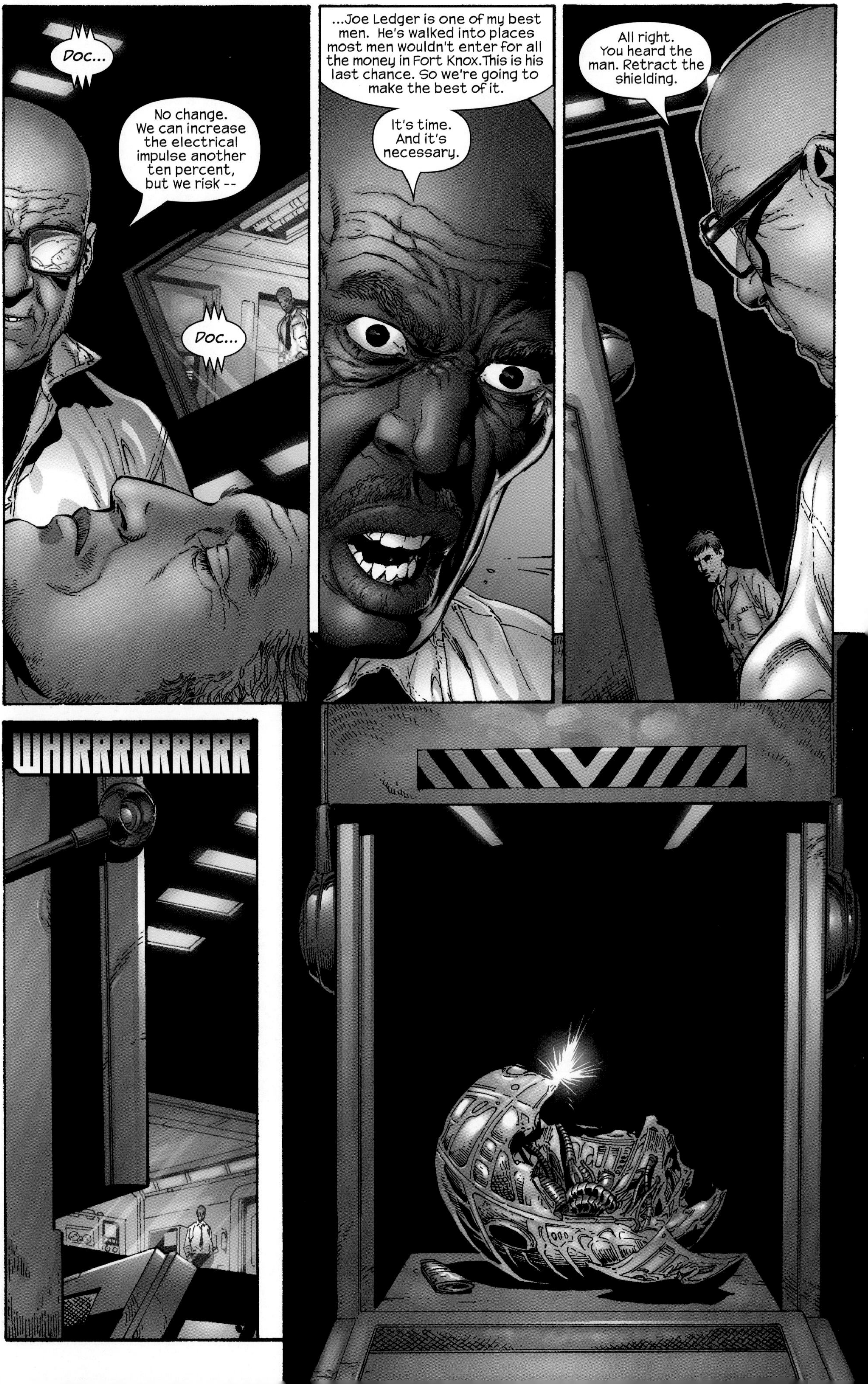
Doc...
No change. We can increase the electrical impulse another ten percent, but we risk --
Doc...
...Joe Ledger is one of my best men. He's walked into places most men wouldn't enter for all the money in Fort Knox. This is his last chance. So we're going to make the best of it.
It's time. And it's necessary.
All right. You heard the man. Retract the shielding.
WHIRRRRRRRRR

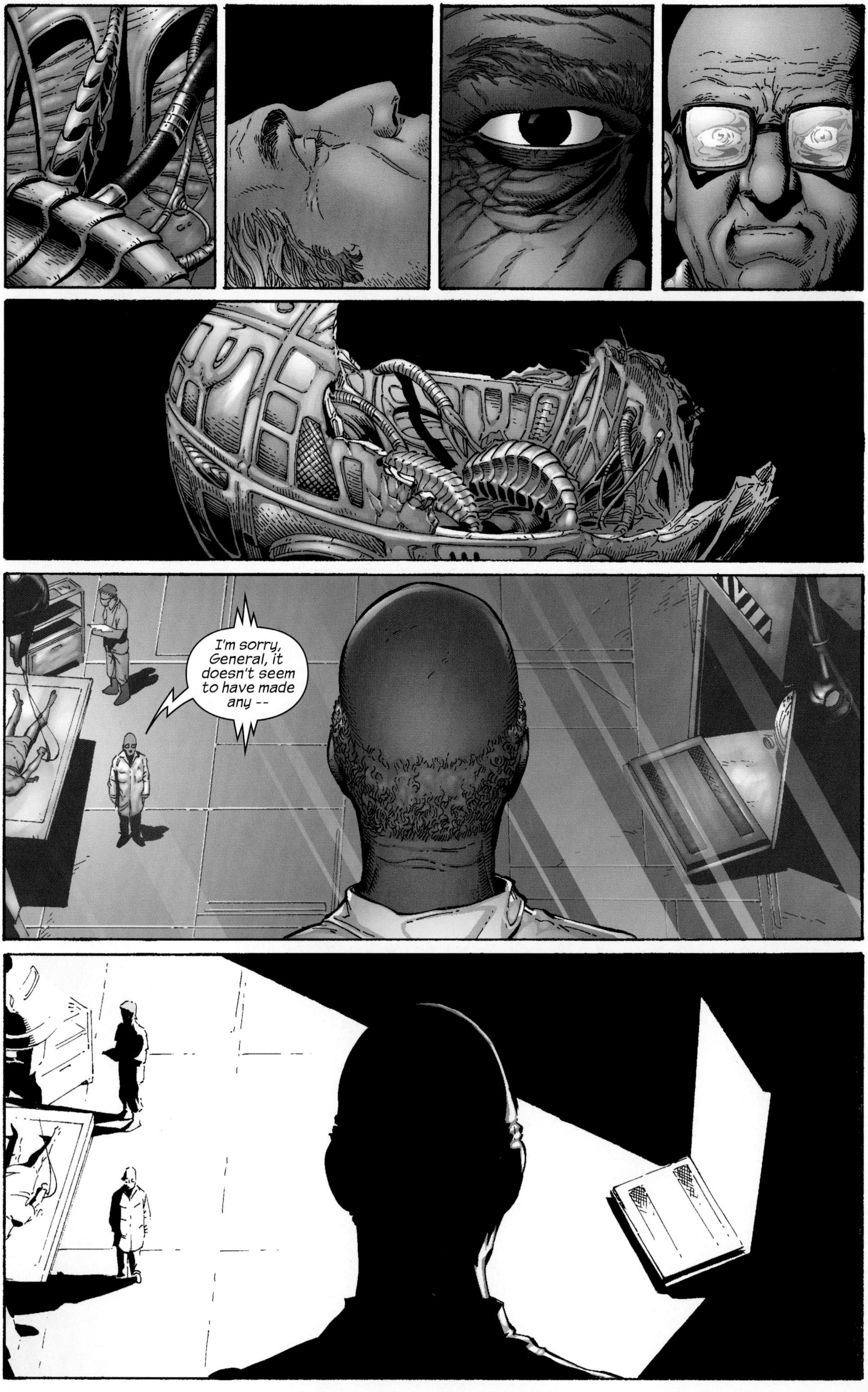
I'm sorry, General, it doesn't seem to have made any --

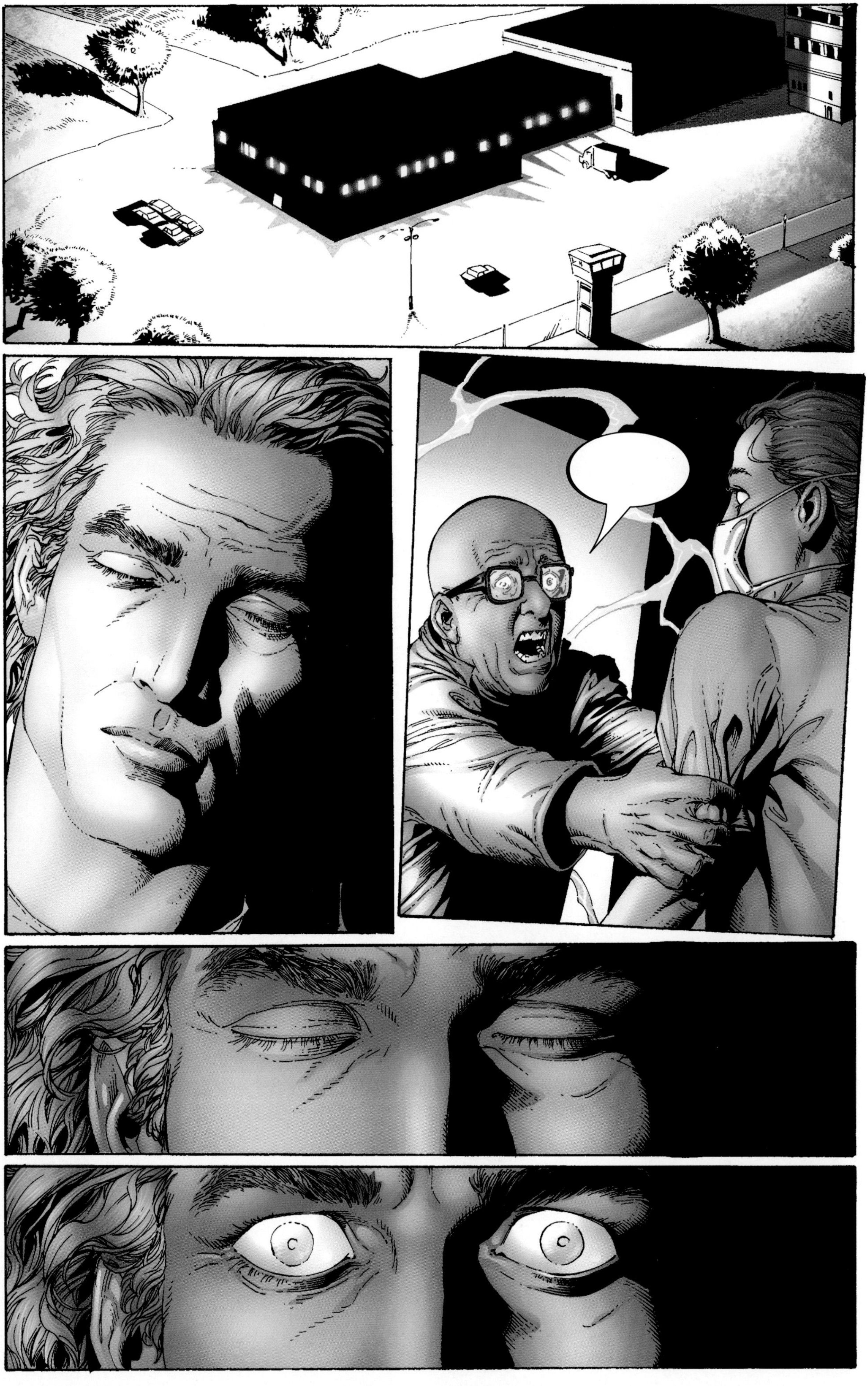

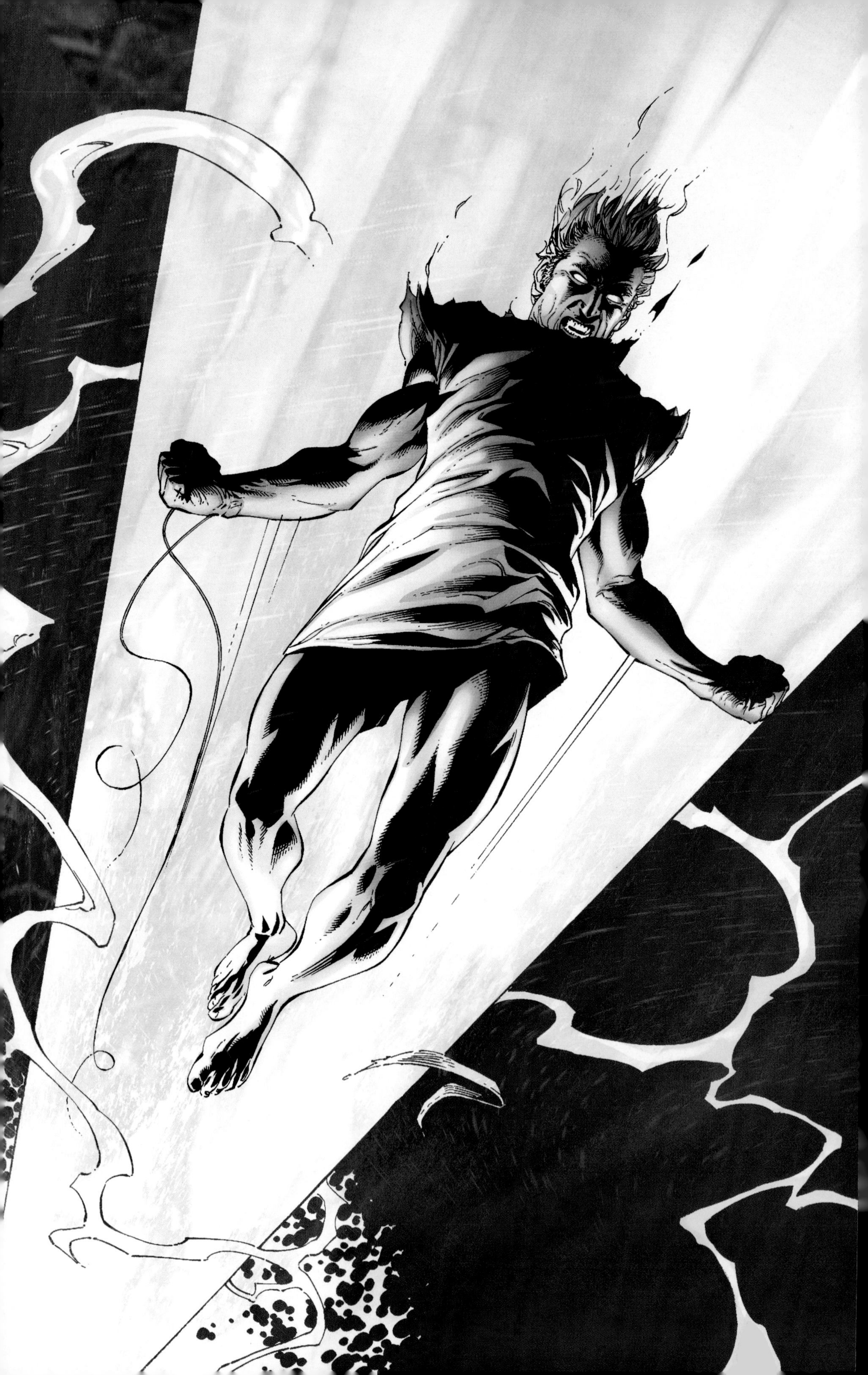

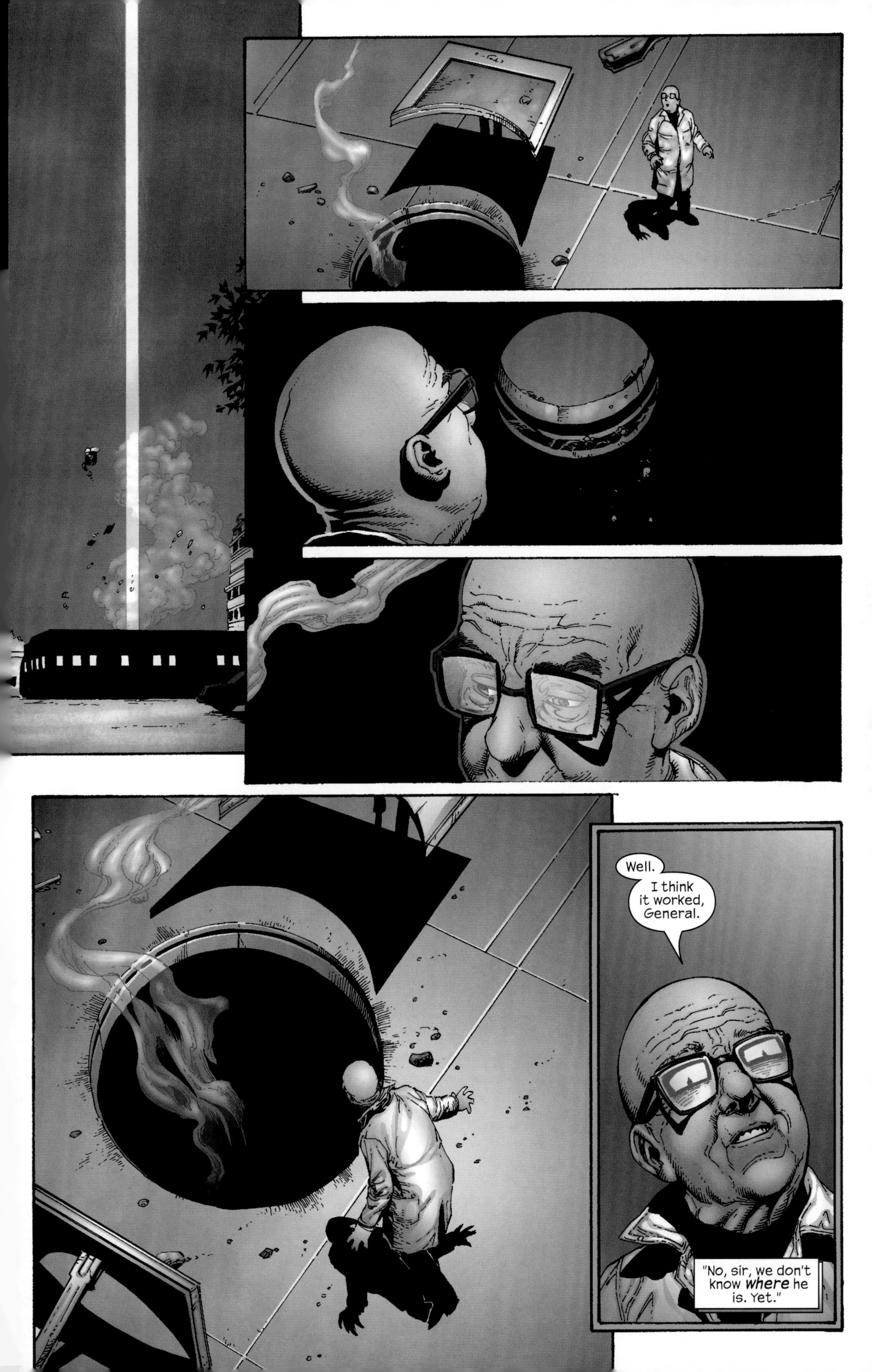
Well.
I think it worked, General.
"No, sir, we don't know *where* he is. Yet."

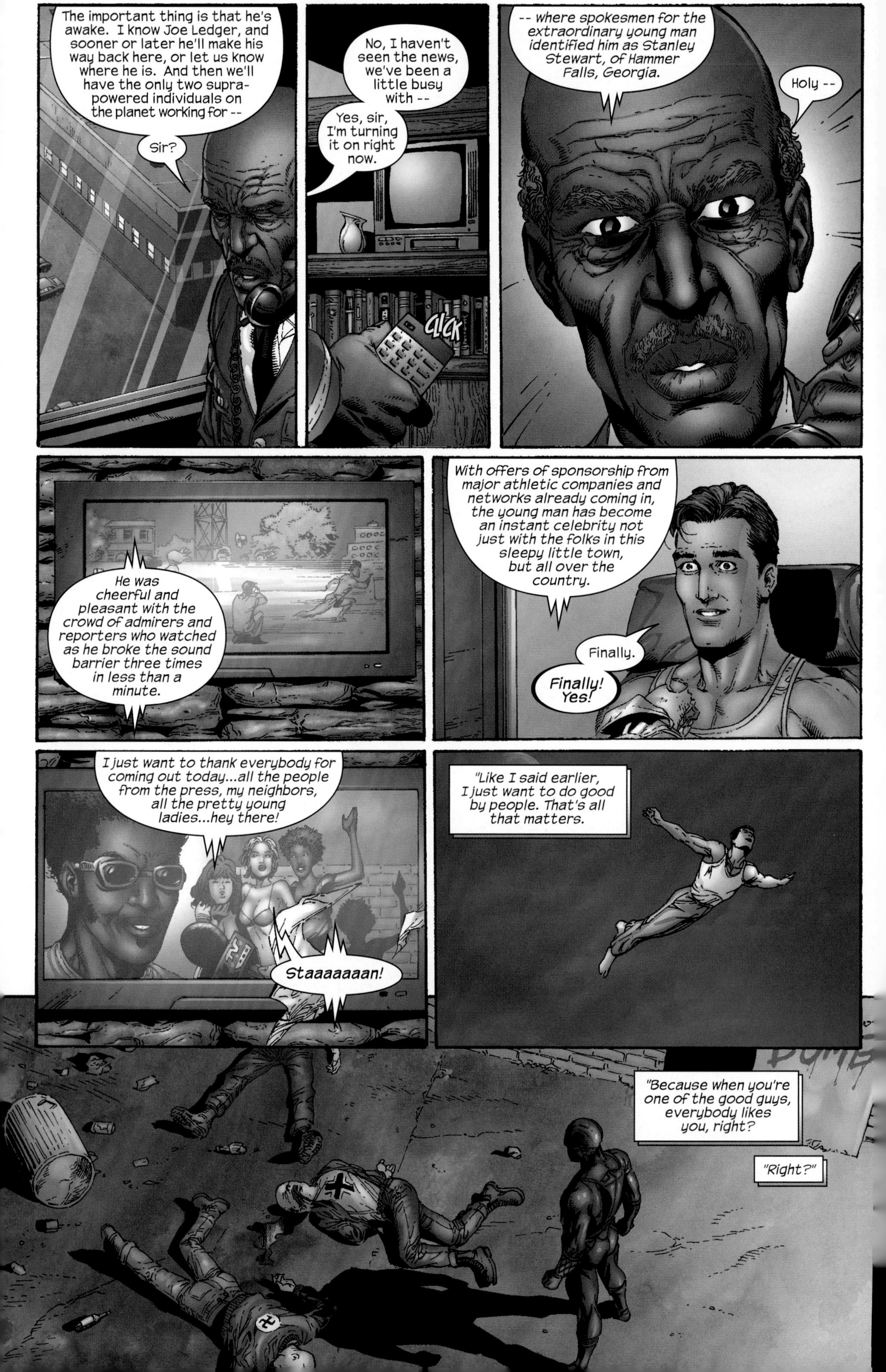
The important thing is that he's awake. I know Joe Ledger, and sooner or later he'll make his way back here, or let us know where he is. And then we'll have the only two supra-powered individuals on the planet working for --
Sir?
No, I haven't seen the news, we've been a little busy with --
Yes, sir, I'm turning it on right now.
CLICK
-- where spokesmen for the extraordinary young man identified him as Stanley Stewart, of Hammer Falls, Georgia.
Holy --
He was cheerful and pleasant with the crowd of admirers and reporters who watched as he broke the sound barrier three times in less than a minute.
With offers of sponsorship from major athletic companies and networks already coming in, the young man has become an instant celebrity not just with the folks in this sleepy little town, but all over the country.
Finally.
Finally! Yes!
I just want to thank everybody for coming out today...all the people from the press, my neighbors, all the pretty young ladies...hey there!
Staaaaaaan!
"Like I said earlier, I just want to do good by people. That's all that matters.
"Because when you're one of the good guys, everybody likes you, right?
"Right?"

Questions of Perspective

#6

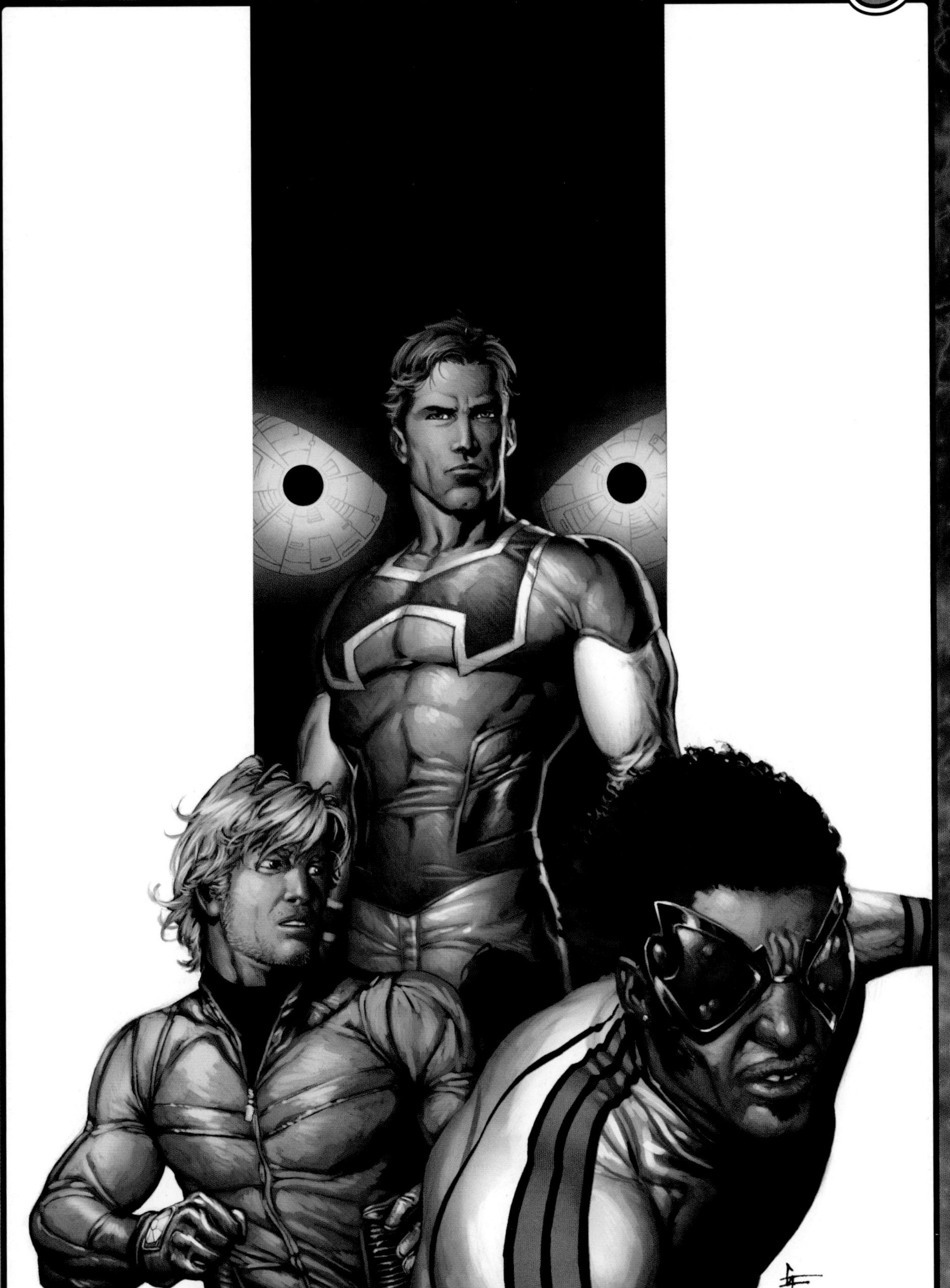
ISANOVE

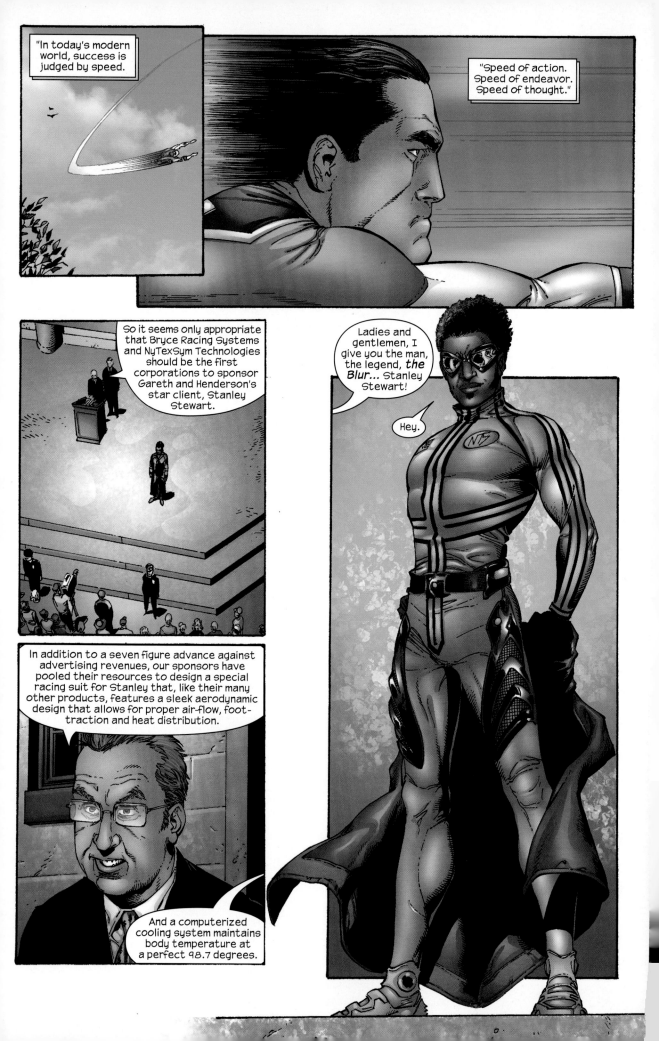

"In today's modern world, success is judged by speed.

"Speed of action. Speed of endeavor. Speed of thought."

So it seems only appropriate that Bryce Racing Systems and NyTexSym Technologies should be the first corporations to sponsor Gareth and Henderson's star client, Stanley Stewart.

Ladies and gentlemen, I give you the man, the legend, *the Blur*... Stanley Stewart!

Hey.

In addition to a seven figure advance against advertising revenues, our sponsors have pooled their resources to design a special racing suit for Stanley that, like their many other products, features a sleek aerodynamic design that allows for proper air-flow, foot-traction and heat distribution.

And a computerized cooling system maintains body temperature at a perfect 98.7 degrees.

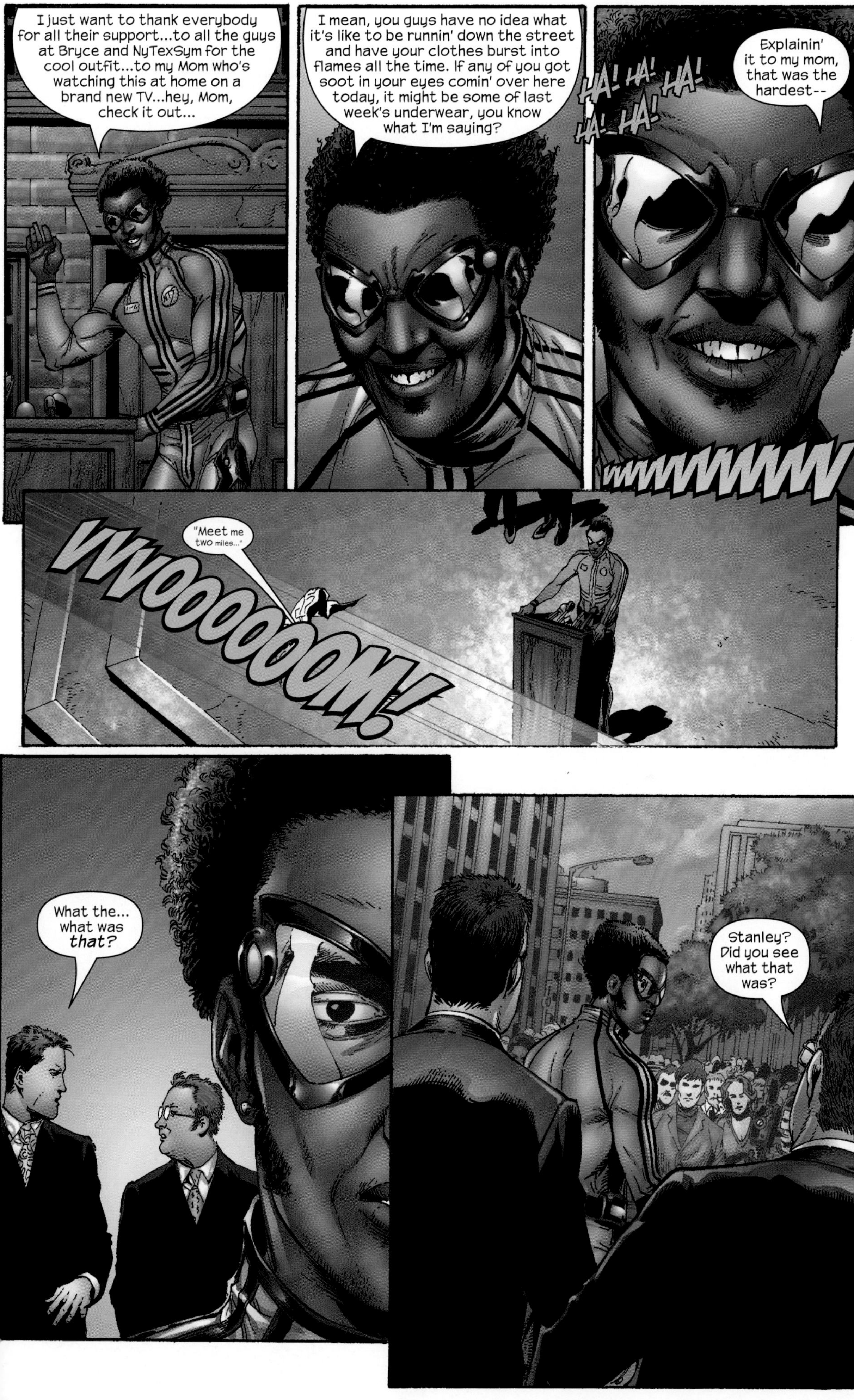

I just want to thank everybody for all their support...to all the guys at Bryce and NyTexSym for the cool outfit...to my Mom who's watching this at home on a brand new TV...hey, Mom, check it out...
I mean, you guys have no idea what it's like to be runnin' down the street and have your clothes burst into flames all the time. If any of you got soot in your eyes comin' over here today, it might be some of last week's underwear, you know what I'm saying?
HA! HA! HA! HA! HA!
Explainin' it to my mom, that was the hardest--
VVVVVVVVVVVVV
VVVOOOOOOOM!
"Meet me two miles..."
What the... what was *that*?
Stanley? Did you see what that was?

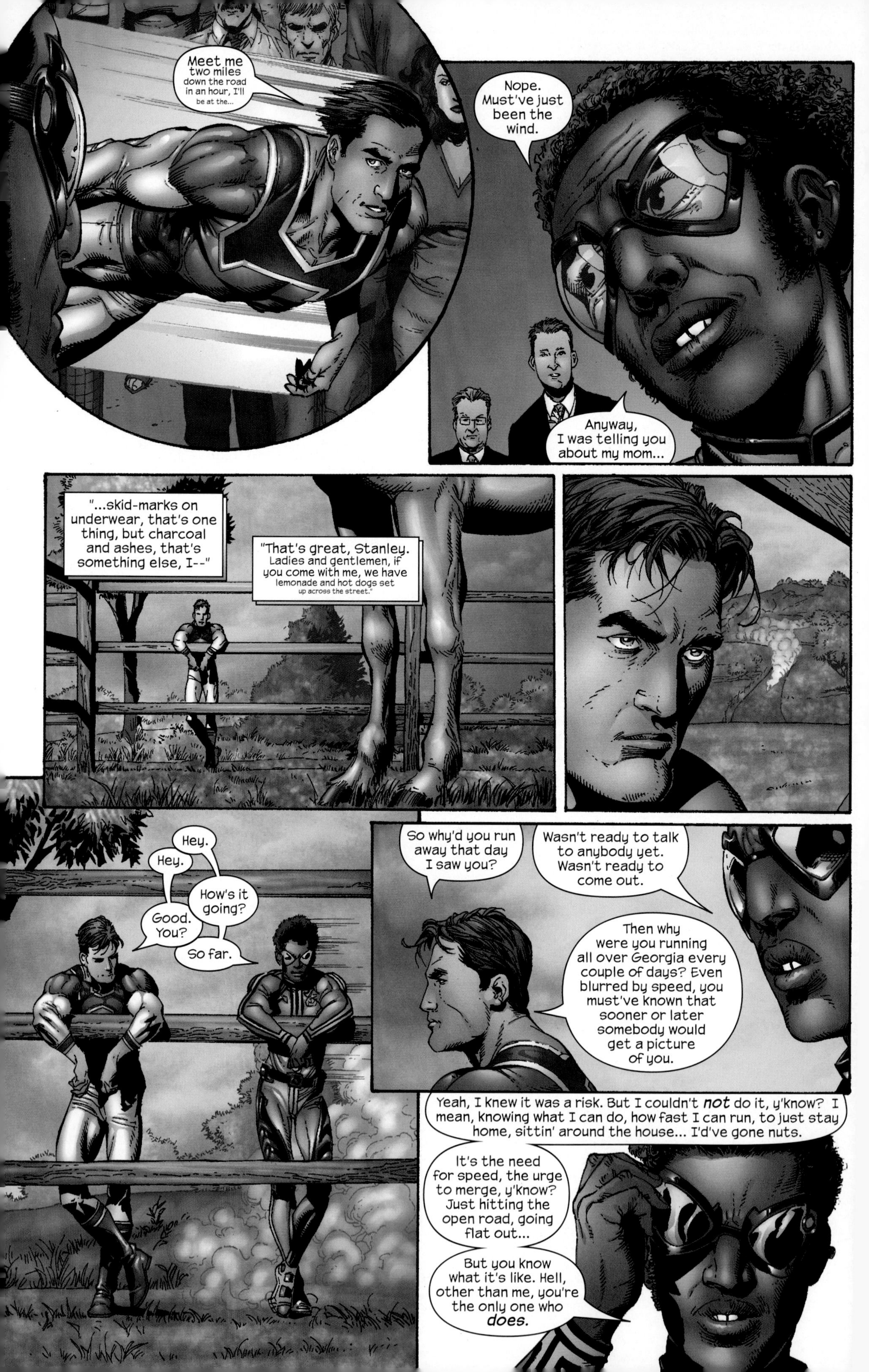

Meet me two miles down the road in an hour, I'll be at the...
Nope. Must've just been the wind.
Anyway, I was telling you about my mom...
"...skid-marks on underwear, that's one thing, but charcoal and ashes, that's something else, I--"
"That's great, Stanley. Ladies and gentlemen, if you come with me, we have lemonade and hot dogs set up across the street."
Hey.
Hey.
How's it going?
Good. You?
So far.
So why'd you run away that day I saw you?
Wasn't ready to talk to anybody yet. Wasn't ready to come out.
Then why were you running all over Georgia every couple of days? Even blurred by speed, you must've known that sooner or later somebody would get a picture of you.
Yeah, I knew it was a risk. But I couldn't *not* do it, y'know? I mean, knowing what I can do, how fast I can run, to just stay home, sittin' around the house... I'd've gone nuts.
It's the need for speed, the urge to merge, y'know? Just hitting the open road, going flat out...
But you know what it's like. Hell, other than me, you're the only one who *does.*

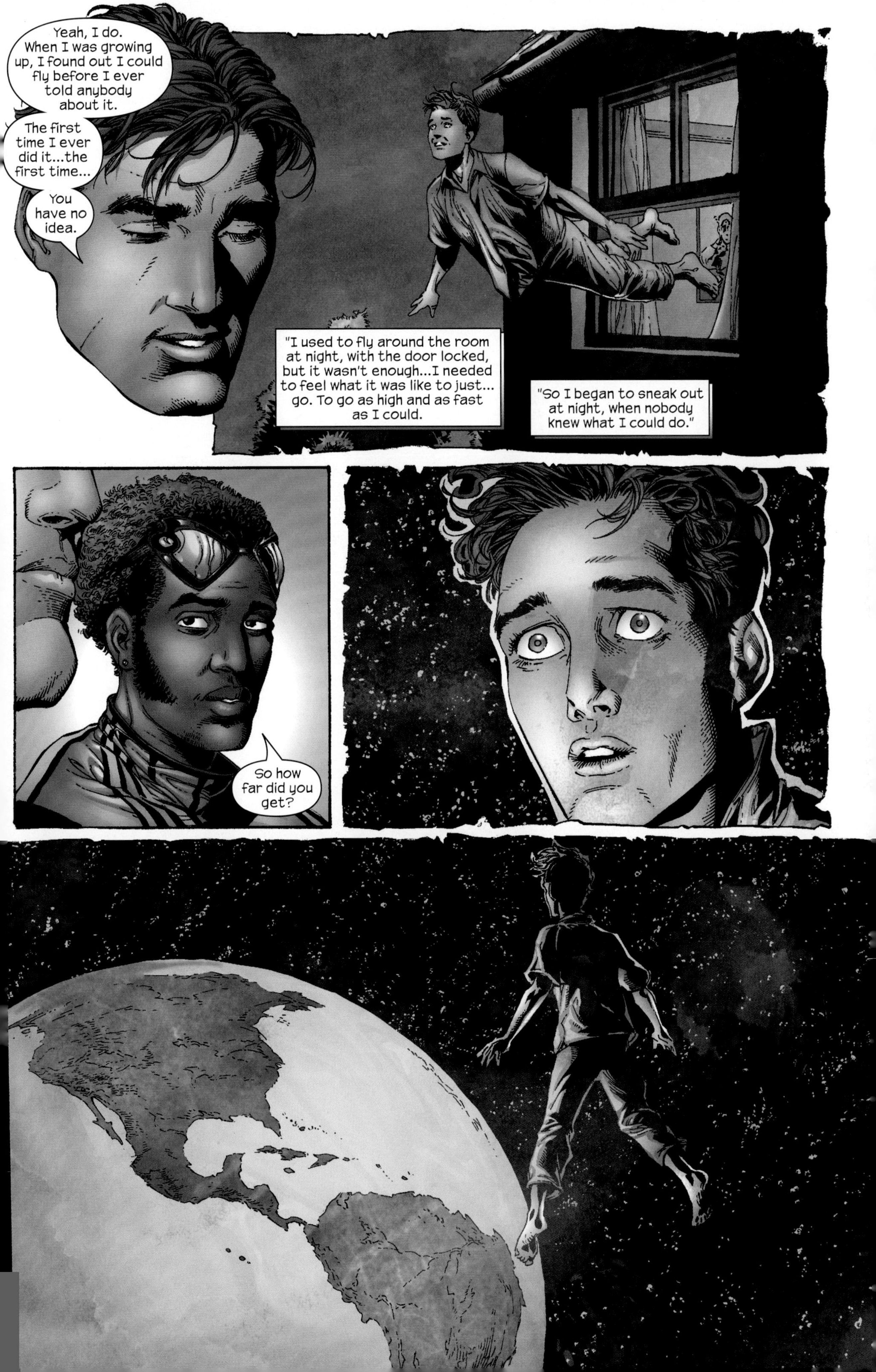
Yeah, I do. When I was growing up, I found out I could fly before I ever told anybody about it.
The first time I ever did it...the first time...
You have no idea.
"I used to fly around the room at night, with the door locked, but it wasn't enough...I needed to feel what it was like to just... go. To go as high and as fast as I could.
"So I began to sneak out at night, when nobody knew what I could do."
So how far did you get?

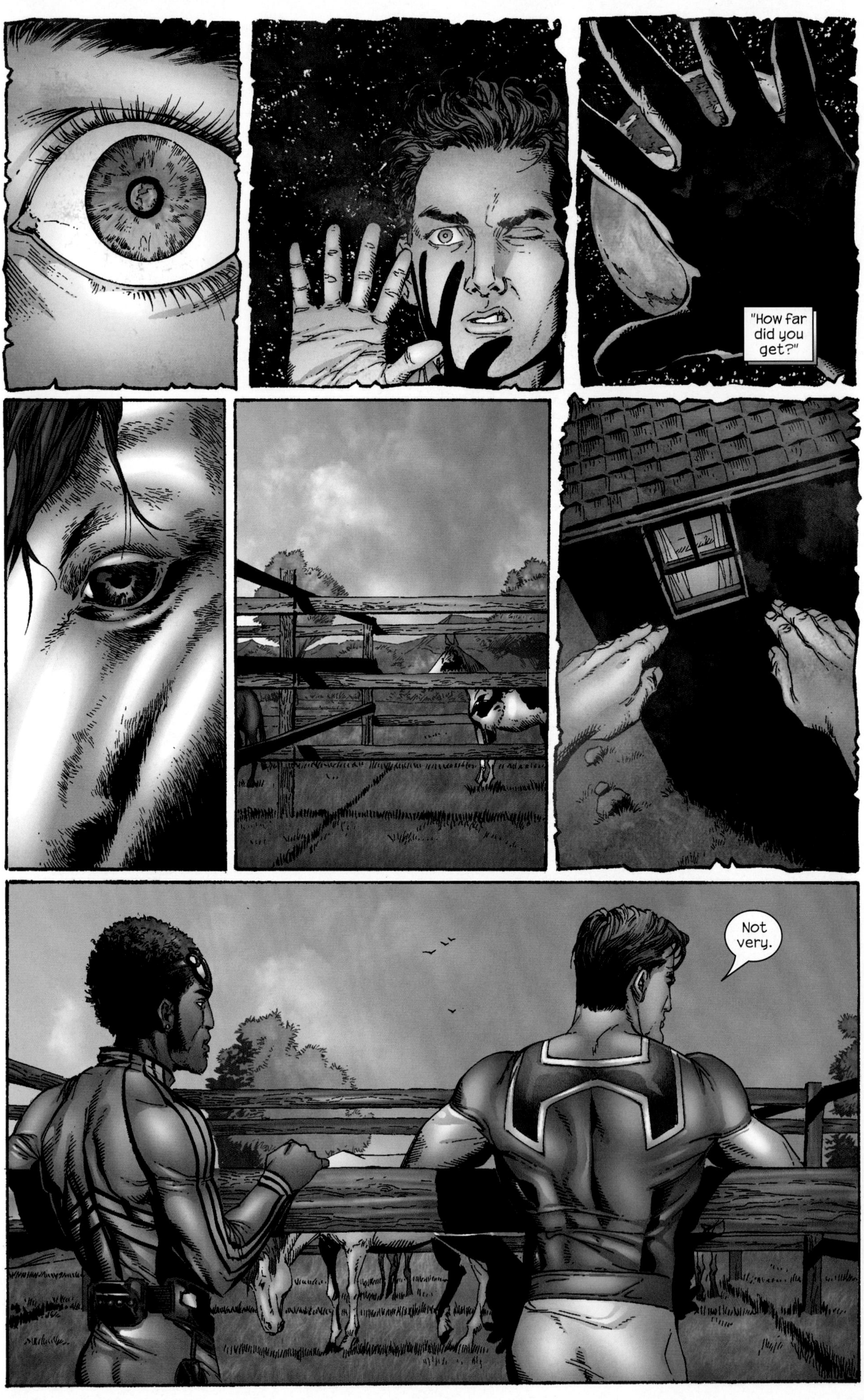
"How far did you get?"
Not very.

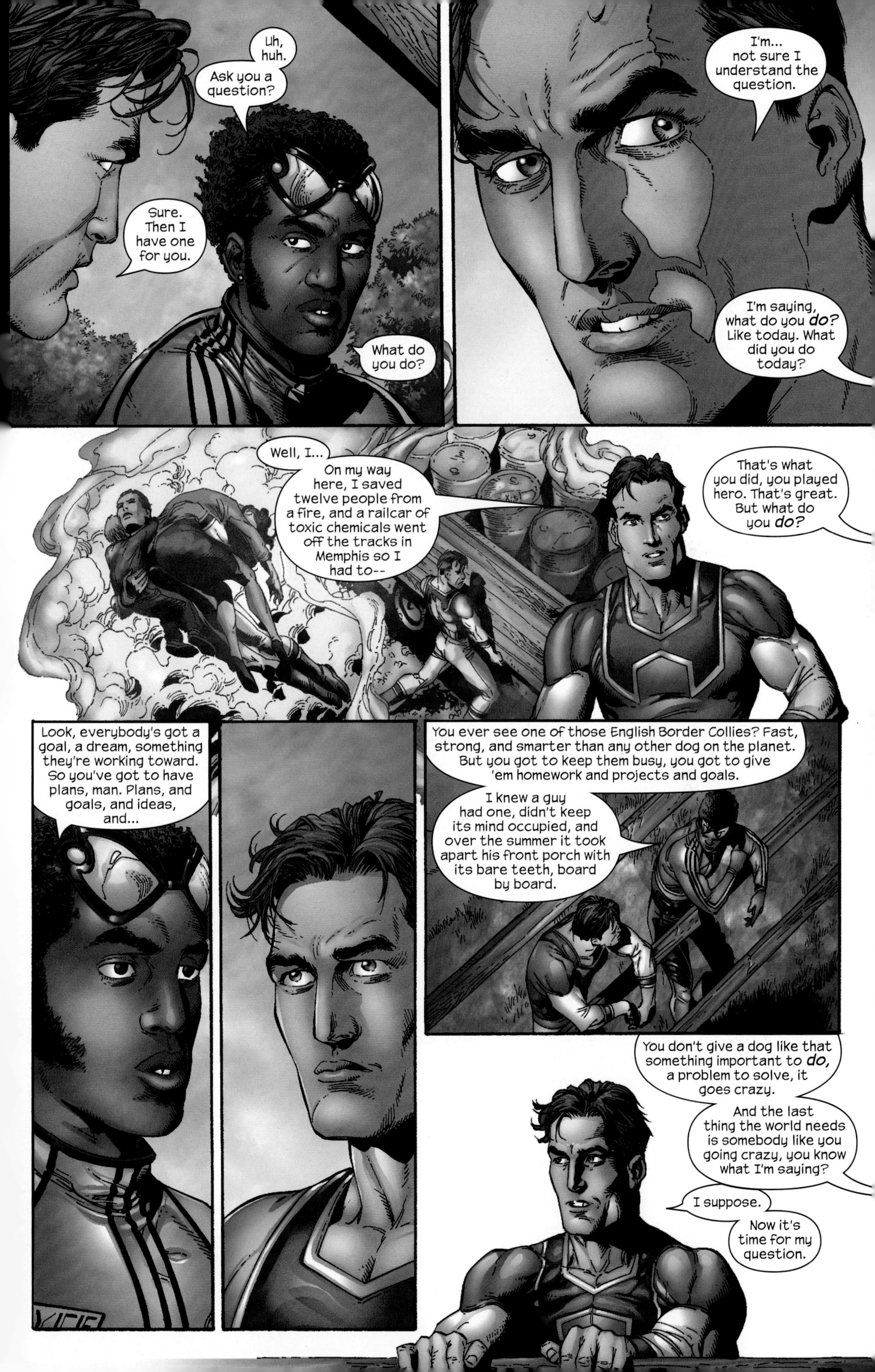
Uh, huh.
Ask you a question?
Sure. Then I have one for you.
What do you do?
I'm... not sure I understand the question.
I'm saying, what do you *do?* Like today. What did you do today?
Well, I...
On my way here, I saved twelve people from a fire, and a railcar of toxic chemicals went off the tracks in Memphis so I had to--
That's what you did, you played hero. That's great. But what do you *do?*
Look, everybody's got a goal, a dream, something they're working toward. So you've got to have plans, man. Plans, and goals, and ideas, and...
You ever see one of those English Border Collies? Fast, strong, and smarter than any other dog on the planet. But you got to keep them busy, you got to give 'em homework and projects and goals.
I knew a guy had one, didn't keep its mind occupied, and over the summer it took apart his front porch with its bare teeth, board by board.
You don't give a dog like that something important to *do,* a problem to solve, it goes crazy.
And the last thing the world needs is somebody like you going crazy, you know what I'm saying?
I suppose.
Now it's time for my question.

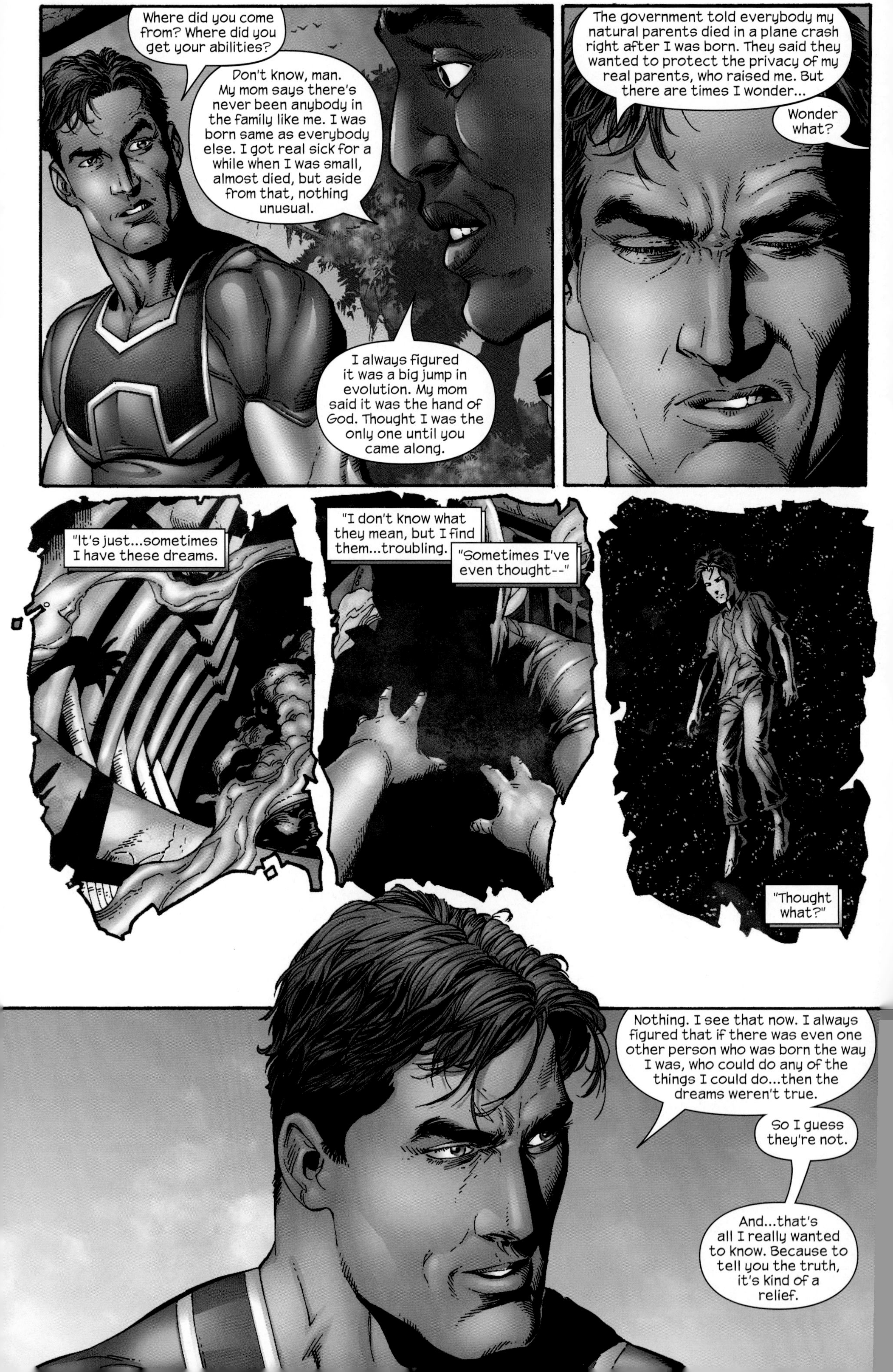
Where did you come from? Where did you get your abilities?
Don't know, man. My mom says there's never been anybody in the family like me. I was born same as everybody else. I got real sick for a while when I was small, almost died, but aside from that, nothing unusual.
I always figured it was a big jump in evolution. My mom said it was the hand of God. Thought I was the only one until you came along.
The government told everybody my natural parents died in a plane crash right after I was born. They said they wanted to protect the privacy of my real parents, who raised me. But there are times I wonder...
Wonder what?
"It's just...sometimes I have these dreams.
"I don't know what they mean, but I find them...troubling.
"Sometimes I've even thought--"
"Thought what?"
Nothing. I see that now. I always figured that if there was even one other person who was born the way I was, who could do any of the things I could do...then the dreams weren't true.
So I guess they're not.
And...that's all I really wanted to know. Because to tell you the truth, it's kind of a relief.

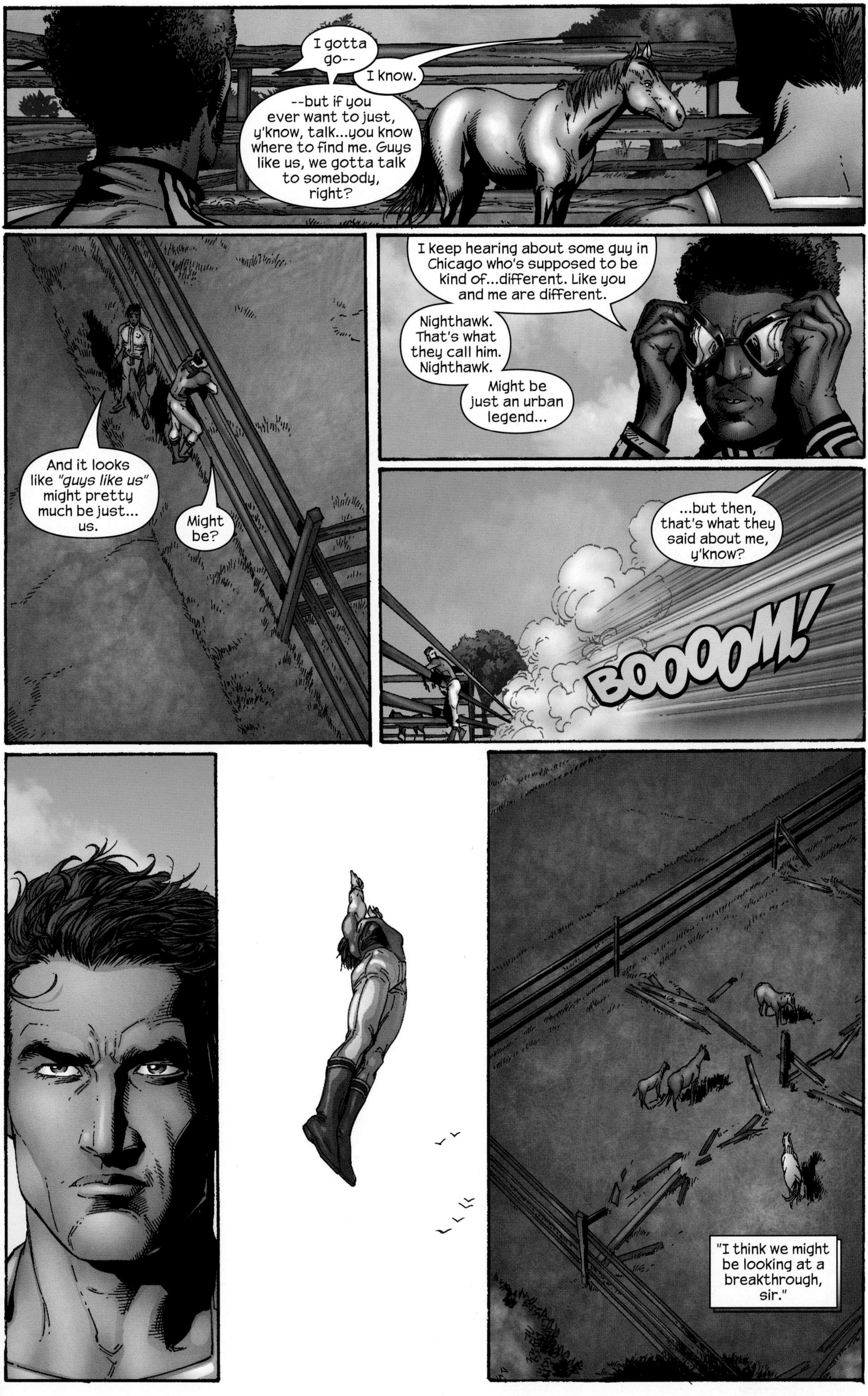

I gotta go--
I know.
--but if you ever want to just, y'know, talk...you know where to find me. Guys like us, we gotta talk to somebody, right?
I keep hearing about some guy in Chicago who's supposed to be kind of...different. Like you and me are different.
Nighthawk. That's what they call him. Nighthawk.
Might be just an urban legend...
And it looks like *"guys like us"* might pretty much be just... us.
Might be?
...but then, that's what they said about me, y'know?
BOOOOM!
"I think we might be looking at a breakthrough, sir."

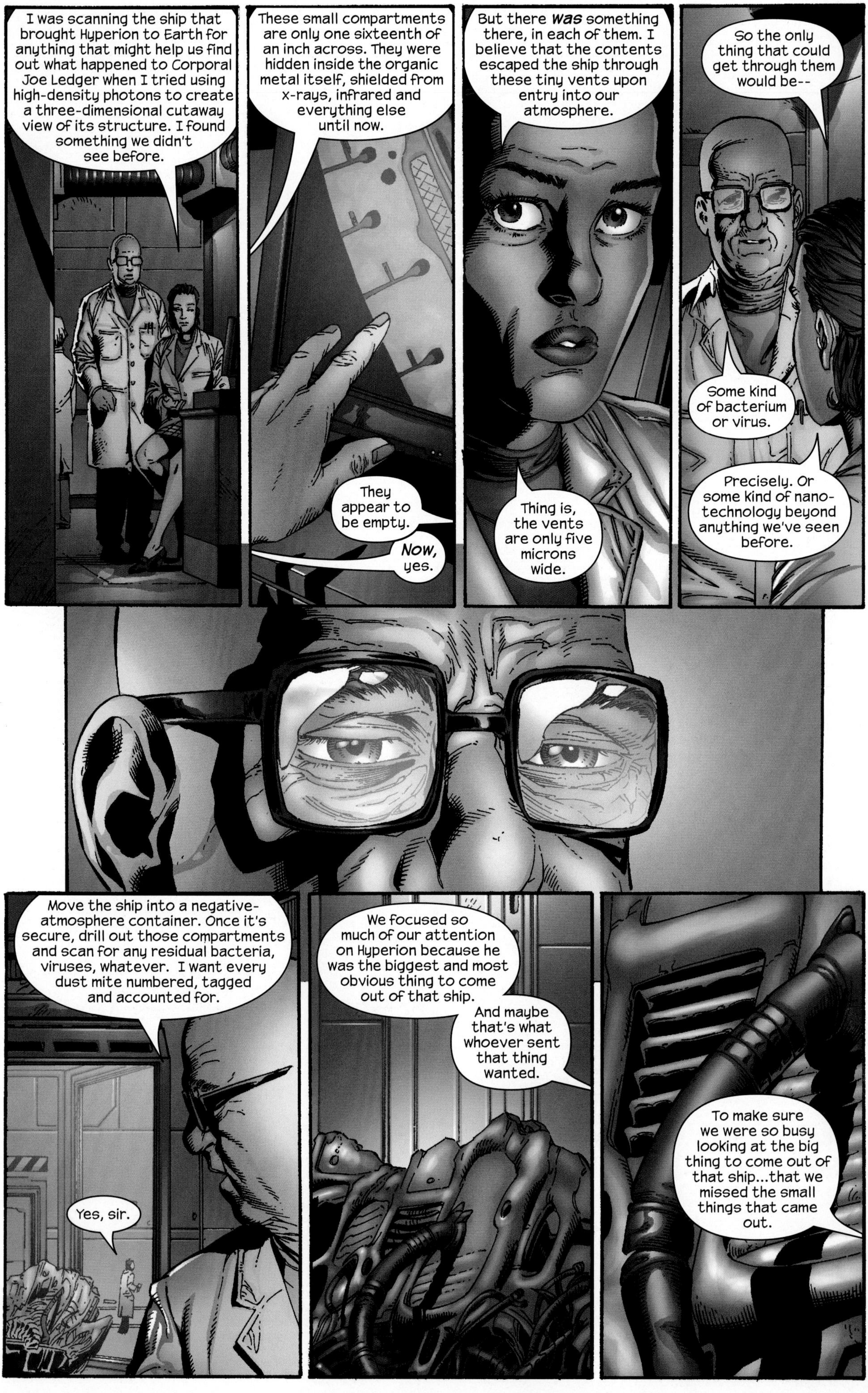
I was scanning the ship that brought Hyperion to Earth for anything that might help us find out what happened to Corporal Joe Ledger when I tried using high-density photons to create a three-dimensional cutaway view of its structure. I found something we didn't see before.
These small compartments are only one sixteenth of an inch across. They were hidden inside the organic metal itself, shielded from x-rays, infrared and everything else until now.
They appear to be empty.
NOW, yes.
But there *WAS* something there, in each of them. I believe that the contents escaped the ship through these tiny vents upon entry into our atmosphere.
Thing is, the vents are only five microns wide.
So the only thing that could get through them would be--
Some kind of bacterium or virus.
Precisely. Or some kind of nano-technology beyond anything we've seen before.
Move the ship into a negative-atmosphere container. Once it's secure, drill out those compartments and scan for any residual bacteria, viruses, whatever. I want every dust mite numbered, tagged and accounted for.
Yes, sir.
We focused so much of our attention on Hyperion because he was the biggest and most obvious thing to come out of that ship.
And maybe that's what whoever sent that thing wanted.
To make sure we were so busy looking at the big thing to come out of that ship...that we missed the small things that came out.

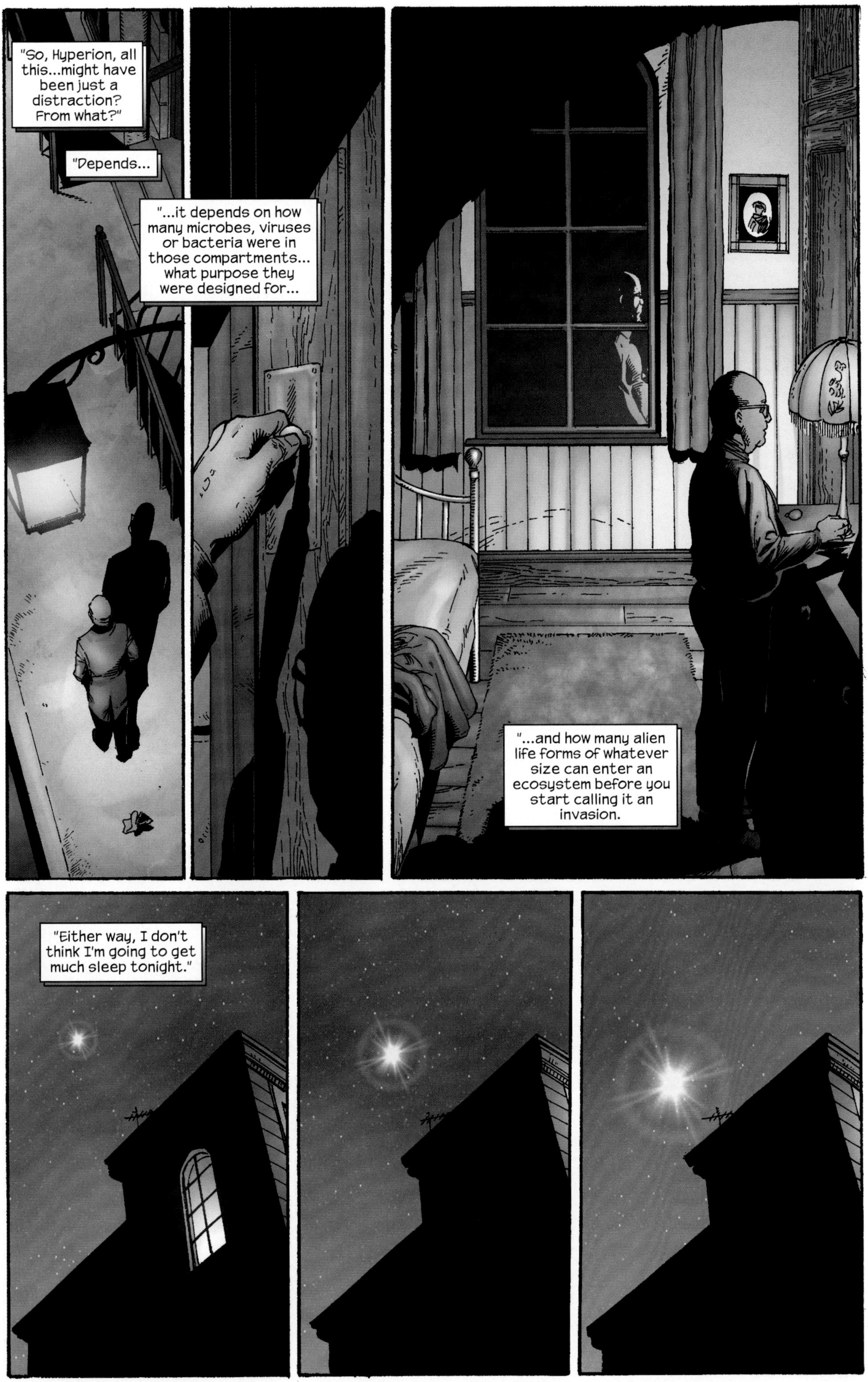
"So, Hyperion, all this...might have been just a distraction? From what?"
"Depends...
"...it depends on how many microbes, viruses or bacteria were in those compartments... what purpose they were designed for...
"...and how many alien life forms of whatever size can enter an ecosystem before you start calling it an invasion.
"Either way, I don't think I'm going to get much sleep tonight."

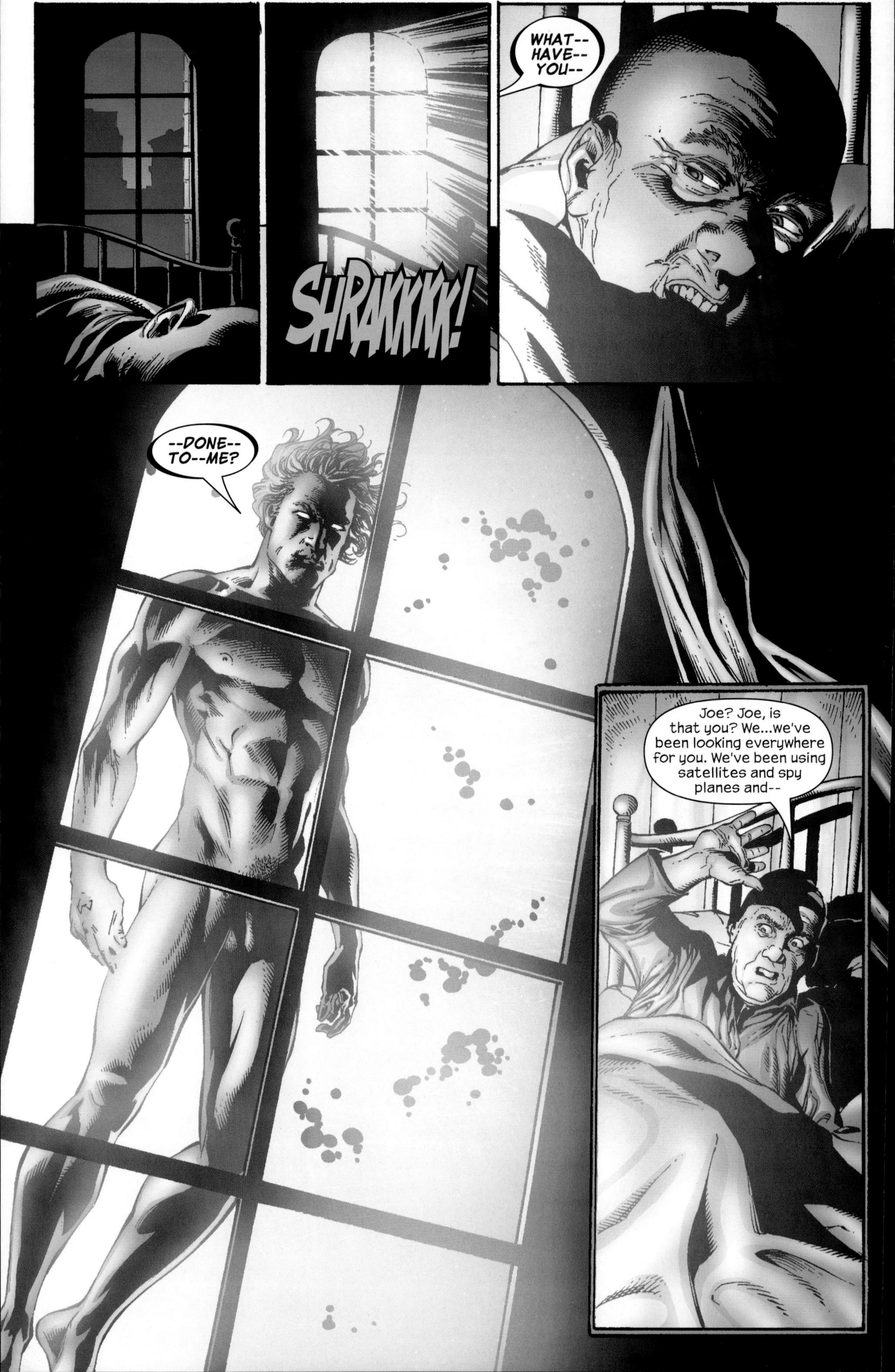

SHRAKKKK!
WHAT--
HAVE--
YOU--
--DONE--
TO--ME?
Joe? Joe, is that you? We...we've been looking everywhere for you. We've been using satellites and spy planes and--

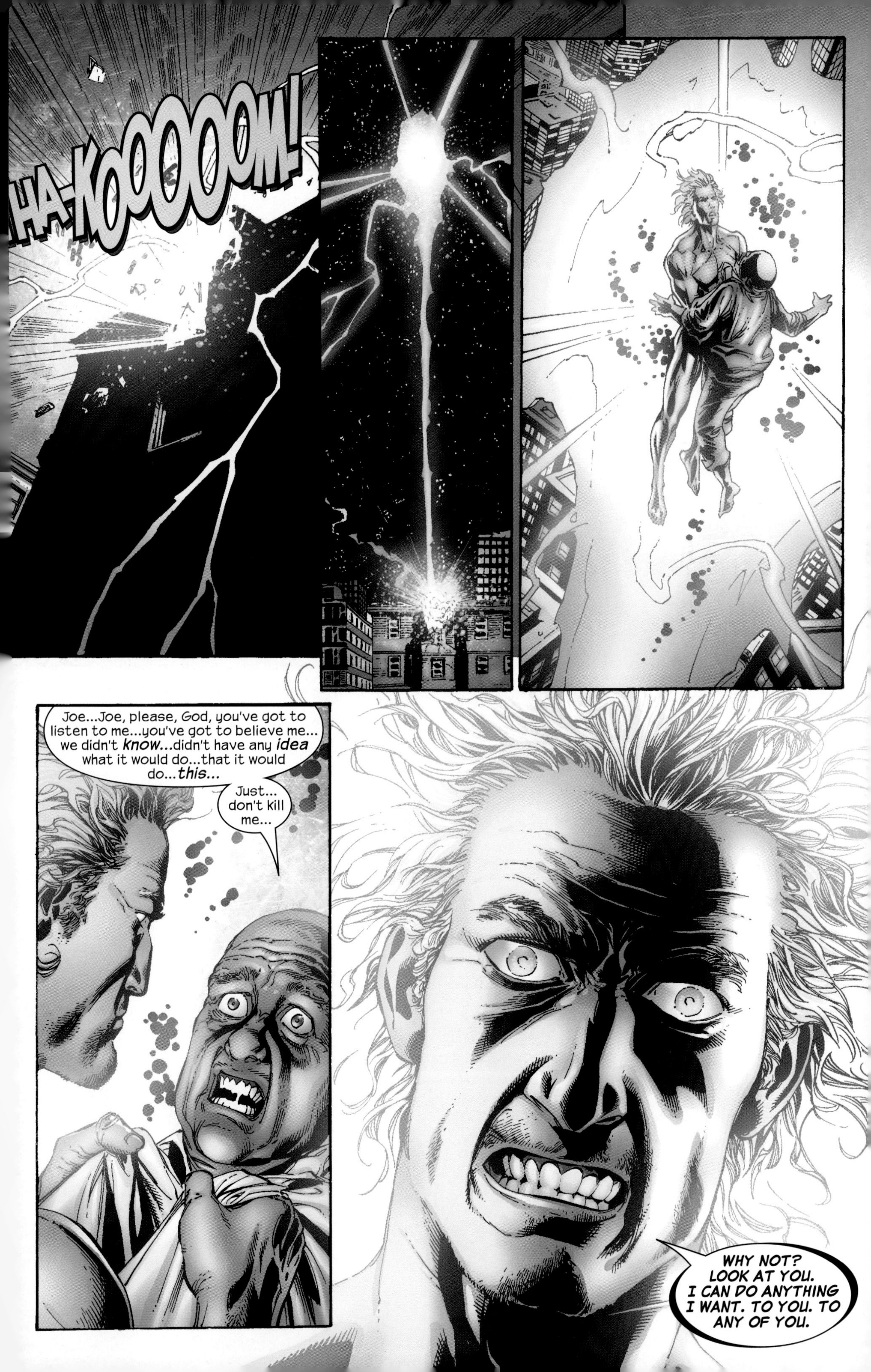
HA-KOOOOOM!
Joe...Joe, please, God, you've got to listen to me...you've got to believe me... we didn't *know*...didn't have any *idea* what it would do...that it would do...*this*...
Just... don't kill me...
WHY NOT? LOOK AT YOU. I CAN DO ANYTHING I WANT. TO YOU. TO ANY OF YOU.

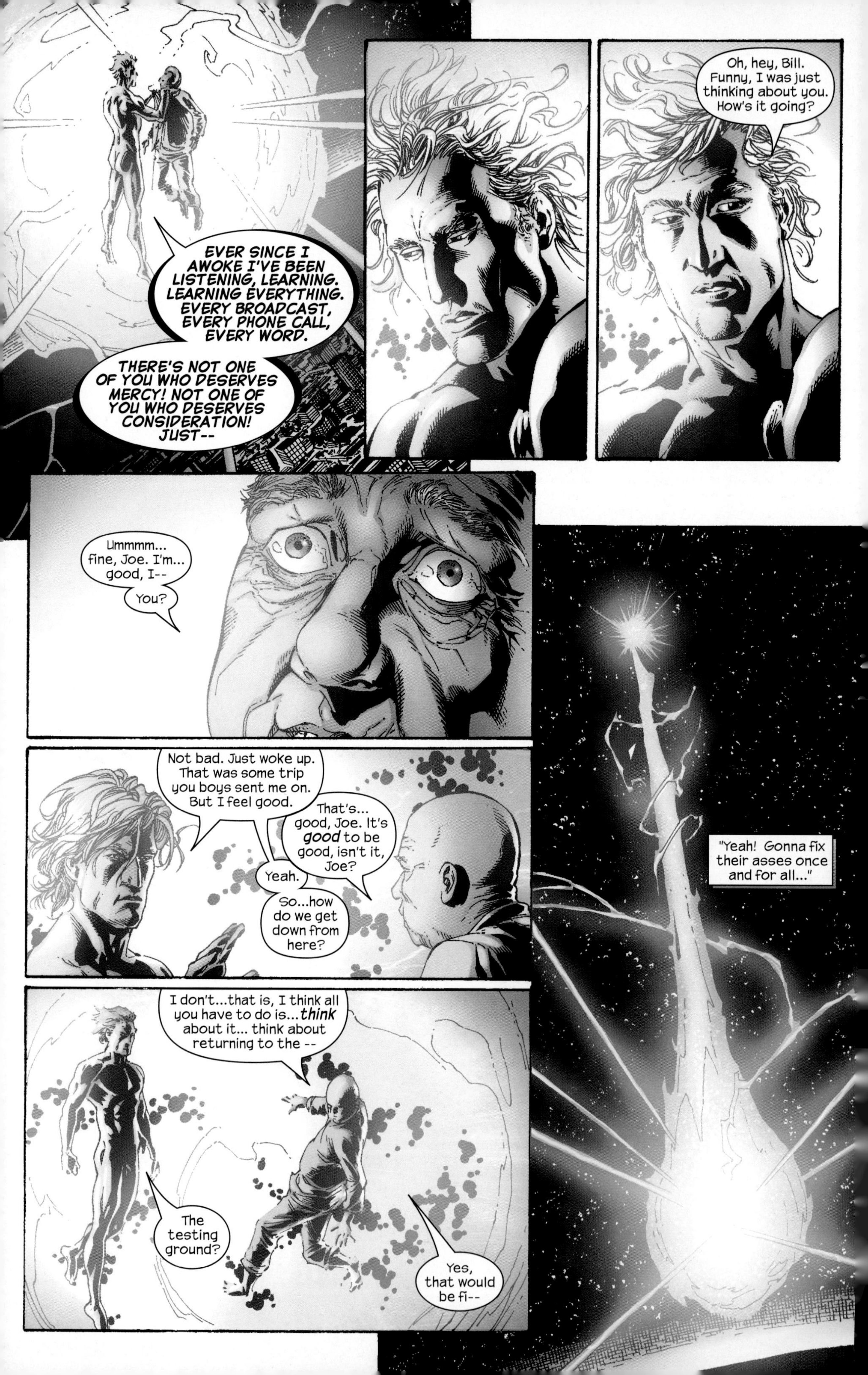
EVER SINCE I AWOKE I'VE BEEN LISTENING, LEARNING. LEARNING EVERYTHING. EVERY BROADCAST, EVERY PHONE CALL, EVERY WORD.
THERE'S NOT ONE OF YOU WHO DESERVES MERCY! NOT ONE OF YOU WHO DESERVES CONSIDERATION! JUST--
Oh, hey, Bill. Funny, I was just thinking about you. How's it going?
Ummmm... fine, Joe. I'm... good, I--
You?
Not bad. Just woke up. That was some trip you boys sent me on. But I feel good.
That's... good, Joe. It's *good* to be good, isn't it, Joe?
Yeah.
So...how do we get down from here?
I don't...that is, I think all you have to do is...*think* about it... think about returning to the --
The testing ground?
Yes, that would be fi--
"Yeah! Gonna fix their asses once and for all..."

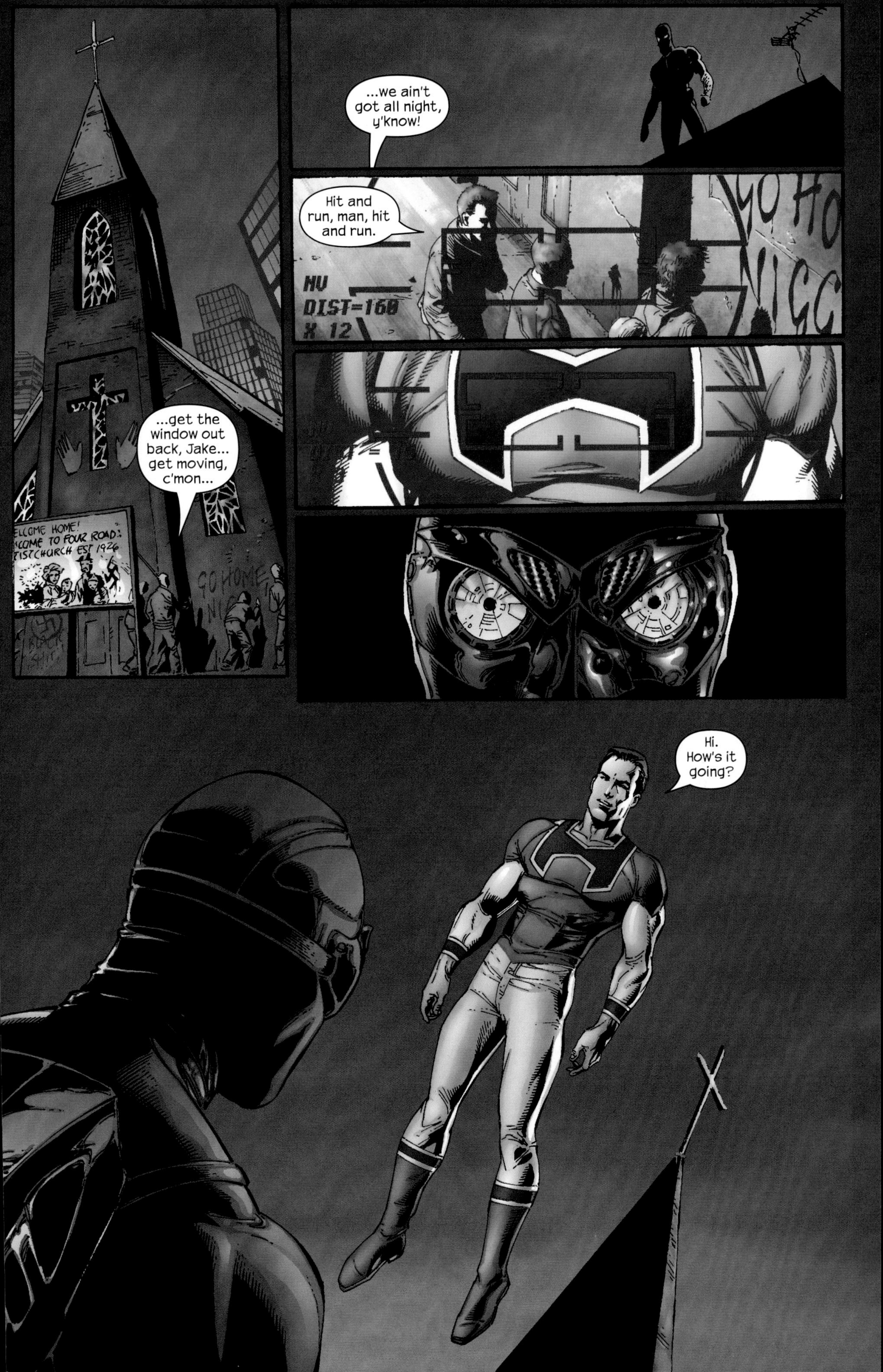
...get the window out back, Jake... get moving, c'mon...
...we ain't got all night, y'know!
Hit and run, man, hit and run.
MV
DIST=160
X 12
Hi. How's it going?

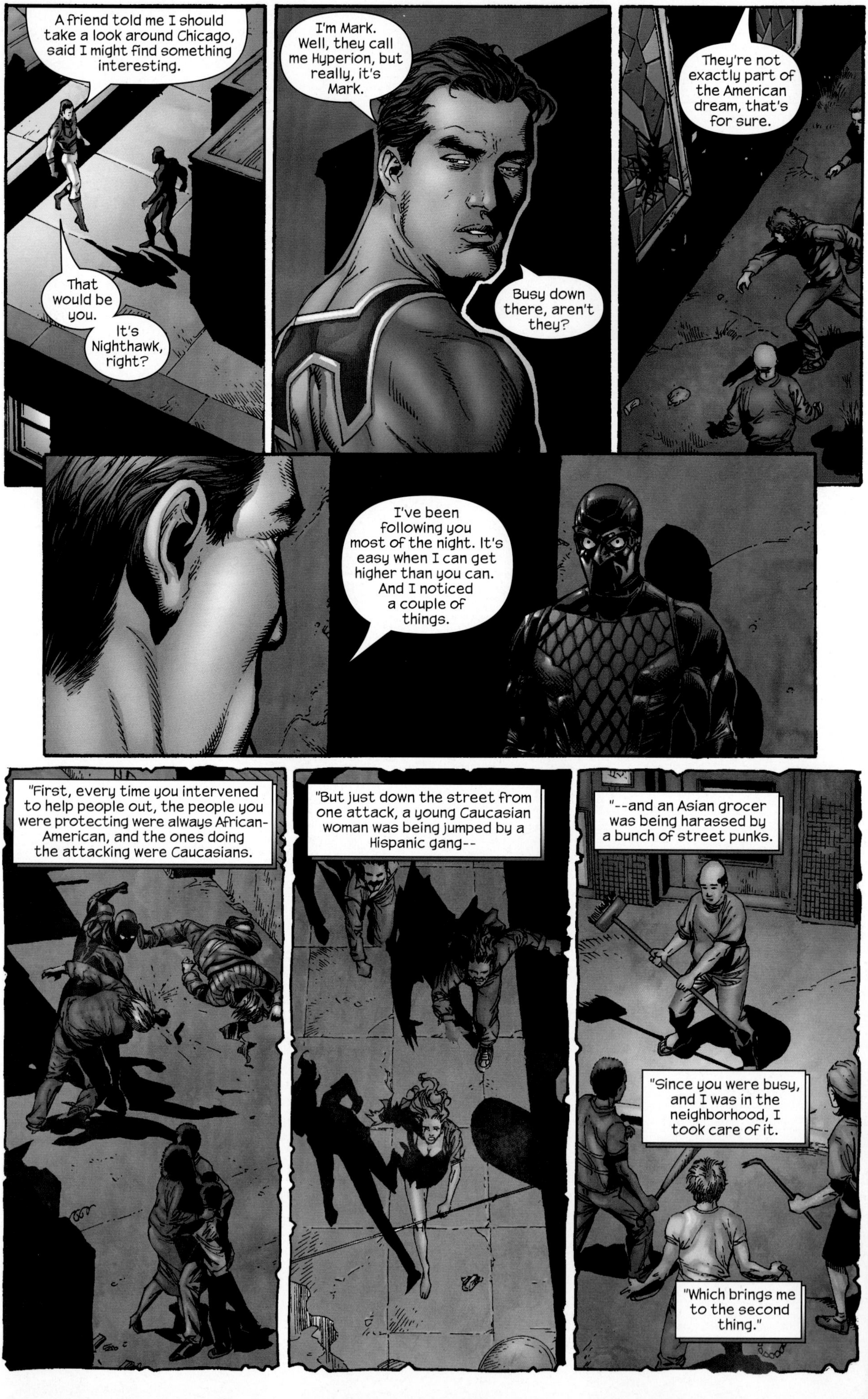
A friend told me I should take a look around Chicago, said I might find something interesting.
That would be you.
It's Nighthawk, right?
I'm Mark. Well, they call me Hyperion, but really, it's Mark.
Busy down there, aren't they?
They're not exactly part of the American dream, that's for sure.
I've been following you most of the night. It's easy when I can get higher than you can. And I noticed a couple of things.
"First, every time you intervened to help people out, the people you were protecting were always African-American, and the ones doing the attacking were Caucasians.
"But just down the street from one attack, a young Caucasian woman was being jumped by a Hispanic gang--
"--and an Asian grocer was being harassed by a bunch of street punks.
"Since you were busy, and I was in the neighborhood, I took care of it.
"Which brings me to the second thing."

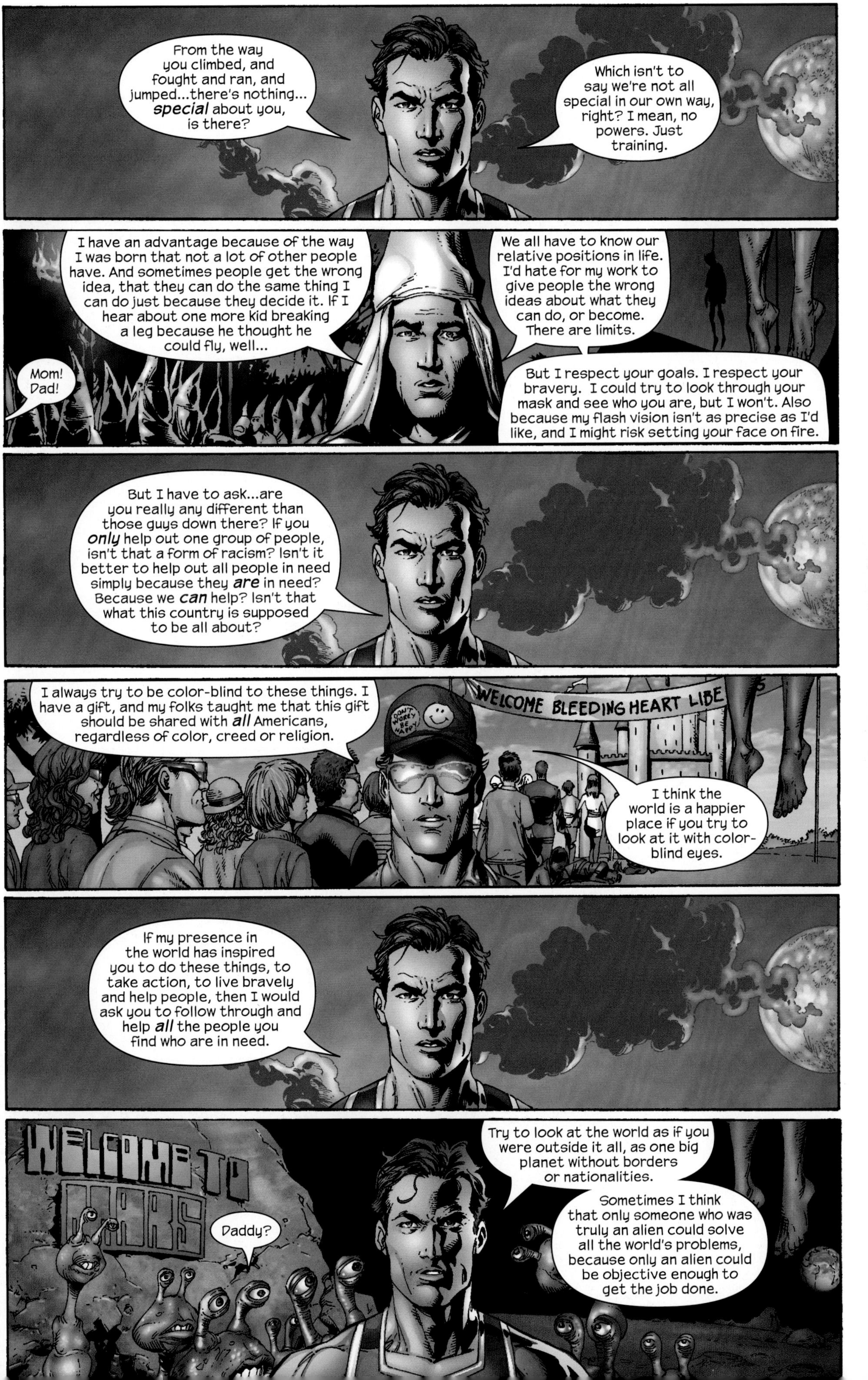

From the way you climbed, and fought and ran, and jumped...there's nothing... *special* about you, is there?
Which isn't to say we're not all special in our own way, right? I mean, no powers. Just training.
I have an advantage because of the way I was born that not a lot of other people have. And sometimes people get the wrong idea, that they can do the same thing I can do just because they decide it. If I hear about one more kid breaking a leg because he thought he could fly, well...
Mom! Dad!
We all have to know our relative positions in life. I'd hate for my work to give people the wrong ideas about what they can do, or become. There are limits.
But I respect your goals. I respect your bravery. I could try to look through your mask and see who you are, but I won't. Also because my flash vision isn't as precise as I'd like, and I might risk setting your face on fire.
But I have to ask...are you really any different than those guys down there? If you *only* help out one group of people, isn't that a form of racism? Isn't it better to help out all people in need simply because they *are* in need? Because we *can* help? Isn't that what this country is supposed to be all about?
I always try to be color-blind to these things. I have a gift, and my folks taught me that this gift should be shared with *all* Americans, regardless of color, creed or religion.
WELCOME BLEEDING HEART LIBE
I think the world is a happier place if you try to look at it with color-blind eyes.
If my presence in the world has inspired you to do these things, to take action, to live bravely and help people, then I would ask you to follow through and help *all* the people you find who are in need.
WELCOME TO MARS
Daddy?
Try to look at the world as if you were outside it all, as one big planet without borders or nationalities.
Sometimes I think that only someone who was truly an alien could solve all the world's problems, because only an alien could be objective enough to get the job done.

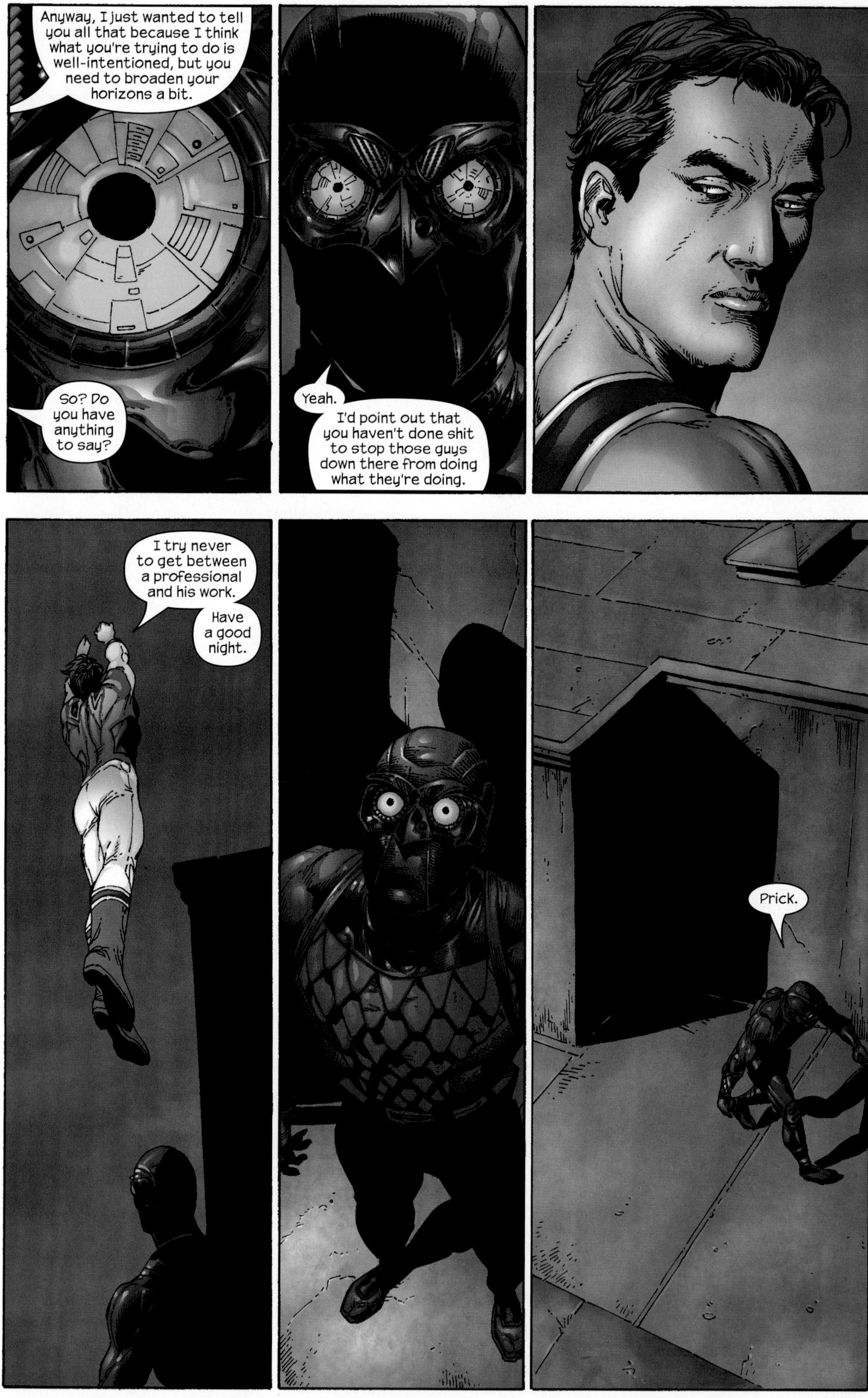

Anyway, I just wanted to tell you all that because I think what you're trying to do is well-intentioned, but you need to broaden your horizons a bit.
So? Do you have anything to say?
Yeah.
I'd point out that you haven't done shit to stop those guys down there from doing what they're doing.
I try never to get between a professional and his work.
Have a good night.
Prick.

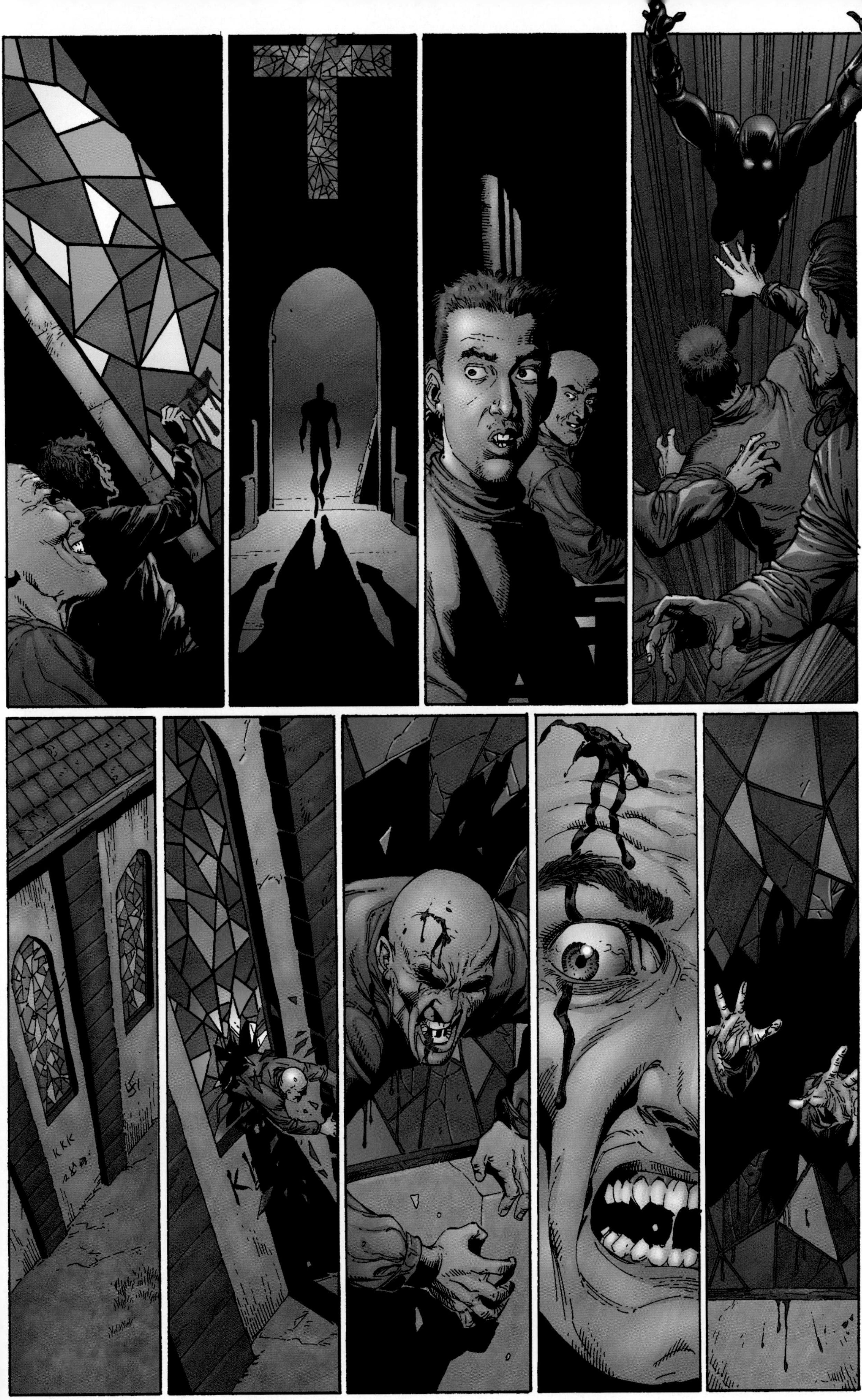
KKK

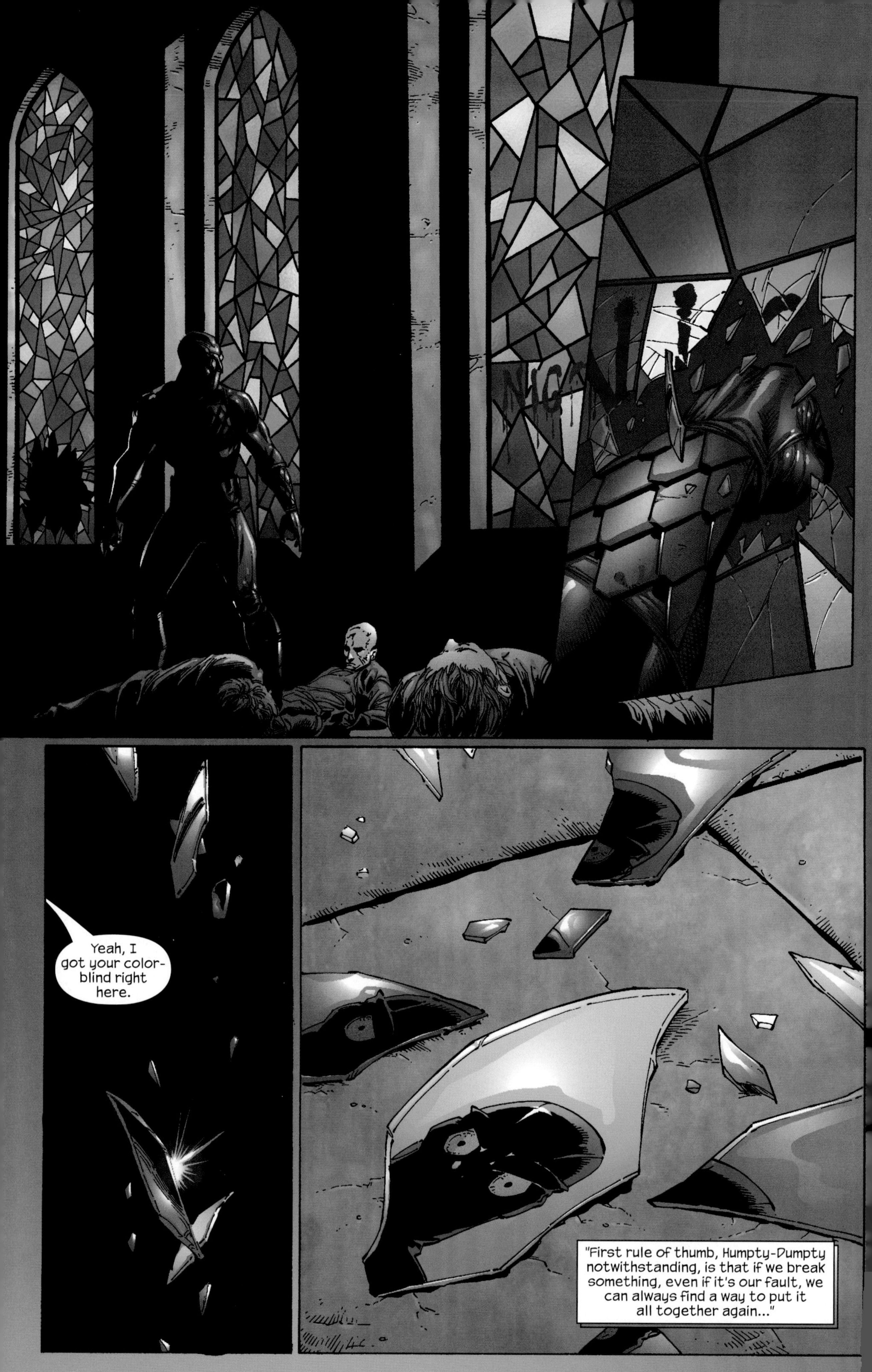
Yeah, I got your color-blind right here.
"First rule of thumb, Humpty-Dumpty notwithstanding, is that if we break something, even if it's our fault, we can always find a way to put it all together again..."

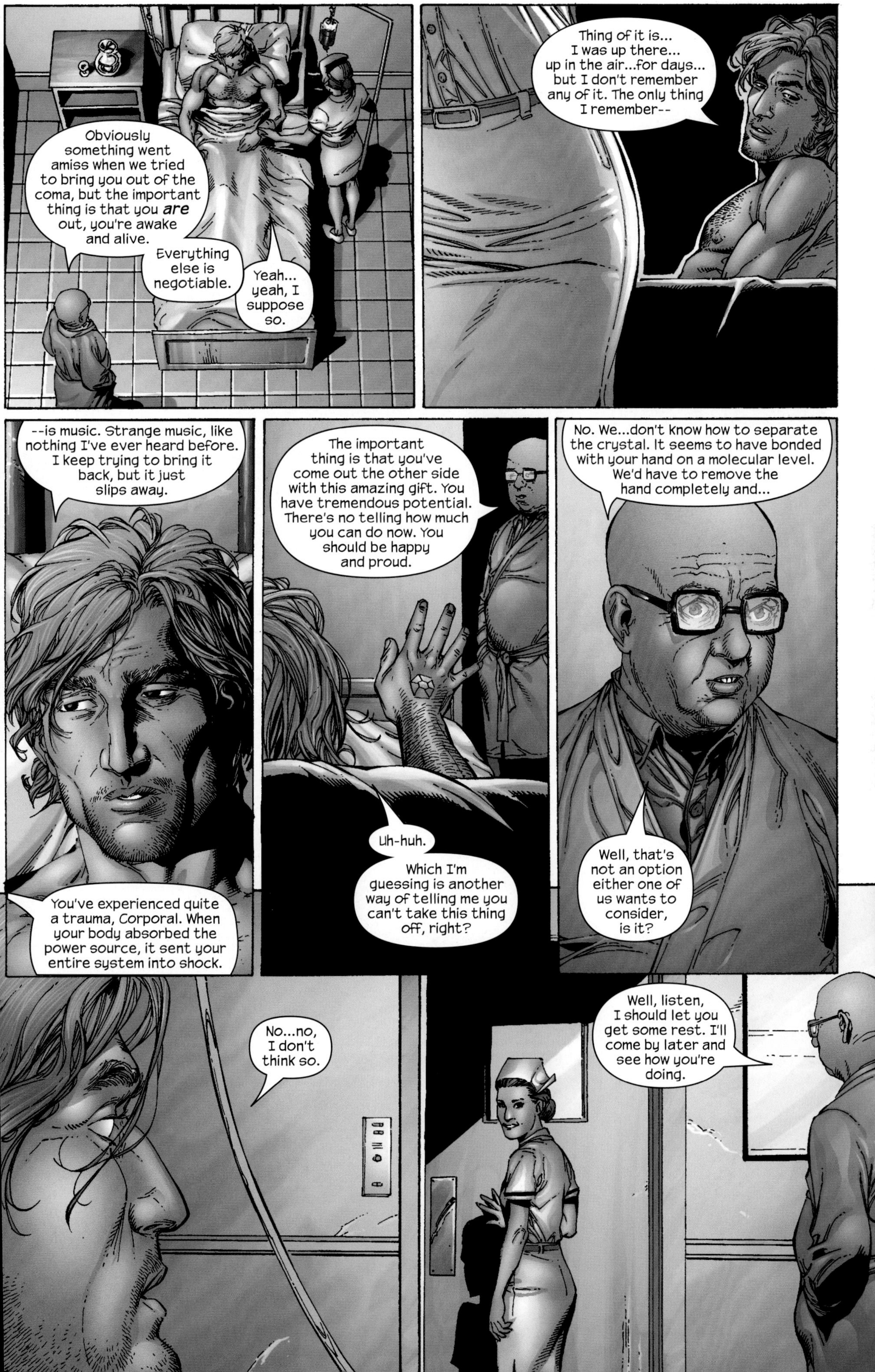
Obviously something went amiss when we tried to bring you out of the coma, but the important thing is that you *are* out, you're awake and alive.
Everything else is negotiable.
Yeah... yeah, I suppose so.
Thing of it is... I was up there... up in the air...for days... but I don't remember any of it. The only thing I remember--
--is music. Strange music, like nothing I've ever heard before. I keep trying to bring it back, but it just slips away.
You've experienced quite a trauma, Corporal. When your body absorbed the power source, it sent your entire system into shock.
The important thing is that you've come out the other side with this amazing gift. You have tremendous potential. There's no telling how much you can do now. You should be happy and proud.
Uh-huh.
Which I'm guessing is another way of telling me you can't take this thing off, right?
No. We...don't know how to separate the crystal. It seems to have bonded with your hand on a molecular level. We'd have to remove the hand completely and...
Well, that's not an option either one of us wants to consider, is it?
No...no, I don't think so.
Well, listen, I should let you get some rest. I'll come by later and see how you're doing.

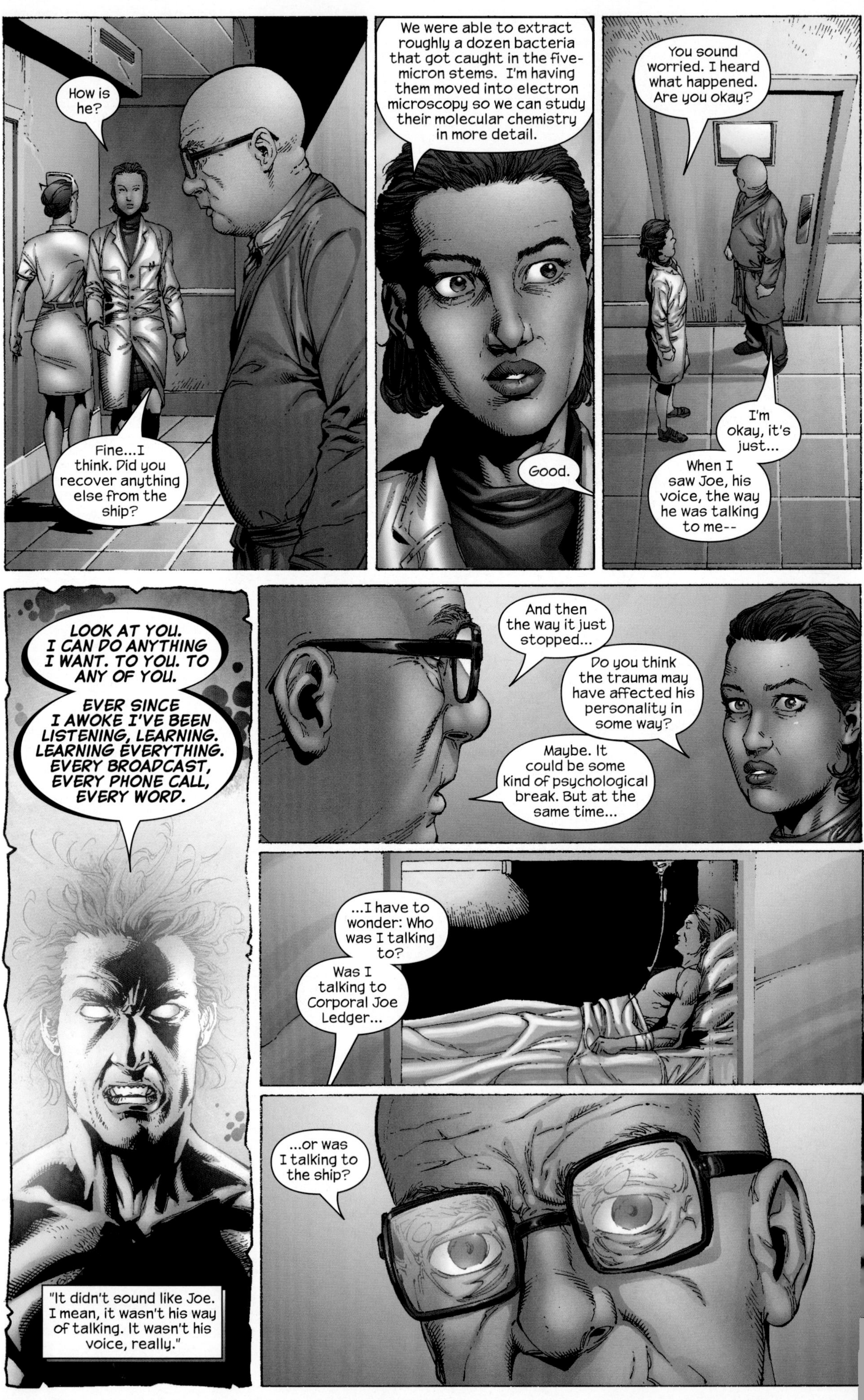
How is he?
Fine...I think. Did you recover anything else from the ship?
We were able to extract roughly a dozen bacteria that got caught in the five-micron stems. I'm having them moved into electron microscopy so we can study their molecular chemistry in more detail.
Good.
You sound worried. I heard what happened. Are you okay?
I'm okay, it's just...
When I saw Joe, his voice, the way he was talking to me--
LOOK AT YOU. I CAN DO ANYTHING I WANT. TO YOU. TO ANY OF YOU.
EVER SINCE I AWOKE I'VE BEEN LISTENING, LEARNING. LEARNING EVERYTHING. EVERY BROADCAST, EVERY PHONE CALL, EVERY WORD.
"It didn't sound like Joe. I mean, it wasn't his way of talking. It wasn't his voice, really."
And then the way it just stopped...
Do you think the trauma may have affected his personality in some way?
Maybe. It could be some kind of psychological break. But at the same time...
...I have to wonder: Who was I talking to?
Was I talking to Corporal Joe Ledger...
...or was I talking to the ship?

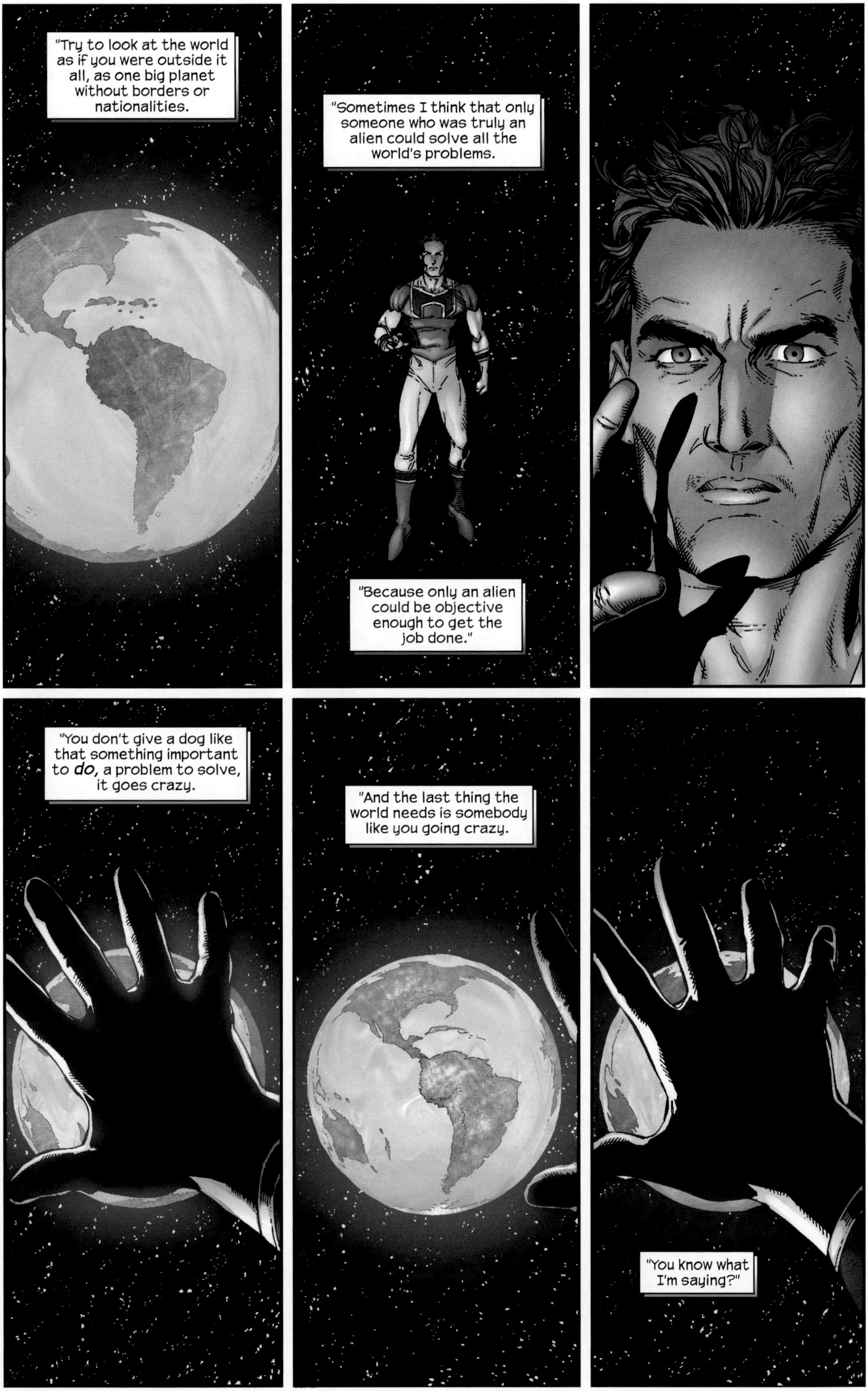
"Try to look at the world as if you were outside it all, as one big planet without borders or nationalities.
"Sometimes I think that only someone who was truly an alien could solve all the world's problems.
"Because only an alien could be objective enough to get the job done."
"You don't give a dog like that something important to *do,* a problem to solve, it goes crazy.
"And the last thing the world needs is somebody like you going crazy.
"You know what I'm saying?"

#7 Powers and Principalities

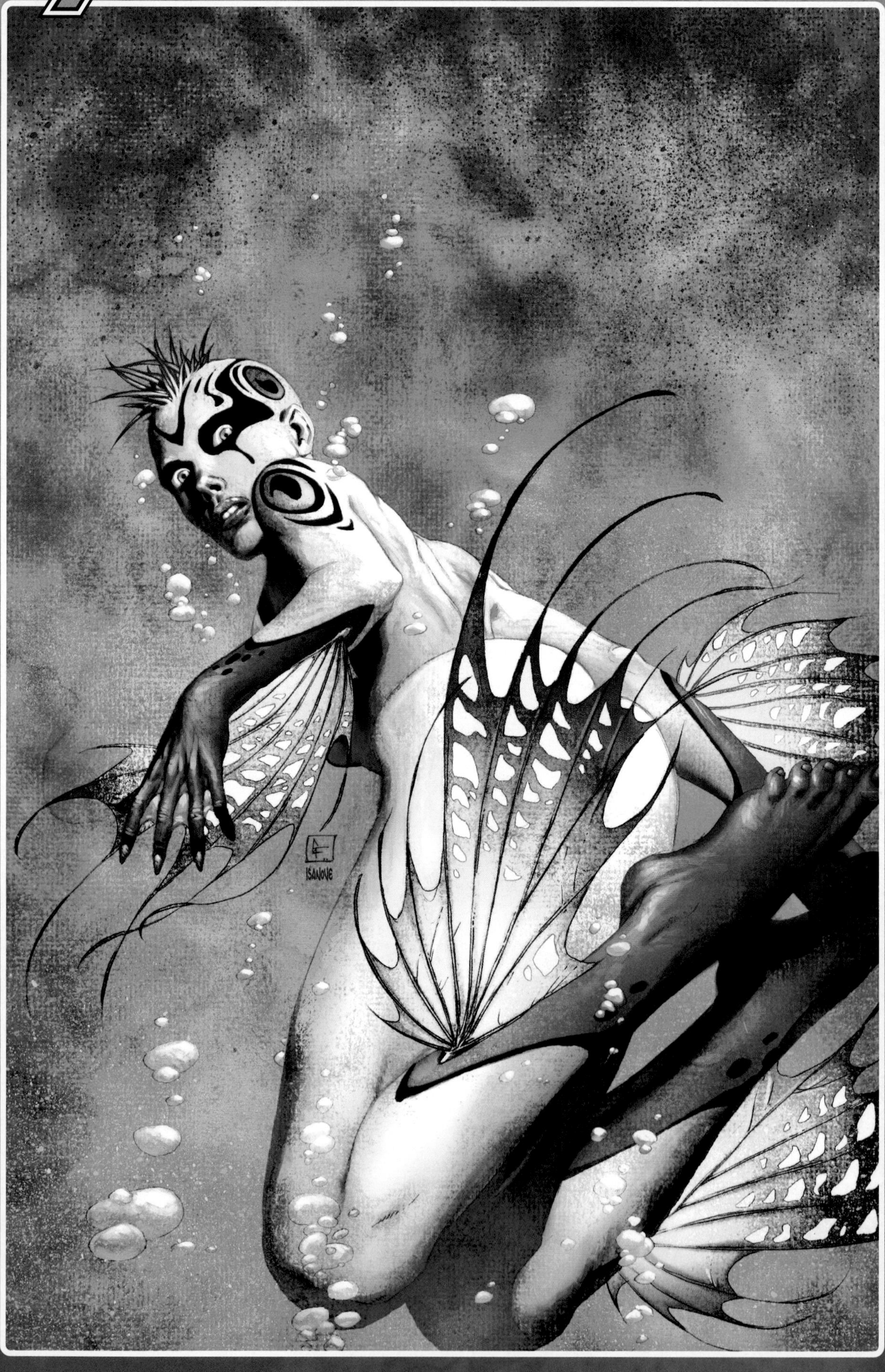
ISANOVE

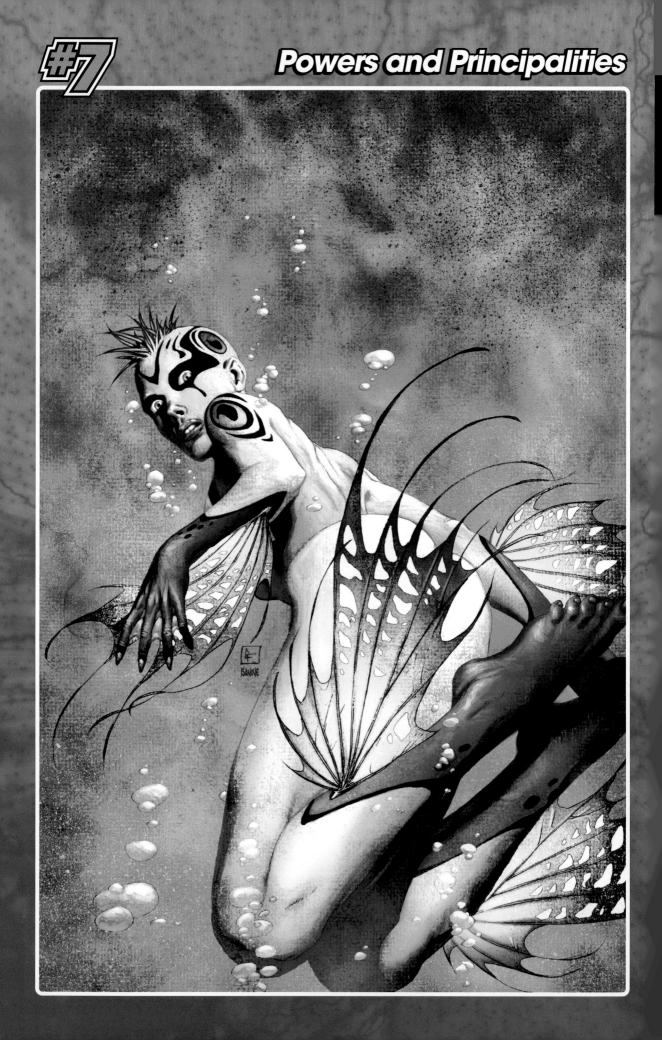

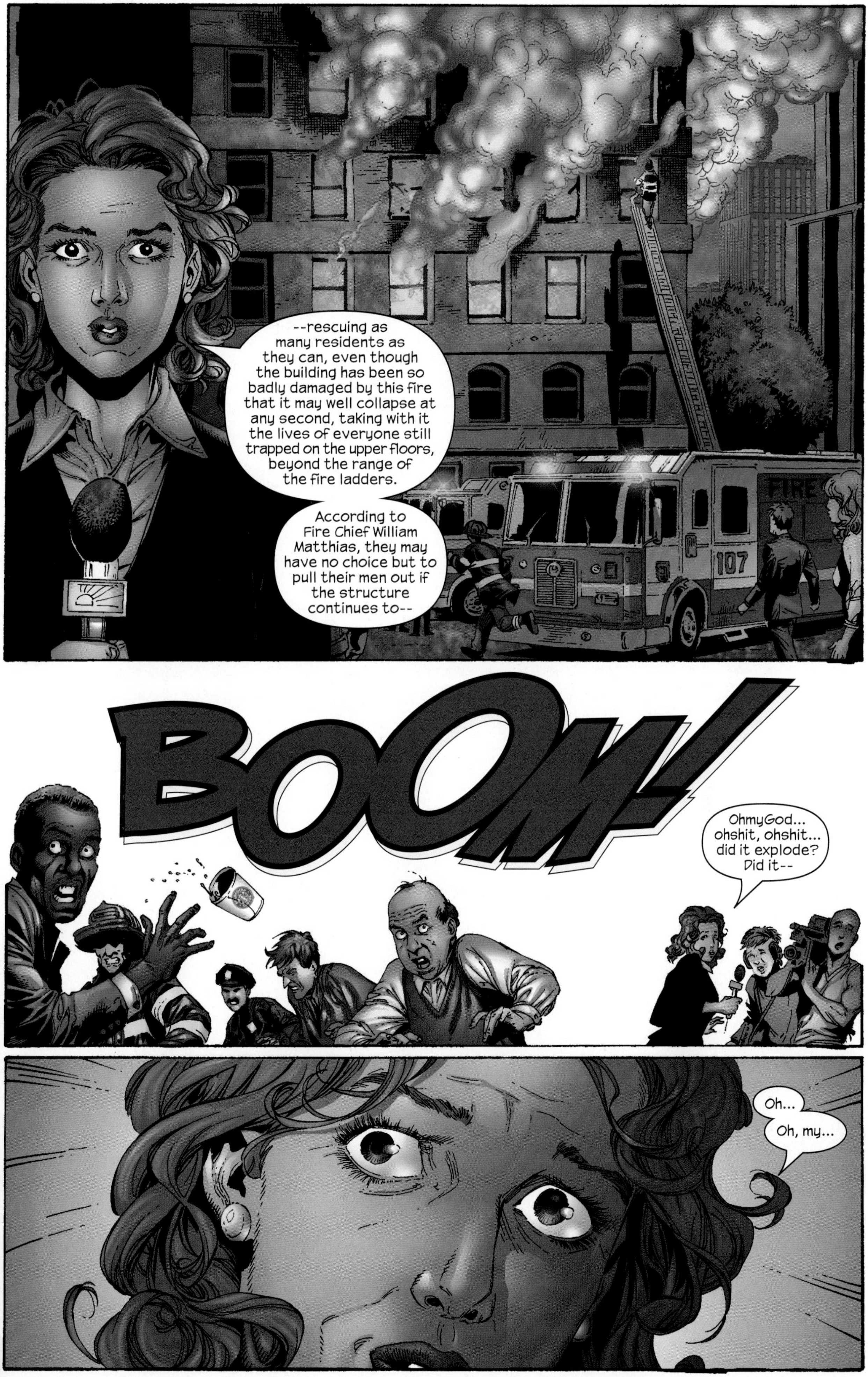
--rescuing as many residents as they can, even though the building has been so badly damaged by this fire that it may well collapse at any second, taking with it the lives of everyone still trapped on the upper floors, beyond the range of the fire ladders.
According to Fire Chief William Matthias, they may have no choice but to pull their men out if the structure continues to--
FIRE
107
BOOM!
OhmyGod... ohshit, ohshit... did it explode? Did it--
Oh...
Oh, my...

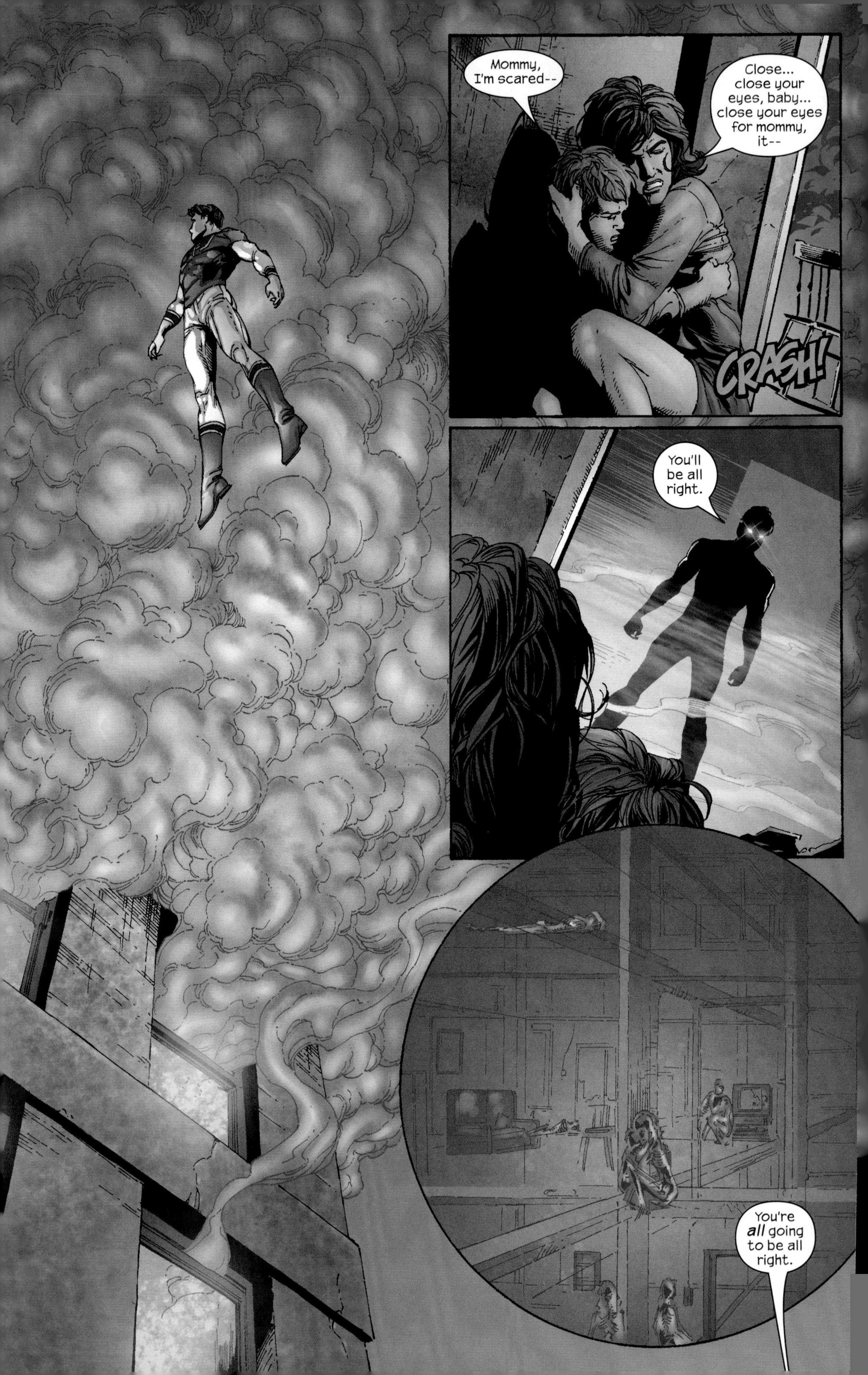
Mommy, I'm scared--
Close... close your eyes, baby... close your eyes for mommy, it--
CRASH!
You'll be all right.
You're *all* going to be all right.

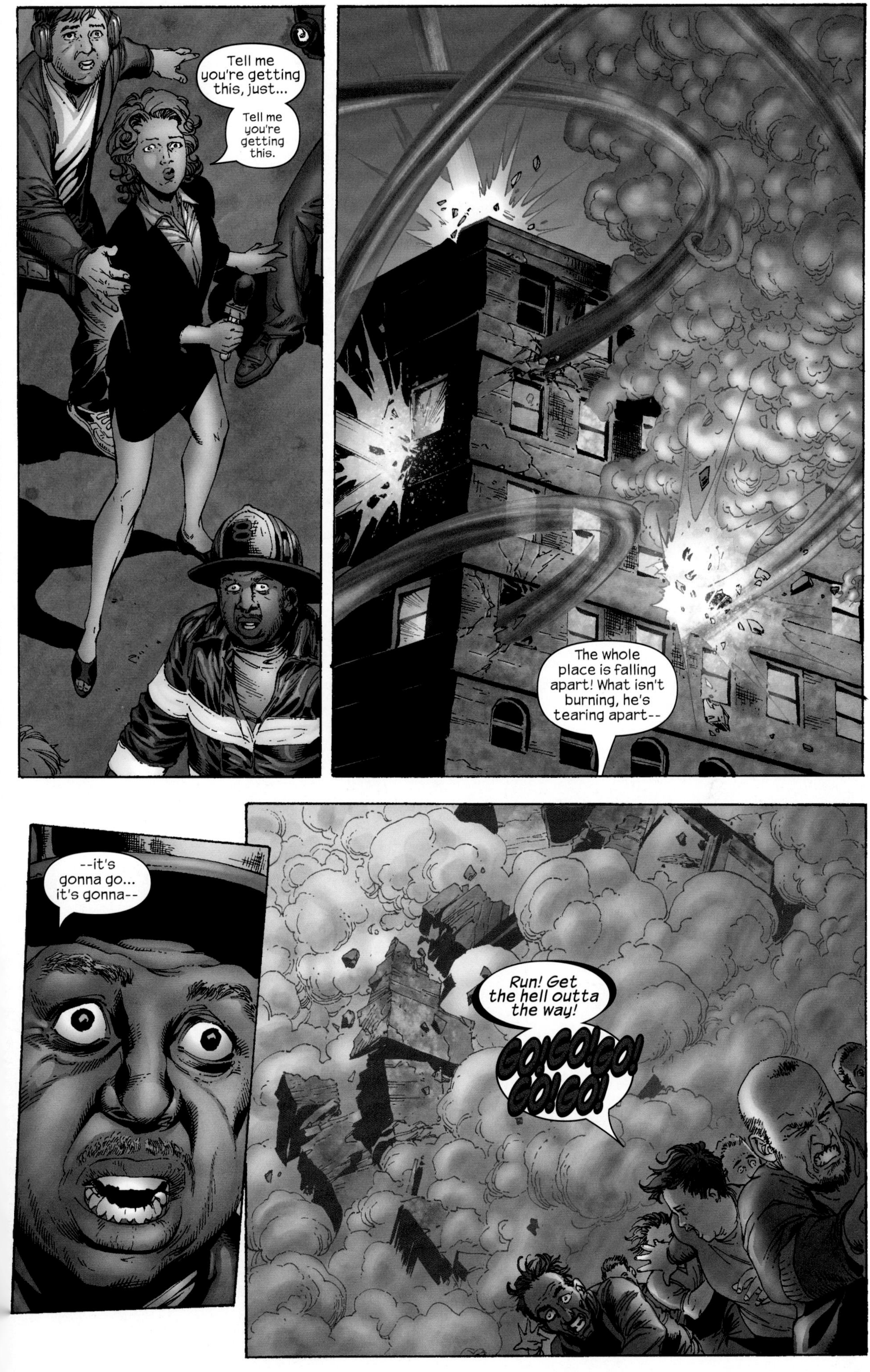
Tell me you're getting this, just...
Tell me you're getting this.
The whole place is falling apart! What isn't burning, he's tearing apart--
--it's gonna go... it's gonna--
Run! Get the hell outta the way!
GO! GO! GO! GO! GO!

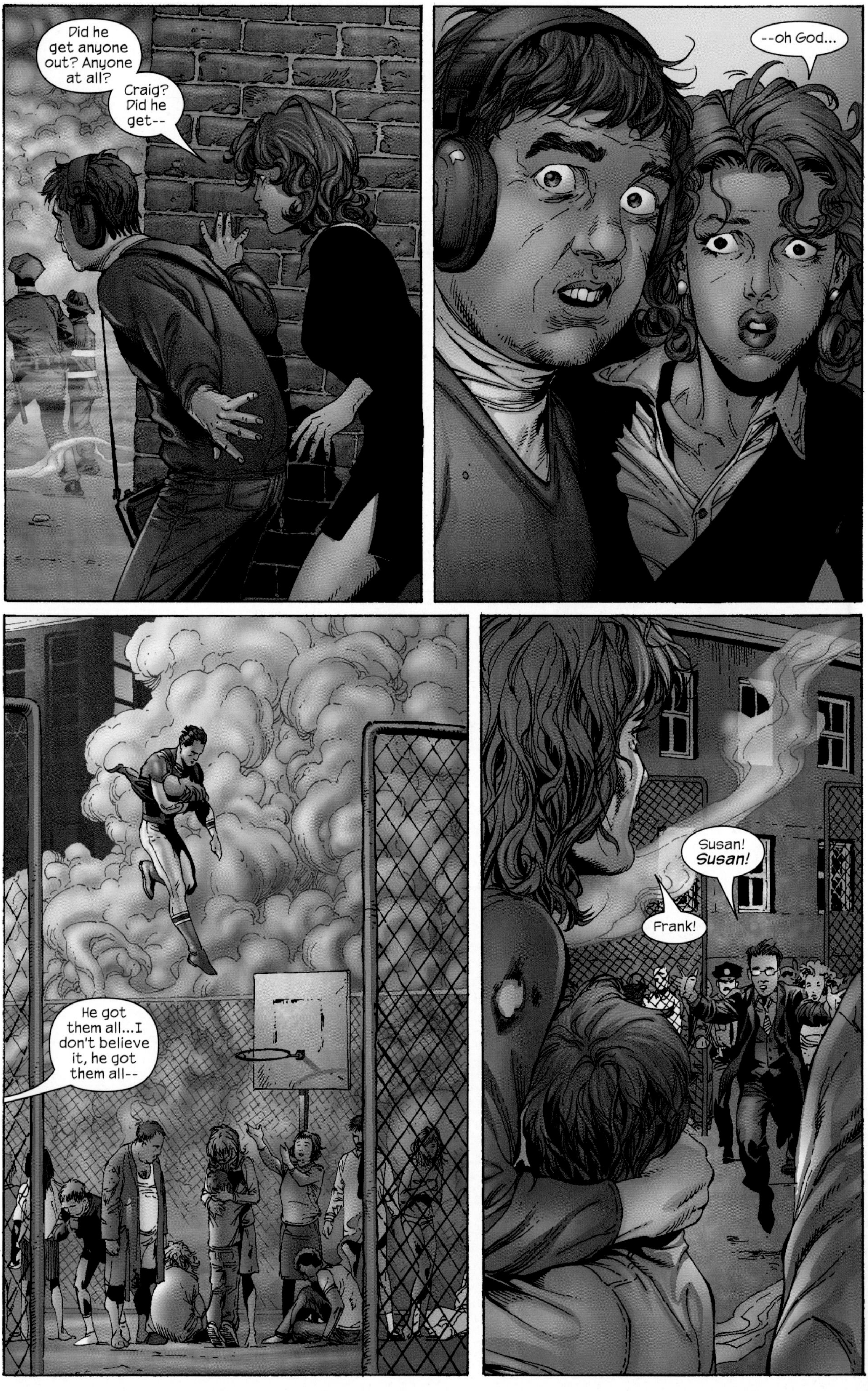
Did he get anyone out? Anyone at all?
Craig? Did he get--
--oh God...
He got them all...I don't believe it, he got them all--
Susan! *Susan!*
Frank!

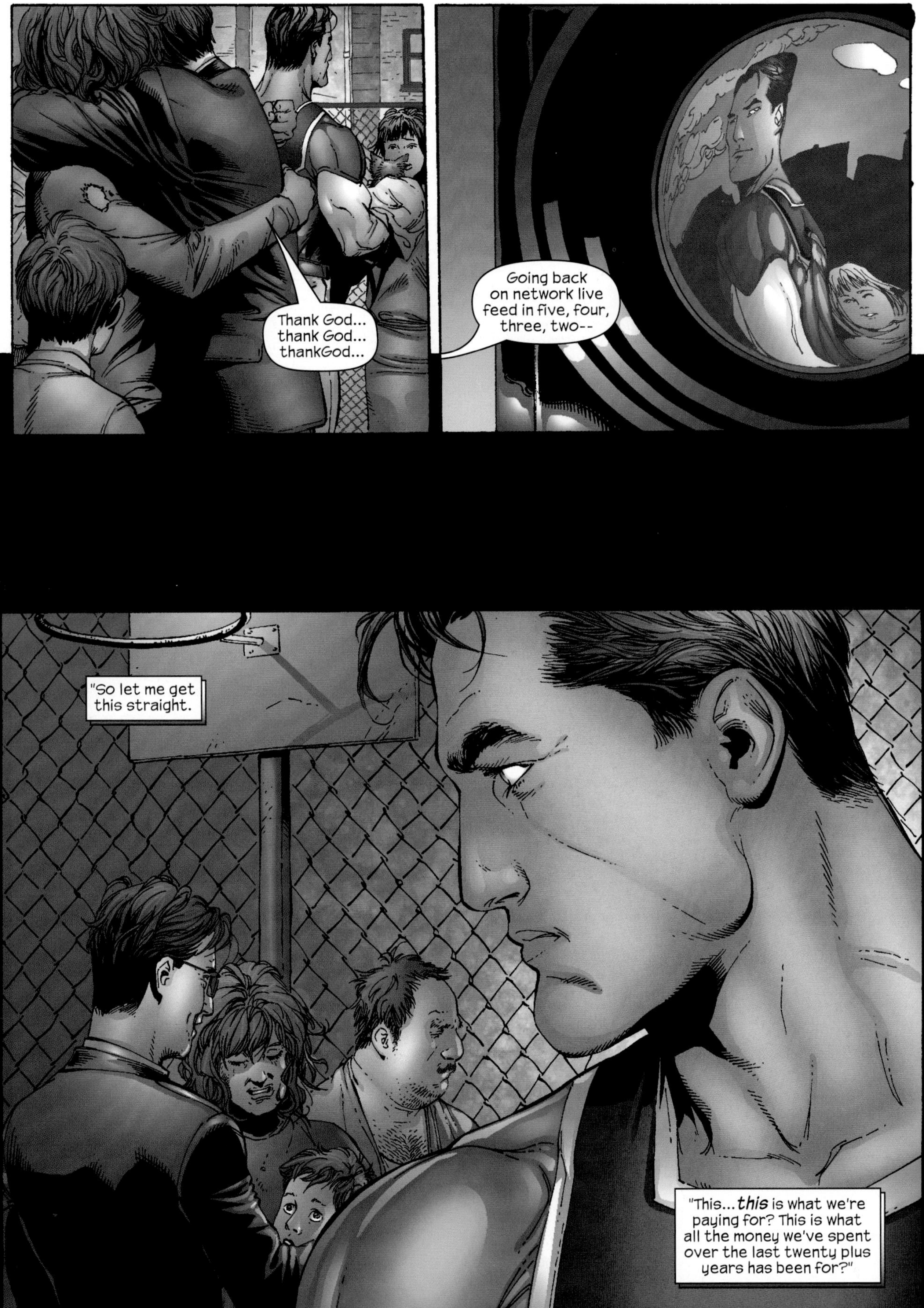

Thank God...
thank God...
thankGod...
Going back on network live feed in five, four, three, two--
"So let me get this straight.
"This... ***this*** is what we're paying for? This is what all the money we've spent over the last twenty plus years has been for?"

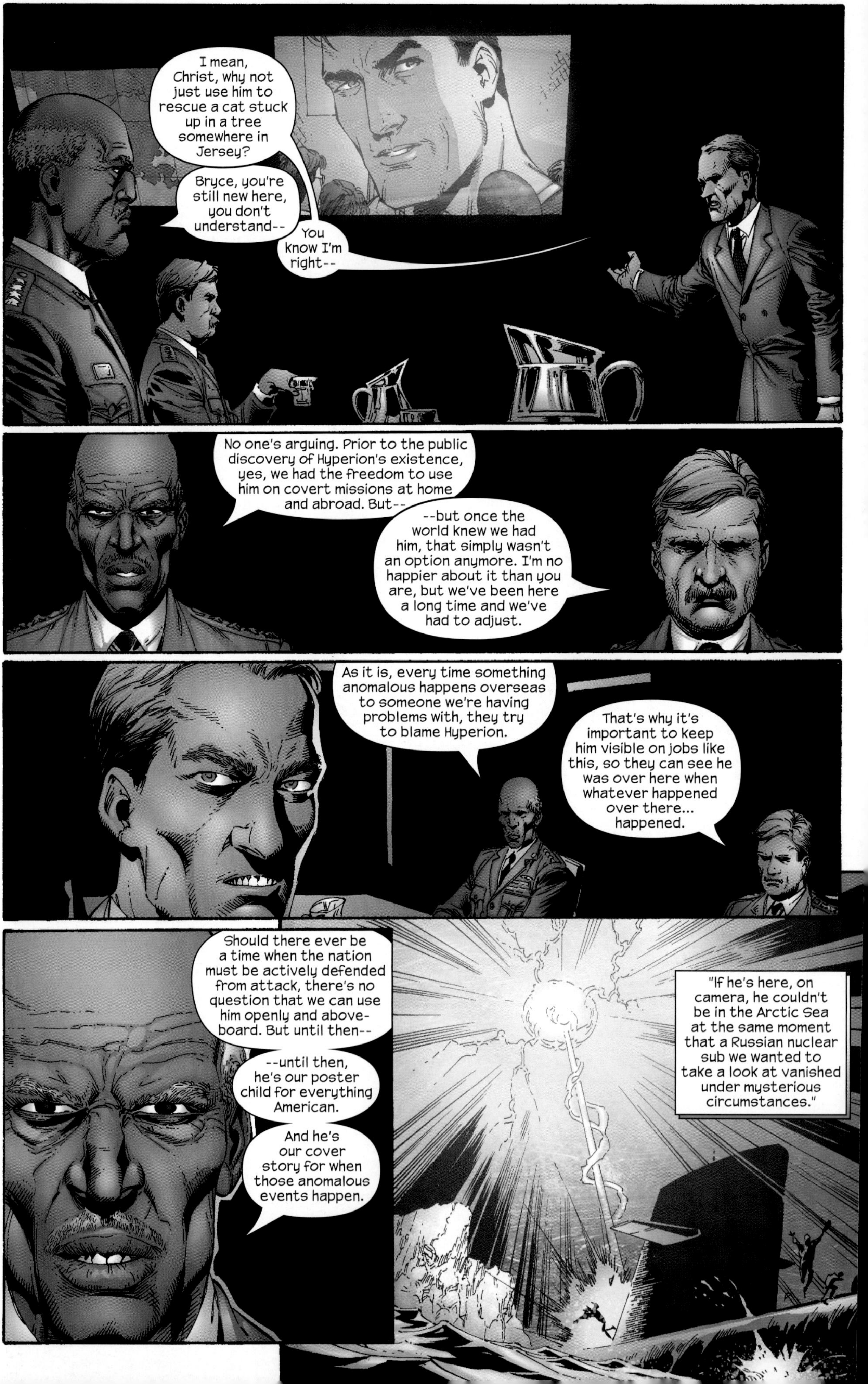
I mean, Christ, why not just use him to rescue a cat stuck up in a tree somewhere in Jersey?
Bryce, you're still new here, you don't understand--
You know I'm right--
No one's arguing. Prior to the public discovery of Hyperion's existence, yes, we had the freedom to use him on covert missions at home and abroad. But--
--but once the world knew we had him, that simply wasn't an option anymore. I'm no happier about it than you are, but we've been here a long time and we've had to adjust.
As it is, every time something anomalous happens overseas to someone we're having problems with, they try to blame Hyperion.
That's why it's important to keep him visible on jobs like this, so they can see he was over here when whatever happened over there... happened.
Should there ever be a time when the nation must be actively defended from attack, there's no question that we can use him openly and above-board. But until then--
--until then, he's our poster child for everything American.
And he's our cover story for when those anomalous events happen.
"If he's here, on camera, he couldn't be in the Arctic Sea at the same moment that a Russian nuclear sub we wanted to take a look at vanished under mysterious circumstances."

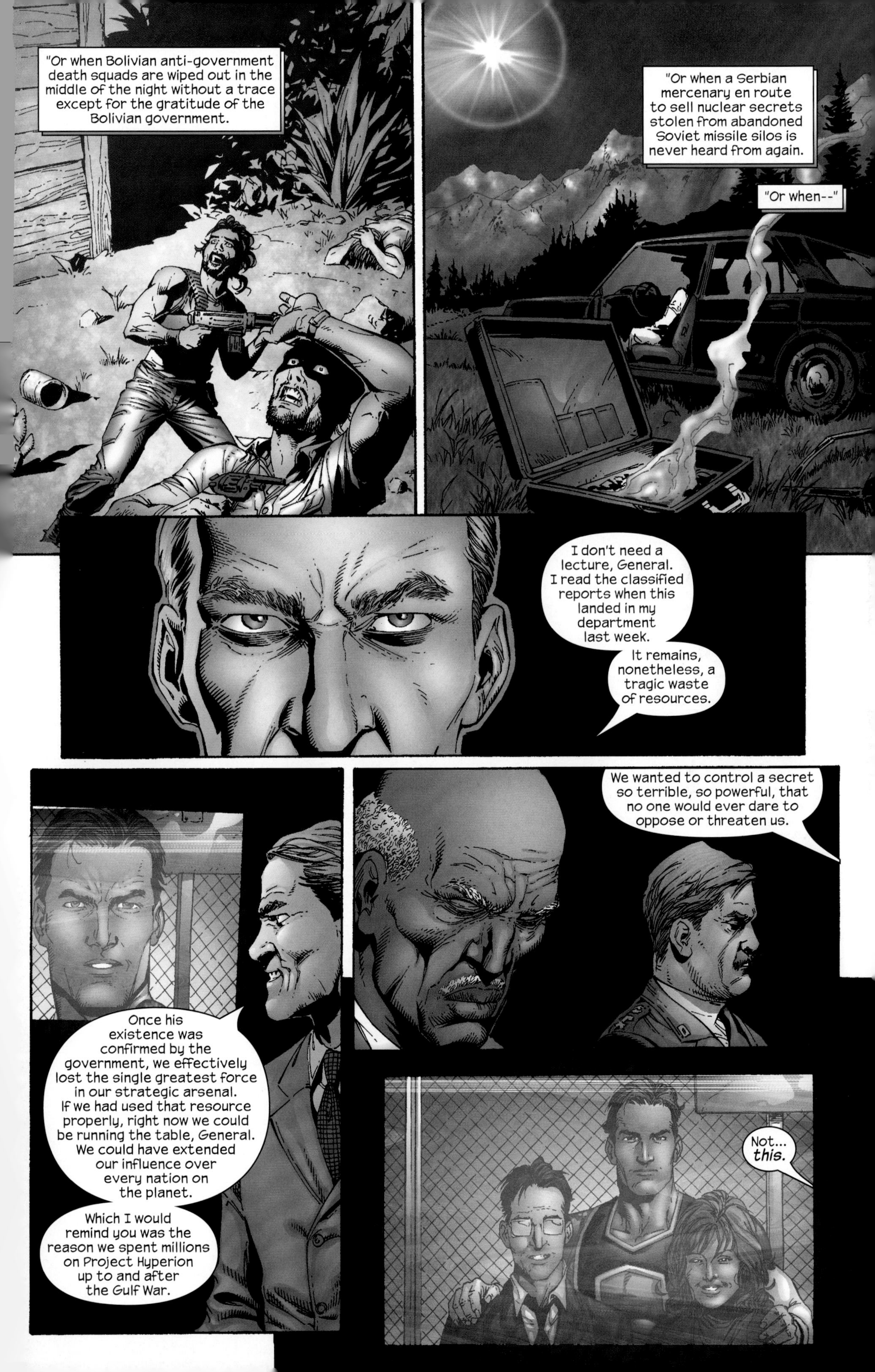
"Or when Bolivian anti-government death squads are wiped out in the middle of the night without a trace except for the gratitude of the Bolivian government.
"Or when a Serbian mercenary en route to sell nuclear secrets stolen from abandoned Soviet missile silos is never heard from again.
"Or when--"
I don't need a lecture, General. I read the classified reports when this landed in my department last week.
It remains, nonetheless, a tragic waste of resources.
Once his existence was confirmed by the government, we effectively lost the single greatest force in our strategic arsenal. If we had used that resource properly, right now we could be running the table, General. We could have extended our influence over every nation on the planet.
Which I would remind you was the reason we spent millions on Project Hyperion up to and after the Gulf War.
We wanted to control a secret so terrible, so powerful, that no one would ever dare to oppose or threaten us.
Not... *this.*

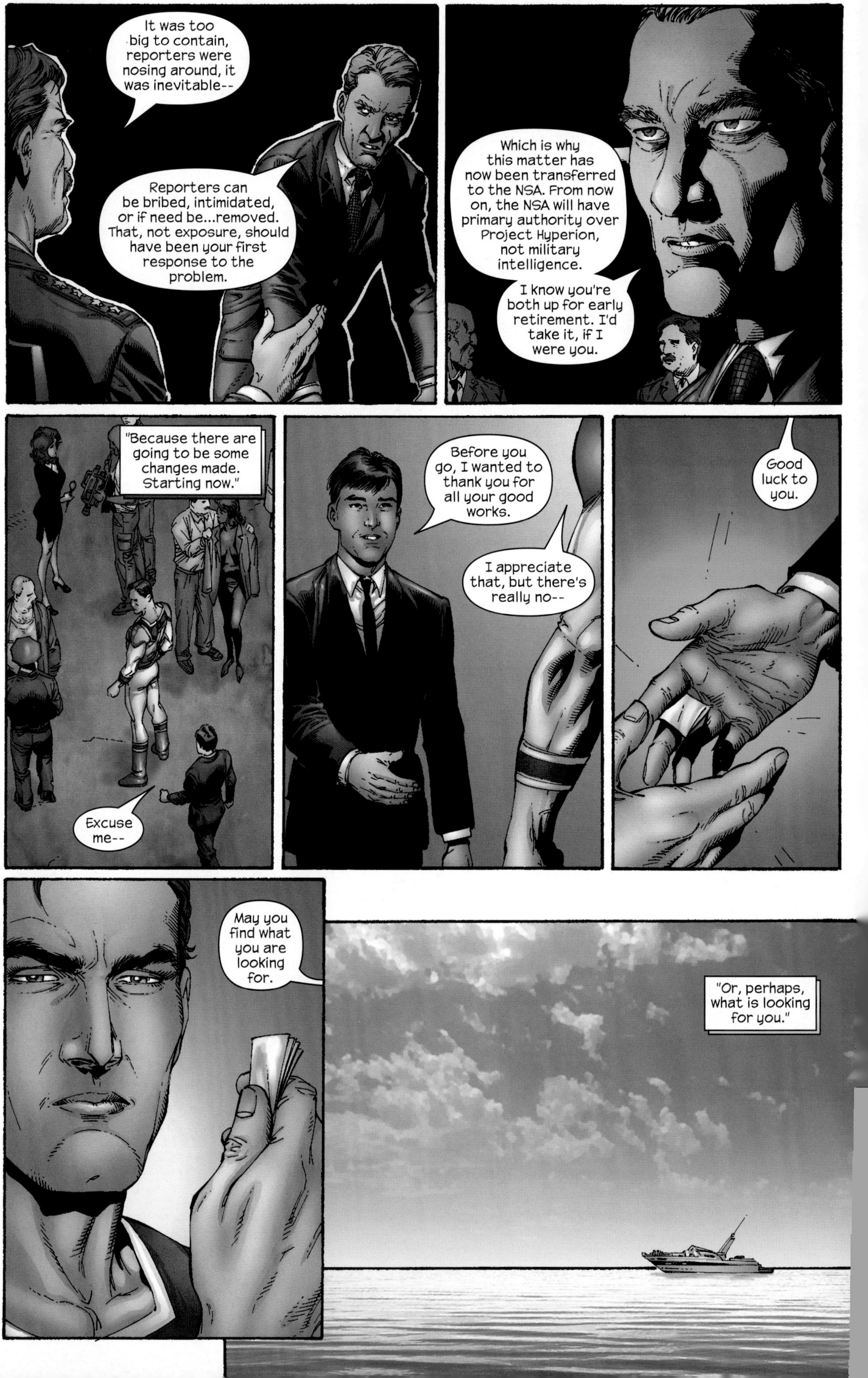
It was too big to contain, reporters were nosing around, it was inevitable--
Reporters can be bribed, intimidated, or if need be...removed. That, not exposure, should have been your first response to the problem.
Which is why this matter has now been transferred to the NSA. From now on, the NSA will have primary authority over Project Hyperion, not military intelligence.
I know you're both up for early retirement. I'd take it, if I were you.
"Because there are going to be some changes made. Starting now."
Excuse me--
Before you go, I wanted to thank you for all your good works.
I appreciate that, but there's really no--
Good luck to you.
May you find what you are looking for.
"Or, perhaps, what is looking for you."

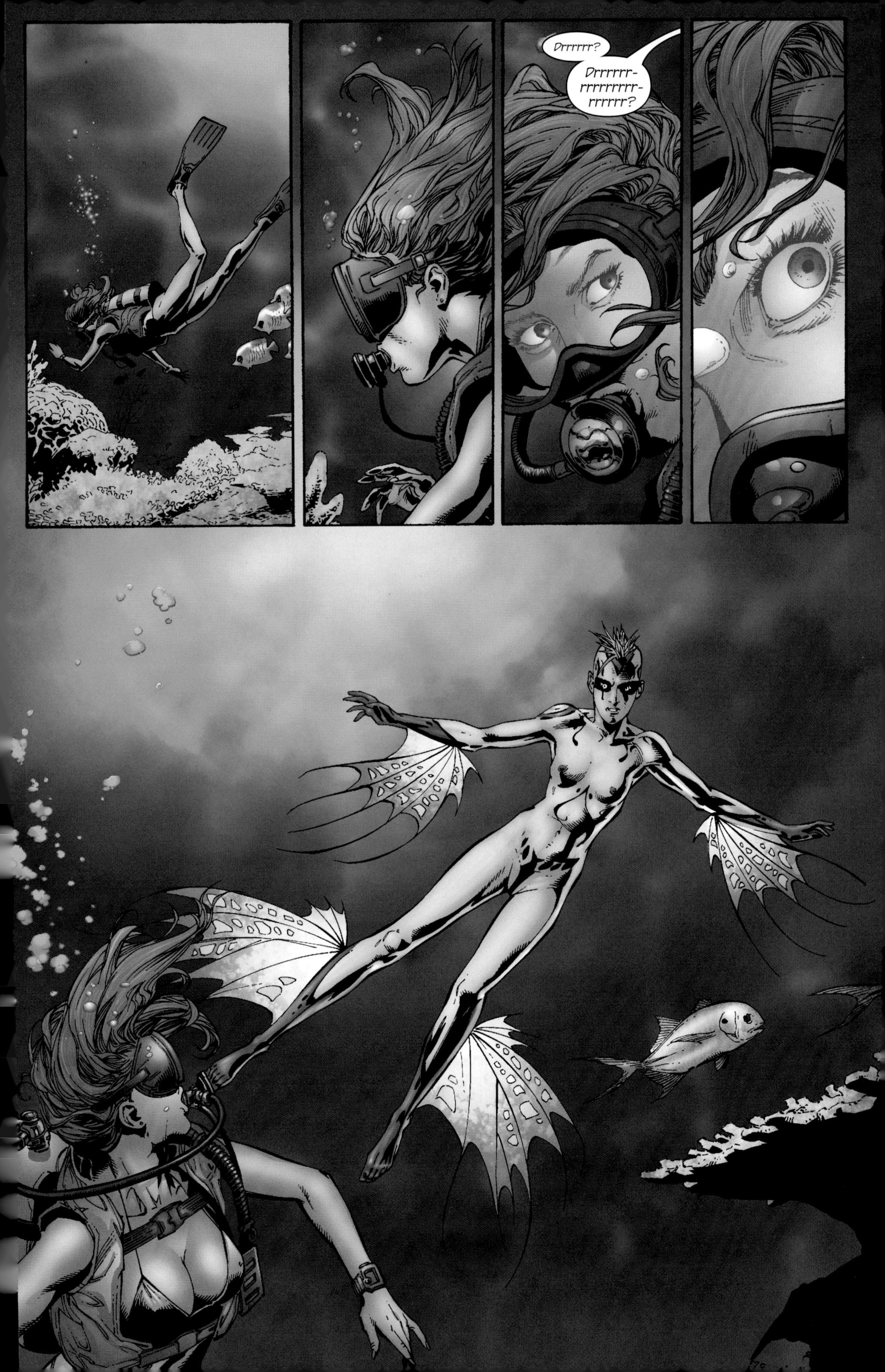
Drrrrrr?
Drrrrrr-rrrrrrrrr-rrrrrr?

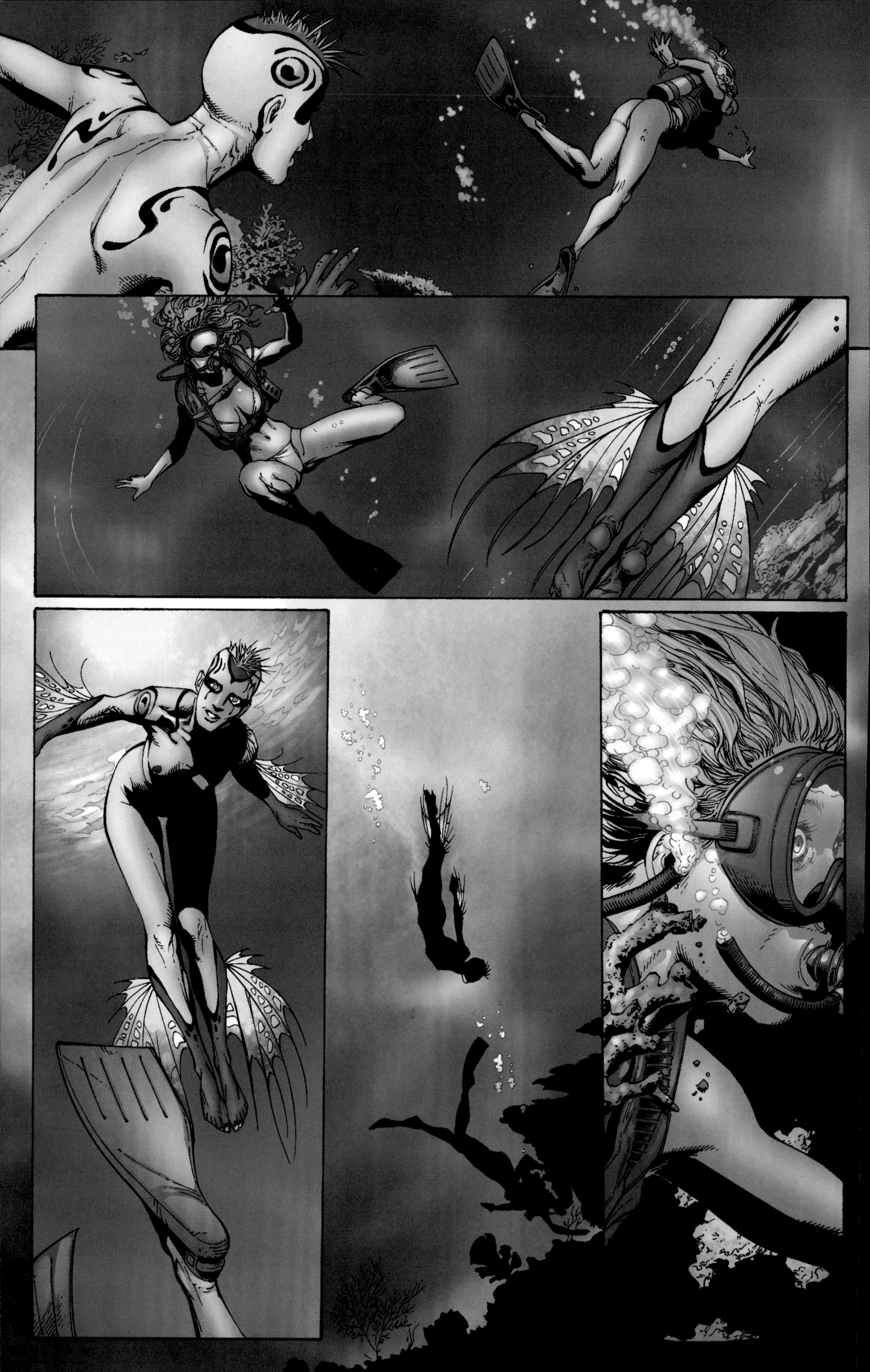

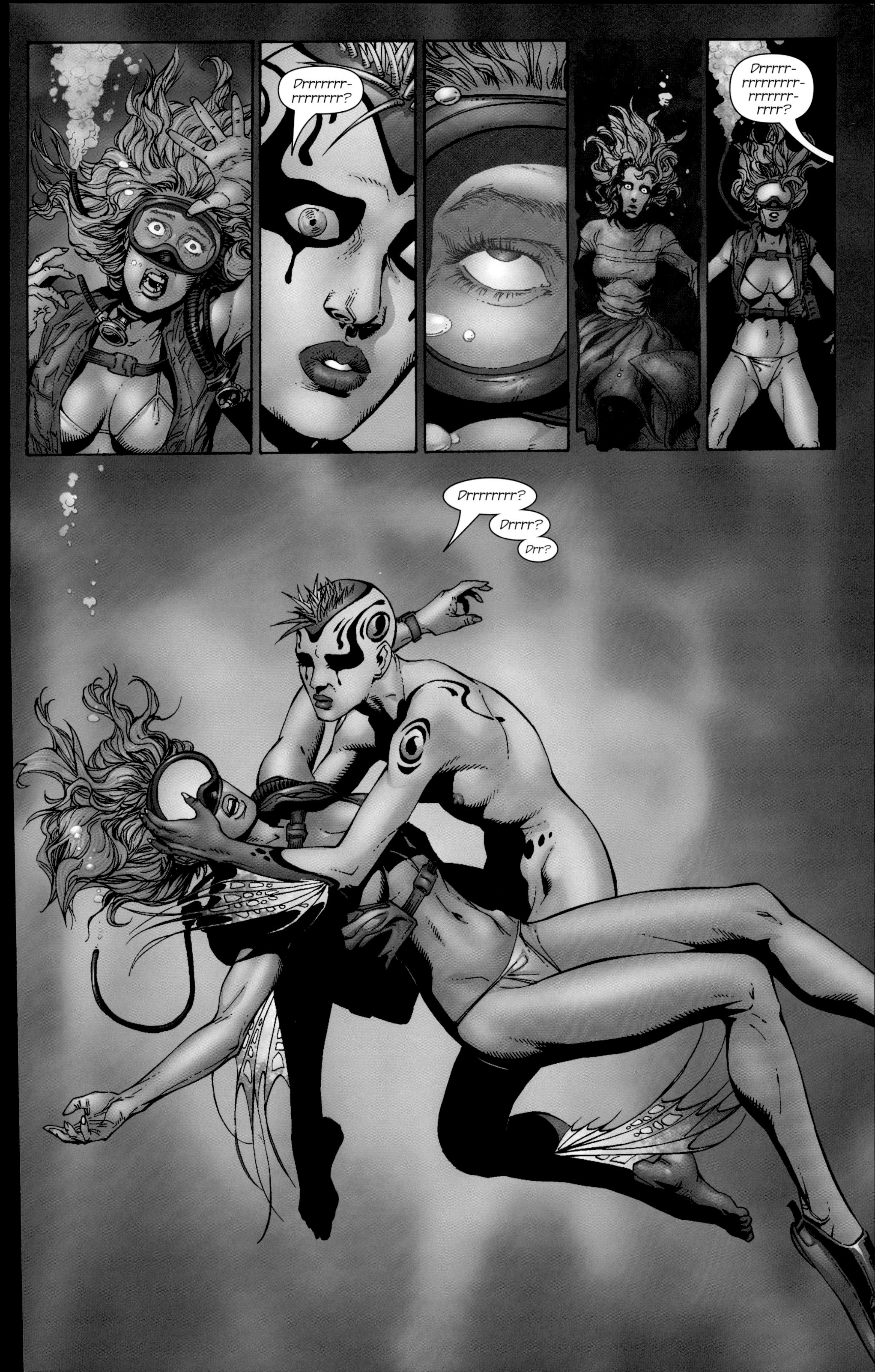
Drrrrrrr-rrrrrrrrr?
Drrrrr-rrrrrrrrrr-rrrrrrrr-rrrr?
Drrrrrrrr?
Drrrr?
Drr?

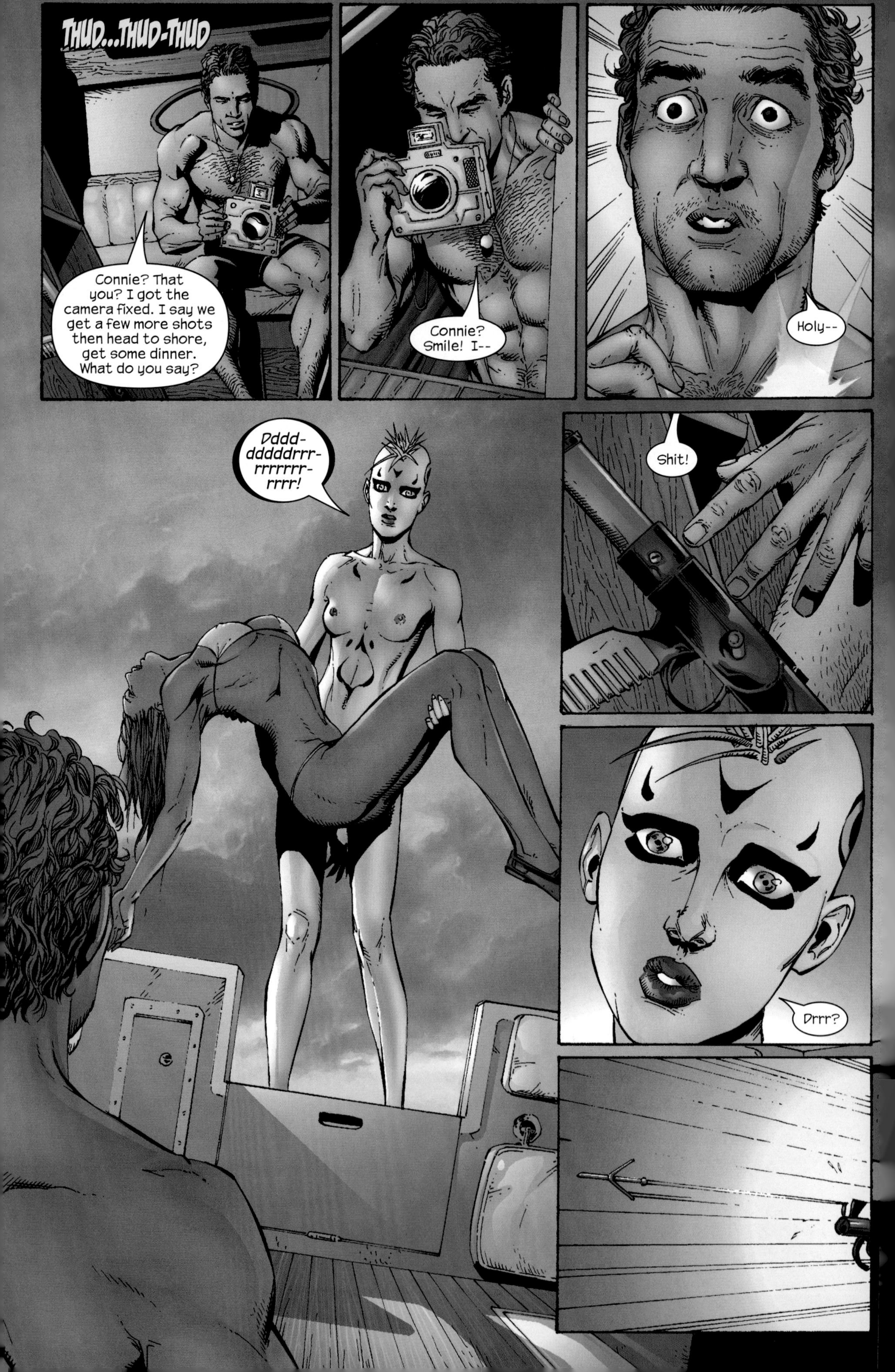
THUD...THUD-THUD
Connie? That you? I got the camera fixed. I say we get a few more shots then head to shore, get some dinner. What do you say?
Connie? Smile! I--
Holy--
Dddd-ddddddrrr-rrrrrrr-rrrr!
Shit!
Drrr?

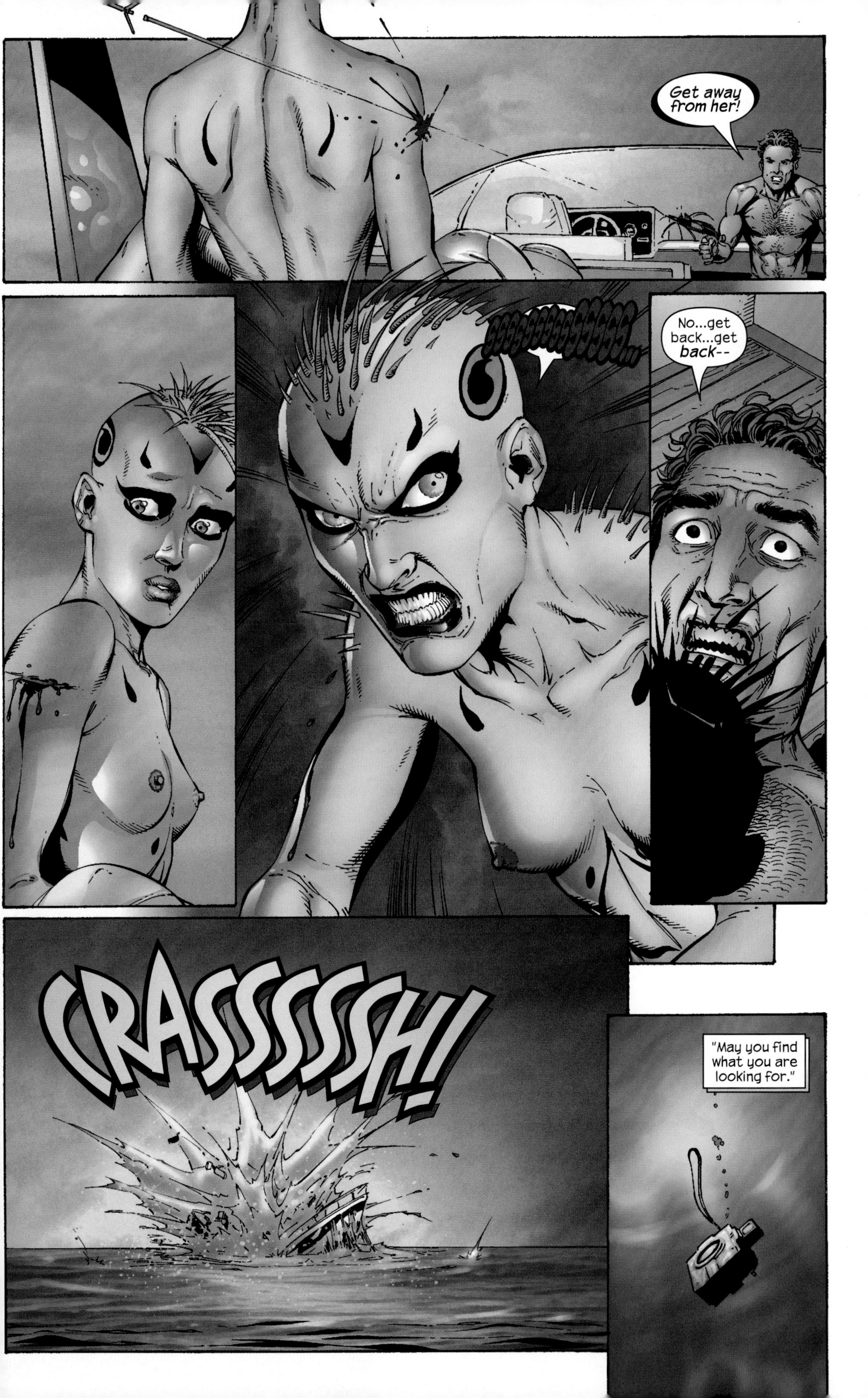
Get away from her!
SSSSSSSSSSSSSS...
No...get back...get *back*--
CRASSSSSH!
"May you find what you are looking for."

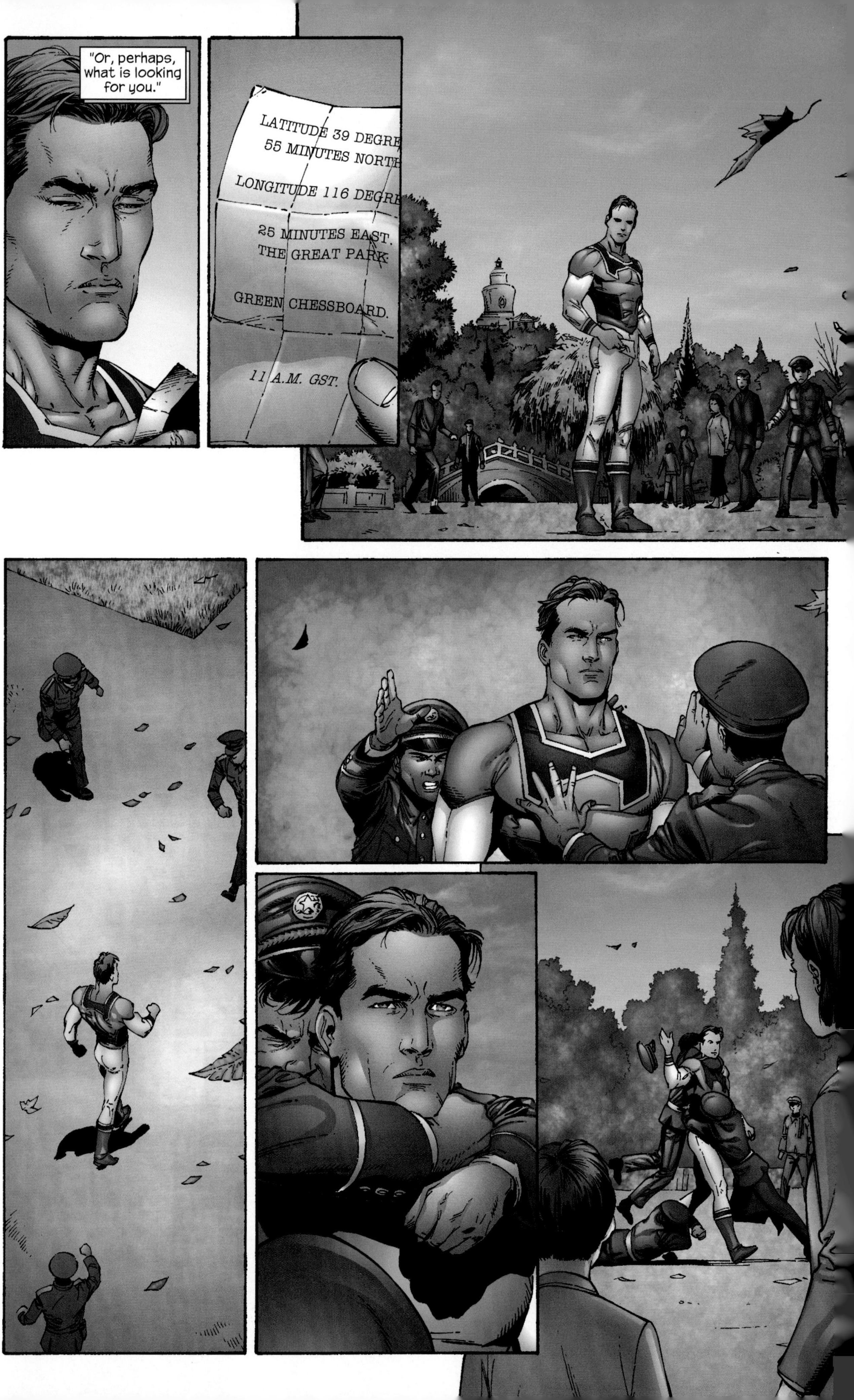
"Or, perhaps, what is looking for you."
LATITUDE 39 DEGRE
55 MINUTES NORTH
LONGITUDE 116 DEGRE
25 MINUTES EAST.
THE GREAT PARK
GREEN CHESSBOARD.
11 A.M. GST.

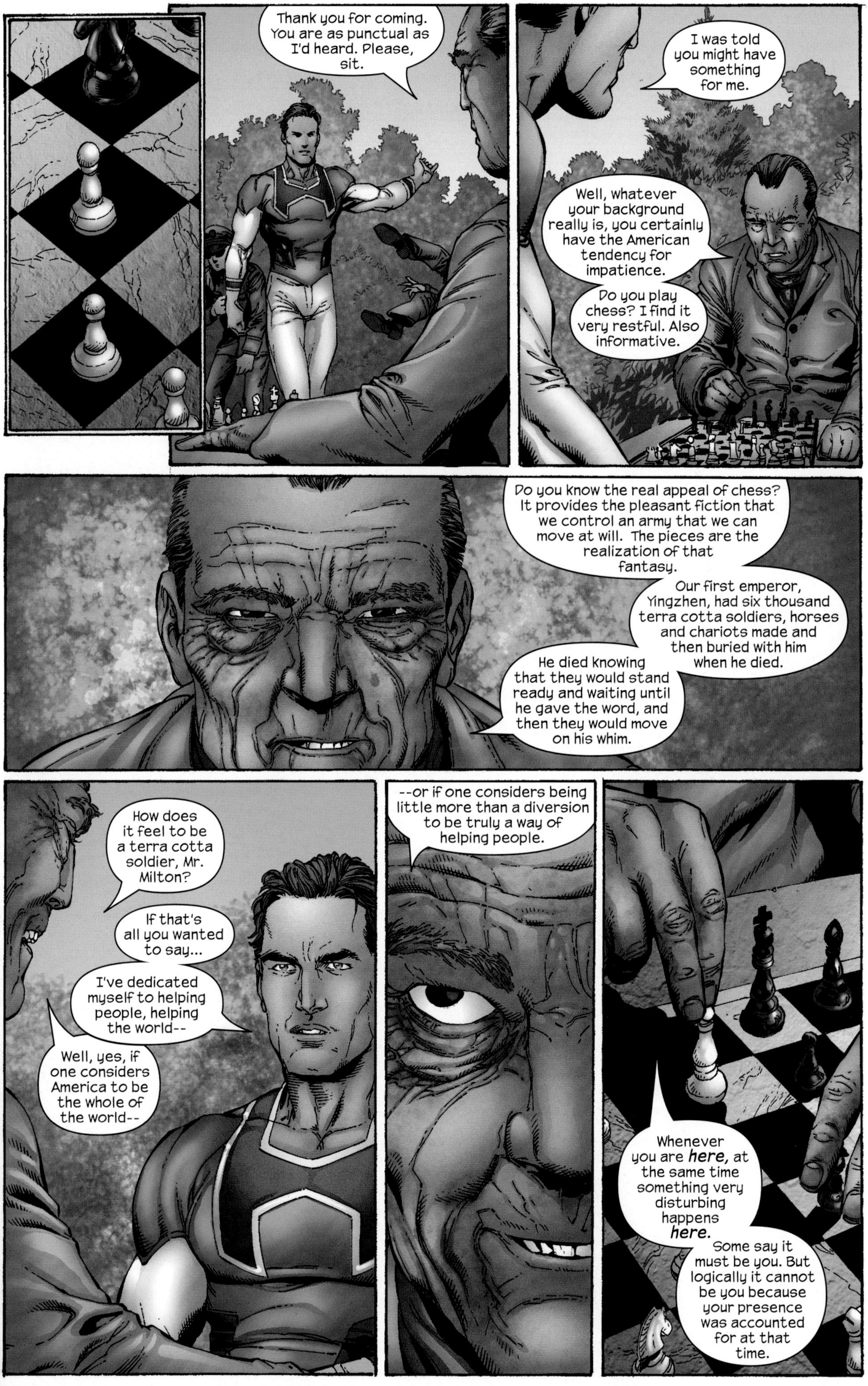
Thank you for coming. You are as punctual as I'd heard. Please, sit.
I was told you might have something for me.
Well, whatever your background really is, you certainly have the American tendency for impatience.
Do you play chess? I find it very restful. Also informative.
Do you know the real appeal of chess? It provides the pleasant fiction that we control an army that we can move at will. The pieces are the realization of that fantasy.
Our first emperor, Yingzhen, had six thousand terra cotta soldiers, horses and chariots made and then buried with him when he died.
He died knowing that they would stand ready and waiting until he gave the word, and then they would move on his whim.
How does it feel to be a terra cotta soldier, Mr. Milton?
If that's all you wanted to say...
I've dedicated myself to helping people, helping the world--
Well, yes, if one considers America to be the whole of the world--
--or if one considers being little more than a diversion to be truly a way of helping people.
Whenever you are *here,* at the same time something very disturbing happens *here.*
Some say it must be you. But logically it cannot be you because your presence was accounted for at that time.

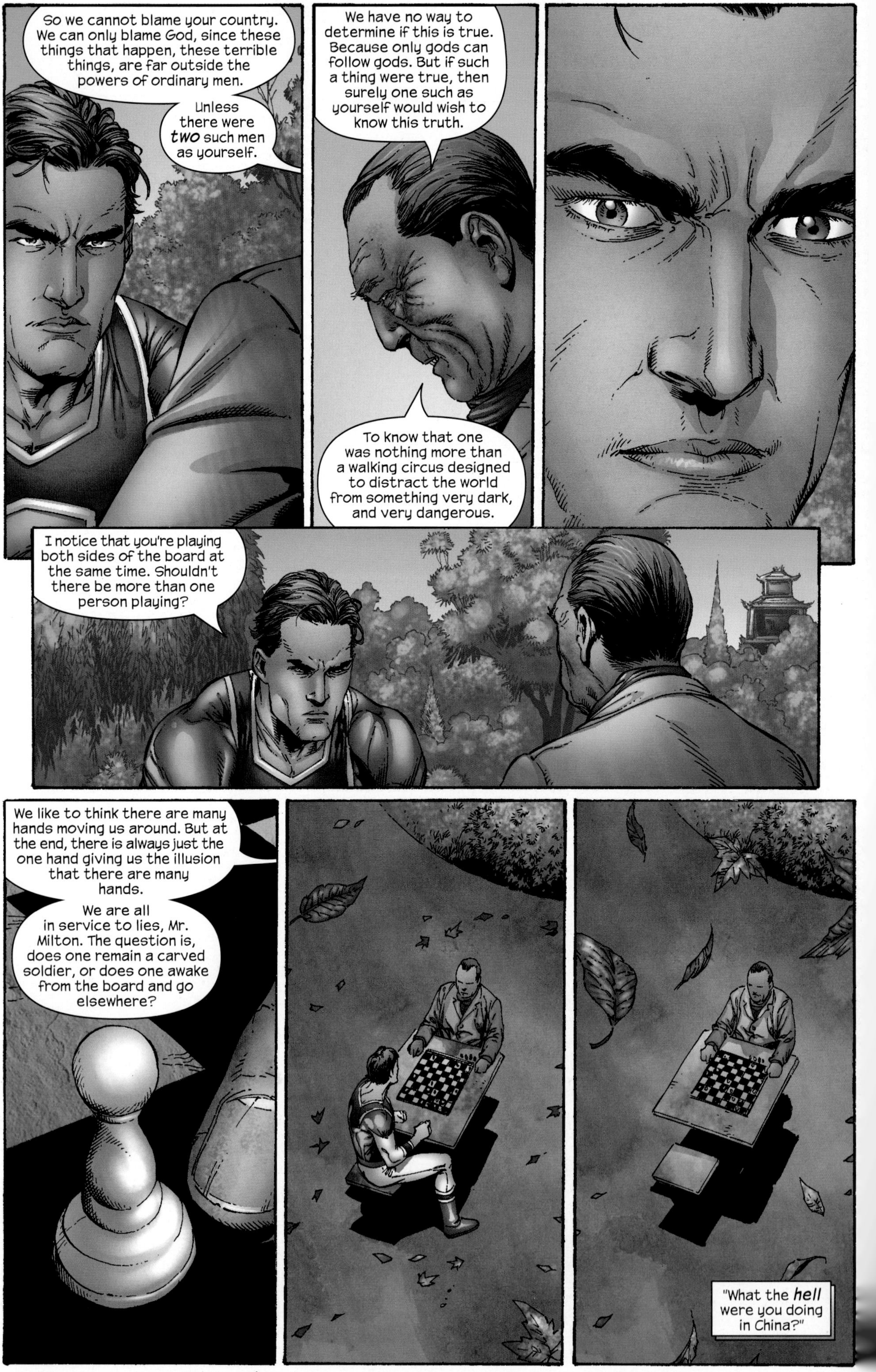

So we cannot blame your country. We can only blame God, since these things that happen, these terrible things, are far outside the powers of ordinary men.
Unless there were *two* such men as yourself.
We have no way to determine if this is true. Because only gods can follow gods. But if such a thing were true, then surely one such as yourself would wish to know this truth.
To know that one was nothing more than a walking circus designed to distract the world from something very dark, and very dangerous.
I notice that you're playing both sides of the board at the same time. Shouldn't there be more than one person playing?
We like to think there are many hands moving us around. But at the end, there is always just the one hand giving us the illusion that there are many hands.
We are all in service to lies, Mr. Milton. The question is, does one remain a carved soldier, or does one awake from the board and go elsewhere?
"What the *hell* were you doing in China?"

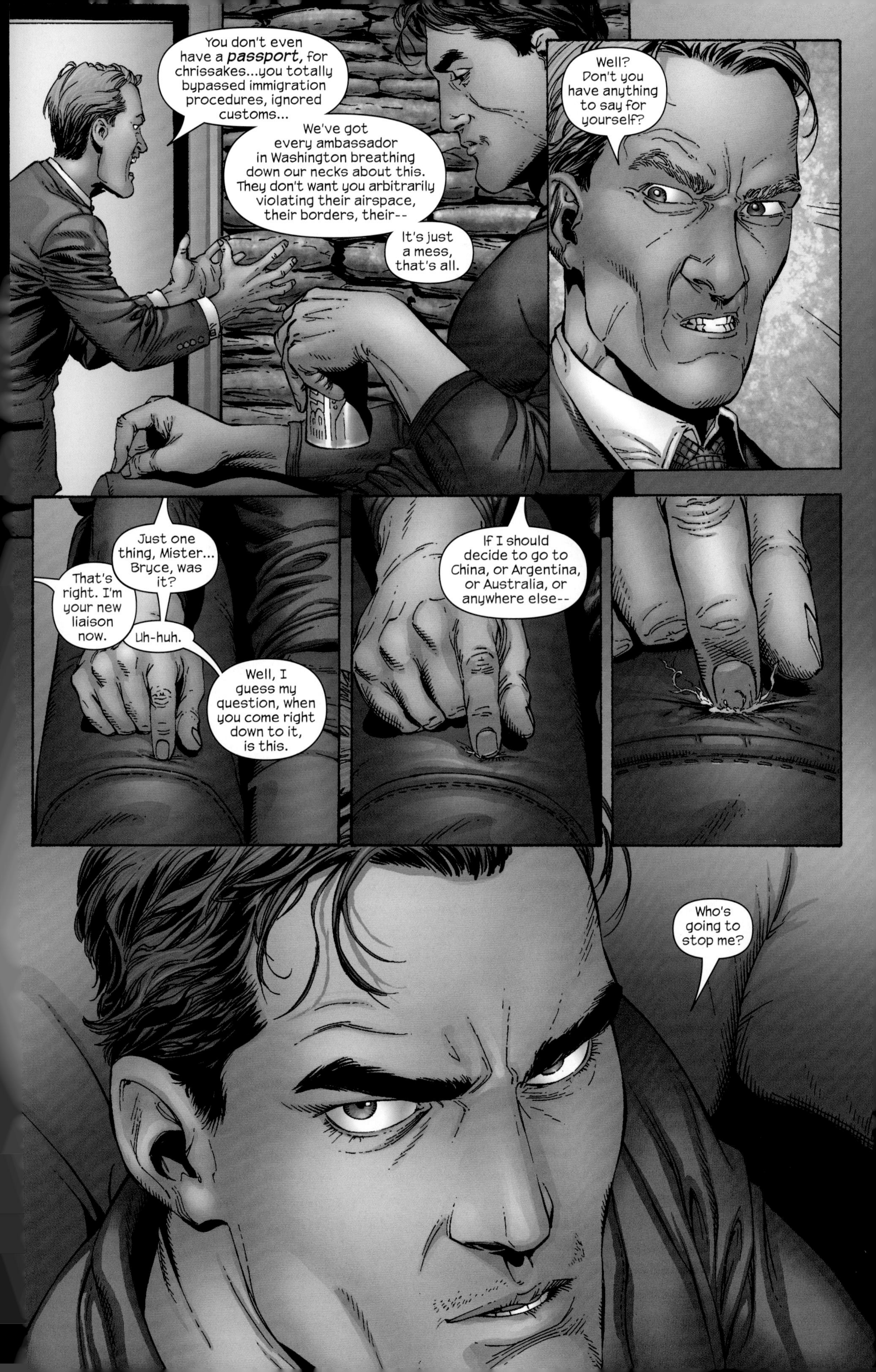

You don't even have a *passport*, for chrissakes...you totally bypassed immigration procedures, ignored customs...
We've got every ambassador in Washington breathing down our necks about this. They don't want you arbitrarily violating their airspace, their borders, their--
It's just a mess, that's all.
Well? Don't you have anything to say for yourself?
Just one thing, Mister... Bryce, was it?
That's right. I'm your new liaison now.
Uh-huh.
Well, I guess my question, when you come right down to it, is this.
If I should decide to go to China, or Argentina, or Australia, or anywhere else--
Who's going to stop me?

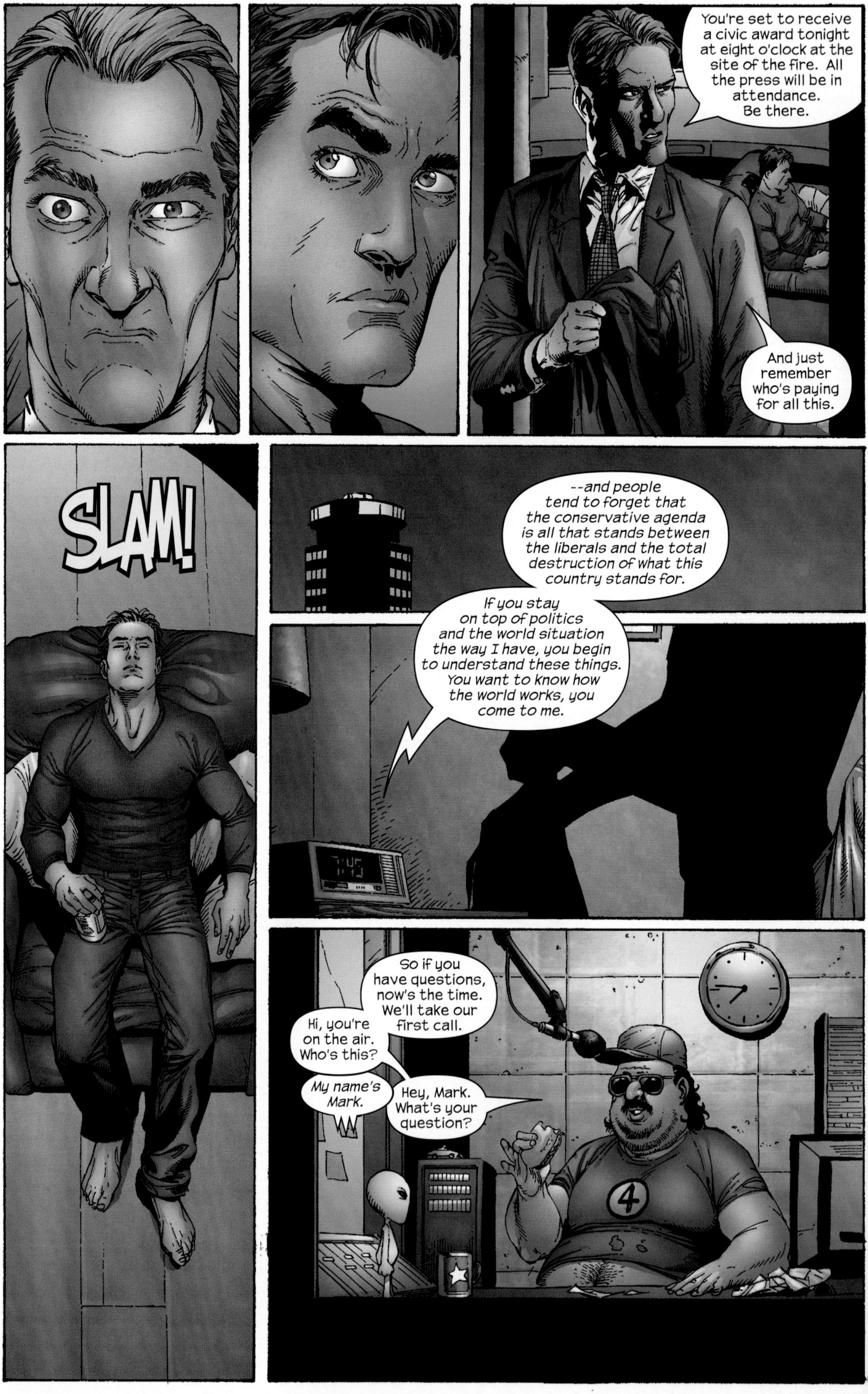
You're set to receive a civic award tonight at eight o'clock at the site of the fire. All the press will be in attendance. Be there.
And just remember who's paying for all this.
SLAM!
--and people tend to forget that the conservative agenda is all that stands between the liberals and the total destruction of what this country stands for.
If you stay on top of politics and the world situation the way I have, you begin to understand these things. You want to know how the world works, you come to me.
So if you have questions, now's the time. We'll take our first call.
Hi, you're on the air. Who's this?
My name's Mark.
Hey, Mark. What's your question?

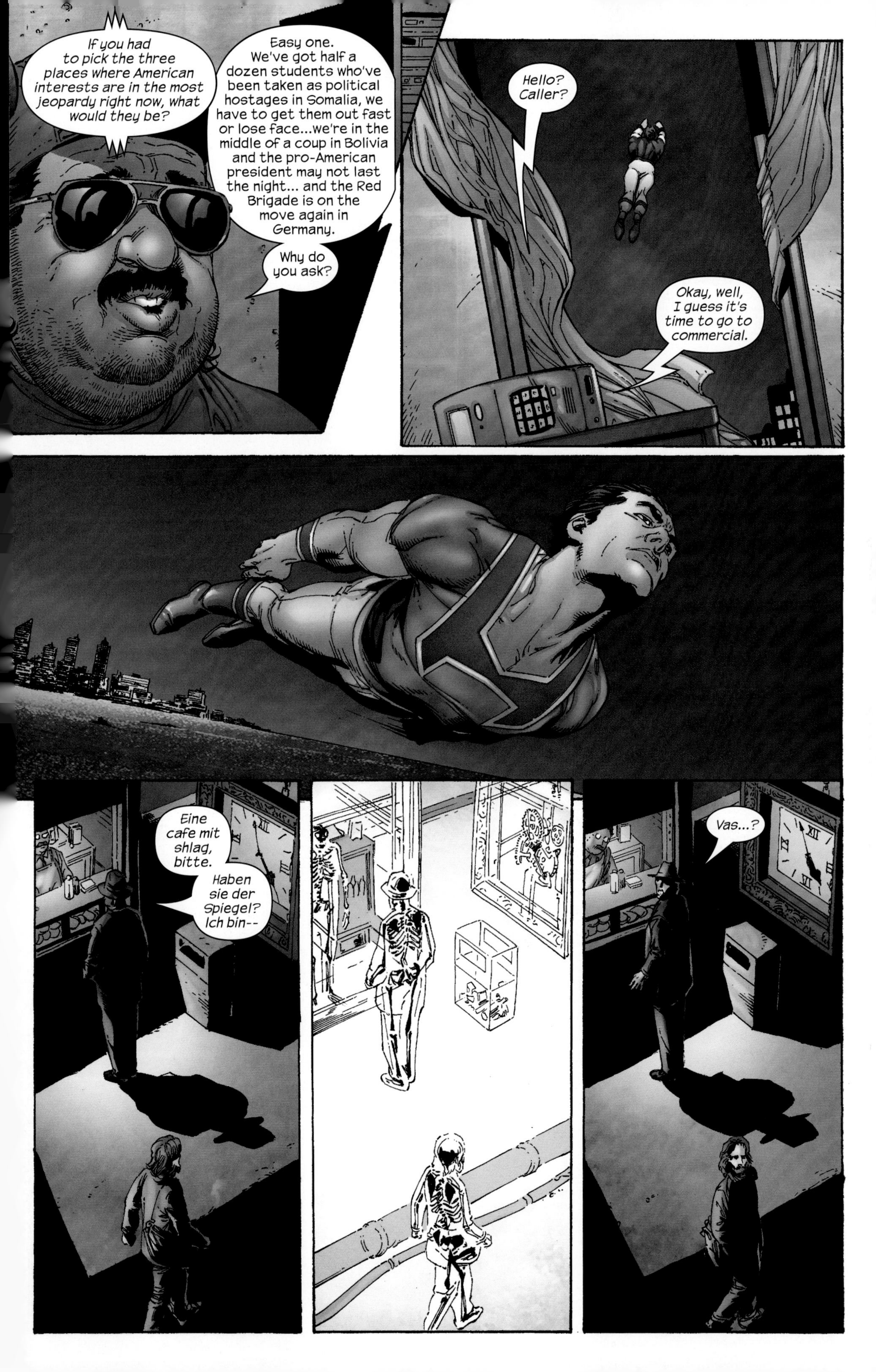
If you had to pick the three places where American interests are in the most jeopardy right now, what would they be?
Easy one. We've got half a dozen students who've been taken as political hostages in Somalia, we have to get them out fast or lose face...we're in the middle of a coup in Bolivia and the pro-American president may not last the night... and the Red Brigade is on the move again in Germany.
Why do you ask?
Hello? Caller?
Okay, well, I guess it's time to go to commercial.
Eine cafe mit shlag, bitte.
Haben sie der Spiegel? Ich bin--
Vas...?

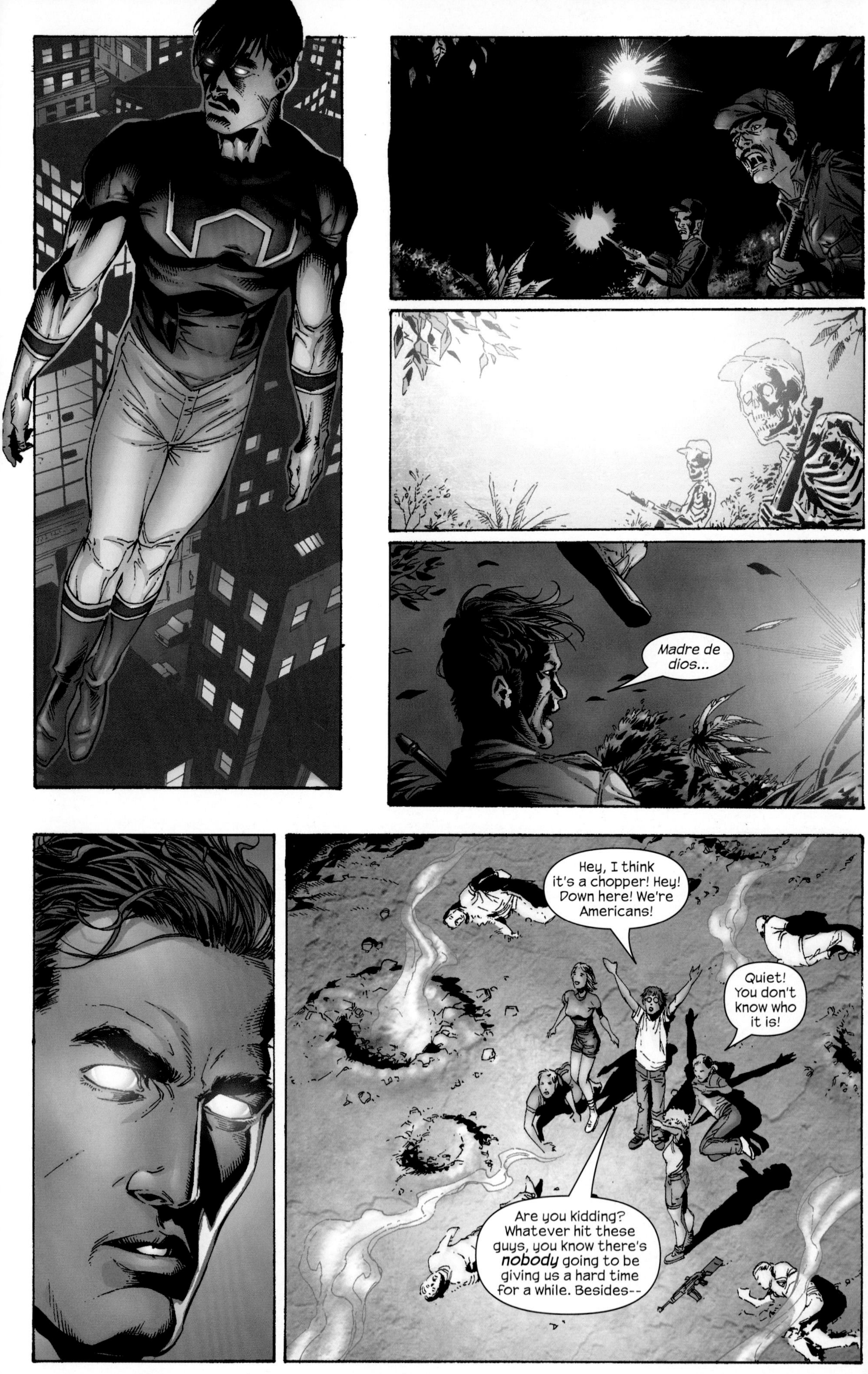
Madre de dios...
Hey, I think it's a chopper! Hey! Down here! We're Americans!
Quiet! You don't know who it is!
Are you kidding? Whatever hit these guys, you know there's nobody going to be giving us a hard time for a while. Besides--

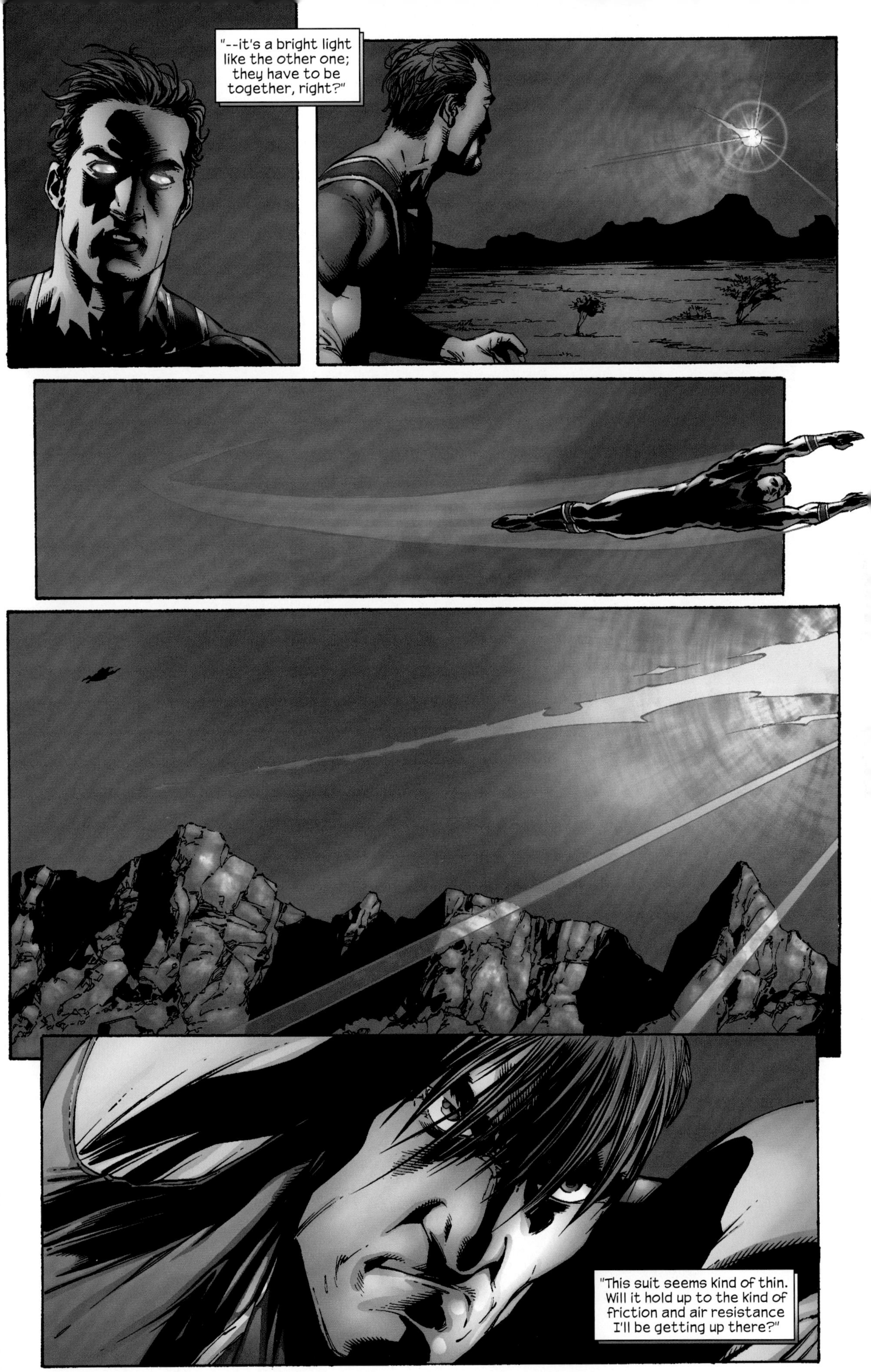
"--it's a bright light like the other one; they have to be together, right?"
"This suit seems kind of thin. Will it hold up to the kind of friction and air resistance I'll be getting up there?"

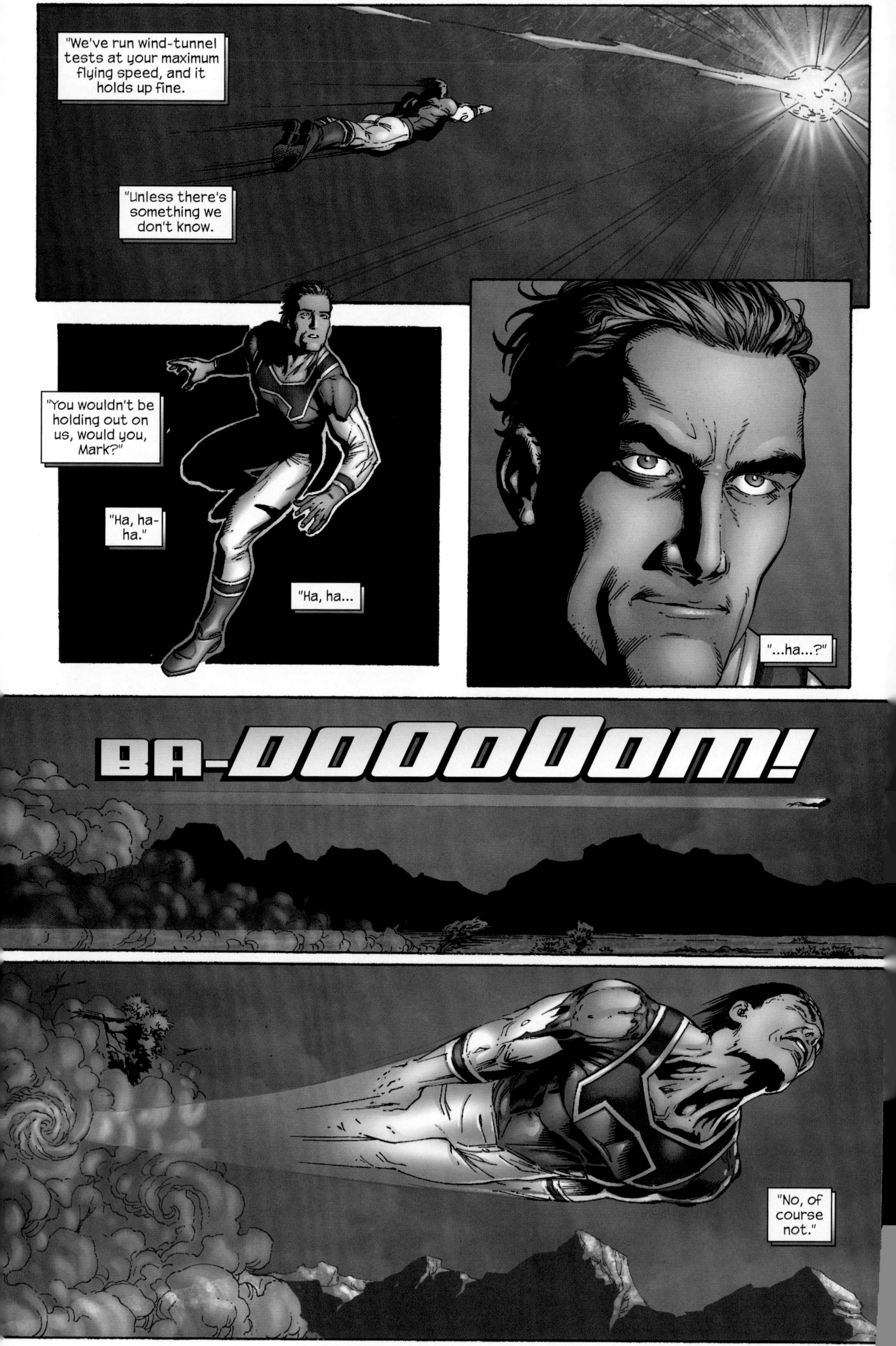
"We've run wind-tunnel tests at your maximum flying speed, and it holds up fine.
"Unless there's something we don't know.
"You wouldn't be holding out on us, would you, Mark?"
"Ha, ha-ha."
"Ha, ha...
"...ha...?"
BA-DOOOOOM!
"No, of course not."

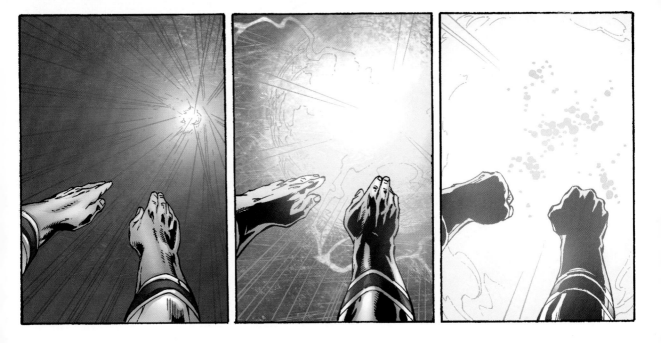

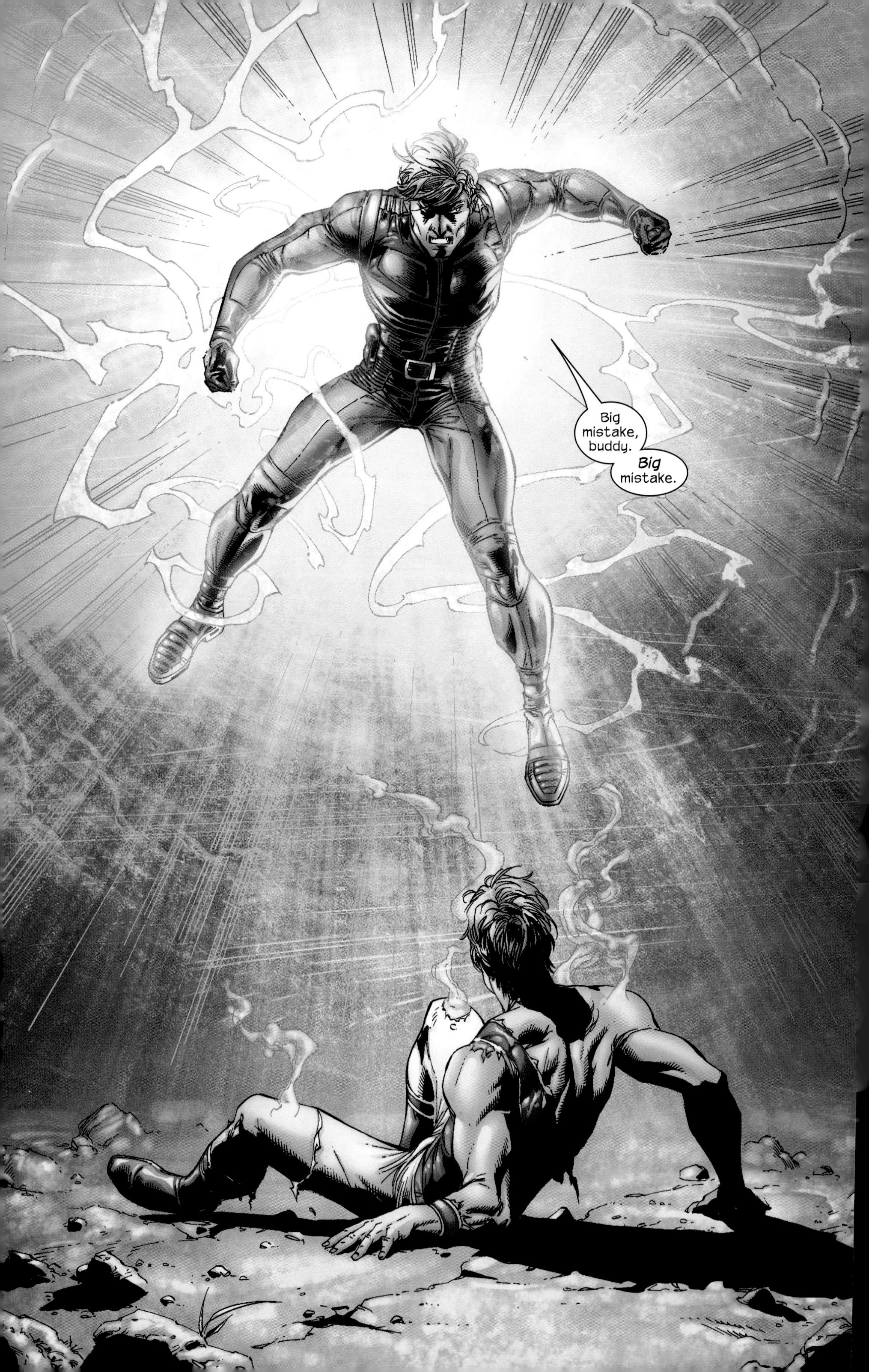
Big mistake, buddy. Big mistake.

"Ubi Dubium, Ibi Libertas"

#8

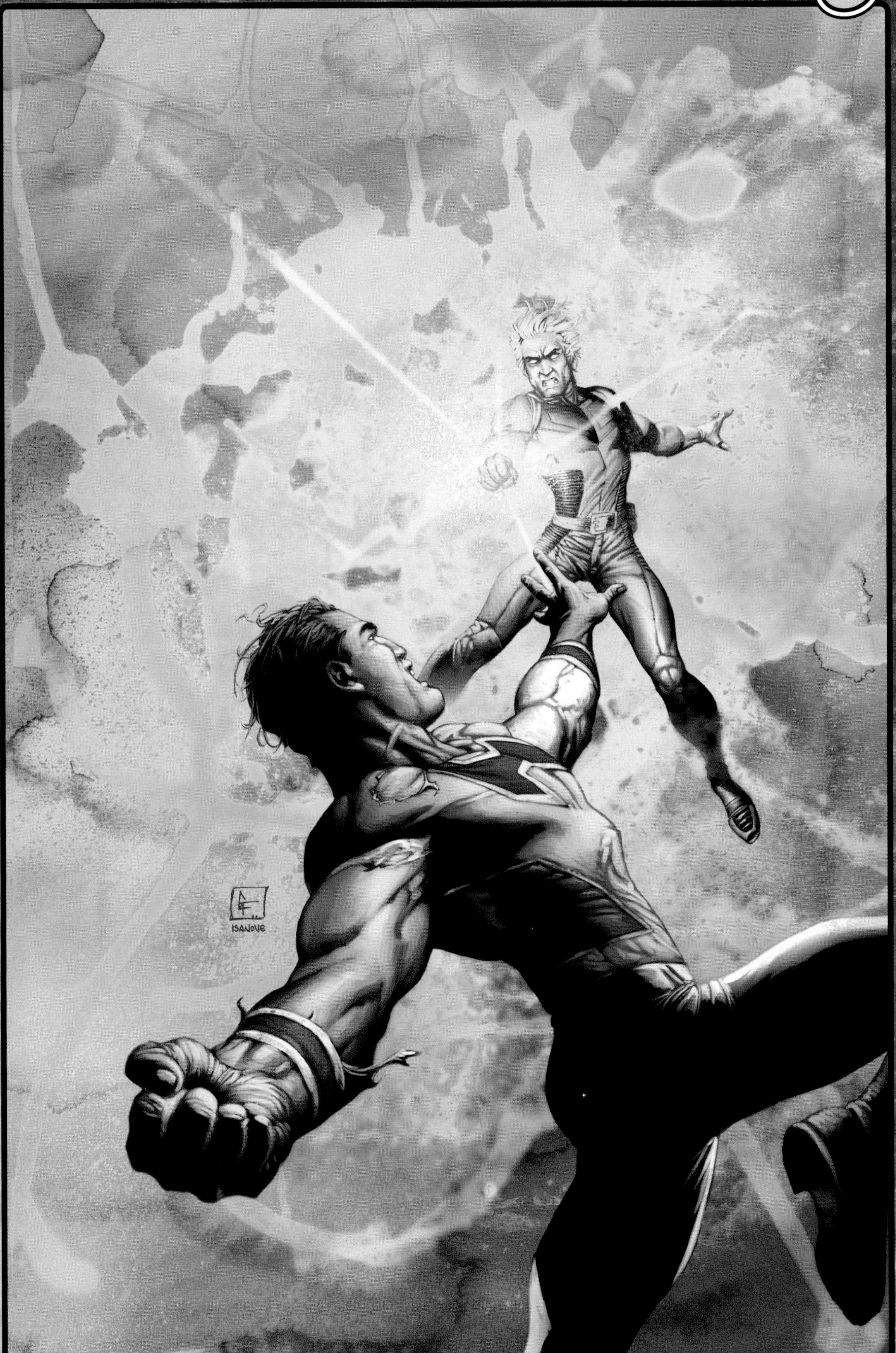
ISANOVE

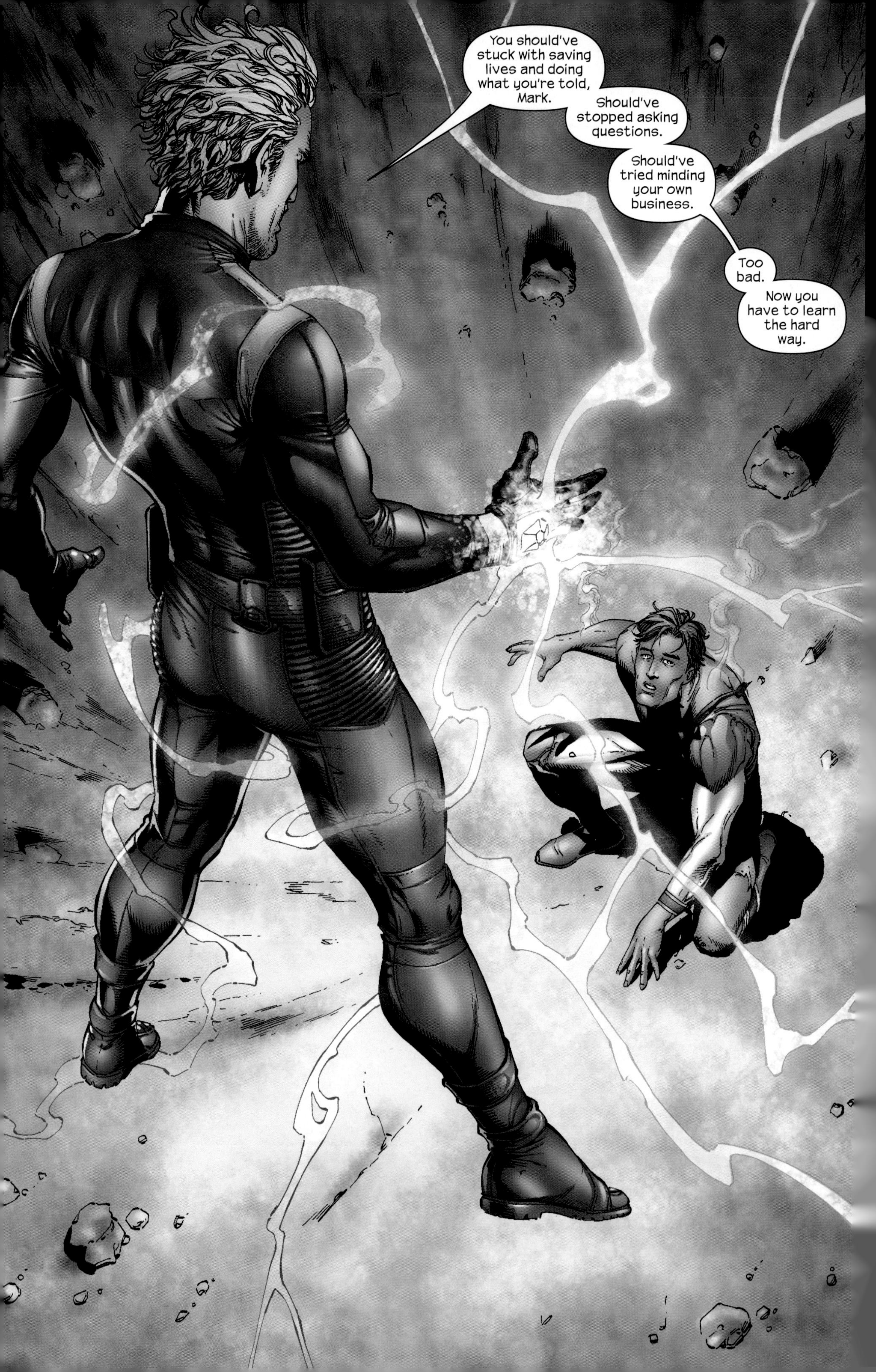
You should've stuck with saving lives and doing what you're told, Mark.
Should've stopped asking questions.
Should've tried minding your own business.
Too bad.
Now you have to learn the hard way.

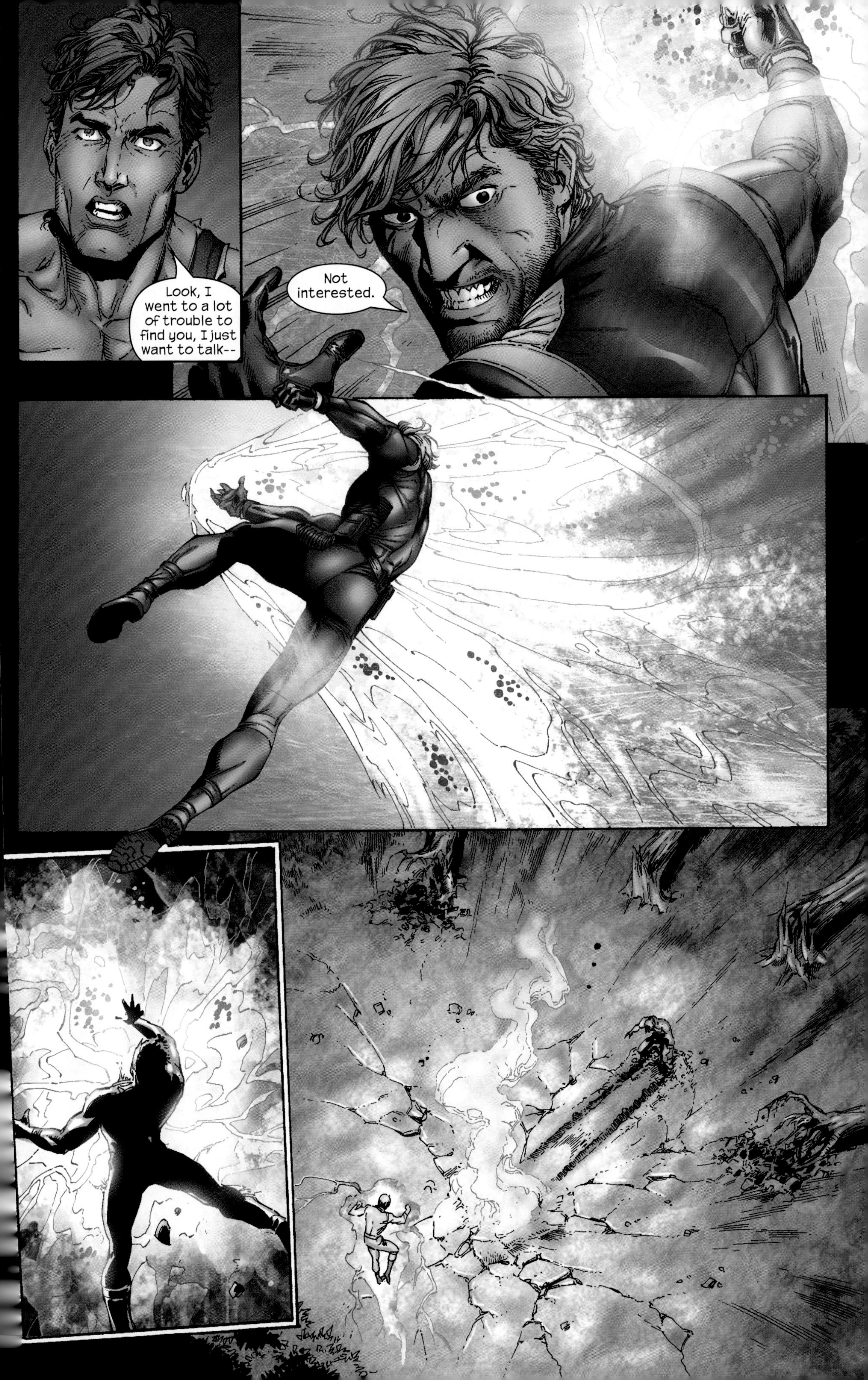
Look, I went to a lot of trouble to find you, I just want to talk--
Not interested.

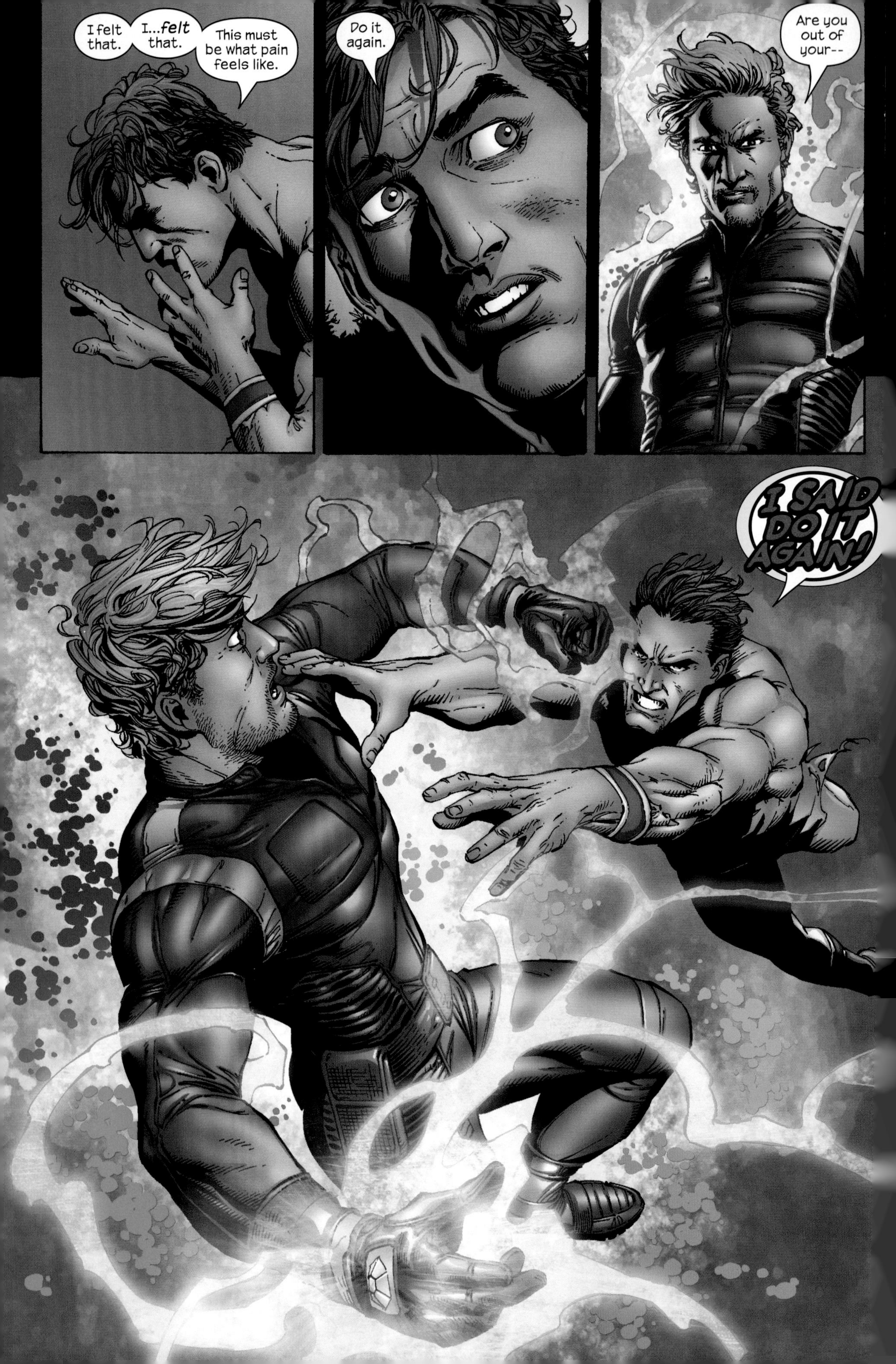
I felt that.
I...felt that.
This must be what pain feels like.
Do it again.
Are you out of your--
I SAID DO IT AGAIN!

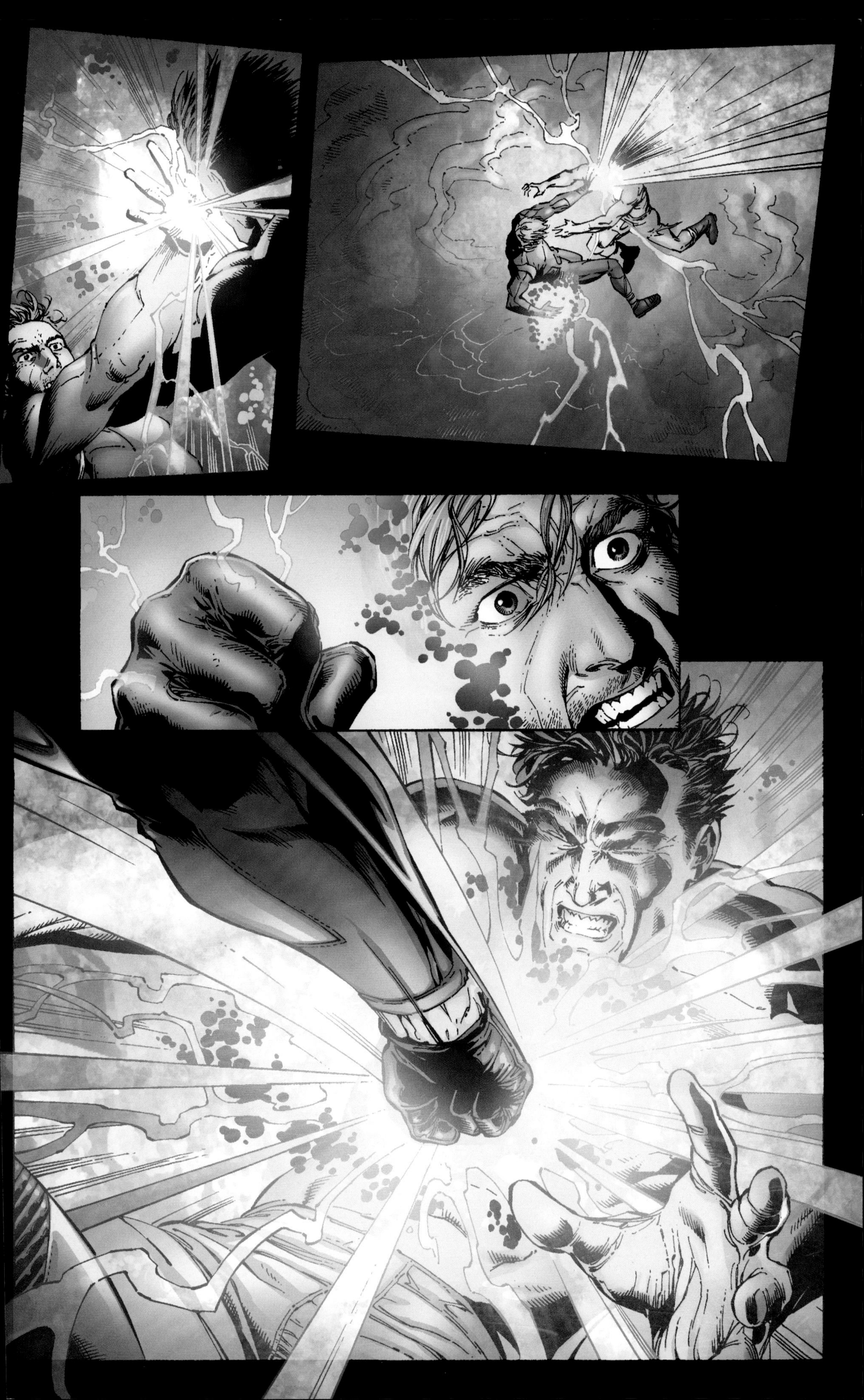

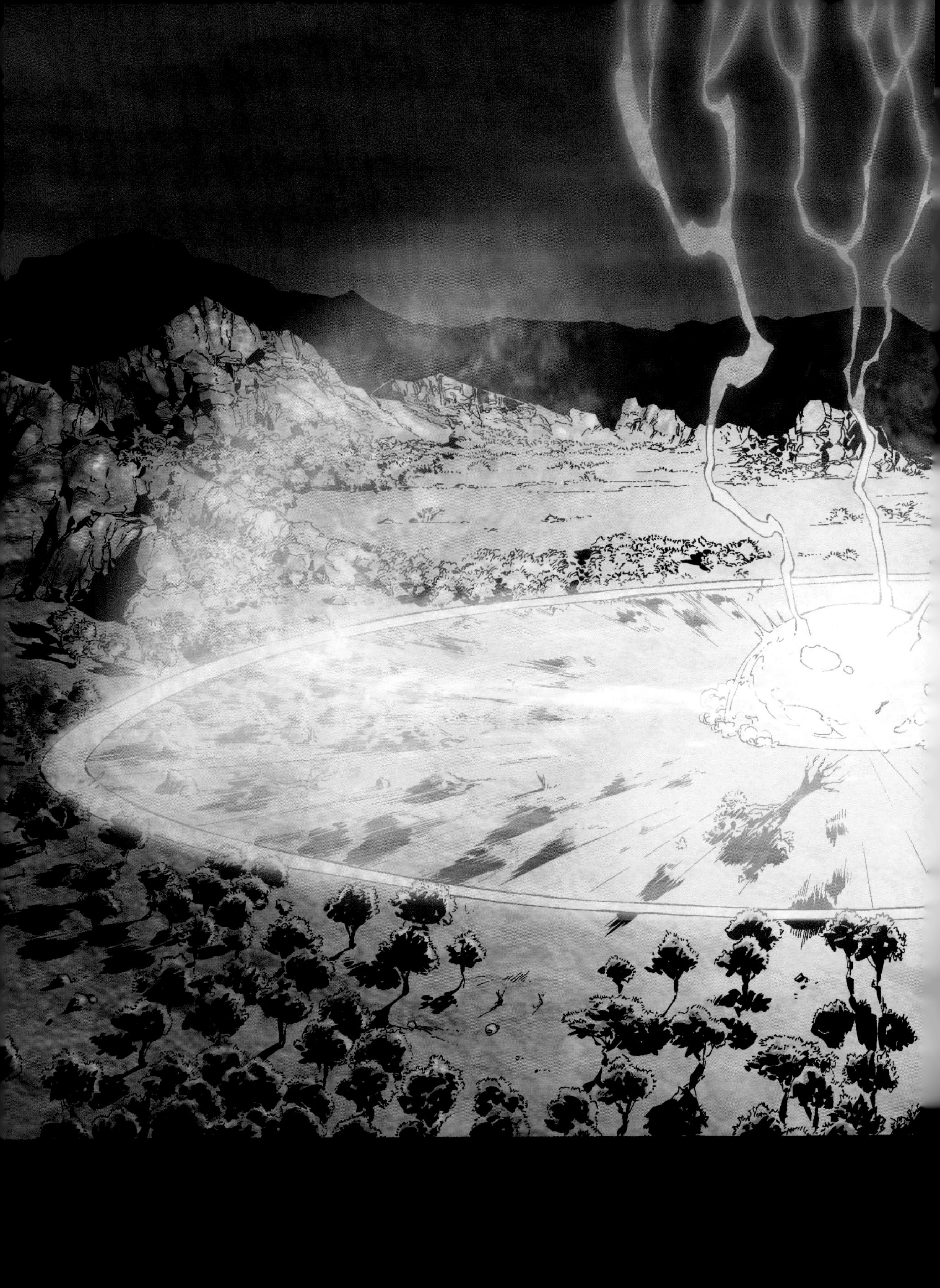

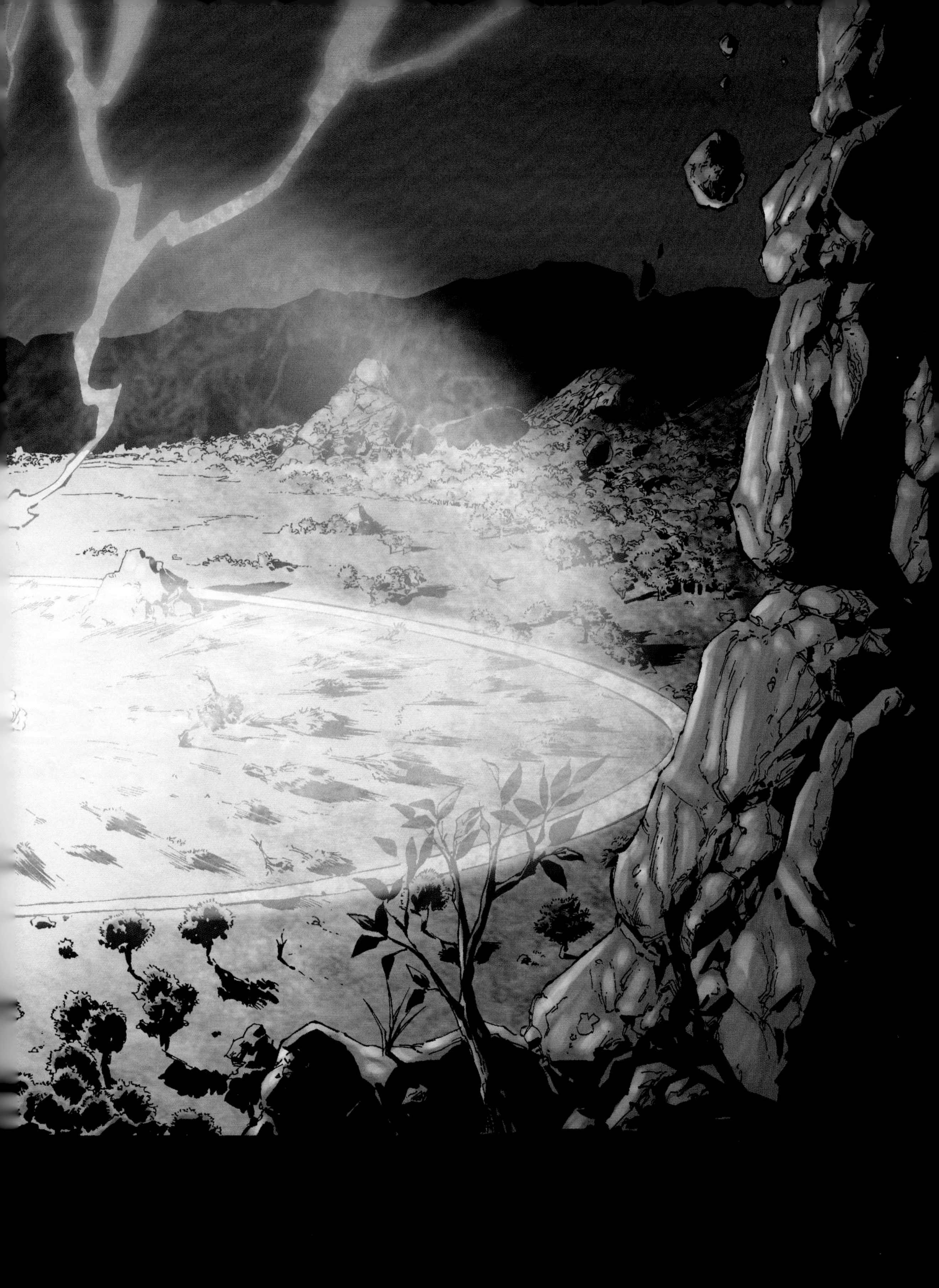

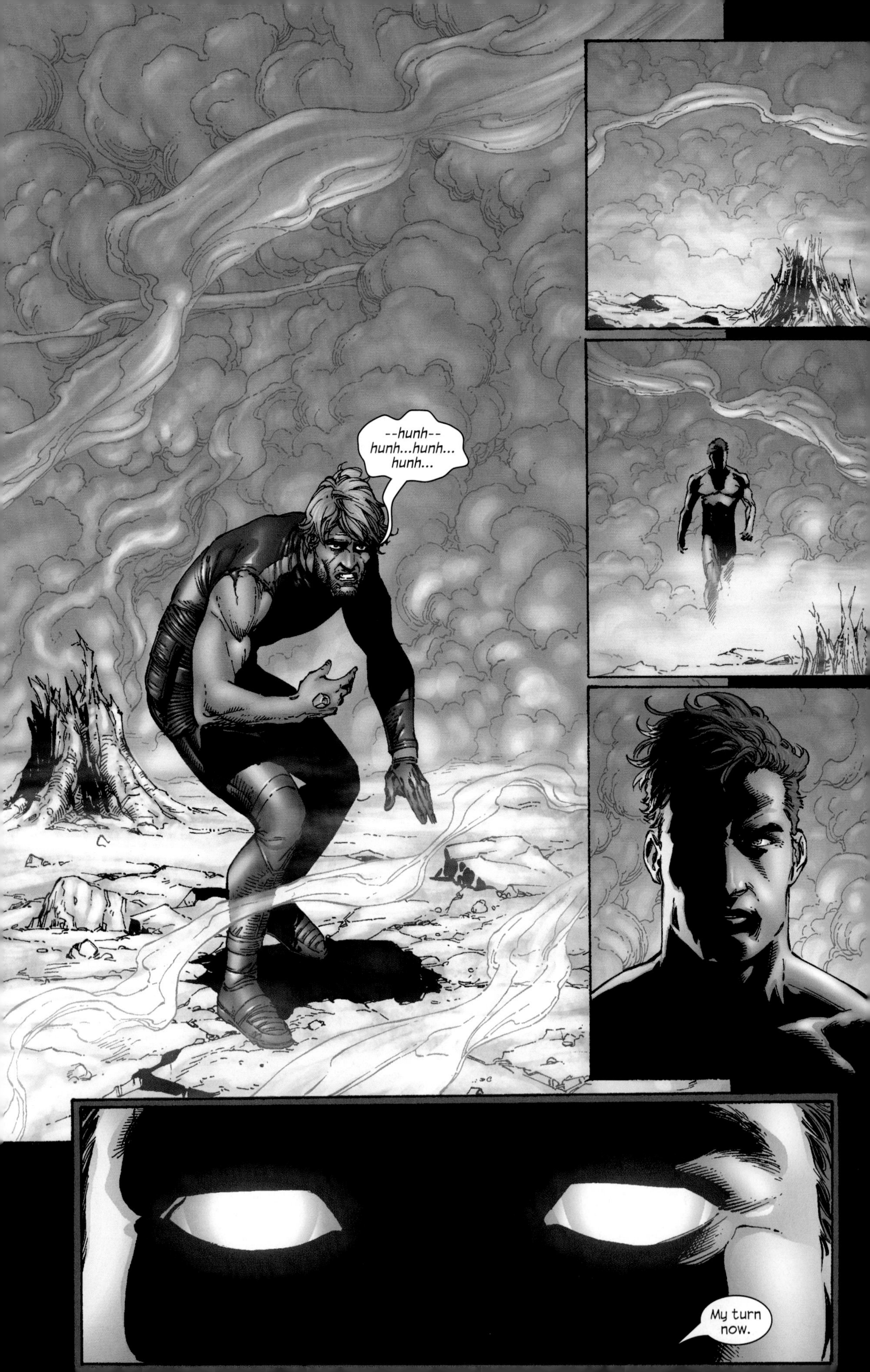
--hunh--
hunh...hunh...
hunh...
My turn now.

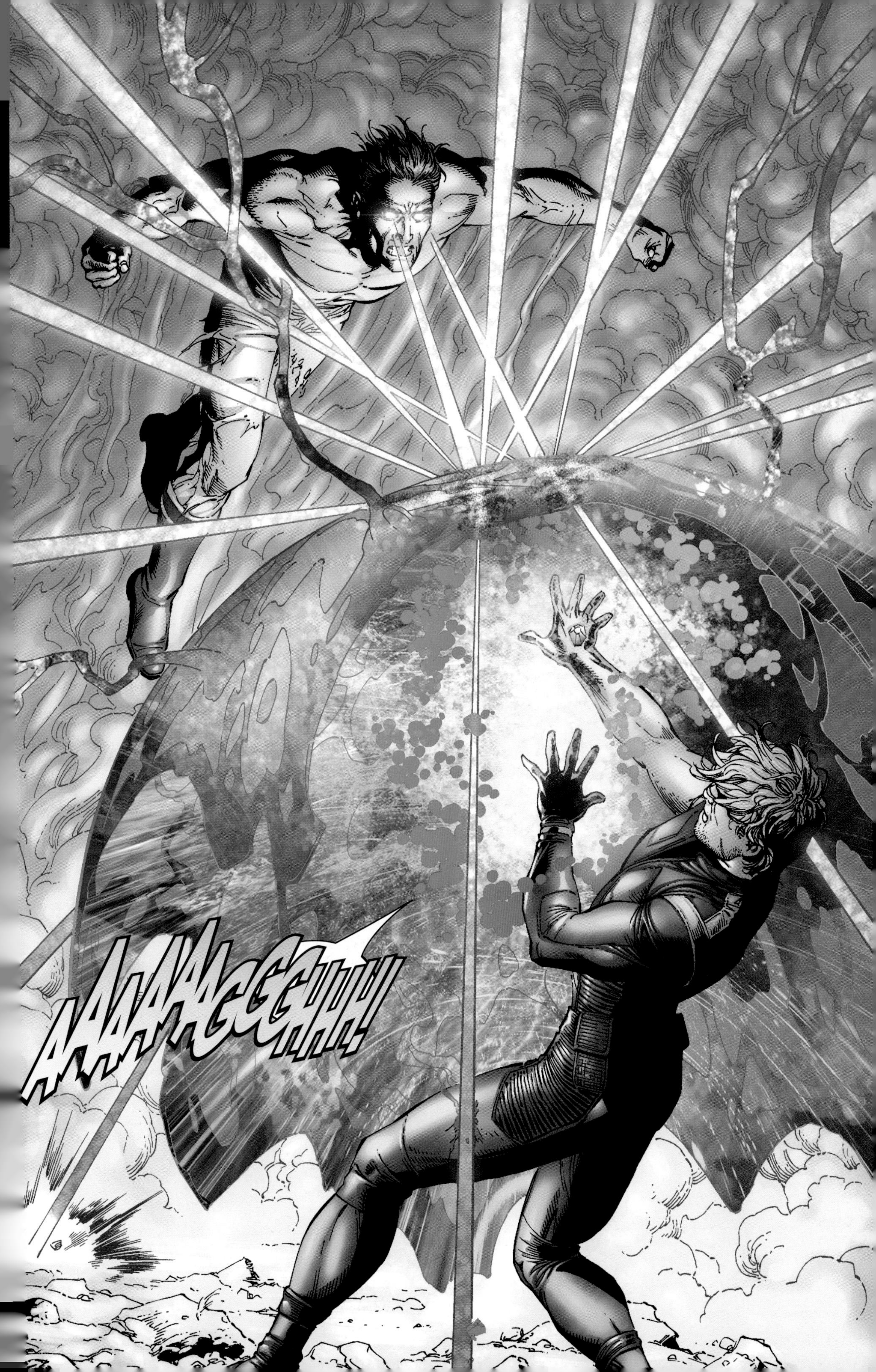
AAAAAGGGHHH!

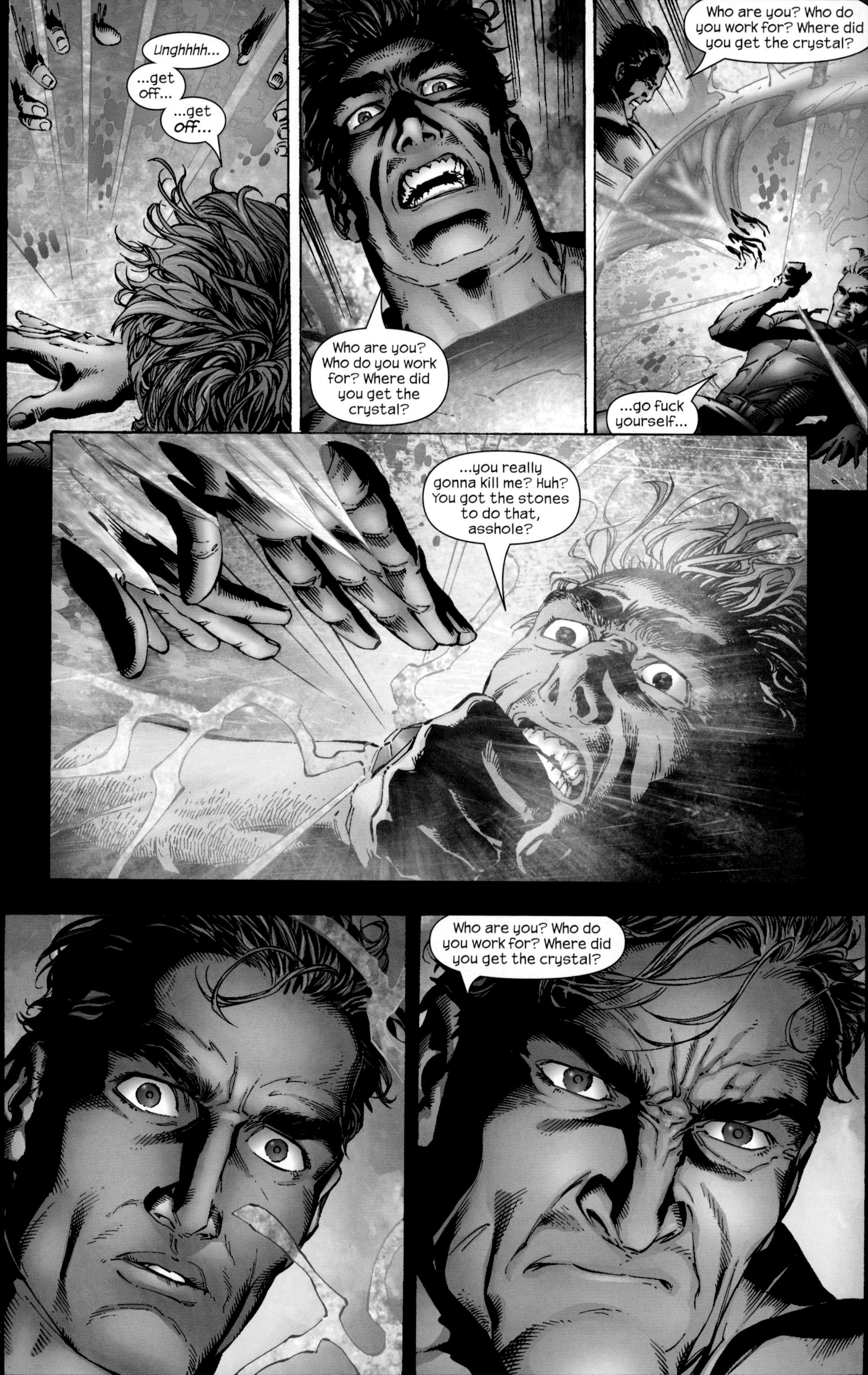
Unghhhh...
...get off...
...get off...
Who are you? Who do you work for? Where did you get the crystal?
Who are you? Who do you work for? Where did you get the crystal?
...go fuck yourself...
...you really gonna kill me? Huh? You got the stones to do that, asshole?
Who are you? Who do you work for? Where did you get the crystal?

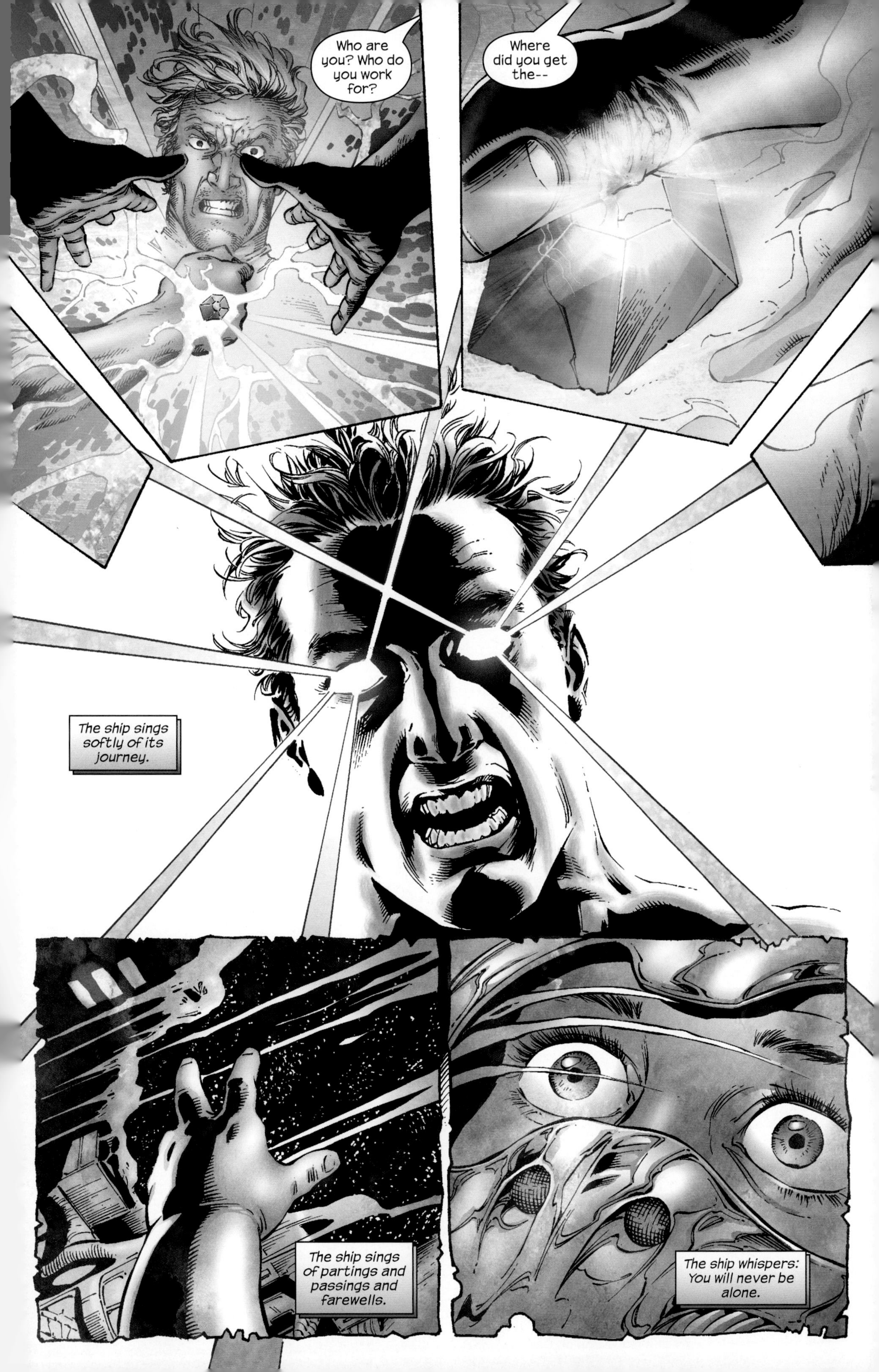
Who are you? Who do you work for?
Where did you get the--
The ship sings softly of its journey.
The ship sings of partings and passings and farewells.
The ship whispers: You will never be alone.

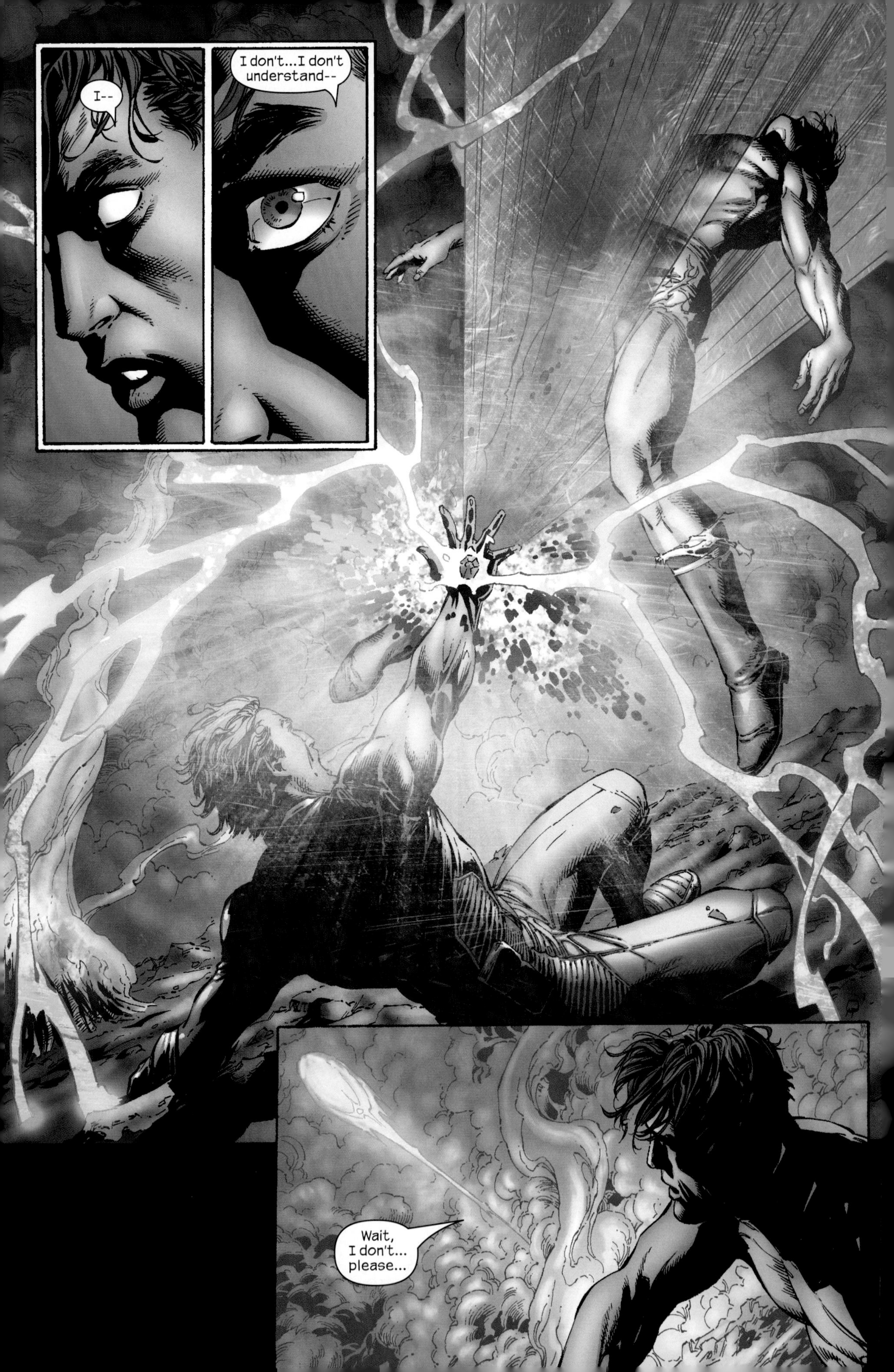
I--
I don't...I don't understand--
Wait, I don't... please...

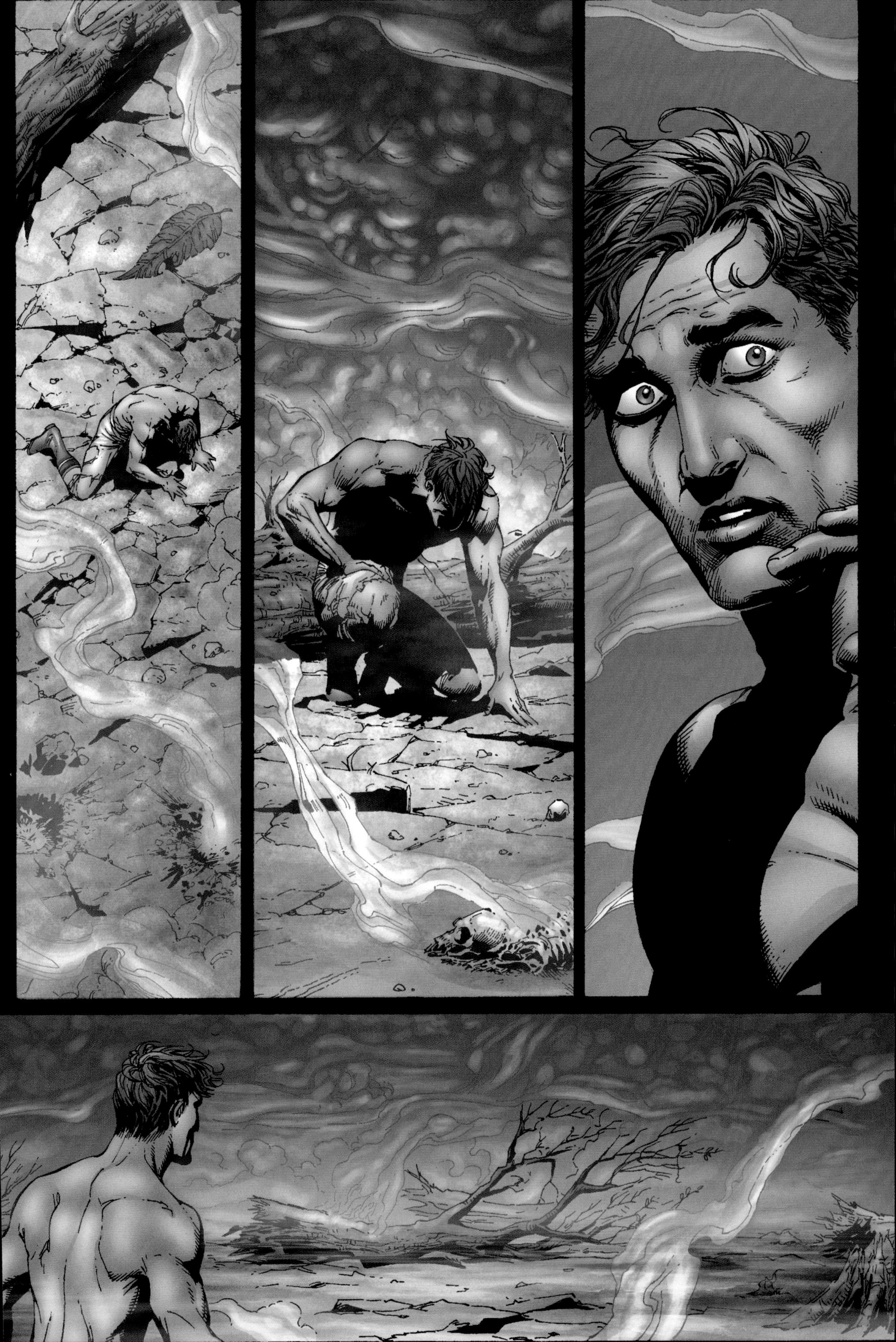

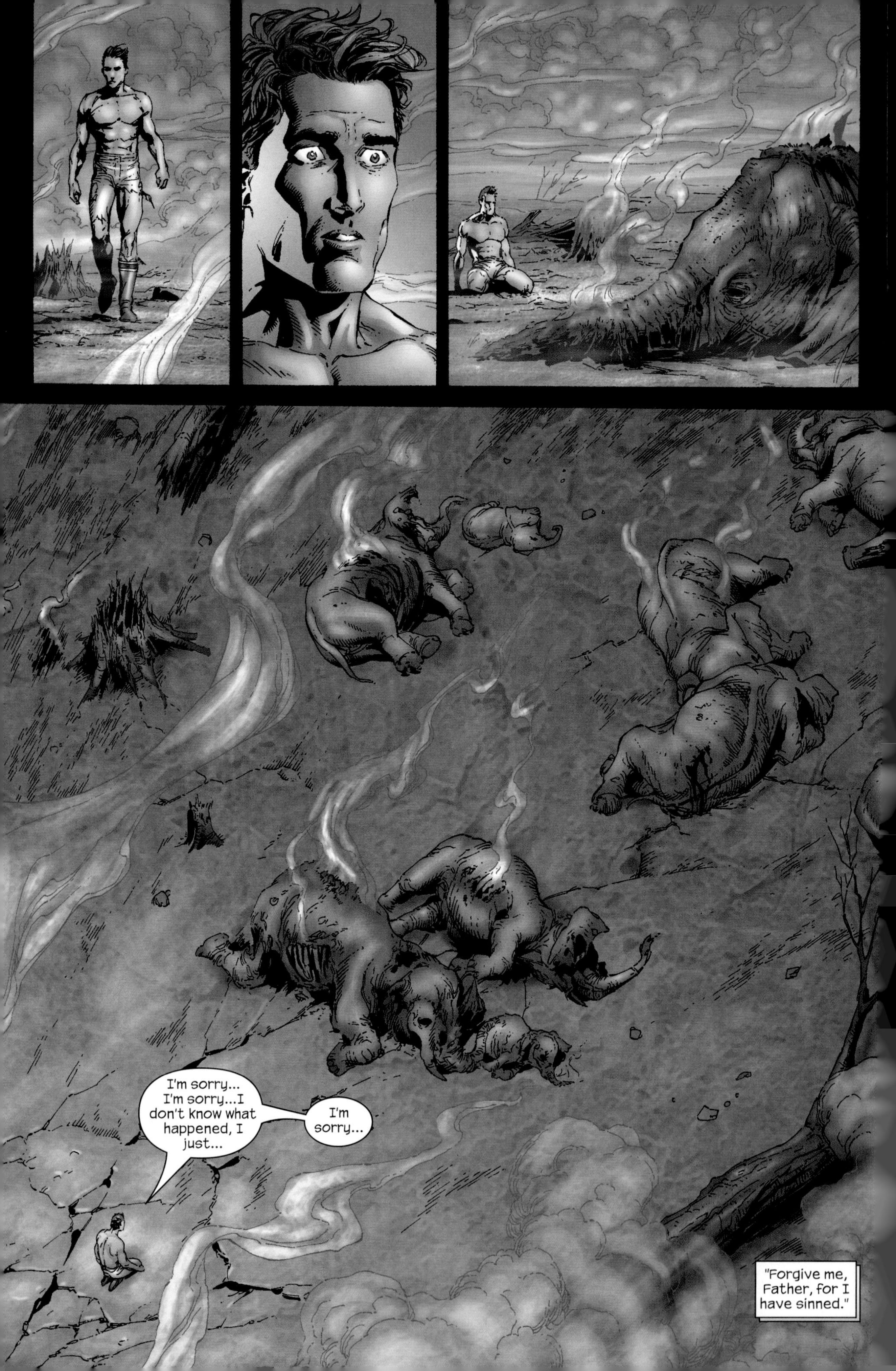
I'm sorry... I'm sorry...I don't know what happened, I just...
I'm sorry...
"Forgive me, Father, for I have sinned."

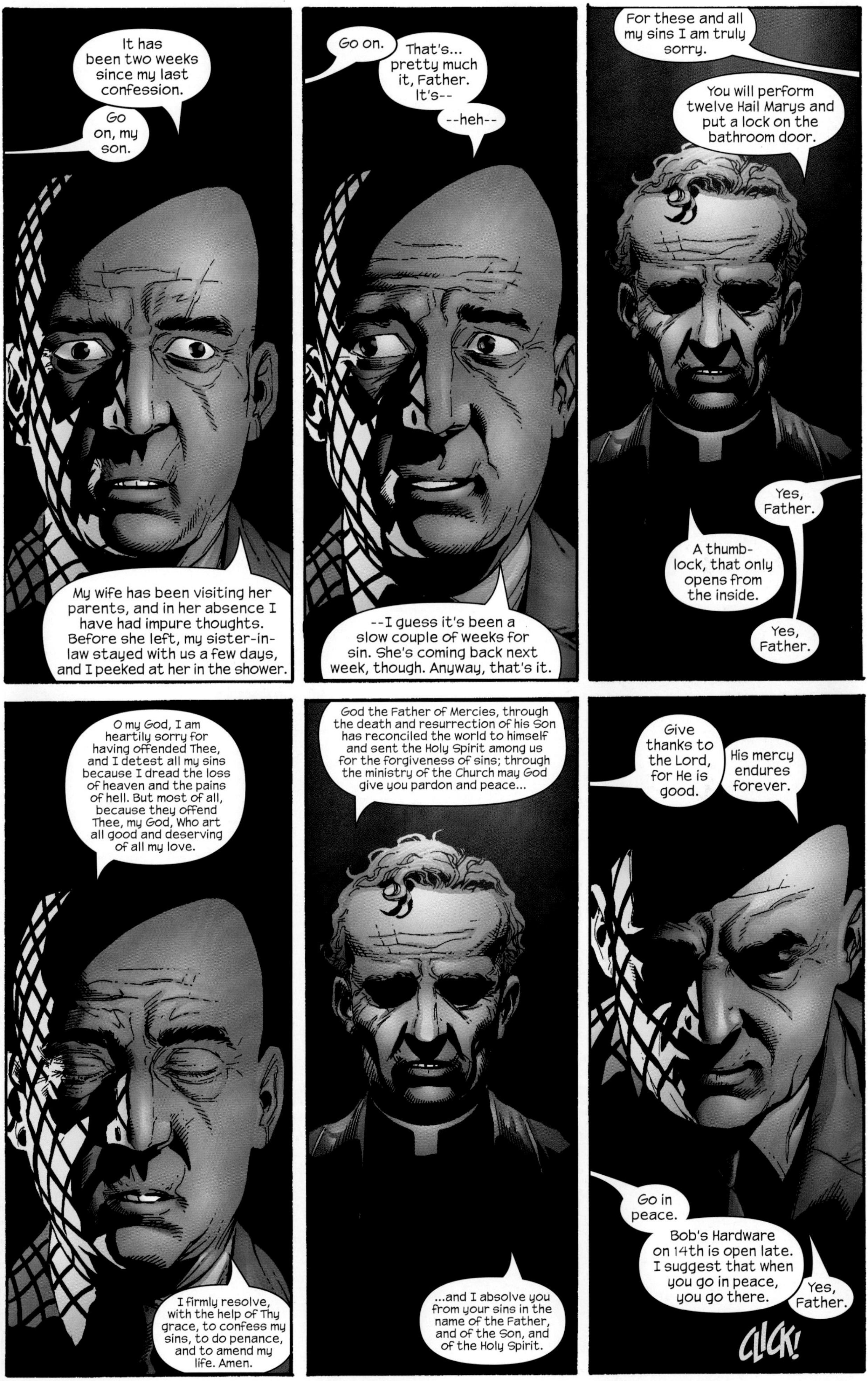
It has been two weeks since my last confession.
Go on, my son.
My wife has been visiting her parents, and in her absence I have had impure thoughts. Before she left, my sister-in-law stayed with us a few days, and I peeked at her in the shower.
Go on.
That's... pretty much it, Father. It's--
--heh--
--I guess it's been a slow couple of weeks for sin. She's coming back next week, though. Anyway, that's it.
For these and all my sins I am truly sorry.
You will perform twelve Hail Marys and put a lock on the bathroom door.
Yes, Father.
A thumb-lock, that only opens from the inside.
Yes, Father.
O my God, I am heartily sorry for having offended Thee, and I detest all my sins because I dread the loss of heaven and the pains of hell. But most of all, because they offend Thee, my God, Who art all good and deserving of all my love.
I firmly resolve, with the help of Thy grace, to confess my sins, to do penance, and to amend my life. Amen.
God the Father of Mercies, through the death and resurrection of his Son has reconciled the world to himself and sent the Holy Spirit among us for the forgiveness of sins; through the ministry of the Church may God give you pardon and peace...
...and I absolve you from your sins in the name of the Father, and of the Son, and of the Holy Spirit.
Give thanks to the Lord, for He is good.
His mercy endures forever.
Go in peace.
Bob's Hardware on 14th is open late. I suggest that when you go in peace, you go there.
Yes, Father.
CLICK!

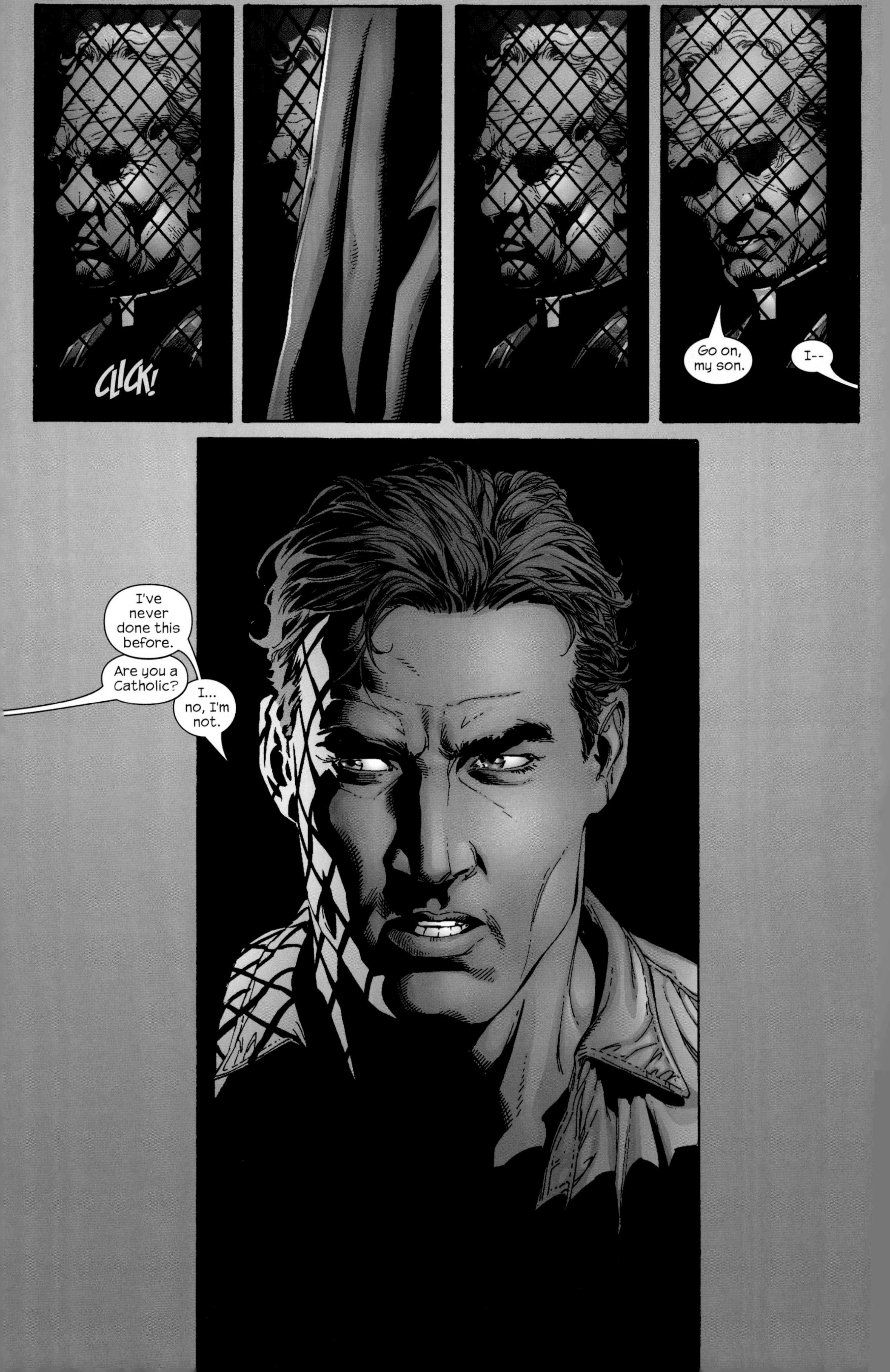
CLICK!
Go on, my son.
I--
I've never done this before.
Are you a Catholic?
I... no, I'm not.

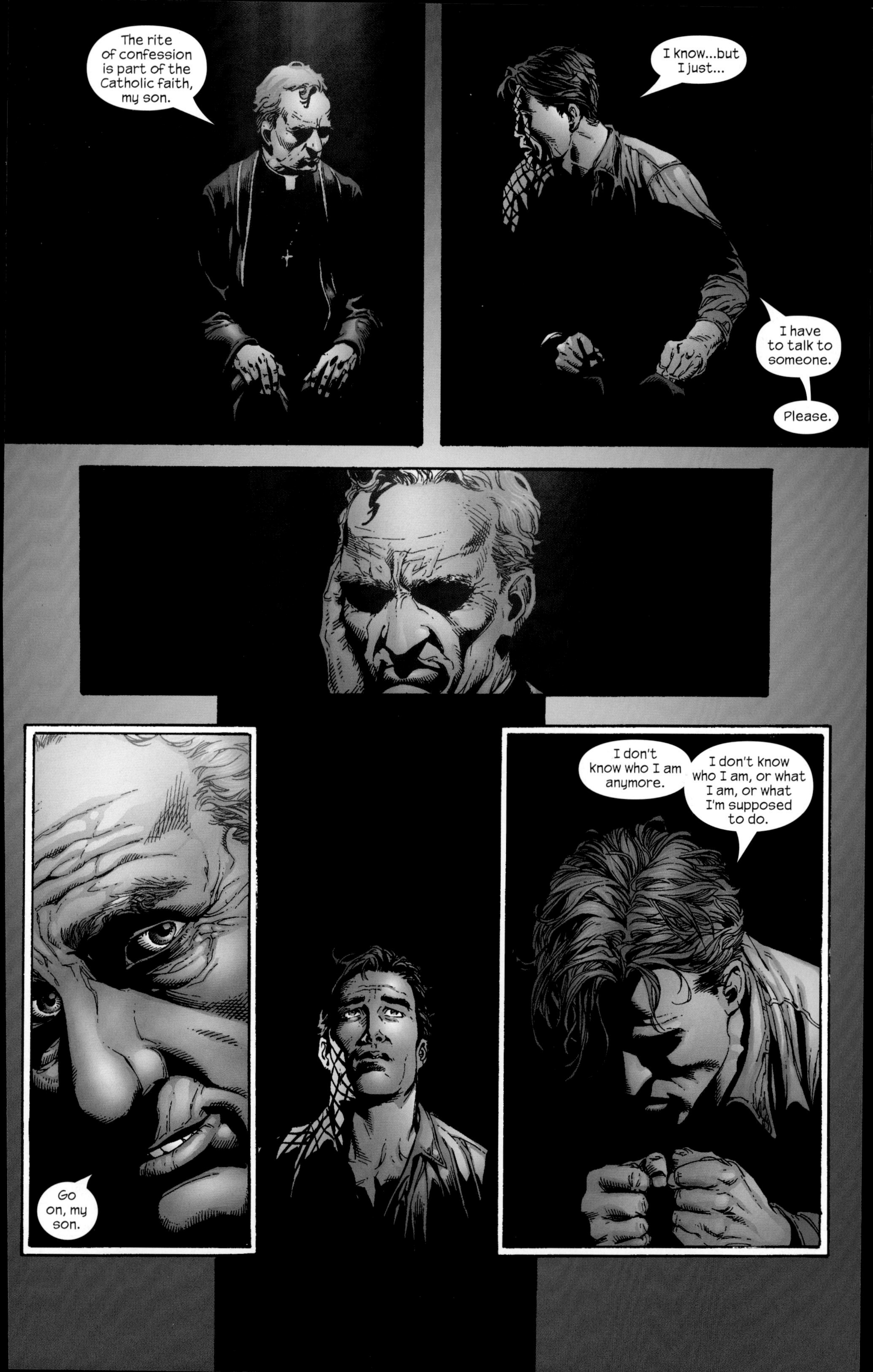
The rite of confession is part of the Catholic faith, my son.
I know...but I just...
I have to talk to someone.
Please.
Go on, my son.
I don't know who I am anymore.
I don't know who I am, or what I am, or what I'm supposed to do.

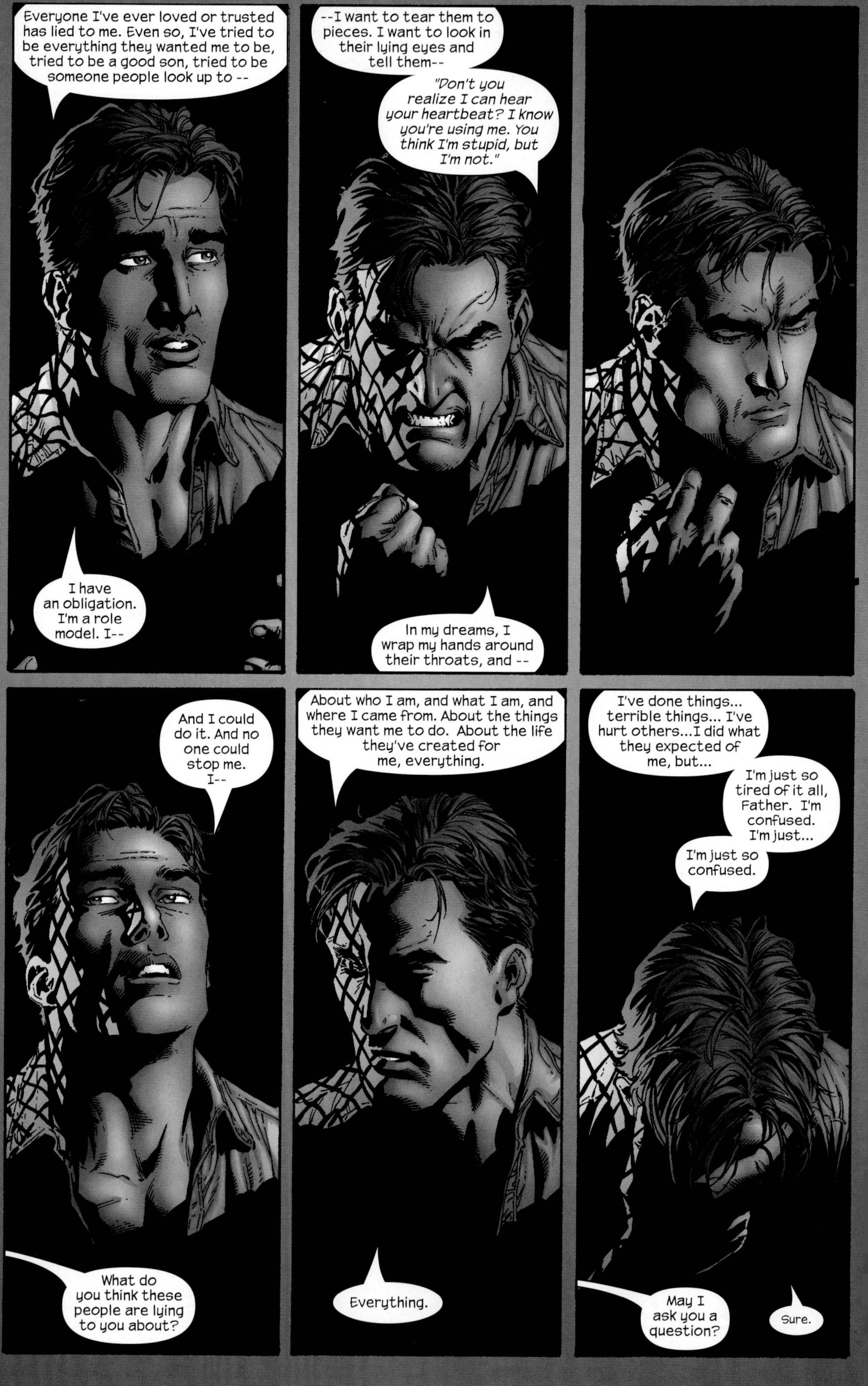
Everyone I've ever loved or trusted has lied to me. Even so, I've tried to be everything they wanted me to be, tried to be a good son, tried to be someone people look up to --
I have an obligation. I'm a role model. I--
--I want to tear them to pieces. I want to look in their lying eyes and tell them--
"Don't you realize I can hear your heartbeat? I know you're using me. You think I'm stupid, but I'm not."
In my dreams, I wrap my hands around their throats, and --
And I could do it. And no one could stop me. I--
What do you think these people are lying to you about?
About who I am, and what I am, and where I came from. About the things they want me to do. About the life they've created for me, everything.
Everything.
I've done things... terrible things... I've hurt others...I did what they expected of me, but...
I'm just so tired of it all, Father. I'm confused. I'm just...
I'm just so confused.
May I ask you a question?
Sure.

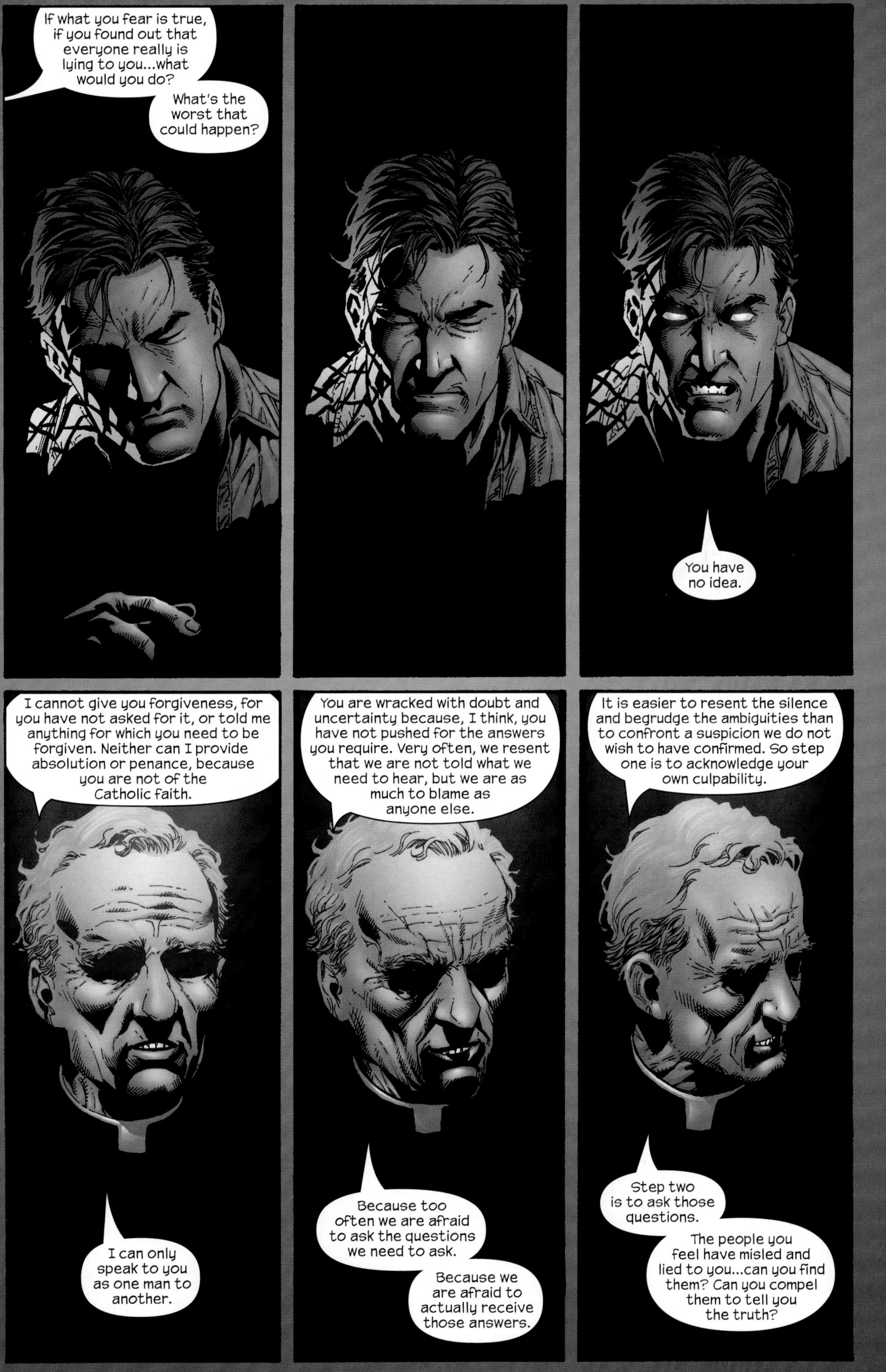

If what you fear is true, if you found out that everyone really is lying to you...what would you do?
What's the worst that could happen?
You have no idea.
I cannot give you forgiveness, for you have not asked for it, or told me anything for which you need to be forgiven. Neither can I provide absolution or penance, because you are not of the Catholic faith.
I can only speak to you as one man to another.
You are wracked with doubt and uncertainty because, I think, you have not pushed for the answers you require. Very often, we resent that we are not told what we need to hear, but we are as much to blame as anyone else.
Because too often we are afraid to ask the questions we need to ask.
Because we are afraid to actually receive those answers.
It is easier to resent the silence and begrudge the ambiguities than to confront a suspicion we do not wish to have confirmed. So step one is to acknowledge your own culpability.
Step two is to ask those questions.
The people you feel have misled and lied to you...can you find them? Can you compel them to tell you the truth?

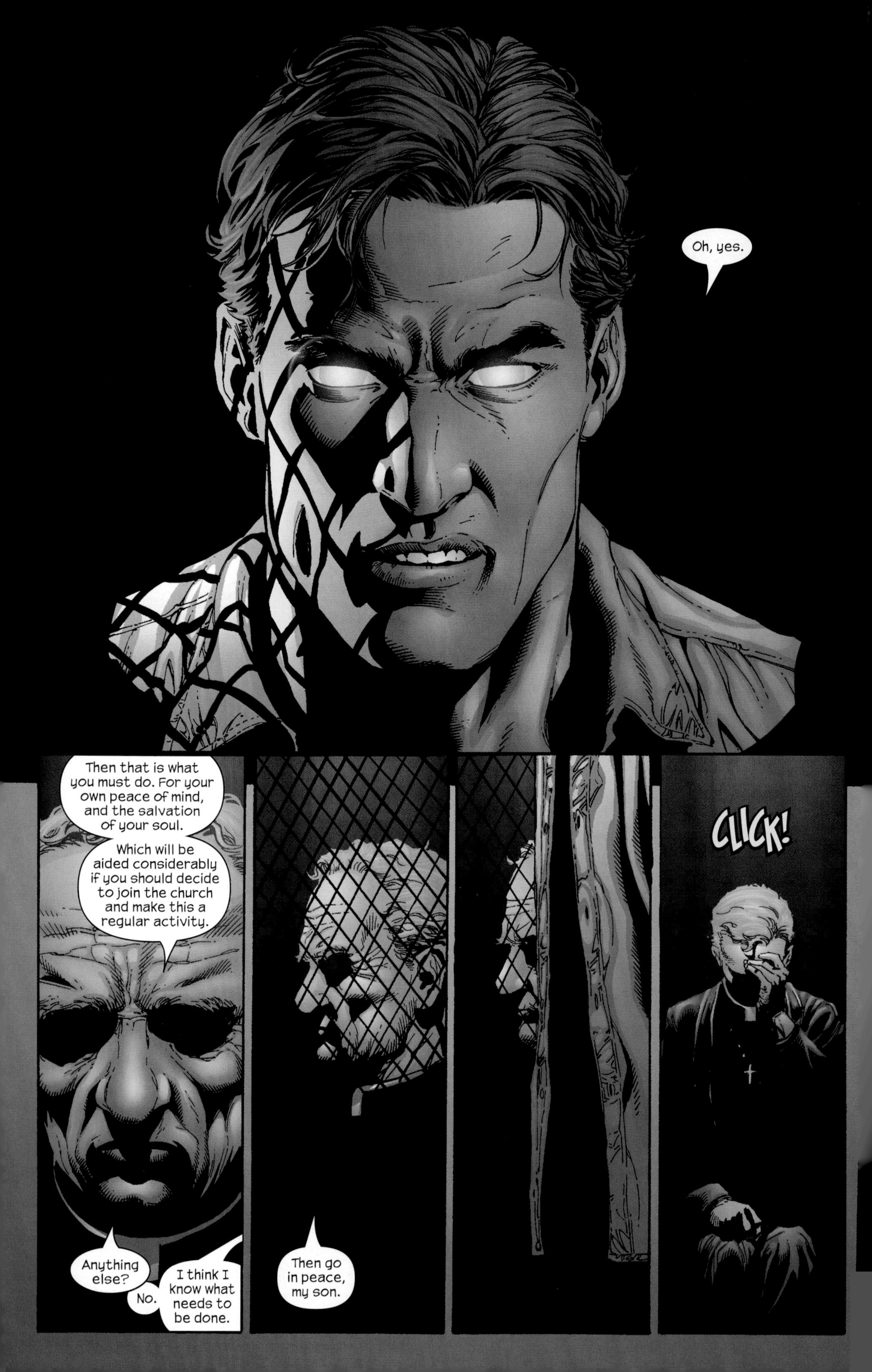
Oh, yes.
Then that is what you must do. For your own peace of mind, and the salvation of your soul.
Which will be aided considerably if you should decide to join the church and make this a regular activity.
Anything else?
No.
I think I know what needs to be done.
Then go in peace, my son.
CLICK!

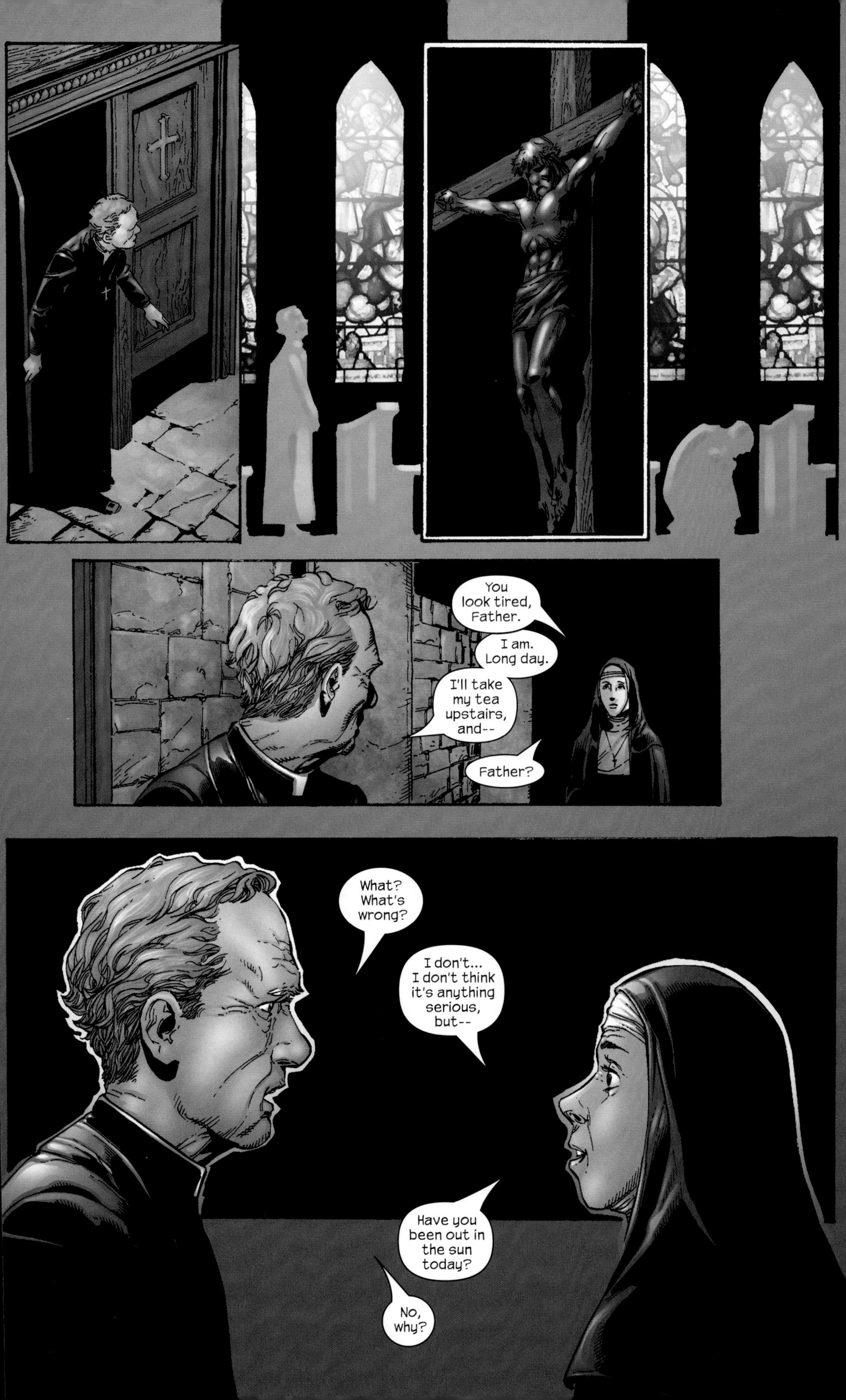

You look tired, Father.
I am. Long day.
I'll take my tea upstairs, and--
Father?
What? What's wrong?
I don't... I don't think it's anything serious, but--
Have you been out in the sun today?
No, why?

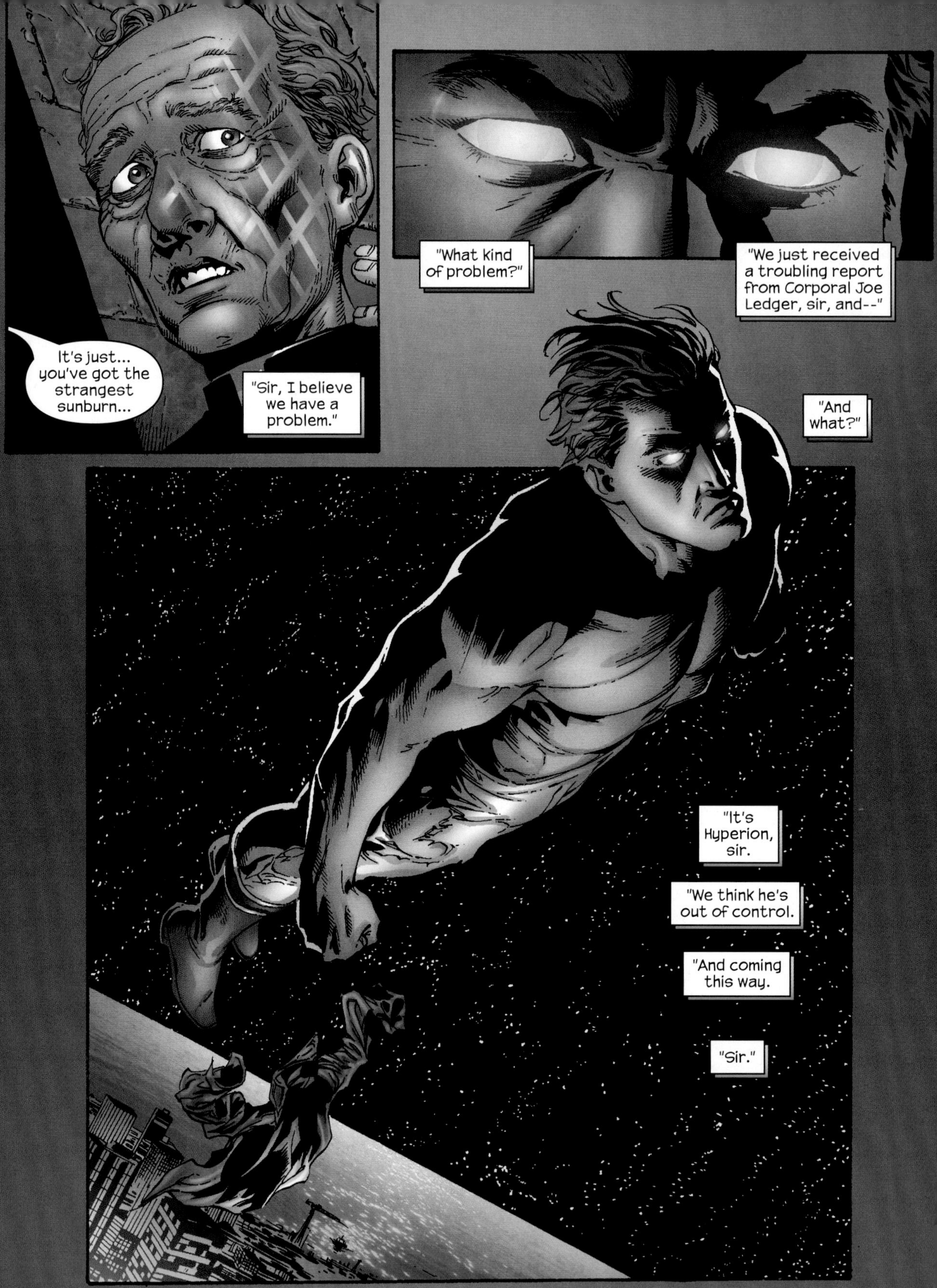
It's just... you've got the strangest sunburn...
"Sir, I believe we have a problem."
"What kind of problem?"
"We just received a troubling report from Corporal Joe Ledger, sir, and--"
"And what?"
"It's Hyperion, sir.
"We think he's out of control.
"And coming this way.
"Sir."

UBI DUBIUM, IBI LIBERTAS

WHERE THERE IS DOUBT, THERE IS FREEDOM

Ten O'Clock

#9

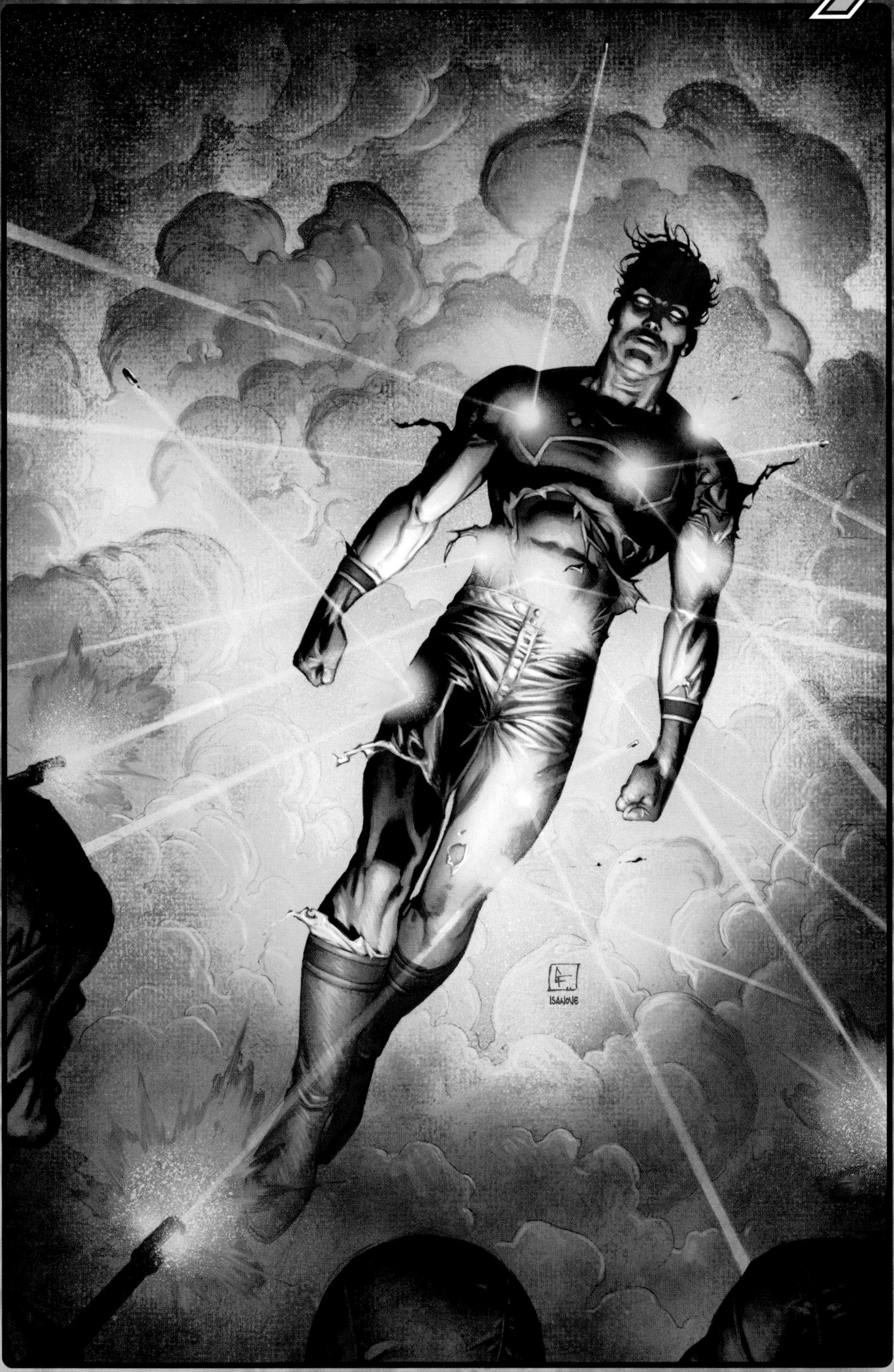

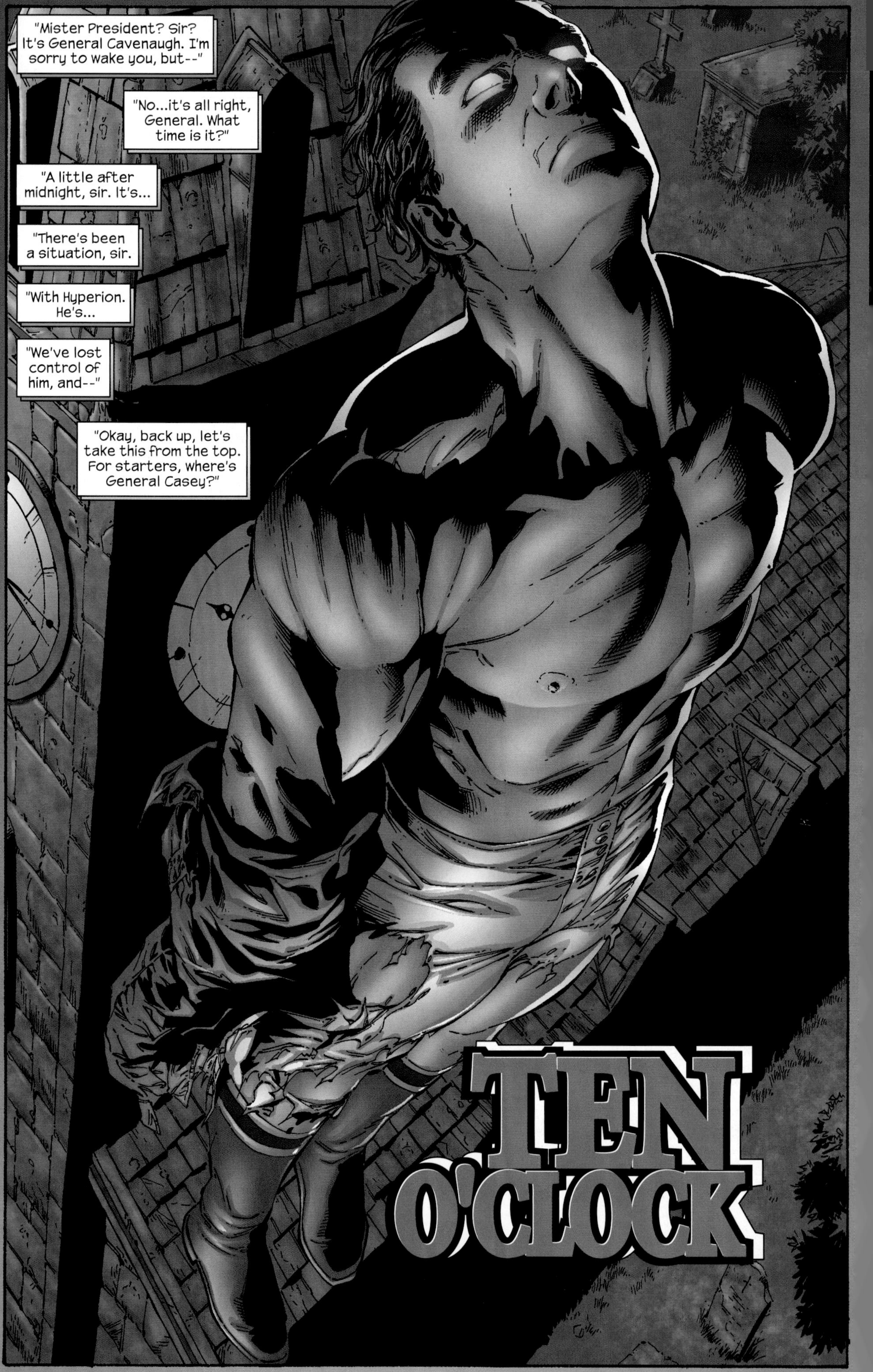
"Mister President? Sir? It's General Cavenaugh. I'm sorry to wake you, but--"
"No...it's all right, General. What time is it?"
"A little after midnight, sir. It's...
"There's been a situation, sir.
"With Hyperion. He's...
"We've lost control of him, and--"
"Okay, back up, let's take this from the top. For starters, where's General Casey?"
TEN O'CLOCK

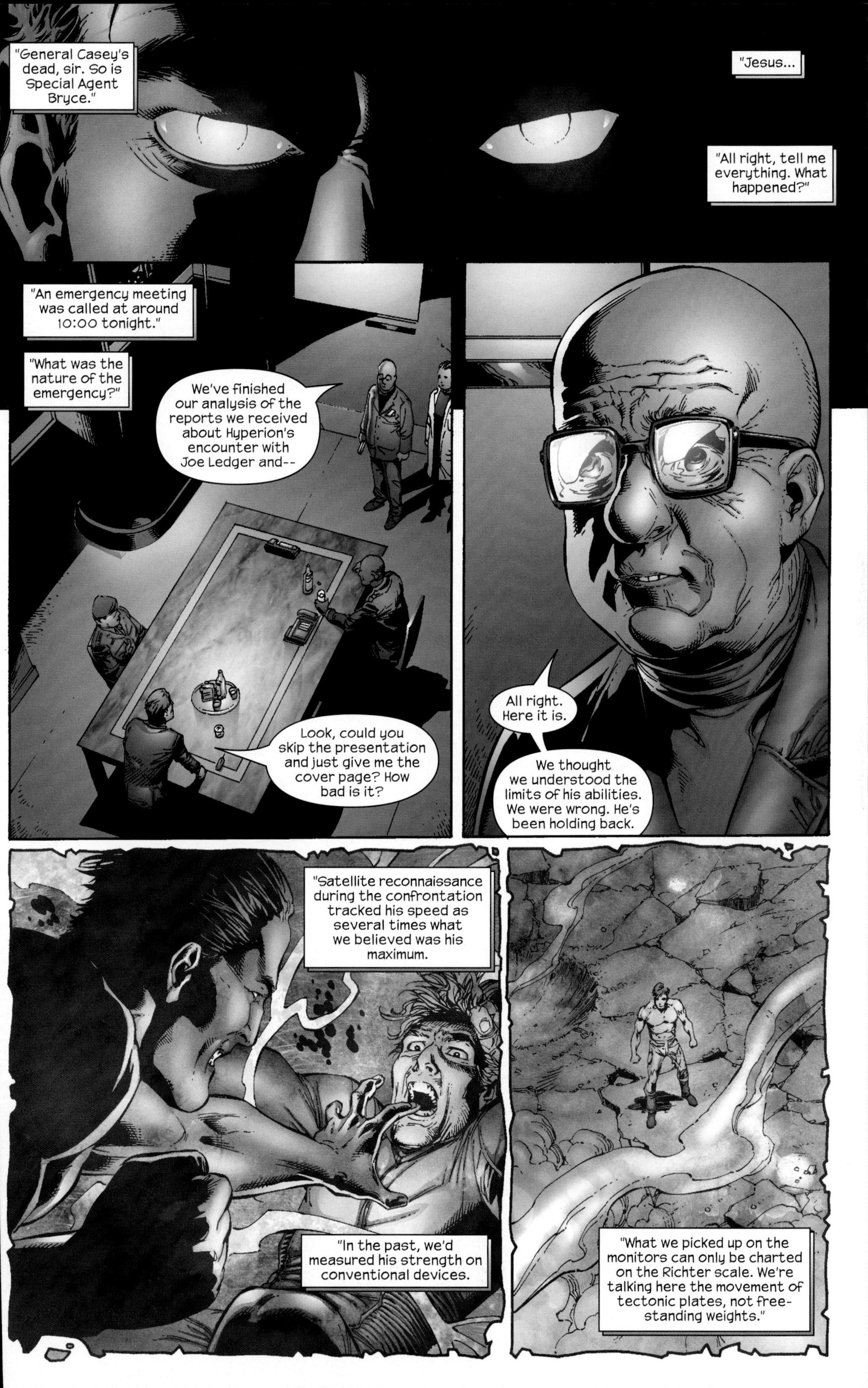
"General Casey's dead, sir. So is Special Agent Bryce."
"Jesus...
"All right, tell me everything. What happened?"
"An emergency meeting was called at around 10:00 tonight."
"What was the nature of the emergency?"
We've finished our analysis of the reports we received about Hyperion's encounter with Joe Ledger and--
Look, could you skip the presentation and just give me the cover page? How bad is it?
All right. Here it is.
We thought we understood the limits of his abilities. We were wrong. He's been holding back.
"Satellite reconnaissance during the confrontation tracked his speed as several times what we believed was his maximum.
"In the past, we'd measured his strength on conventional devices.
"What we picked up on the monitors can only be charted on the Richter scale. We're talking here the movement of tectonic plates, not free-standing weights."

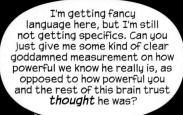

I'm getting fancy language here, but I'm still not getting specifics. Can you just give me some kind of clear goddamned measurement on how powerful we know he really is, as opposed to how powerful you and the rest of this brain trust *thought* he was?
CA
AZ
NM
OK
AR
MS
AL
TX
LA
AK
The only mathematical expression that works is to calculate his ability in megadeaths.
"If he were to begin an attack at his peak ability in a randomly selected urban city on the Eastern Seaboard--
VT
NH
MA
RI
CT
NJ
DE
MD
DC
MI
PA
IN
OH
WV
KY
NC
SC
GA
MS
PR
"He could conceivably eliminate a minimum of two thousand people per hour."

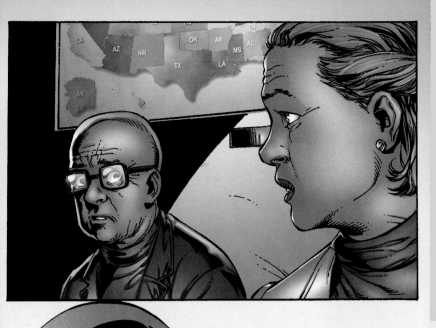

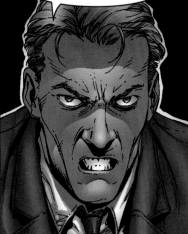

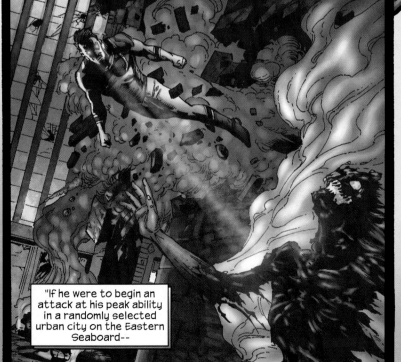

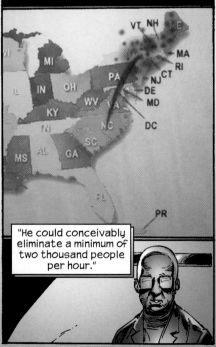

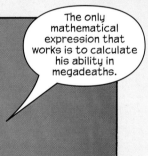

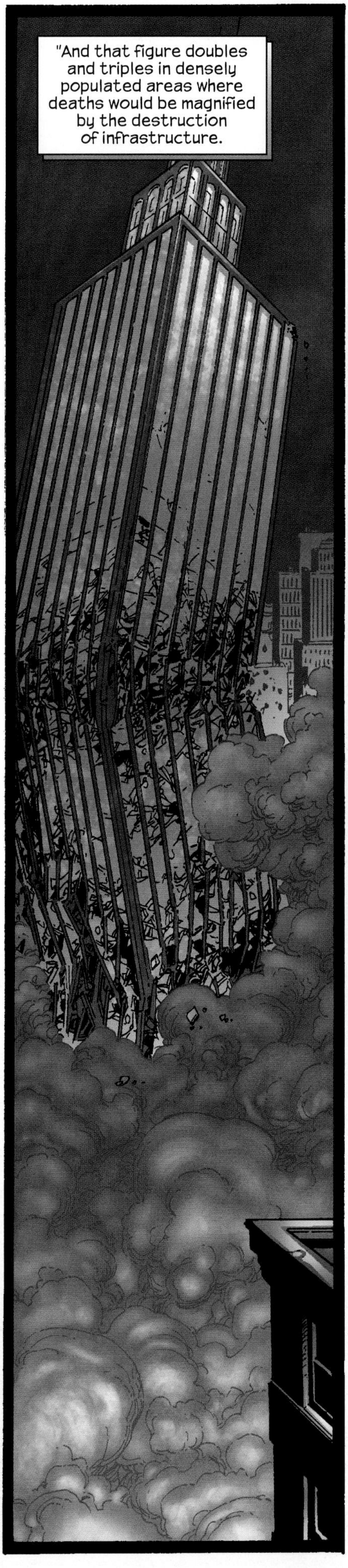
"And that figure doubles and triples in densely populated areas where deaths would be magnified by the destruction of infrastructure.

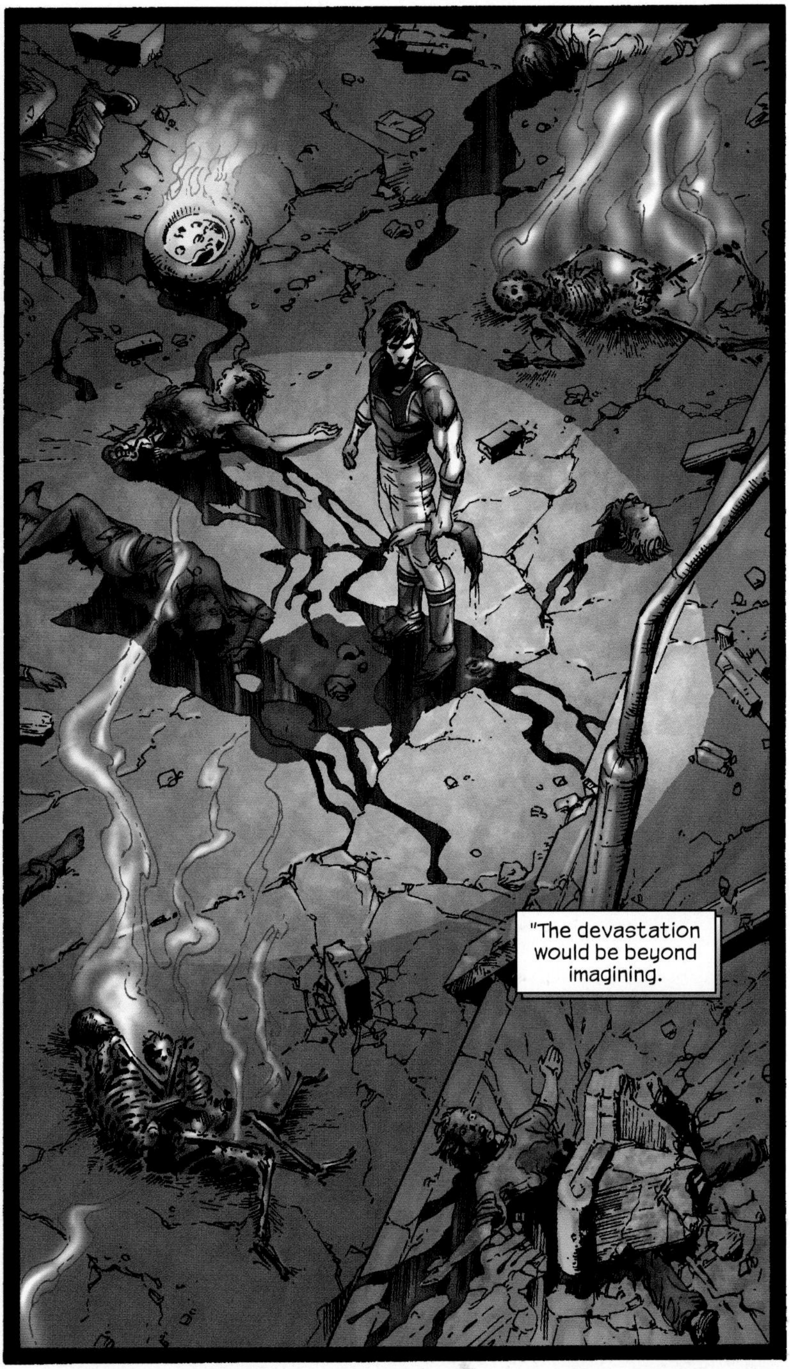
"The devastation would be beyond imagining.

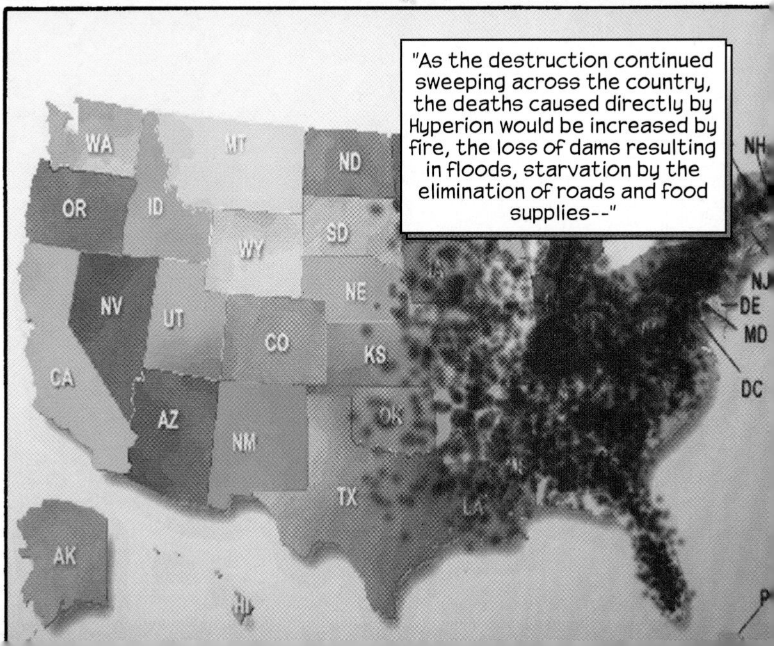
"As the destruction continued sweeping across the country, the deaths caused directly by Hyperion would be increased by fire, the loss of dams resulting in floods, starvation by the elimination of roads and food supplies--"
WA
MT
ND
OR
ID
SD
WY
NE
NV
UT
CO
KS
CA
AZ
NM
OK
TX
LA
AK
NH
NJ
DE
MD
DC

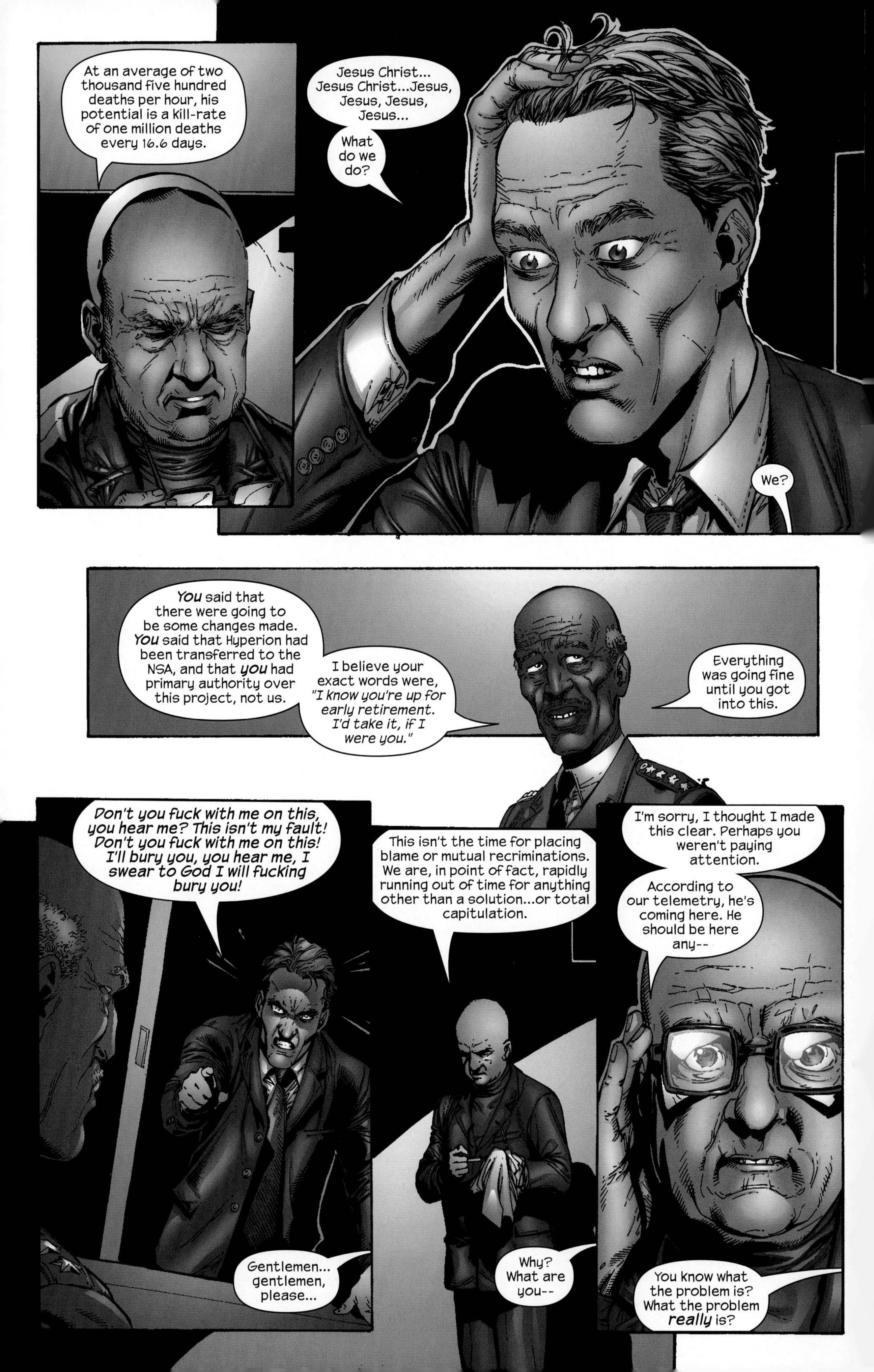

At an average of two thousand five hundred deaths per hour, his potential is a kill-rate of one million deaths every 16.6 days.
Jesus Christ... Jesus Christ...Jesus, Jesus, Jesus, Jesus...
What do we do?
We?
You said that there were going to be some changes made. You said that Hyperion had been transferred to the NSA, and that you had primary authority over this project, not us.
I believe your exact words were, "I know you're up for early retirement. I'd take it, if I were you."
Everything was going fine until you got into this.
Don't you fuck with me on this, you hear me? This isn't my fault! Don't you fuck with me on this! I'll bury you, you hear me, I swear to God I will fucking bury you!
Gentlemen... gentlemen, please...
This isn't the time for placing blame or mutual recriminations. We are, in point of fact, rapidly running out of time for anything other than a solution...or total capitulation.
Why? What are you--
I'm sorry, I thought I made this clear. Perhaps you weren't paying attention.
According to our telemetry, he's coming here. He should be here any--
You know what the problem is? What the problem really is?

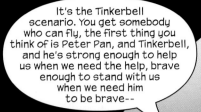

It's the Tinkerbell scenario. You get somebody who can fly, the first thing you think of is Peter Pan, and Tinkerbell, and he's strong enough to help us when we need the help, brave enough to stand with us when we need him to be brave--

Then one day you find out he's been holding back on you. And you realize that there's nowhere you can run that he can't get to. Like the old gospel song says, there's no hiding place...no hiding place down here.

Look, this is all premature--

We don't *know* that he's coming here to start trouble. He...he might just be coming here to talk. To ask the questions we knew were coming sooner or later. He --

He's coming because he's not stupid and he's figured out we've been lying to him. You saw the satellite photos, you saw what he did in his fight with Ledger.

"That look to you like a man who just wants to come and talk?"

If I had that kind of power, and I found out the people I'd believed, the people I trusted for the last twenty years, had been lying to me, I'd kill anybody who stood between me and those answers.

I was always afraid a day like this might come. You remember, right, Bill?

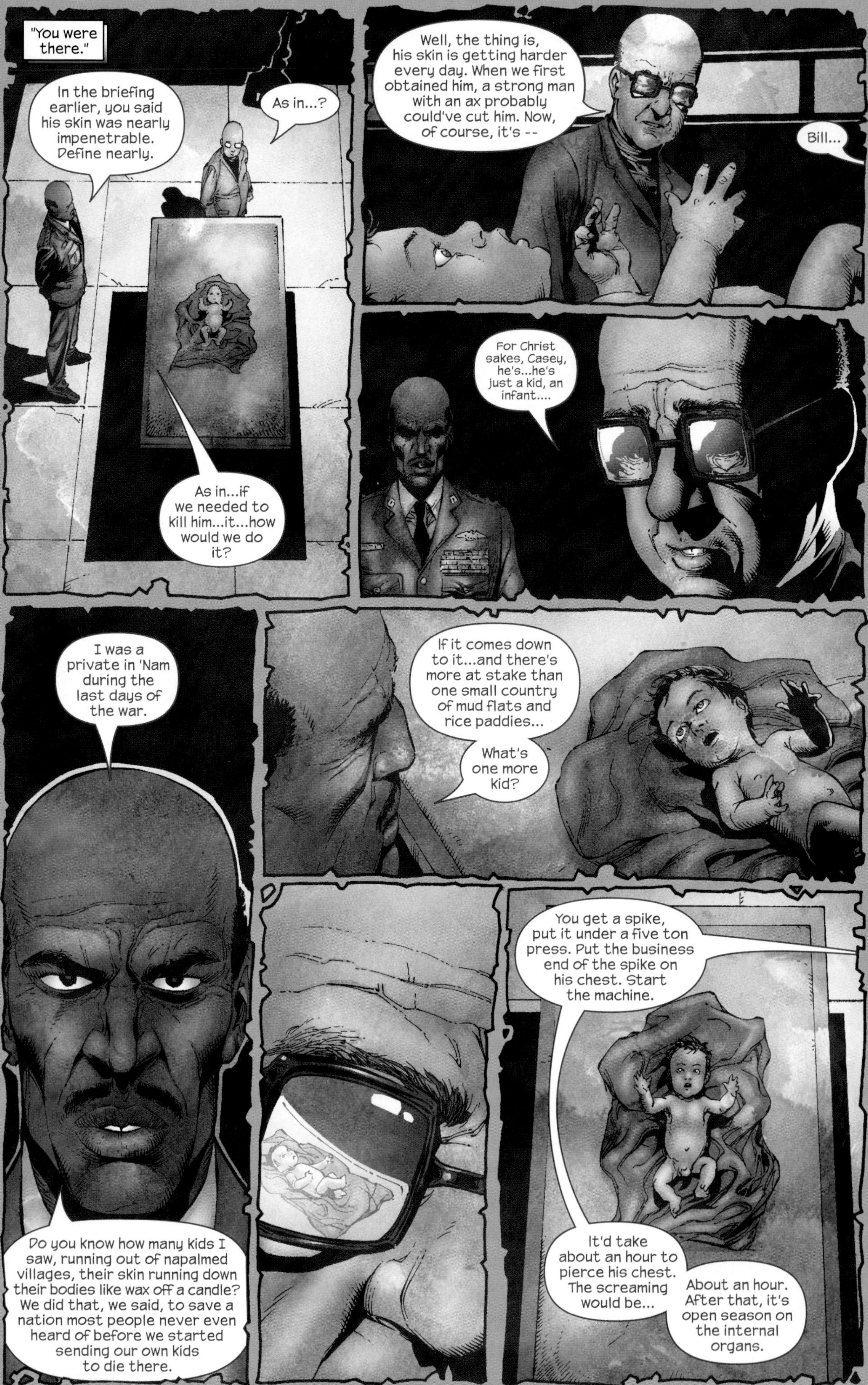
"You were there."
In the briefing earlier, you said his skin was nearly impenetrable. Define nearly.
As in...?
As in...if we needed to kill him...it...how would we do it?
Well, the thing is, his skin is getting harder every day. When we first obtained him, a strong man with an ax probably could've cut him. Now, of course, it's --
Bill...
For Christ sakes, Casey, he's...he's just a kid, an infant....
I was a private in 'Nam during the last days of the war.
Do you know how many kids I saw, running out of napalmed villages, their skin running down their bodies like wax off a candle? We did that, we said, to save a nation most people never even heard of before we started sending our own kids to die there.
If it comes down to it...and there's more at stake than one small country of mud flats and rice paddies...
What's one more kid?
You get a spike, put it under a five ton press. Put the business end of the spike on his chest. Start the machine.
It'd take about an hour to pierce his chest. The screaming would be...
About an hour. After that, it's open season on the internal organs.

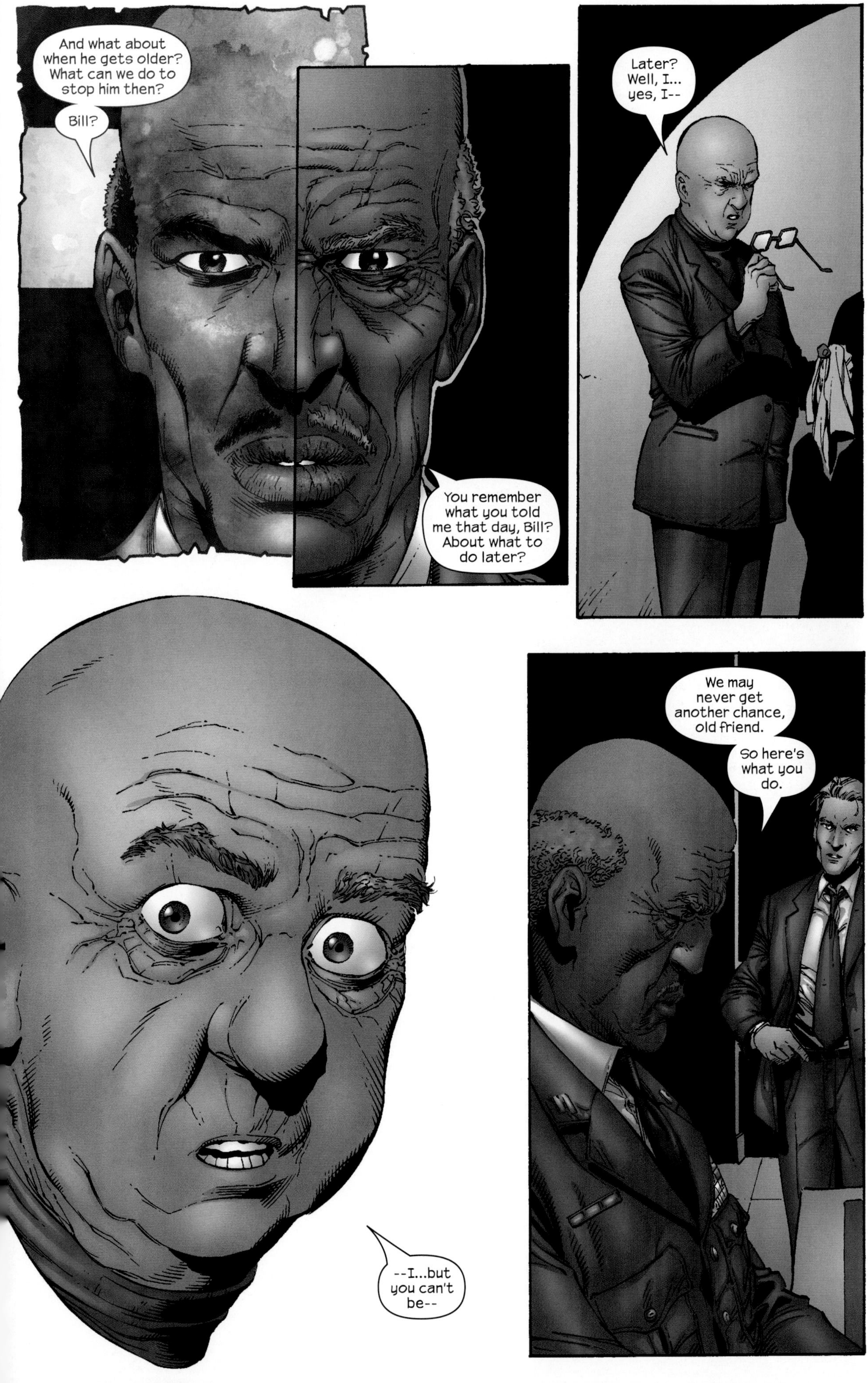
And what about when he gets older? What can we do to stop him then?
Bill?
You remember what you told me that day, Bill? About what to do later?
Later? Well, I... yes, I--
--I...but you can't be--
We may never get another chance, old friend.
So here's what you do.

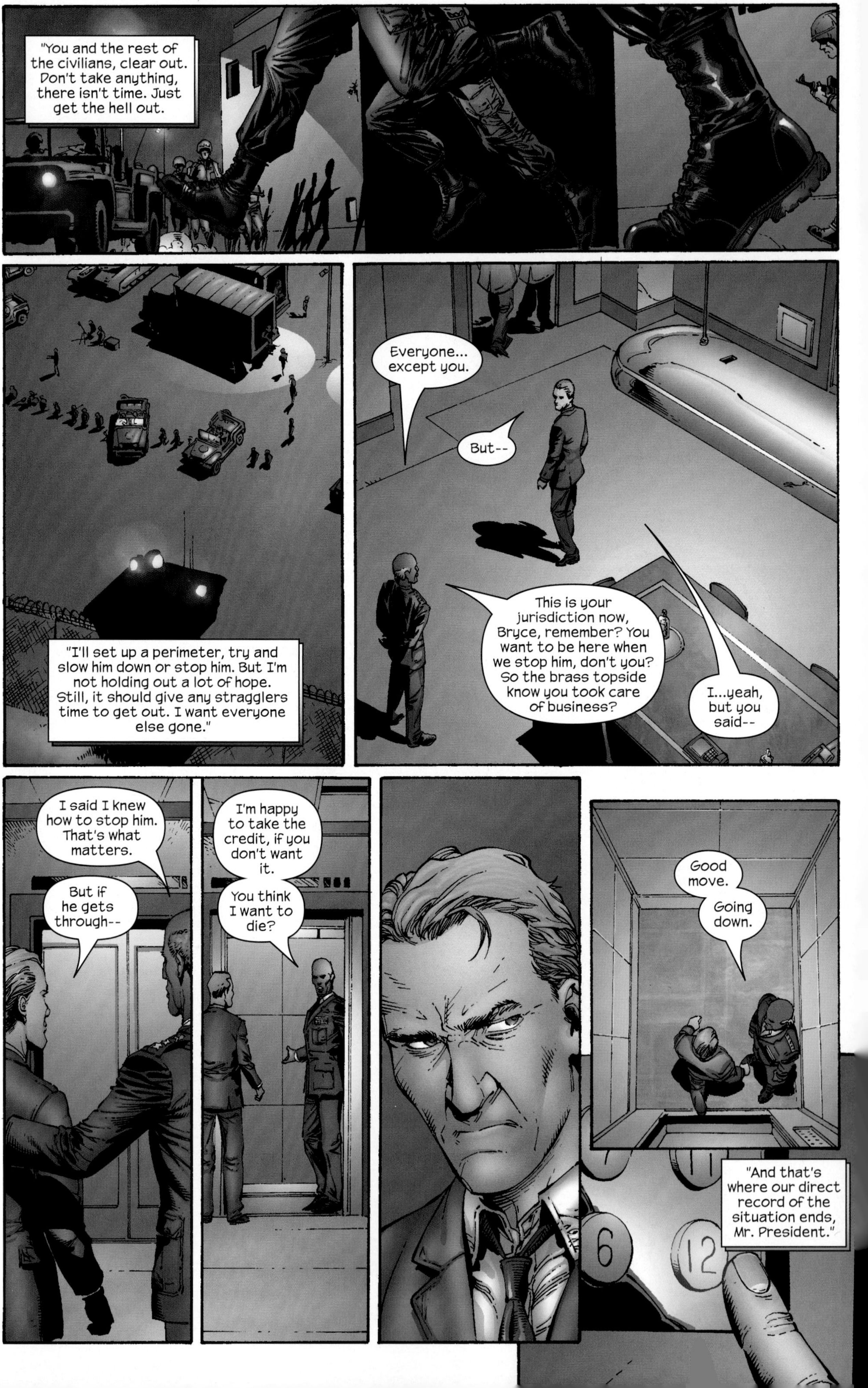
"You and the rest of the civilians, clear out. Don't take anything, there isn't time. Just get the hell out.
"I'll set up a perimeter, try and slow him down or stop him. But I'm not holding out a lot of hope. Still, it should give any stragglers time to get out. I want everyone else gone."
Everyone... except you.
But--
This is your jurisdiction now, Bryce, remember? You want to be here when we stop him, don't you? So the brass topside know you took care of business?
I...yeah, but you said--
I said I knew how to stop him. That's what matters.
But if he gets through--
I'm happy to take the credit, if you don't want it.
You think I want to die?
Good move.
Going down.
"And that's where our direct record of the situation ends, Mr. President."

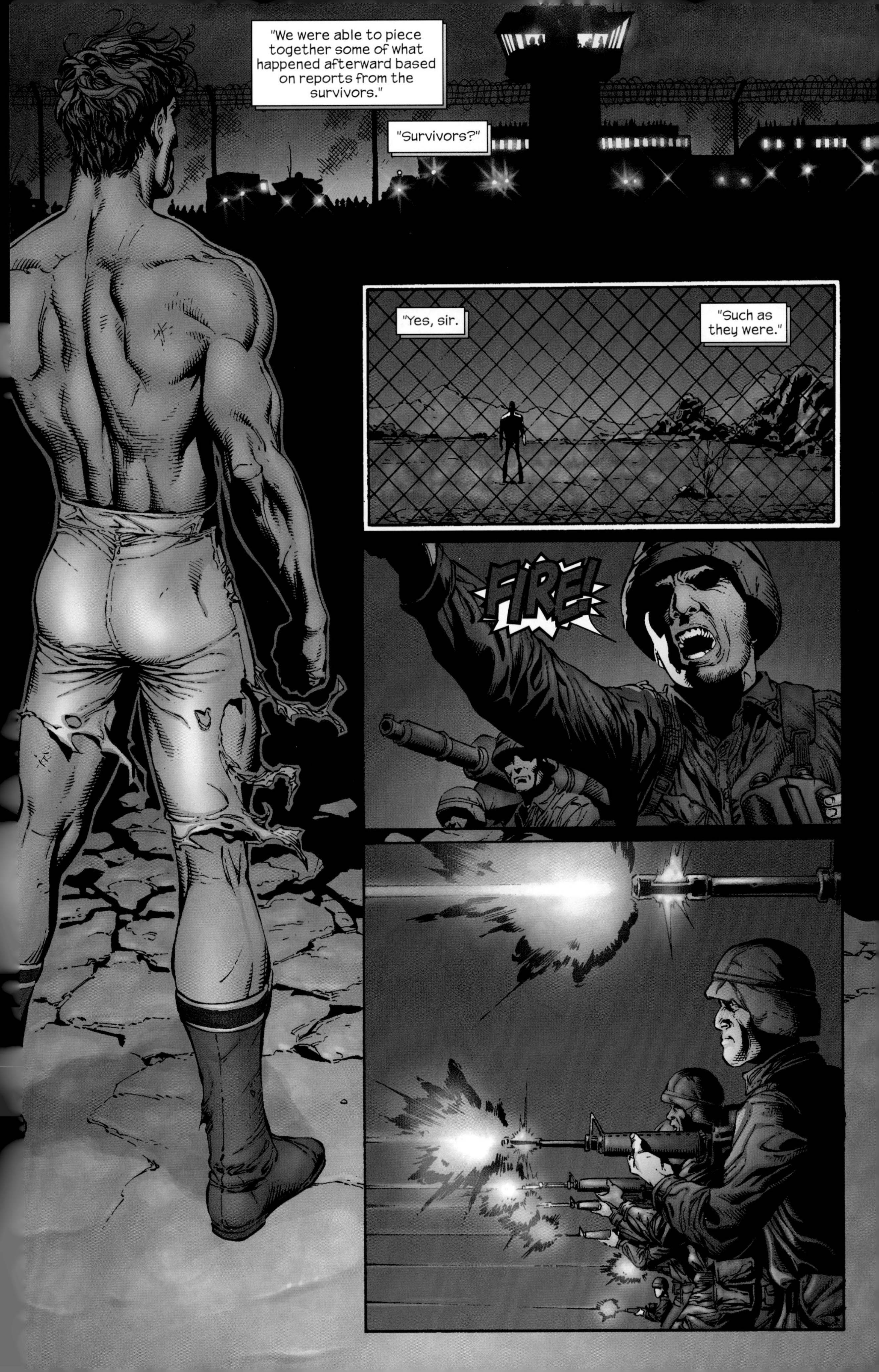
"We were able to piece together some of what happened afterward based on reports from the survivors."
"Survivors?"
"Yes, sir.
"Such as they were."
FIRE!

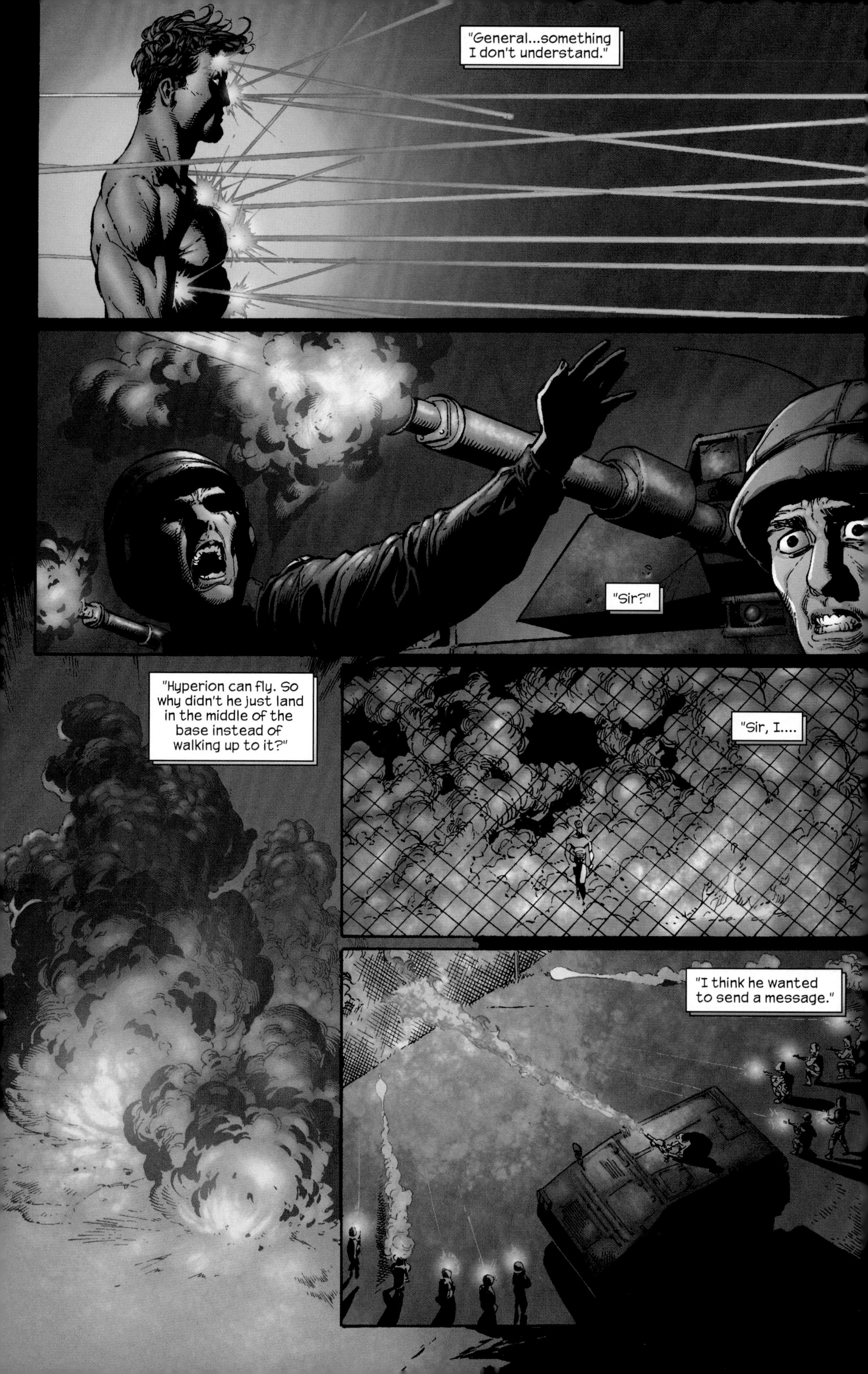
"General...something I don't understand."
"Sir?"
"Hyperion can fly. So why didn't he just land in the middle of the base instead of walking up to it?"
"Sir, I....
"I think he wanted to send a message."

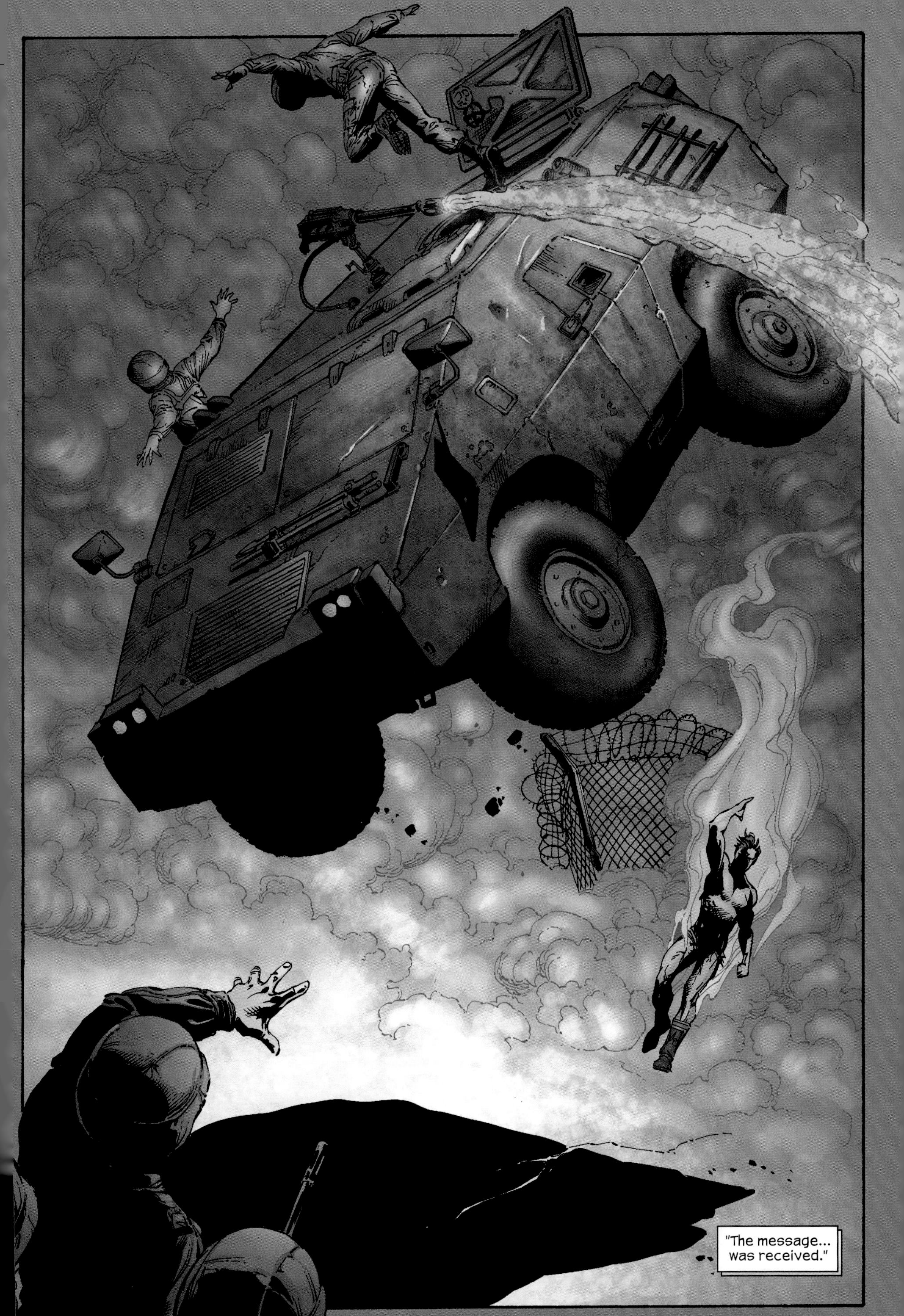
"The message... was received."

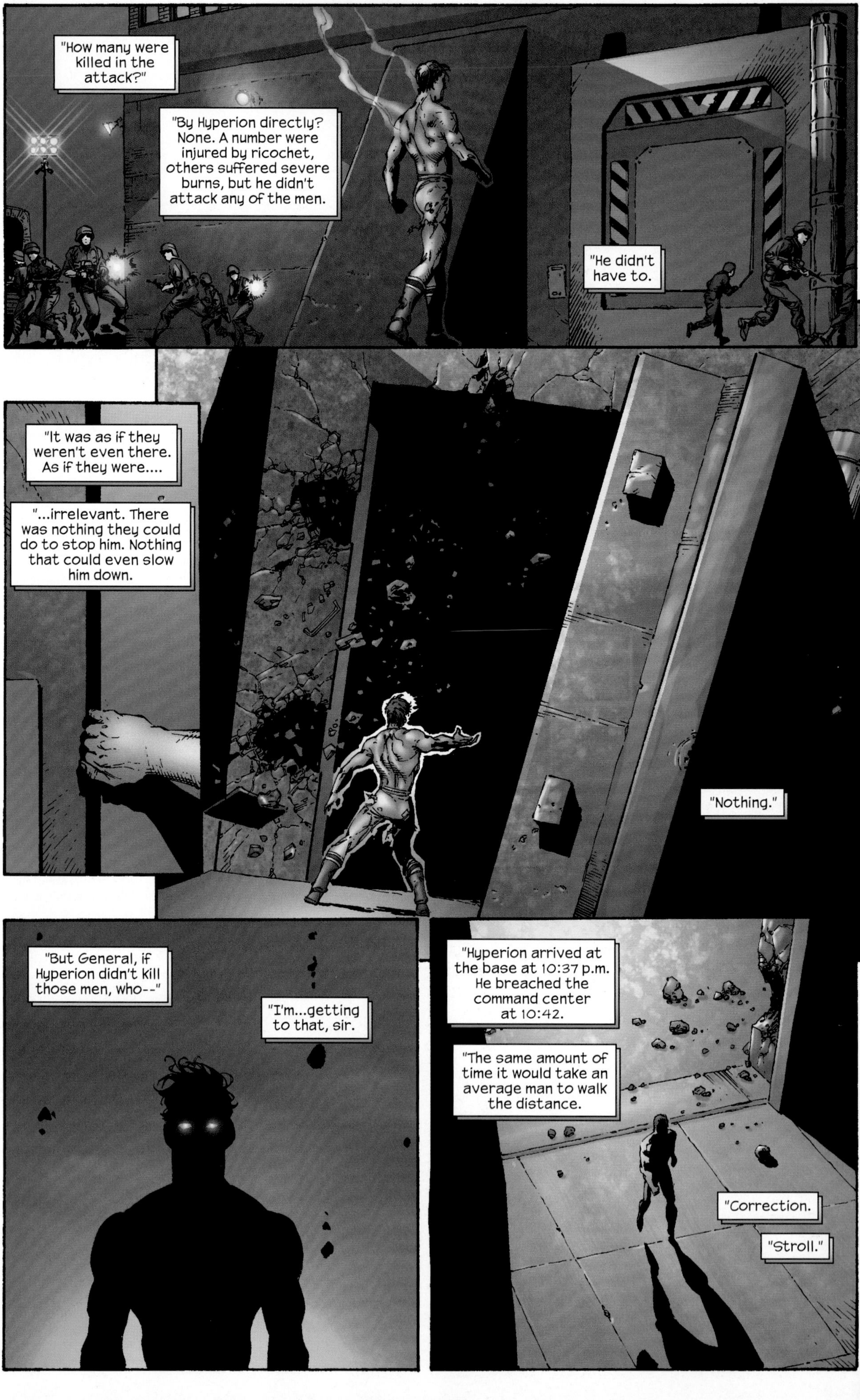
"How many were killed in the attack?"
"By Hyperion directly? None. A number were injured by ricochet, others suffered severe burns, but he didn't attack any of the men.
"He didn't have to.
"It was as if they weren't even there. As if they were....
"...irrelevant. There was nothing they could do to stop him. Nothing that could even slow him down.
"Nothing."
"But General, if Hyperion didn't kill those men, who--"
"I'm...getting to that, sir.
"Hyperion arrived at the base at 10:37 p.m. He breached the command center at 10:42.
"The same amount of time it would take an average man to walk the distance.
"Correction.
"Stroll."

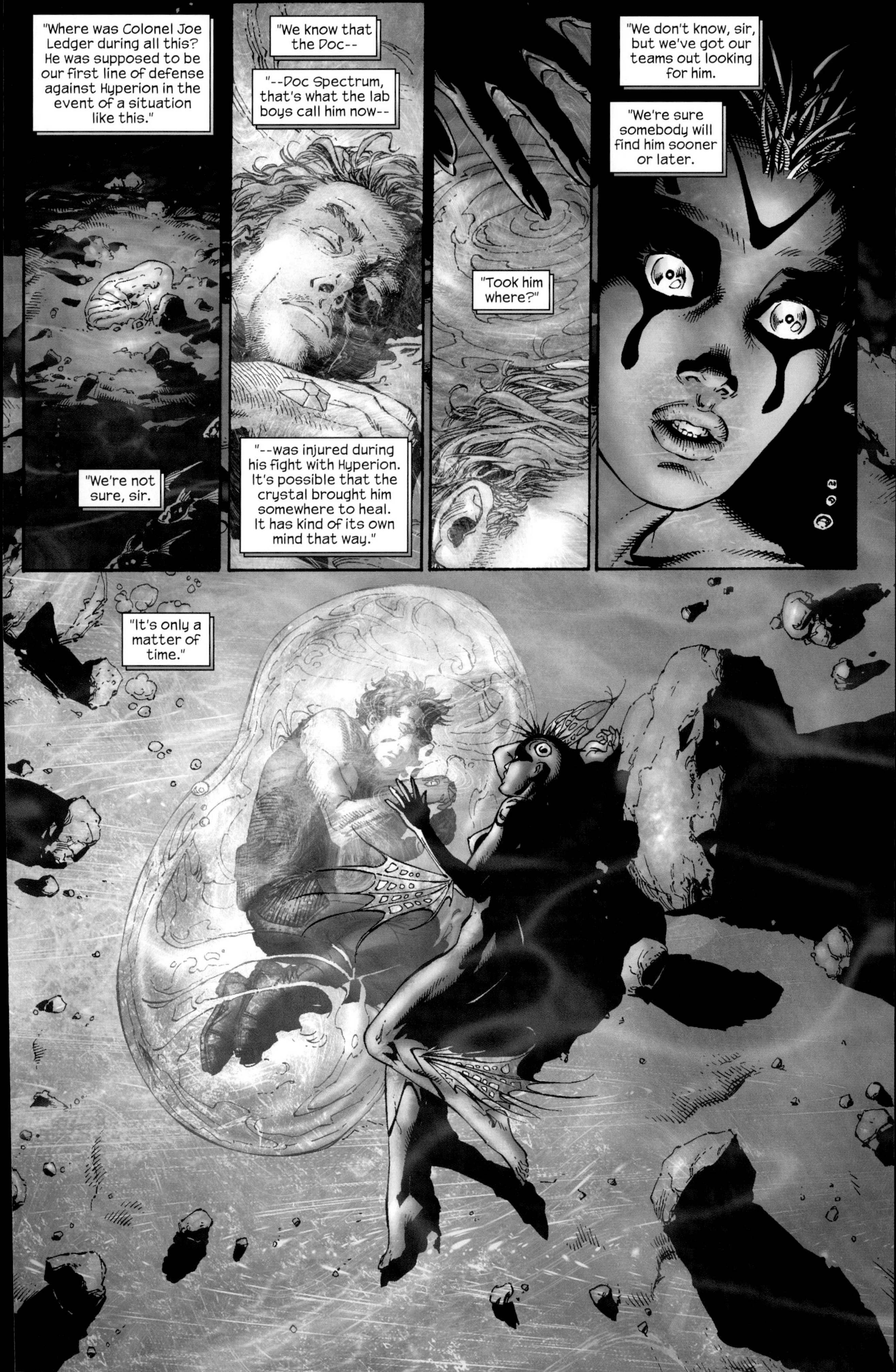
"Where was Colonel Joe Ledger during all this? He was supposed to be our first line of defense against Hyperion in the event of a situation like this."
"We're not sure, sir.
"We know that the Doc--
"--Doc Spectrum, that's what the lab boys call him now--
"--was injured during his fight with Hyperion. It's possible that the crystal brought him somewhere to heal. It has kind of its own mind that way."
"Took him where?"
"We don't know, sir, but we've got our teams out looking for him.
"We're sure somebody will find him sooner or later.
"It's only a matter of time."

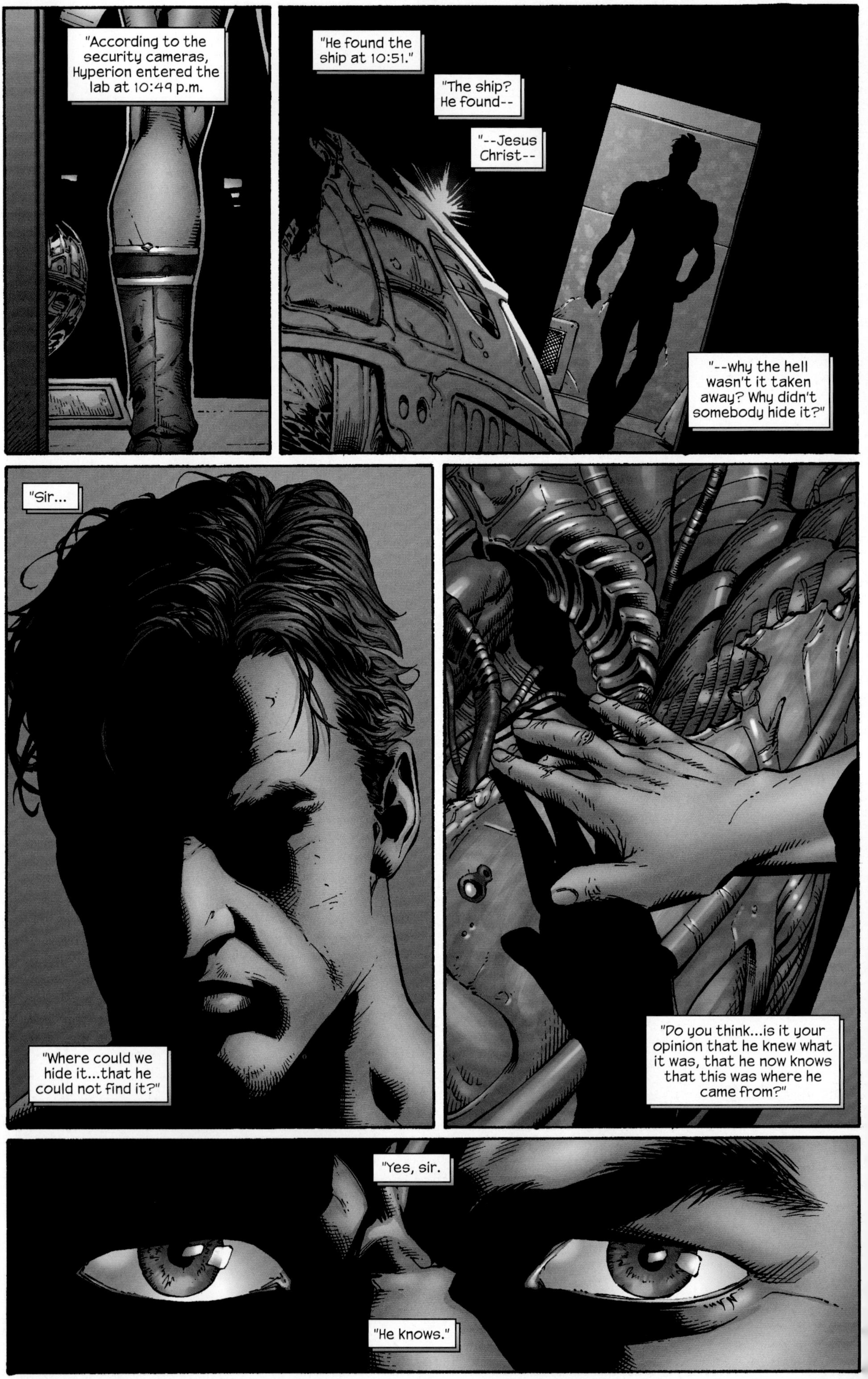
"According to the security cameras, Hyperion entered the lab at 10:49 p.m.
"He found the ship at 10:51."
"The ship? He found--
"--Jesus Christ--
"--why the hell wasn't it taken away? Why didn't somebody hide it?"
"Sir...
"Where could we hide it...that he could not find it?"
"Do you think...is it your opinion that he knew what it was, that he now knows that this was where he came from?"
"Yes, sir.
"He knows."

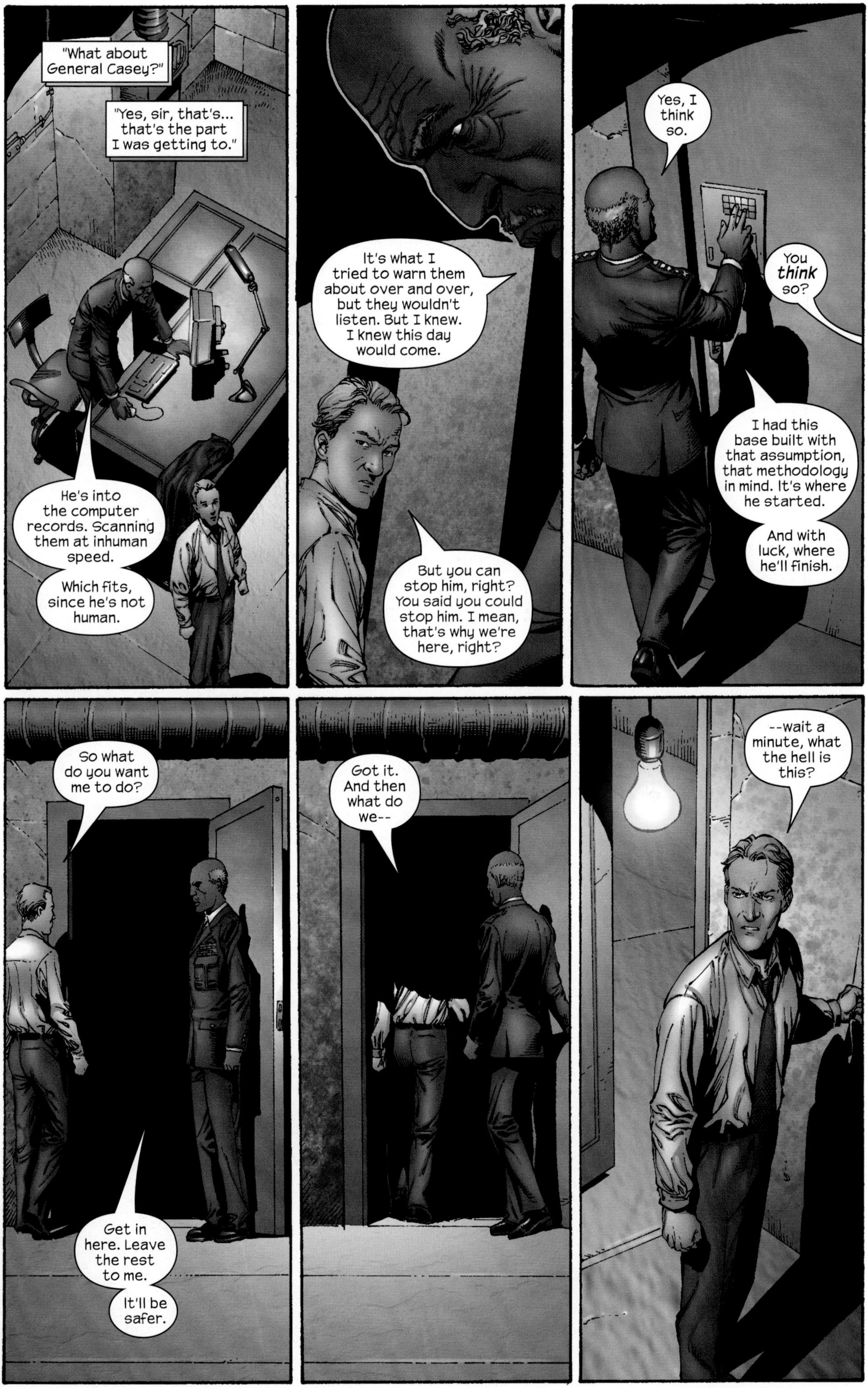
"What about General Casey?"
"Yes, sir, that's... that's the part I was getting to."
He's into the computer records. Scanning them at inhuman speed.
Which fits, since he's not human.
It's what I tried to warn them about over and over, but they wouldn't listen. But I knew. I knew this day would come.
But you can stop him, right? You said you could stop him. I mean, that's why we're here, right?
Yes, I think so.
You *think* so?
I had this base built with that assumption, that methodology in mind. It's where he started.
And with luck, where he'll finish.
So what do you want me to do?
Get in here. Leave the rest to me.
It'll be safer.
Got it. And then what do we--
--wait a minute, what the hell is this?

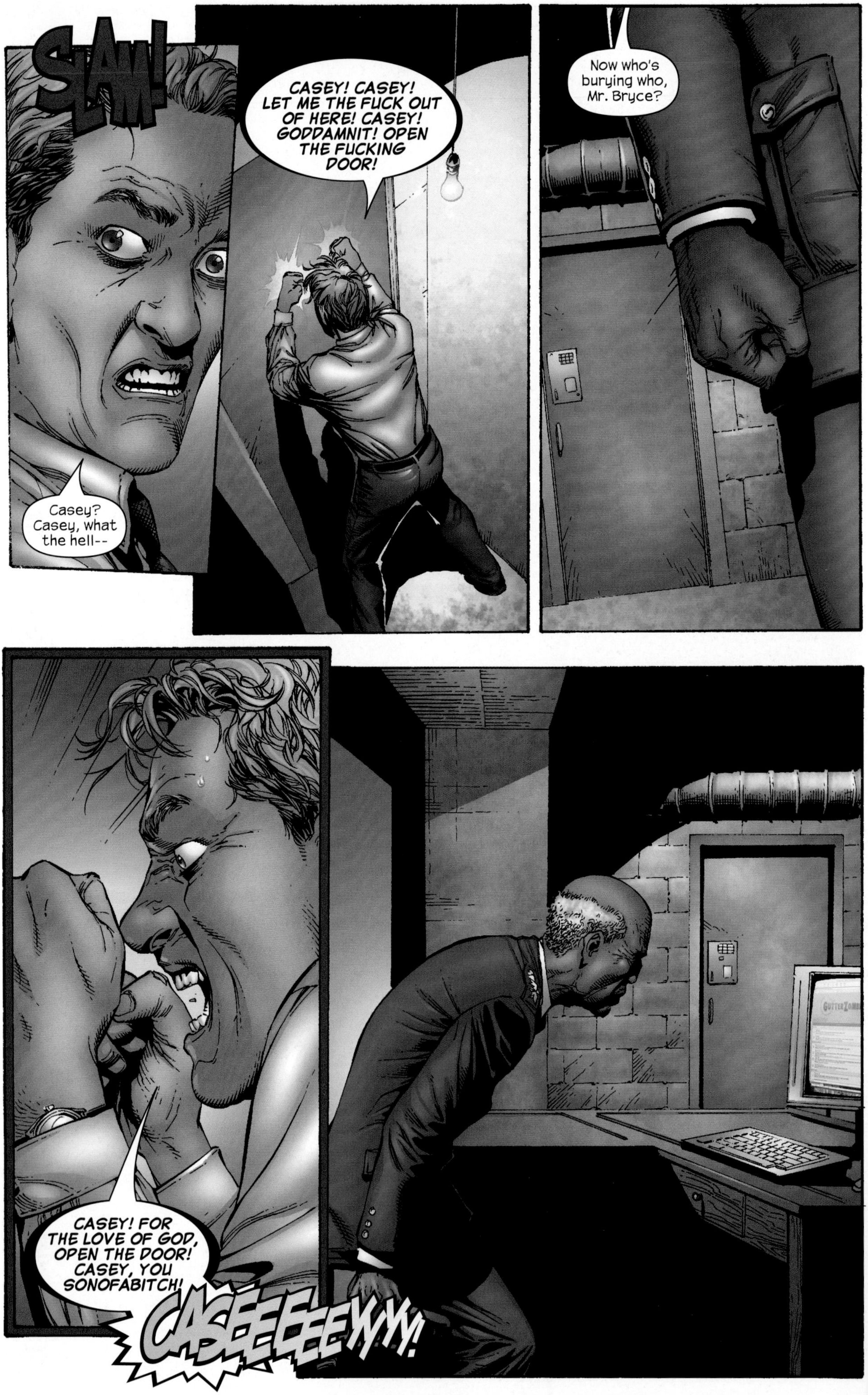
SLAM!
Casey? Casey, what the hell--
CASEY! CASEY! LET ME THE FUCK OUT OF HERE! CASEY! GODDAMNIT! OPEN THE FUCKING DOOR!
Now who's burying who, Mr. Bryce?
CASEY! FOR THE LOVE OF GOD, OPEN THE DOOR! CASEY, YOU SONOFABITCH!
CASEEEEEYYYY!

SYSTEM STAND-BY.
SYSTEM ARMED.
RELEASE REMOTE TO ACTIVATE
Ready when you are, you son of a bitch.

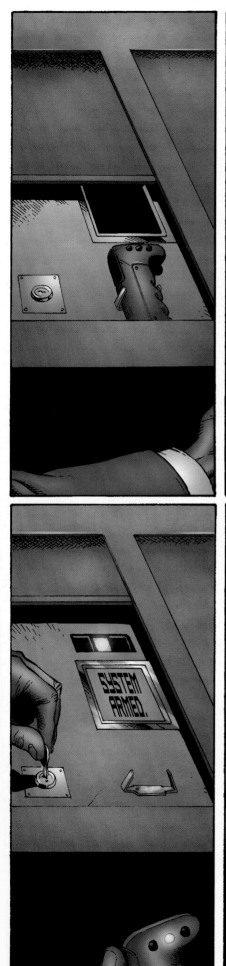

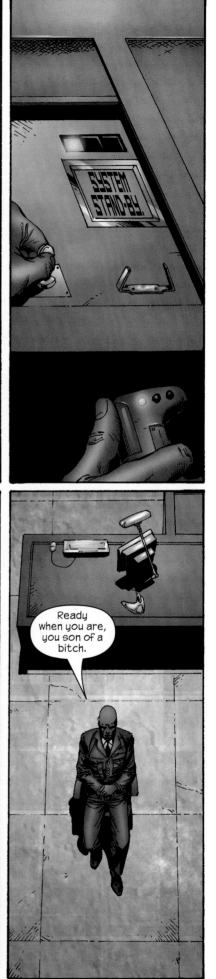

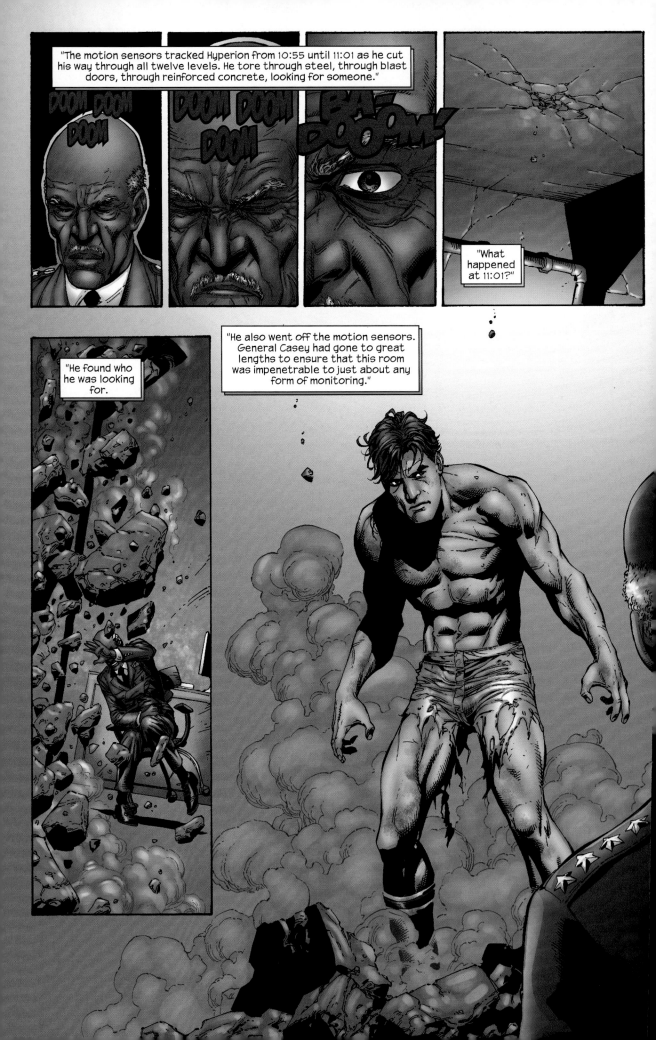

"The motion sensors tracked Hyperion from 10:55 until 11:01 as he cut his way through all twelve levels. He tore through steel, through blast doors, through reinforced concrete, looking for someone."

DOOM DOOM DOOM

DOOM DOOM DOOM

B-A-DOOOM!

"What happened at 11:01?"

"He also went off the motion sensors. General Casey had gone to great lengths to ensure that this room was impenetrable to just about any form of monitoring."

"He found who he was looking for."

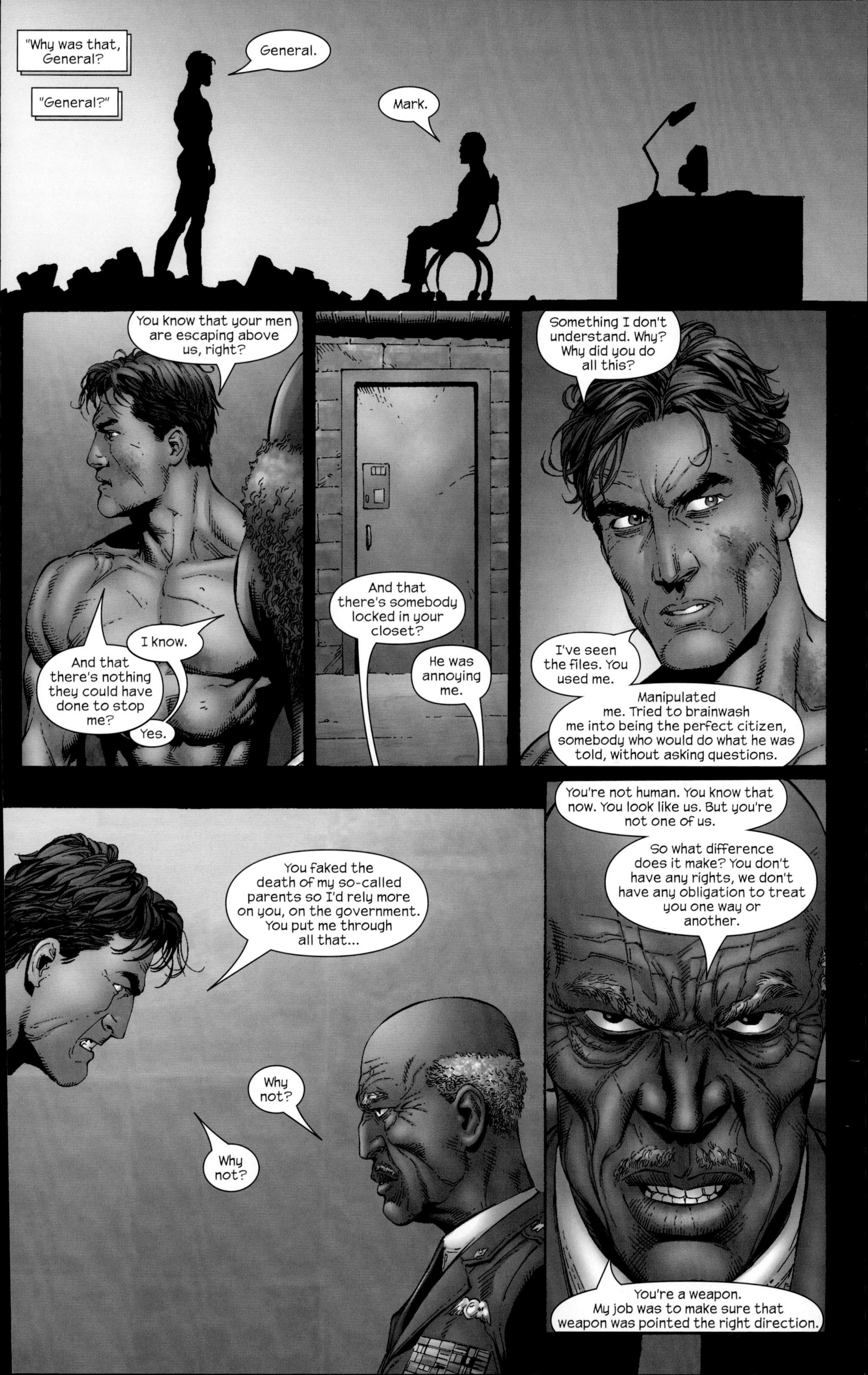
"Why was that, General?
General.
"General?"
Mark.
You know that your men are escaping above us, right?
I know.
And that there's nothing they could have done to stop me?
Yes.
And that there's somebody locked in your closet?
He was annoying me.
Something I don't understand. Why? Why did you do all this?
I've seen the files. You used me.
Manipulated me. Tried to brainwash me into being the perfect citizen, somebody who would do what he was told, without asking questions.
You faked the death of my so-called parents so I'd rely more on you, on the government. You put me through all that...
Why not?
Why not?
You're not human. You know that now. You look like us. But you're not one of us.
So what difference does it make? You don't have any rights, we don't have any obligation to treat you one way or another.
You're a weapon. My job was to make sure that weapon was pointed the right direction.

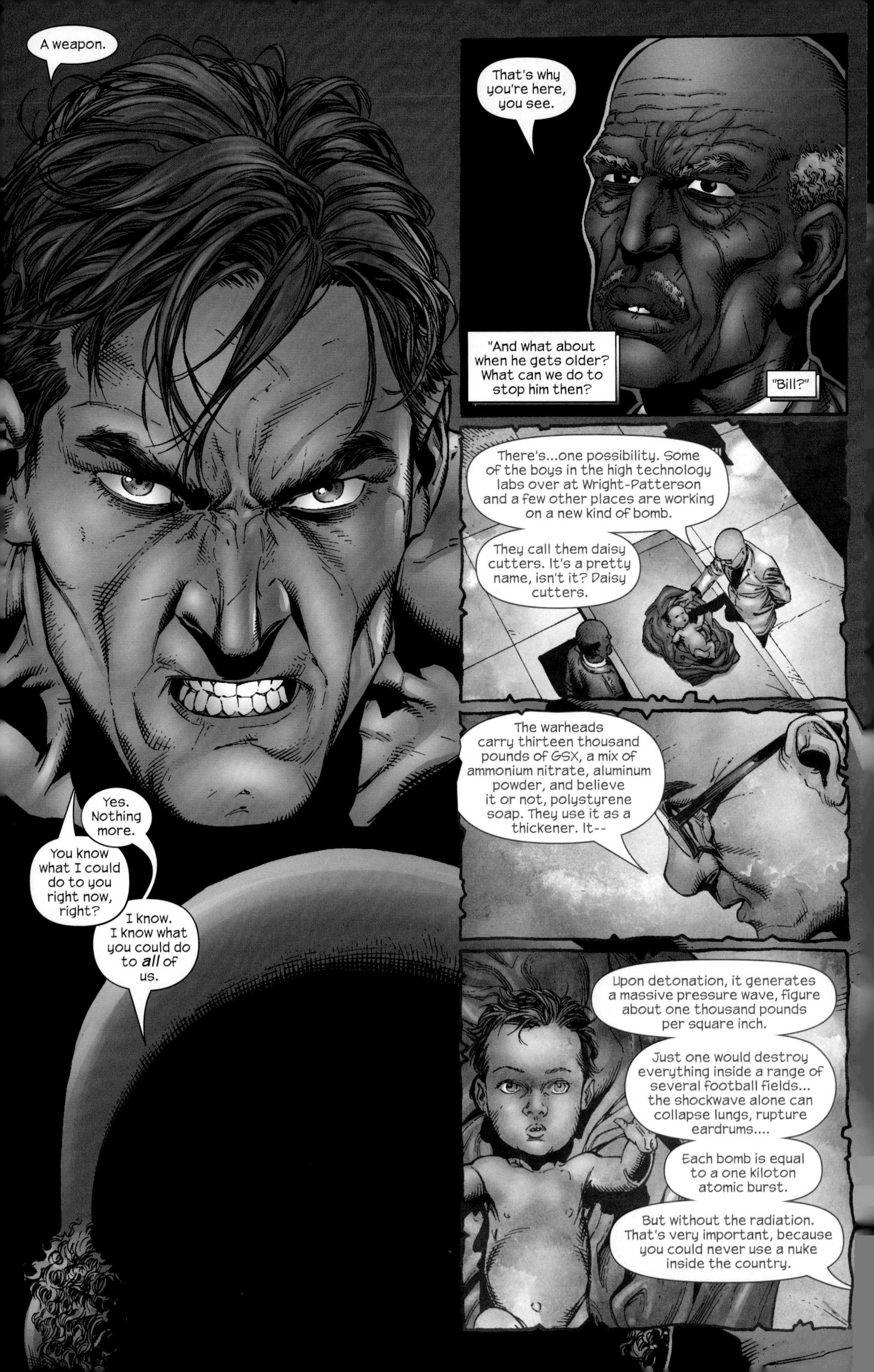

A weapon.
That's why you're here, you see.
"And what about when he gets older? What can we do to stop him then?
"Bill?"
There's...one possibility. Some of the boys in the high technology labs over at Wright-Patterson and a few other places are working on a new kind of bomb.
They call them daisy cutters. It's a pretty name, isn't it? Daisy cutters.
The warheads carry thirteen thousand pounds of GSX, a mix of ammonium nitrate, aluminum powder, and believe it or not, polystyrene soap. They use it as a thickener. It--
Upon detonation, it generates a massive pressure wave, figure about one thousand pounds per square inch.
Just one would destroy everything inside a range of several football fields... the shockwave alone can collapse lungs, rupture eardrums....
Each bomb is equal to a one kiloton atomic burst.
But without the radiation. That's very important, because you could never use a nuke inside the country.
Yes. Nothing more.
You know what I could do to you right now, right?
I know. I know what you could do to *all* of us.

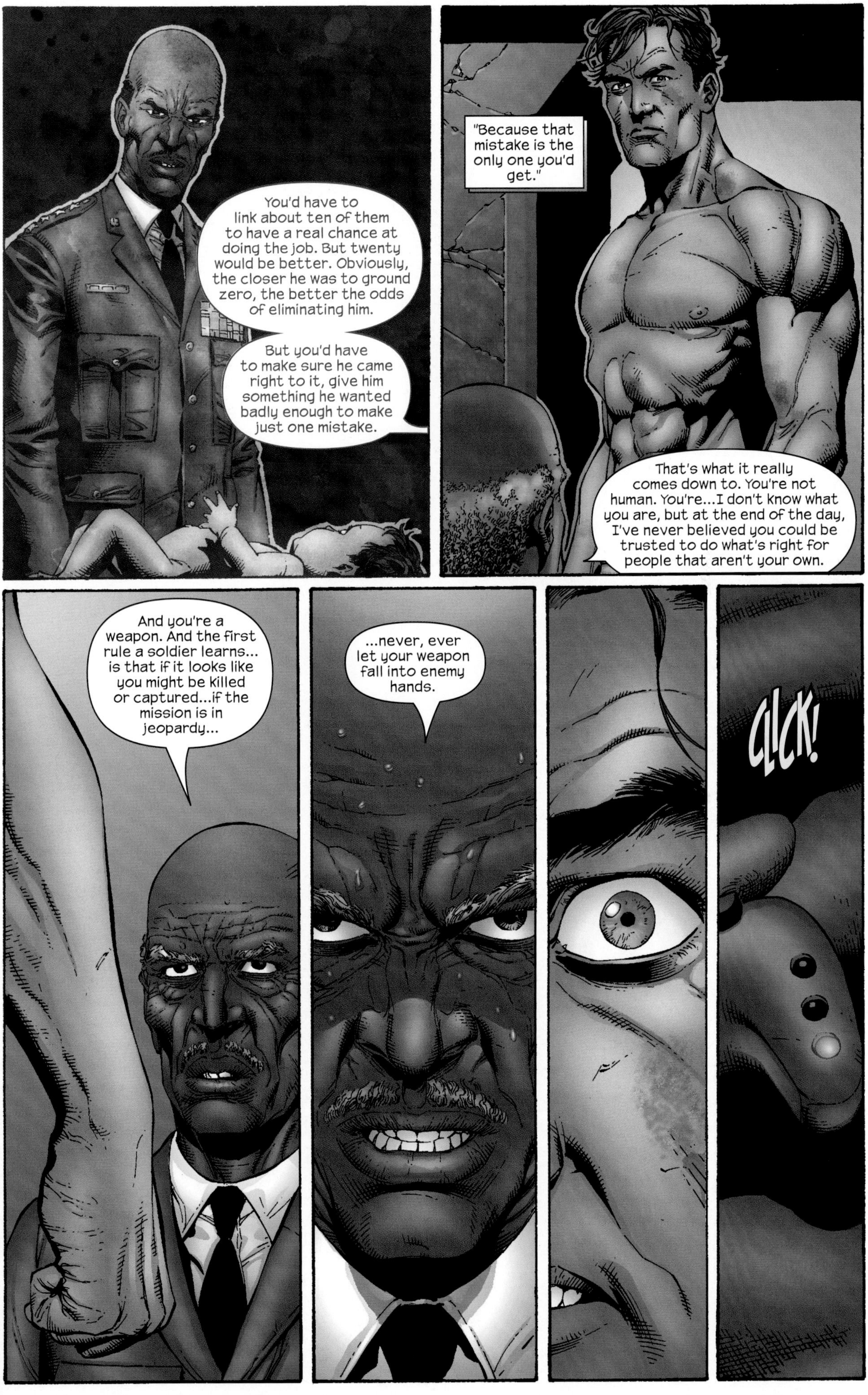
You'd have to link about ten of them to have a real chance at doing the job. But twenty would be better. Obviously, the closer he was to ground zero, the better the odds of eliminating him.
But you'd have to make sure he came right to it, give him something he wanted badly enough to make just one mistake.
"Because that mistake is the only one you'd get."
That's what it really comes down to. You're not human. You're...I don't know what you are, but at the end of the day, I've never believed you could be trusted to do what's right for people that aren't your own.
And you're a weapon. And the first rule a soldier learns... is that if it looks like you might be killed or captured...if the mission is in jeopardy...
...never, ever let your weapon fall into enemy hands.
CLICK!

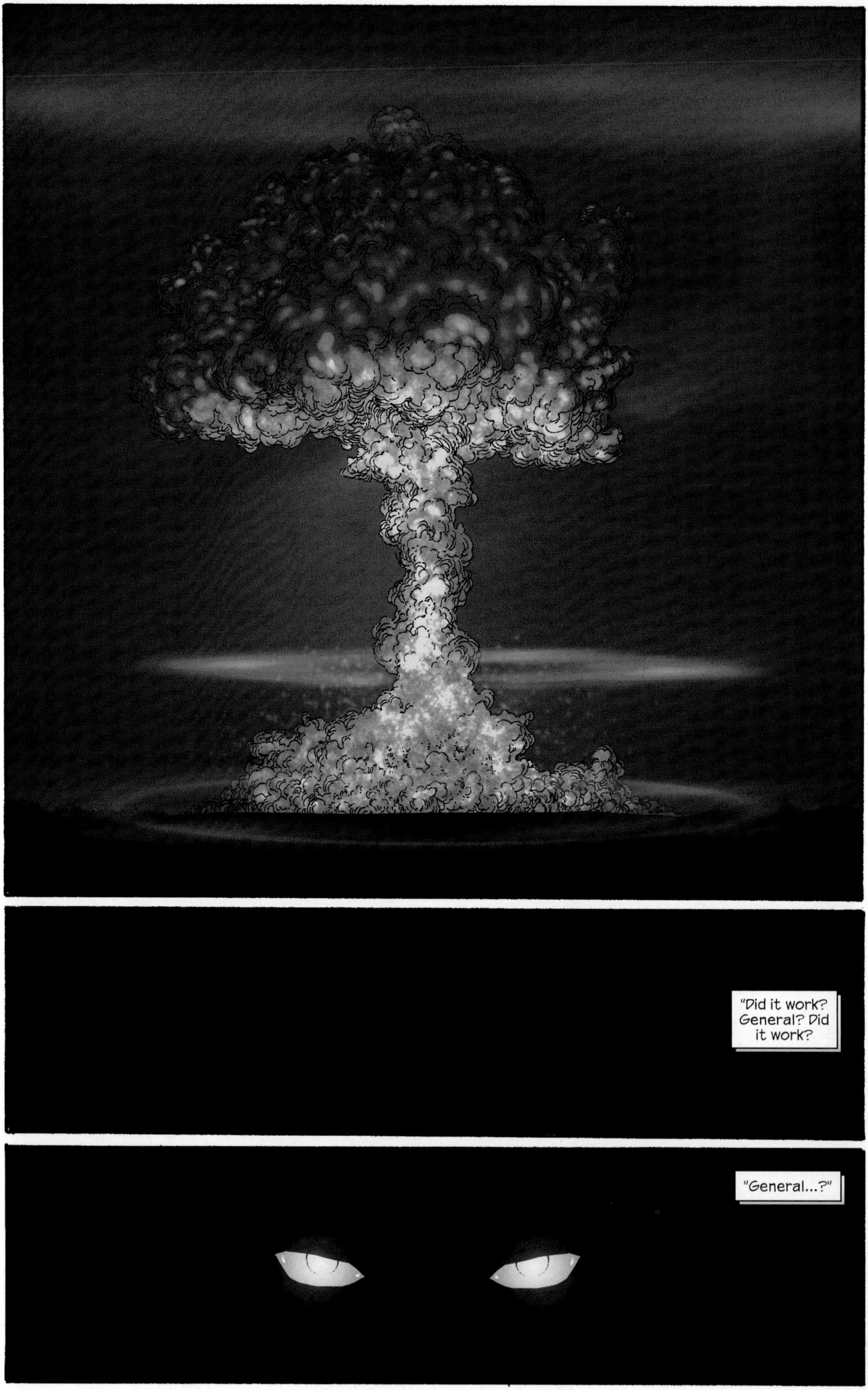
"Did it work? General? Did it work?
"General...?"

Ladies' Night

#10

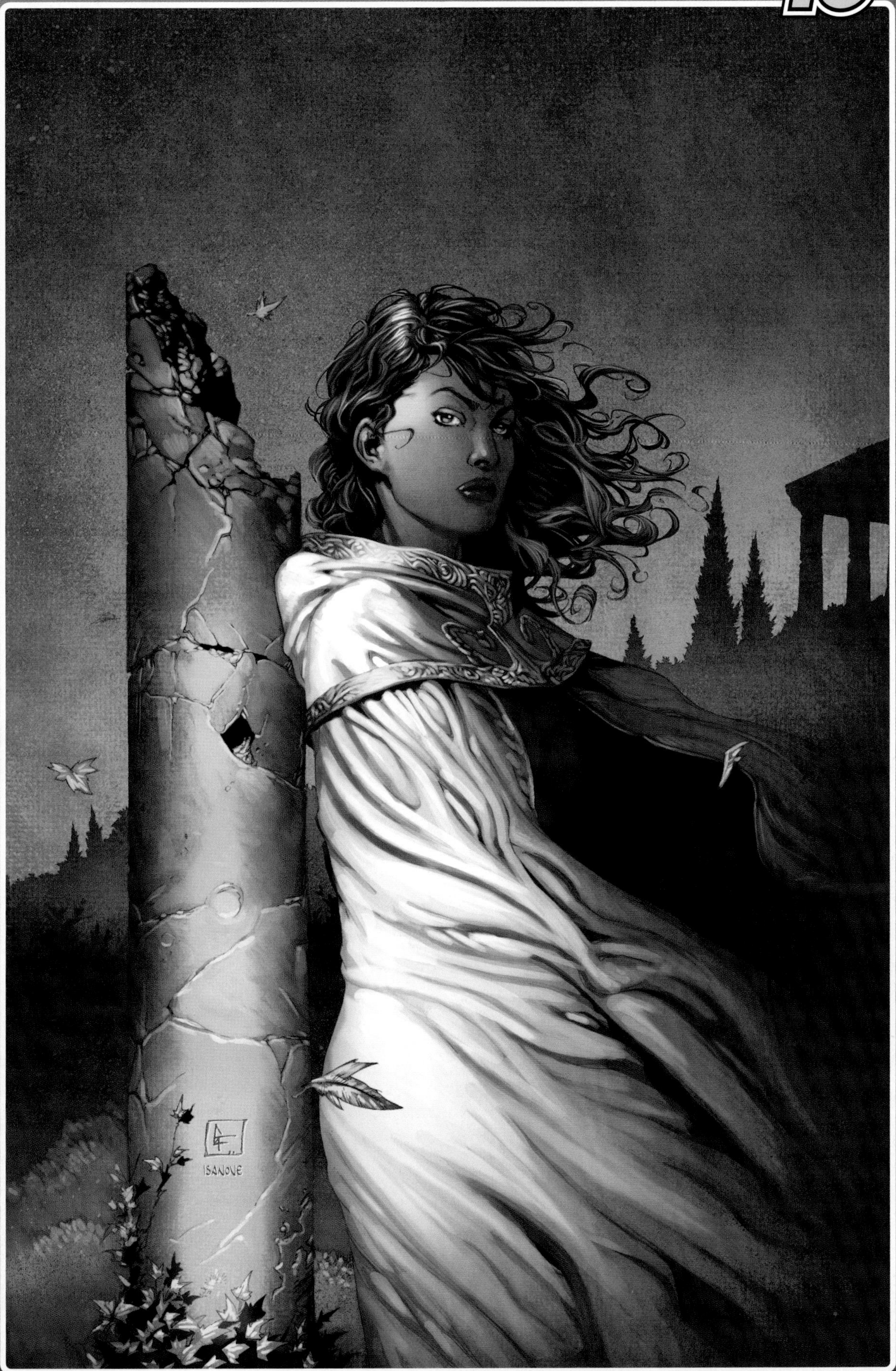
ISANOVE

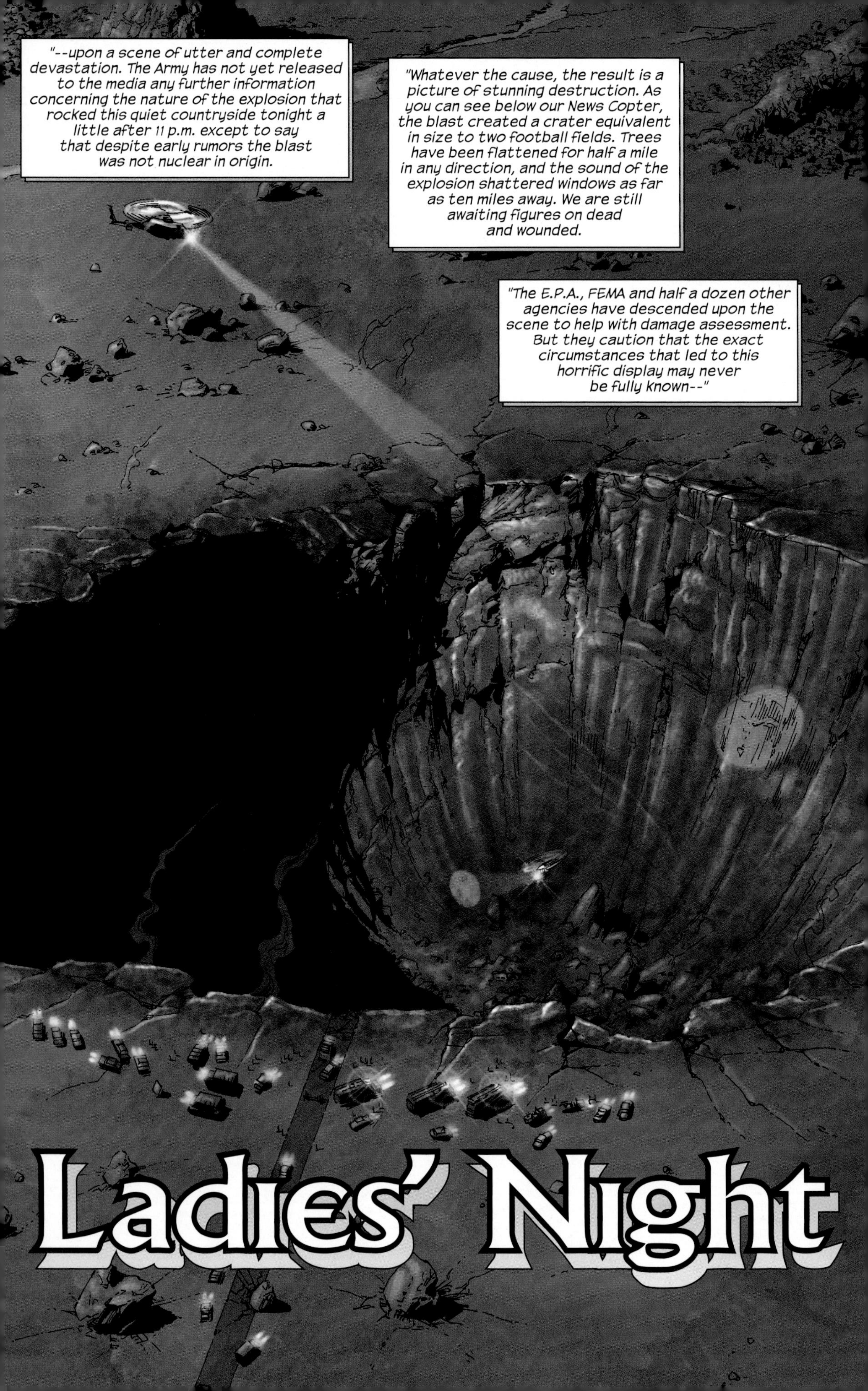
"--upon a scene of utter and complete devastation. The Army has not yet released to the media any further information concerning the nature of the explosion that rocked this quiet countryside tonight a little after 11 p.m. except to say that despite early rumors the blast was not nuclear in origin.
"Whatever the cause, the result is a picture of stunning destruction. As you can see below our News Copter, the blast created a crater equivalent in size to two football fields. Trees have been flattened for half a mile in any direction, and the sound of the explosion shattered windows as far as ten miles away. We are still awaiting figures on dead and wounded.
"The E.P.A., FEMA and half a dozen other agencies have descended upon the scene to help with damage assessment. But they caution that the exact circumstances that led to this horrific display may never be fully known--"
Ladies' Night

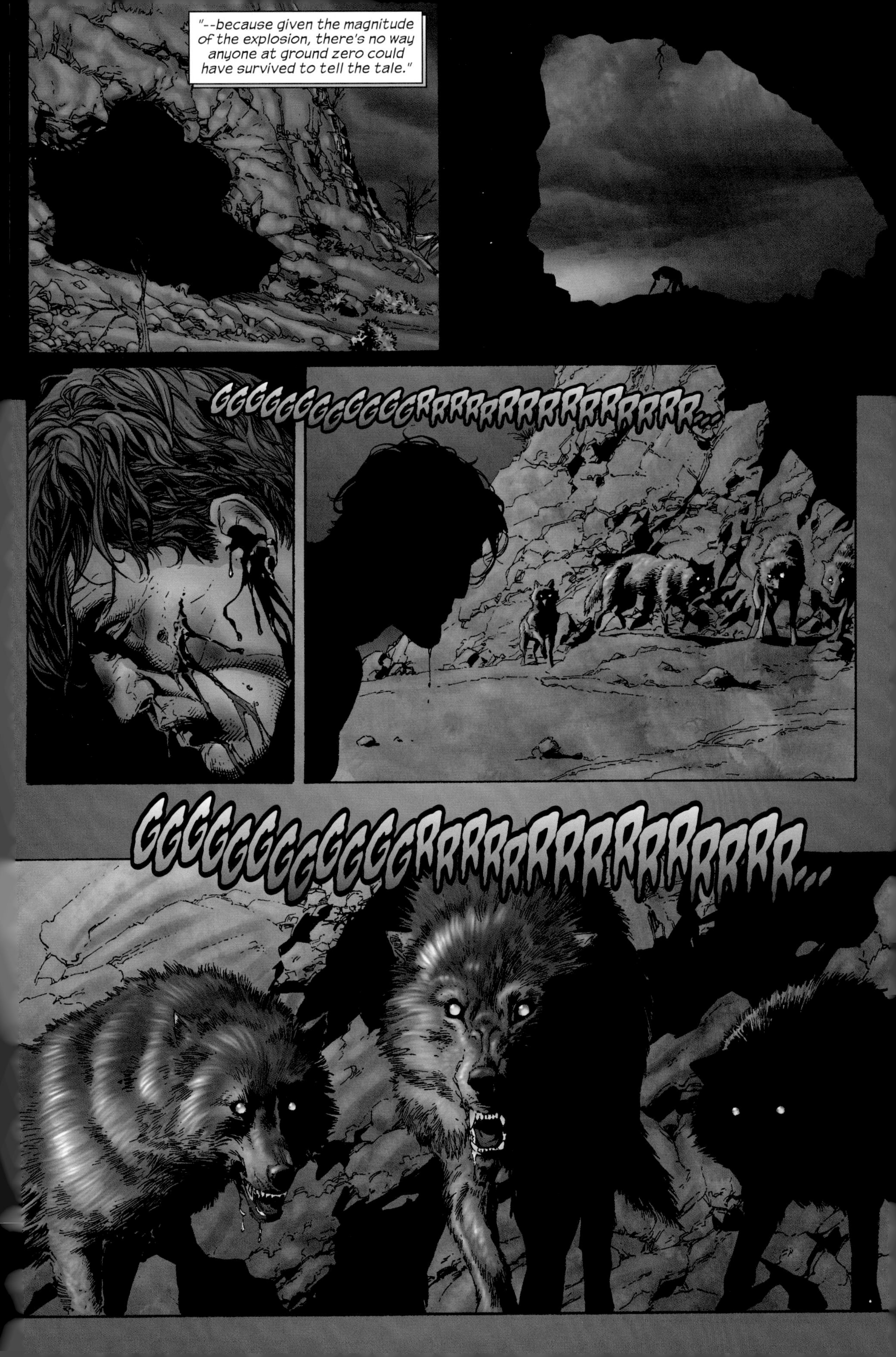
"--because given the magnitude of the explosion, there's no way anyone at ground zero could have survived to tell the tale."
GGGGGGGGGGGRRRRRRRRRRRRRRR...
GGGGGGGGGGGRRRRRRRRRRRRRRR...

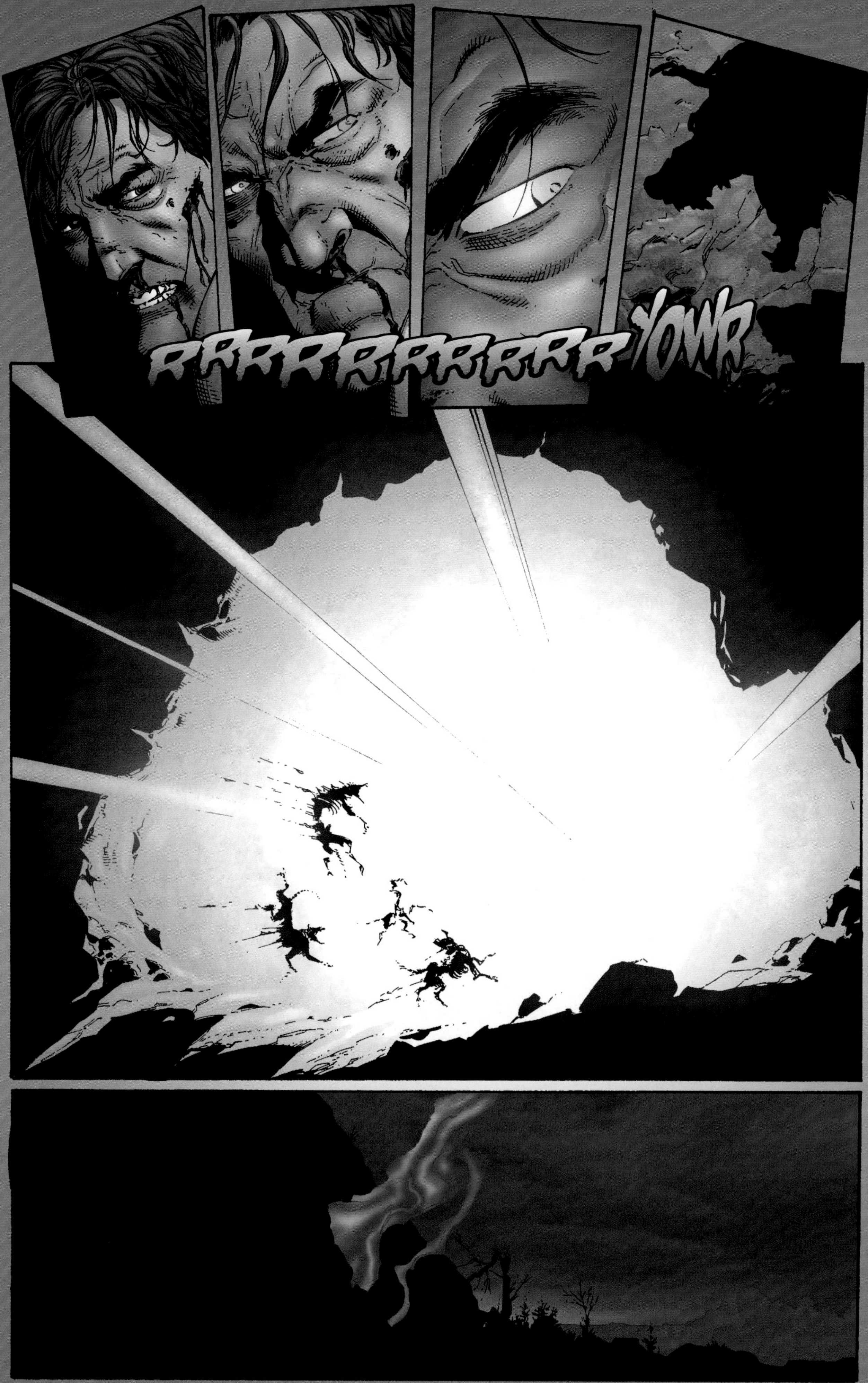
RRRRRRRRRRRRYOWR

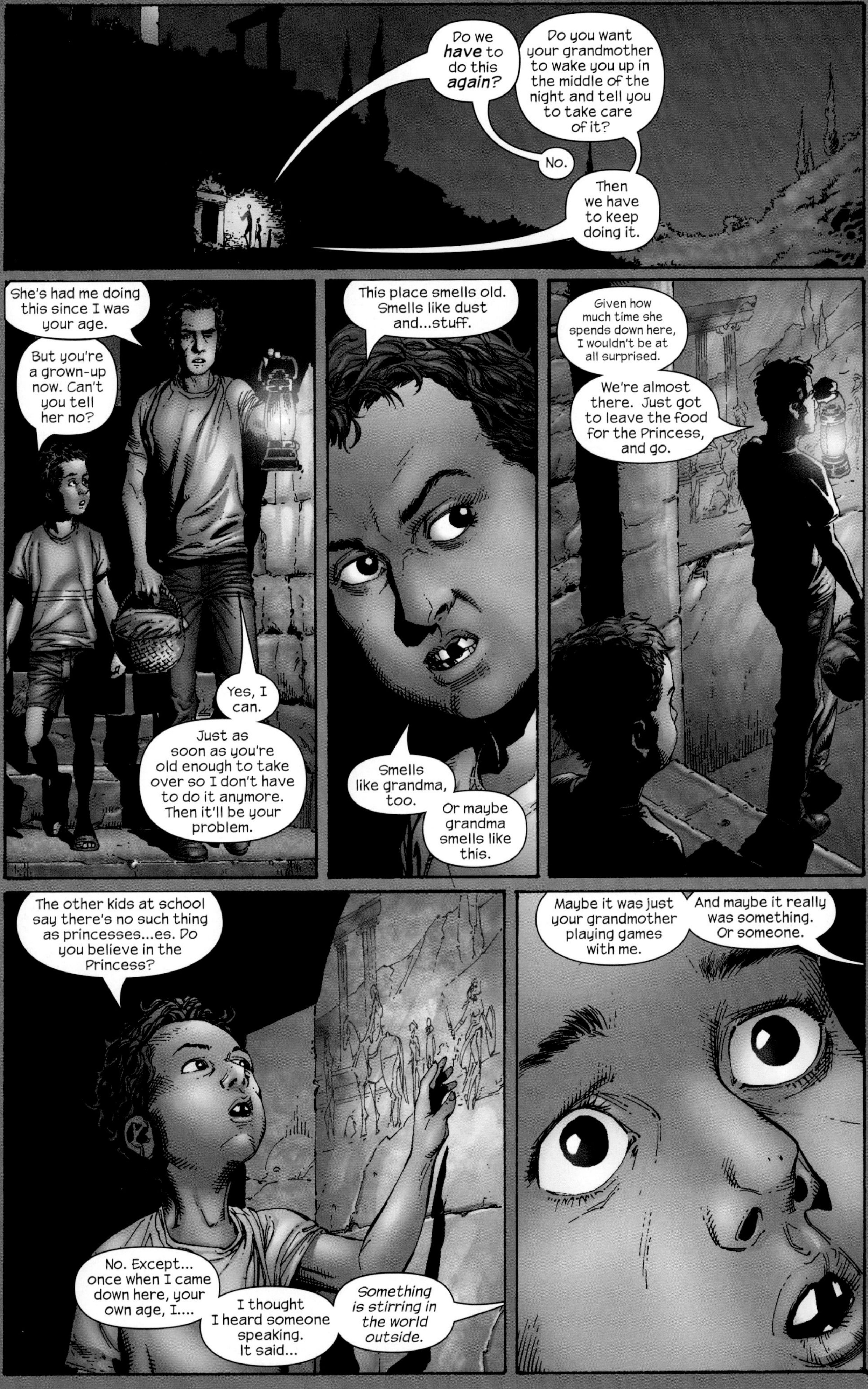
Do we *have* to do this *again*?
Do you want your grandmother to wake you up in the middle of the night and tell you to take care of it?
No.
Then we have to keep doing it.
She's had me doing this since I was your age.
But you're a grown-up now. Can't you tell her no?
Yes, I can.
Just as soon as you're old enough to take over so I don't have to do it anymore. Then it'll be your problem.
This place smells old. Smells like dust and...stuff.
Smells like grandma, too.
Or maybe grandma smells like this.
Given how much time she spends down here, I wouldn't be at all surprised.
We're almost there. Just got to leave the food for the Princess, and go.
The other kids at school say there's no such thing as princesses...es. Do you believe in the Princess?
No. Except... once when I came down here, your own age, I....
I thought I heard someone speaking. It said...
Something is stirring in the world outside.
Maybe it was just your grandmother playing games with me.
And maybe it really was something. Or someone.

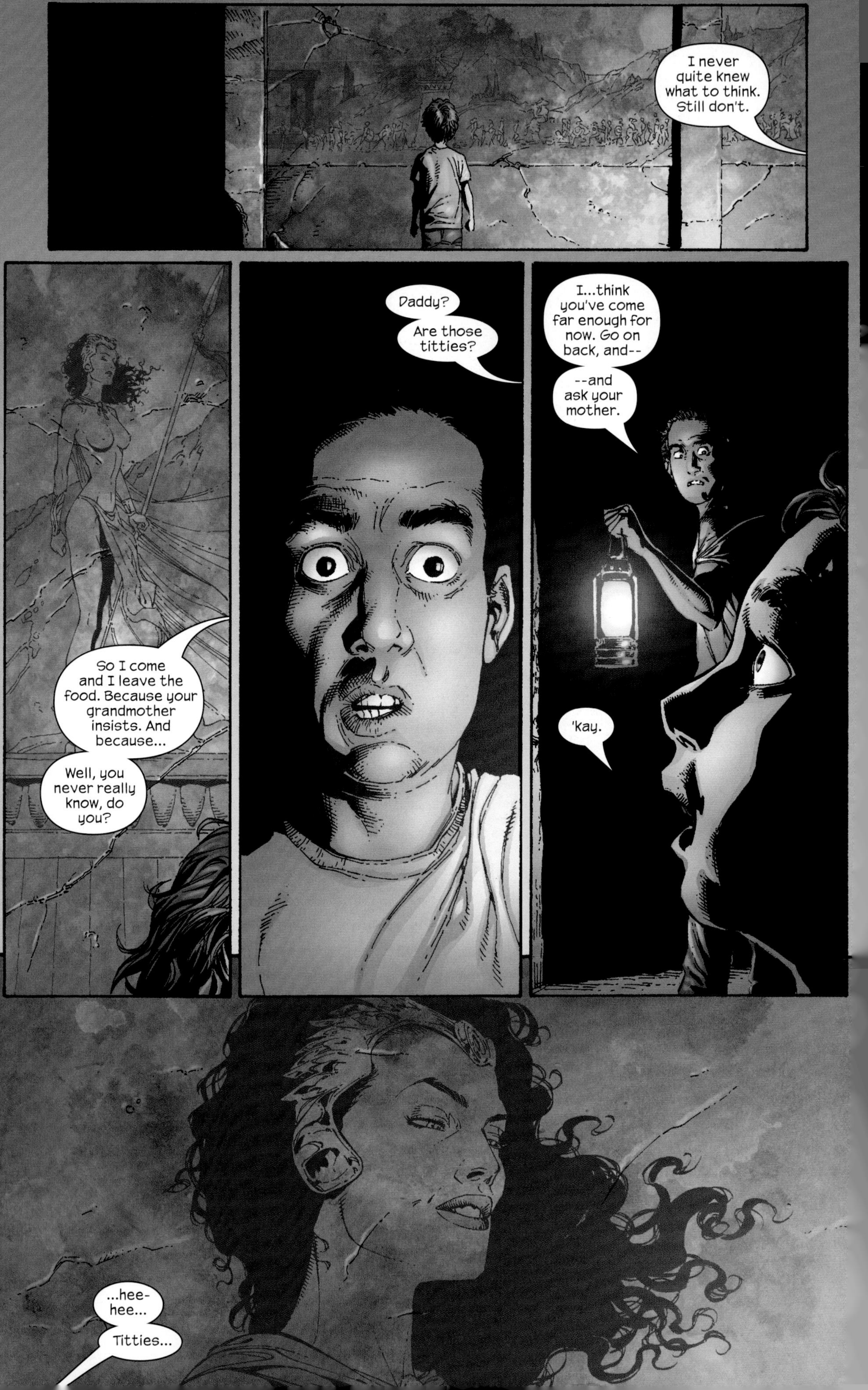
I never quite knew what to think. Still don't.
So I come and I leave the food. Because your grandmother insists. And because...
Well, you never really know, do you?
Daddy?
Are those titties?
I...think you've come far enough for now. Go on back, and--
--and ask your mother.
'kay.
...hee-hee...
Titties...

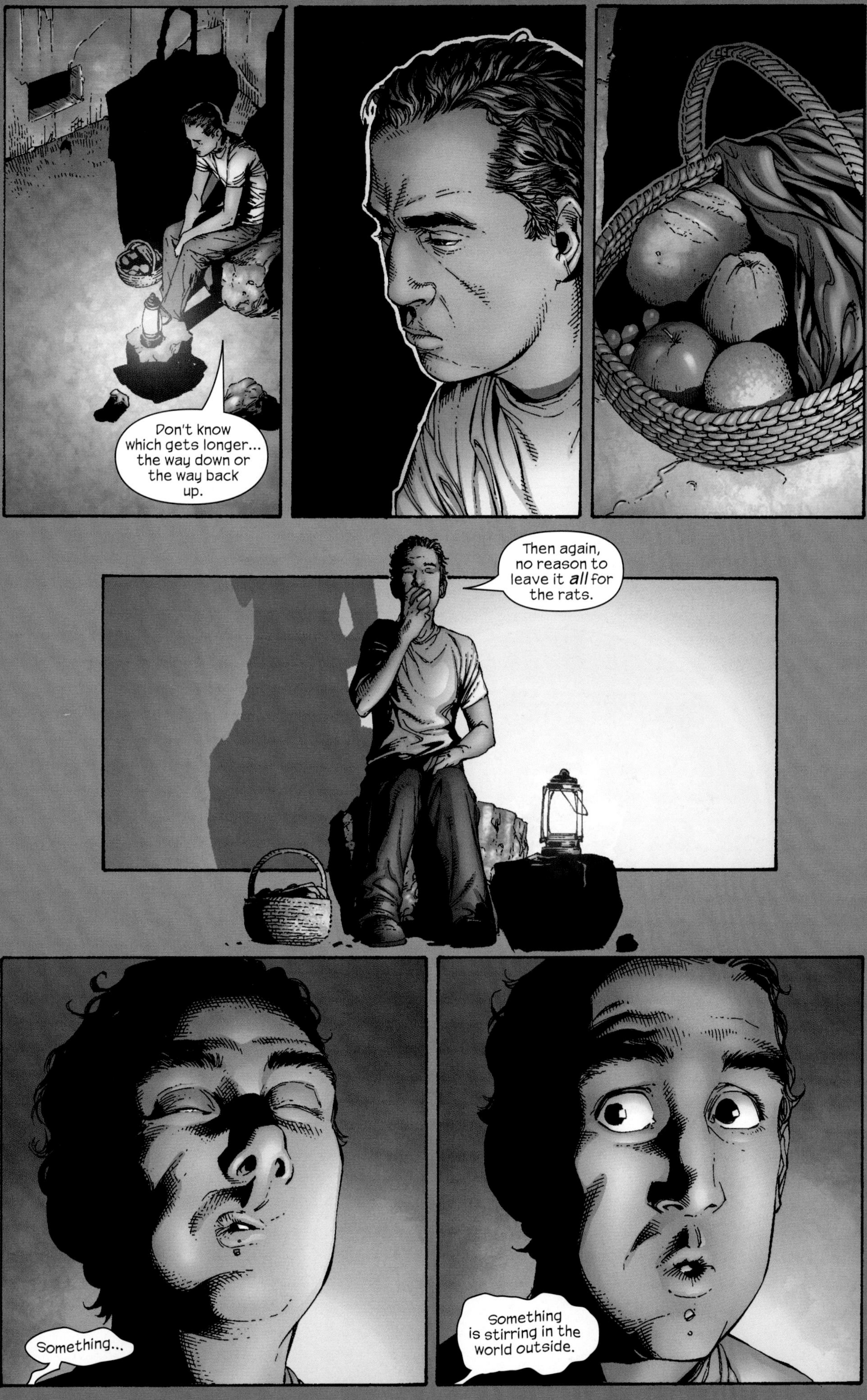
Don't know which gets longer... the way down or the way back up.
Then again, no reason to leave it *all* for the rats.
Something...
Something is stirring in the world outside.

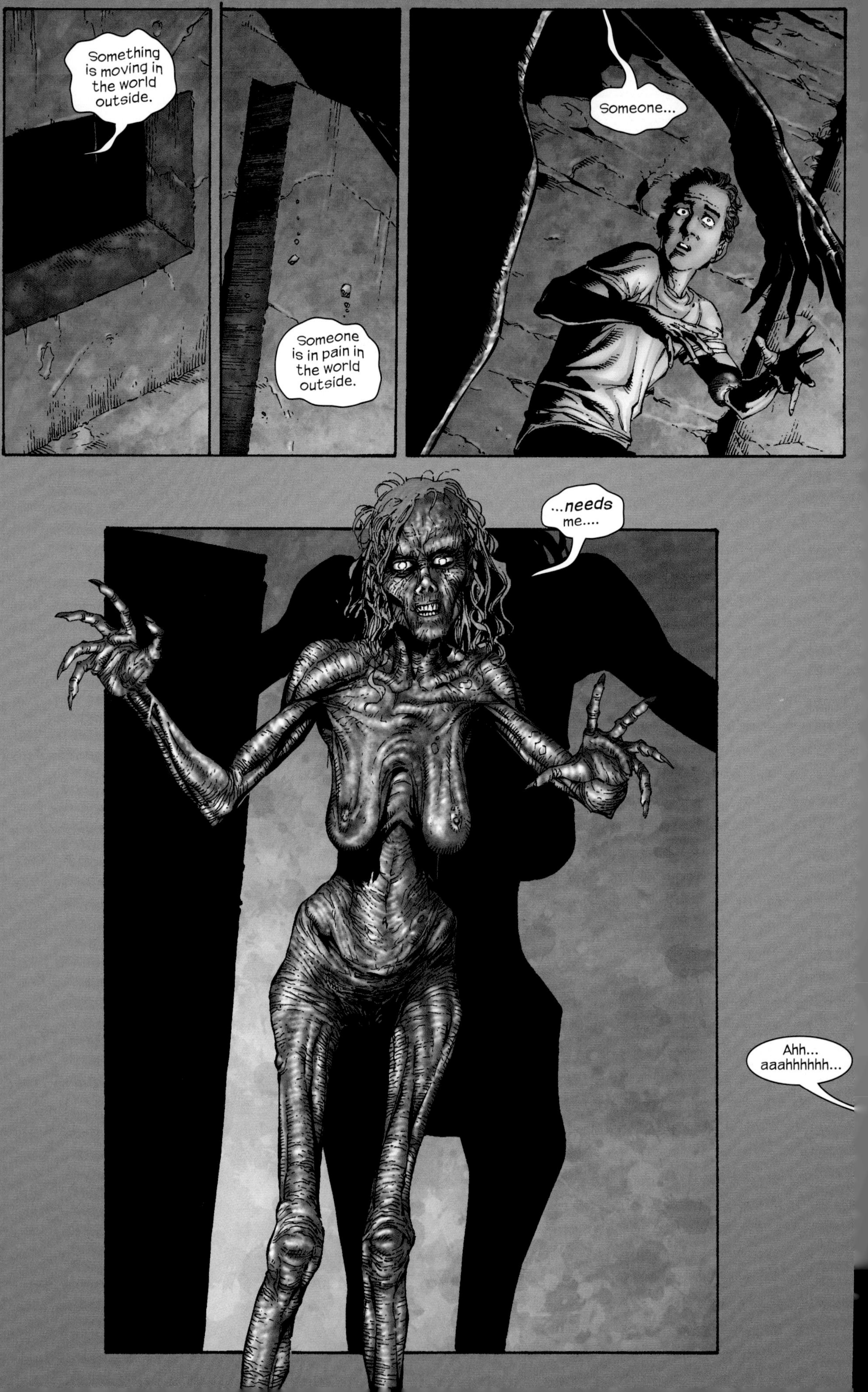
Something is moving in the world outside.
Someone is in pain in the world outside.
Someone...
...needs me....
Ahh... aaahhhhhh...

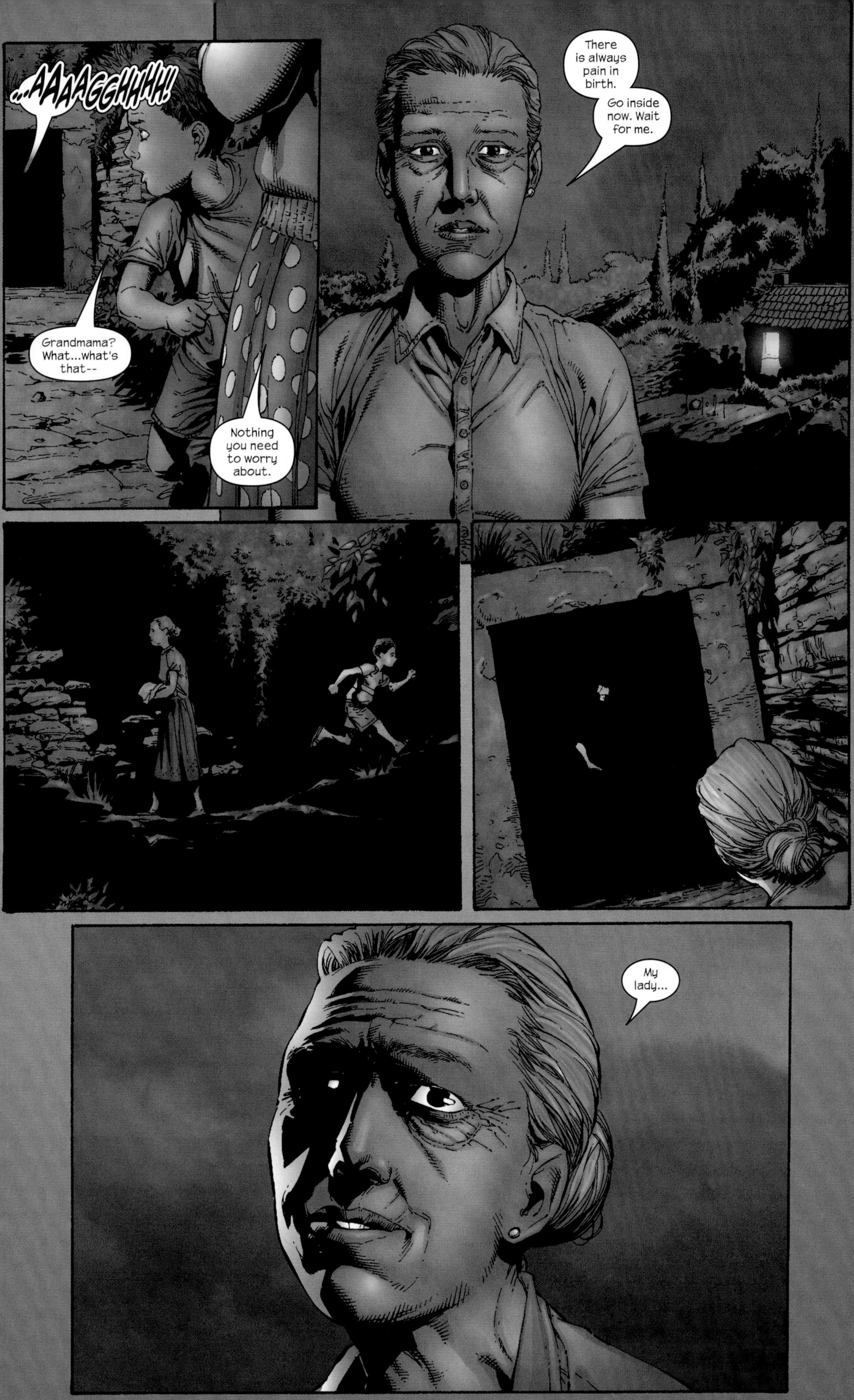
..AAAAGGHHHH!
Grandmama? What...what's that--
Nothing you need to worry about.
There is always pain in birth.
Go inside now. Wait for me.
My lady...

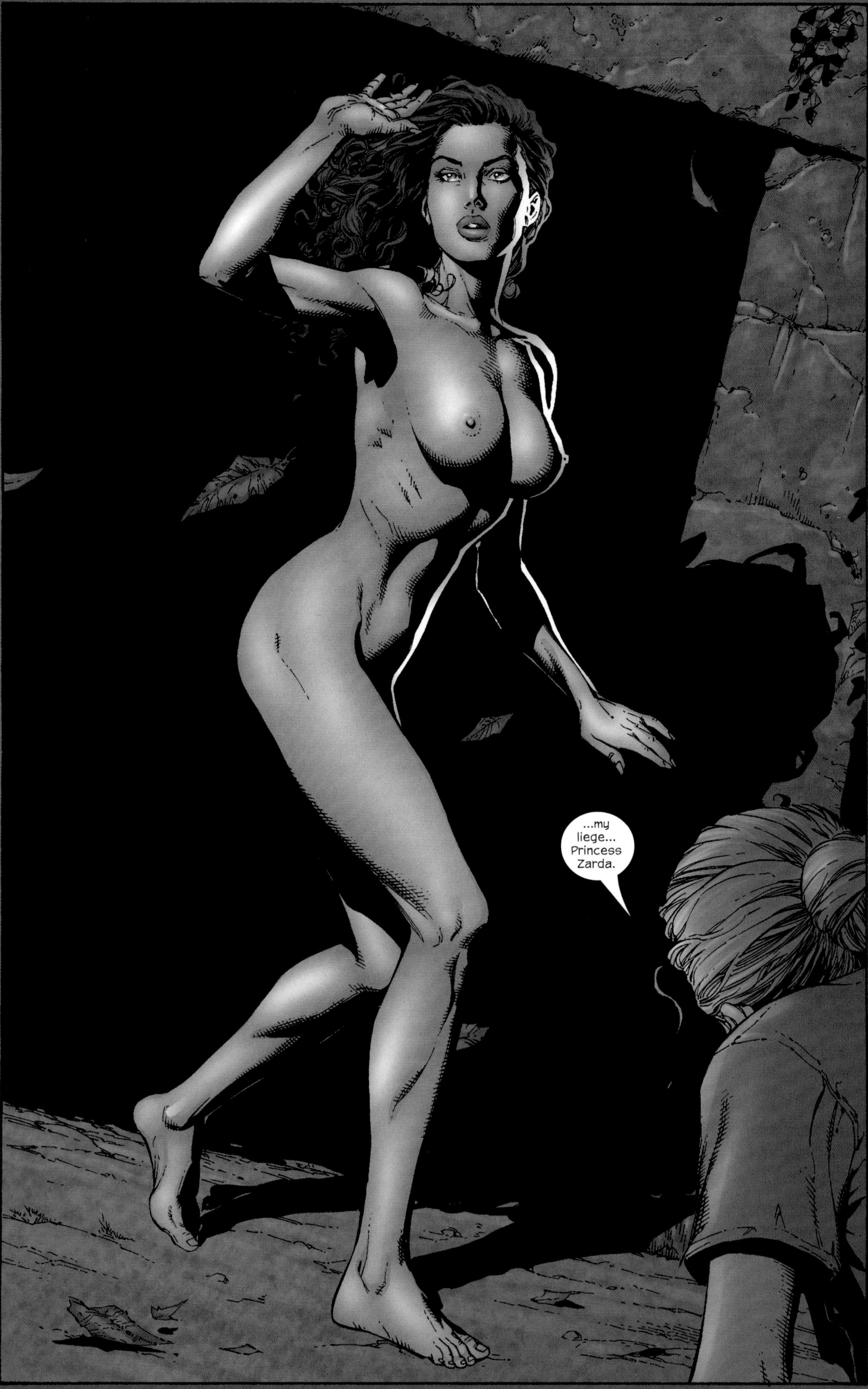
...my liege... Princess Zarda.

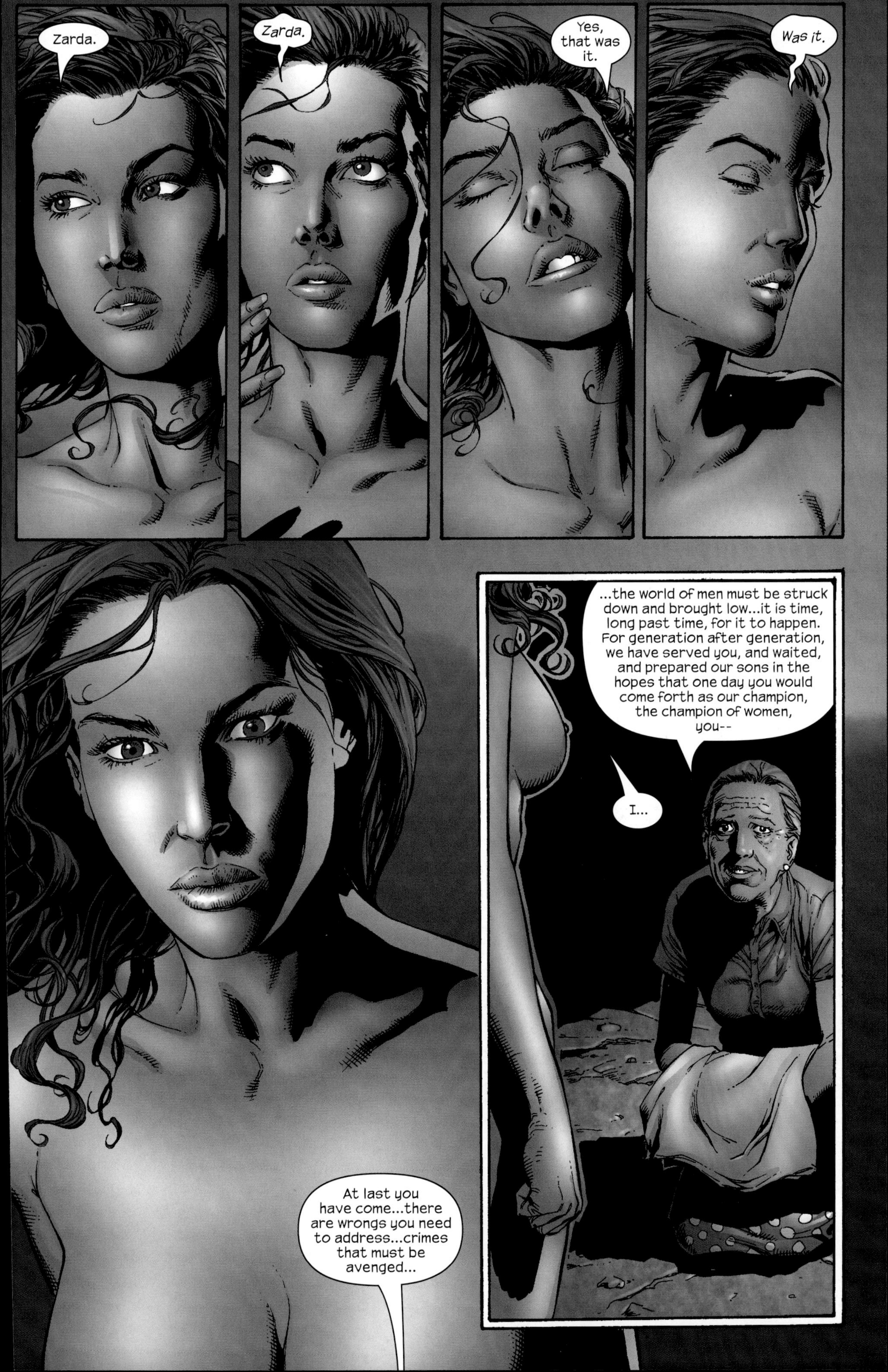
Zarda.
Zarda.
Yes, that was it.
Was it.
...the world of men must be struck down and brought low...it is time, long past time, for it to happen. For generation after generation, we have served you, and waited, and prepared our sons in the hopes that one day you would come forth as our champion, the champion of women, you--
I...
At last you have come...there are wrongs you need to address...crimes that must be avenged...

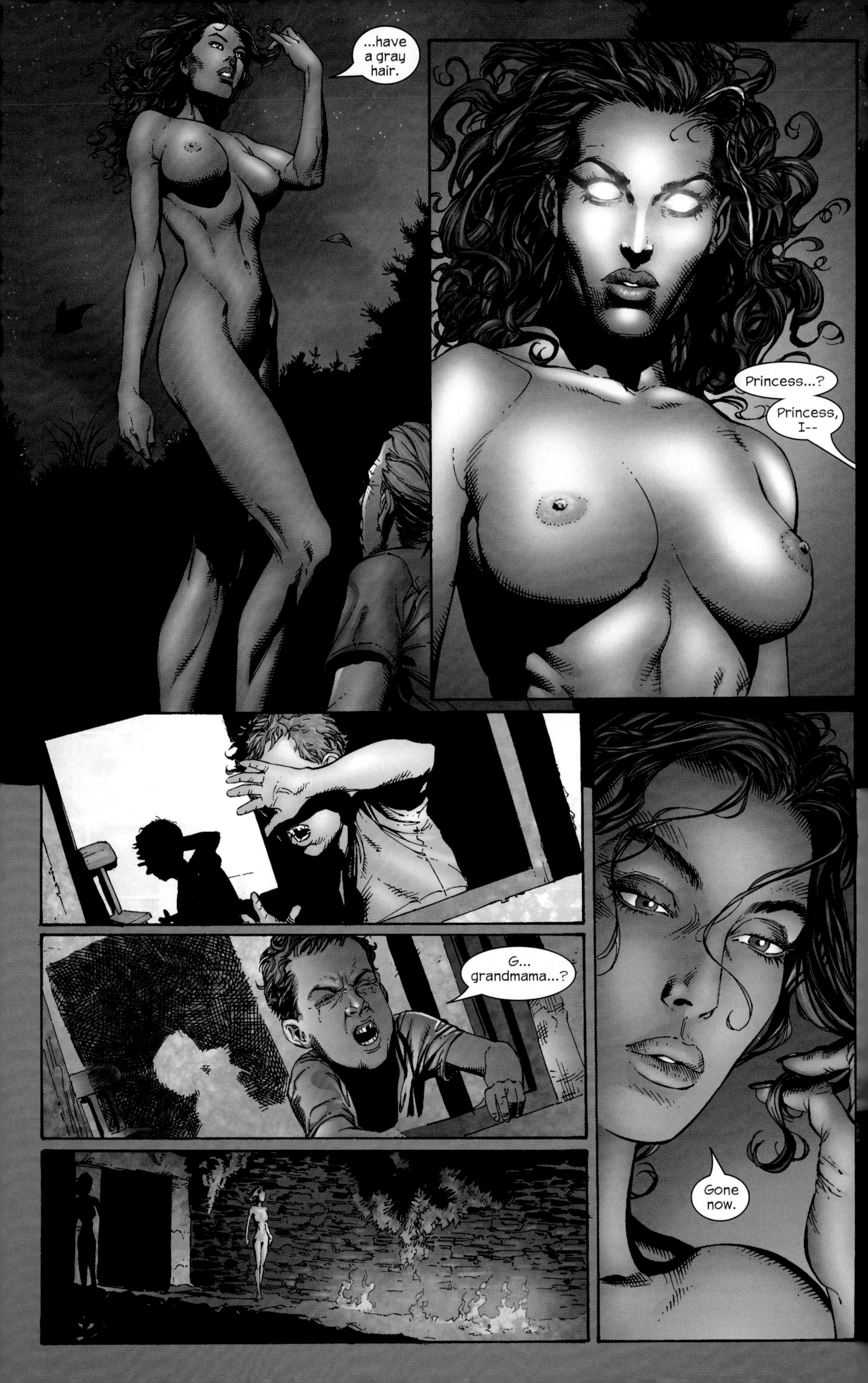
...have a gray hair.
Princess...?
Princess, I--
G... grandmama...?
Gone now.

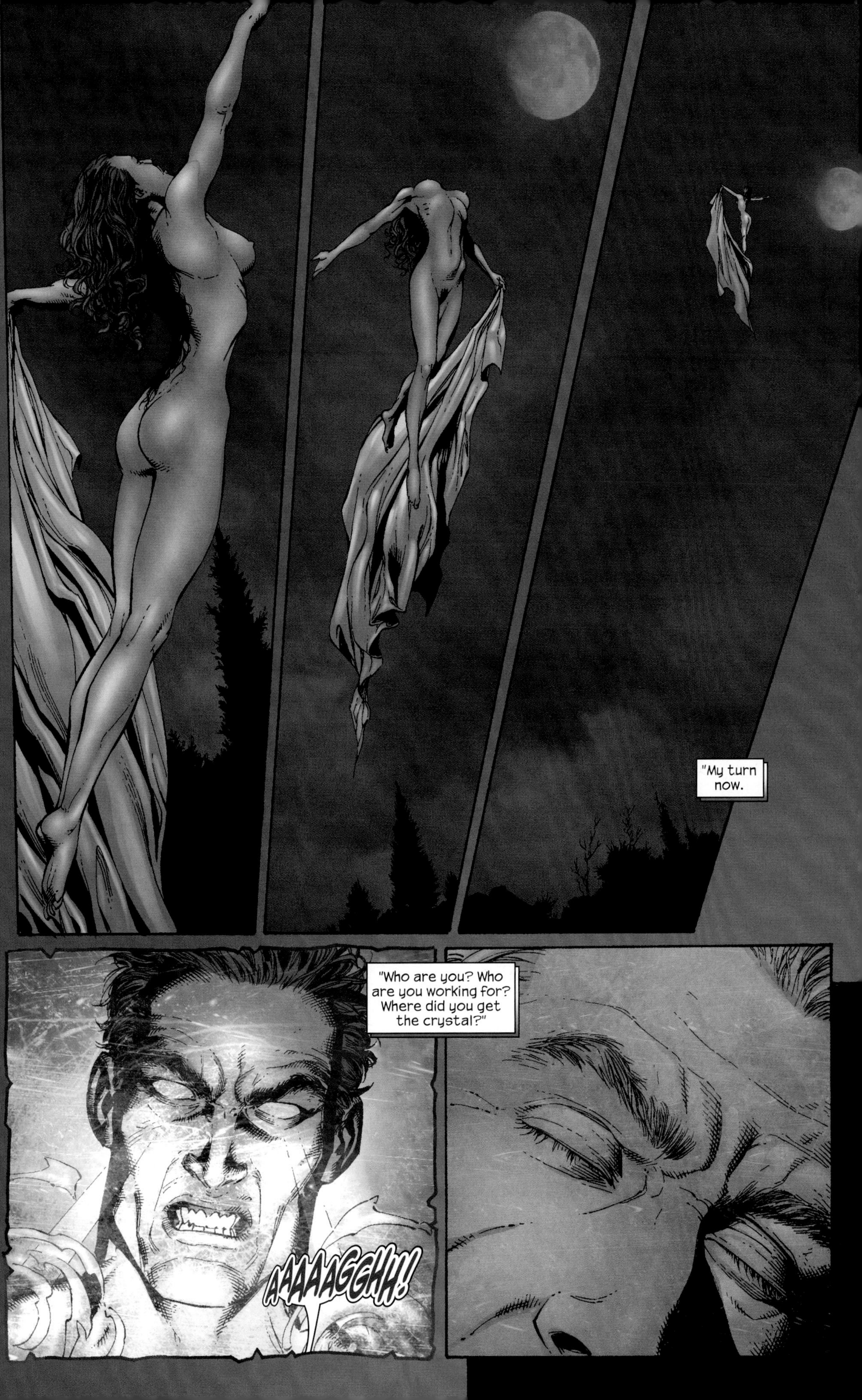
"My turn now.
"Who are you? Who are you working for? Where did you get the crystal?"
AAAAAGGHH!

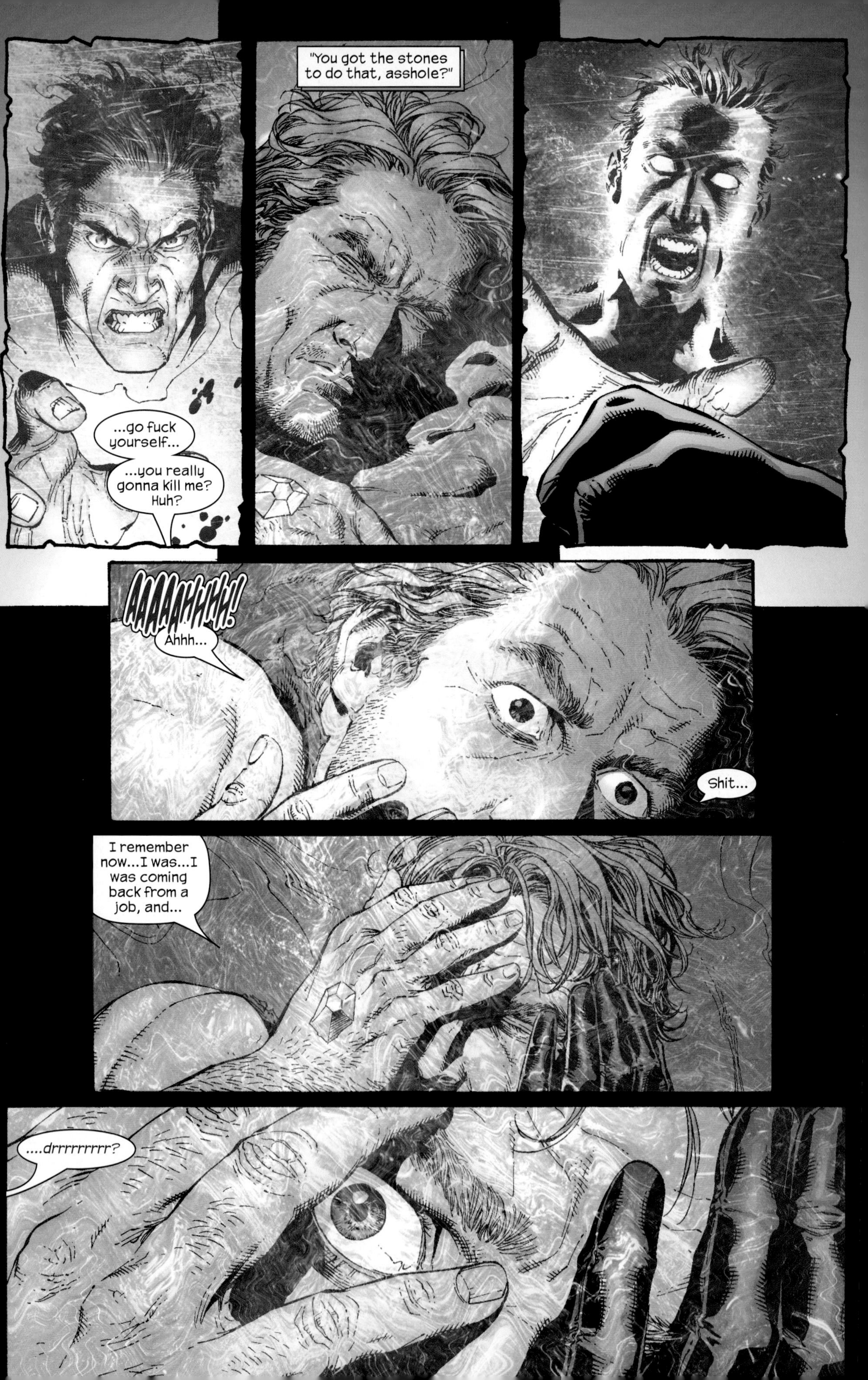
...go fuck yourself...
...you really gonna kill me? Huh?
"You got the stones to do that, asshole?"
AAAAAHHHH!
Ahhh...
Shit...
I remember now...I was...I was coming back from a job, and...
....drrrrrrrrr?

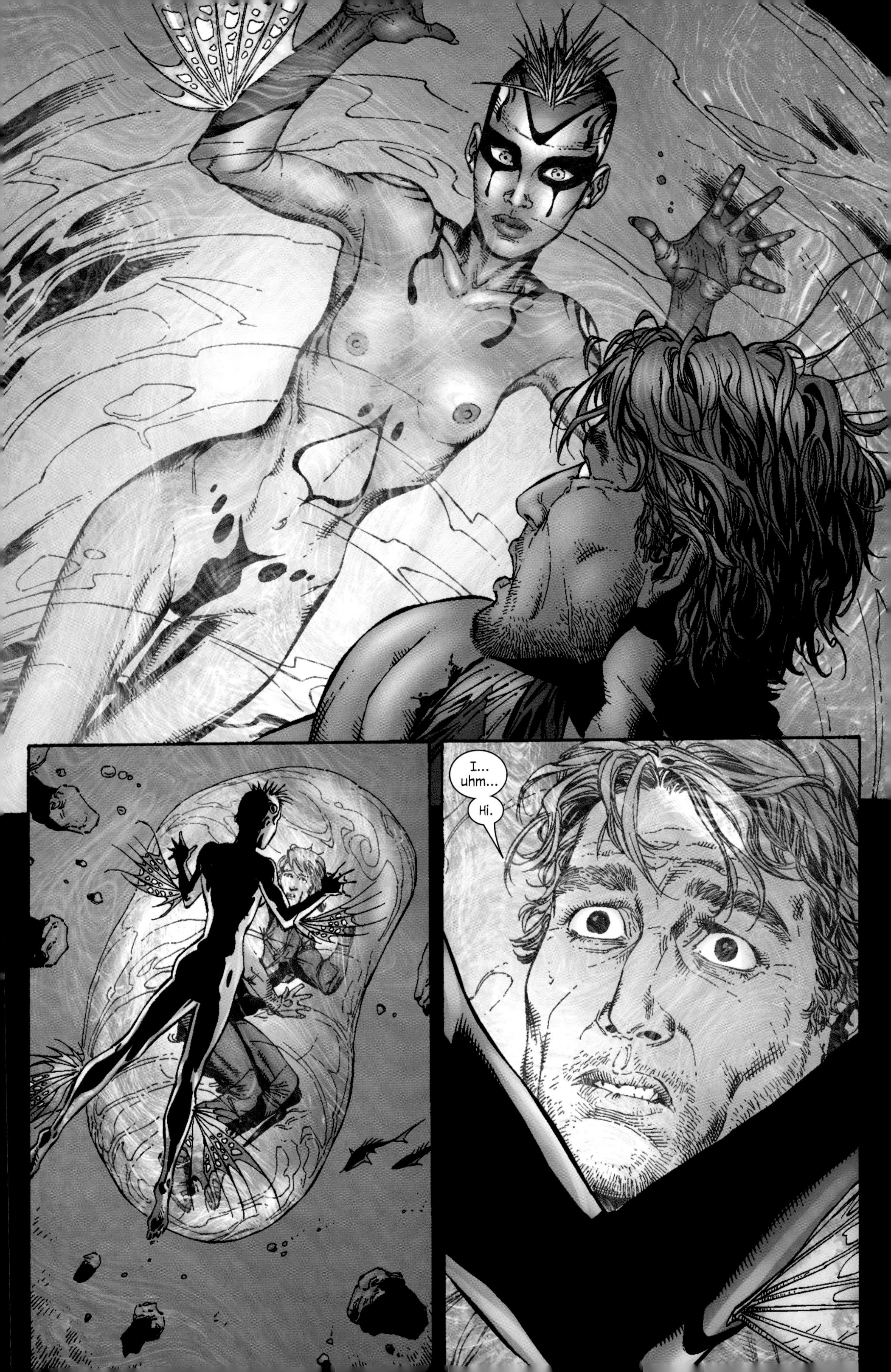
I... uhm...
Hi.

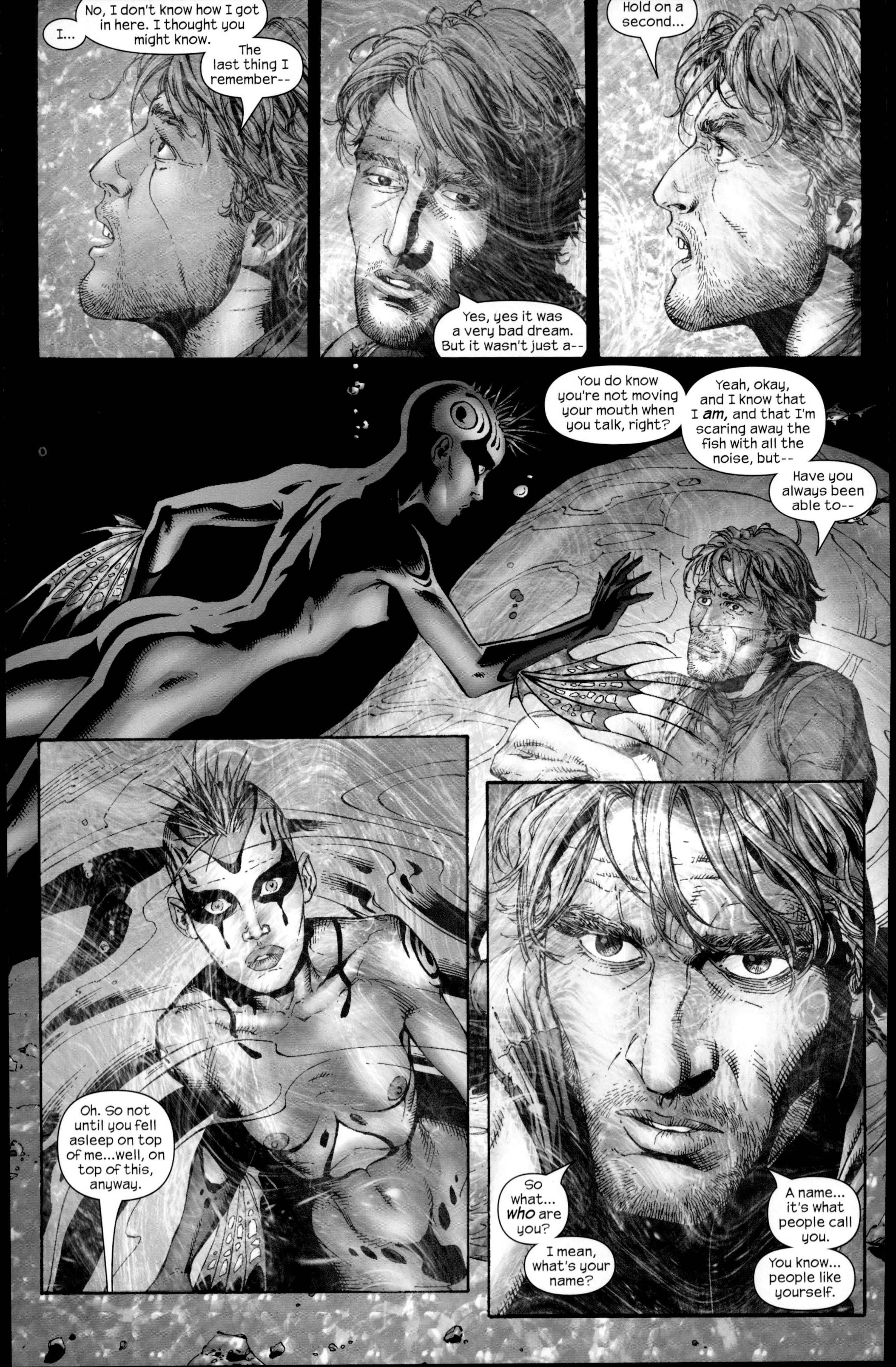

I...
No, I don't know how I got in here. I thought you might know.
The last thing I remember--
Yes, yes it was a very bad dream. But it wasn't just a--
Hold on a second...
You do know you're not moving your mouth when you talk, right?
Yeah, okay, and I know that I *am,* and that I'm scaring away the fish with all the noise, but--
Have you always been able to--
Oh. So not until you fell asleep on top of me...well, on top of this, anyway.
So what... *who* are you?
I mean, what's your name?
A name... it's what people call you.
You know... people like yourself.

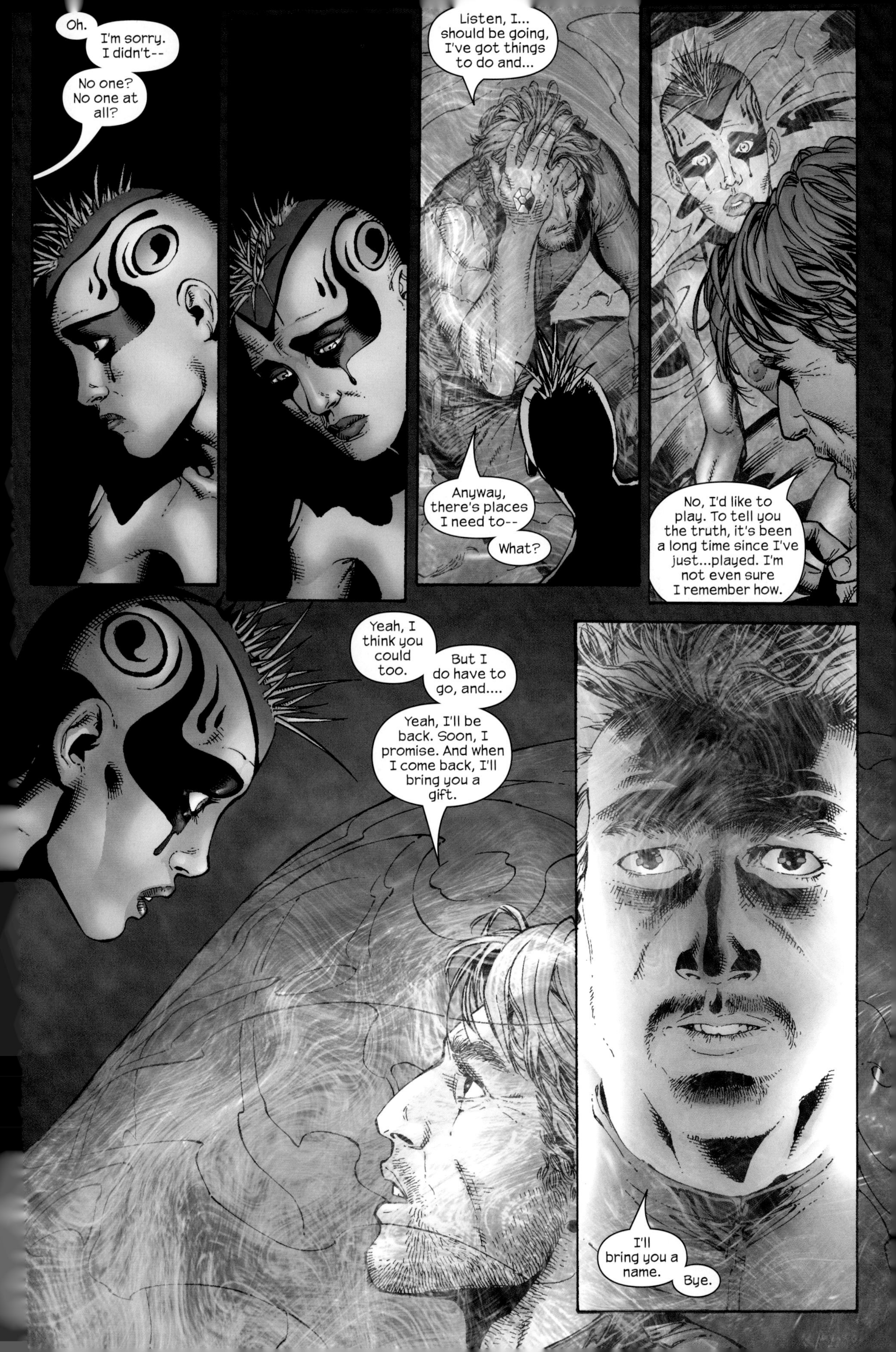
Oh.
I'm sorry. I didn't--
No one? No one at all?
Listen, I... should be going, I've got things to do and...
Anyway, there's places I need to--
What?
No, I'd like to play. To tell you the truth, it's been a long time since I've just...played. I'm not even sure I remember how.
Yeah, I think you could too.
But I do have to go, and....
Yeah, I'll be back. Soon, I promise. And when I come back, I'll bring you a gift.
I'll bring you a name.
Bye.

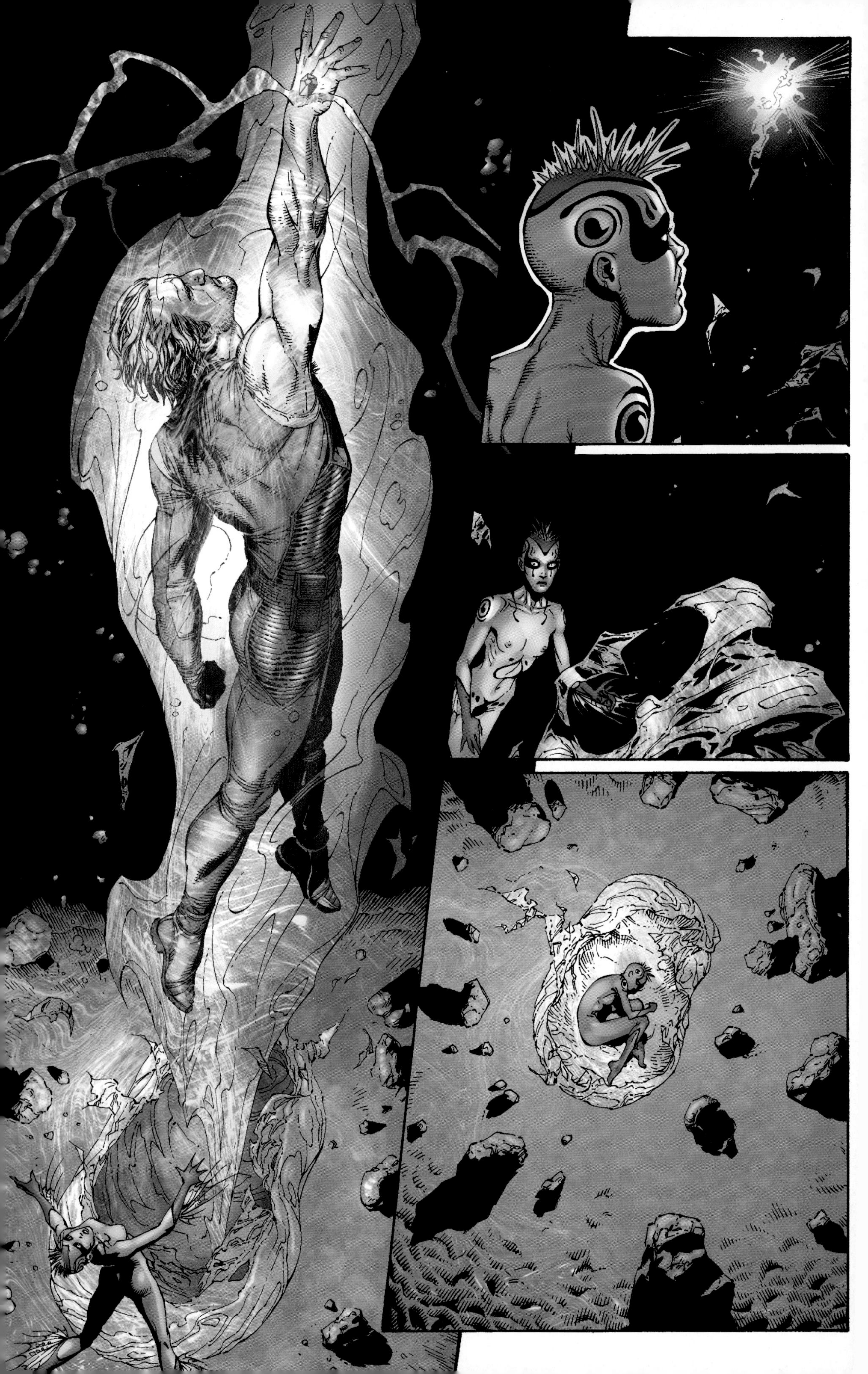

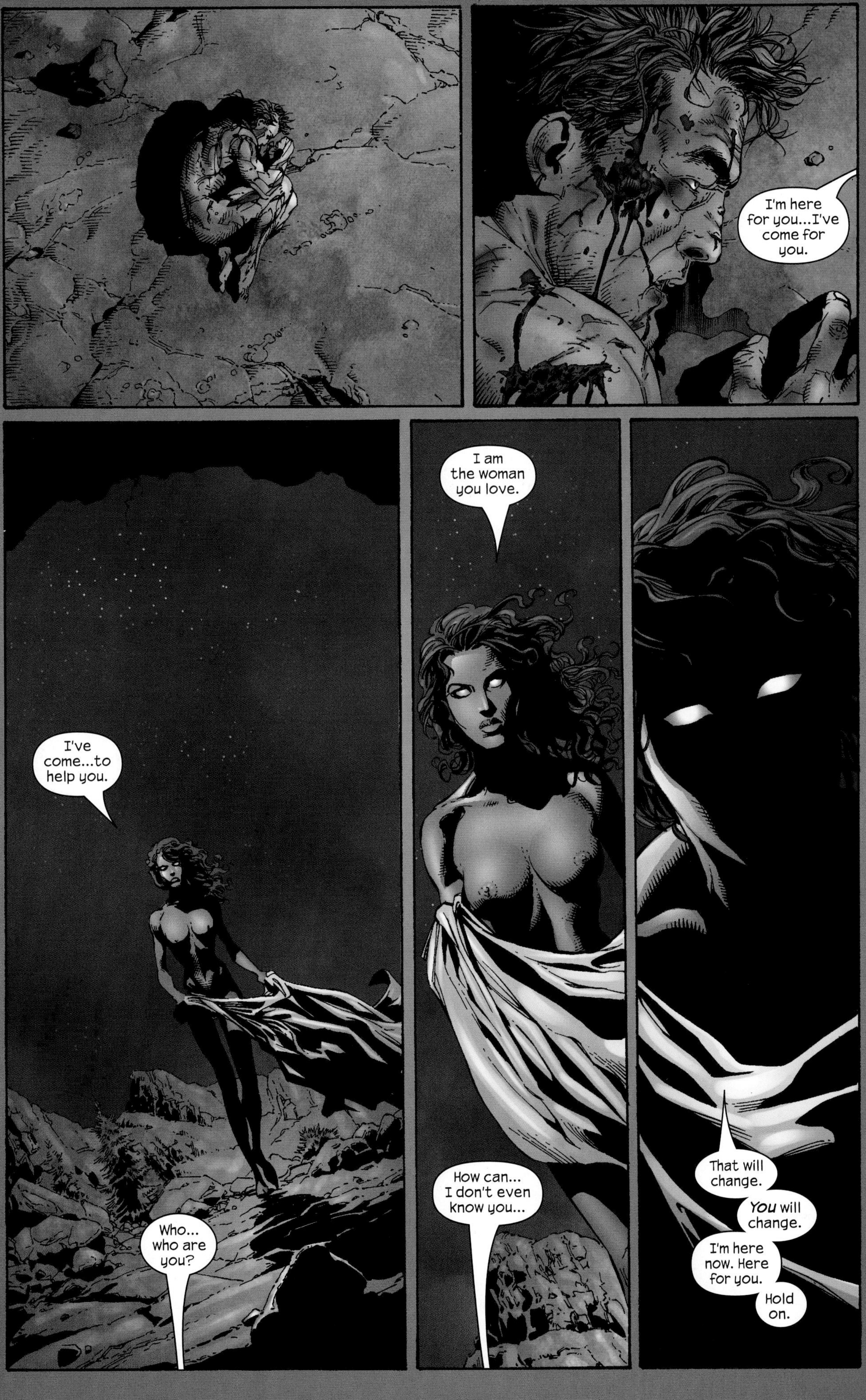
I'm here for you...I've come for you.
I've come...to help you.
Who... who are you?
I am the woman you love.
How can... I don't even know you...
That will change.
YOU will change.
I'm here now. Here for you.
Hold on.

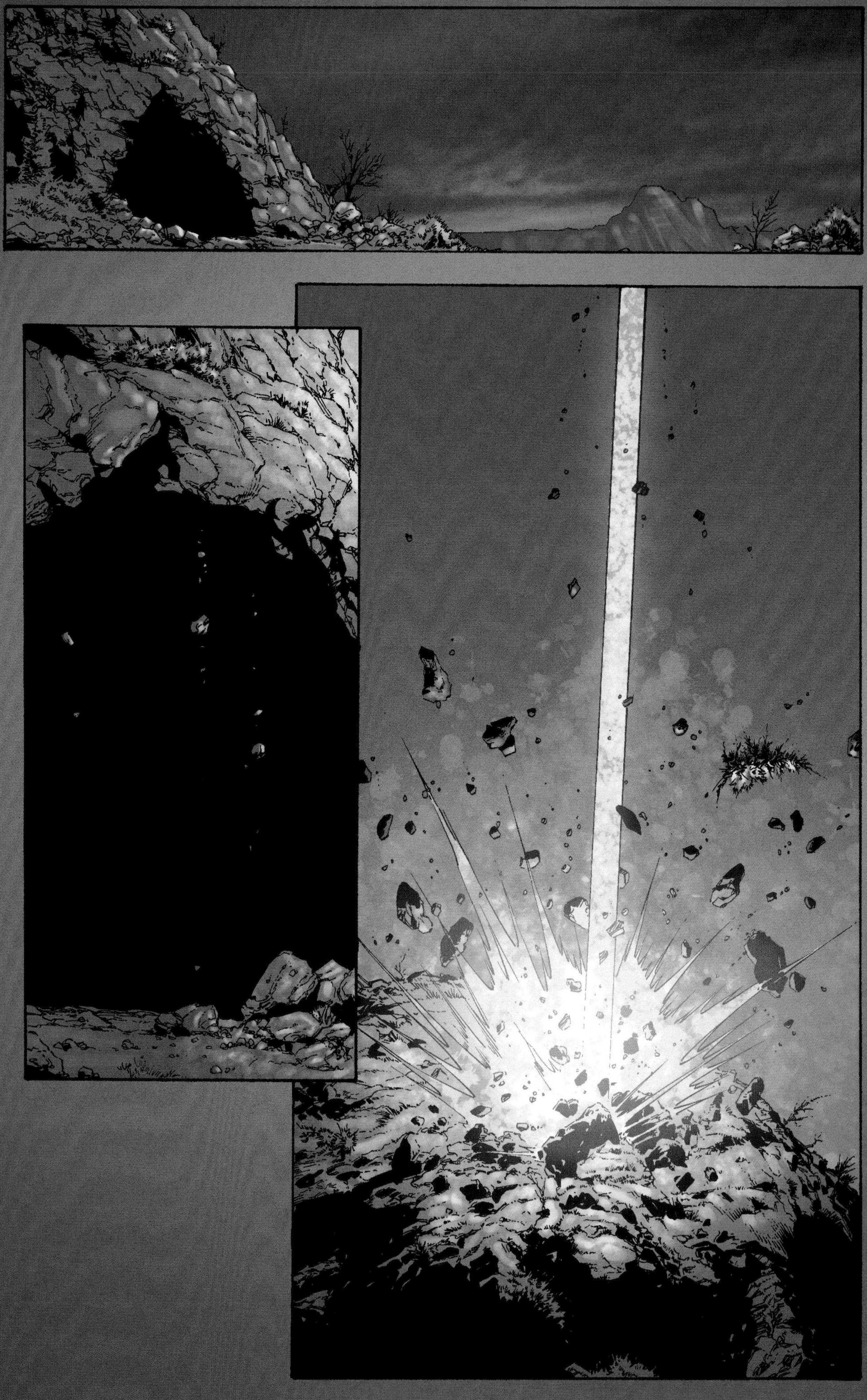

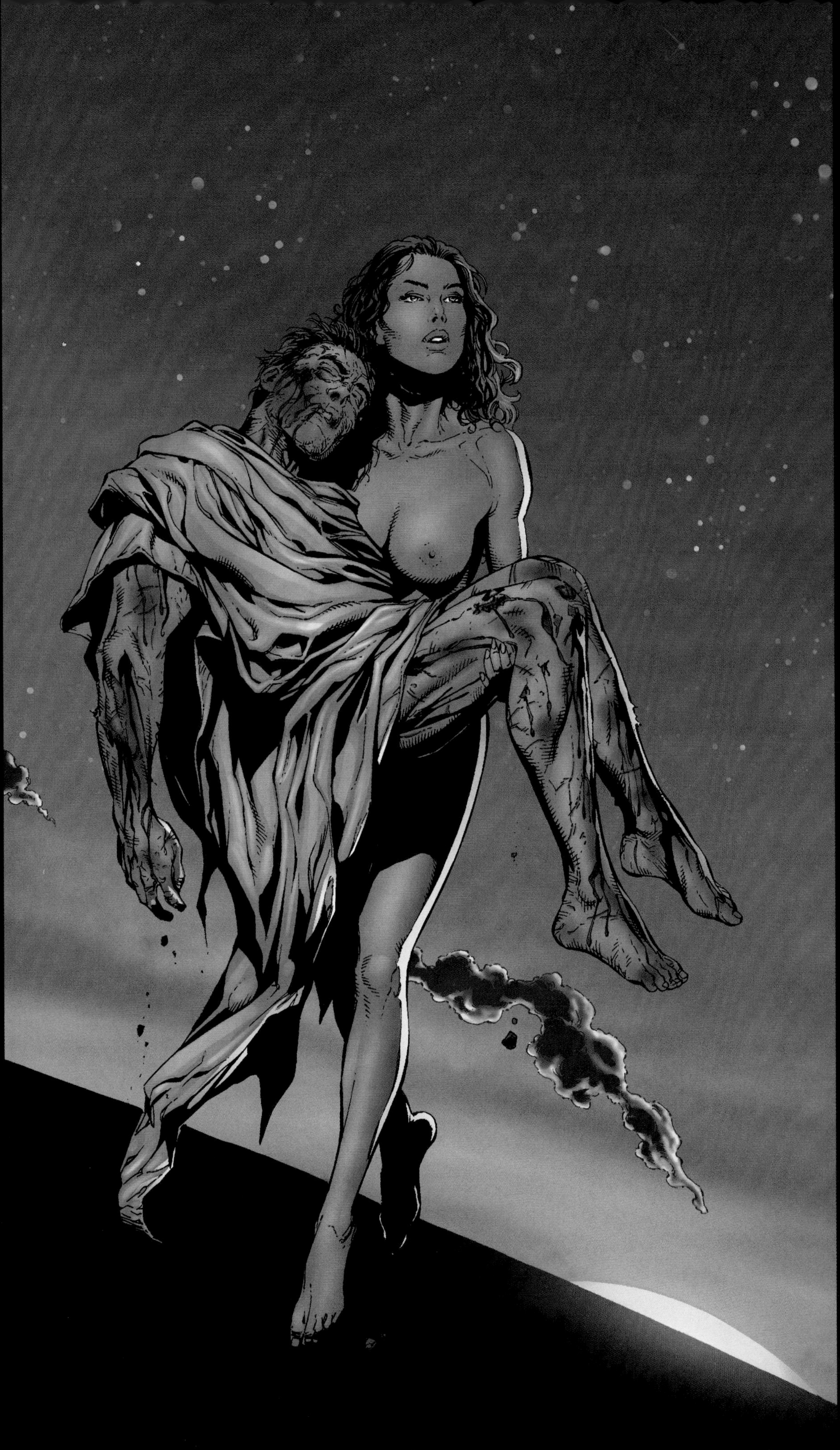

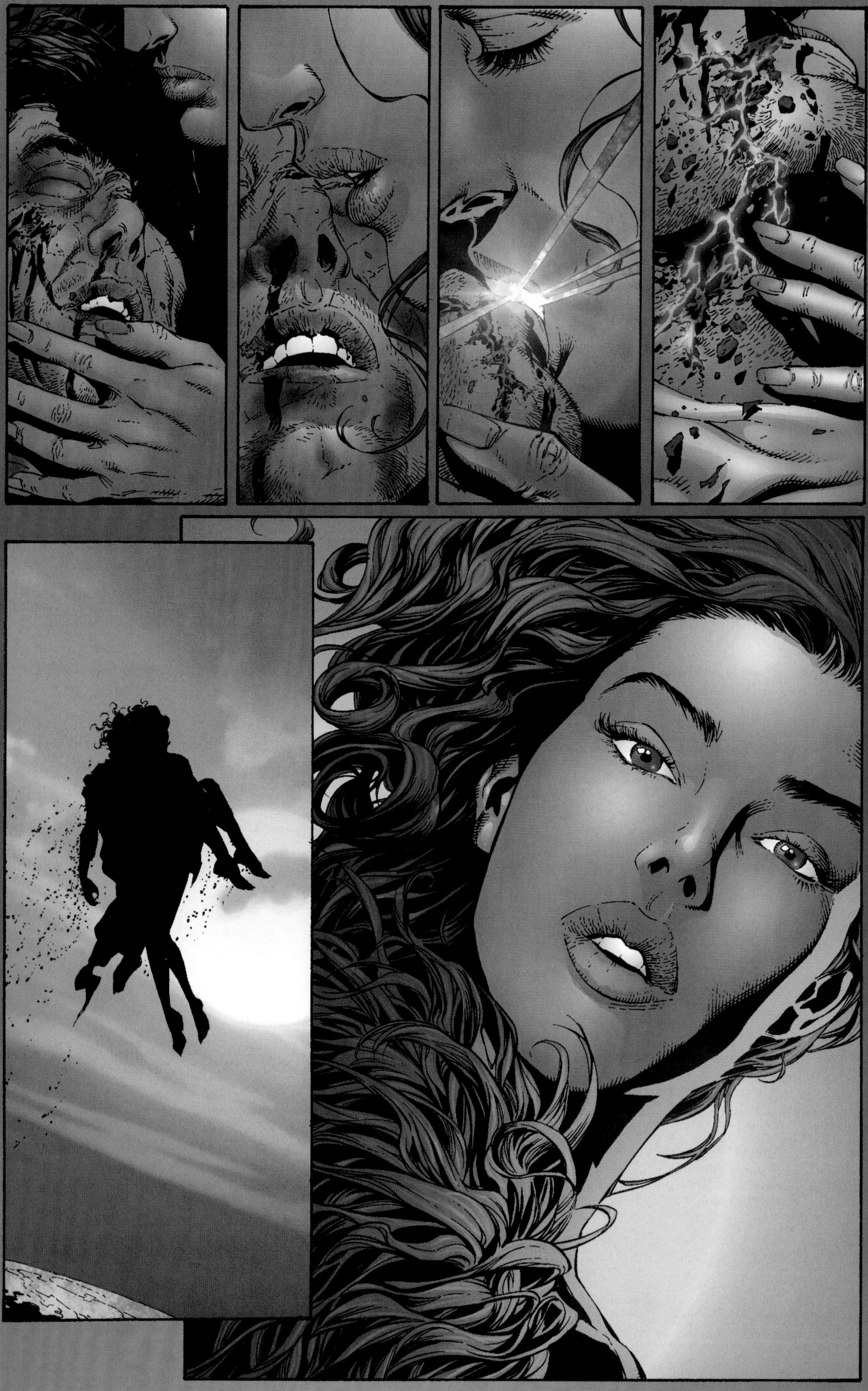

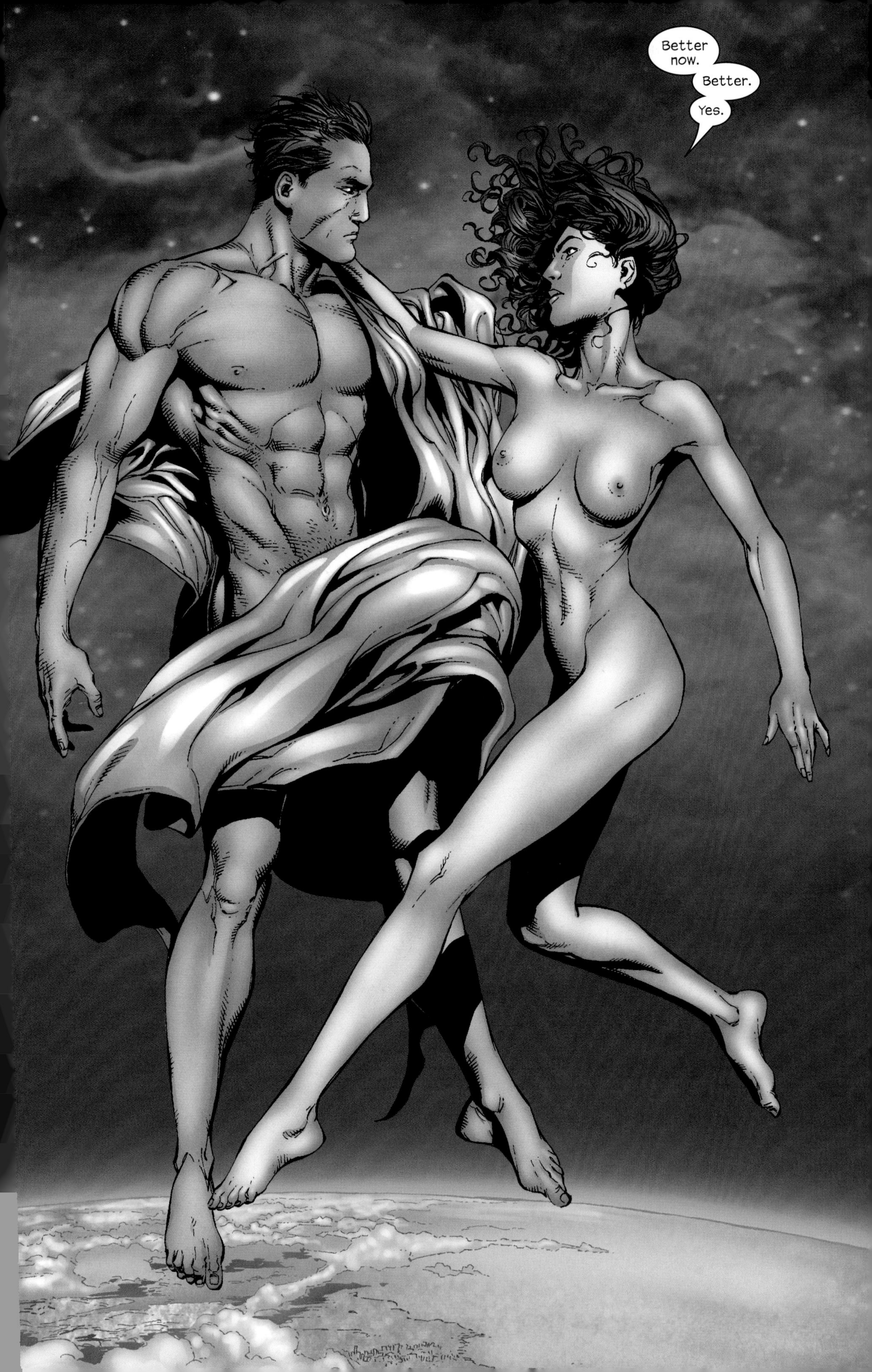
Better now.
Better.
Yes.

#11

Never Alone

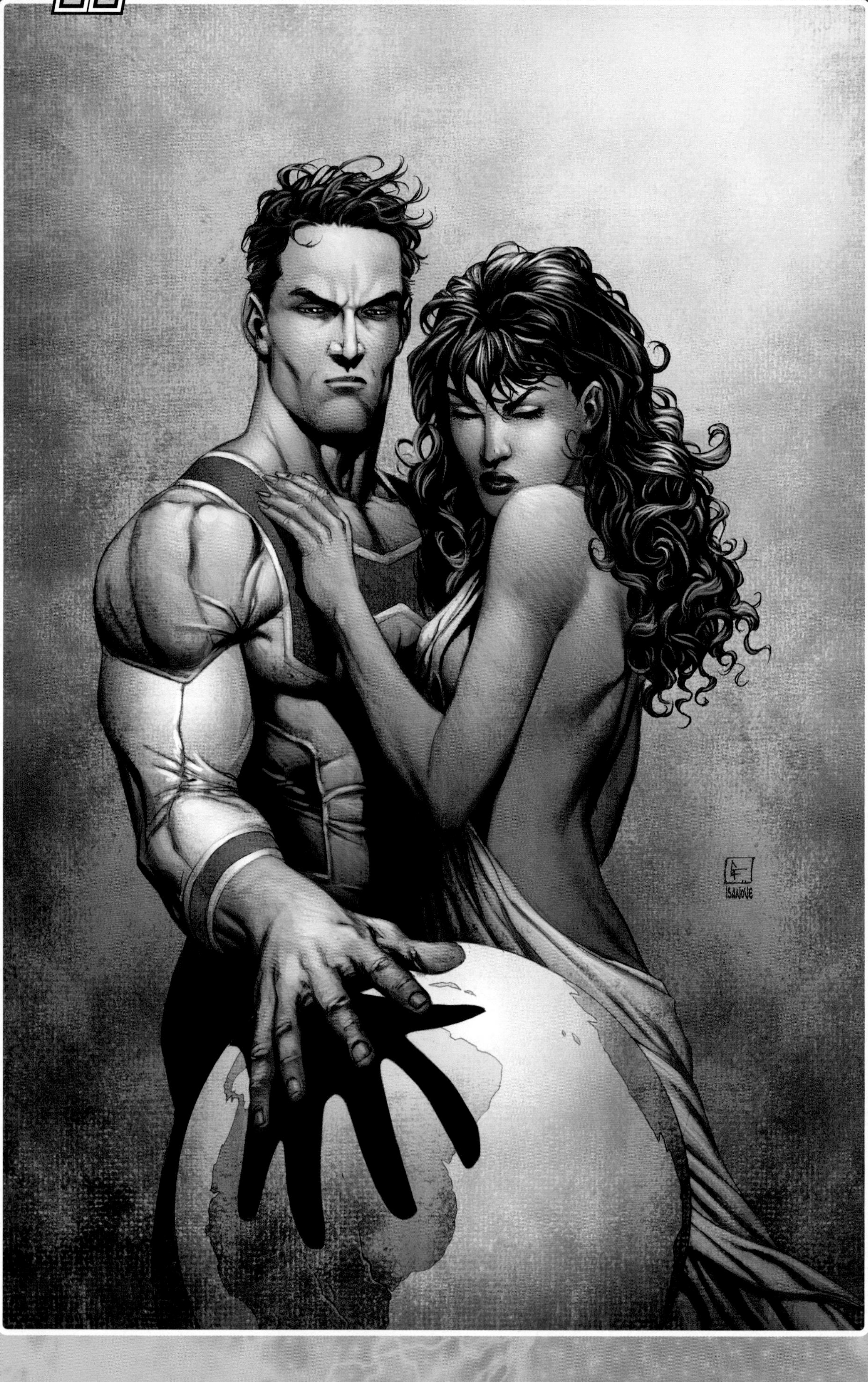

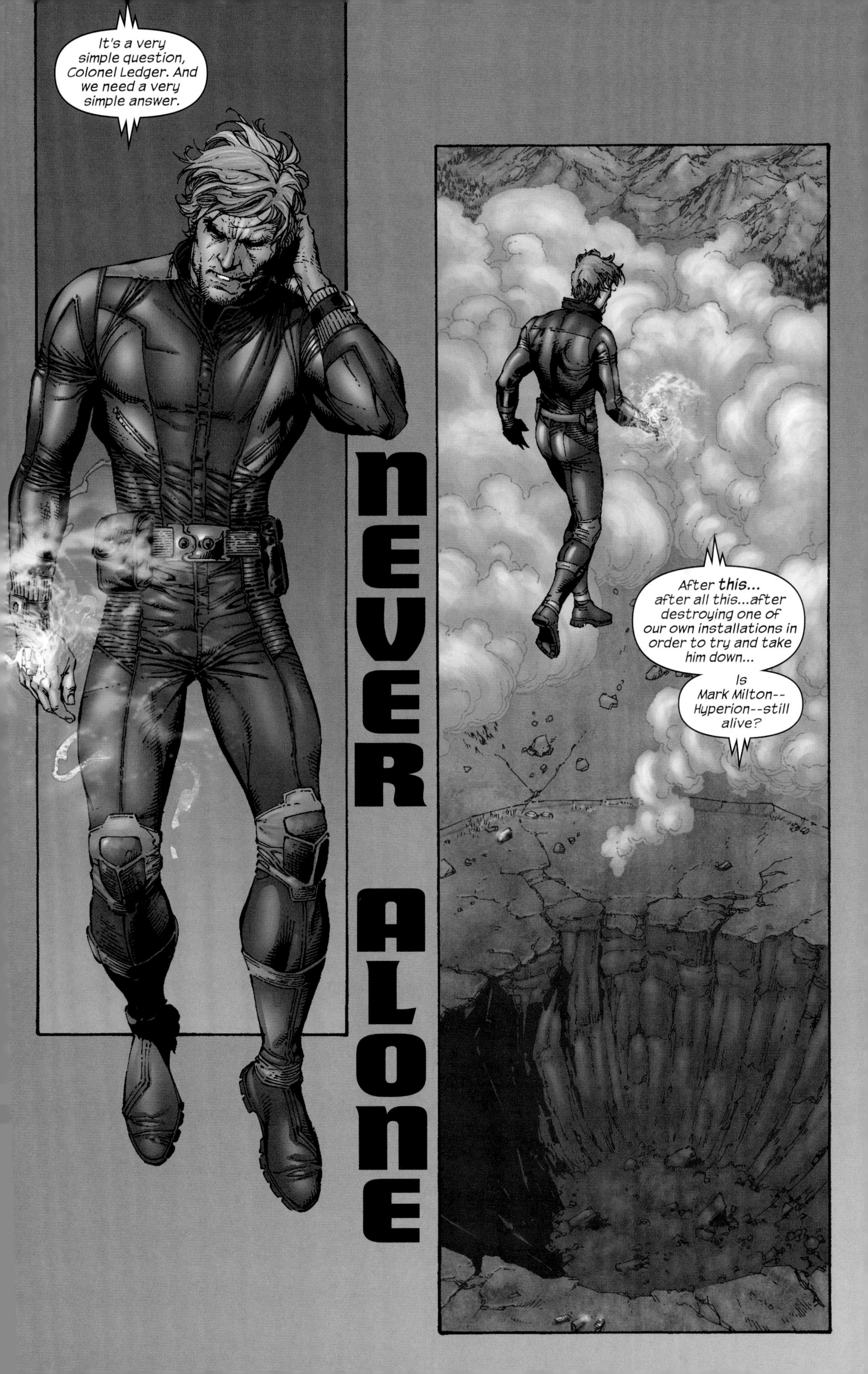
It's a very simple question, Colonel Ledger. And we need a very simple answer.
NEVER ALONE
After this... after all this...after destroying one of our own installations in order to try and take him down...
Is Mark Milton--Hyperion--still alive?

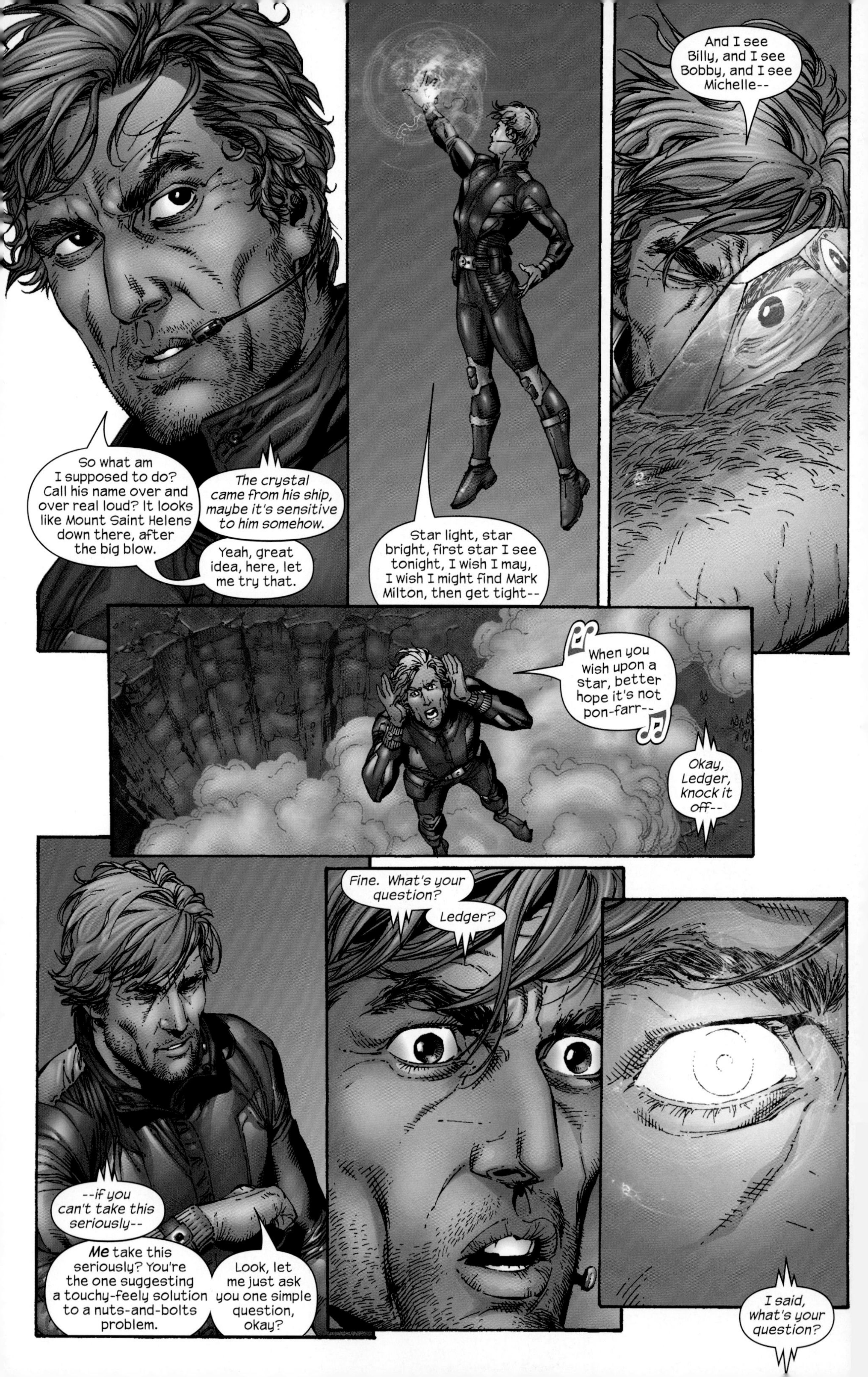

So what am I supposed to do? Call his name over and over real loud? It looks like Mount Saint Helens down there, after the big blow.
The crystal came from his ship, maybe it's sensitive to him somehow.
Yeah, great idea, here, let me try that.
Star light, star bright, first star I see tonight, I wish I may, I wish I might find Mark Milton, then get tight--
And I see Billy, and I see Bobby, and I see Michelle--
When you wish upon a star, better hope it's not pon-farr--
Okay, Ledger, knock it off--
--if you can't take this seriously--
Me take this seriously? You're the one suggesting a touchy-feely solution to a nuts-and-bolts problem.
Look, let me just ask you one simple question, okay?
Fine. What's your question?
Ledger?
I said, what's your question?

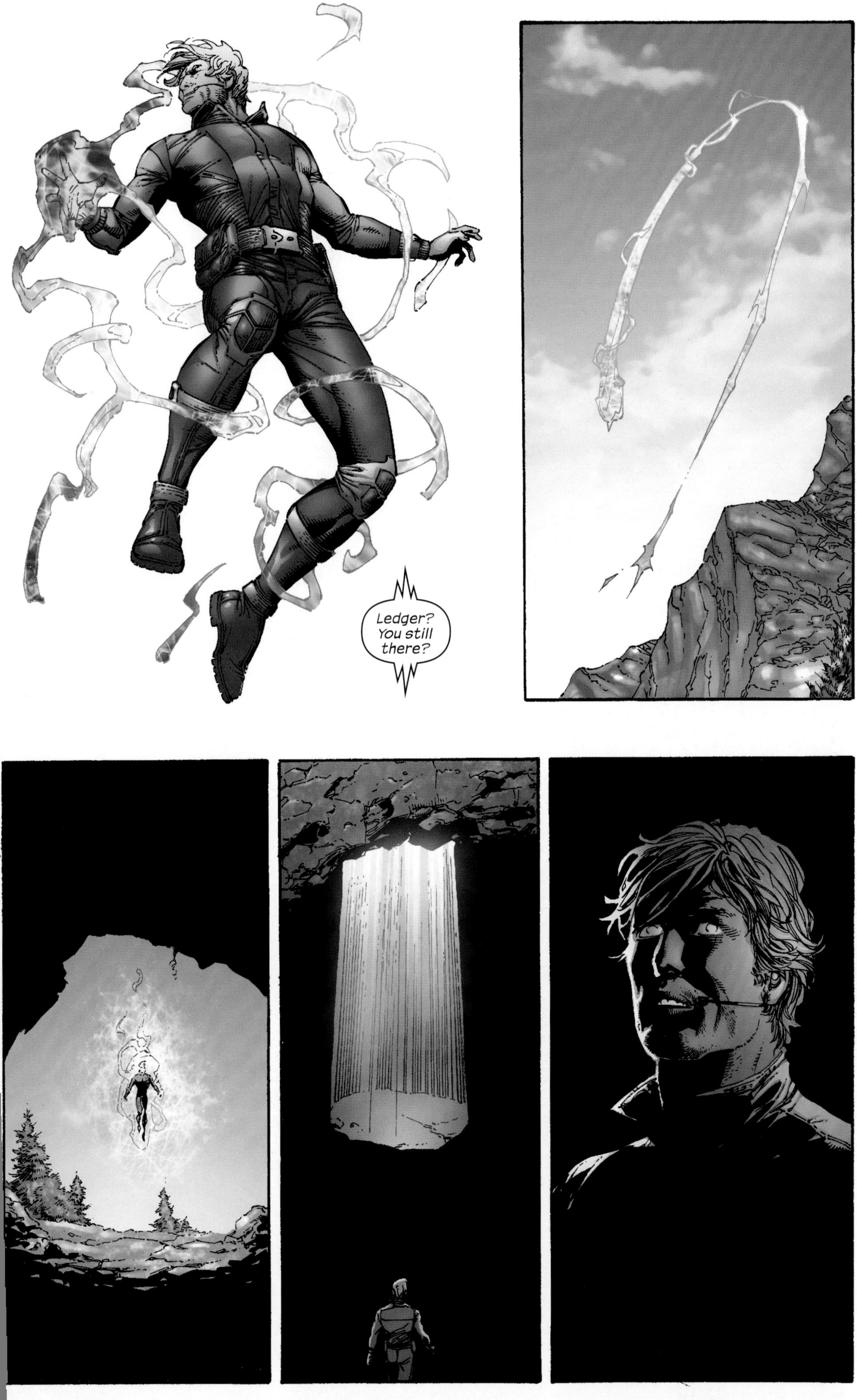
Ledger? You still there?

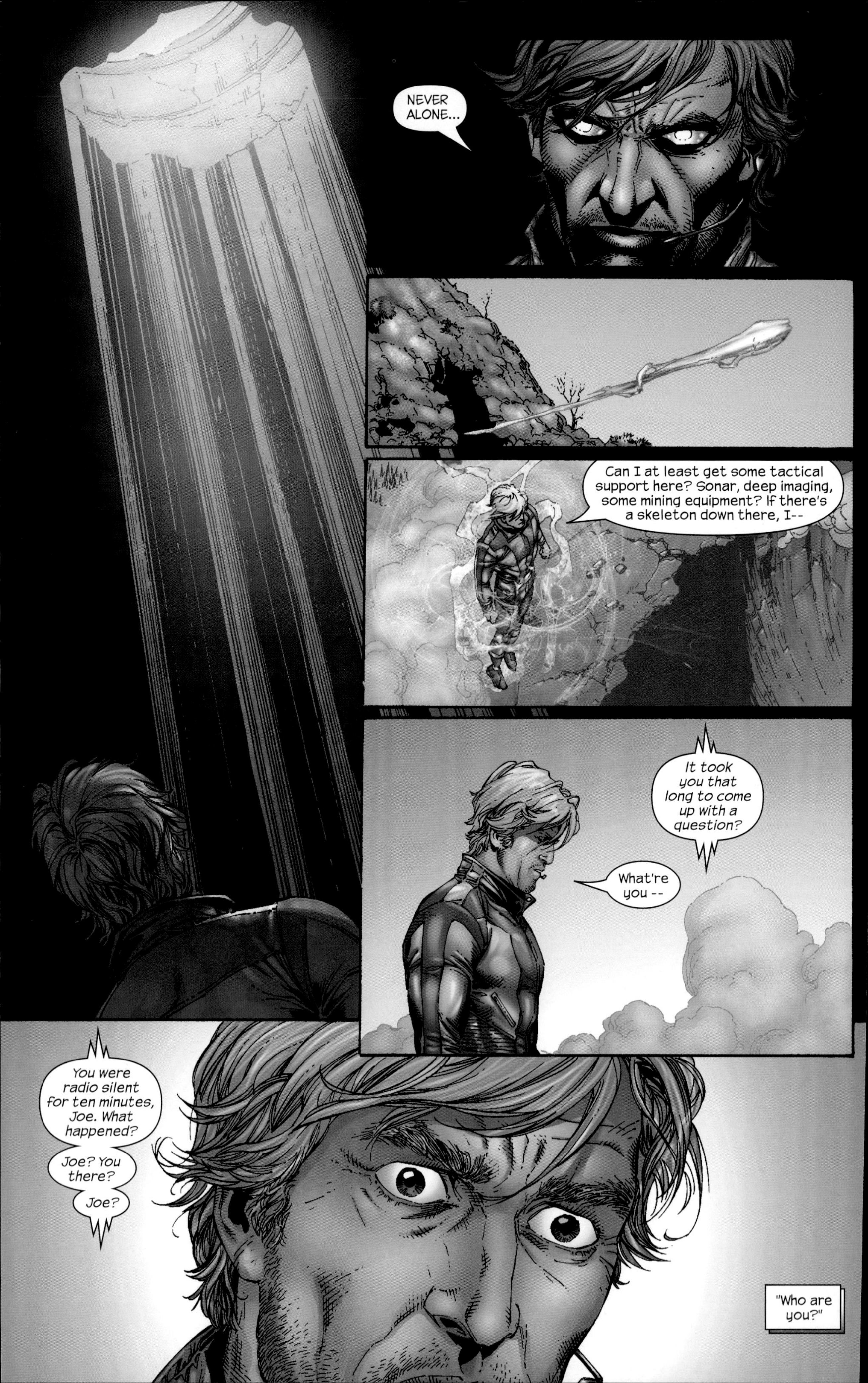
NEVER ALONE...
Can I at least get some tactical support here? Sonar, deep imaging, some mining equipment? If there's a skeleton down there, I--
It took you that long to come up with a question?
What're you --
You were radio silent for ten minutes, Joe. What happened?
Joe? You there?
Joe?
"Who are you?"

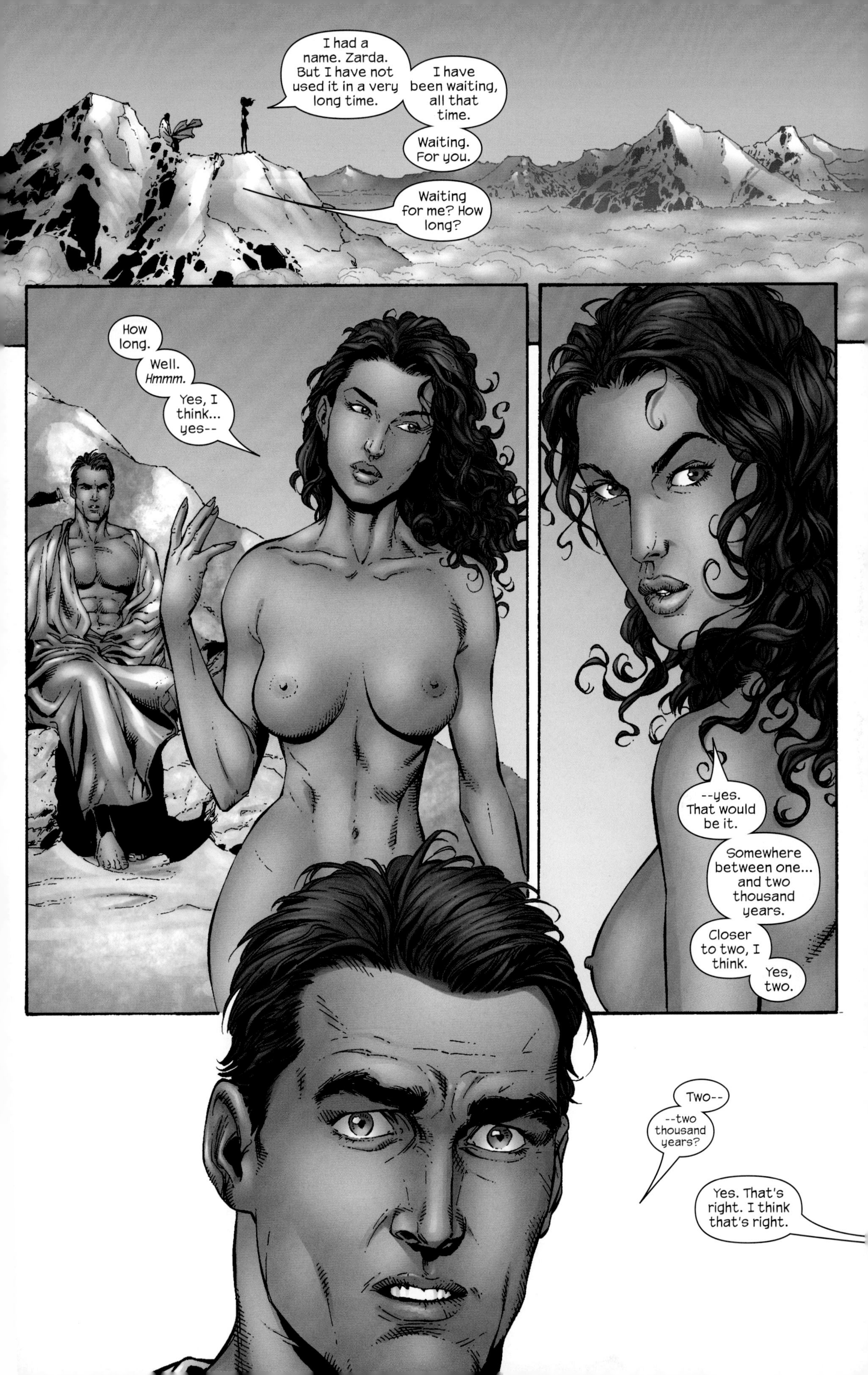
I had a name. Zarda. But I have not used it in a very long time.
I have been waiting, all that time.
Waiting. For you.
Waiting for me? How long?
How long.
Well. *Hmmm.*
Yes, I think... yes--
--yes. That would be it.
Somewhere between one... and two thousand years.
Closer to two, I think.
Yes, two.
Two--
--two thousand years?
Yes. That's right. I think that's right.

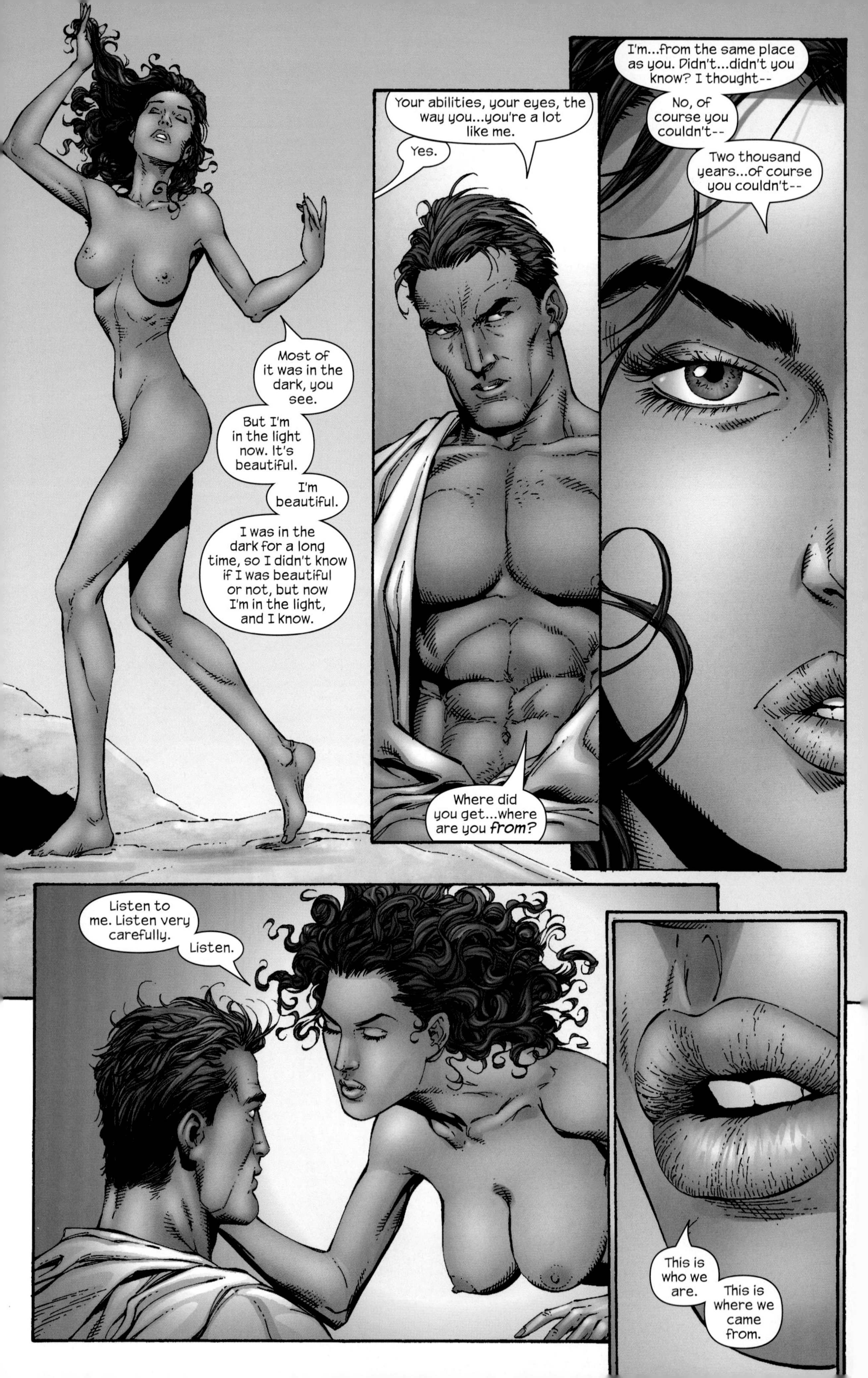

Most of it was in the dark, you see.
But I'm in the light now. It's beautiful.
I'm beautiful.
I was in the dark for a long time, so I didn't know if I was beautiful or not, but now I'm in the light, and I know.
Your abilities, your eyes, the way you...you're a lot like me.
Yes.
Where did you get...where are you *from?*
I'm...from the same place as you. Didn't...didn't you know? I thought--
No, of course you couldn't--
Two thousand years...of course you couldn't--
Listen to me. Listen very carefully.
Listen.
This is who we are.
This is where we came from.

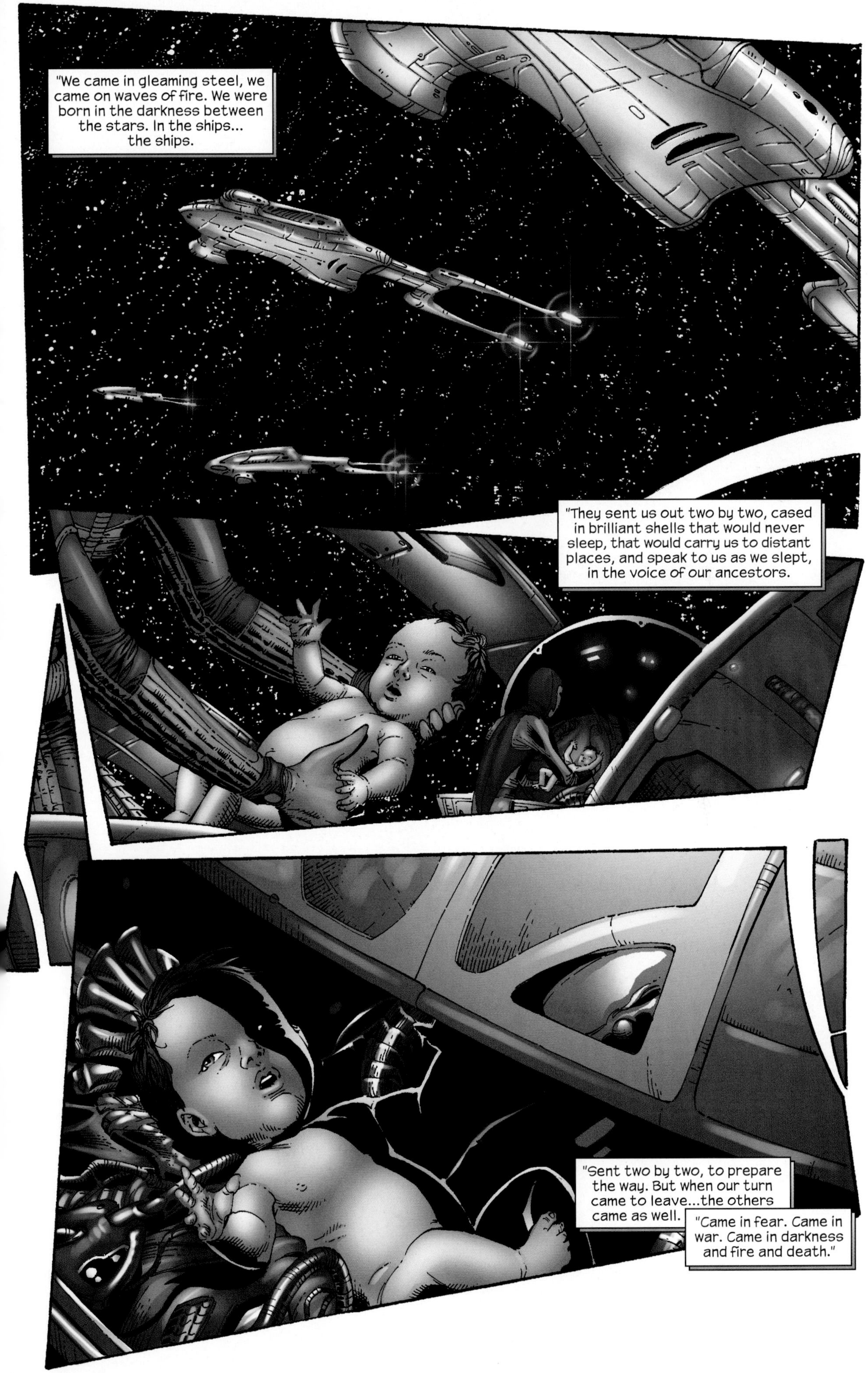
"We came in gleaming steel, we came on waves of fire. We were born in the darkness between the stars. In the ships... the ships.
"They sent us out two by two, cased in brilliant shells that would never sleep, that would carry us to distant places, and speak to us as we slept, in the voice of our ancestors.
"Sent two by two, to prepare the way. But when our turn came to leave...the others came as well.
"Came in fear. Came in war. Came in darkness and fire and death."

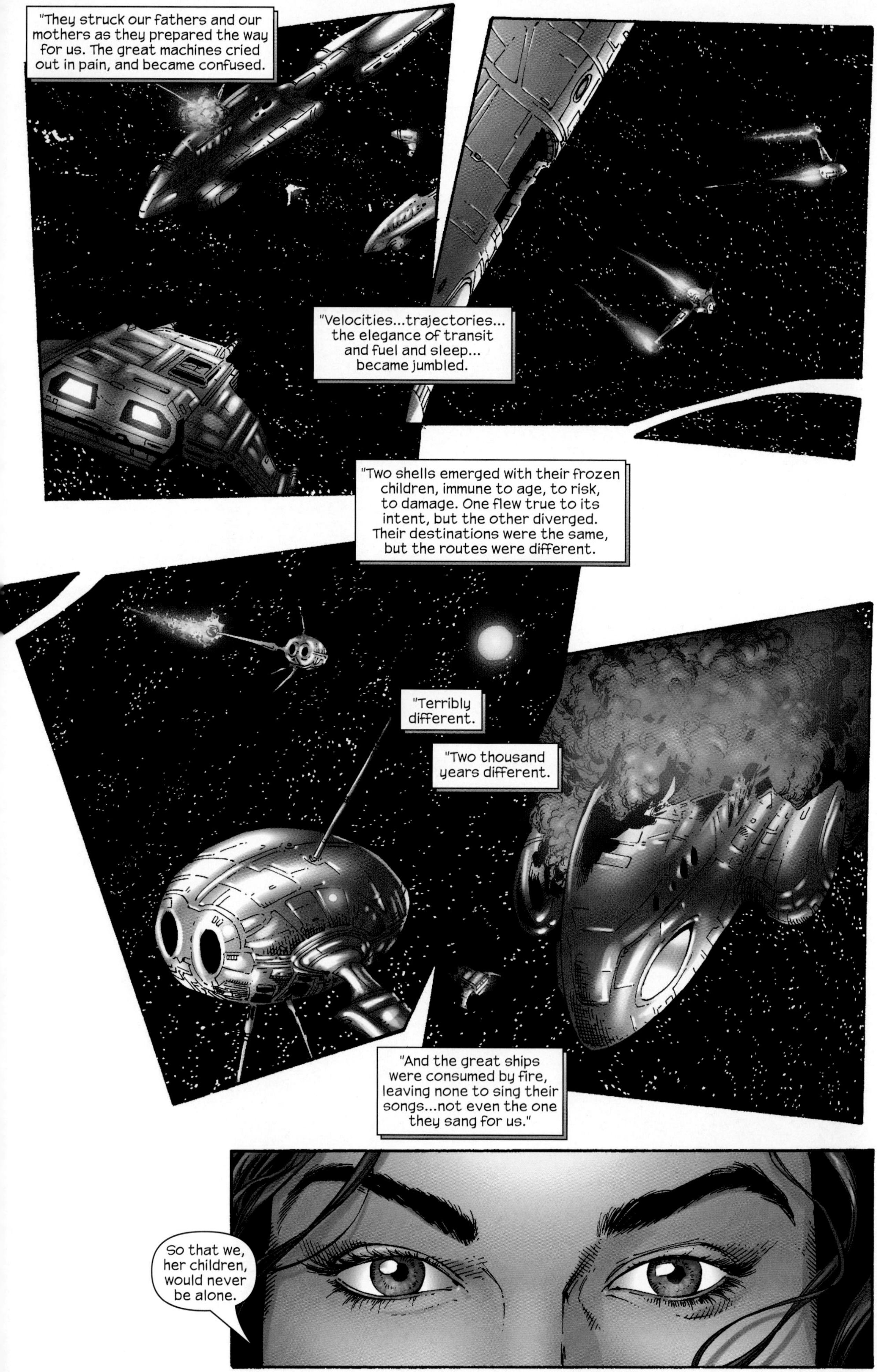
"They struck our fathers and our mothers as they prepared the way for us. The great machines cried out in pain, and became confused.
"Velocities...trajectories... the elegance of transit and fuel and sleep... became jumbled.
"Two shells emerged with their frozen children, immune to age, to risk, to damage. One flew true to its intent, but the other diverged. Their destinations were the same, but the routes were different.
"Terribly different.
"Two thousand years different.
"And the great ships were consumed by fire, leaving none to sing their songs...not even the one they sang for us."
So that we, her children, would never be alone.

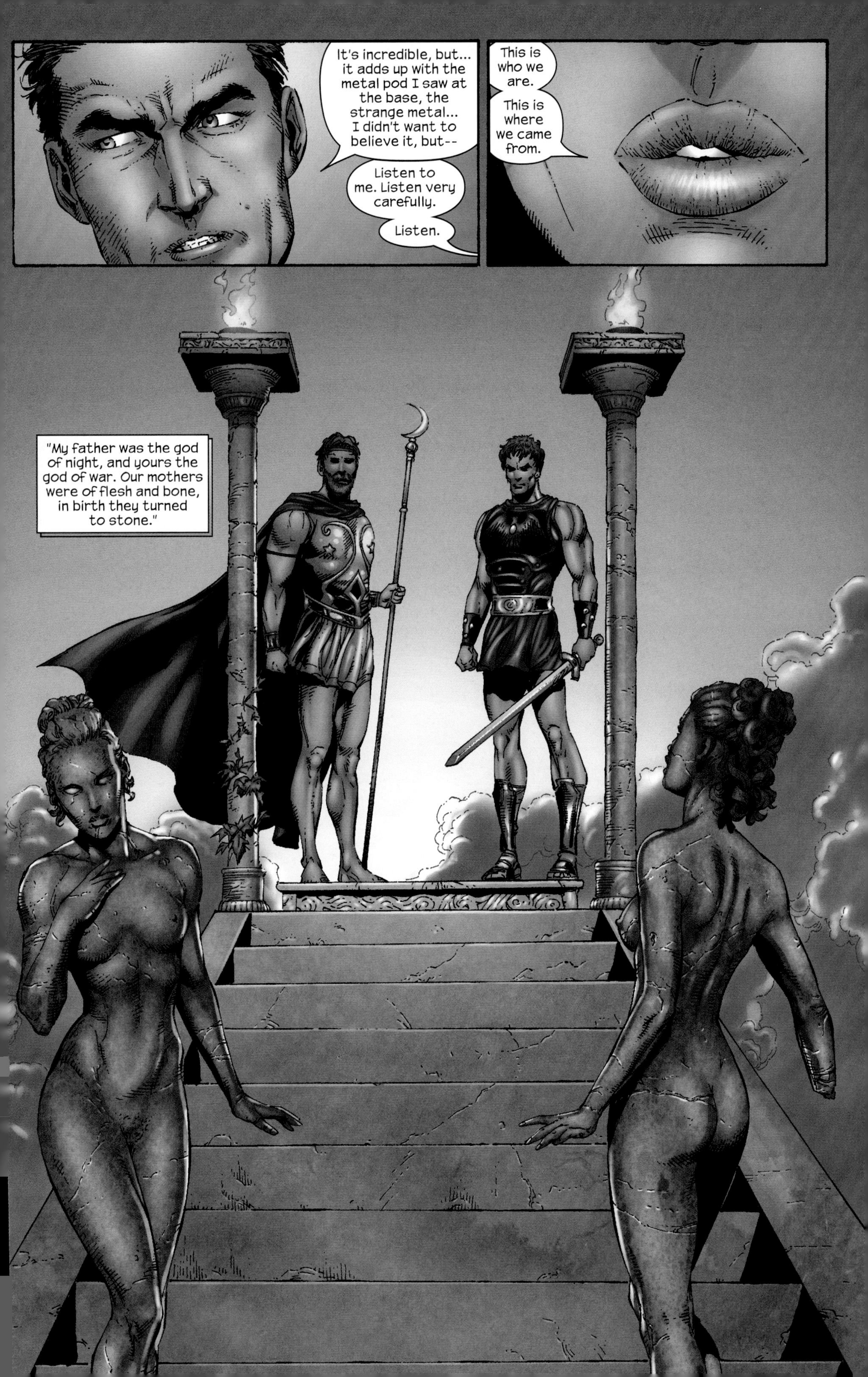
It's incredible, but... it adds up with the metal pod I saw at the base, the strange metal... I didn't want to believe it, but--
Listen to me. Listen very carefully.
Listen.
This is who we are.
This is where we came from.
"My father was the god of night, and yours the god of war. Our mothers were of flesh and bone, in birth they turned to stone."

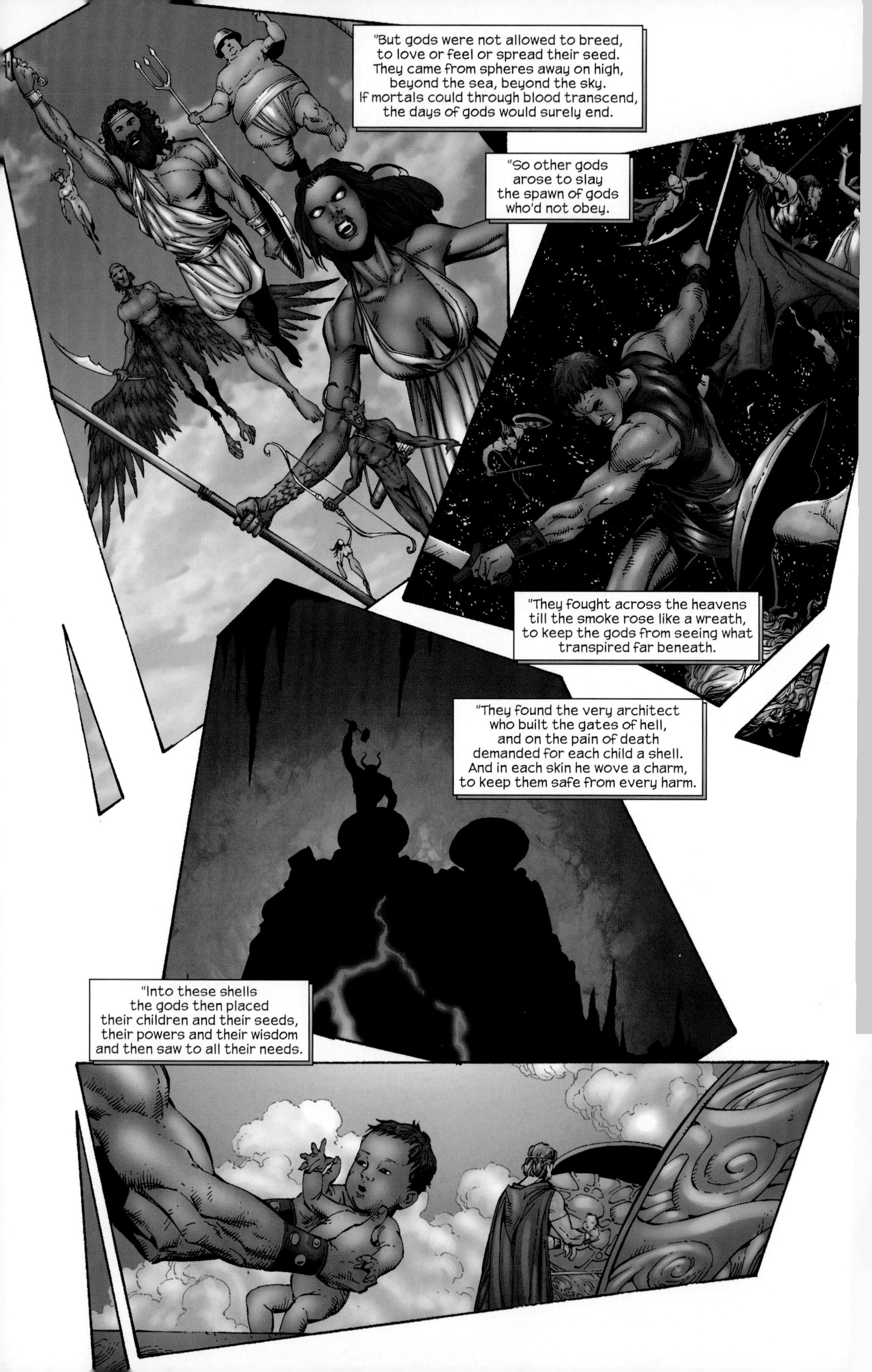
"But gods were not allowed to breed, to love or feel or spread their seed. They came from spheres away on high, beyond the sea, beyond the sky. If mortals could through blood transcend, the days of gods would surely end.
"So other gods arose to slay the spawn of gods who'd not obey.
"They fought across the heavens till the smoke rose like a wreath, to keep the gods from seeing what transpired far beneath.
"They found the very architect who built the gates of hell, and on the pain of death demanded for each child a shell. And in each skin he wove a charm, to keep them safe from every harm.
"Into these shells the gods then placed their children and their seeds, their powers and their wisdom and then saw to all their needs.

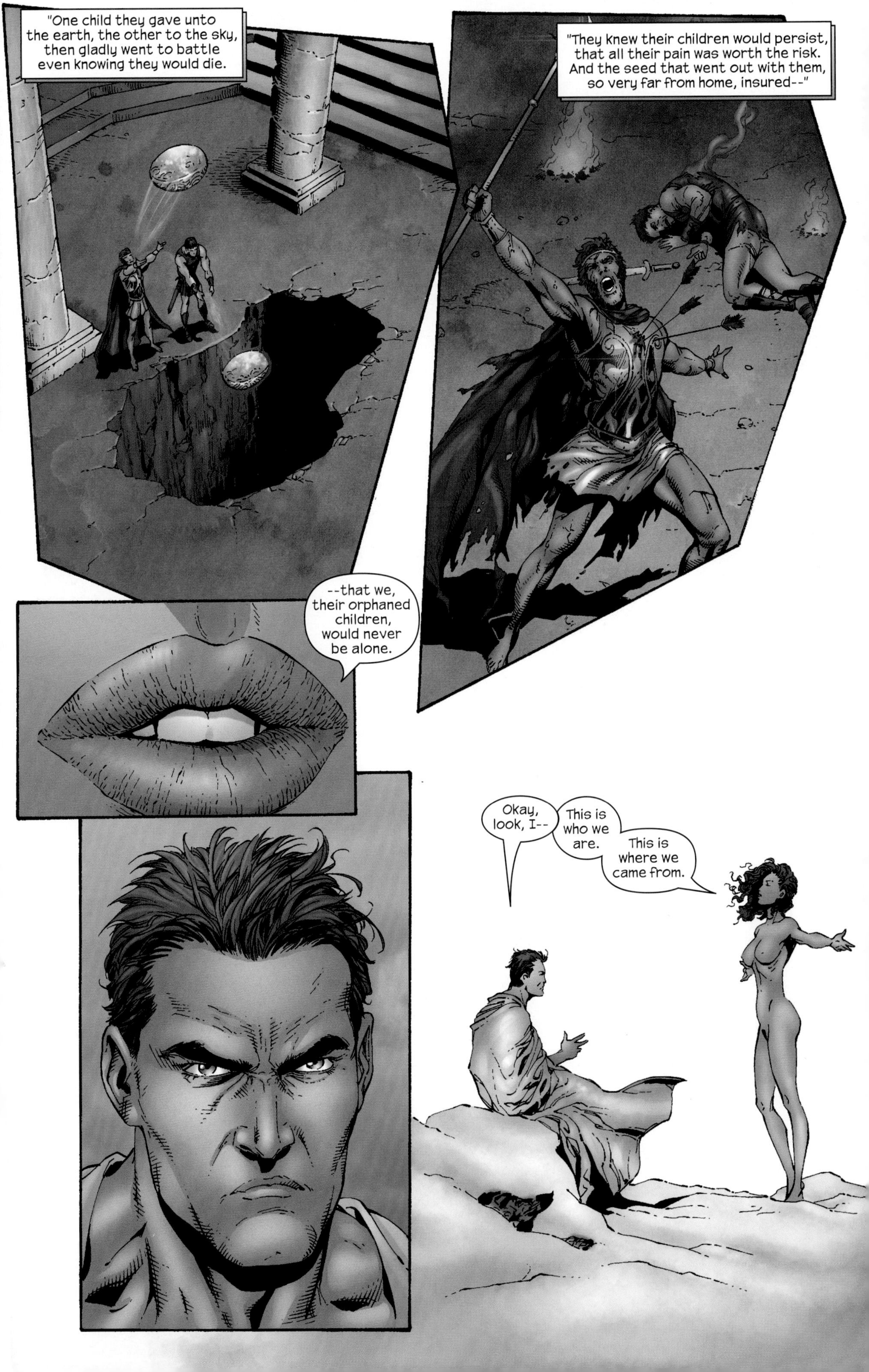
"One child they gave unto the earth, the other to the sky, then gladly went to battle even knowing they would die.
"They knew their children would persist, that all their pain was worth the risk. And the seed that went out with them, so very far from home, insured--"
--that we, their orphaned children, would never be alone.
Okay, look, I--
This is who we are.
This is where we came from.

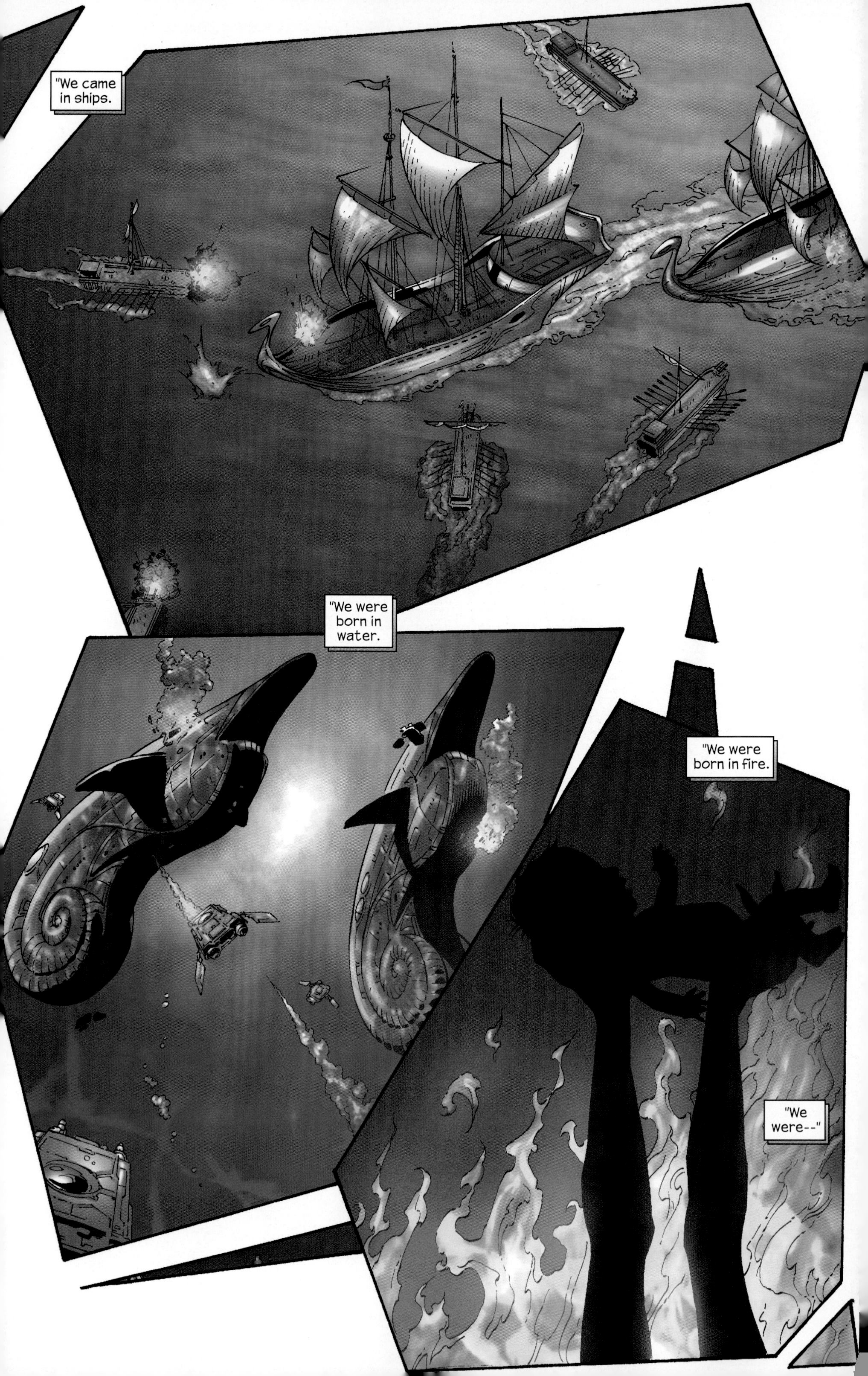
"We came in ships.
"We were born in water.
"We were born in fire.
"We were--"

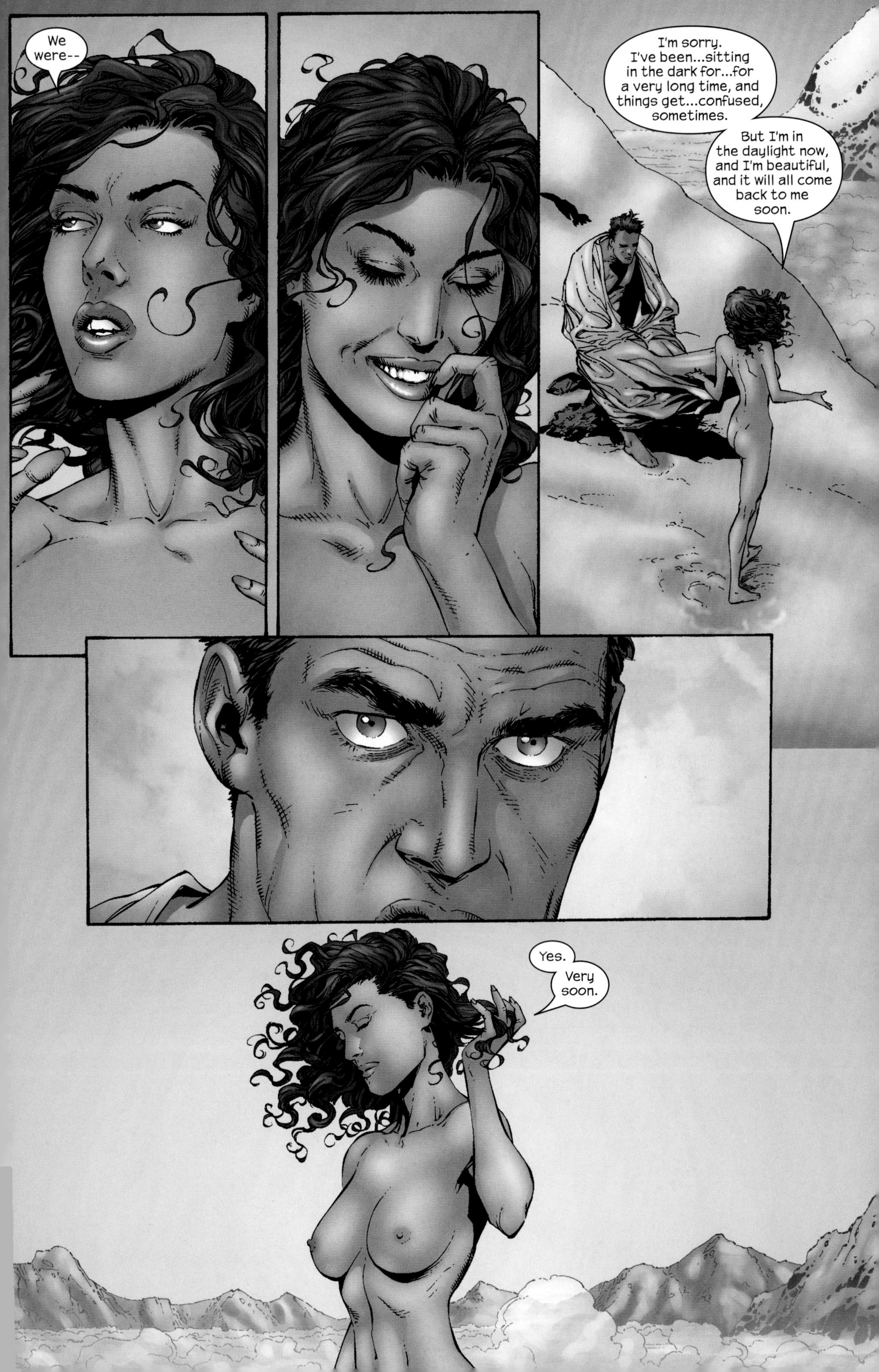
We were--
I'm sorry. I've been...sitting in the dark for...for a very long time, and things get...confused, sometimes.
But I'm in the daylight now, and I'm beautiful, and it will all come back to me soon.
Yes.
Very soon.

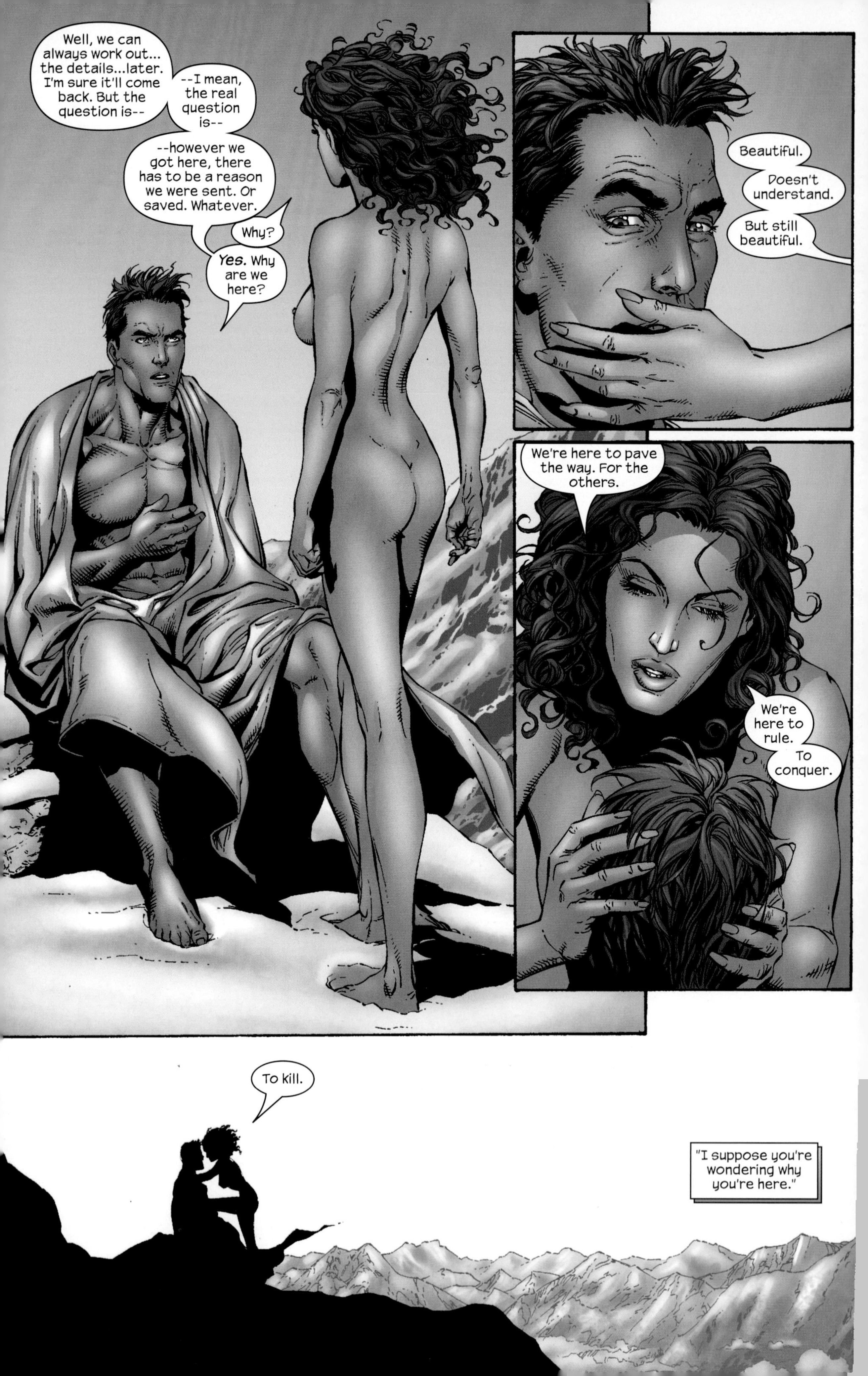
Well, we can always work out... the details...later. I'm sure it'll come back. But the question is--
--I mean, the real question is--
--however we got here, there has to be a reason we were sent. Or saved. Whatever.
Why?
Yes. Why are we here?
Beautiful.
Doesn't understand.
But still beautiful.
We're here to pave the way. For the others.
We're here to rule.
To conquer.
To kill.
"I suppose you're wondering why you're here."

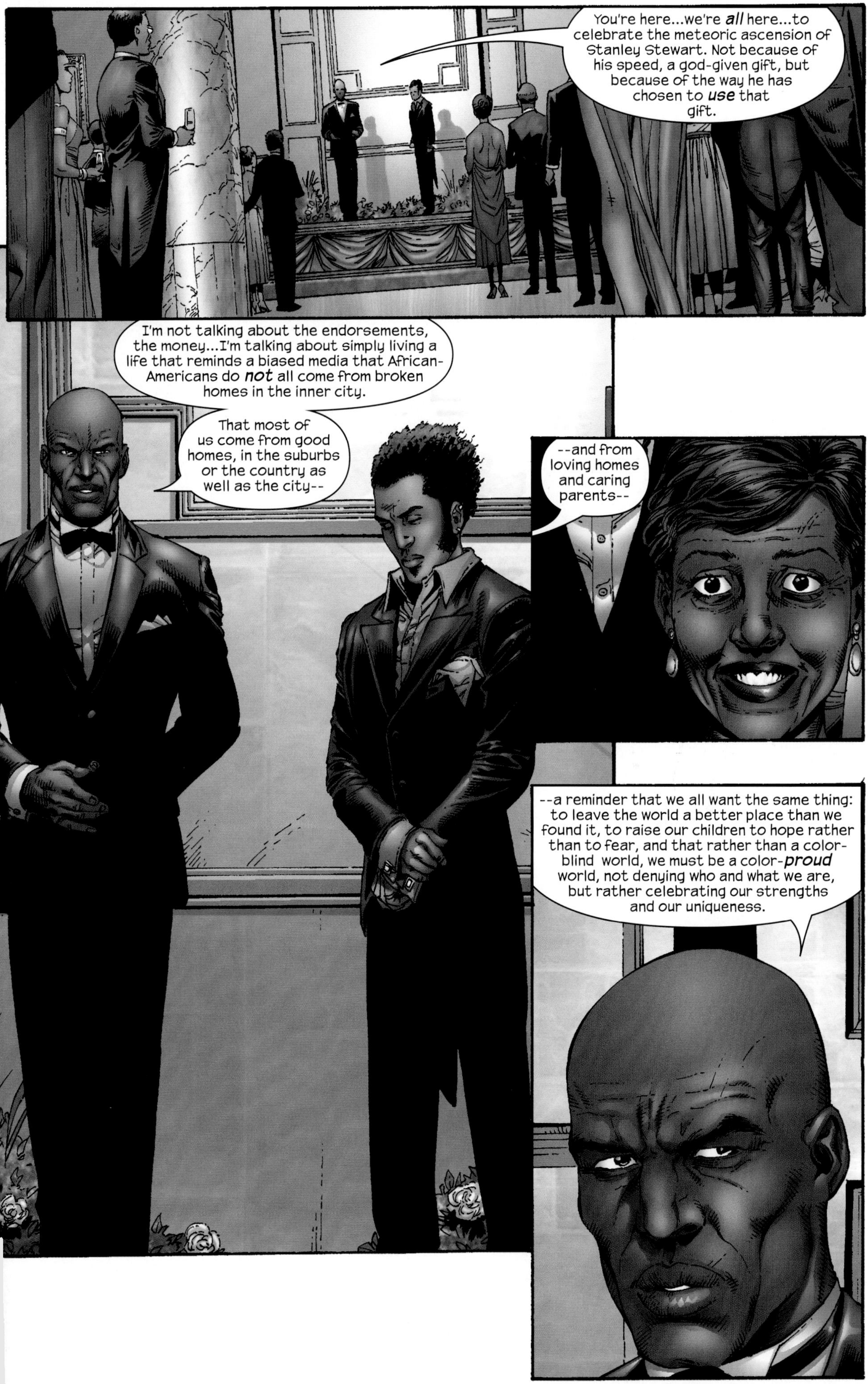
You're here...we're *all* here...to celebrate the meteoric ascension of Stanley Stewart. Not because of his speed, a god-given gift, but because of the way he has chosen to *use* that gift.
I'm not talking about the endorsements, the money...I'm talking about simply living a life that reminds a biased media that African-Americans do *not* all come from broken homes in the inner city.
That most of us come from good homes, in the suburbs or the country as well as the city--
--and from loving homes and caring parents--
--a reminder that we all want the same thing: to leave the world a better place than we found it, to raise our children to hope rather than to fear, and that rather than a color-blind world, we must be a color-*proud* world, not denying who and what we are, but rather celebrating our strengths and our uniqueness.

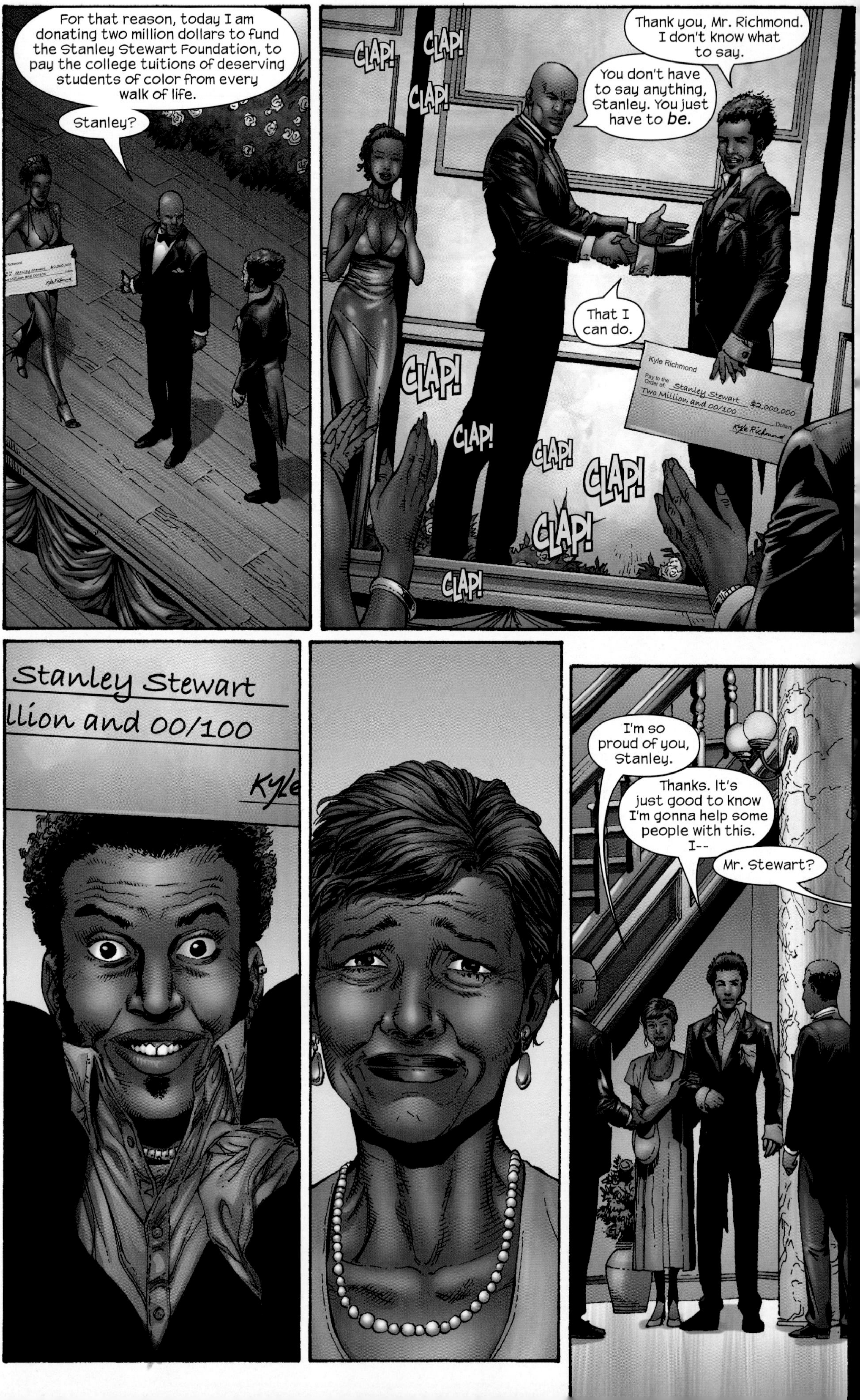
For that reason, today I am donating two million dollars to fund the Stanley Stewart Foundation, to pay the college tuitions of deserving students of color from every walk of life.
Stanley?
CLAP! CLAP!
CLAP!
Thank you, Mr. Richmond. I don't know what to say.
You don't have to say anything, Stanley. You just have to *be.*
That I can do.
Kyle Richmond
Pay to the Order of: Stanley Stewart $2,000,000
Two Million and 00/100 Dollars
Kyle Richmond
CLAP!
CLAP!
CLAP!
CLAP!
CLAP!
CLAP!
Stanley Stewart
llion and 00/100
Kyle
I'm so proud of you, Stanley.
Thanks. It's just good to know I'm gonna help some people with this. I--
Mr. Stewart?

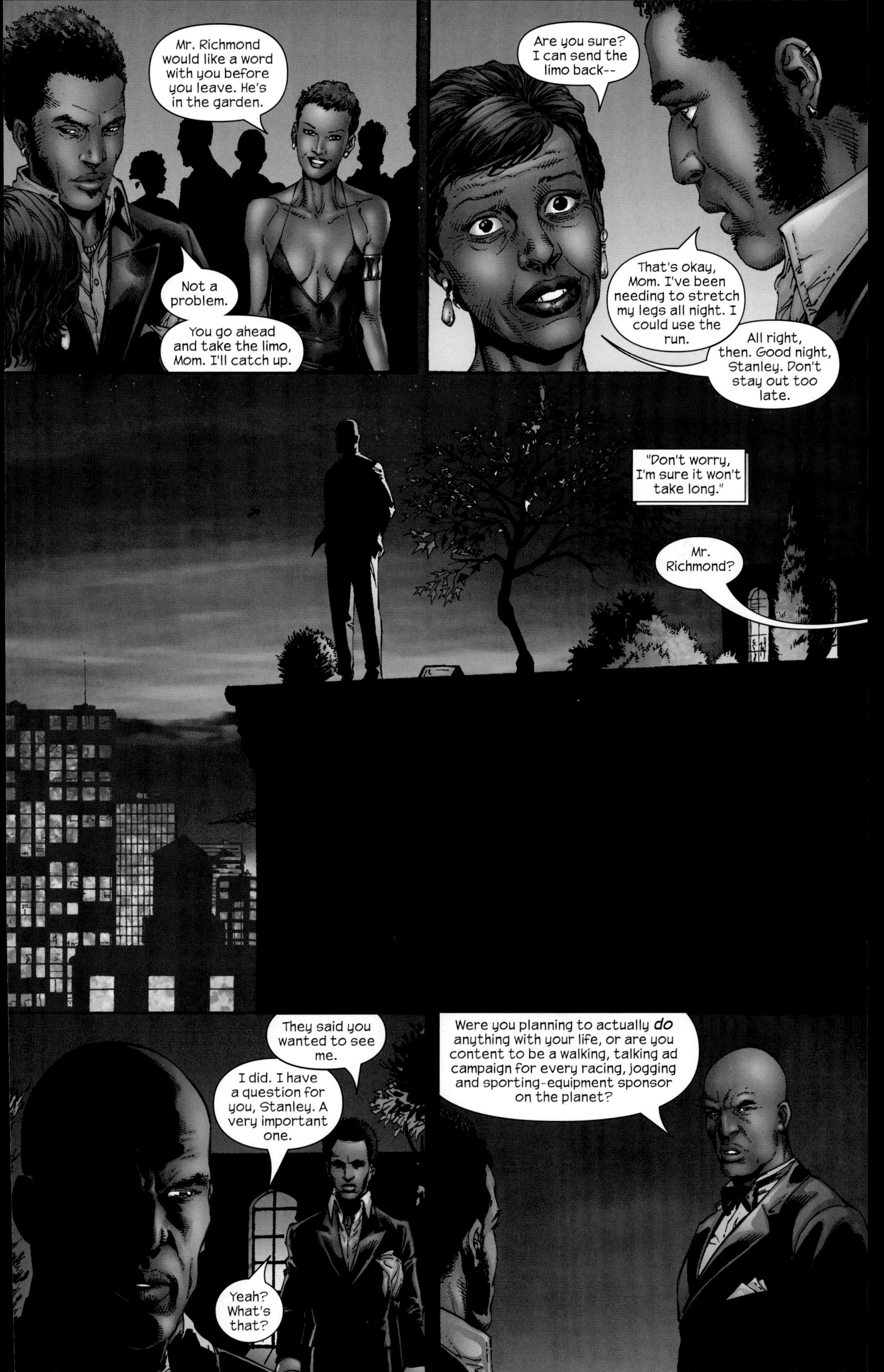
Mr. Richmond would like a word with you before you leave. He's in the garden.
Not a problem.
You go ahead and take the limo, Mom. I'll catch up.
Are you sure? I can send the limo back--
That's okay, Mom. I've been needing to stretch my legs all night. I could use the run.
All right, then. Good night, Stanley. Don't stay out too late.
"Don't worry, I'm sure it won't take long."
Mr. Richmond?
They said you wanted to see me.
I did. I have a question for you, Stanley. A very important one.
Yeah? What's that?
Were you planning to actually *do* anything with your life, or are you content to be a walking, talking ad campaign for every racing, jogging and sporting-equipment sponsor on the planet?

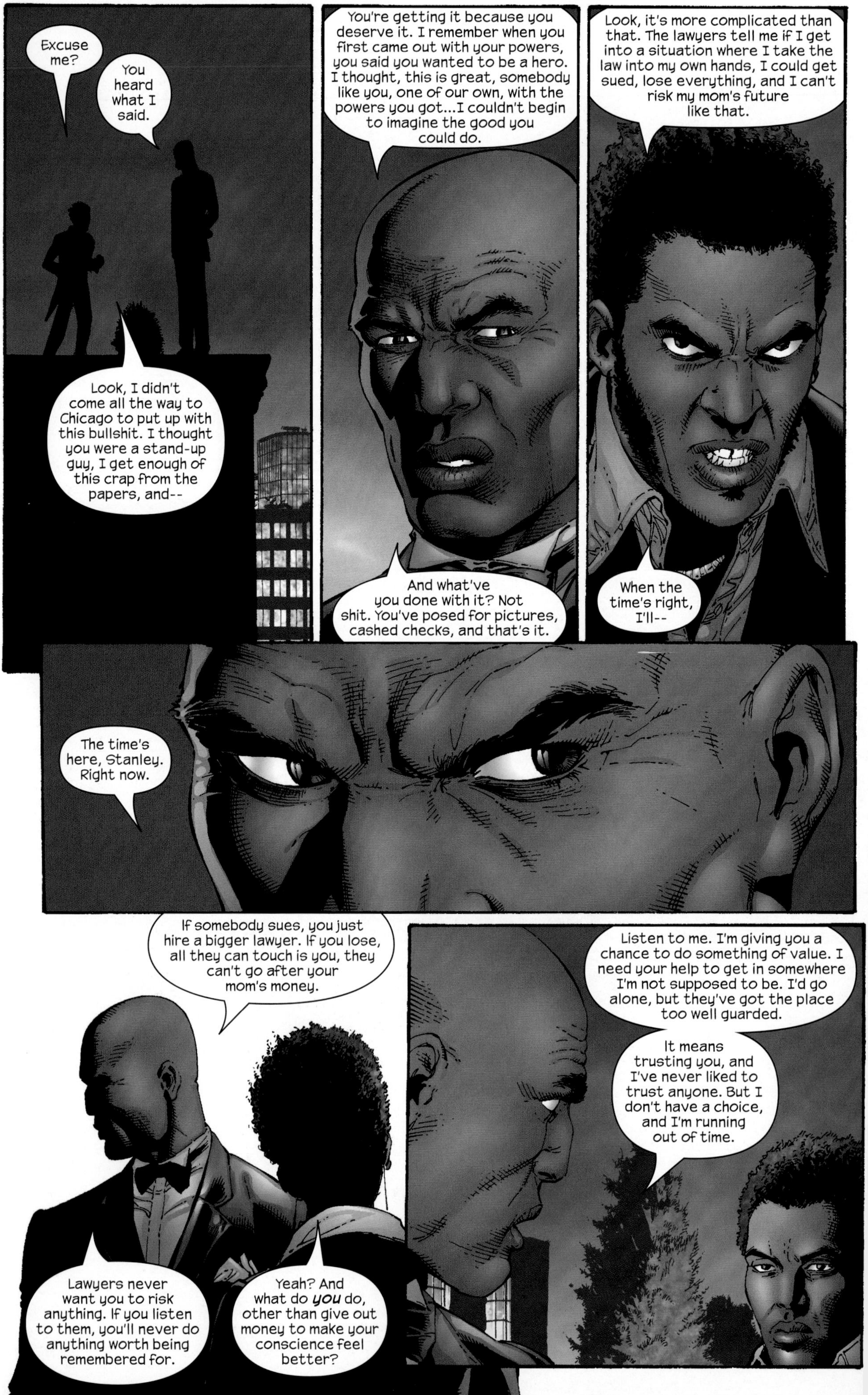
Excuse me?
You heard what I said.
Look, I didn't come all the way to Chicago to put up with this bullshit. I thought you were a stand-up guy, I get enough of this crap from the papers, and--
You're getting it because you deserve it. I remember when you first came out with your powers, you said you wanted to be a hero. I thought, this is great, somebody like you, one of our own, with the powers you got...I couldn't begin to imagine the good you could do.
And what've you done with it? Not shit. You've posed for pictures, cashed checks, and that's it.
Look, it's more complicated than that. The lawyers tell me if I get into a situation where I take the law into my own hands, I could get sued, lose everything, and I can't risk my mom's future like that.
When the time's right, I'll--
The time's here, Stanley. Right now.
If somebody sues, you just hire a bigger lawyer. If you lose, all they can touch is you, they can't go after your mom's money.
Lawyers never want you to risk anything. If you listen to them, you'll never do anything worth being remembered for.
Yeah? And what do *you* do, other than give out money to make your conscience feel better?
Listen to me. I'm giving you a chance to do something of value. I need your help to get in somewhere I'm not supposed to be. I'd go alone, but they've got the place too well guarded.
It means trusting you, and I've never liked to trust anyone. But I don't have a choice, and I'm running out of time.

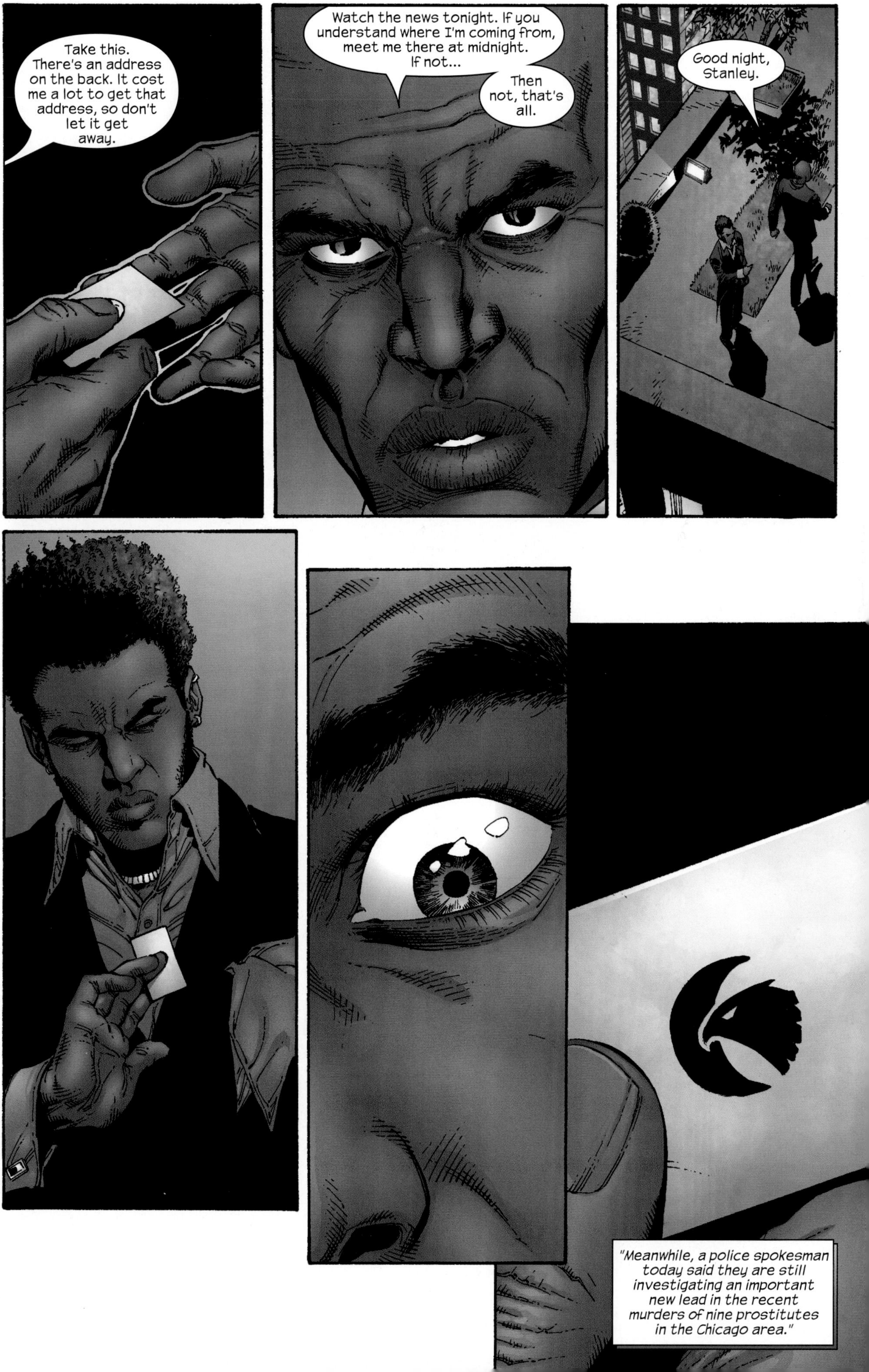
Take this. There's an address on the back. It cost me a lot to get that address, so don't let it get away.
Watch the news tonight. If you understand where I'm coming from, meet me there at midnight. If not...
Then not, that's all.
Good night, Stanley.
"Meanwhile, a police spokesman today said they are still investigating an important new lead in the recent murders of nine prostitutes in the Chicago area."

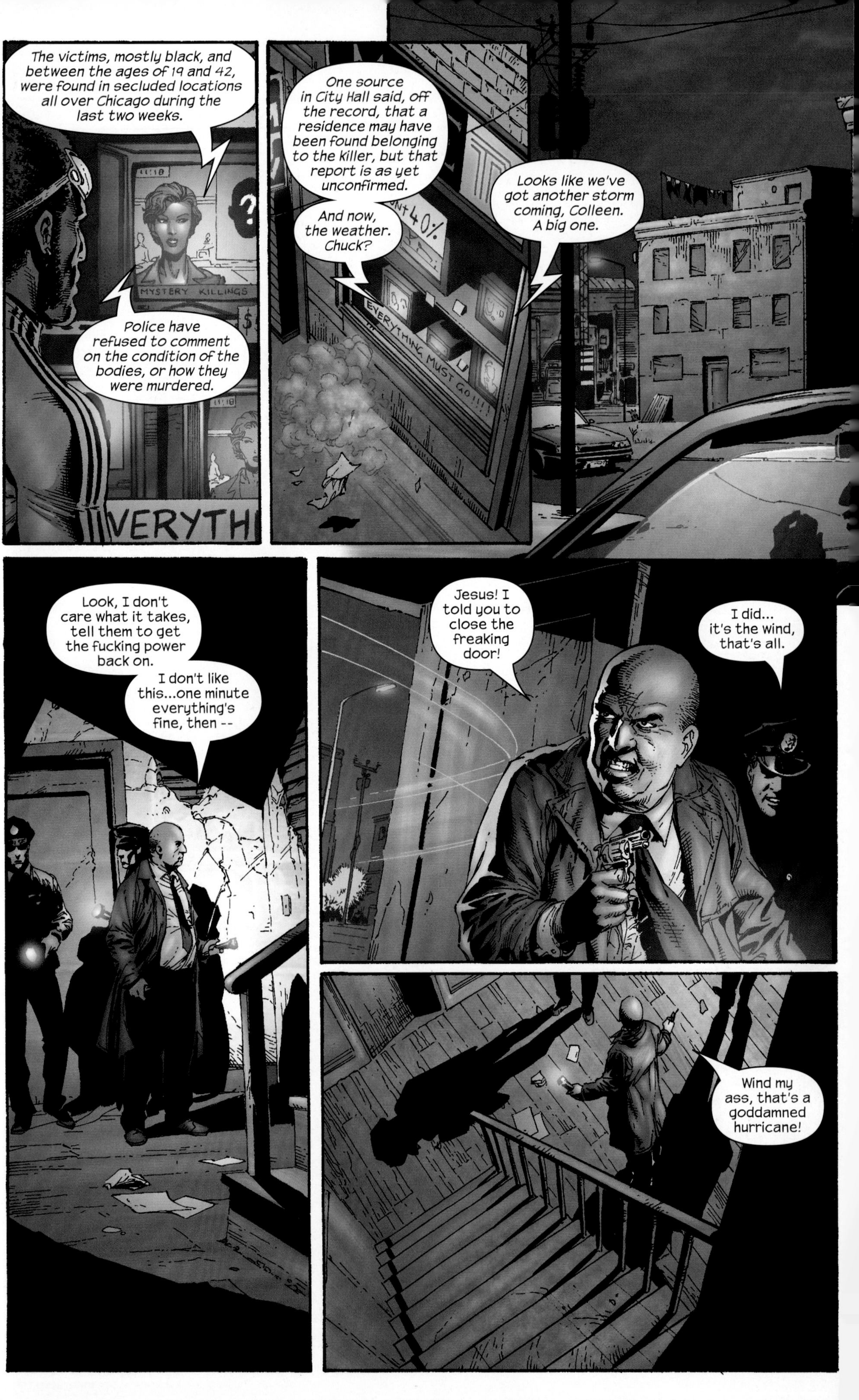
The victims, mostly black, and between the ages of 19 and 42, were found in secluded locations all over Chicago during the last two weeks.
11:18
MYSTERY KILLINGS
Police have refused to comment on the condition of the bodies, or how they were murdered.
VERYTH
One source in City Hall said, off the record, that a residence may have been found belonging to the killer, but that report is as yet unconfirmed.
And now, the weather. Chuck?
EVERYTHING MUST GO!!!
Looks like we've got another storm coming, Colleen. A big one.
Look, I don't care what it takes, tell them to get the fucking power back on.
I don't like this...one minute everything's fine, then --
Jesus! I told you to close the freaking door!
I did... it's the wind, that's all.
Wind my ass, that's a goddamned hurricane!

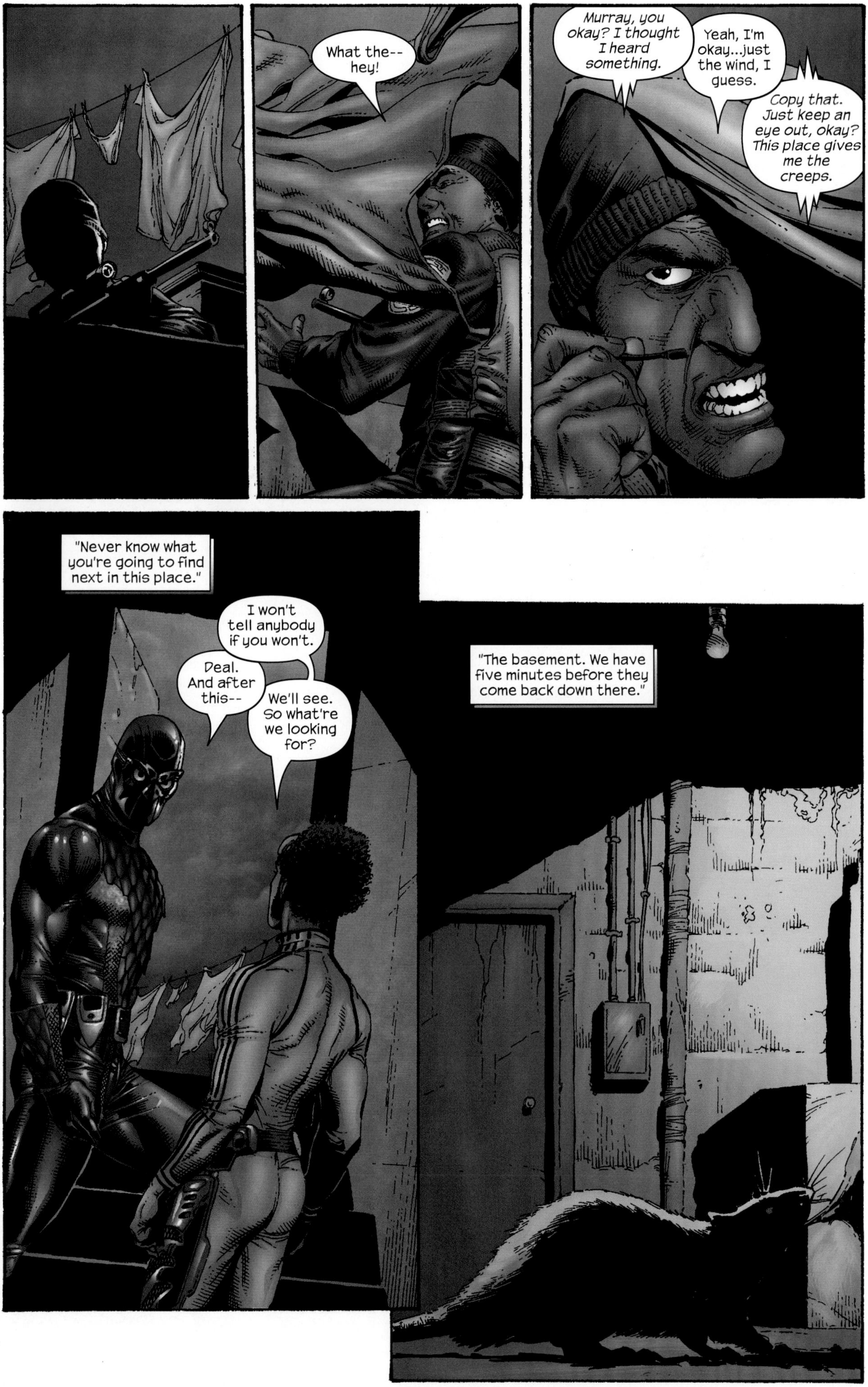
What the-- hey!
Murray, you okay? I thought I heard something.
Yeah, I'm okay...just the wind, I guess.
Copy that. Just keep an eye out, okay? This place gives me the creeps.
"Never know what you're going to find next in this place."
I won't tell anybody if you won't.
Deal. And after this--
We'll see. So what're we looking for?
"The basement. We have five minutes before they come back down there."

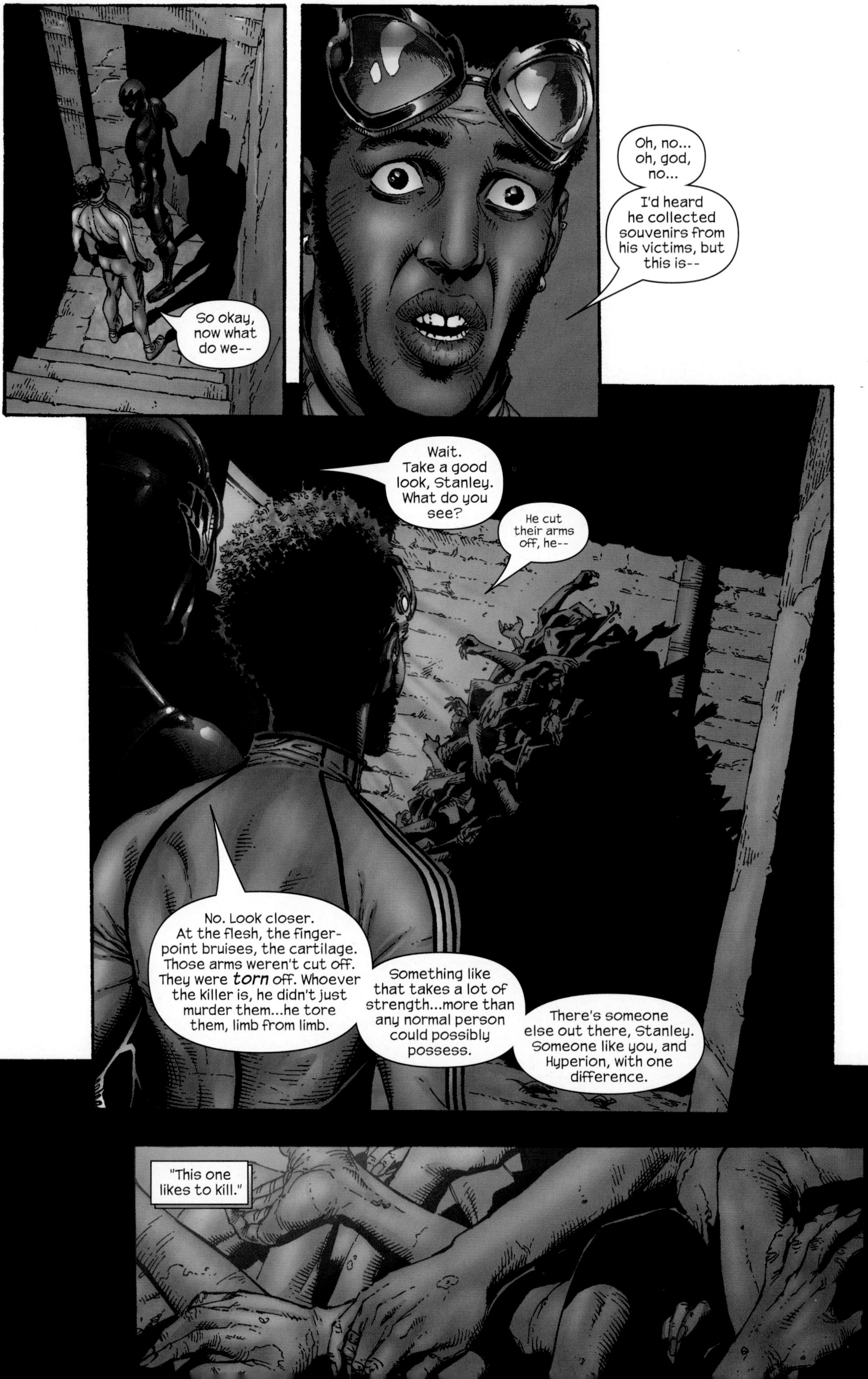
So okay, now what do we--
Oh, no... oh, god, no...
I'd heard he collected souvenirs from his victims, but this is--
Wait. Take a good look, Stanley. What do you see?
He cut their arms off, he--
No. Look closer. At the flesh, the finger-point bruises, the cartilage. Those arms weren't cut off. They were torn off. Whoever the killer is, he didn't just murder them...he tore them, limb from limb.
Something like that takes a lot of strength...more than any normal person could possibly possess.
There's someone else out there, Stanley. Someone like you, and Hyperion, with one difference.
"This one likes to kill."

Ominous Tidings Expressed as Four-Part Harmony

#12

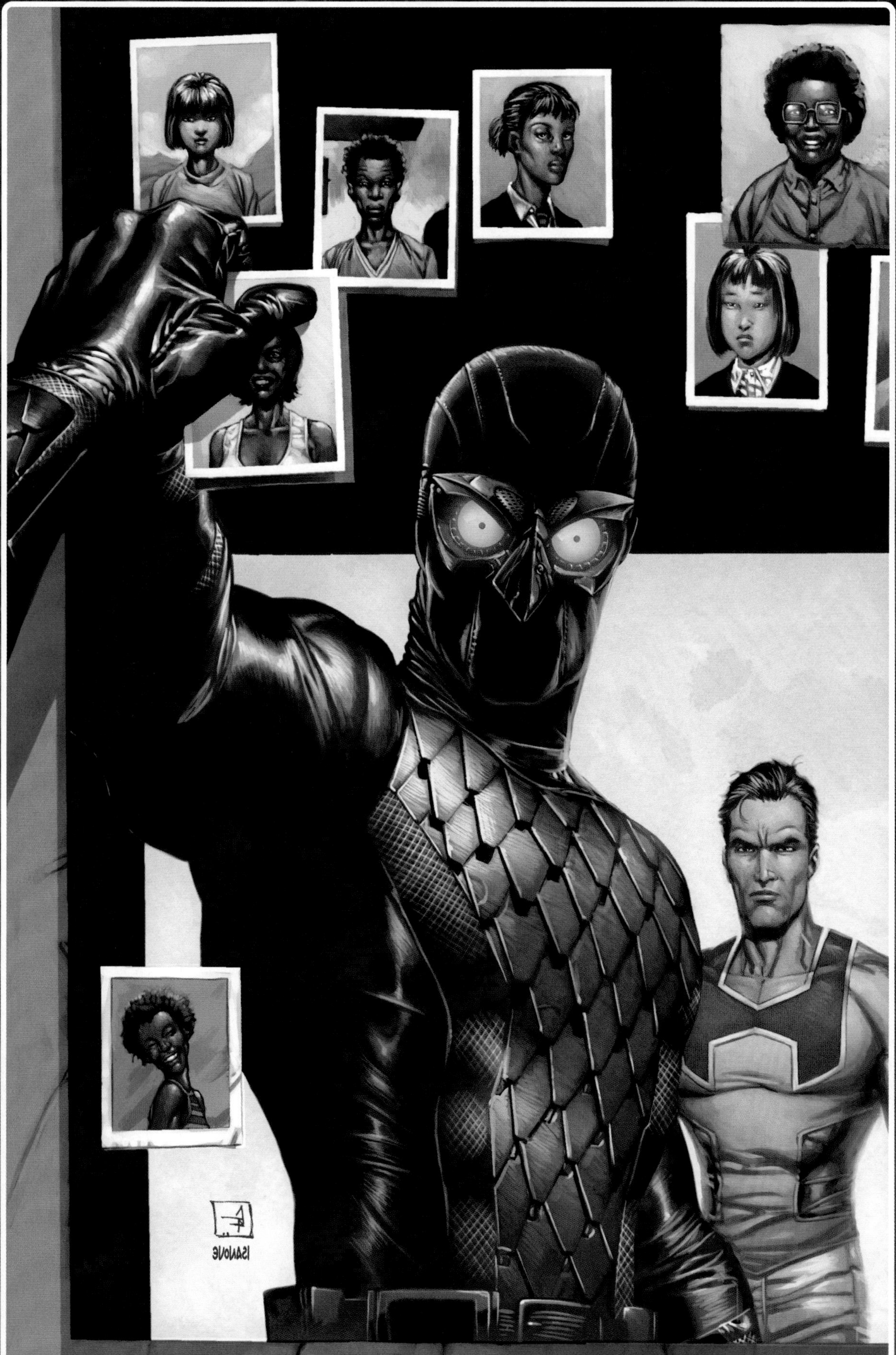

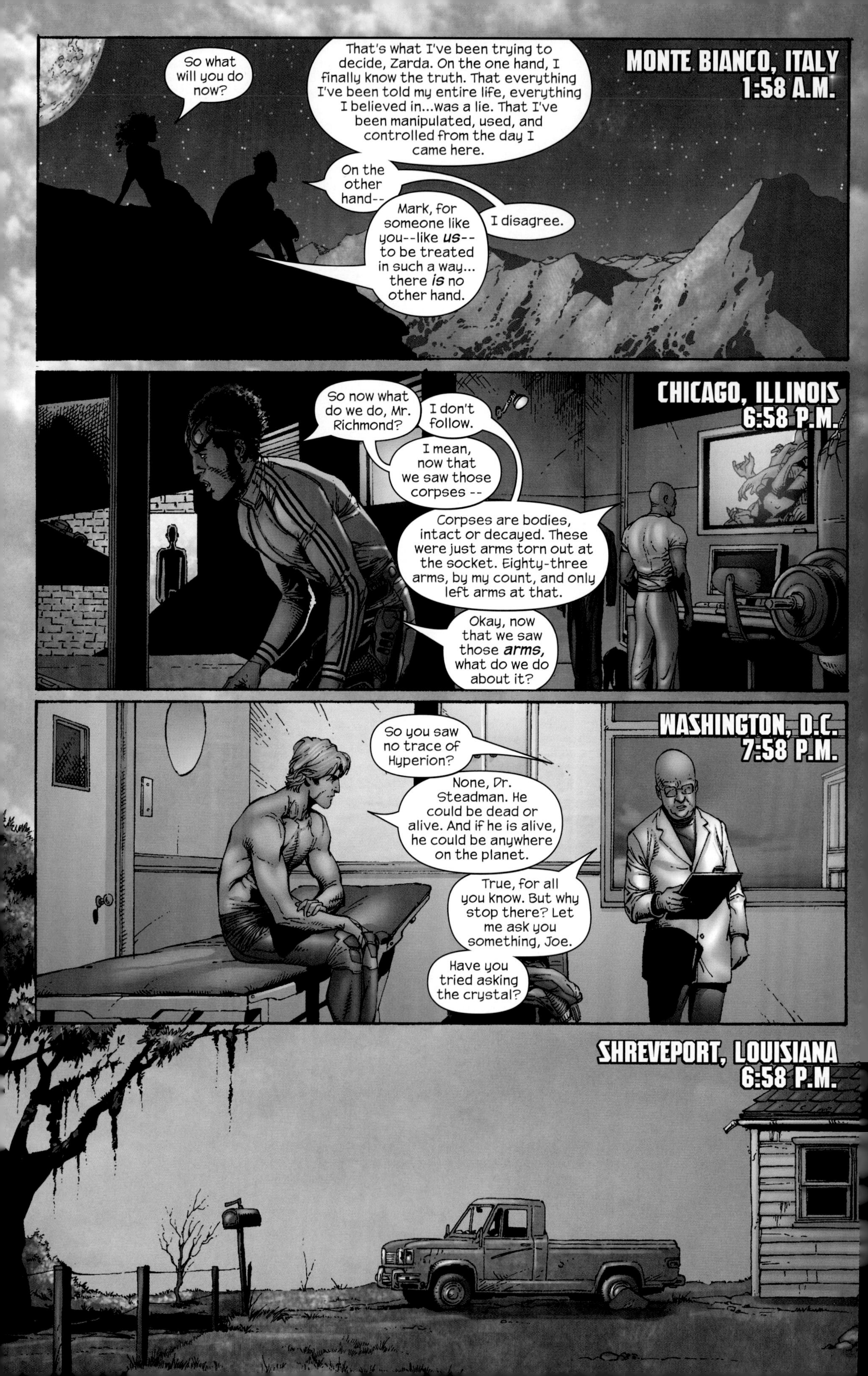
MONTE BIANCO, ITALY
1:58 A.M.
So what will you do now?
That's what I've been trying to decide, Zarda. On the one hand, I finally know the truth. That everything I've been told my entire life, everything I believed in...was a lie. That I've been manipulated, used, and controlled from the day I came here.
On the other hand--
I disagree.
Mark, for someone like you--like *us*--to be treated in such a way... there *is* no other hand.
CHICAGO, ILLINOIS
6:58 P.M.
So now what do we do, Mr. Richmond?
I don't follow.
I mean, now that we saw those corpses --
Corpses are bodies, intact or decayed. These were just arms torn out at the socket. Eighty-three arms, by my count, and only left arms at that.
Okay, now that we saw those *arms,* what do we do about it?
WASHINGTON, D.C.
7:58 P.M.
So you saw no trace of Hyperion?
None, Dr. Steadman. He could be dead or alive. And if he is alive, he could be anywhere on the planet.
True, for all you know. But why stop there? Let me ask you something, Joe.
Have you tried asking the crystal?
SHREVEPORT, LOUISIANA
6:58 P.M.

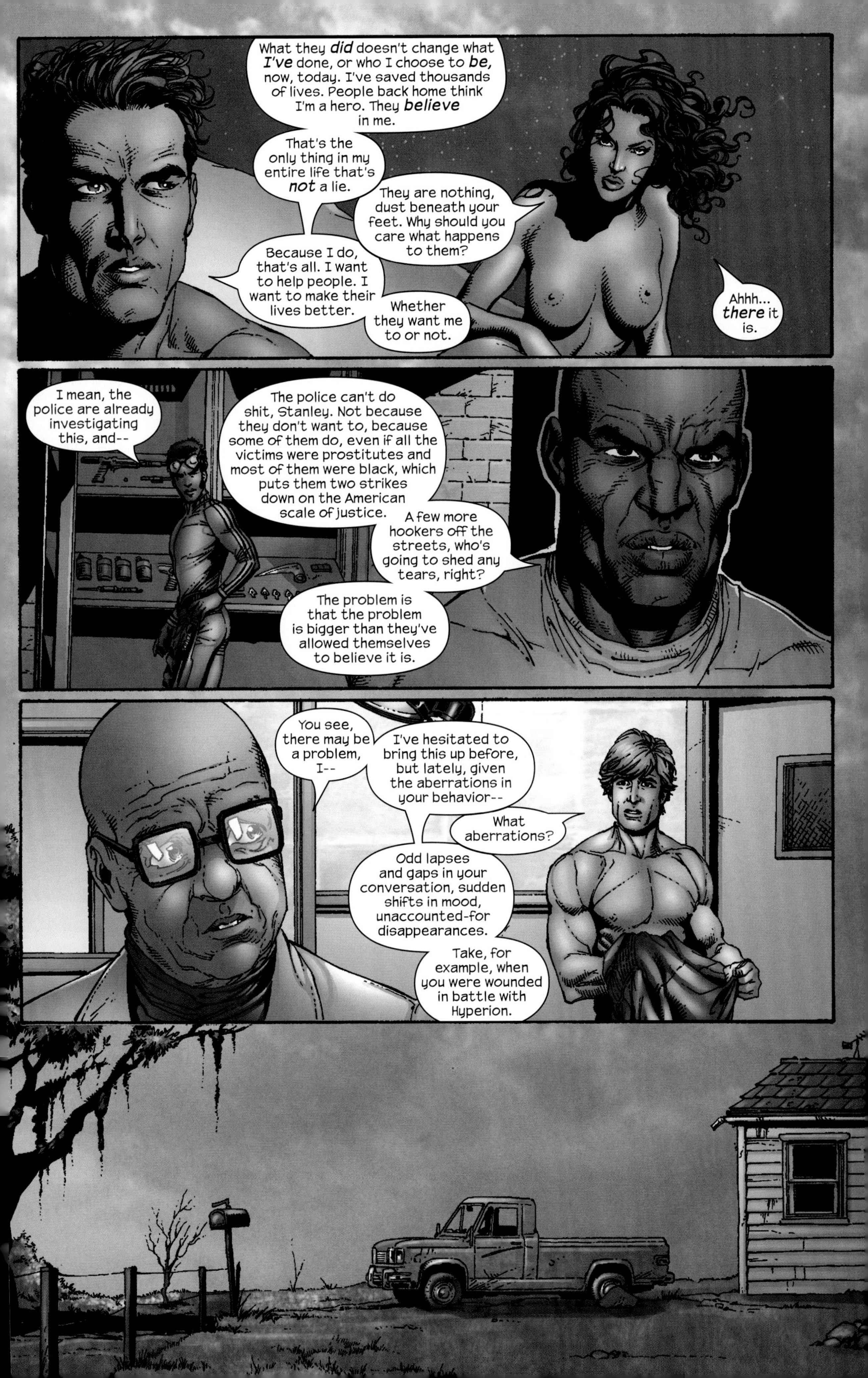
What they *did* doesn't change what *I've* done, or who I choose to *be,* now, today. I've saved thousands of lives. People back home think I'm a hero. They *believe* in me.
That's the only thing in my entire life that's *not* a lie.
They are nothing, dust beneath your feet. Why should you care what happens to them?
Because I do, that's all. I want to help people. I want to make their lives better.
Whether they want me to or not.
Ahhh... *there* it is.
I mean, the police are already investigating this, and--
The police can't do shit, Stanley. Not because they don't want to, because some of them do, even if all the victims were prostitutes and most of them were black, which puts them two strikes down on the American scale of justice.
A few more hookers off the streets, who's going to shed any tears, right?
The problem is that the problem is bigger than they've allowed themselves to believe it is.
You see, there may be a problem, I--
I've hesitated to bring this up before, but lately, given the aberrations in your behavior--
What aberrations?
Odd lapses and gaps in your conversation, sudden shifts in mood, unaccounted-for disappearances.
Take, for example, when you were wounded in battle with Hyperion.

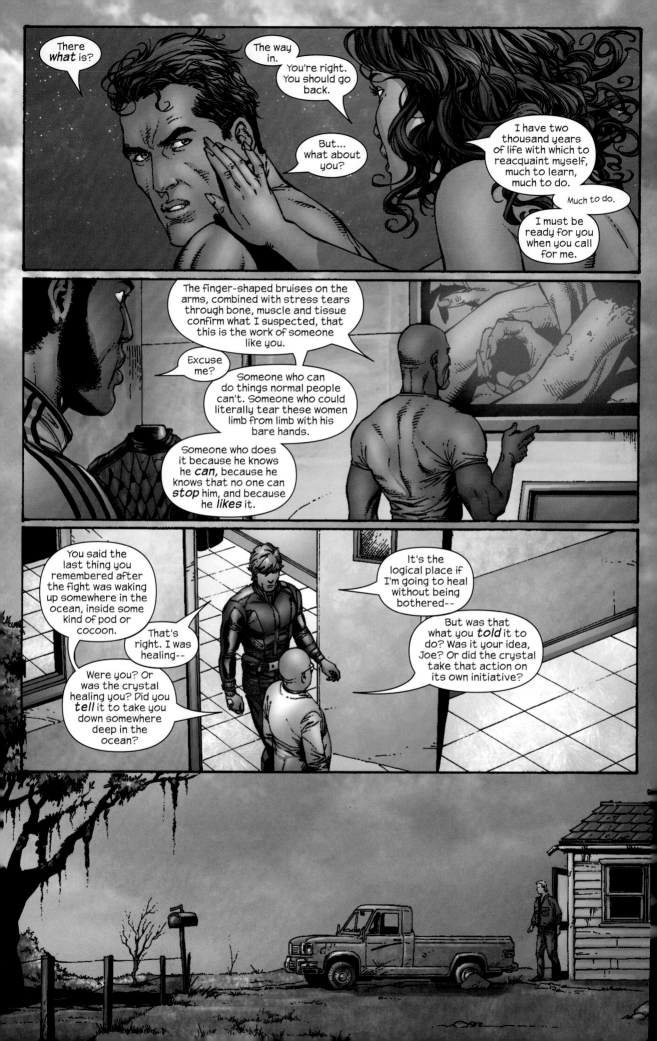

There *what* is?

The way in. You're right. You should go back.

But... what about you?

I have two thousand years of life with which to reacquaint myself, much to learn, much to do.

Much to do.

I must be ready for you when you call for me.

The finger-shaped bruises on the arms, combined with stress tears through bone, muscle and tissue confirm what I suspected, that this is the work of someone like you.

Excuse me?

Someone who can do things normal people can't. Someone who could literally tear these women limb from limb with his bare hands.

Someone who does it because he knows he *can*, because he knows that no one can *stop* him, and because he *likes* it.

You said the last thing you remembered after the fight was waking up somewhere in the ocean, inside some kind of pod or cocoon.

That's right. I was healing--

Were you? Or was the crystal healing you? Did you *tell* it to take you down somewhere deep in the ocean?

It's the logical place if I'm going to heal without being bothered--

But was that what you *told* it to do? Was it your idea, Joe? Or did the crystal take that action on its own initiative?

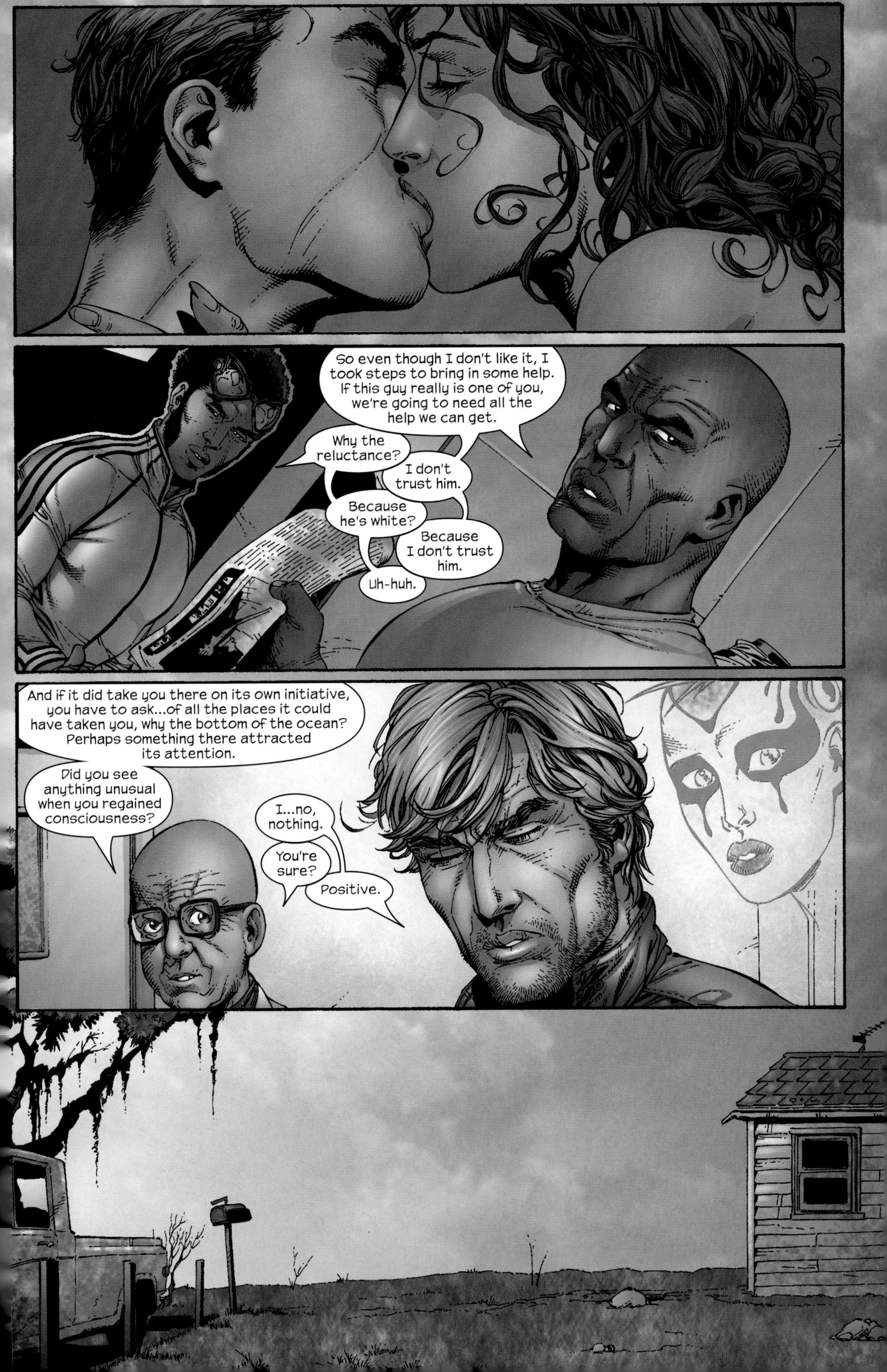
So even though I don't like it, I took steps to bring in some help. If this guy really is one of you, we're going to need all the help we can get.
Why the reluctance?
I don't trust him.
Because he's white?
Because I don't trust him.
Uh-huh.
And if it did take you there on its own initiative, you have to ask...of all the places it could have taken you, why the bottom of the ocean? Perhaps something there attracted its attention.
Did you see anything unusual when you regained consciousness?
I...no, nothing.
You're sure?
Positive.

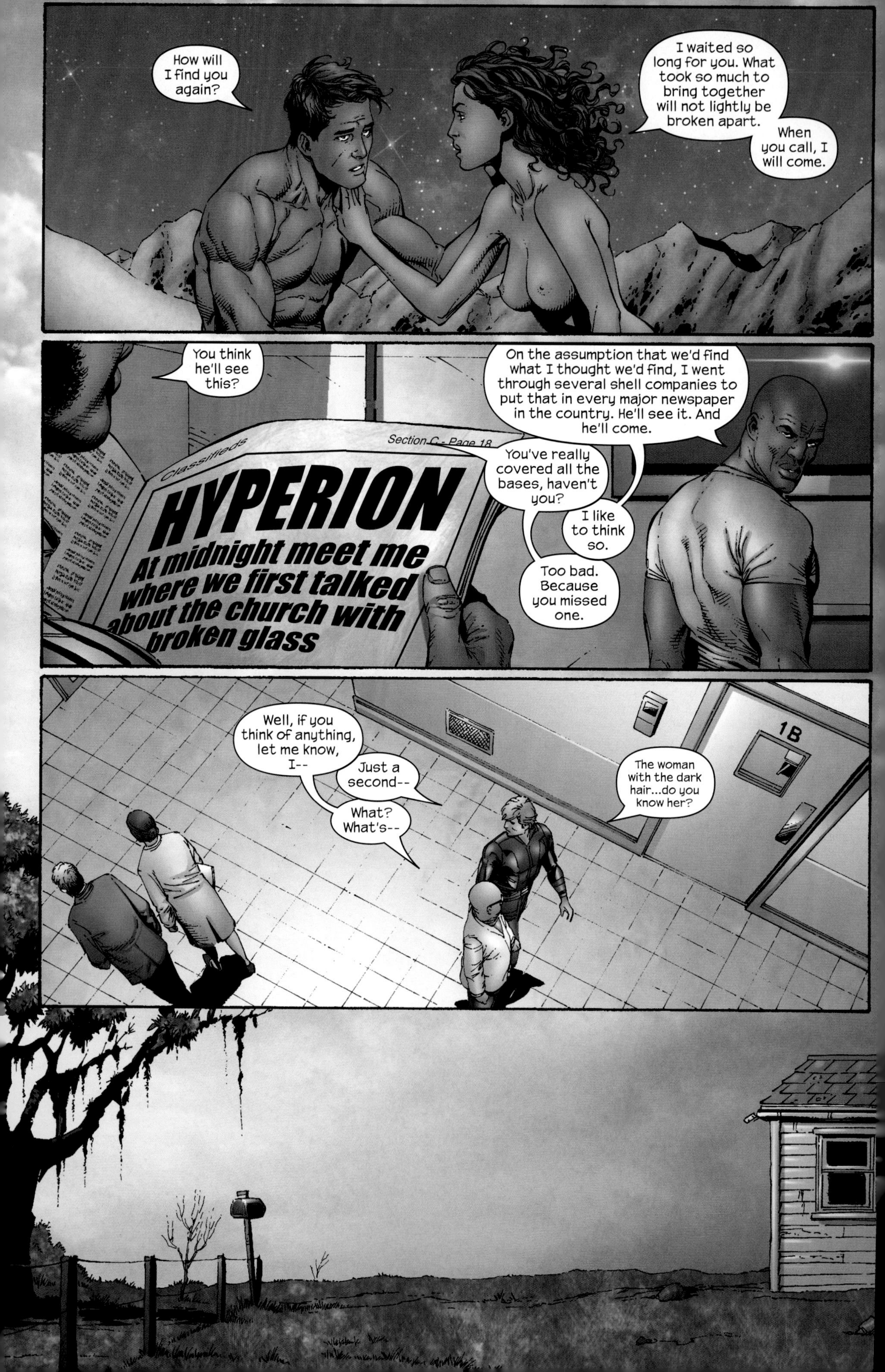
How will I find you again?
I waited so long for you. What took so much to bring together will not lightly be broken apart.
When you call, I will come.
You think he'll see this?
Classifieds
Section C - Page 18
HYPERION
At midnight meet me where we first talked about the church with broken glass
On the assumption that we'd find what I thought we'd find, I went through several shell companies to put that in every major newspaper in the country. He'll see it. And he'll come.
You've really covered all the bases, haven't you?
I like to think so.
Too bad. Because you missed one.
Well, if you think of anything, let me know, I--
Just a second--
What? What's--
1B
The woman with the dark hair...do you know her?

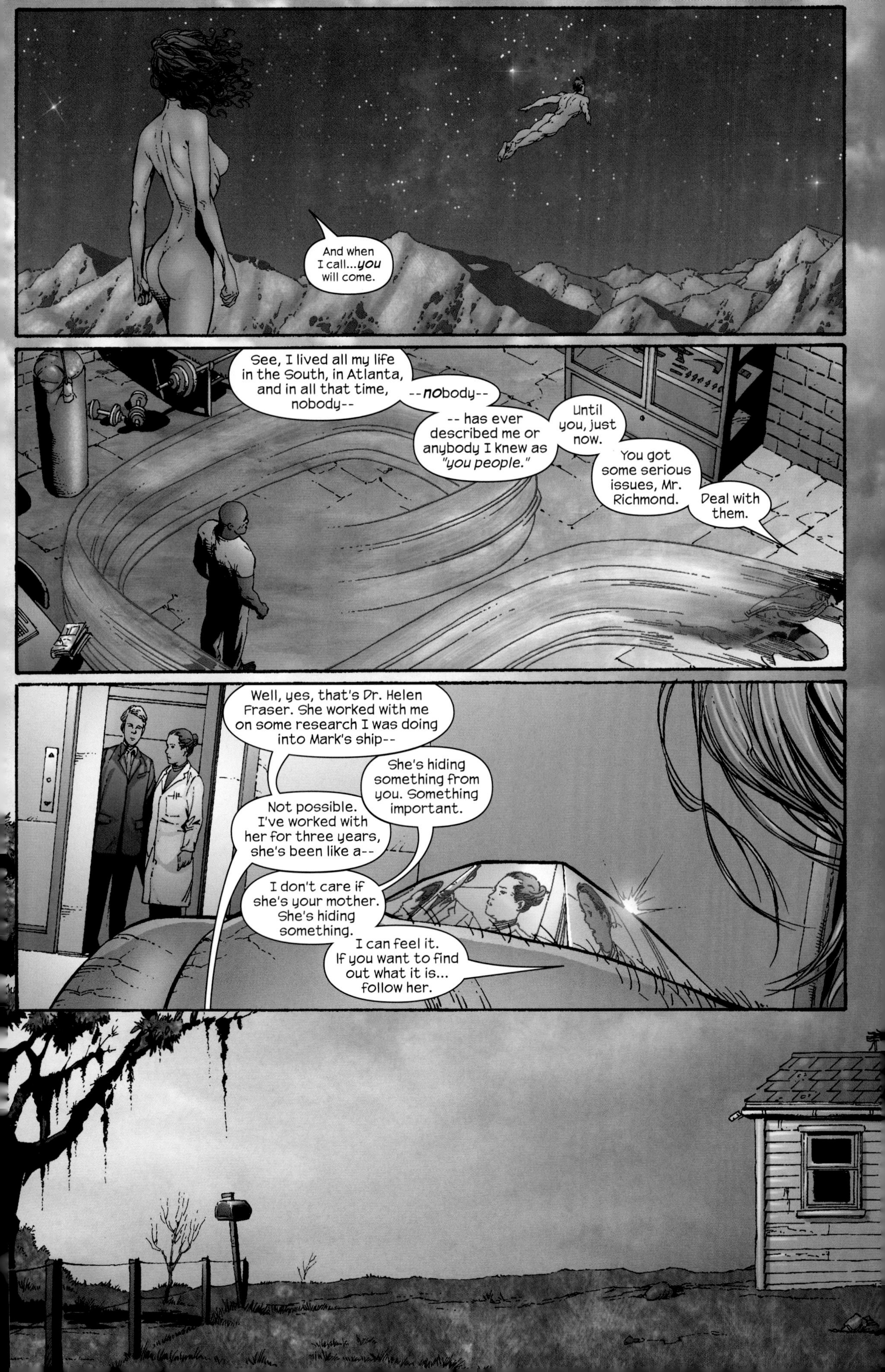
And when I call...*you* will come.
See, I lived all my life in the South, in Atlanta, and in all that time, nobody--
--*NO*body--
-- has ever described me or anybody I knew as *"you people."*
Until you, just now.
You got some serious issues, Mr. Richmond.
Deal with them.
Well, yes, that's Dr. Helen Fraser. She worked with me on some research I was doing into Mark's ship--
She's hiding something from you. Something important.
Not possible. I've worked with her for three years, she's been like a--
I don't care if she's your mother. She's hiding something.
I can feel it. If you want to find out what it is... follow her.

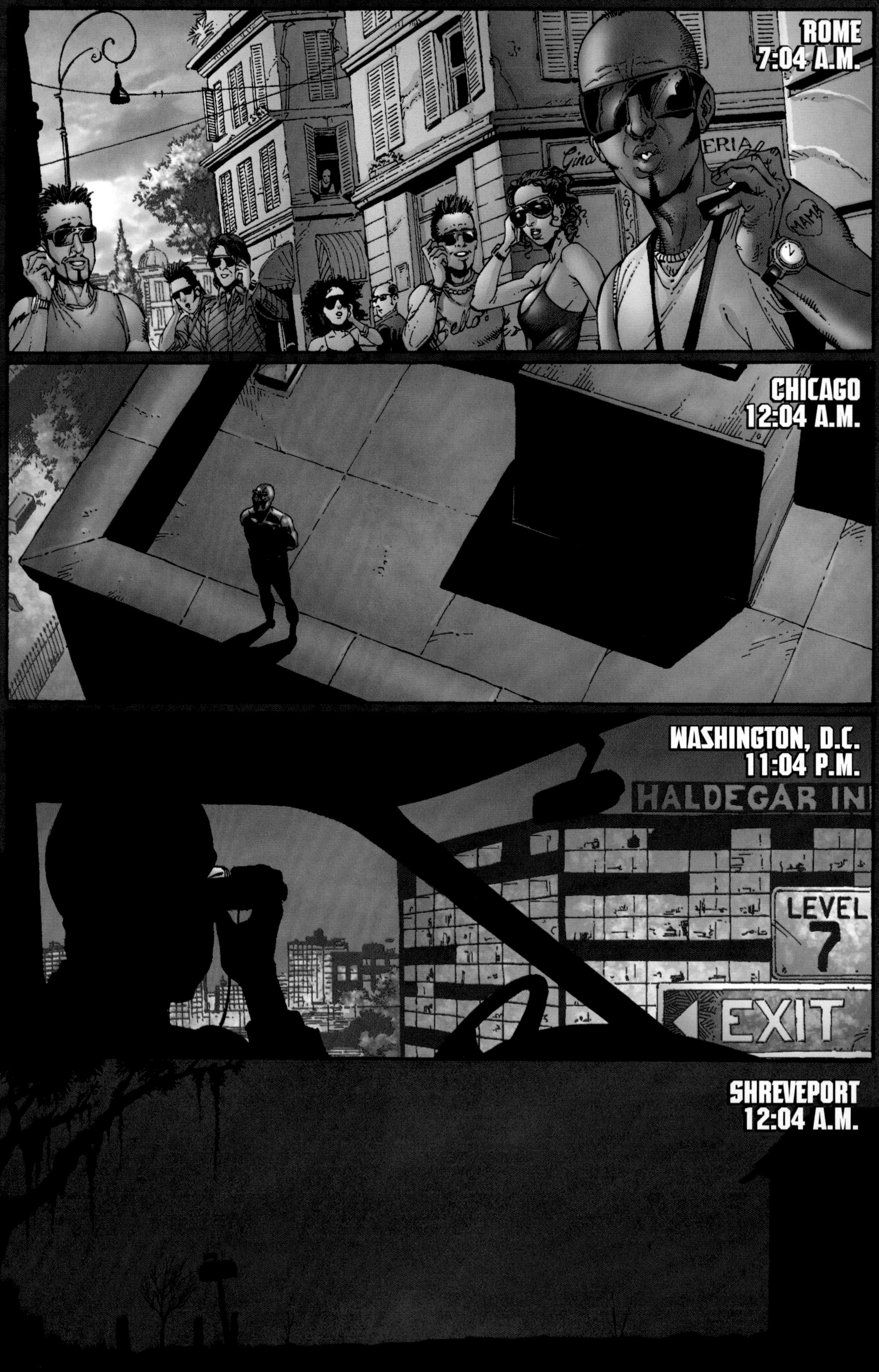
ROME
7:04 A.M.
Gina
Bello
MAMA
CHICAGO
12:04 A.M.
WASHINGTON, D.C.
11:04 P.M.
HALDEGAR IN
LEVEL
7
EXIT
SHREVEPORT
12:04 A.M.

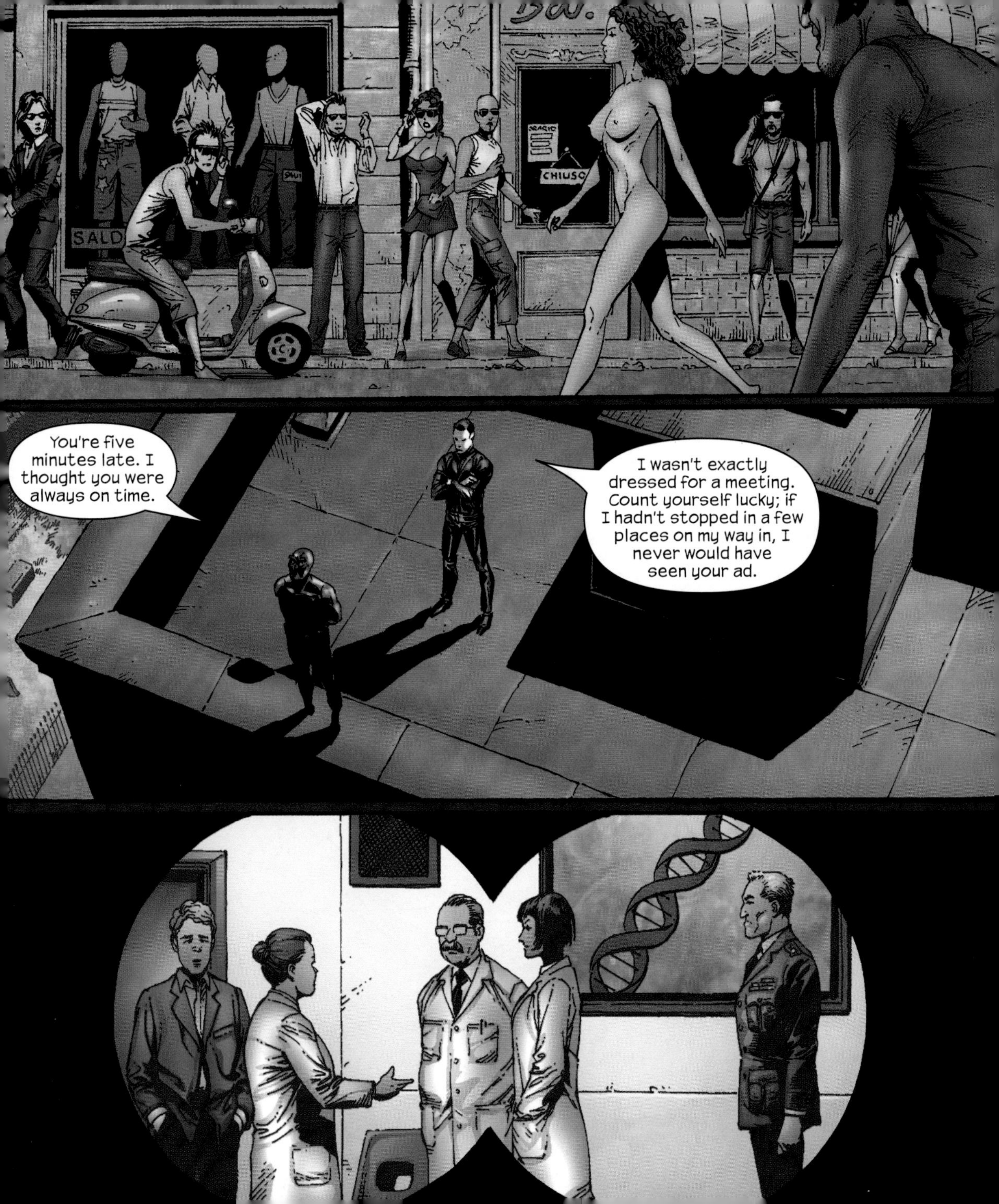
CHIUSO
You're five minutes late. I thought you were always on time.
I wasn't exactly dressed for a meeting. Count yourself lucky; if I hadn't stopped in a few places on my way in, I never would have seen your ad.

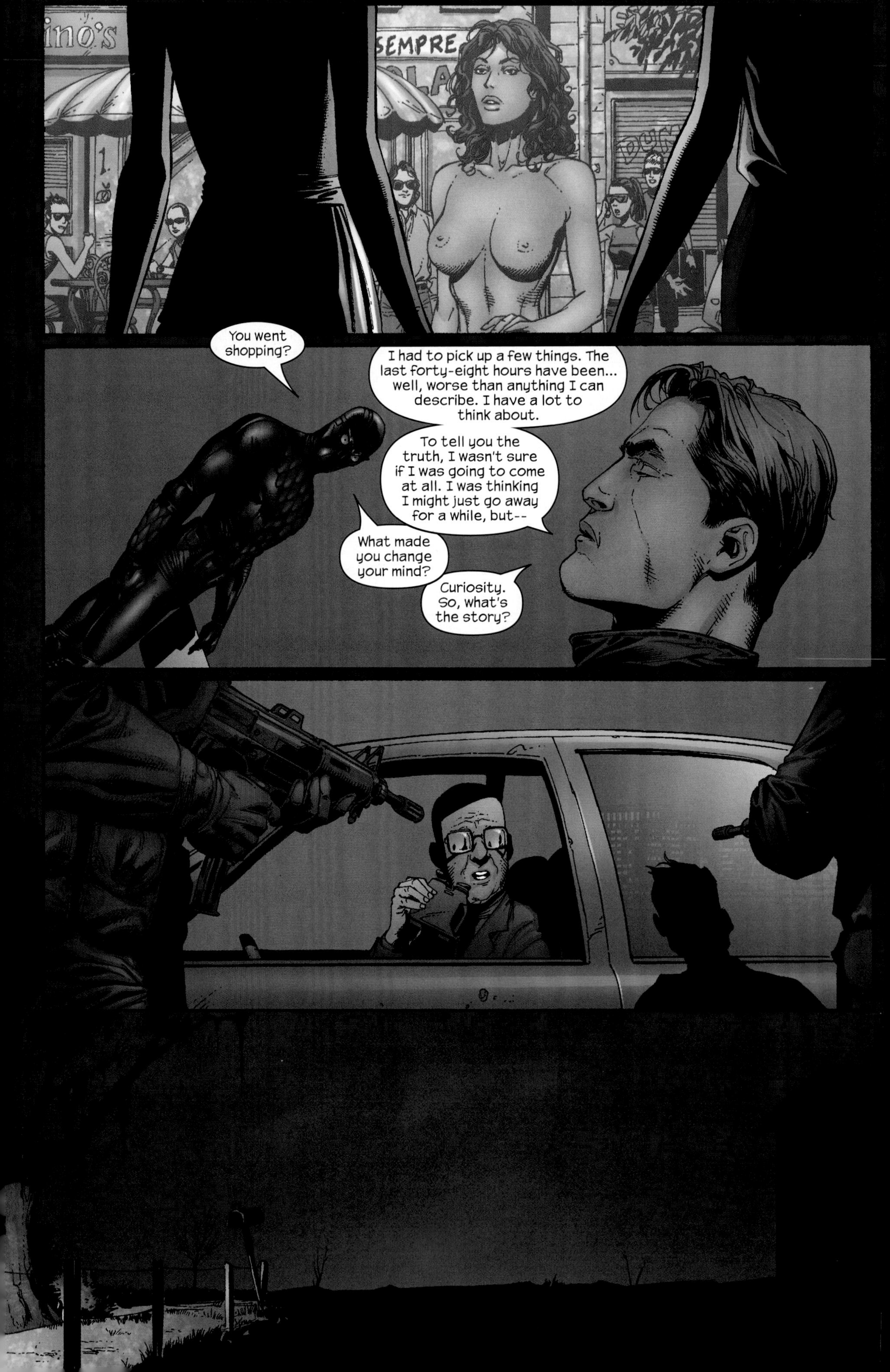
SEMPRE
You went shopping?
I had to pick up a few things. The last forty-eight hours have been... well, worse than anything I can describe. I have a lot to think about.
To tell you the truth, I wasn't sure if I was going to come at all. I was thinking I might just go away for a while, but--
What made you change your mind?
Curiosity. So, what's the story?

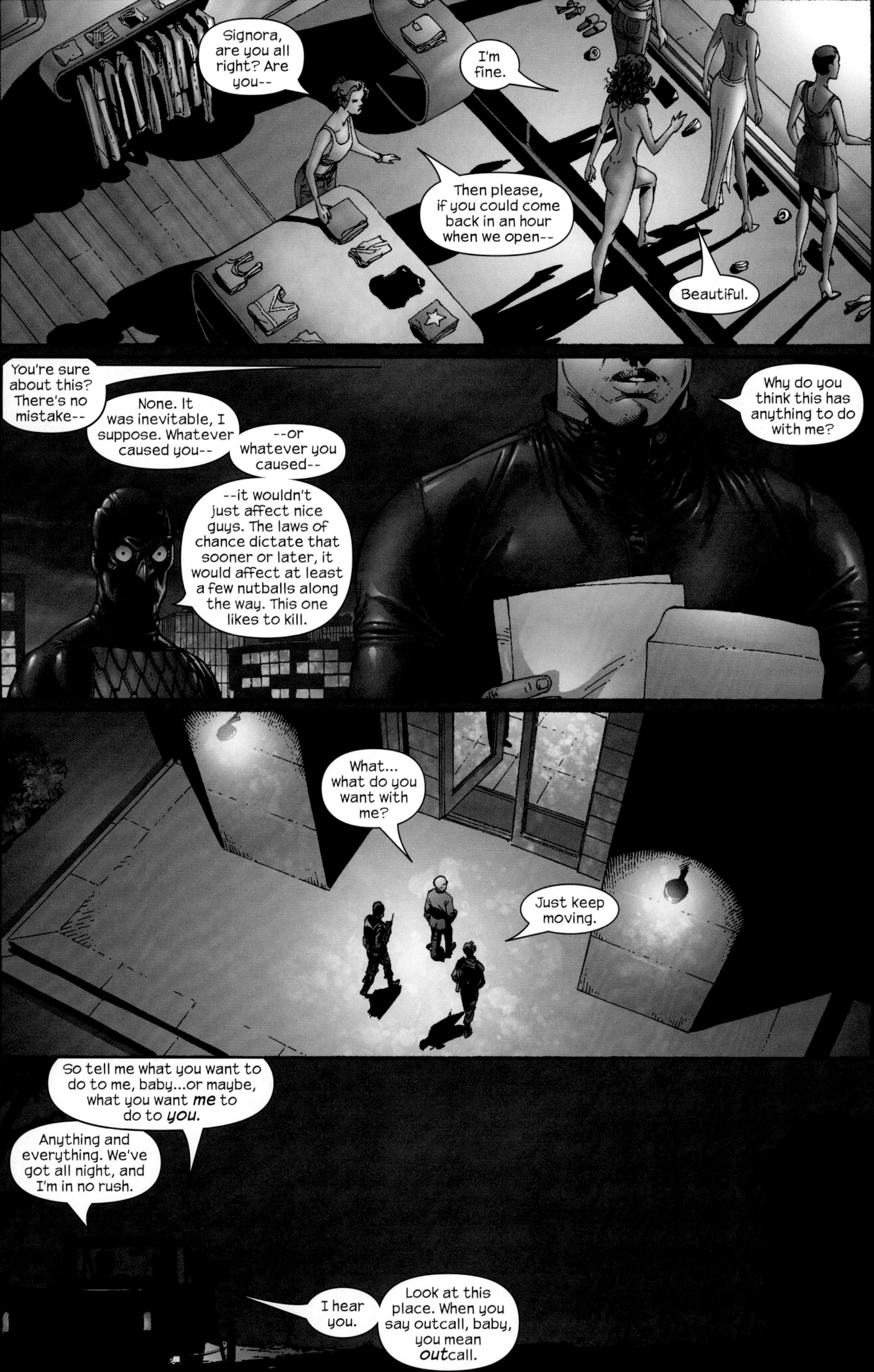
Signora, are you all right? Are you--
I'm fine.
Then please, if you could come back in an hour when we open--
Beautiful.
You're sure about this? There's no mistake--
None. It was inevitable, I suppose. Whatever caused you--
--or whatever you caused--
--it wouldn't just affect nice guys. The laws of chance dictate that sooner or later, it would affect at least a few nutballs along the way. This one likes to kill.
Why do you think this has anything to do with me?
What... what do you want with me?
Just keep moving.
So tell me what you want to do to me, baby...or maybe, what you want me to do to you.
Anything and everything. We've got all night, and I'm in no rush.
I hear you.
Look at this place. When you say outcall, baby, you mean outcall.

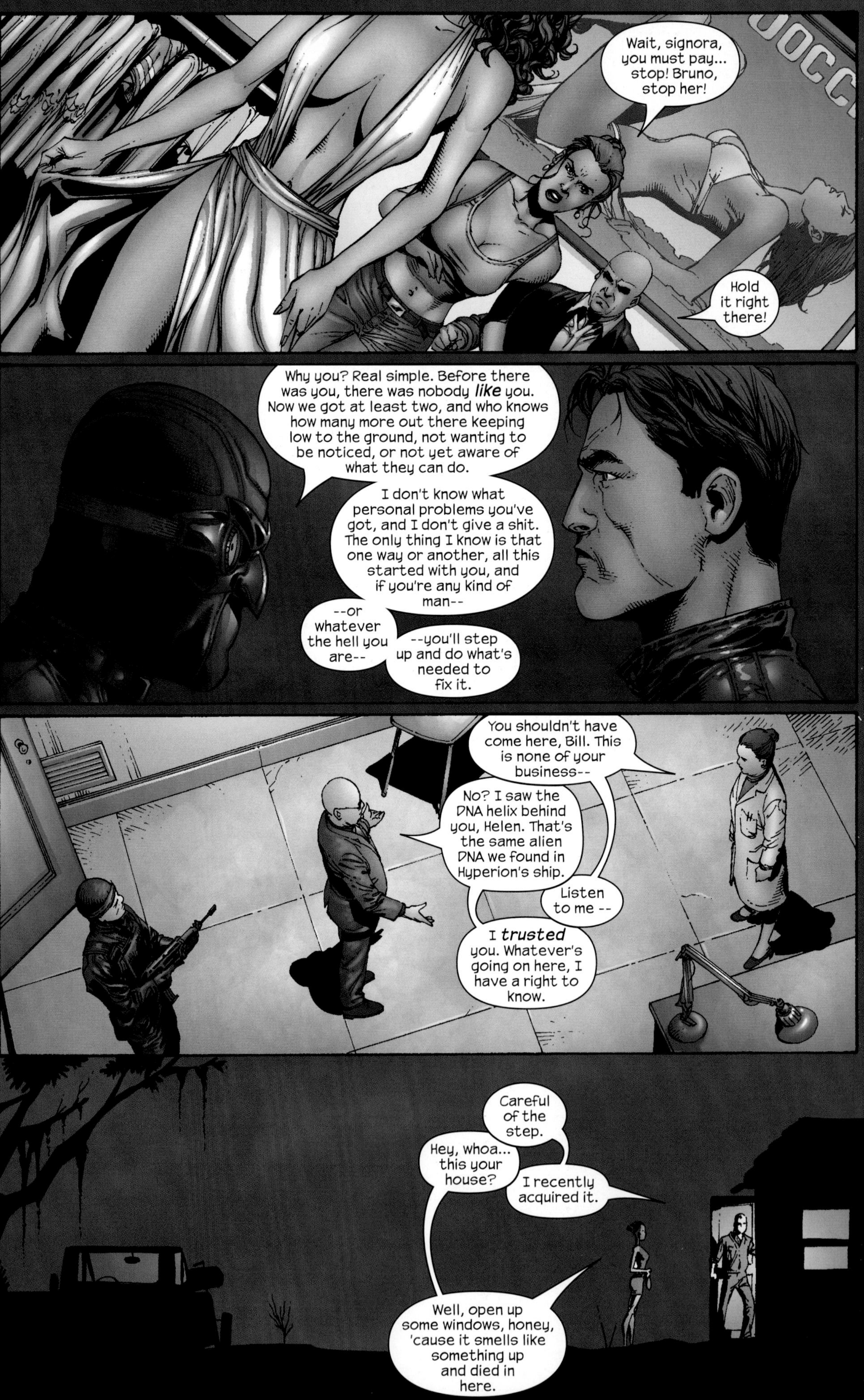

Wait, signora, you must pay... stop! Bruno, stop her!
Hold it right there!
Why you? Real simple. Before there was you, there was nobody *like* you. Now we got at least two, and who knows how many more out there keeping low to the ground, not wanting to be noticed, or not yet aware of what they can do.
I don't know what personal problems you've got, and I don't give a shit. The only thing I know is that one way or another, all this started with you, and if you're any kind of man--
--or whatever the hell you are--
--you'll step up and do what's needed to fix it.
You shouldn't have come here, Bill. This is none of your business--
No? I saw the DNA helix behind you, Helen. That's the same alien DNA we found in Hyperion's ship.
Listen to me --
I *trusted* you. Whatever's going on here, I have a right to know.
Careful of the step.
Hey, whoa... this your house?
I recently acquired it.
Well, open up some windows, honey, 'cause it smells like something up and died in here.

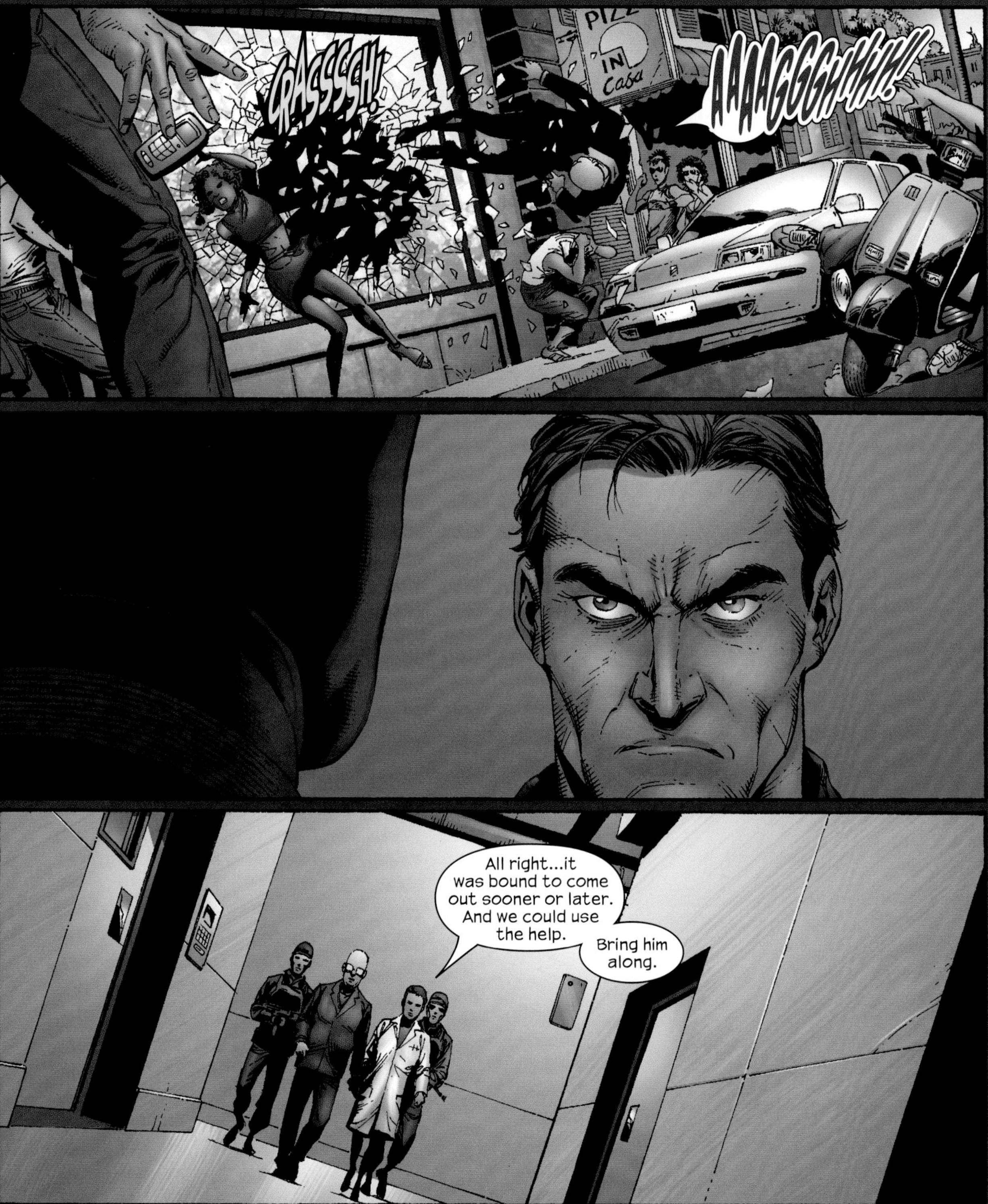
CRASSSSH!
AAAAGGGHHHH!
PIZZ
IN
Casa
All right...it was bound to come out sooner or later. And we could use the help.
Bring him along.

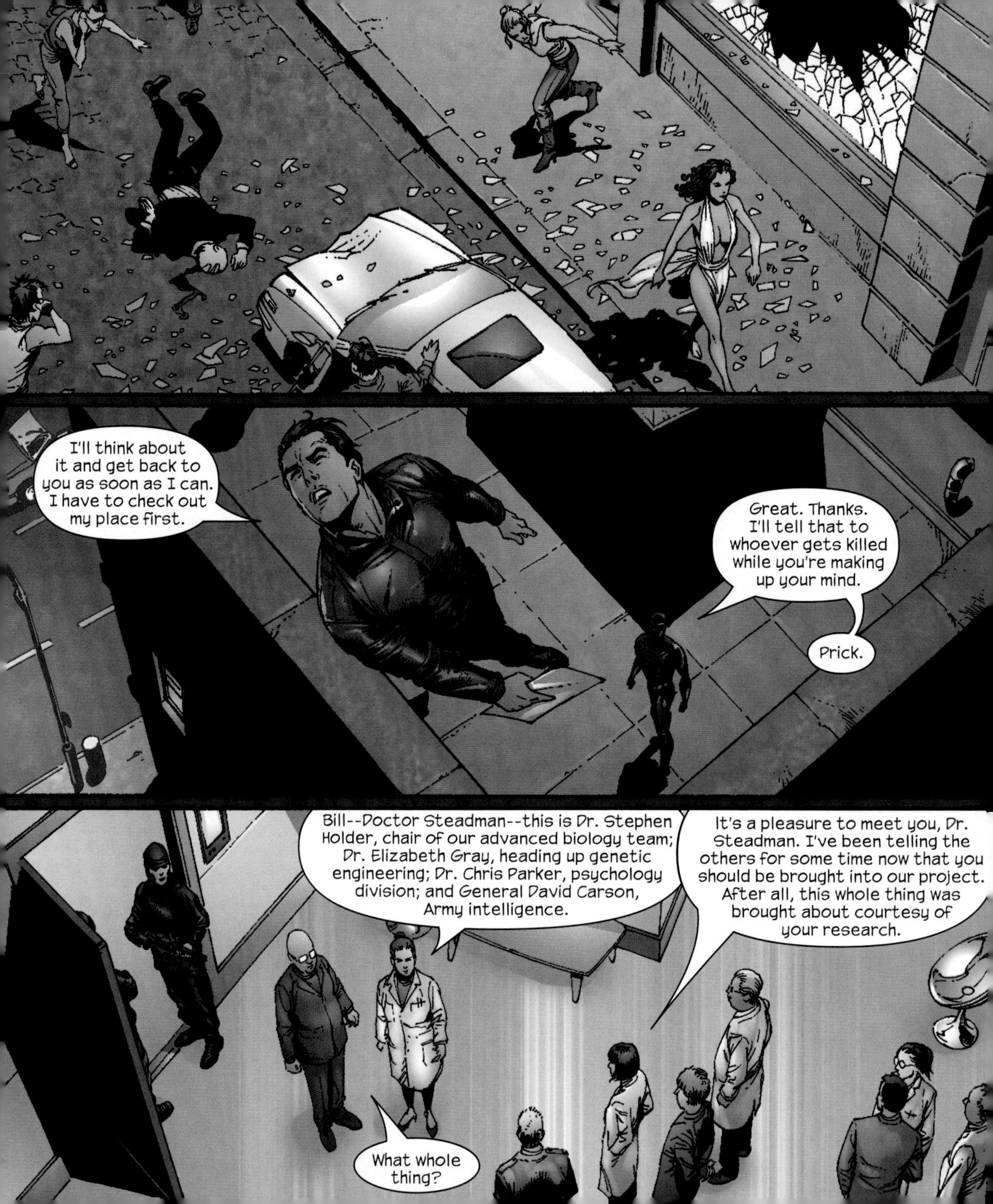

I'll think about it and get back to you as soon as I can. I have to check out my place first.
Great. Thanks. I'll tell that to whoever gets killed while you're making up your mind.
Prick.
Bill--Doctor Steadman--this is Dr. Stephen Holder, chair of our advanced biology team; Dr. Elizabeth Gray, heading up genetic engineering; Dr. Chris Parker, psychology division; and General David Carson, Army intelligence.
It's a pleasure to meet you, Dr. Steadman. I've been telling the others for some time now that you should be brought into our project. After all, this whole thing was brought about courtesy of your research.
What whole thing?

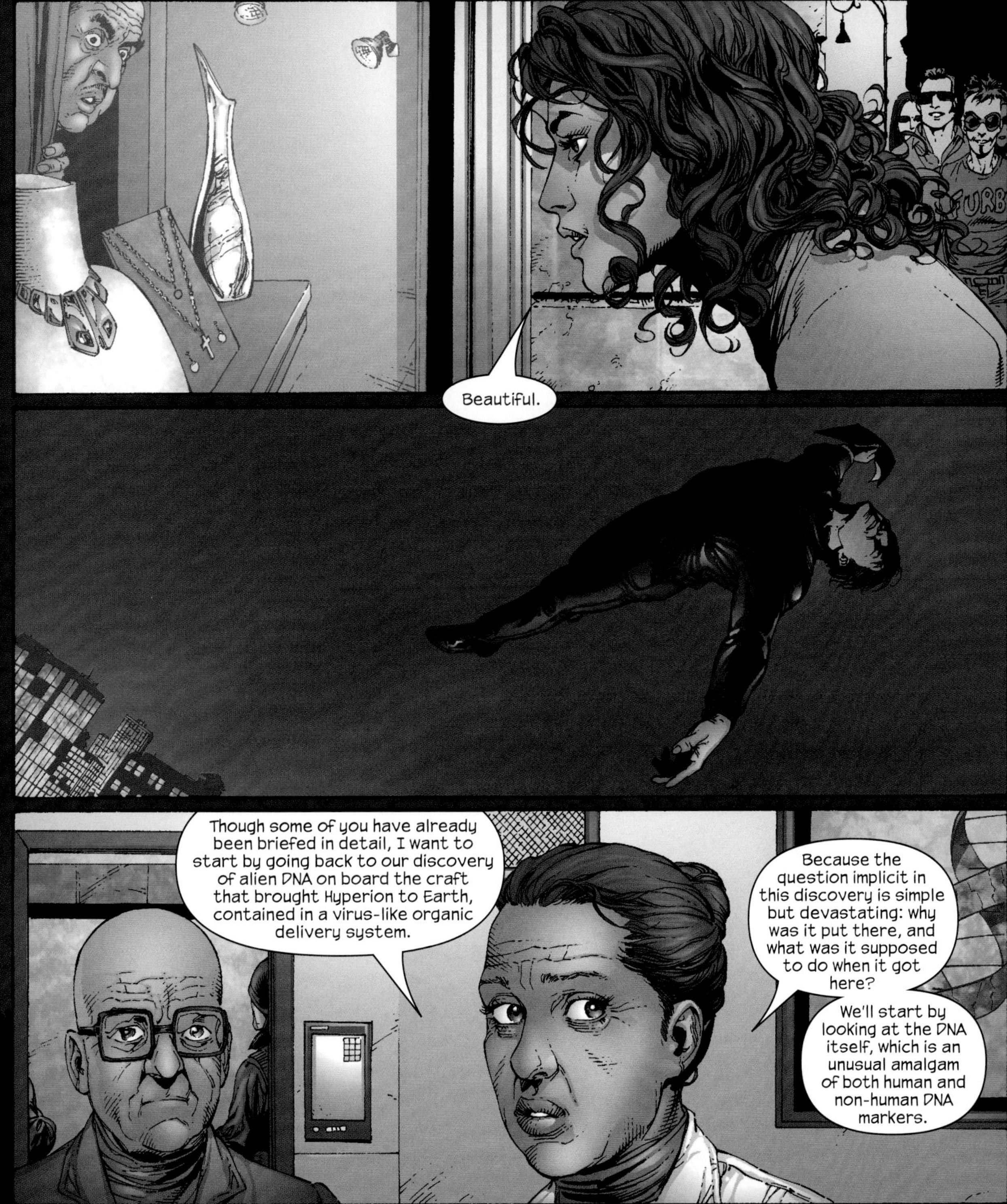
Beautiful.
Though some of you have already been briefed in detail, I want to start by going back to our discovery of alien DNA on board the craft that brought Hyperion to Earth, contained in a virus-like organic delivery system.
Because the question implicit in this discovery is simple but devastating: why was it put there, and what was it supposed to do when it got here?
We'll start by looking at the DNA itself, which is an unusual amalgam of both human and non-human DNA markers.

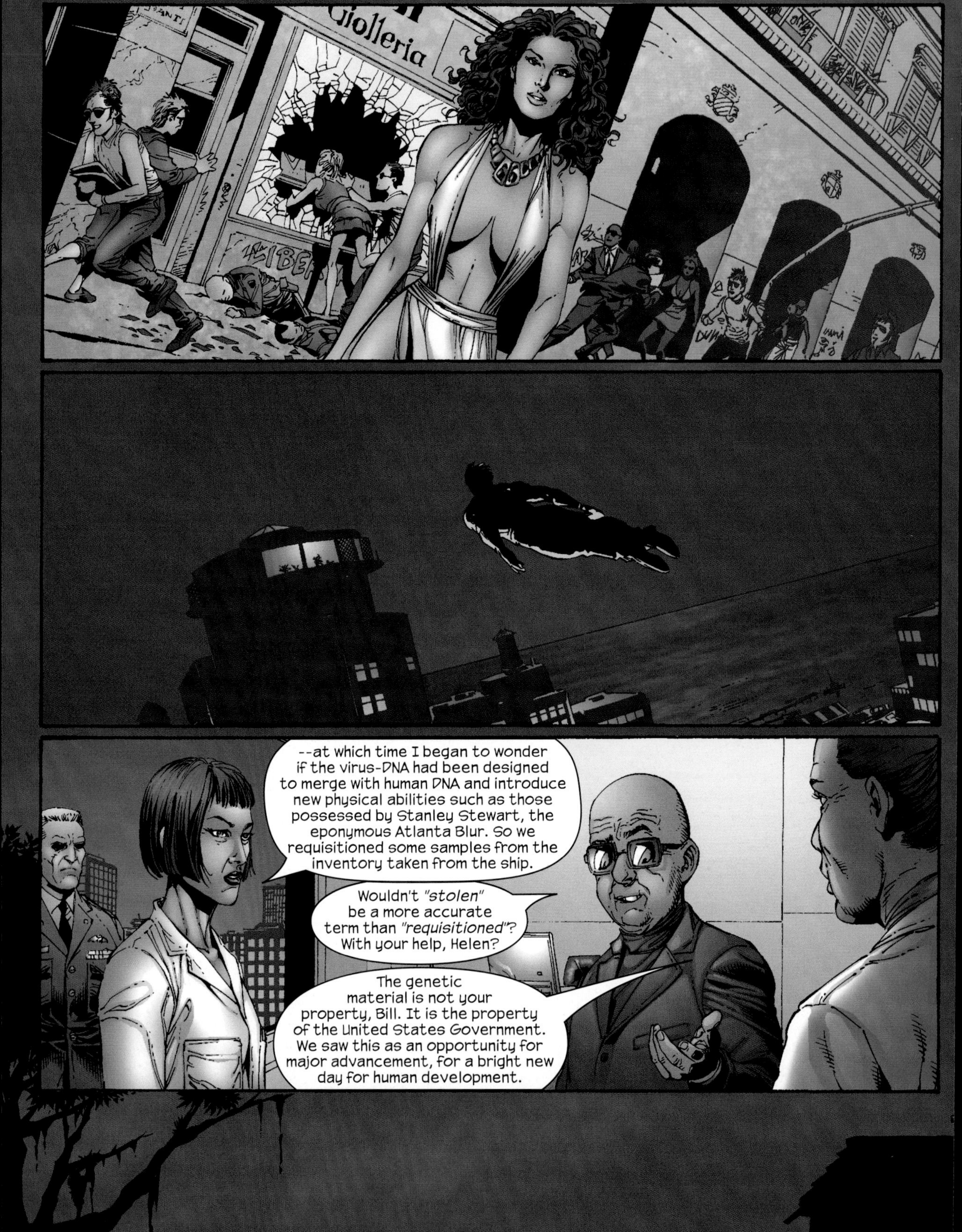

Gioielleria
--at which time I began to wonder if the virus-DNA had been designed to merge with human DNA and introduce new physical abilities such as those possessed by Stanley Stewart, the eponymous Atlanta Blur. So we requisitioned some samples from the inventory taken from the ship.
Wouldn't "stolen" be a more accurate term than "requisitioned"? With your help, Helen?
The genetic material is not your property, Bill. It is the property of the United States Government. We saw this as an opportunity for major advancement, for a bright new day for human development.

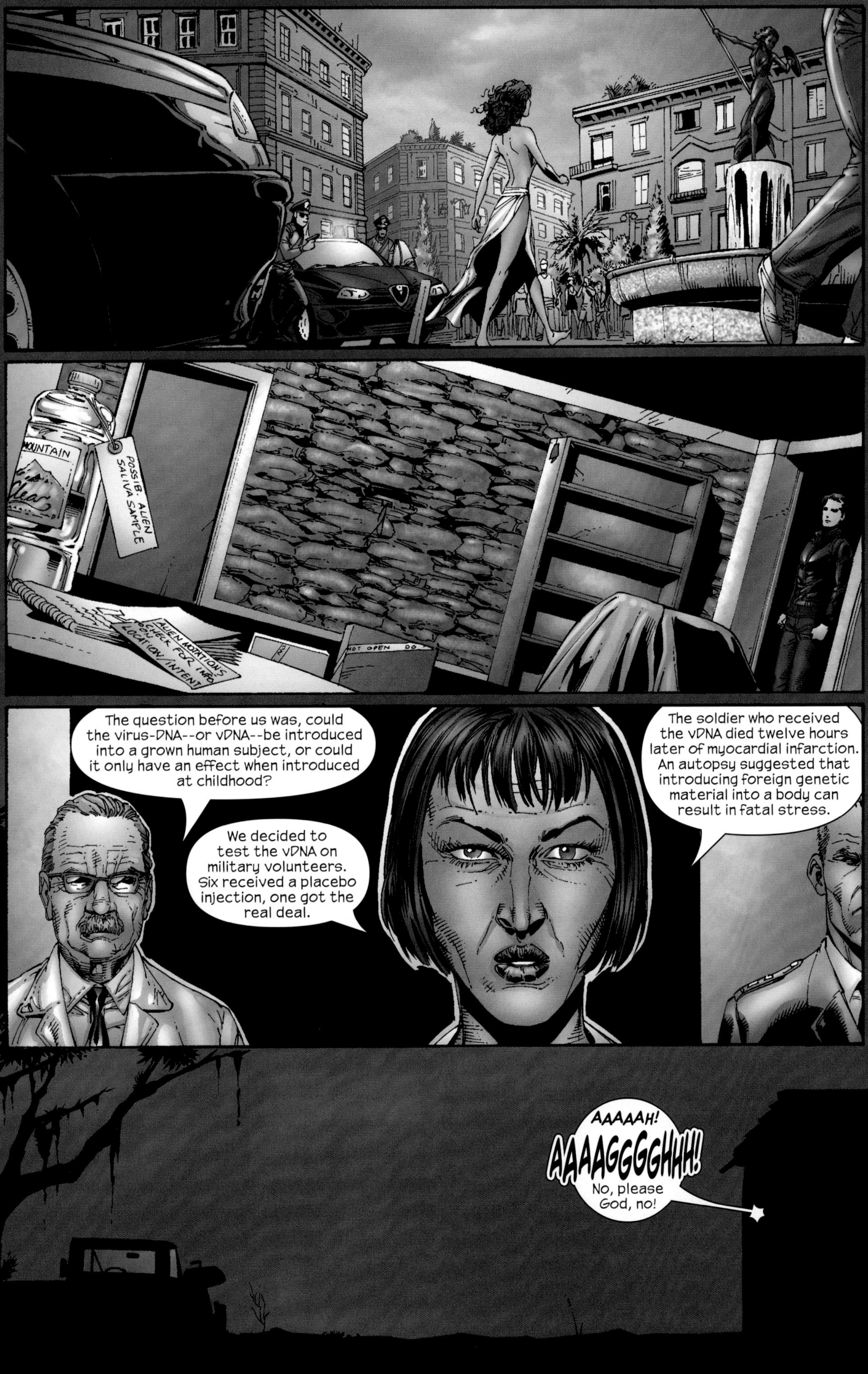
MOUNTAIN
POSSIB. ALIEN SALIVA SAMPLE
ALIEN NOTATIONS? CHECK FOR INFO ON LOCATION/INTENT
The question before us was, could the virus-DNA--or vDNA--be introduced into a grown human subject, or could it only have an effect when introduced at childhood?
We decided to test the vDNA on military volunteers. Six received a placebo injection, one got the real deal.
The soldier who received the vDNA died twelve hours later of myocardial infarction. An autopsy suggested that introducing foreign genetic material into a body can result in fatal stress.
AAAAAH!
AAAAGGGHHH!
No, please God, no!

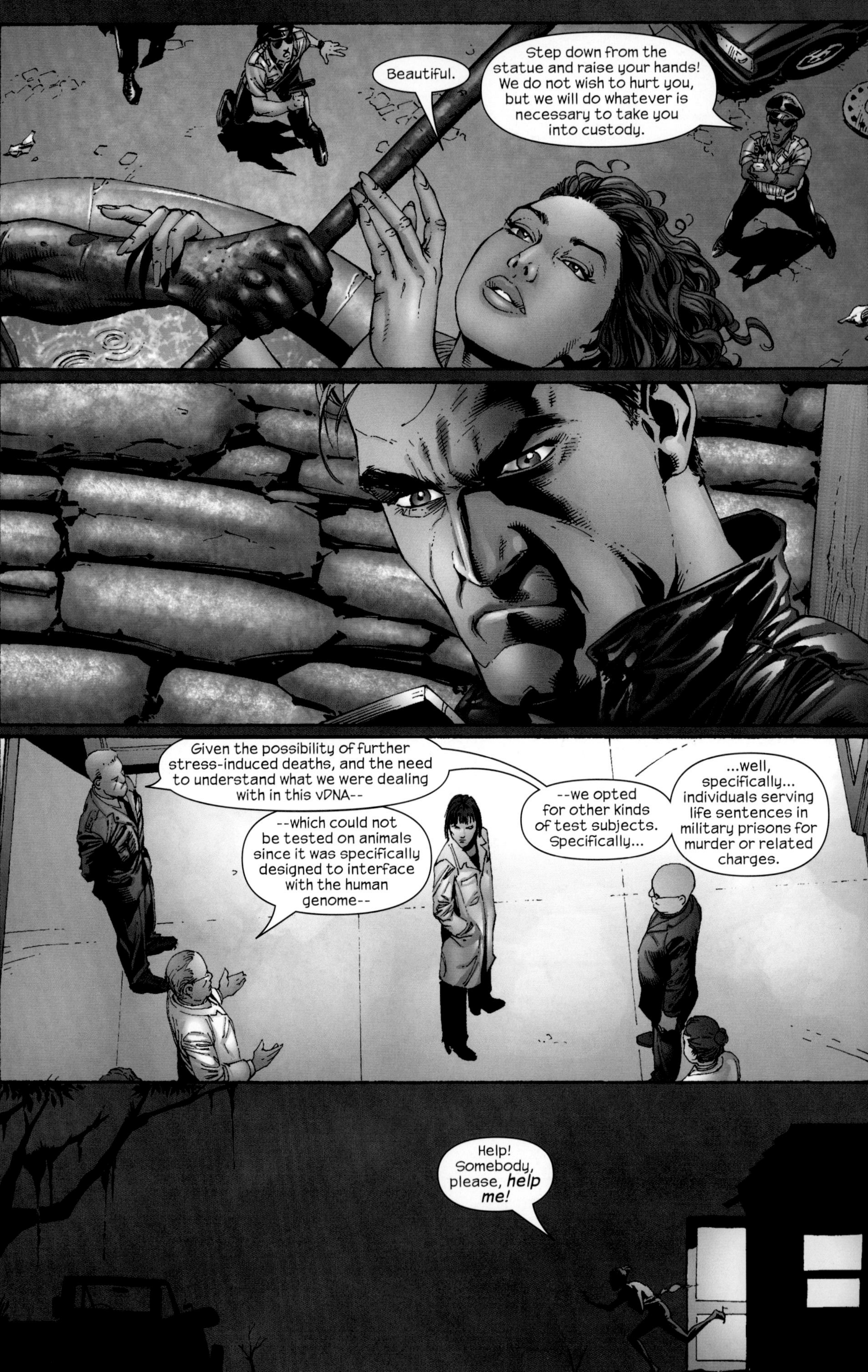
Beautiful.
Step down from the statue and raise your hands! We do not wish to hurt you, but we will do whatever is necessary to take you into custody.
Given the possibility of further stress-induced deaths, and the need to understand what we were dealing with in this vDNA--
--which could not be tested on animals since it was specifically designed to interface with the human genome--
--we opted for other kinds of test subjects. Specifically...
...well, specifically... individuals serving life sentences in military prisons for murder or related charges.
Help! Somebody, please, *help me!*

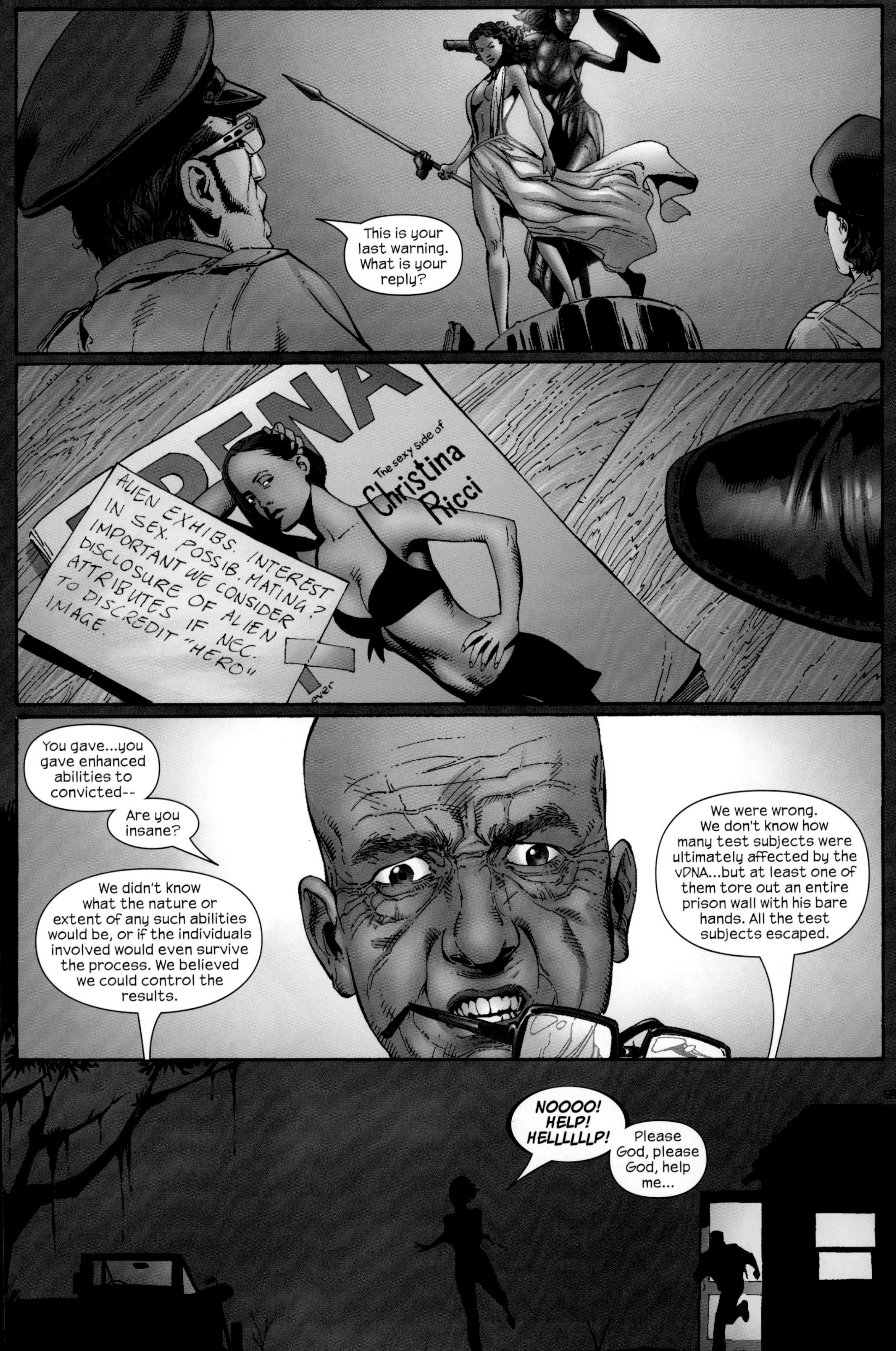

This is your last warning. What is your reply?
The sexy side of Christina Ricci
ALIEN EXHIBS. INTEREST IN SEX. POSSIB. MATING? IMPORTANT WE CONSIDER DISCLOSURE OF ALIEN ATTRIBUTES IF NEC. TO DISCREDIT "HERO" IMAGE.
You gave...you gave enhanced abilities to convicted--
Are you insane?
We didn't know what the nature or extent of any such abilities would be, or if the individuals involved would even survive the process. We believed we could control the results.
We were wrong. We don't know how many test subjects were ultimately affected by the vDNA...but at least one of them tore out an entire prison wall with his bare hands. All the test subjects escaped.
NOOOO! HELP! HELLLLLLP!
Please God, please God, help me...

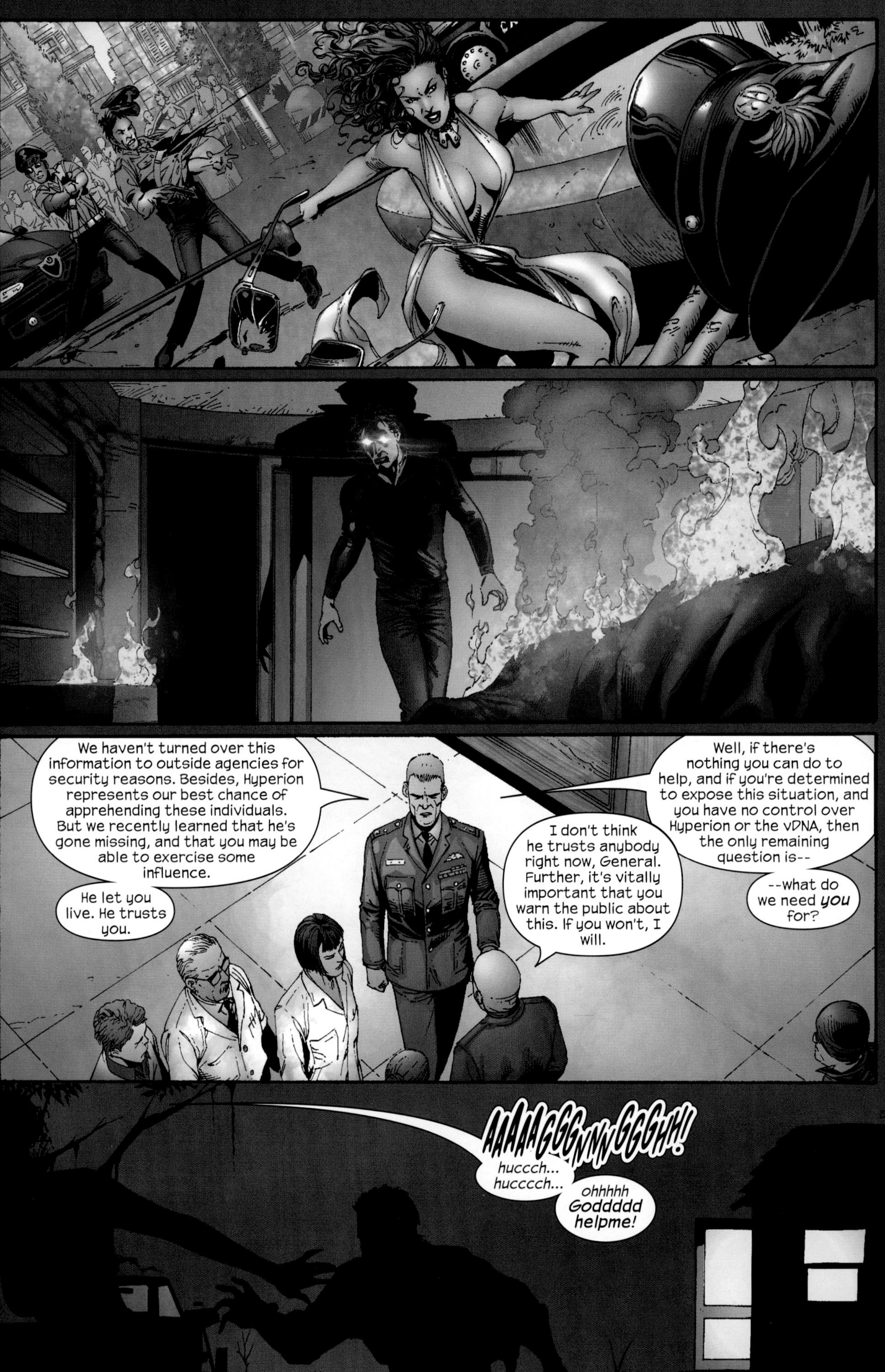
We haven't turned over this information to outside agencies for security reasons. Besides, Hyperion represents our best chance of apprehending these individuals. But we recently learned that he's gone missing, and that you may be able to exercise some influence.
He let you live. He trusts you.
I don't think he trusts anybody right now, General. Further, it's vitally important that you warn the public about this. If you won't, I will.
Well, if there's nothing you can do to help, and if you're determined to expose this situation, and you have no control over Hyperion or the vDNA, then the only remaining question is--
--what do we need **you** for?
AAAAAGGGNNNGGGHH!
hucccch... huccccch...
ohhhhh Godddddd helpme!

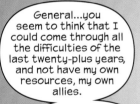

General...you seem to think that I could come through all the difficulties of the last twenty-plus years, and not have my own resources, my own allies.

Do you really think I would come here without precautions?

FEEEEEEIEEE...

SKRUNNNCH

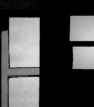

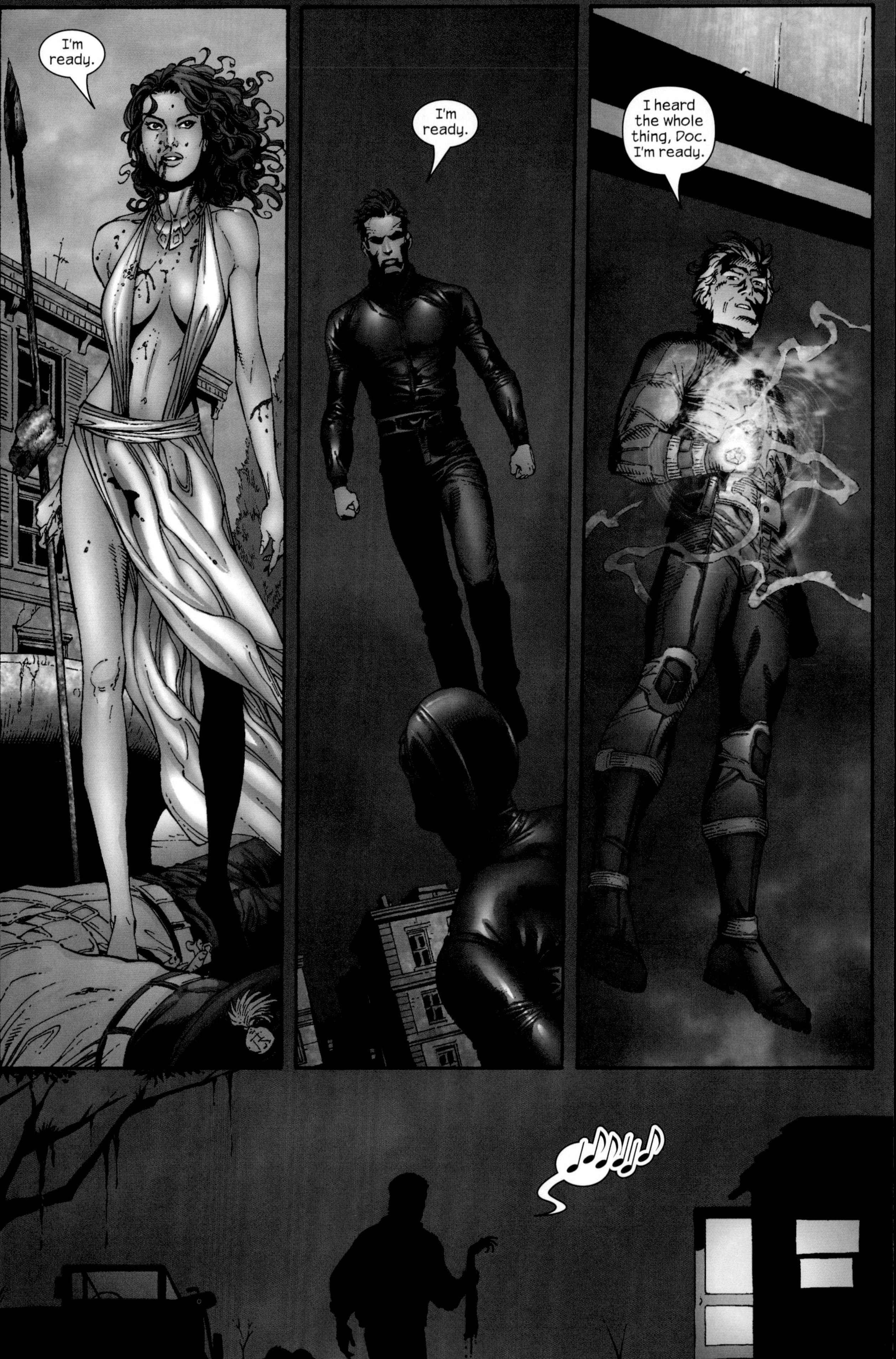
I'm ready.
I'm ready.
I heard the whole thing, Doc. I'm ready.

Supreme Power #1 Special Edition Cover
by Joe Quesada

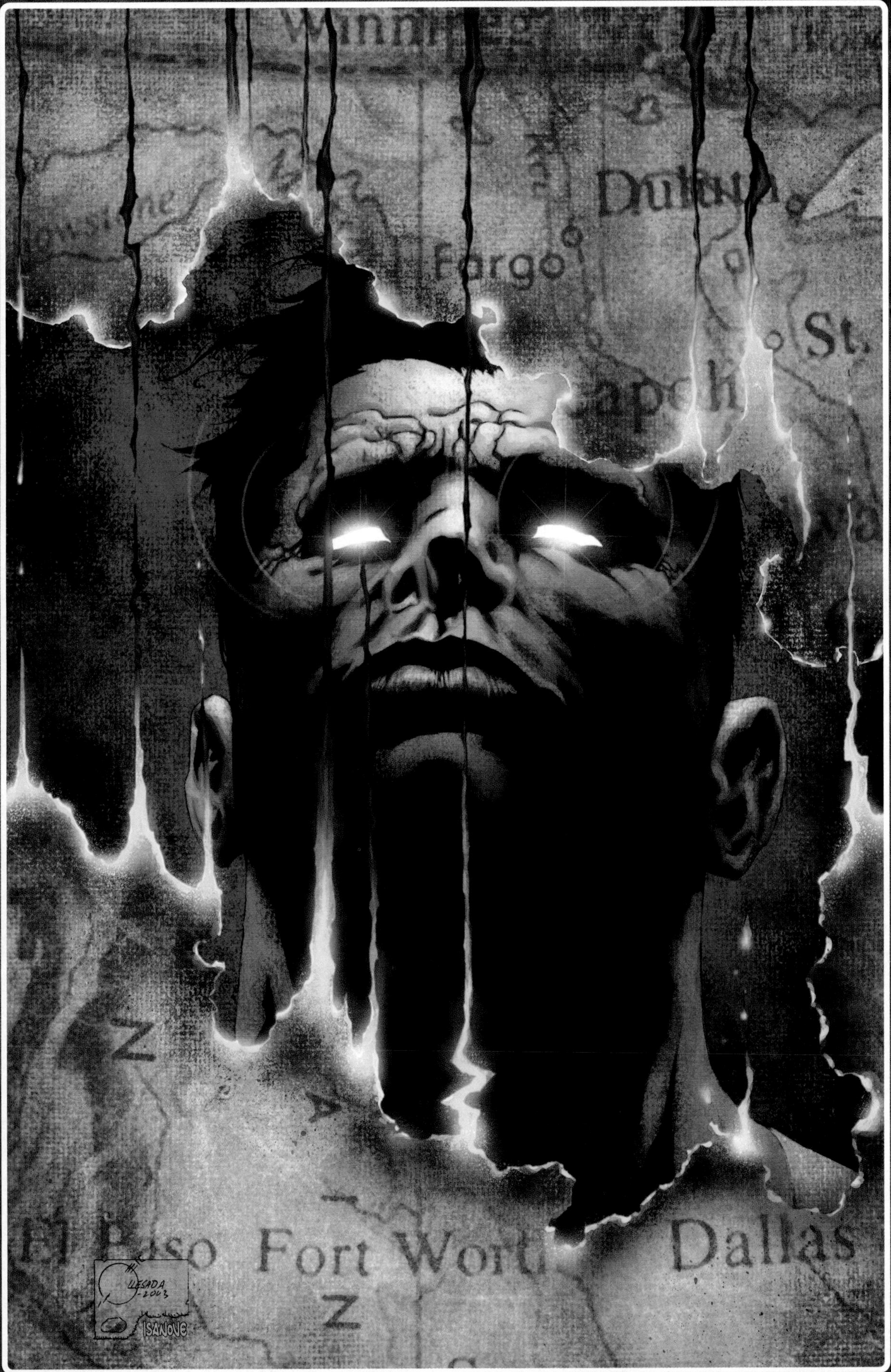
Fargo
St.
Dallas
ISANOVE

Wizard #143 Cover
by Joe Quesada

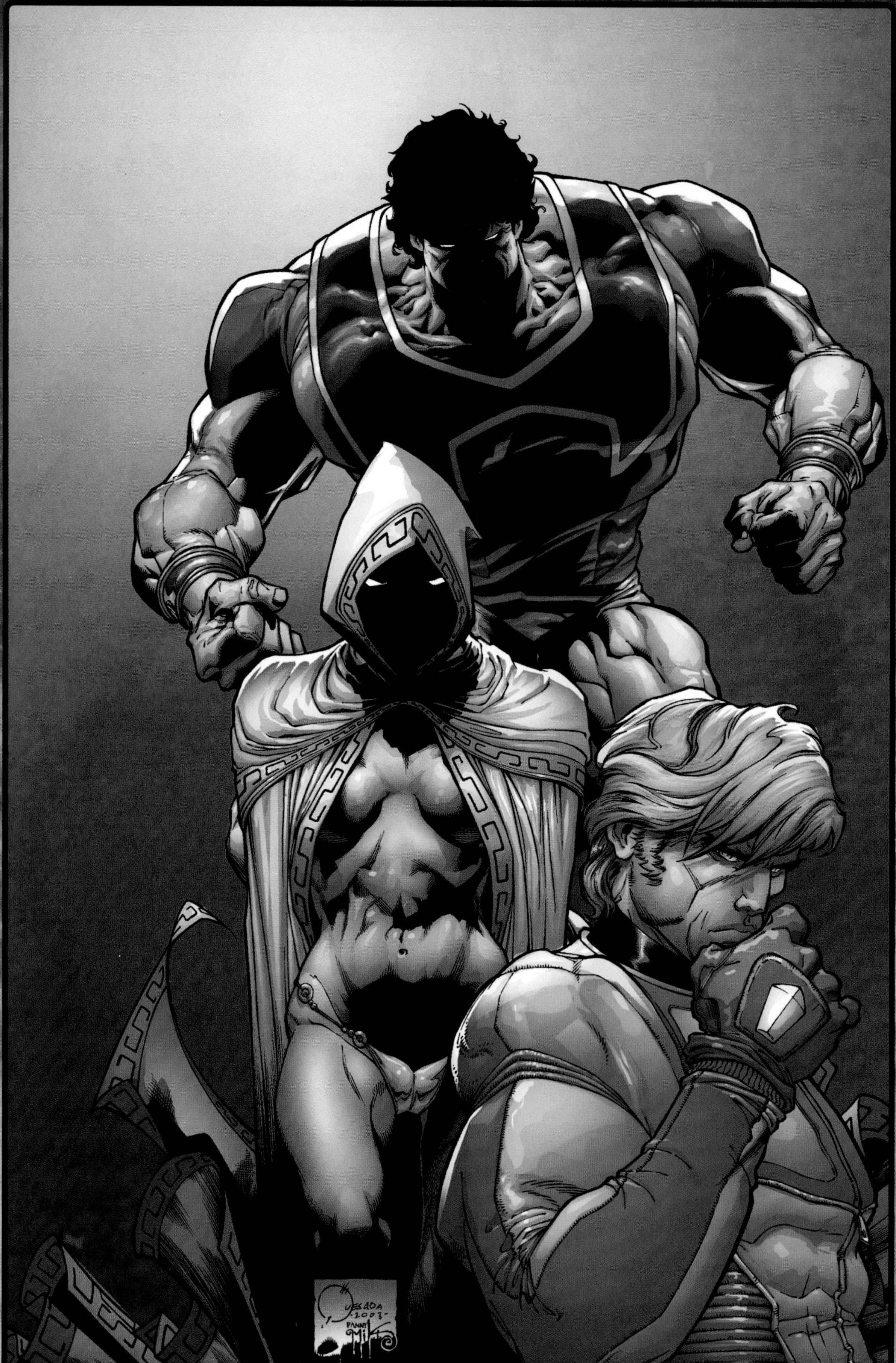

CHARACTER DESIGNS
By Gary Frank

HYPERION

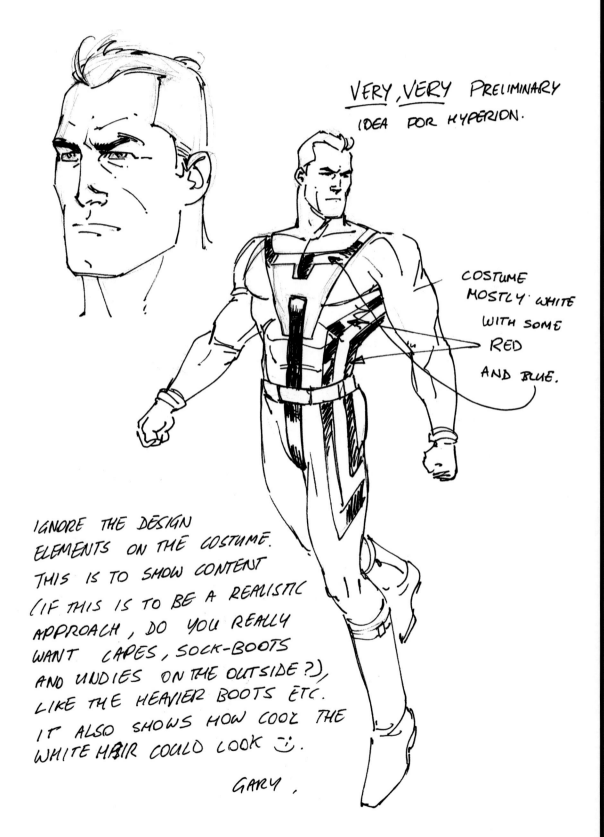

VERY, VERY PRELIMINARY IDEA FOR HYPERION.

COSTUME MOSTLY WHITE WITH SOME RED AND BLUE.

IGNORE THE DESIGN ELEMENTS ON THE COSTUME. THIS IS TO SHOW CONTENT (IF THIS IS TO BE A REALISTIC APPROACH, DO YOU REALLY WANT CAPES, SOCK-BOOTS AND UNDIES ON THE OUTSIDE?), LIKE THE HEAVIER BOOTS ETC. IT ALSO SHOWS HOW COOL THE WHITE HAIR COULD LOOK :).

GARY.

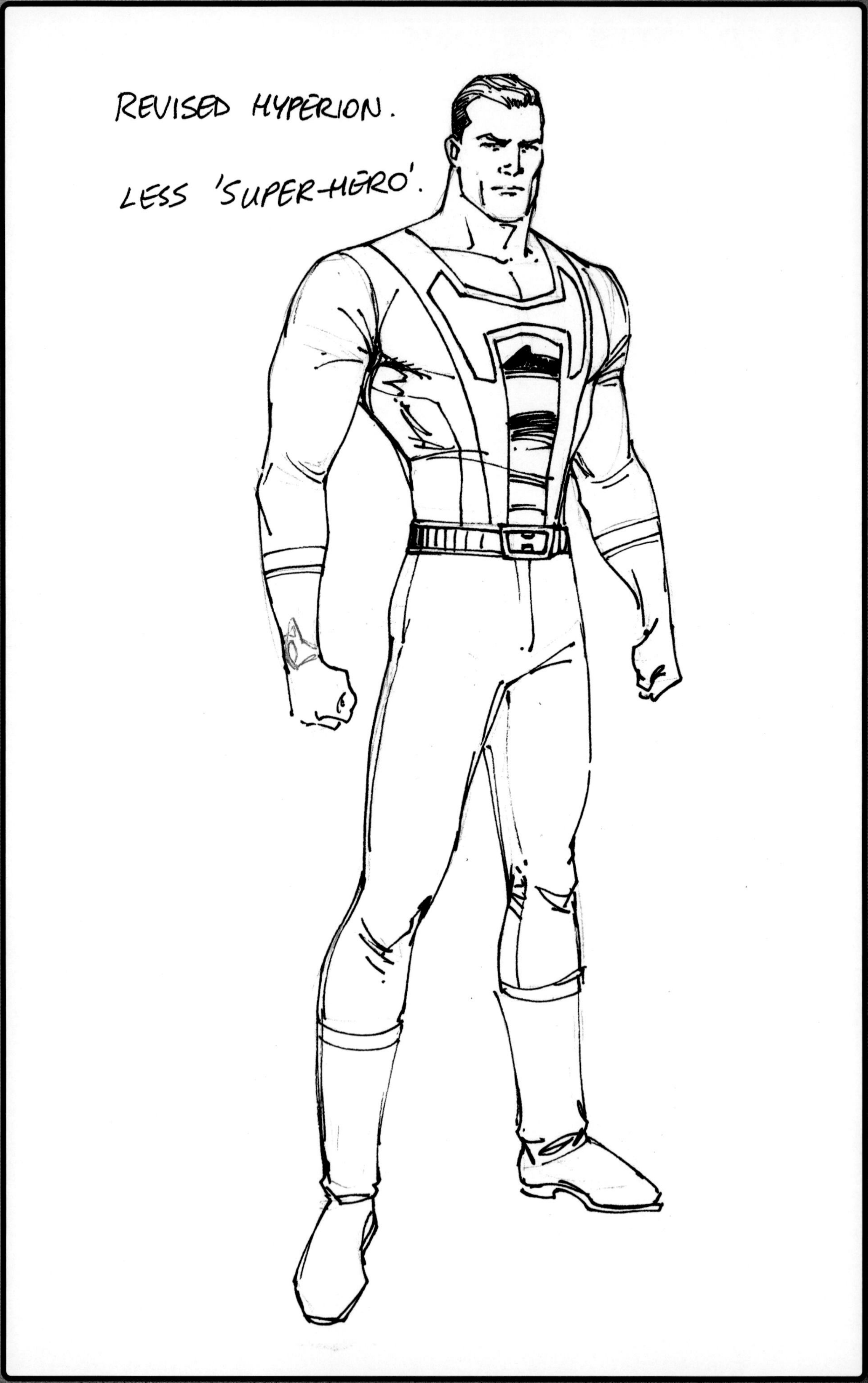
REVISED HYPERION.
LESS 'SUPER-HERO'.

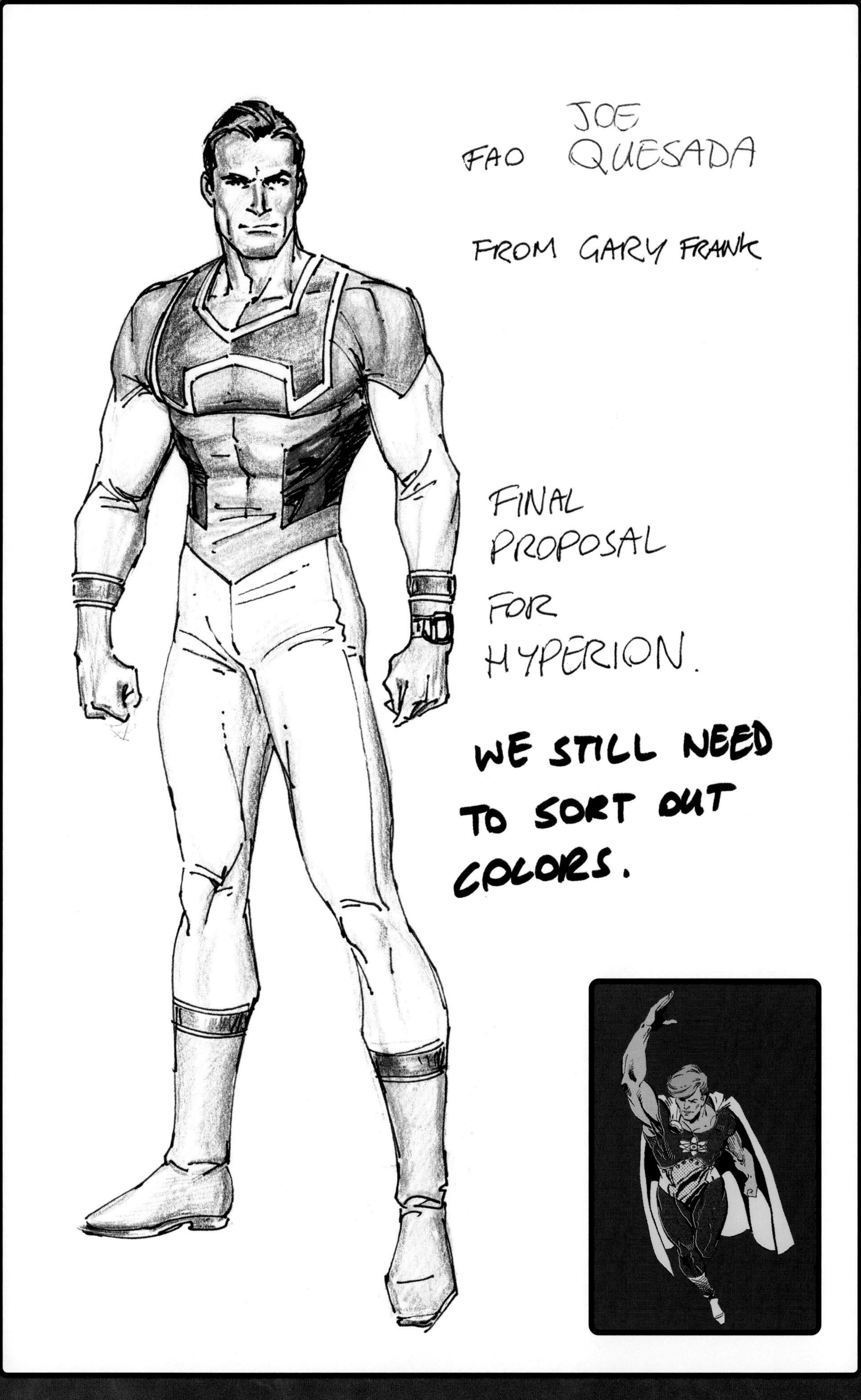
FAO JOE QUESADA
FROM GARY FRANK
FINAL PROPOSAL FOR HYPERION.
WE STILL NEED TO SORT OUT COLORS.

POWER PRINCESS

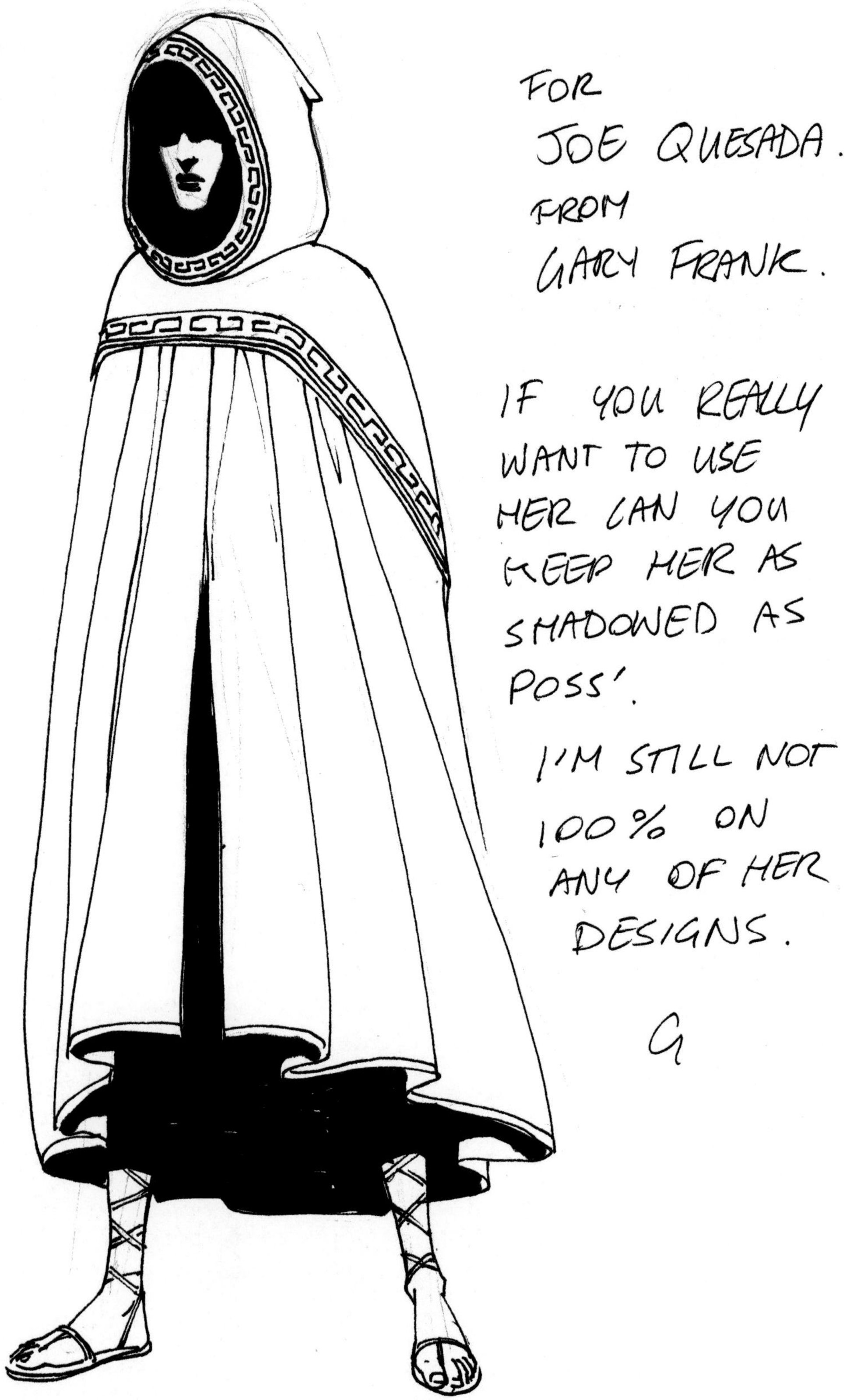
FOR
JOE QUESADA.
FROM
GARY FRANK.
IF YOU REALLY
WANT TO USE
HER CAN YOU
KEEP HER AS
SHADOWED AS
POSS'.
I'M STILL NOT
100% ON
ANY OF HER
DESIGNS.
G

3

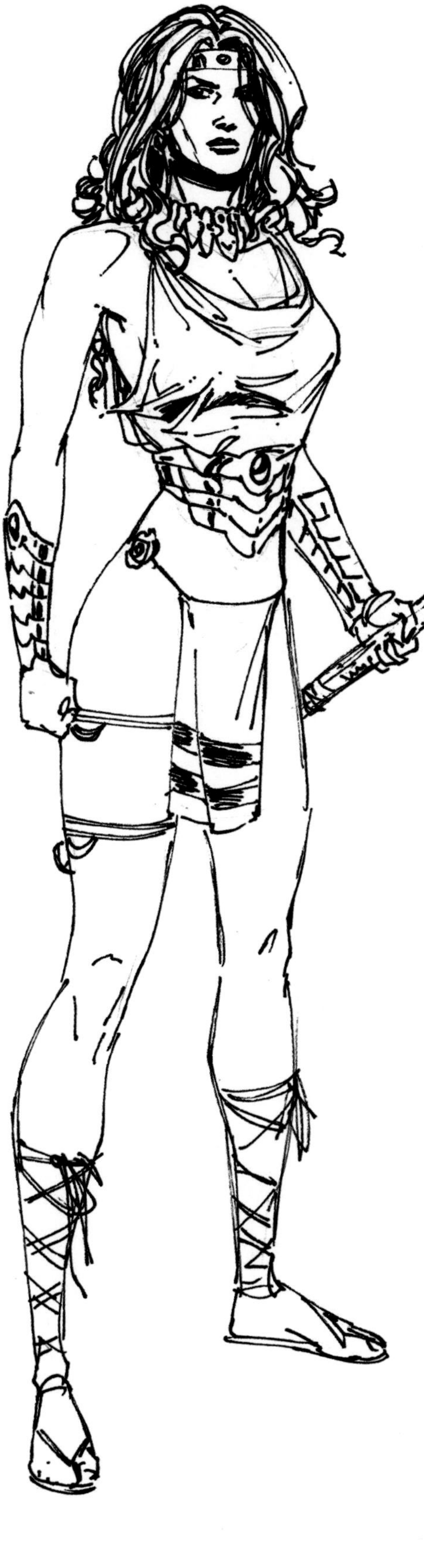

POWERPRINCESS UPON ARRIVAL.

WE CAN GIVE HER SOME MORE SEXY/MODERN THREADS AS THE STORY PROGRESSES.

THE MAIN POINT OF THIS PIC' IS TO RUN THE STAFF IDEA PAST EVERYONE. I THINK I CAN SPEAK FOR US ALL WHEN I SAY THAT WE SHOULD BE ABLE TO DO BETTER THAN A TRANSPARENT SHIELD.

HOW ABOUT A (COLLAPSABLE) STAFF THAT SHE COULD USE AS A WEAPON AND TO DEFLECT BULLETS ETC A LA WONDER WOMAN'S BRACELETS?

FAO JMS

FROM

GARY FRANK

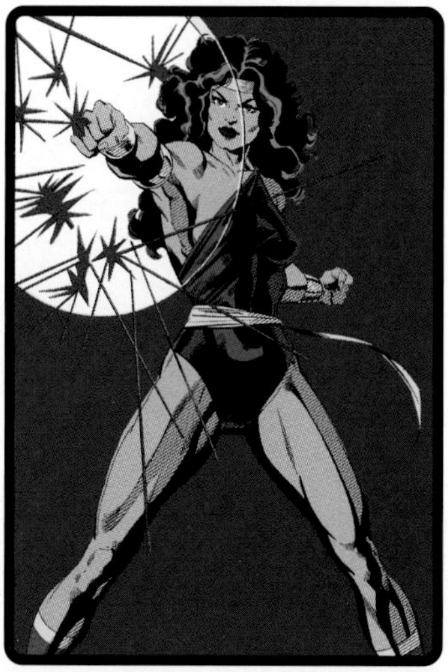

POWER PRINCESS.

I'D LIKE TO GET HER TO
SOMETHING LIKE THIS EVENTUALLY.
THE COLORIST WOULD NEED TO
GO SHINY ON THE COSTUME
TO MAKE LOOK LIKE RUBBER
OR PVC.
   AS I SAID BEFORE, I'D
LIKE TO CHANGE THE COSTUME
OFTEN, KEEPING A FEW ELEMENTS
SUCH AS ♀ AND THE PALETTE.
RED/BLACK OR PINK/BLACK
       FOR EXTRA KITSCH.
JMS

   ANDREW SAID THAT HE THOUGHT
P.P. WAS GOING TO LOOK
A BIT "DIRTIER" THAN THIS,
SO COULD YOU GIVE ME A
LITTLE MORE GUIDANCE?
   THANKS

GARY
(BY THE WAY, I'M THINKING ALONG
THE LINES OF "SUPERHEROINE"
COSTUME THAT A STRIPPER
WOULD WEAR IN HER ACT)

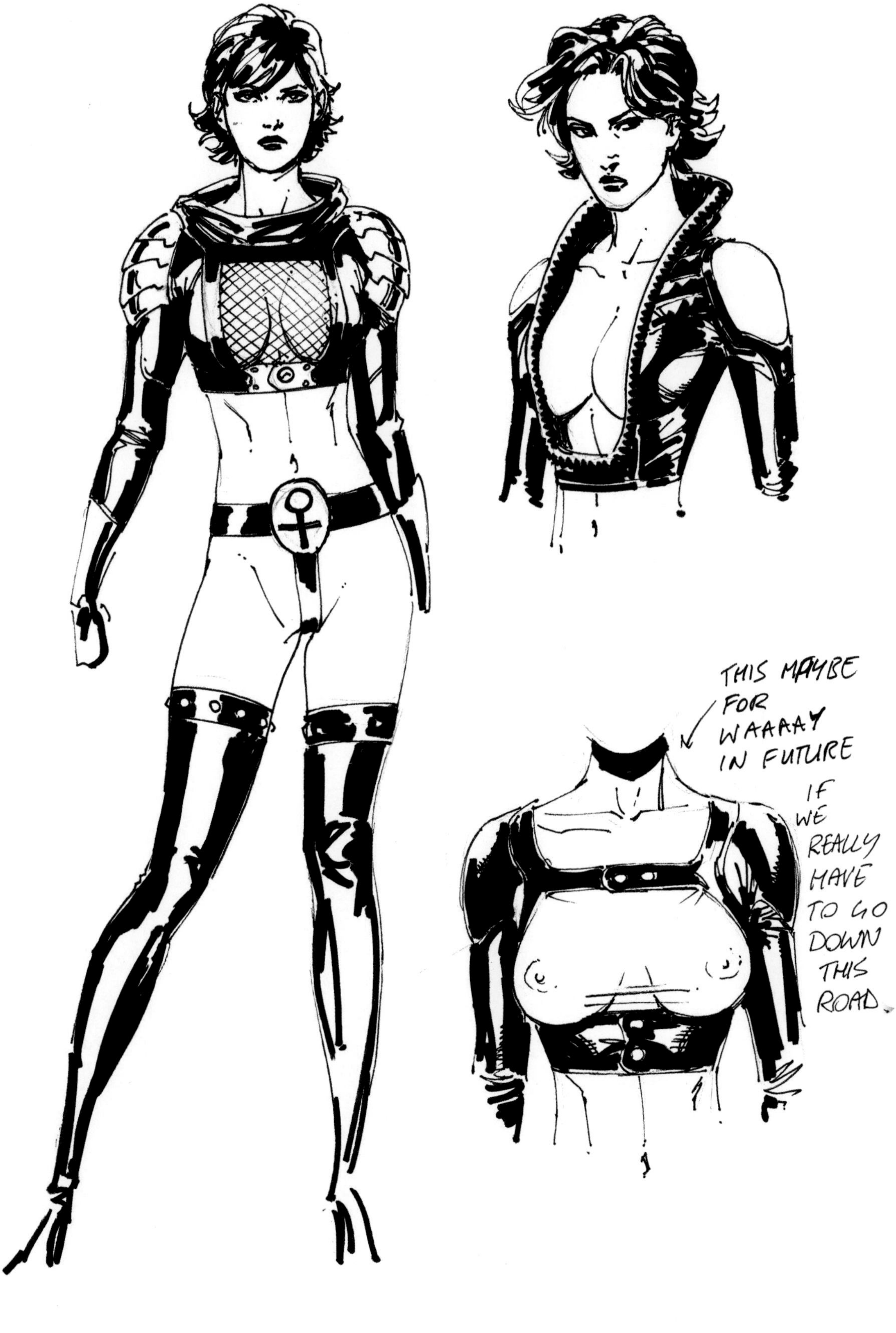
THIS MAYBE FOR WAAAAY IN FUTURE
IF WE REALLY HAVE TO GO DOWN THIS ROAD.

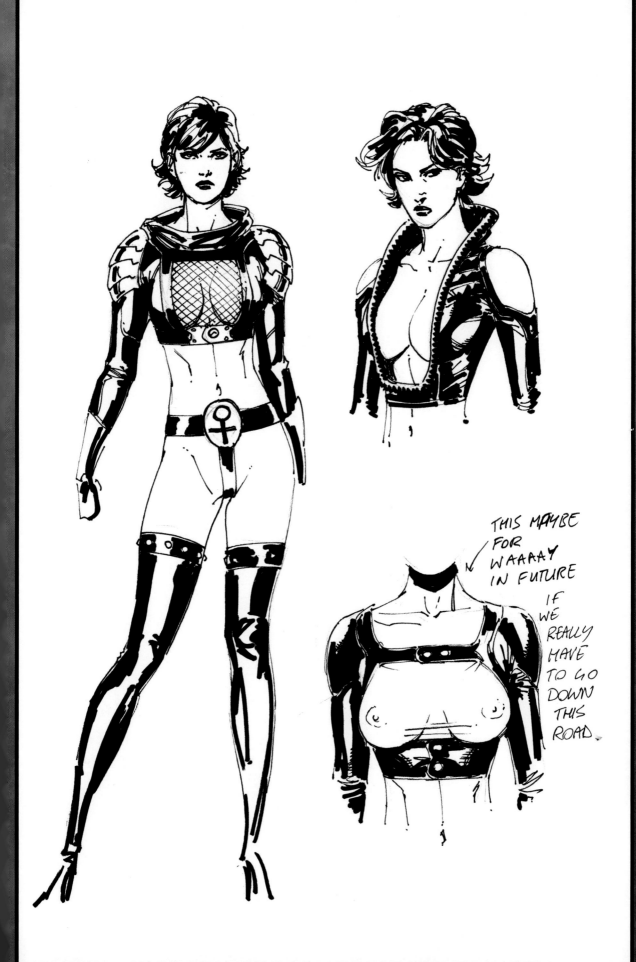

NIGHTHAWK

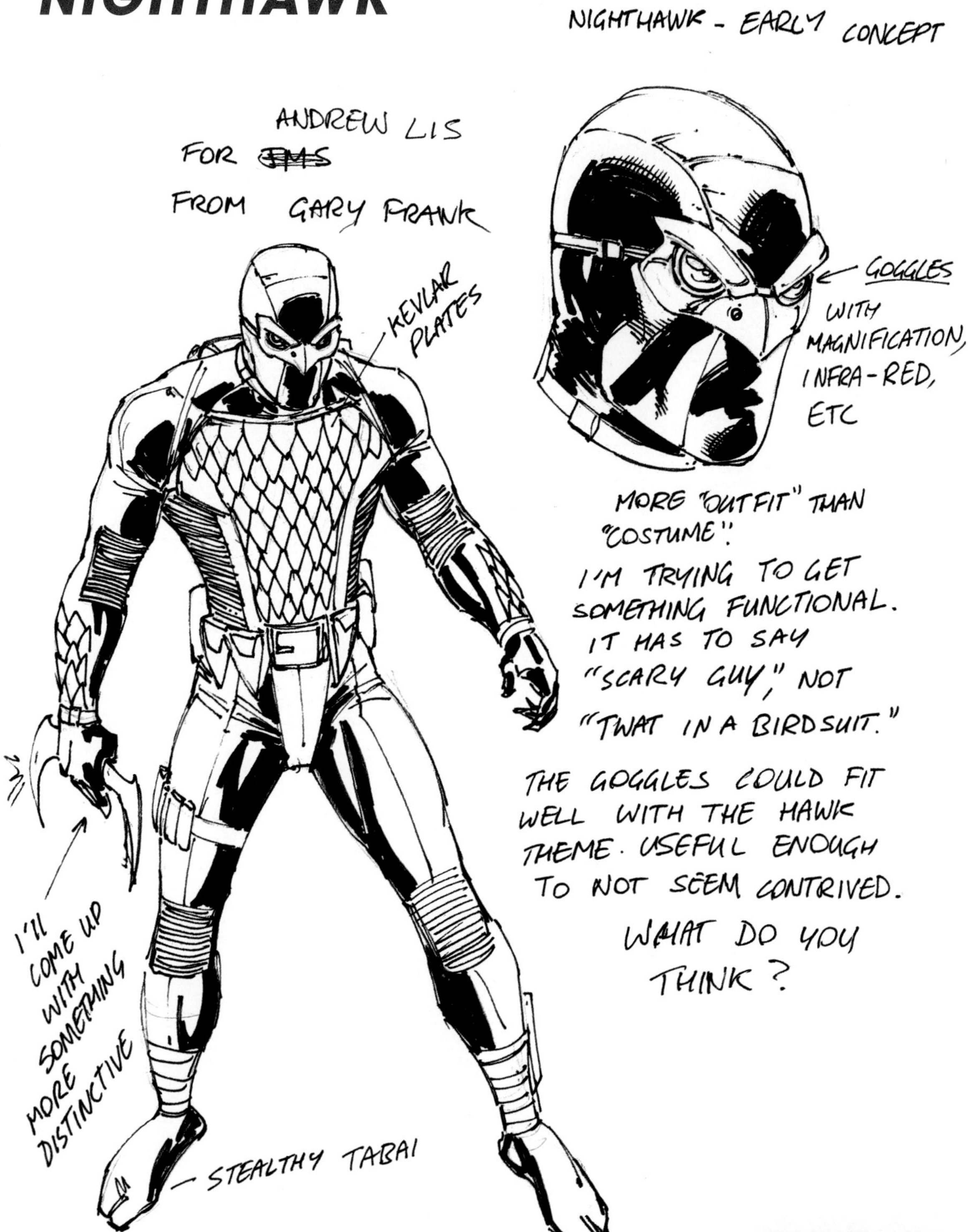
NIGHTHAWK - EARLY CONCEPT
ANDREW LIS
FOR ~~JMS~~
FROM GARY FRANK
KEVLAR PLATES
GOGGLES
WITH MAGNIFICATION, INFRA-RED, ETC
MORE "OUTFIT" THAN "COSTUME".
I'M TRYING TO GET SOMETHING FUNCTIONAL. IT HAS TO SAY "SCARY GUY," NOT "TWAT IN A BIRDSUIT."
THE GOGGLES COULD FIT WELL WITH THE HAWK THEME. USEFUL ENOUGH TO NOT SEEM CONTRIVED.
WHAT DO YOU THINK?
I'LL COME UP WITH SOMETHING MORE DISTINCTIVE
STEALTHY TABAI

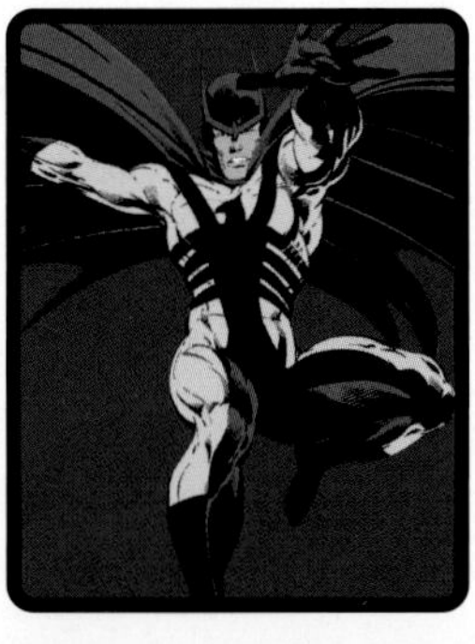

DOCTOR SPECTRUM

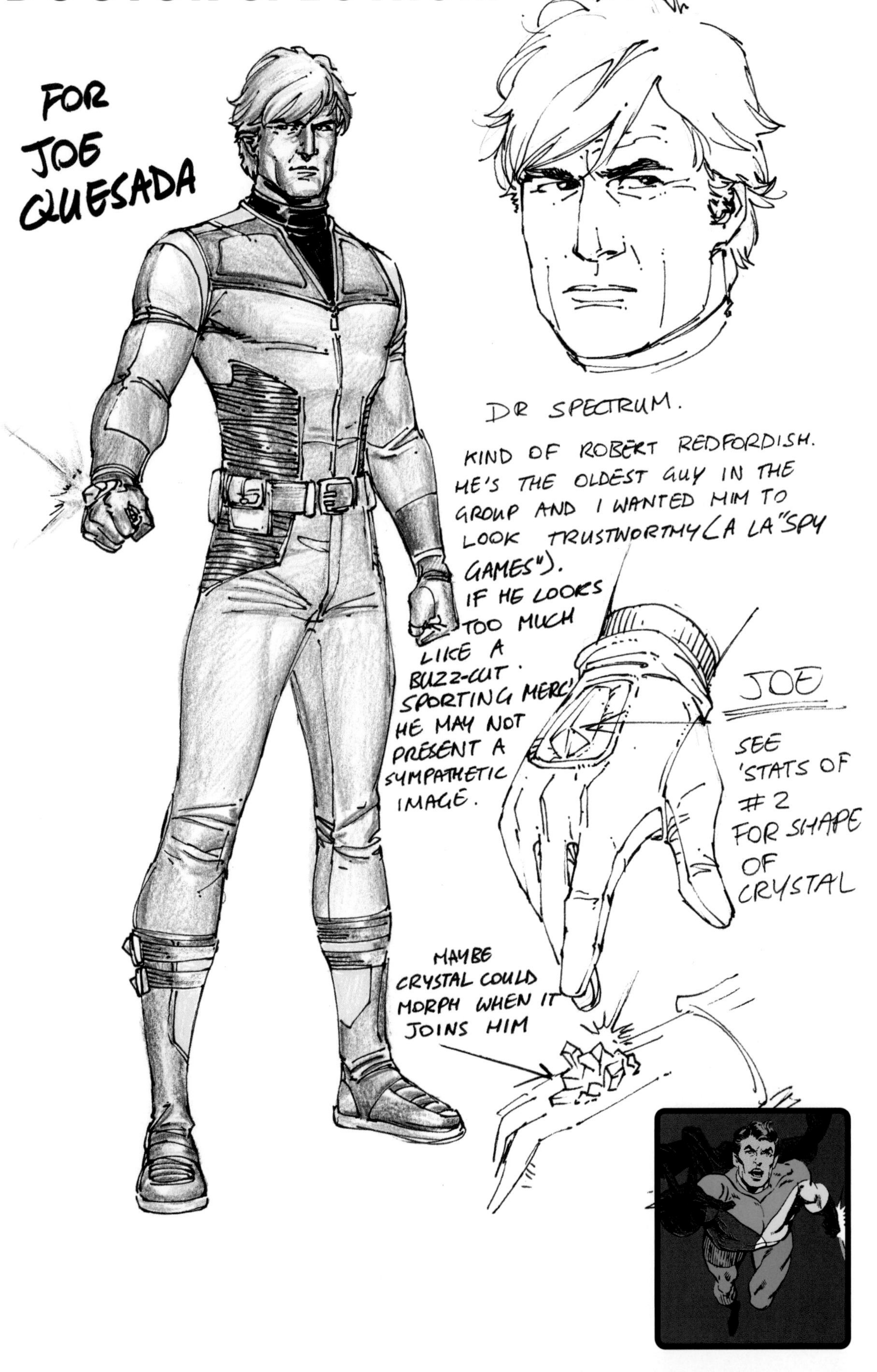
FOR JOE QUESADA
DR SPECTRUM.
KIND OF ROBERT REDFORDISH. HE'S THE OLDEST GUY IN THE GROUP AND I WANTED HIM TO LOOK TRUSTWORTHY (A LA "SPY GAMES").
IF HE LOOKS TOO MUCH LIKE A BUZZ-CUT SPORTING MERC HE MAY NOT PRESENT A SYMPATHETIC IMAGE.
JOE
SEE 'STATS OF #2 FOR SHAPE OF CRYSTAL
MAYBE CRYSTAL COULD MORPH WHEN IT JOINS HIM

NUKE

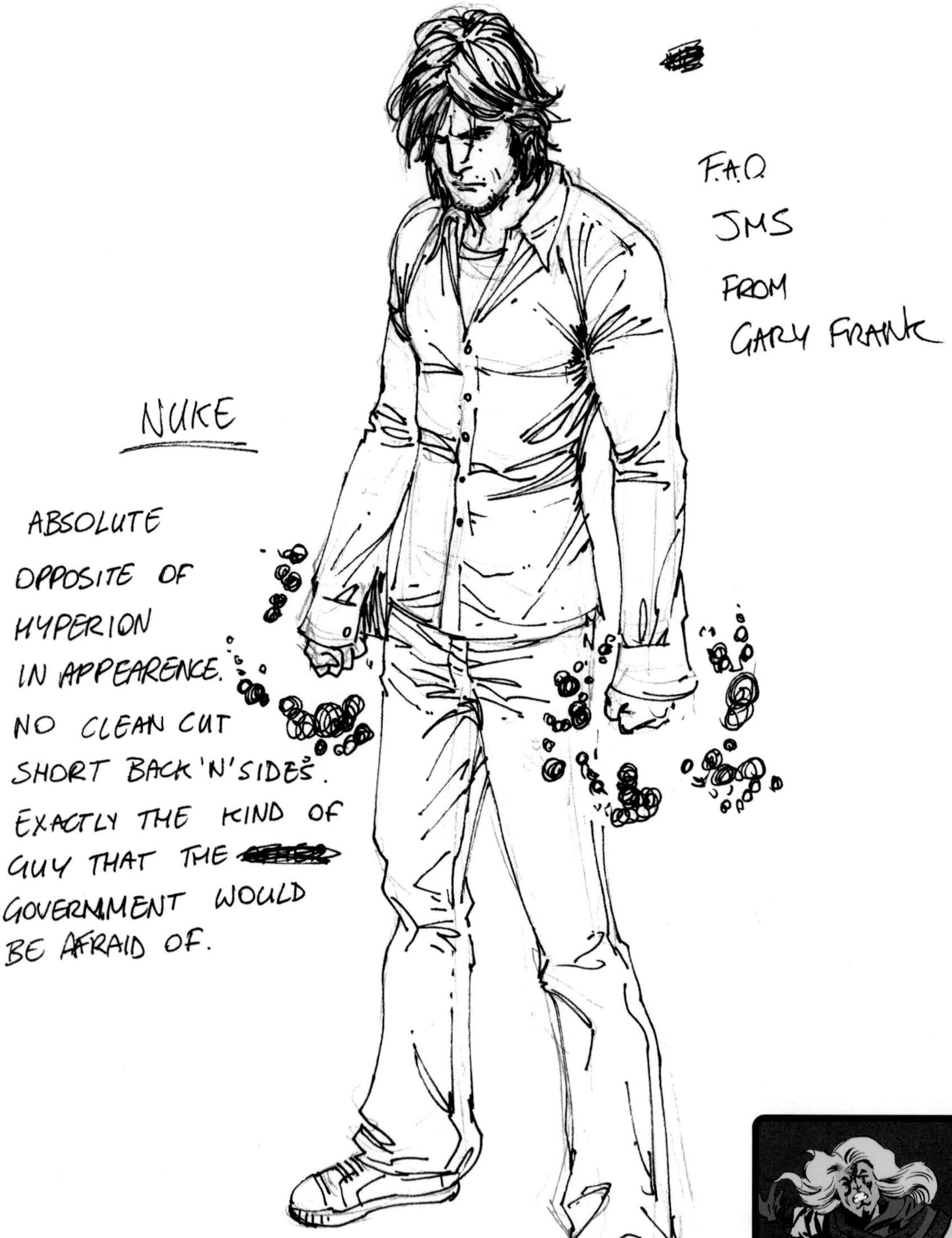
F.A.O
JMS
FROM
GARY FRANK
NUKE
ABSOLUTE
OPPOSITE OF
HYPERION
IN APPEARENCE.
NO CLEAN CUT
SHORT BACK'N'SIDES.
EXACTLY THE KIND OF
GUY THAT THE
GOVERNMENT WOULD
BE AFRAID OF.

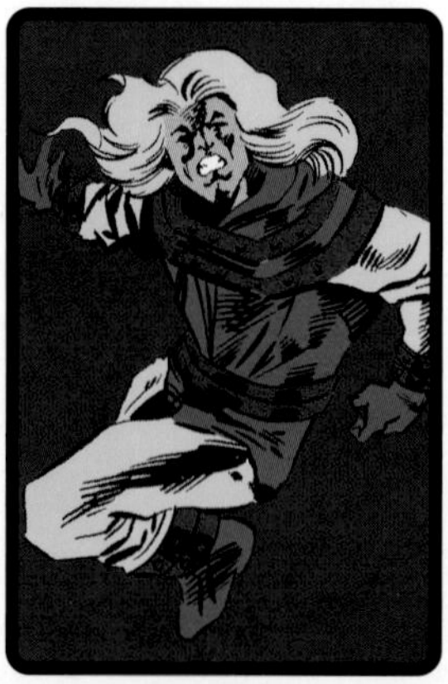

AMPHIBIAN

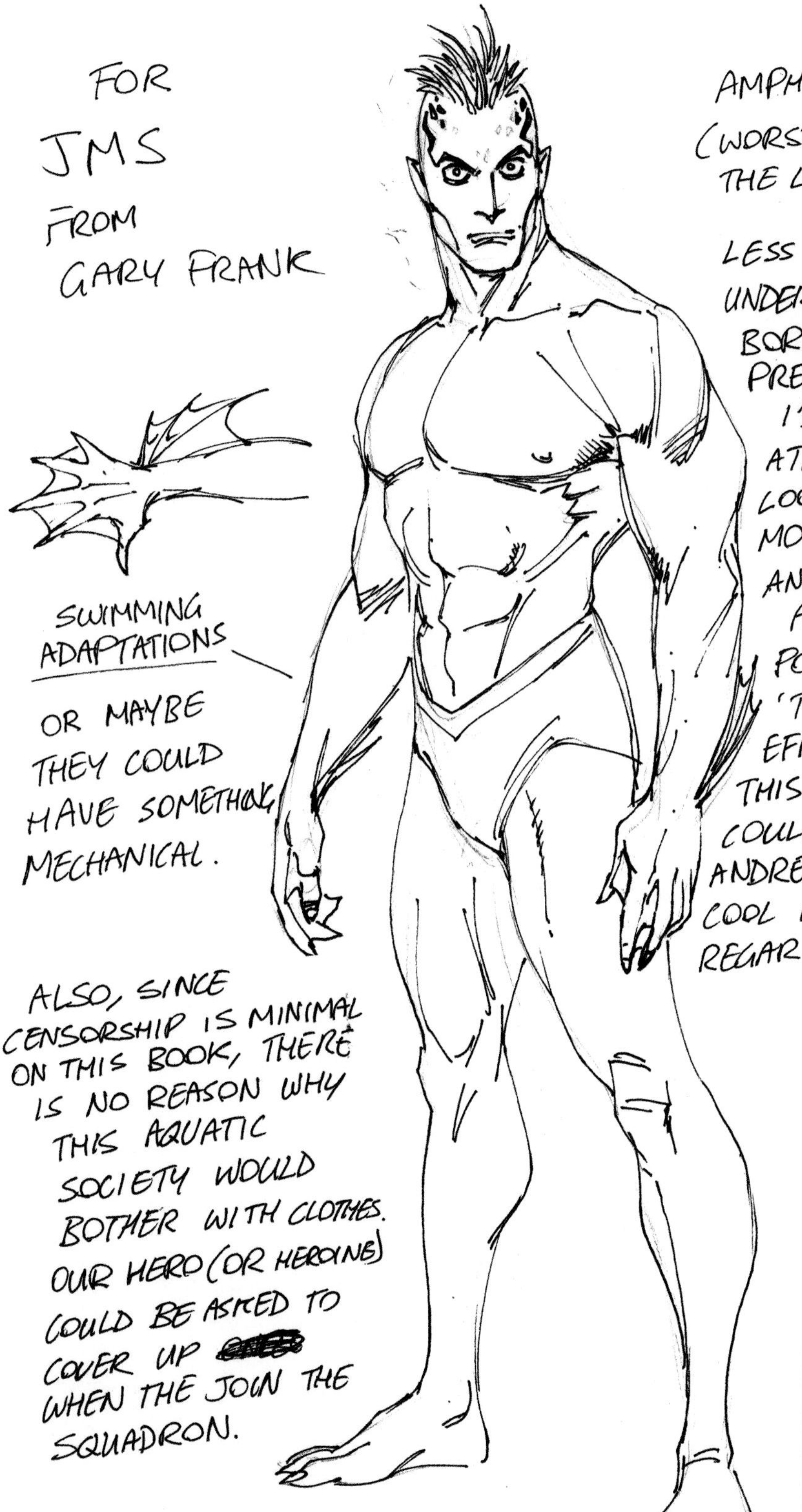
FOR
JMS
FROM
GARY FRANK
SWIMMING ADAPTATIONS
OR MAYBE THEY COULD HAVE SOMETHING MECHANICAL.
ALSO, SINCE CENSORSHIP IS MINIMAL ON THIS BOOK, THERE IS NO REASON WHY THIS AQUATIC SOCIETY WOULD BOTHER WITH CLOTHES. OUR HERO (OR HEROINE) COULD BE ASKED TO COVER UP [redacted] WHEN THE JOIN THE SQUADRON.
AMPHIBIAN (WORST NAME OF THE LOT?)
LESS LIKE AN UNDERWATER BJORN BORG THAN PREDECESSORS. I'D LIKE THE ATLANTIANS TO LOOK A LITTLE MORE EVOLVED AND STRANGE. ALSO, TO AVOID POWER PRINCESS'S 'TOKEN FEMALE' EFFECT, MAYBE THIS CHARACTER COULD BE A WOMAN(?) ANDREW HAD SOME COOL IDEAS IN THIS REGARD.

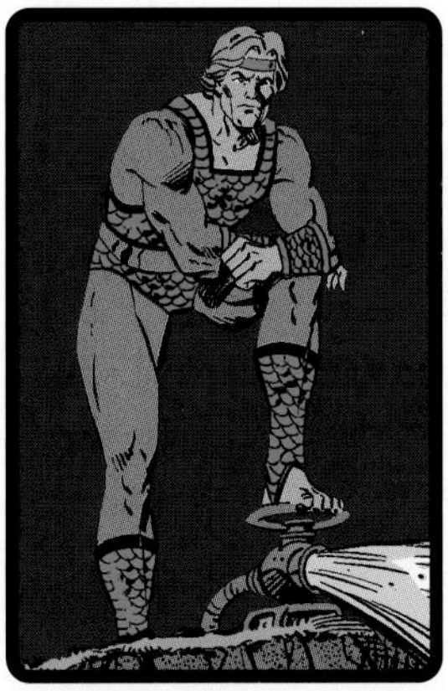

COVER SKETCHES & COVER PENCILS
By Gary Frank

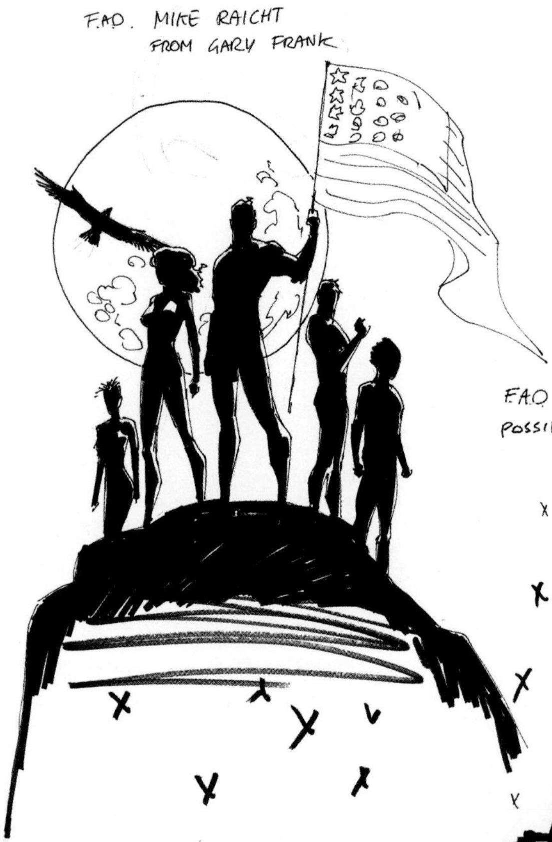
F.A.O. MIKE RAICHT
FROM GARY FRANK

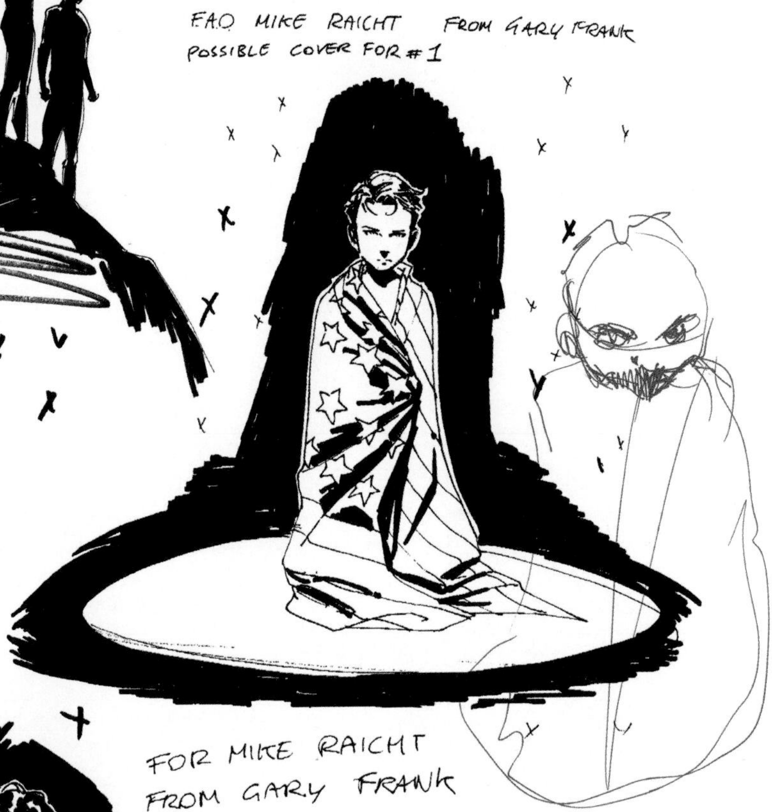
F.A.O MIKE RAICHT FROM GARY FRANK
POSSIBLE COVER FOR #1

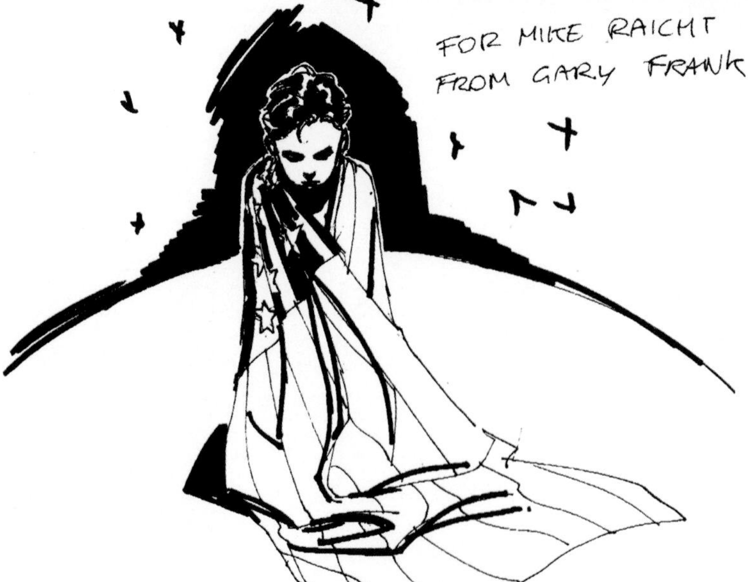
FOR MIKE RAICHT
FROM GARY FRANK

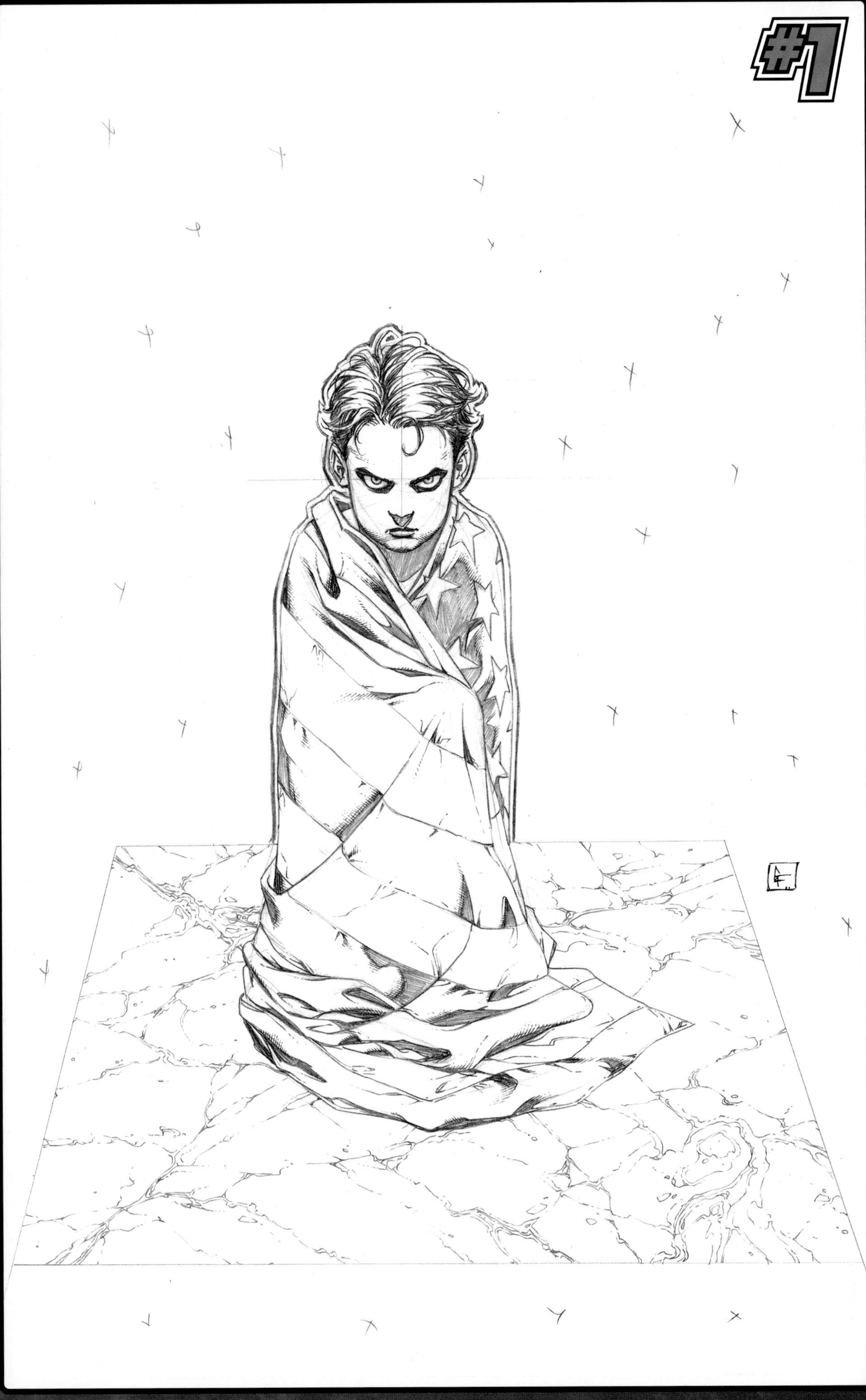
#1

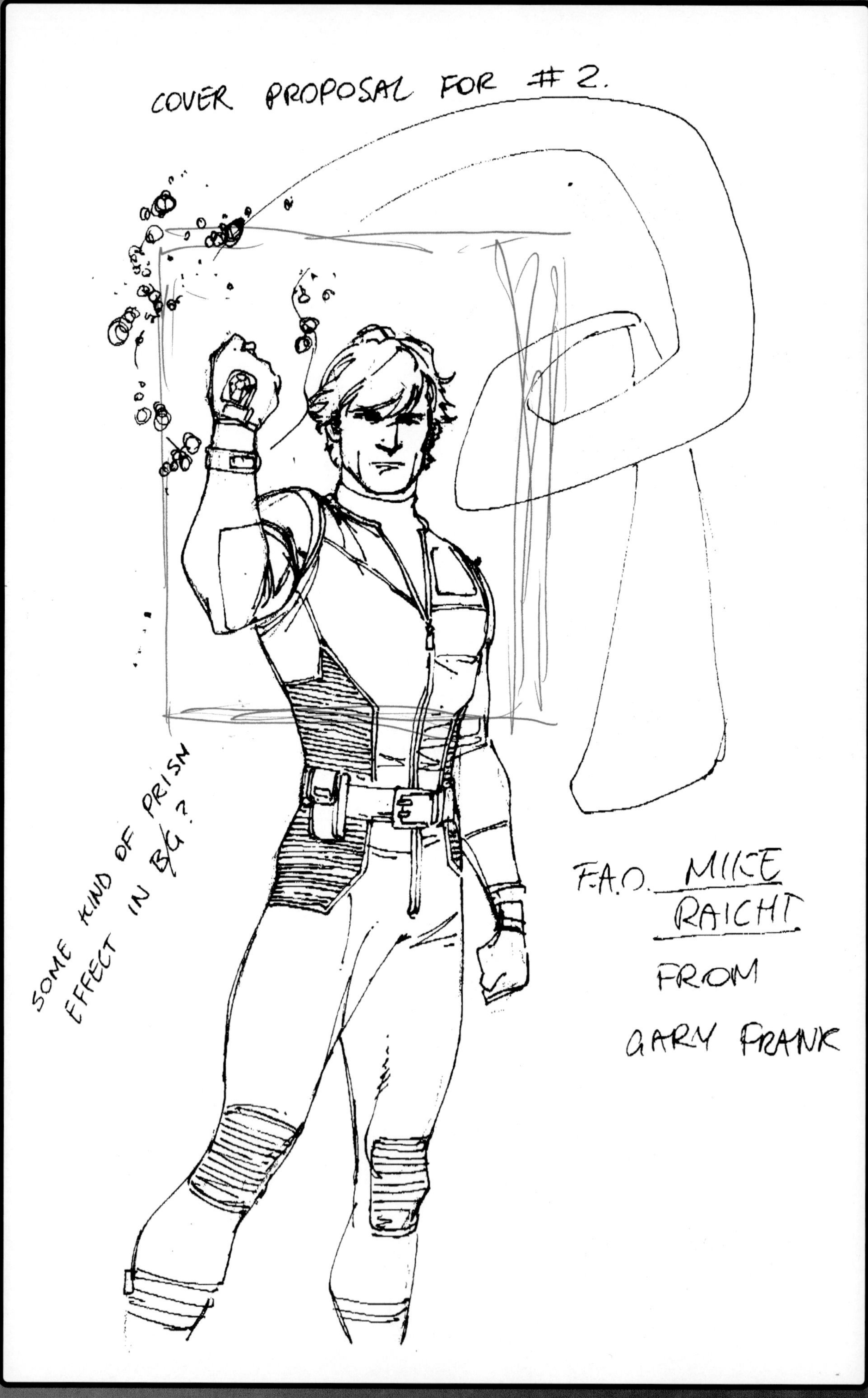
COVER PROPOSAL FOR #2.
SOME KIND OF PRISM EFFECT IN B/G?
F.A.O. MIKE RAICHT
FROM GARY FRANK

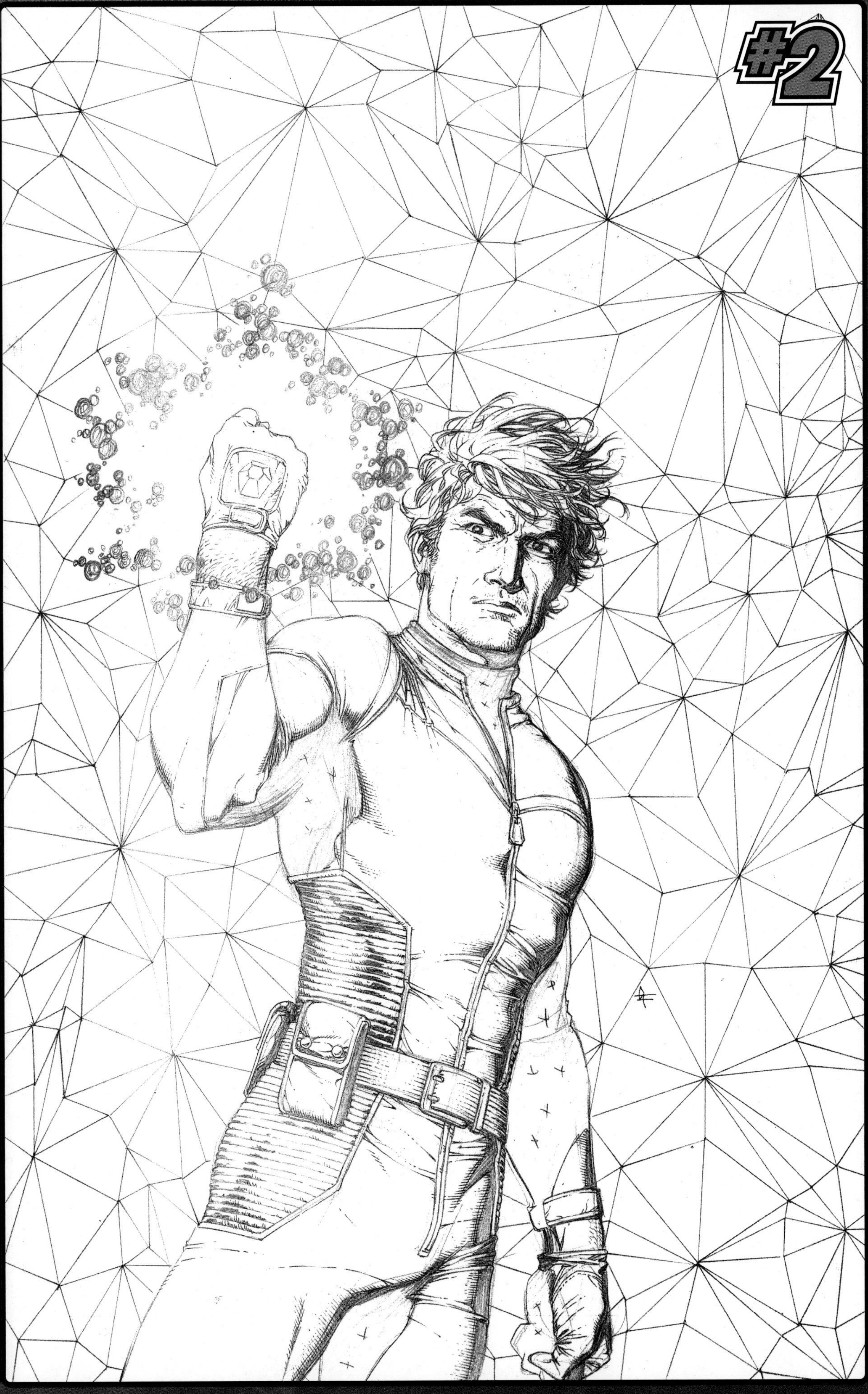
#2

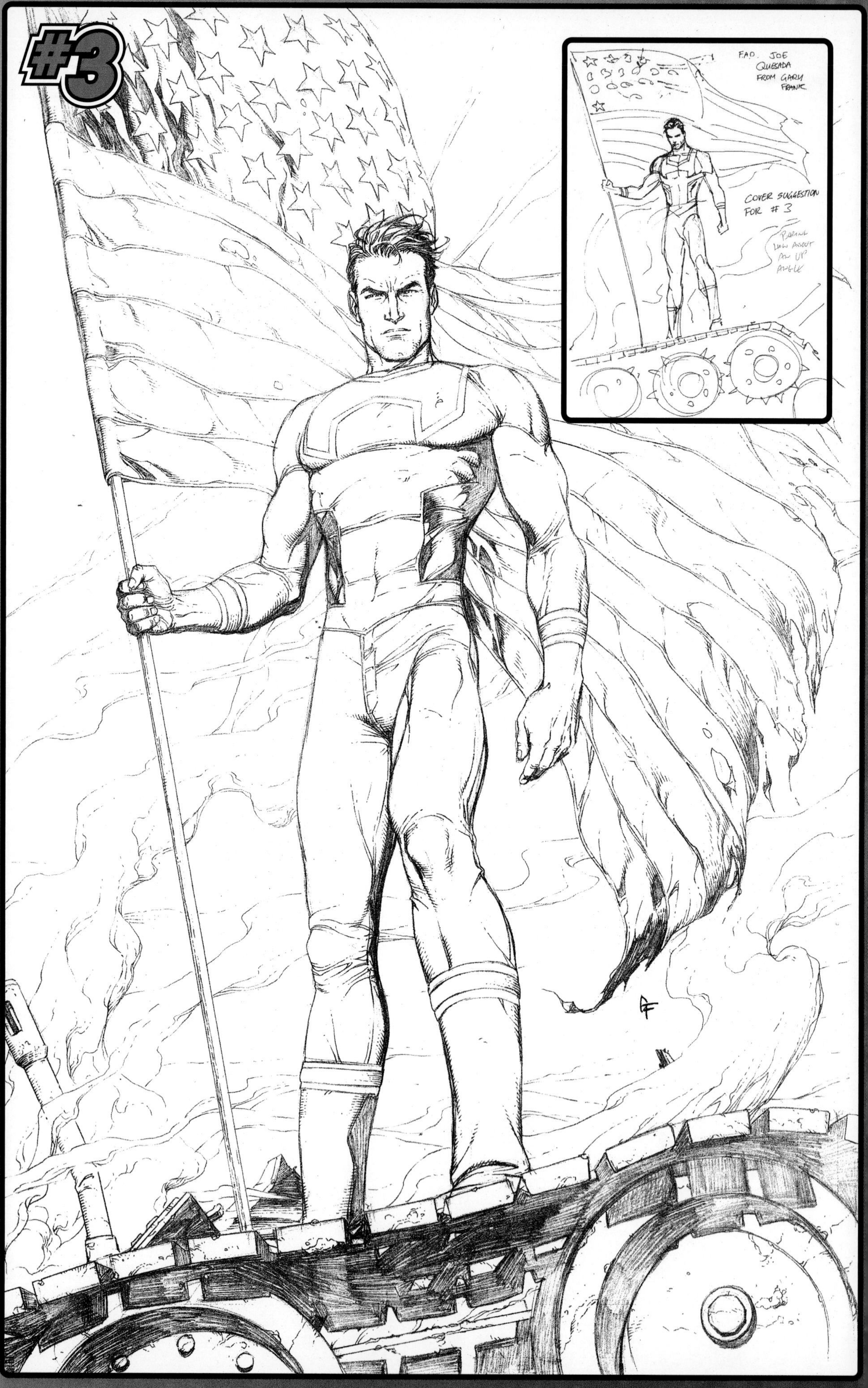

#3
F.A.O. JOE QUESADA FROM GARY FRANK
COVER SUGGESTION FOR # 3
HOW ABOUT AN UP ANGLE

#4

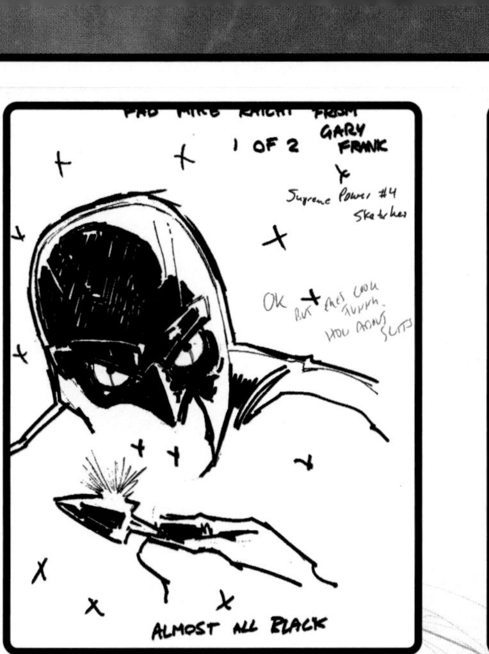
1 OF 2
GARY FRANK
Supreme Power #4 Sketches
OK
ALMOST ALL BLACK

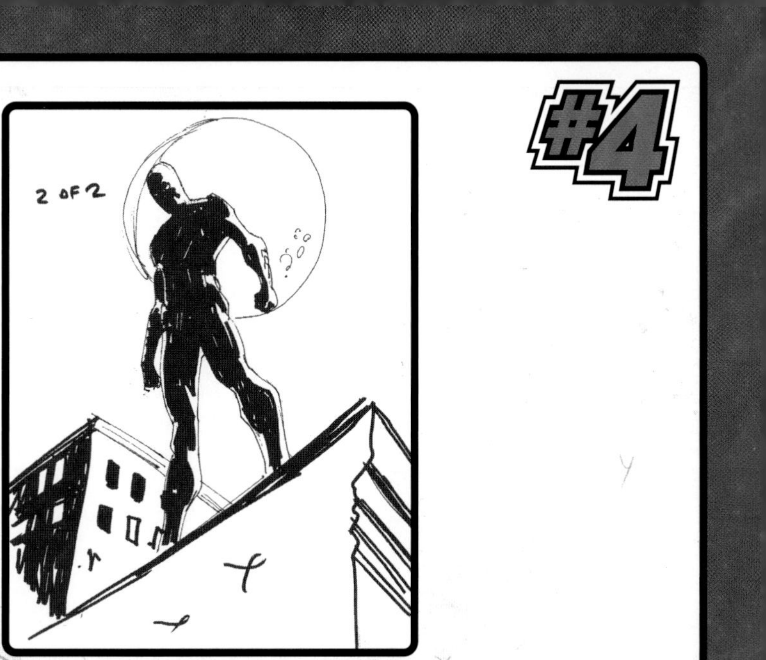
2 OF 2

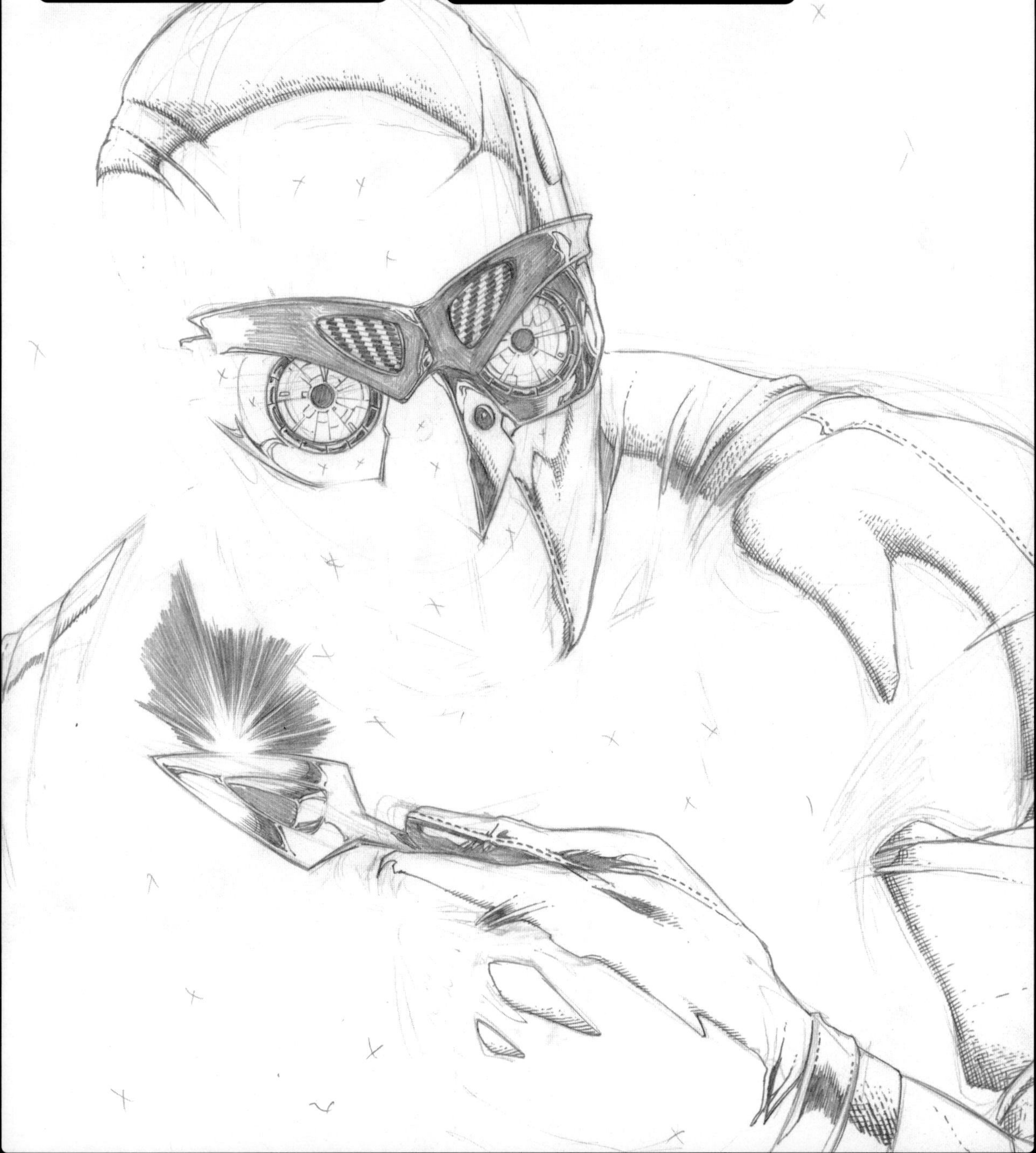

#5

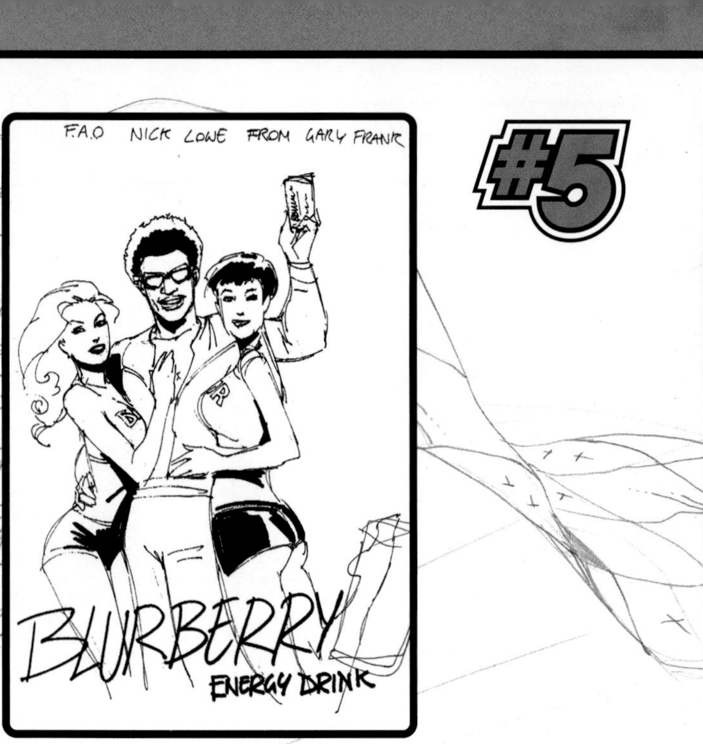
F.A.O NICK LOWE FROM GARY FRANK
BLURBERRY
ENERGY DRINK

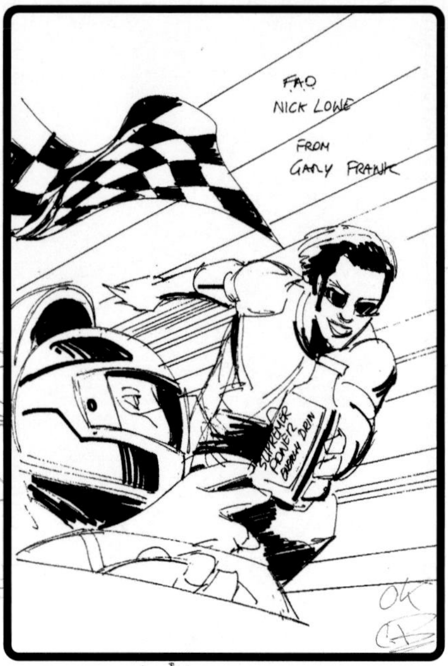
F.A.O
NICK LOWE
FROM
GARY FRANK
OK

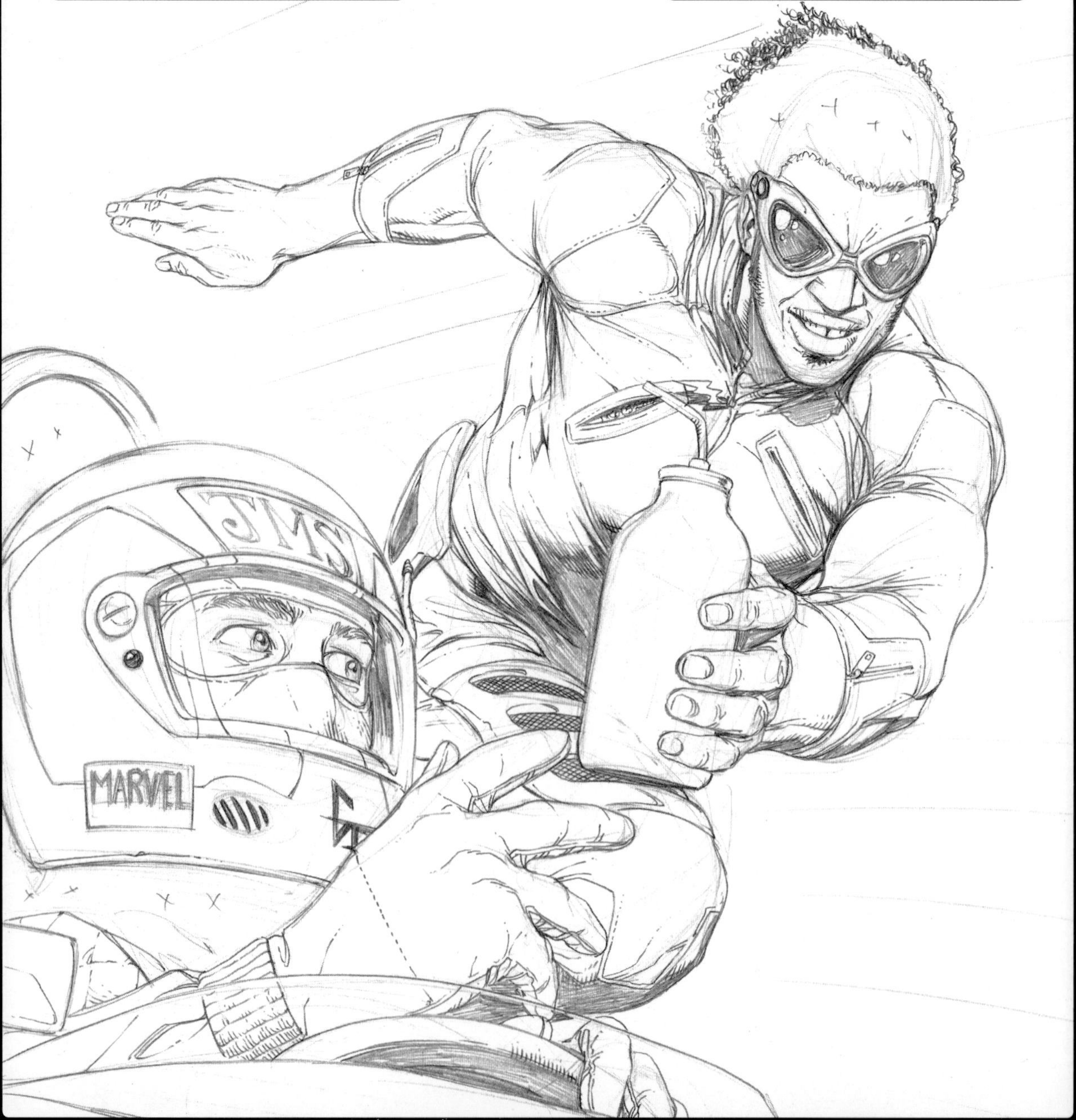
JMS
MARVEL

#6

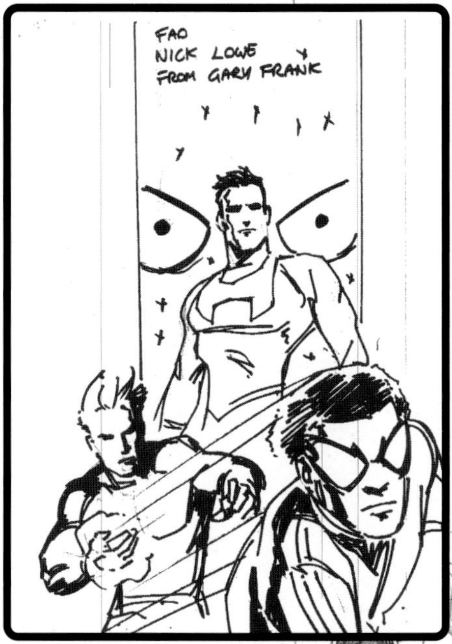
FAO
NICK LOWE
FROM GARY FRANK

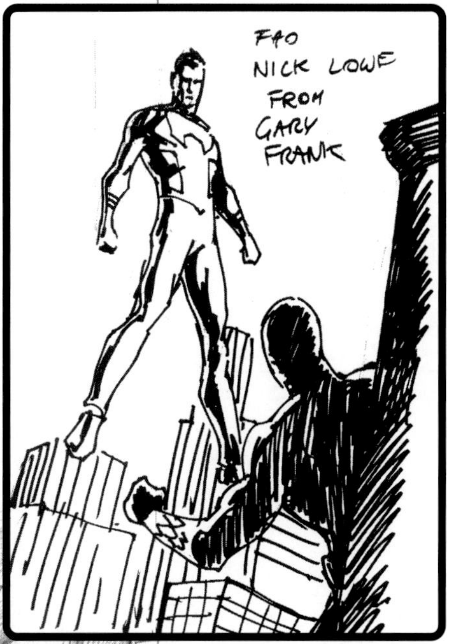
FAO
NICK LOWE
FROM
GARY
FRANK

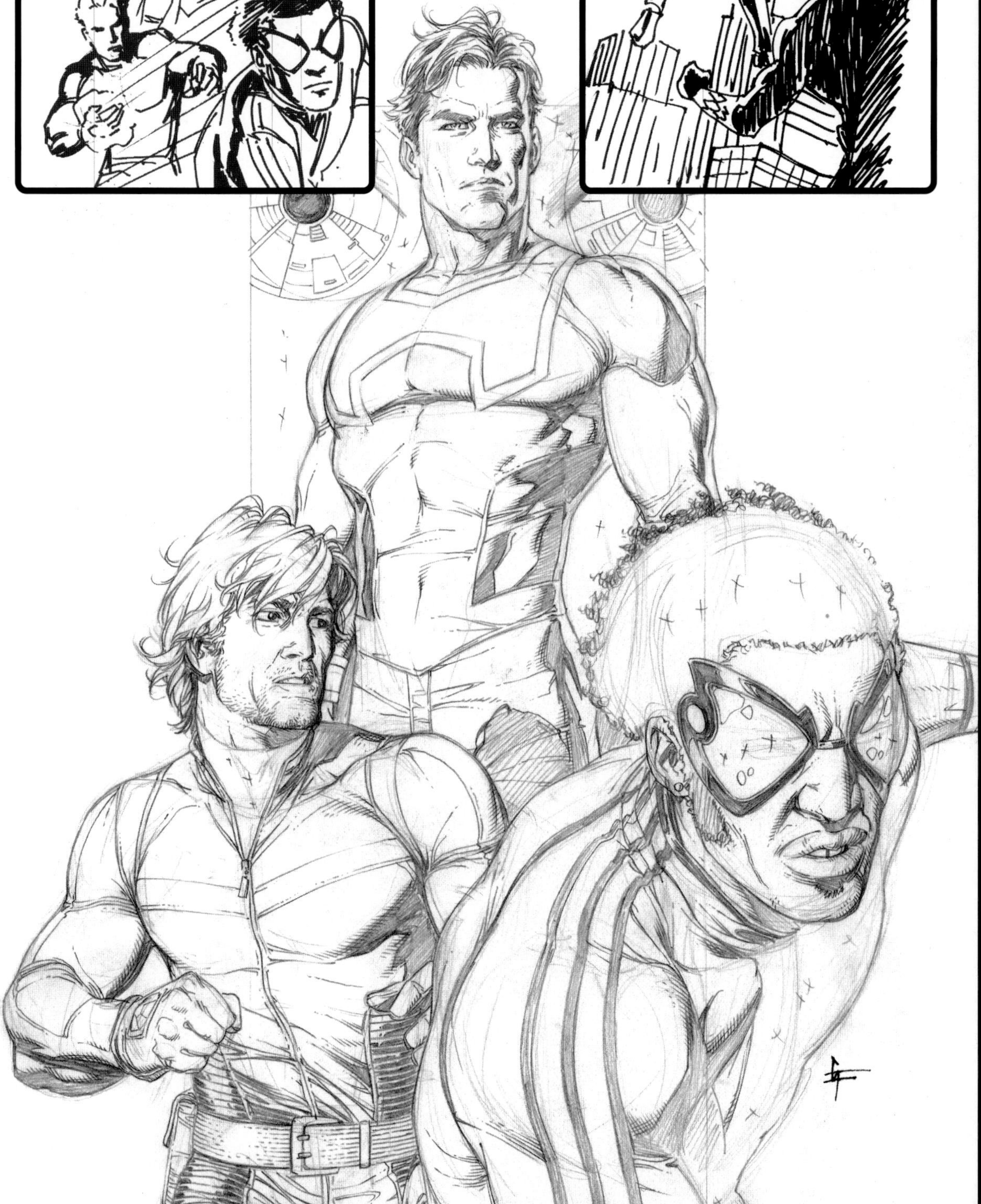

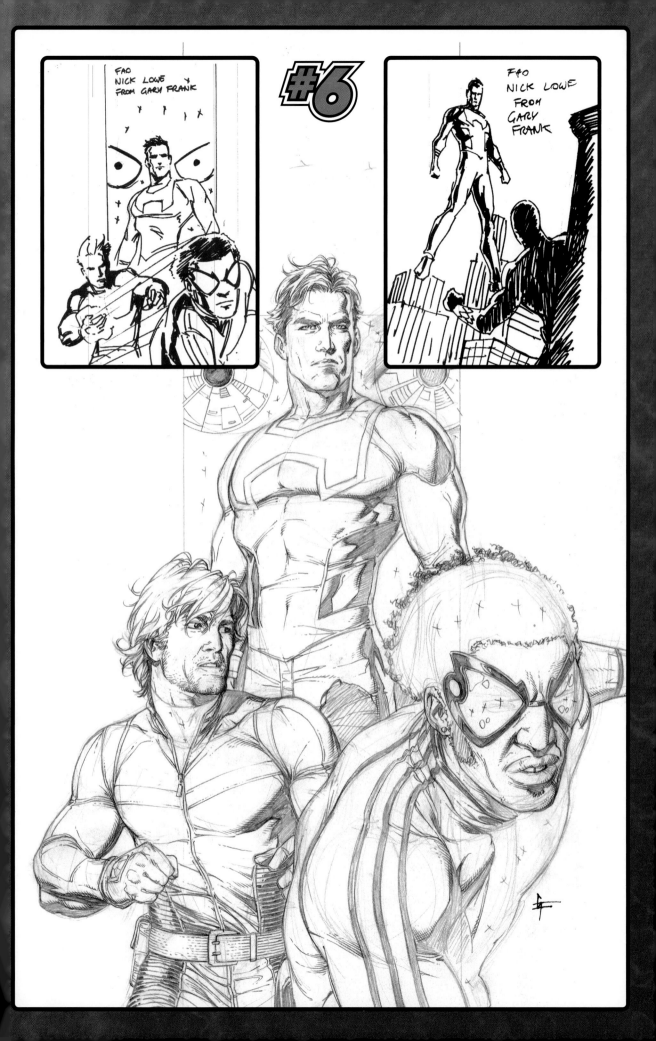

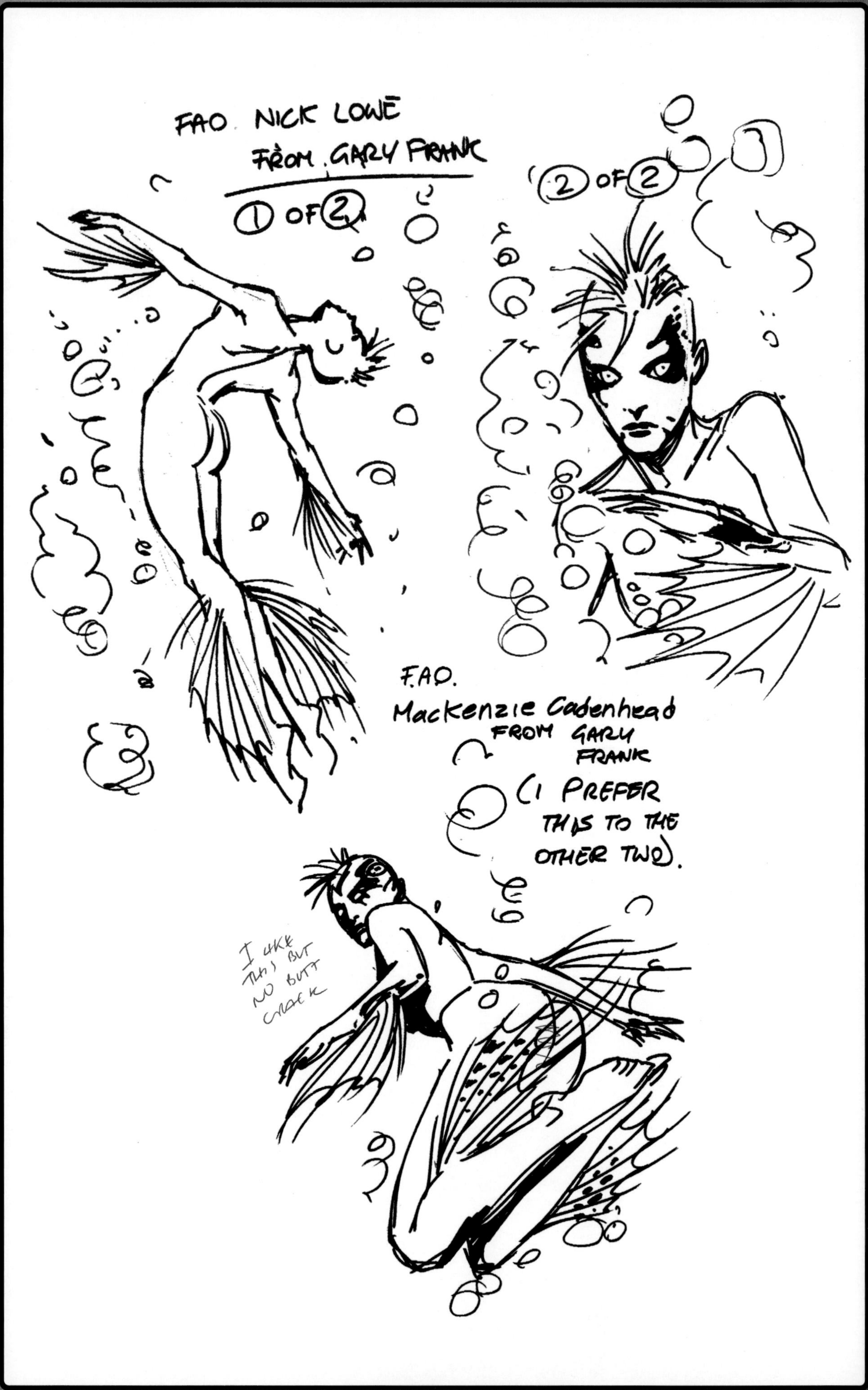
FAO NICK LOWE
FROM GARY FRANK
1 OF 2
2 OF 2
F.A.O.
Mackenzie Cadenhead
FROM GARY FRANK
(I PREFER THIS TO THE OTHER TWO).
I LIKE THIS BUT NO BUTT CRACK

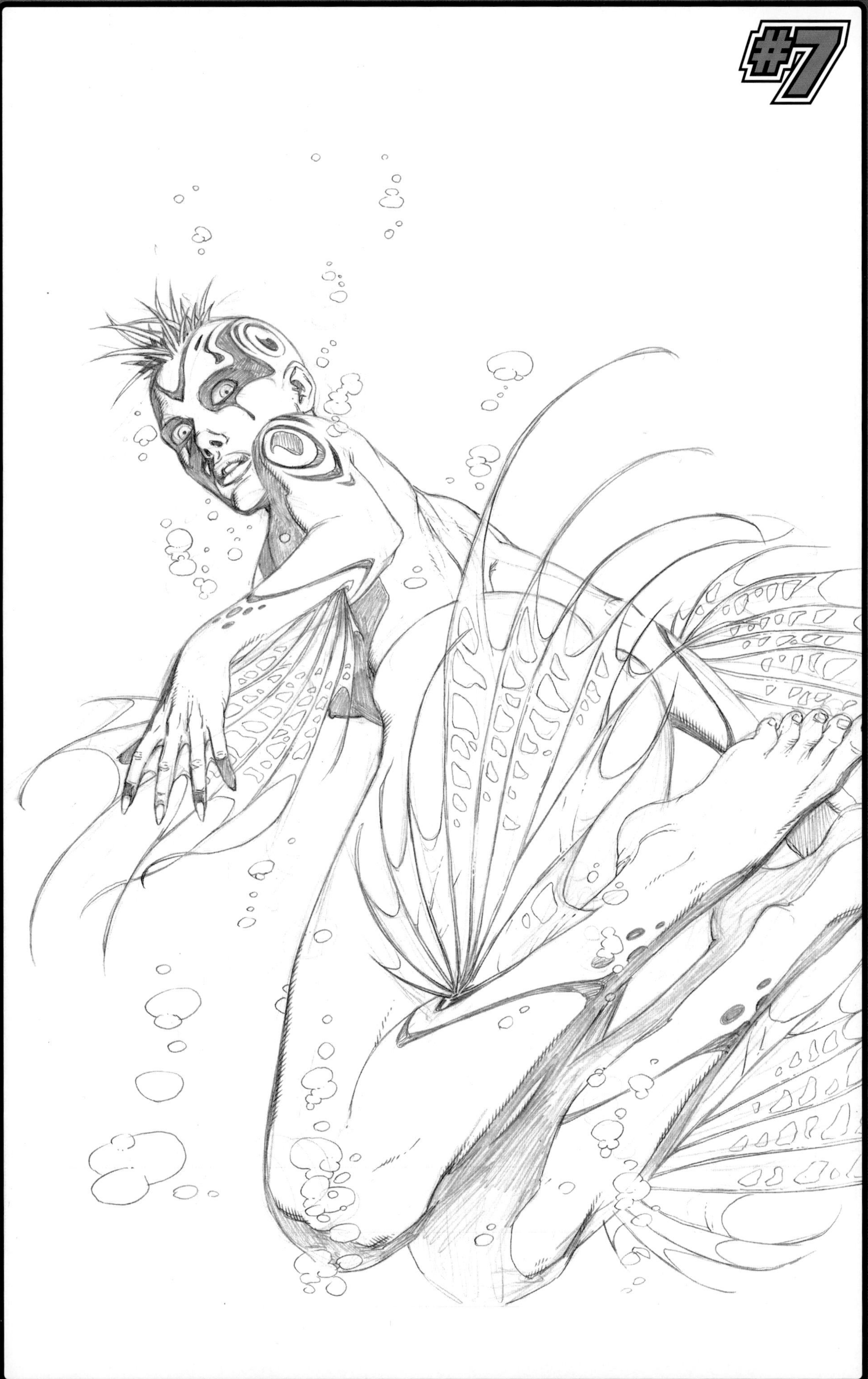
#7

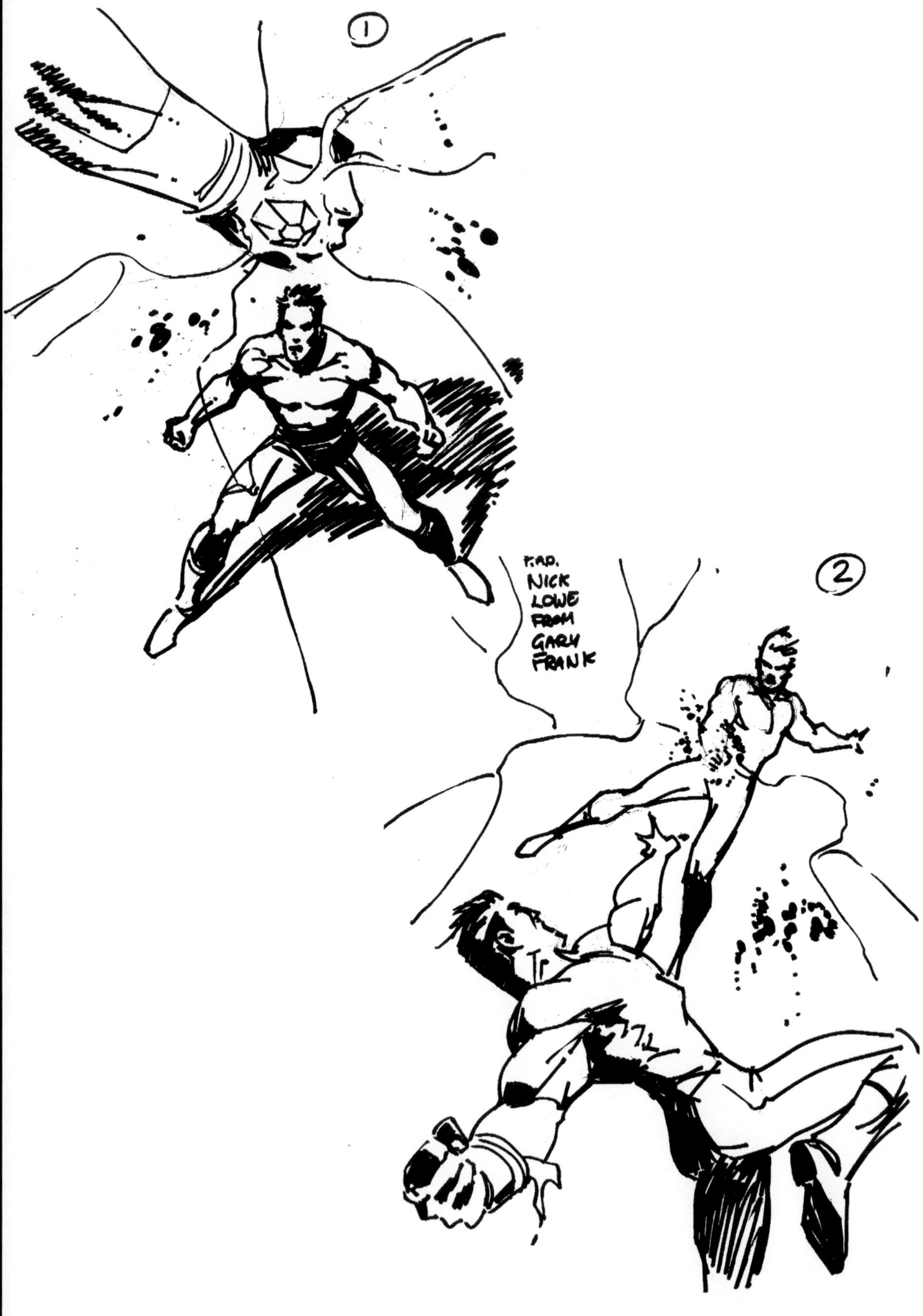
1
F.A.O.
NICK
LOWE
FROM
GARY
FRANK
2

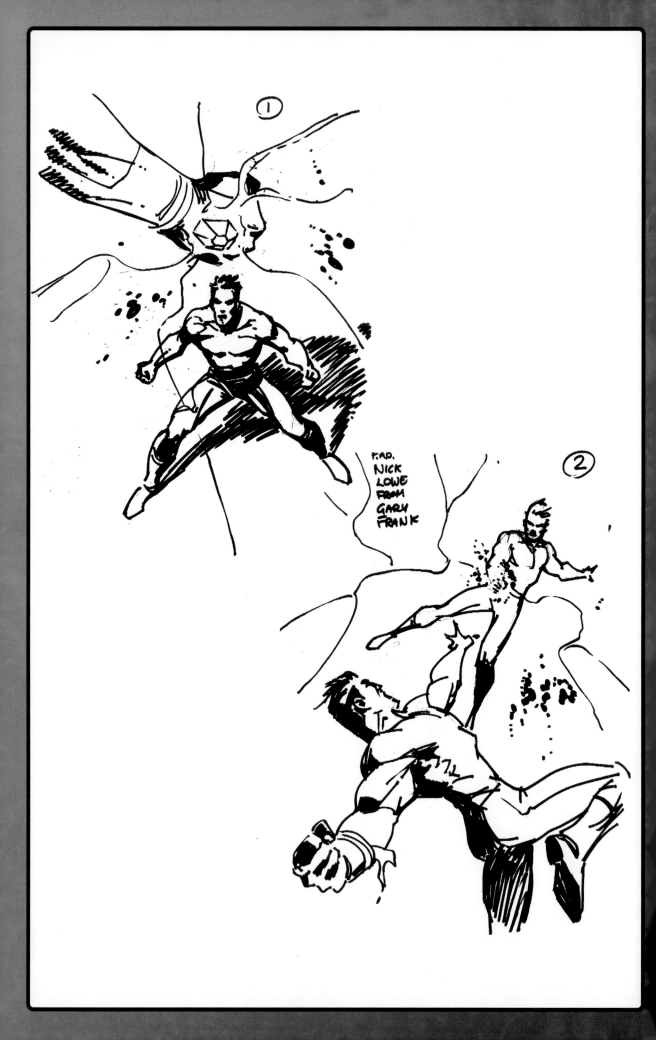

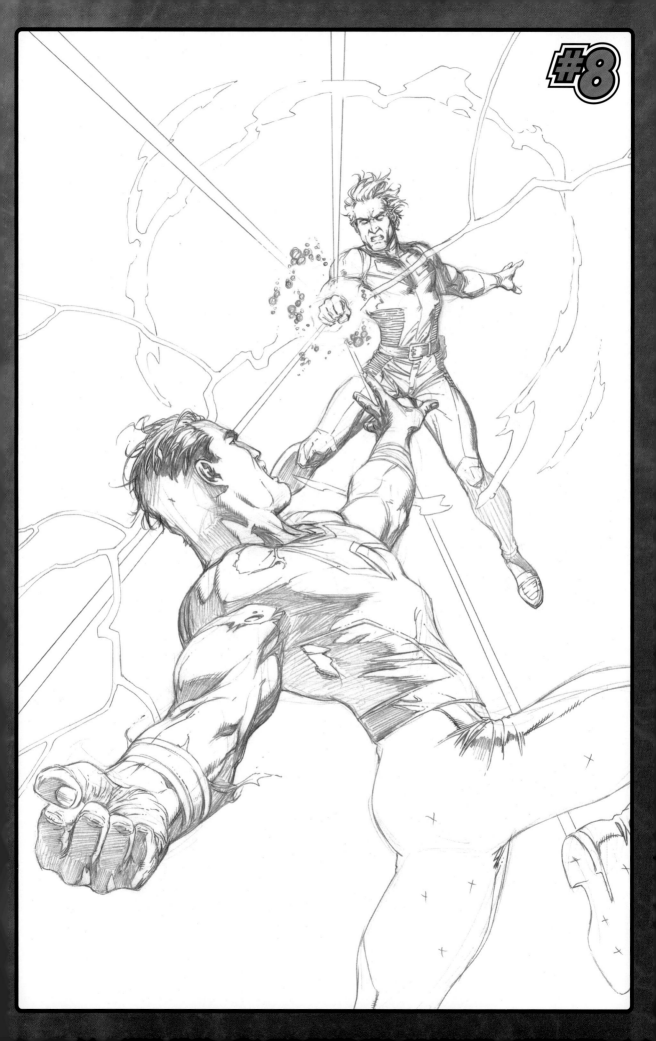

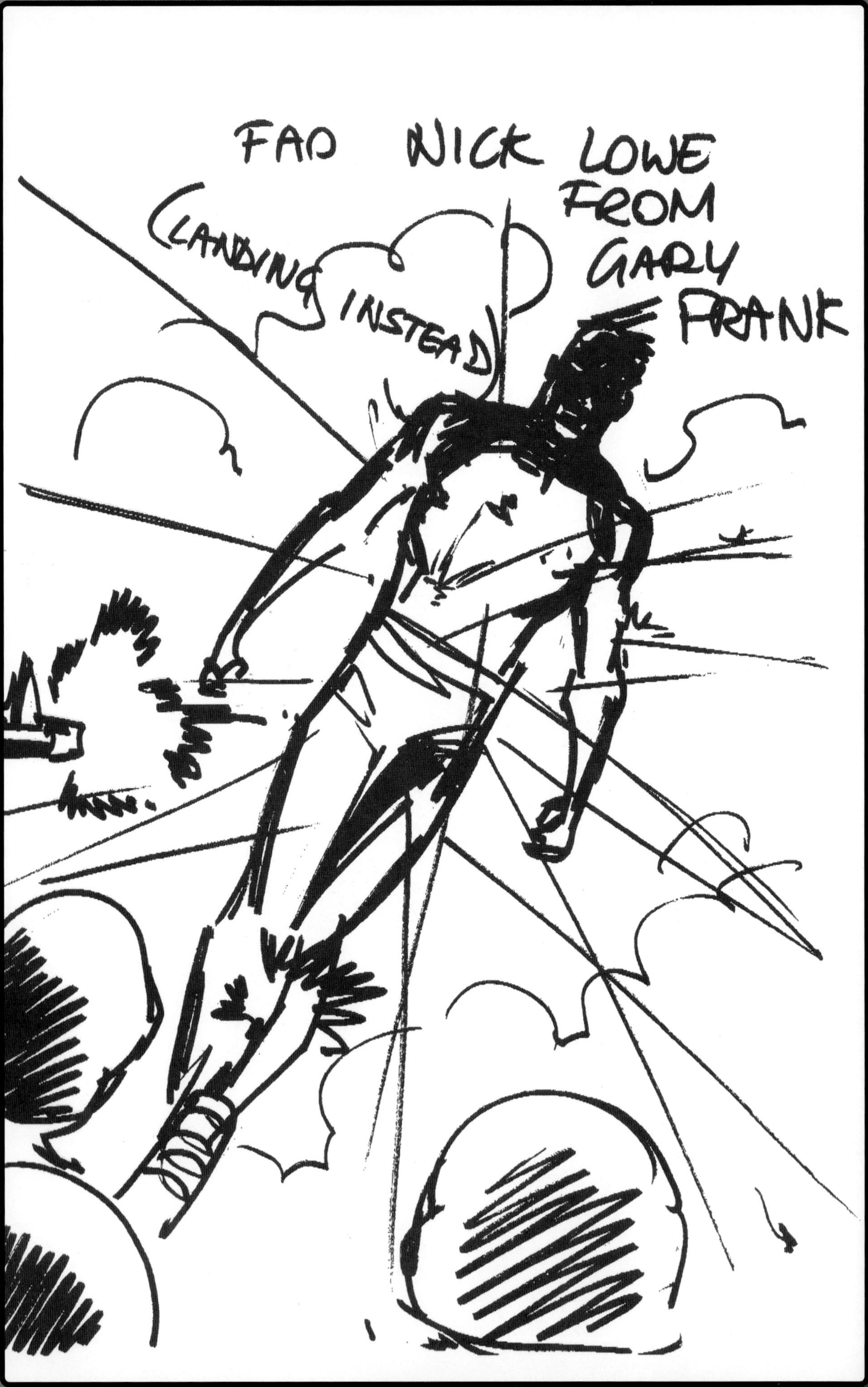
FAO NICK LOWE FROM GARY FRANK
(LANDING INSTEAD)

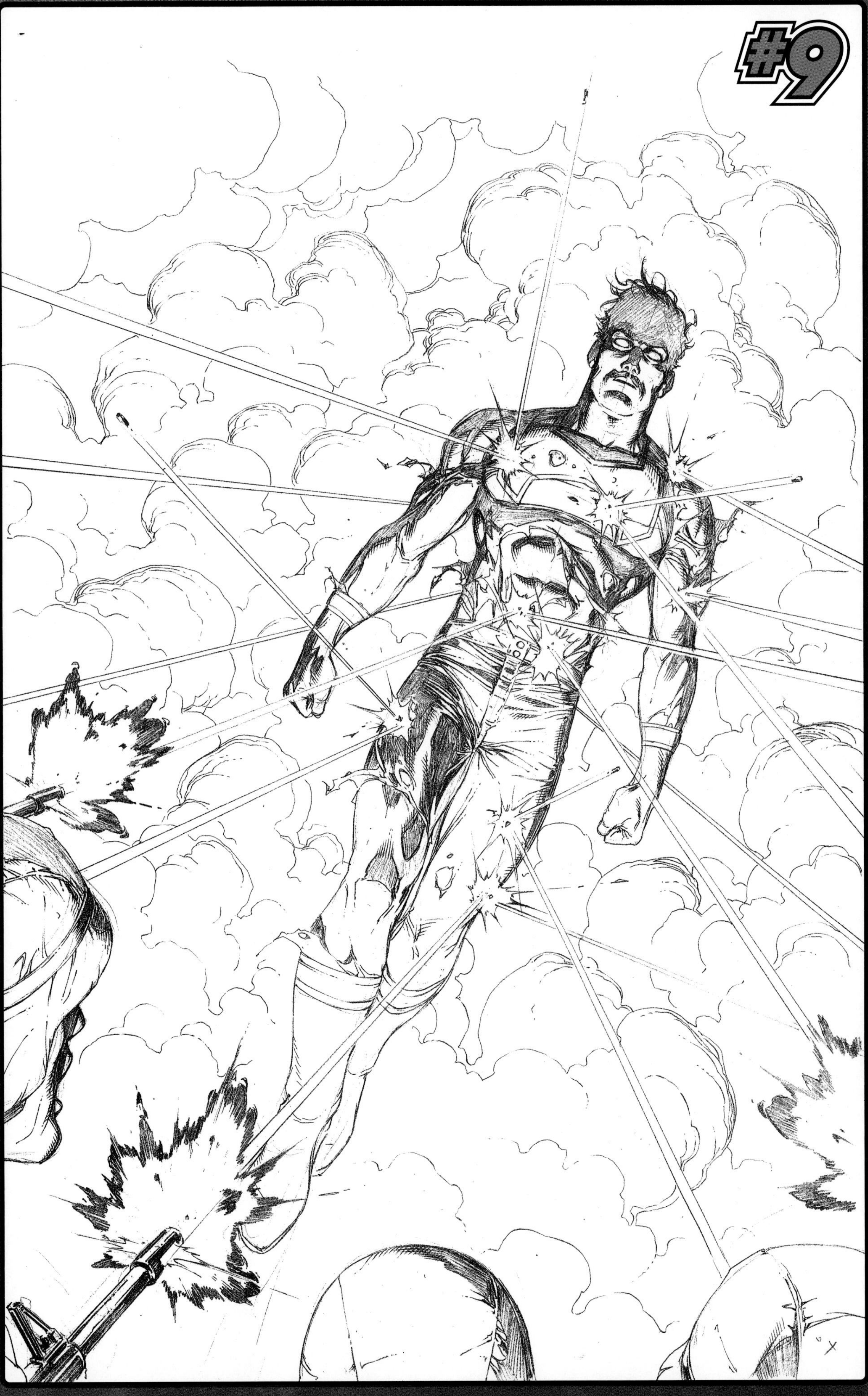
#9

#10

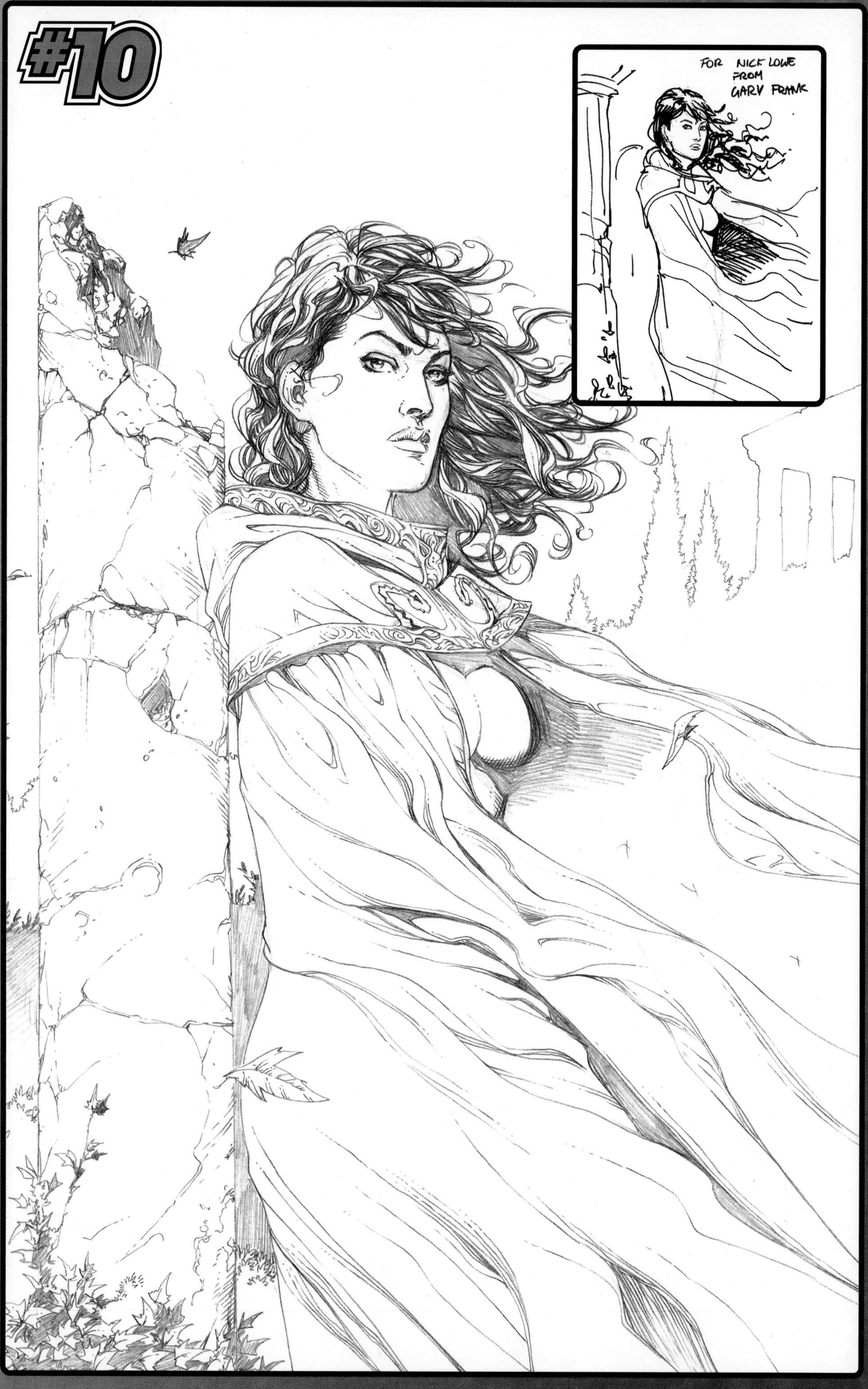
FOR NICK LOWE
FROM
GARY FRANK

#11

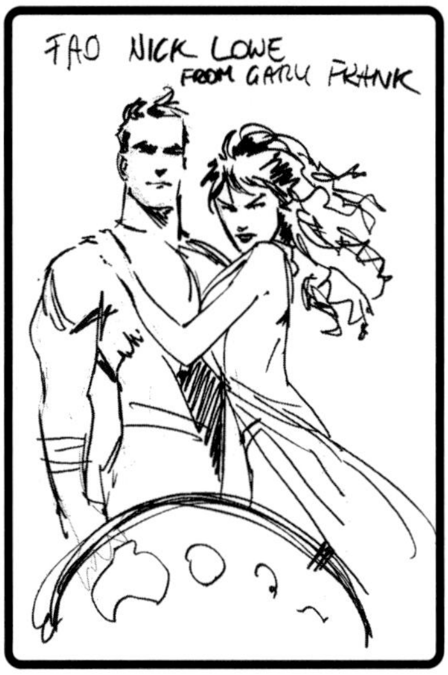
FAO NICK LOWE
FROM GARY FRANK

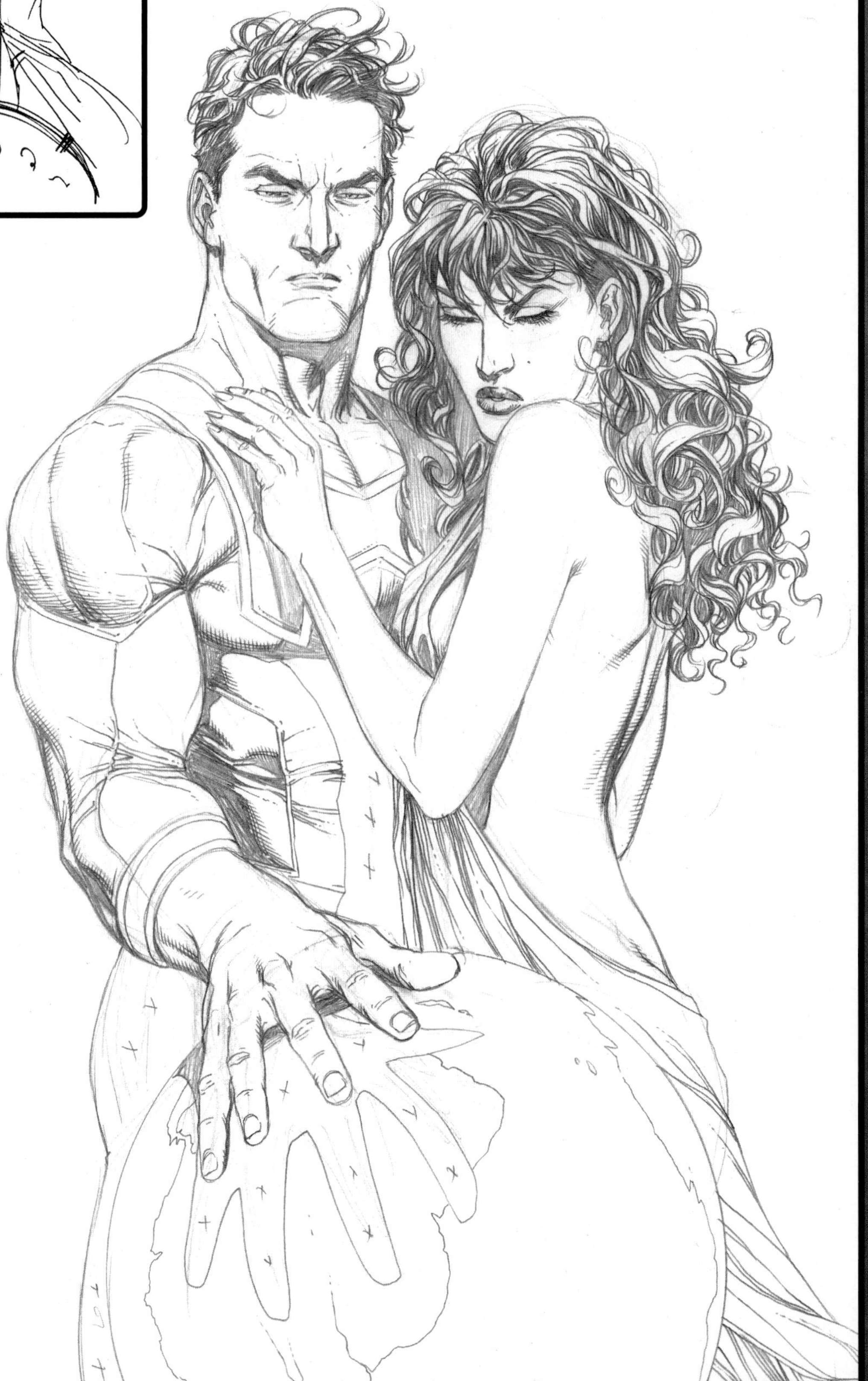

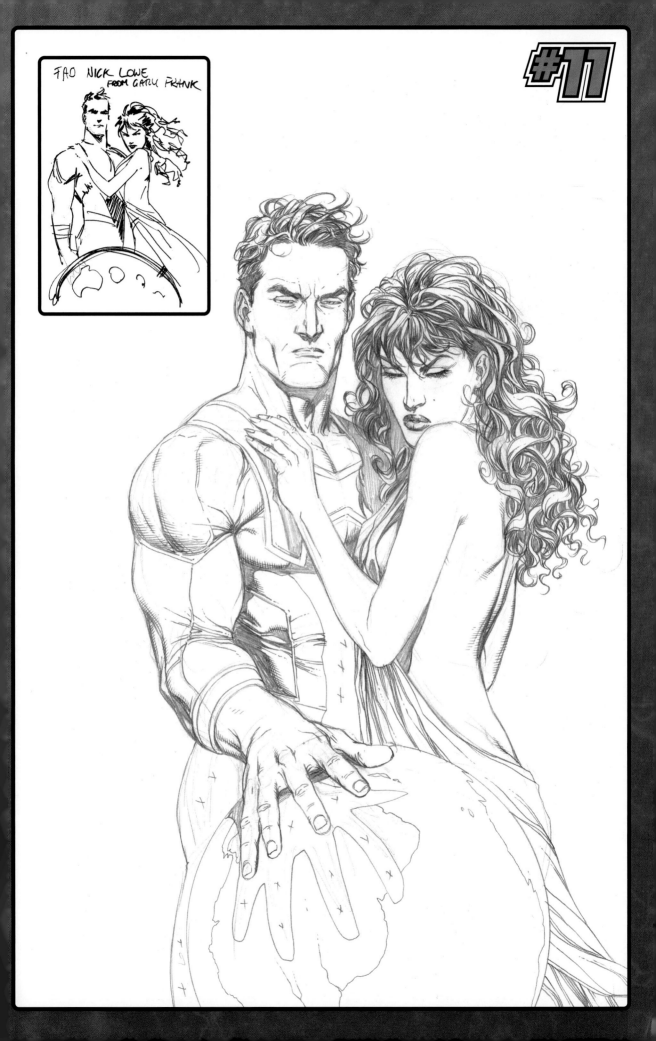

HISTORY LESSON

Marvel readers got their first glimpse of the Squadron Supreme in the two fine issues of *Avengers* reprinted here. It was a strange case of Earth's Mightiest Heroes meeting—Earth's Mightiest Heroes. And that was okay with me because the more super heroes packed in a story, the better! Scripter Roy Thomas had stunningly introduced a brand-new array of characters in the Marvel pantheon. With names such as Nighthawk, Hyperion and Doctor Spectrum, you knew these guys were cool. Especially because they were based on an already-existing group of baddies called the Squadron Sinister, also the brainchild of Mr. T.

And did they catch on! The Squadron Supreme has appeared numerous times in *Avengers*, always giving as good as it got. Individual members have popped up in various Marvel titles through the decades. A version of Nighthawk became a permanent member of another super group: the Defenders. Notably, the Squadron even received its own twelve-issue limited series in the 1980s, brilliantly written by the late Mark Gruenwald and edited by yours truly.

Why do writers keep coming back to these figures? What characteristics do they possess that continually attract generation after generation of creators? I believe it has to do with power. Pure and simple. Collectively, they're a match for the Avengers, the X-Men or the Fantastic Four. Hyperion, alone, is on par with our Thunder God, the Mighty Thor himself. And, the bottom line is, who has the most power is what super-hero comics are all about.

I can't say what was going through Roy's mind when he created the Squadron Supreme. But I can tell you what Mark and I were thinking when we conceived the *Squadron Supreme* limited series. We wanted to explore the theme of absolute power corrupting absolutely. The Squadron had become the rulers of their world. Their word was law. And even though they had the people's best interests at heart, weren't they truly despots in colorful costumes—benevolent or otherwise?

It appears *Amazing Spider-Man* scribe J. Michael Straczynski has found a motherlode of themes to examine with his own take on the Squadron called *Supreme Power*. J. Michael is striking out in a bold new direction. Here is the Squadron for the 21st century. Here is a startling twist on perhaps the most famous origin in all comicdom, complete with enough duplicity and paranoia to make espionage author John LeCarre green with envy.

More than thirty years separates the reprinted *Avengers* and the first issue of *Supreme Power*. Roy Thomas' initial genius of creation has been reimagined for a new generation of comics readers by the scintillating talent of Straczynski and artist Gary Frank. It remains a fresh, vital, relevant group of characters. And it's your turn to experience them in all their troubled glory. Now...

Up, up and awaaaaaaaaayyyyyy!

I just made that up.

Ralph Macchio

Ralph Macchio

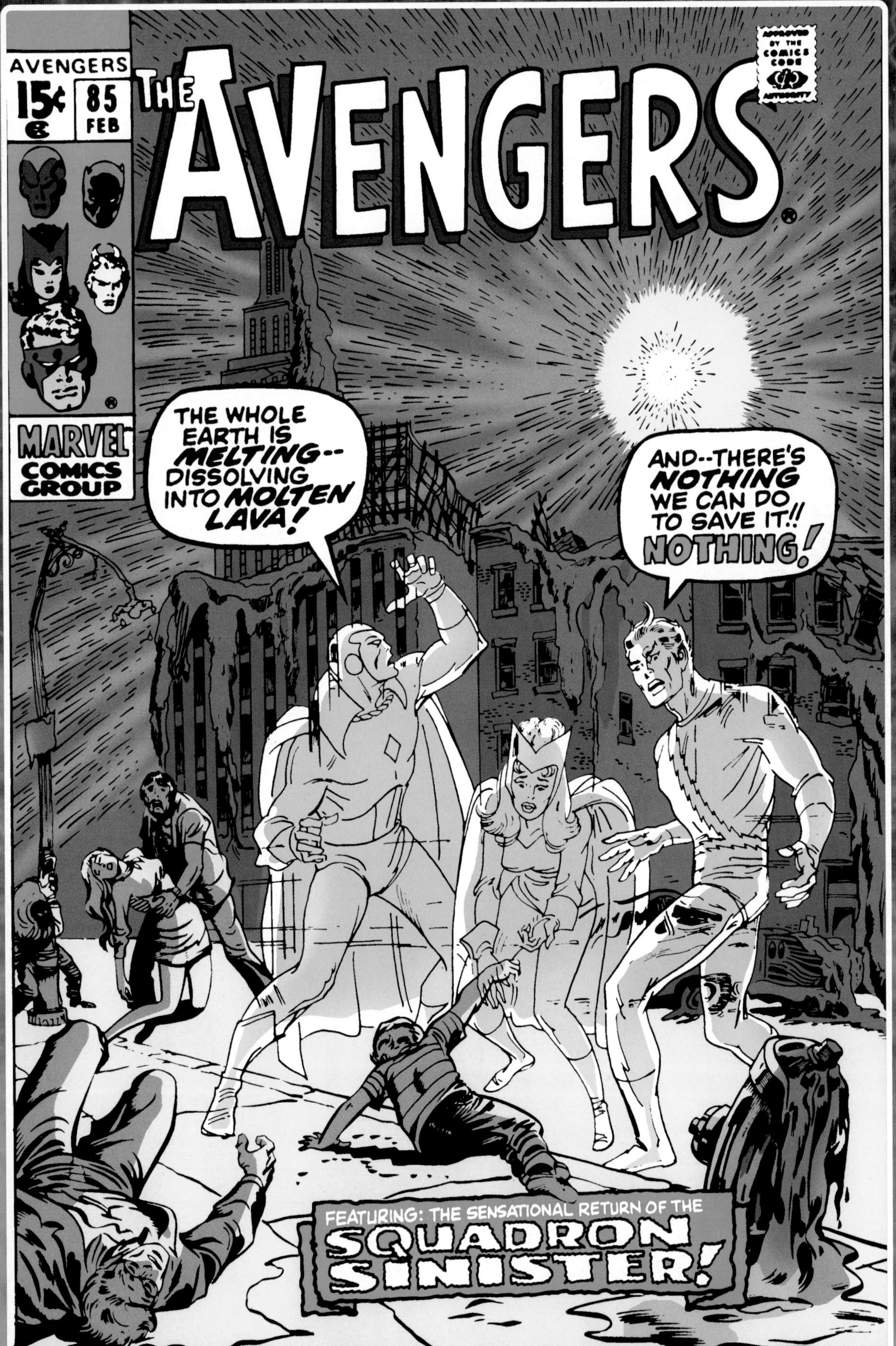
AVENGERS
15¢
85
FEB
THE AVENGERS
MARVEL COMICS GROUP
APPROVED BY THE COMICS CODE AUTHORITY
THE WHOLE EARTH IS MELTING-- DISSOLVING INTO MOLTEN LAVA!
AND--THERE'S NOTHING WE CAN DO TO SAVE IT!! NOTHING!
FEATURING: THE SENSATIONAL RETURN OF THE SQUADRON SINISTER!

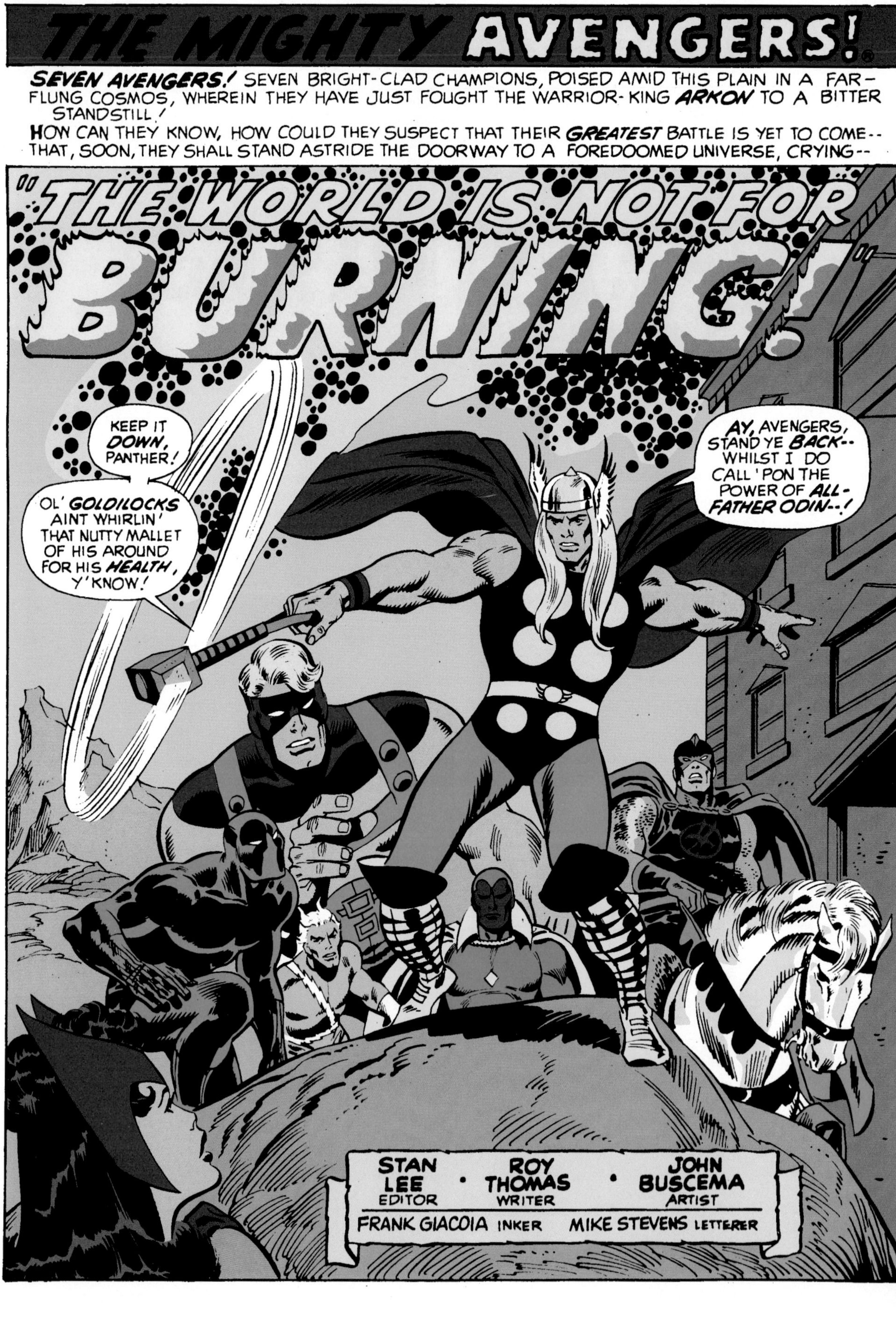
THE MIGHTY AVENGERS!
SEVEN AVENGERS! SEVEN BRIGHT-CLAD CHAMPIONS, POISED AMID THIS PLAIN IN A FAR-FLUNG COSMOS, WHEREIN THEY HAVE JUST FOUGHT THE WARRIOR-KING ARKON TO A BITTER STANDSTILL!
HOW CAN THEY KNOW, HOW COULD THEY SUSPECT THAT THEIR GREATEST BATTLE IS YET TO COME-- THAT, SOON, THEY SHALL STAND ASTRIDE THE DOORWAY TO A FOREDOOMED UNIVERSE, CRYING--
"THE WORLD IS NOT FOR BURNING!"
KEEP IT DOWN, PANTHER!
OL' GOLDILOCKS AINT WHIRLIN' THAT NUTTY MALLET OF HIS AROUND FOR HIS HEALTH, Y'KNOW!
AY, AVENGERS, STAND YE BACK-- WHILST I DO CALL 'PON THE POWER OF ALL-FATHER ODIN--!
STAN LEE EDITOR • ROY THOMAS WRITER • JOHN BUSCEMA ARTIST
FRANK GIACOIA INKER MIKE STEVENS LETTERER

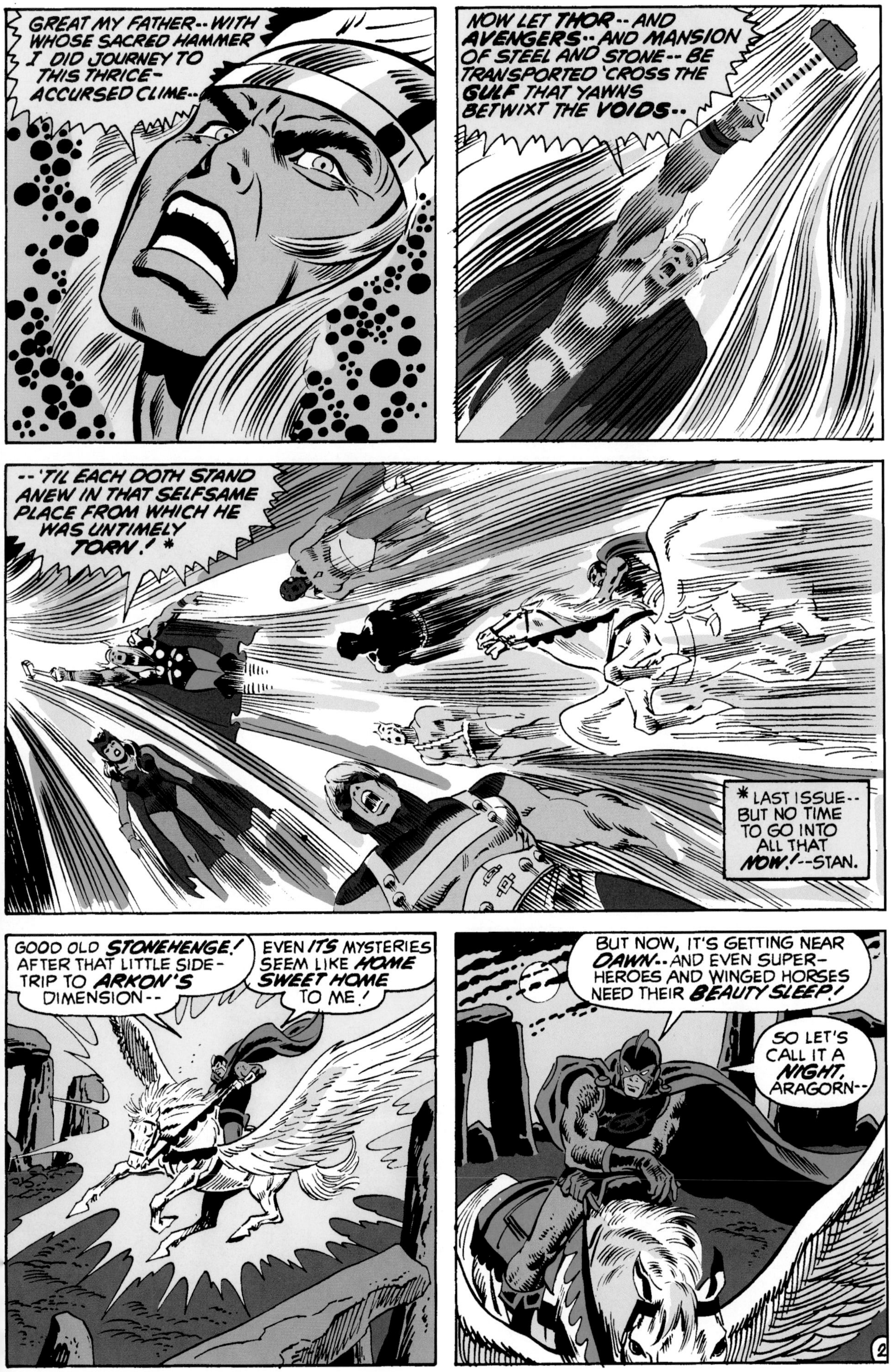
GREAT MY FATHER--WITH WHOSE SACRED HAMMER I DID JOURNEY TO THIS THRICE-ACCURSED CLIME--
NOW LET THOR--AND AVENGERS--AND MANSION OF STEEL AND STONE--BE TRANSPORTED 'CROSS THE GULF THAT YAWNS BETWIXT THE VOIDS--
--'TIL EACH DOTH STAND ANEW IN THAT SELFSAME PLACE FROM WHICH HE WAS UNTIMELY TORN! *
* LAST ISSUE--BUT NO TIME TO GO INTO ALL THAT NOW!--STAN.
GOOD OLD STONEHENGE! AFTER THAT LITTLE SIDE-TRIP TO ARKON'S DIMENSION--
EVEN ITS MYSTERIES SEEM LIKE HOME SWEET HOME TO ME!
BUT NOW, IT'S GETTING NEAR DAWN--AND EVEN SUPER-HEROES AND WINGED HORSES NEED THEIR BEAUTY SLEEP!
SO LET'S CALL IT A NIGHT, ARAGORN--
2

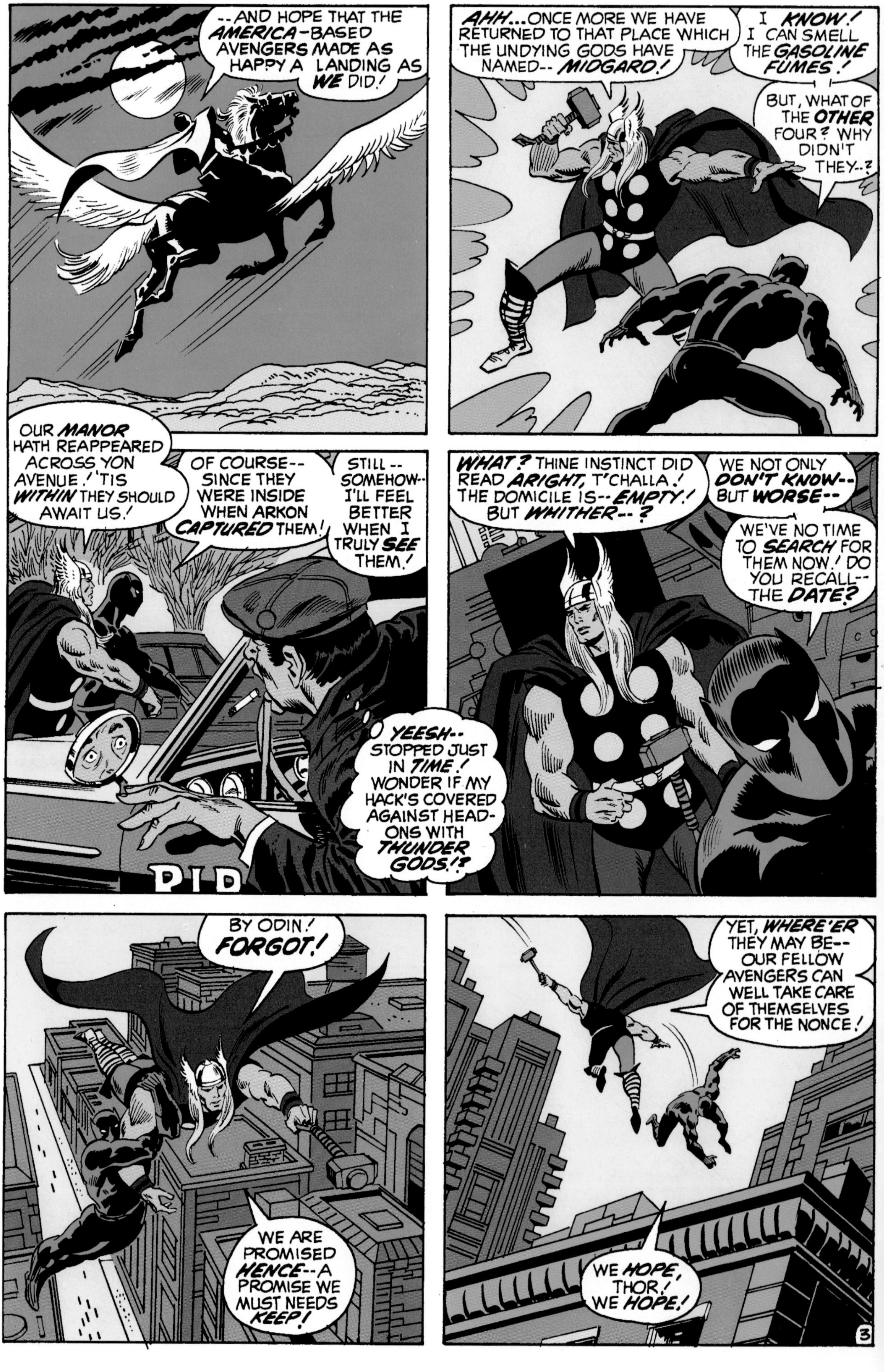

--AND HOPE THAT THE AMERICA-BASED AVENGERS MADE AS HAPPY A LANDING AS WE DID!
AHH...ONCE MORE WE HAVE RETURNED TO THAT PLACE WHICH THE UNDYING GODS HAVE NAMED--MIDGARD!
I KNOW! I CAN SMELL THE GASOLINE FUMES!
BUT, WHAT OF THE OTHER FOUR? WHY DIDN'T THEY--?
OUR MANOR HATH REAPPEARED ACROSS YON AVENUE! 'TIS WITHIN THEY SHOULD AWAIT US!
OF COURSE-- SINCE THEY WERE INSIDE WHEN ARKON CAPTURED THEM!
STILL-- SOMEHOW-- I'LL FEEL BETTER WHEN I TRULY SEE THEM!
YEESH-- STOPPED JUST IN TIME! WONDER IF MY HACK'S COVERED AGAINST HEAD-ONS WITH THUNDER GODS!?
WHAT? THINE INSTINCT DID READ ARIGHT, T'CHALLA! THE DOMICILE IS--EMPTY! BUT WHITHER--?
WE NOT ONLY DON'T KNOW-- BUT WORSE--
WE'VE NO TIME TO SEARCH FOR THEM NOW! DO YOU RECALL-- THE DATE?
BY ODIN! FORGOT!
WE ARE PROMISED HENCE--A PROMISE WE MUST NEEDS KEEP!
YET, WHERE'ER THEY MAY BE-- OUR FELLOW AVENGERS CAN WELL TAKE CARE OF THEMSELVES FOR THE NONCE!
WE HOPE, THOR! WE HOPE!
3

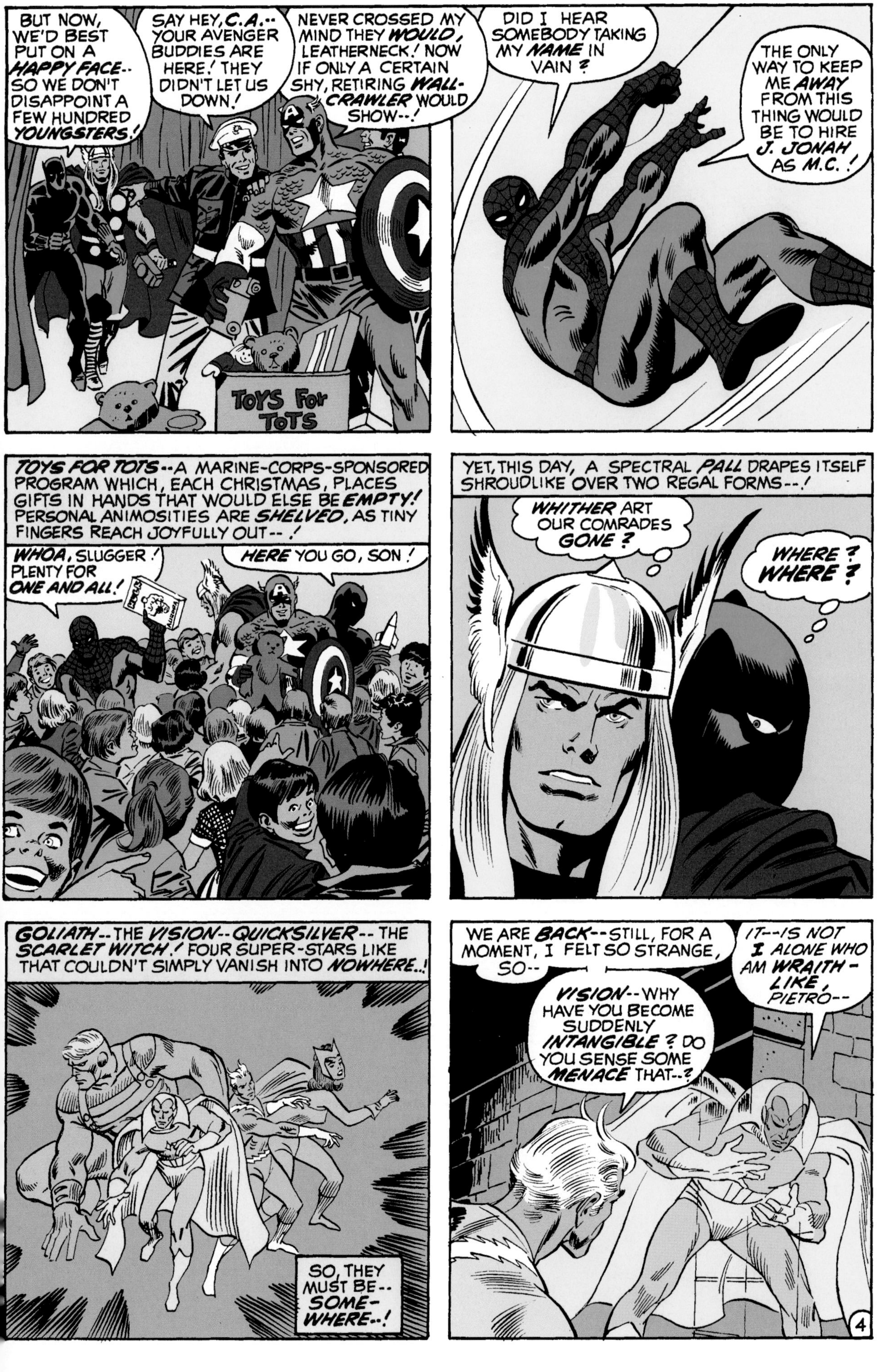

BUT NOW, WE'D BEST PUT ON A HAPPY FACE-- SO WE DON'T DISAPPOINT A FEW HUNDRED YOUNGSTERS!
SAY HEY, C.A.-- YOUR AVENGER BUDDIES ARE HERE! THEY DIDN'T LET US DOWN!
NEVER CROSSED MY MIND THEY WOULD, LEATHERNECK! NOW IF ONLY A CERTAIN SHY, RETIRING WALL-CRAWLER WOULD SHOW--!
TOYS FOR TOTS
DID I HEAR SOMEBODY TAKING MY NAME IN VAIN?
THE ONLY WAY TO KEEP ME AWAY FROM THIS THING WOULD BE TO HIRE J. JONAH AS M.C.!
TOYS FOR TOTS--A MARINE-CORPS-SPONSORED PROGRAM WHICH, EACH CHRISTMAS, PLACES GIFTS IN HANDS THAT WOULD ELSE BE EMPTY! PERSONAL ANIMOSITIES ARE SHELVED, AS TINY FINGERS REACH JOYFULLY OUT--!
WHOA, SLUGGER! PLENTY FOR ONE AND ALL!
HERE YOU GO, SON!
YET, THIS DAY, A SPECTRAL PALL DRAPES ITSELF SHROUDLIKE OVER TWO REGAL FORMS--!
WHITHER ART OUR COMRADES GONE?
WHERE? WHERE?
GOLIATH--THE VISION--QUICKSILVER--THE SCARLET WITCH! FOUR SUPER-STARS LIKE THAT COULDN'T SIMPLY VANISH INTO NOWHERE..!
SO, THEY MUST BE--SOME-WHERE--!
WE ARE BACK--STILL, FOR A MOMENT, I FELT SO STRANGE, SO--
IT--IS NOT I ALONE WHO AM WRAITH-LIKE, PIETRO--
VISION--WHY HAVE YOU BECOME SUDDENLY INTANGIBLE? DO YOU SENSE SOME MENACE THAT--?
4

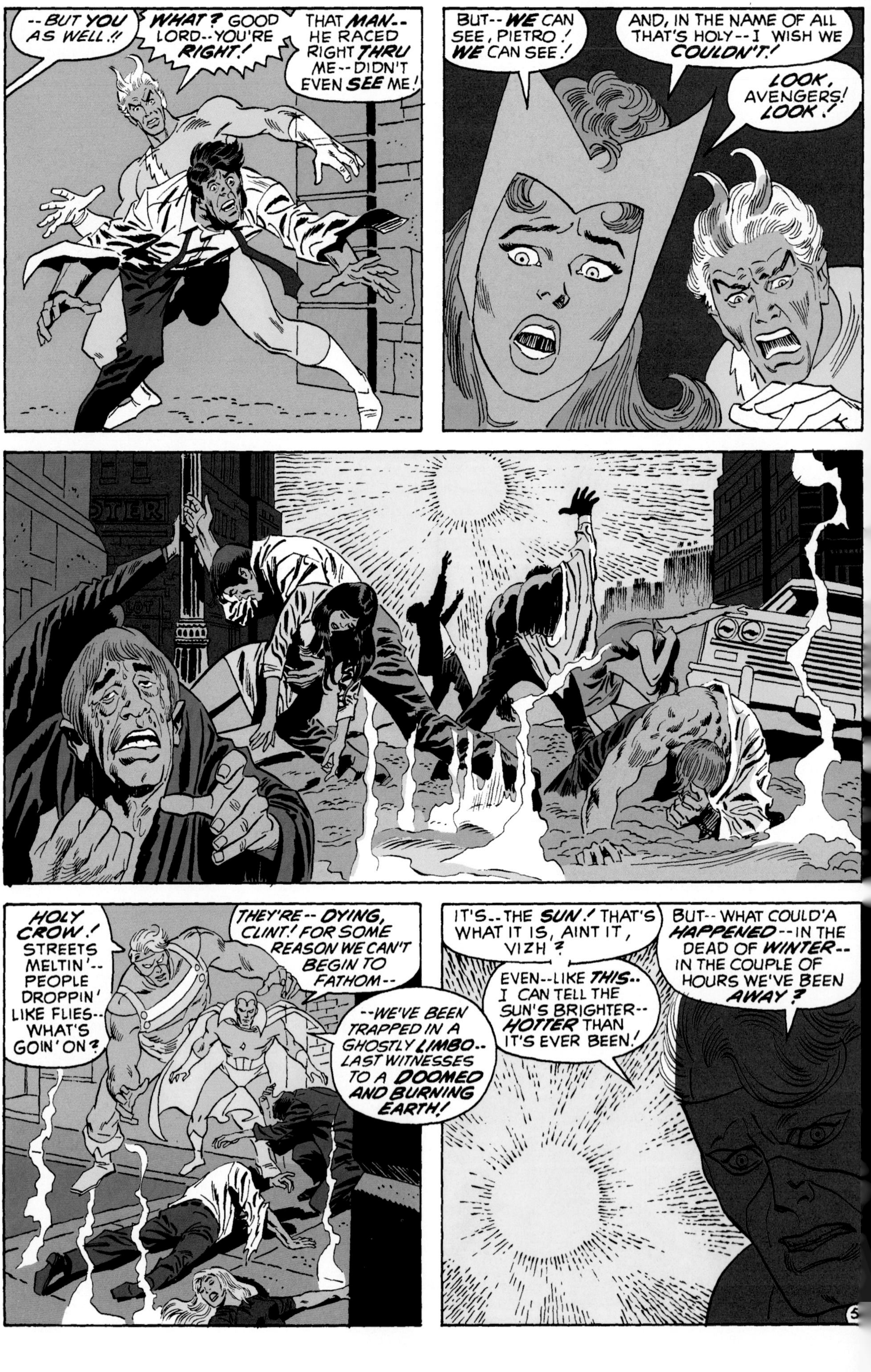

--BUT YOU AS WELL.!!
WHAT? GOOD LORD--YOU'RE RIGHT!
THAT MAN-- HE RACED RIGHT THRU ME--DIDN'T EVEN SEE ME!
BUT--WE CAN SEE, PIETRO! WE CAN SEE!
AND, IN THE NAME OF ALL THAT'S HOLY--I WISH WE COULDN'T!
LOOK, AVENGERS! LOOK!
HOLY CROW! STREETS MELTIN'--PEOPLE DROPPIN' LIKE FLIES--WHAT'S GOIN' ON?
THEY'RE--DYING, CLINT! FOR SOME REASON WE CAN'T BEGIN TO FATHOM--
--WE'VE BEEN TRAPPED IN A GHOSTLY LIMBO--LAST WITNESSES TO A DOOMED AND BURNING EARTH!
IT'S--THE SUN! THAT'S WHAT IT IS, AINT IT, VIZH?
EVEN--LIKE THIS--I CAN TELL THE SUN'S BRIGHTER--HOTTER THAN IT'S EVER BEEN!
BUT--WHAT COULD'A HAPPENED--IN THE DEAD OF WINTER--IN THE COUPLE OF HOURS WE'VE BEEN AWAY?
5

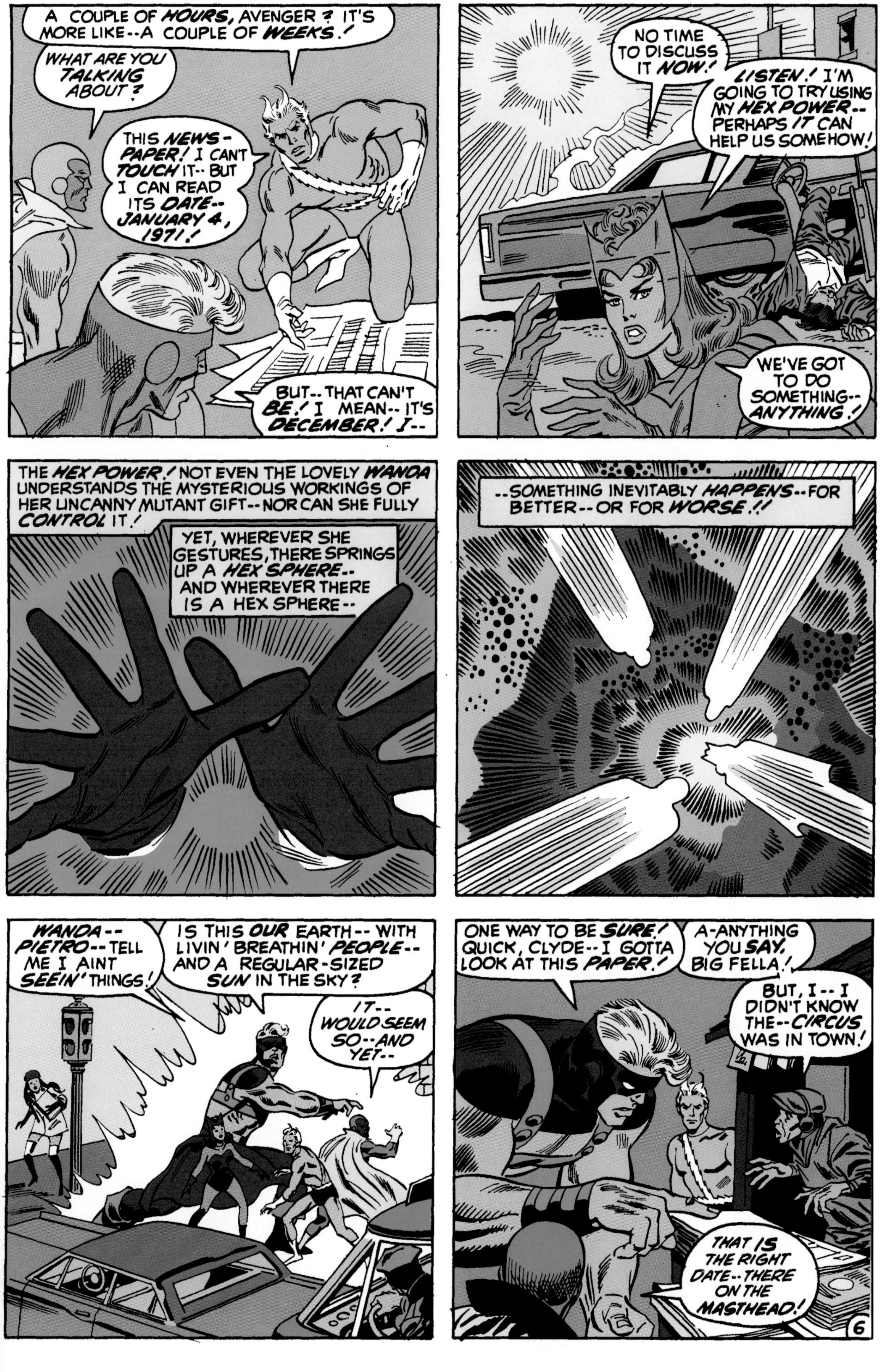
A COUPLE OF HOURS, AVENGER? IT'S MORE LIKE--A COUPLE OF WEEKS.!
WHAT ARE YOU TALKING ABOUT?
THIS NEWS-PAPER! I CAN'T TOUCH IT-- BUT I CAN READ ITS DATE-- JANUARY 4, 1971!
BUT-- THAT CAN'T BE! I MEAN-- IT'S DECEMBER! I--
NO TIME TO DISCUSS IT NOW!
LISTEN! I'M GOING TO TRY USING MY HEX POWER-- PERHAPS IT CAN HELP US SOMEHOW!
WE'VE GOT TO DO SOMETHING-- ANYTHING!
THE HEX POWER! NOT EVEN THE LOVELY WANDA UNDERSTANDS THE MYSTERIOUS WORKINGS OF HER UNCANNY MUTANT GIFT-- NOR CAN SHE FULLY CONTROL IT!
YET, WHEREVER SHE GESTURES, THERE SPRINGS UP A HEX SPHERE-- AND WHEREVER THERE IS A HEX SPHERE--
--SOMETHING INEVITABLY HAPPENS-- FOR BETTER-- OR FOR WORSE!!
WANDA-- PIETRO-- TELL ME I AINT SEEIN' THINGS!
IS THIS OUR EARTH-- WITH LIVIN' BREATHIN' PEOPLE-- AND A REGULAR-SIZED SUN IN THE SKY?
IT-- WOULD SEEM SO-- AND YET--
ONE WAY TO BE SURE! QUICK, CLYDE-- I GOTTA LOOK AT THIS PAPER!
A-ANYTHING YOU SAY, BIG FELLA!
BUT, I-- I DIDN'T KNOW THE-- CIRCUS WAS IN TOWN!
THAT IS THE RIGHT DATE-- THERE ON THE MASTHEAD!
6

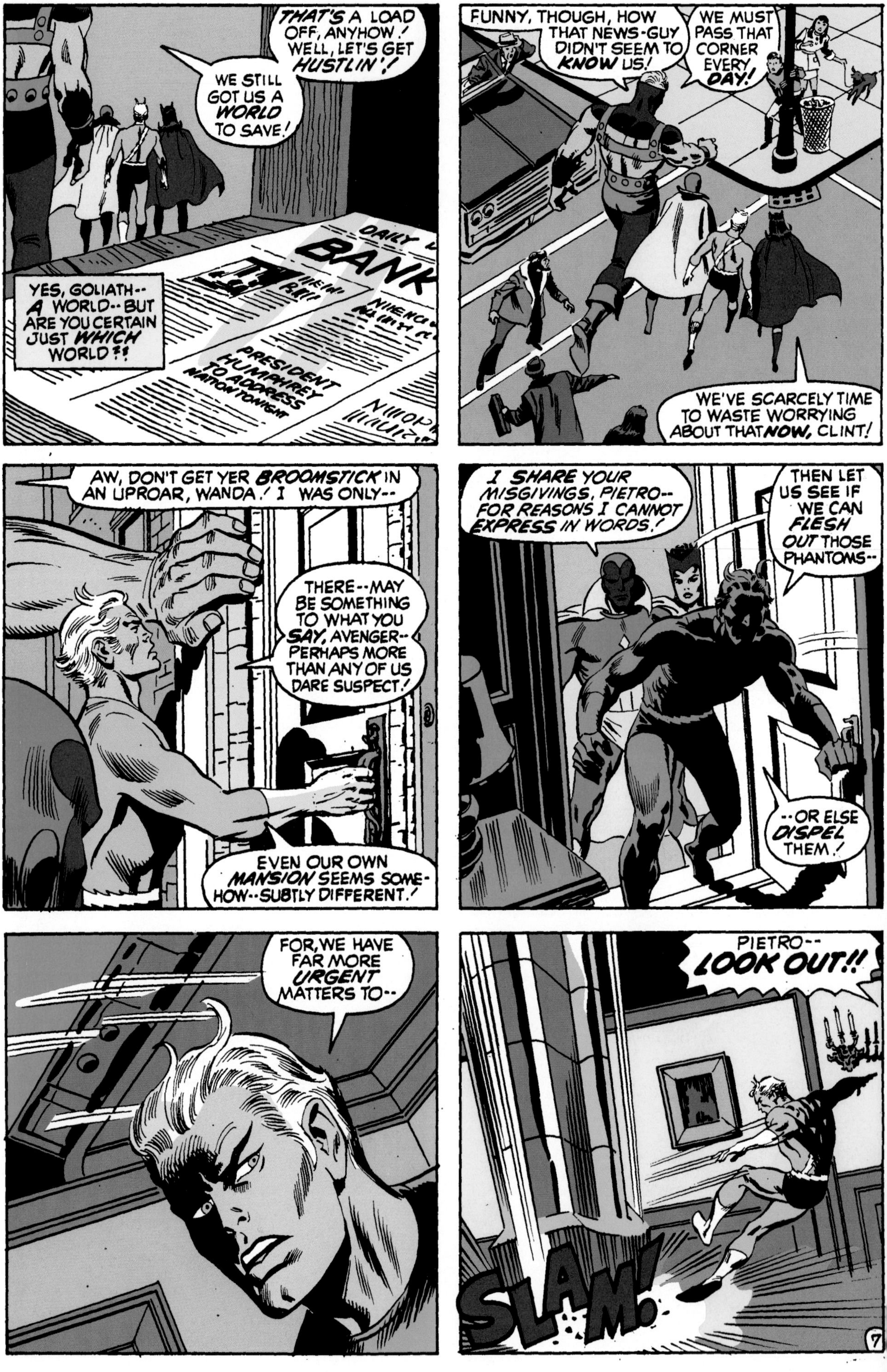
THAT'S A LOAD OFF, ANYHOW! WELL, LET'S GET HUSTLIN'!
WE STILL GOT US A WORLD TO SAVE!
DAILY
BANK
PRESIDENT HUMPHREY TO ADDRESS NATION TONIGHT
YES, GOLIATH-- A WORLD--BUT ARE YOU CERTAIN JUST WHICH WORLD?!
FUNNY, THOUGH, HOW THAT NEWS-GUY DIDN'T SEEM TO KNOW US!
WE MUST PASS THAT CORNER EVERY DAY!
WE'VE SCARCELY TIME TO WASTE WORRYING ABOUT THAT NOW, CLINT!
AW, DON'T GET YER BROOMSTICK IN AN UPROAR, WANDA! I WAS ONLY--
THERE--MAY BE SOMETHING TO WHAT YOU SAY, AVENGER--PERHAPS MORE THAN ANY OF US DARE SUSPECT!
EVEN OUR OWN MANSION SEEMS SOME-HOW--SUBTLY DIFFERENT!
I SHARE YOUR MISGIVINGS, PIETRO-- FOR REASONS I CANNOT EXPRESS IN WORDS!
THEN LET US SEE IF WE CAN FLESH OUT THOSE PHANTOMS--
--OR ELSE DISPEL THEM!
FOR, WE HAVE FAR MORE URGENT MATTERS TO--
PIETRO-- LOOK OUT!!
SLAM!
7

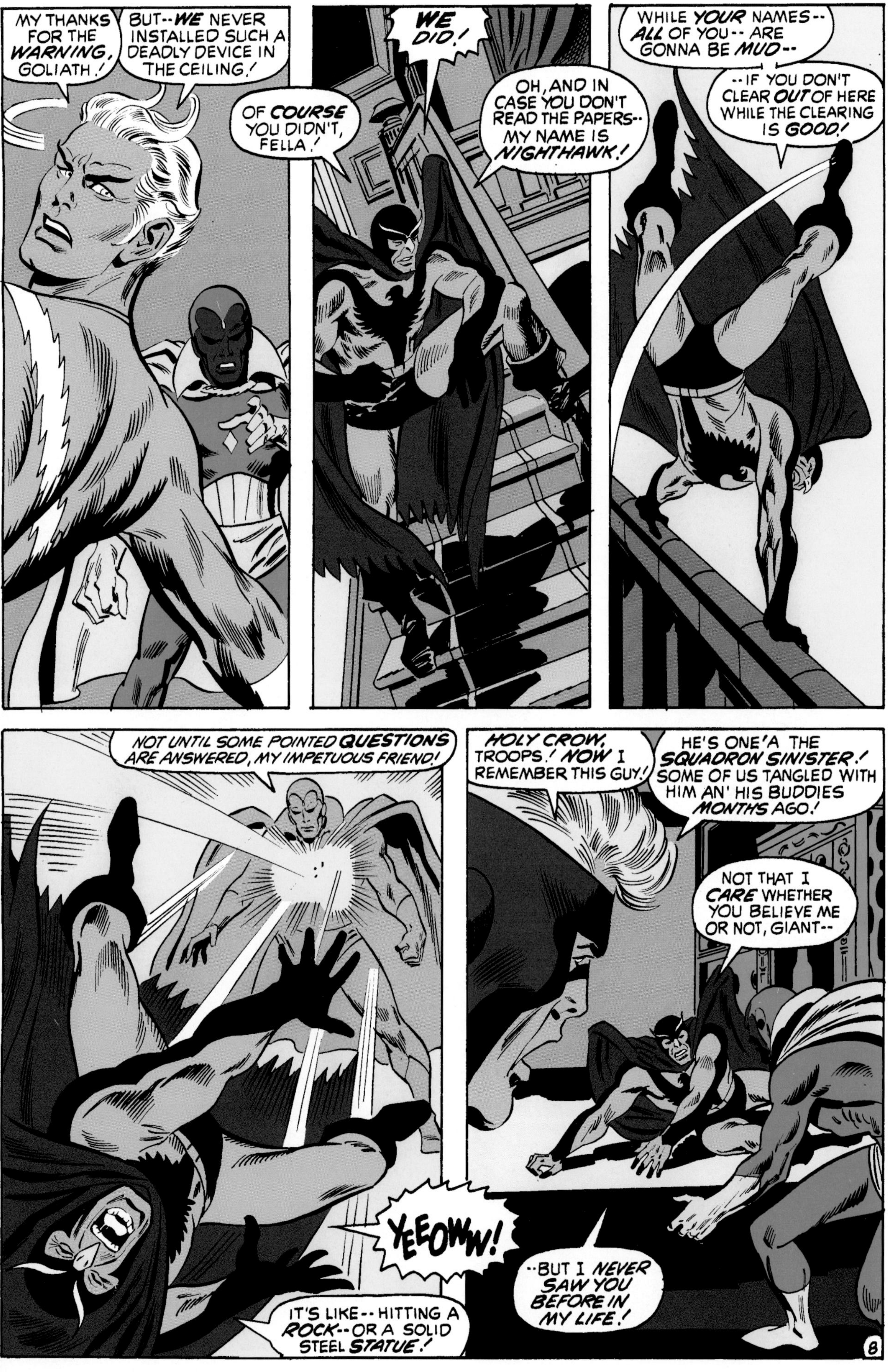
MY THANKS FOR THE WARNING, GOLIATH!
BUT--WE NEVER INSTALLED SUCH A DEADLY DEVICE IN THE CEILING!
OF COURSE YOU DIDN'T, FELLA!
WE DID!
OH, AND IN CASE YOU DON'T READ THE PAPERS-- MY NAME IS NIGHTHAWK!
WHILE YOUR NAMES-- ALL OF YOU-- ARE GONNA BE MUD--
--IF YOU DON'T CLEAR OUT OF HERE WHILE THE CLEARING IS GOOD!
NOT UNTIL SOME POINTED QUESTIONS ARE ANSWERED, MY IMPETUOUS FRIEND!
YEEOWW!
IT'S LIKE--HITTING A ROCK--OR A SOLID STEEL STATUE!
HOLY CROW, TROOPS! NOW I REMEMBER THIS GUY!
HE'S ONE'A THE SQUADRON SINISTER! SOME OF US TANGLED WITH HIM AN' HIS BUDDIES MONTHS AGO!
NOT THAT I CARE WHETHER YOU BELIEVE ME OR NOT, GIANT--
--BUT I NEVER SAW YOU BEFORE IN MY LIFE!
8

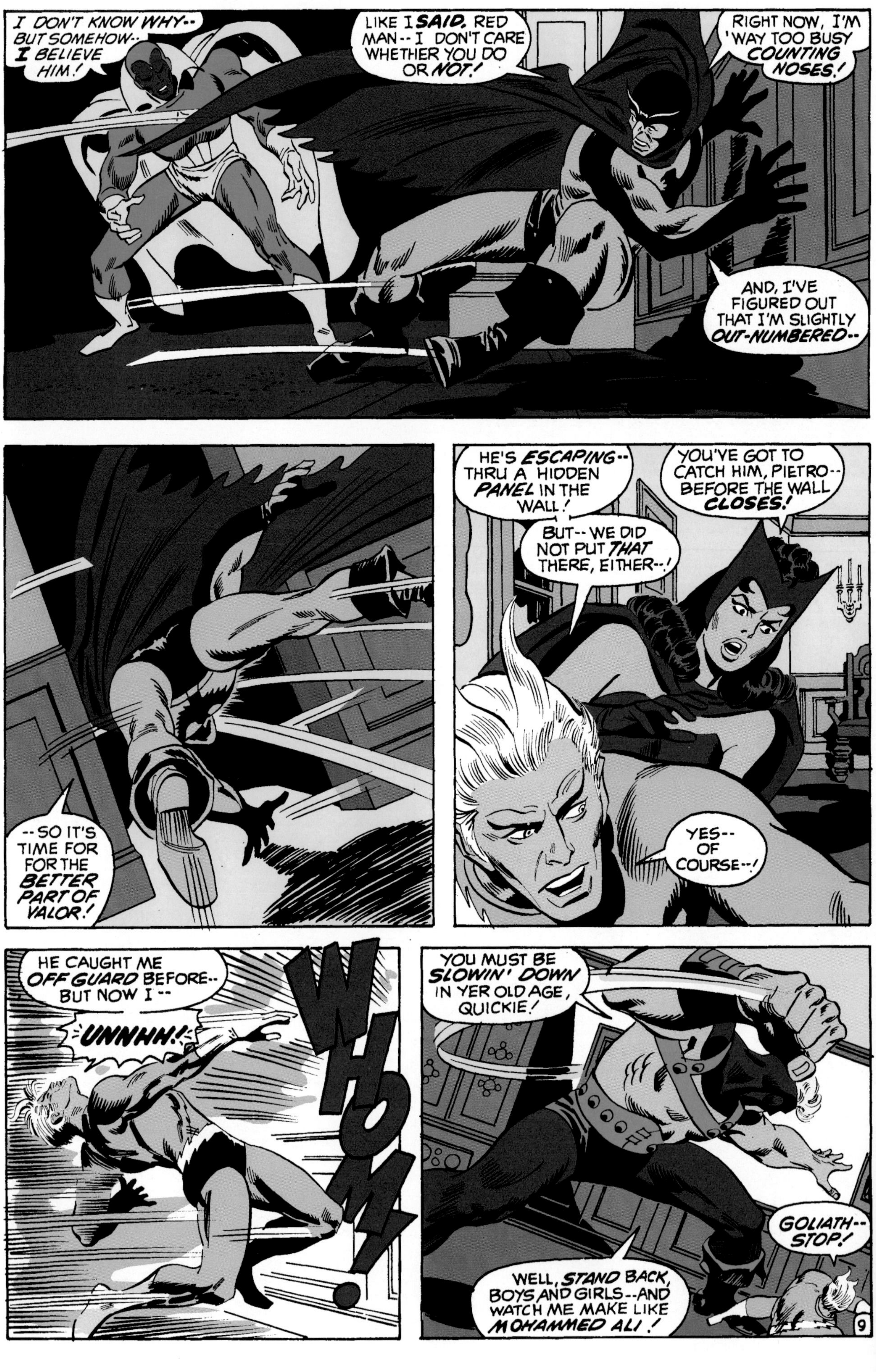
I DON'T KNOW WHY-- BUT SOMEHOW-- I BELIEVE HIM!
LIKE I SAID, RED MAN-- I DON'T CARE WHETHER YOU DO OR NOT!
RIGHT NOW, I'M 'WAY TOO BUSY COUNTING NOSES!
AND, I'VE FIGURED OUT THAT I'M SLIGHTLY OUT-NUMBERED--
--SO IT'S TIME FOR FOR THE BETTER PART OF VALOR!
HE'S ESCAPING-- THRU A HIDDEN PANEL IN THE WALL!
YOU'VE GOT TO CATCH HIM, PIETRO-- BEFORE THE WALL CLOSES!
BUT-- WE DID NOT PUT THAT THERE, EITHER--!
YES-- OF COURSE--!
HE CAUGHT ME OFF GUARD BEFORE-- BUT NOW I --
UNNHH!
WHOM
YOU MUST BE SLOWIN' DOWN IN YER OLD AGE, QUICKIE!
GOLIATH-- STOP!
WELL, STAND BACK, BOYS AND GIRLS--AND WATCH ME MAKE LIKE MOHAMMED ALI!
9

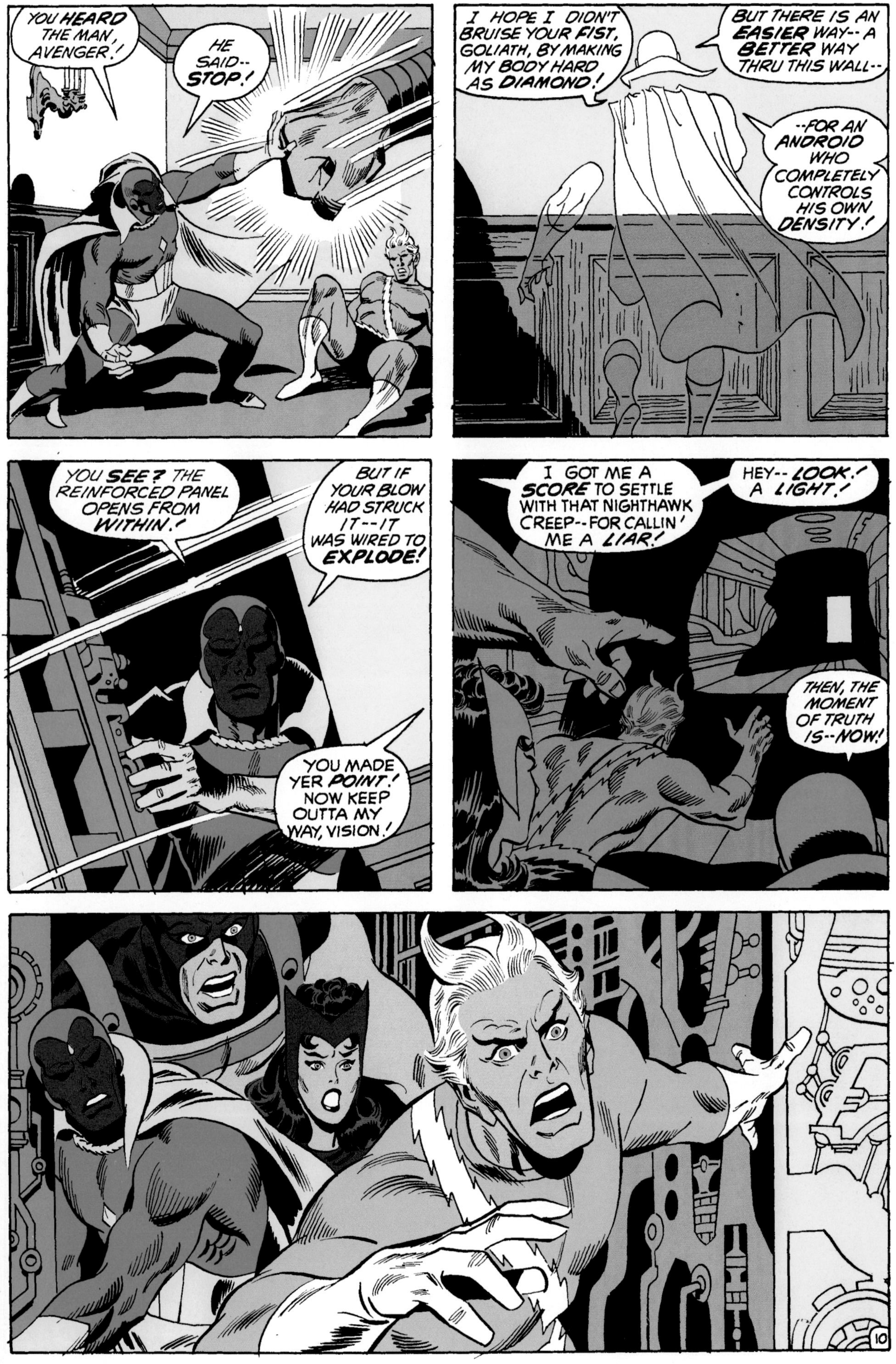
YOU HEARD THE MAN, AVENGER!
HE SAID-- STOP!
I HOPE I DIDN'T BRUISE YOUR FIST, GOLIATH, BY MAKING MY BODY HARD AS DIAMOND!
BUT THERE IS AN EASIER WAY-- A BETTER WAY THRU THIS WALL--
--FOR AN ANDROID WHO COMPLETELY CONTROLS HIS OWN DENSITY!
YOU SEE? THE REINFORCED PANEL OPENS FROM WITHIN!
BUT IF YOUR BLOW HAD STRUCK IT--IT WAS WIRED TO EXPLODE!
YOU MADE YER POINT! NOW KEEP OUTTA MY WAY, VISION!
I GOT ME A SCORE TO SETTLE WITH THAT NIGHTHAWK CREEP--FOR CALLIN' ME A LIAR!
HEY-- LOOK! A LIGHT!
THEN, THE MOMENT OF TRUTH IS--NOW!
10

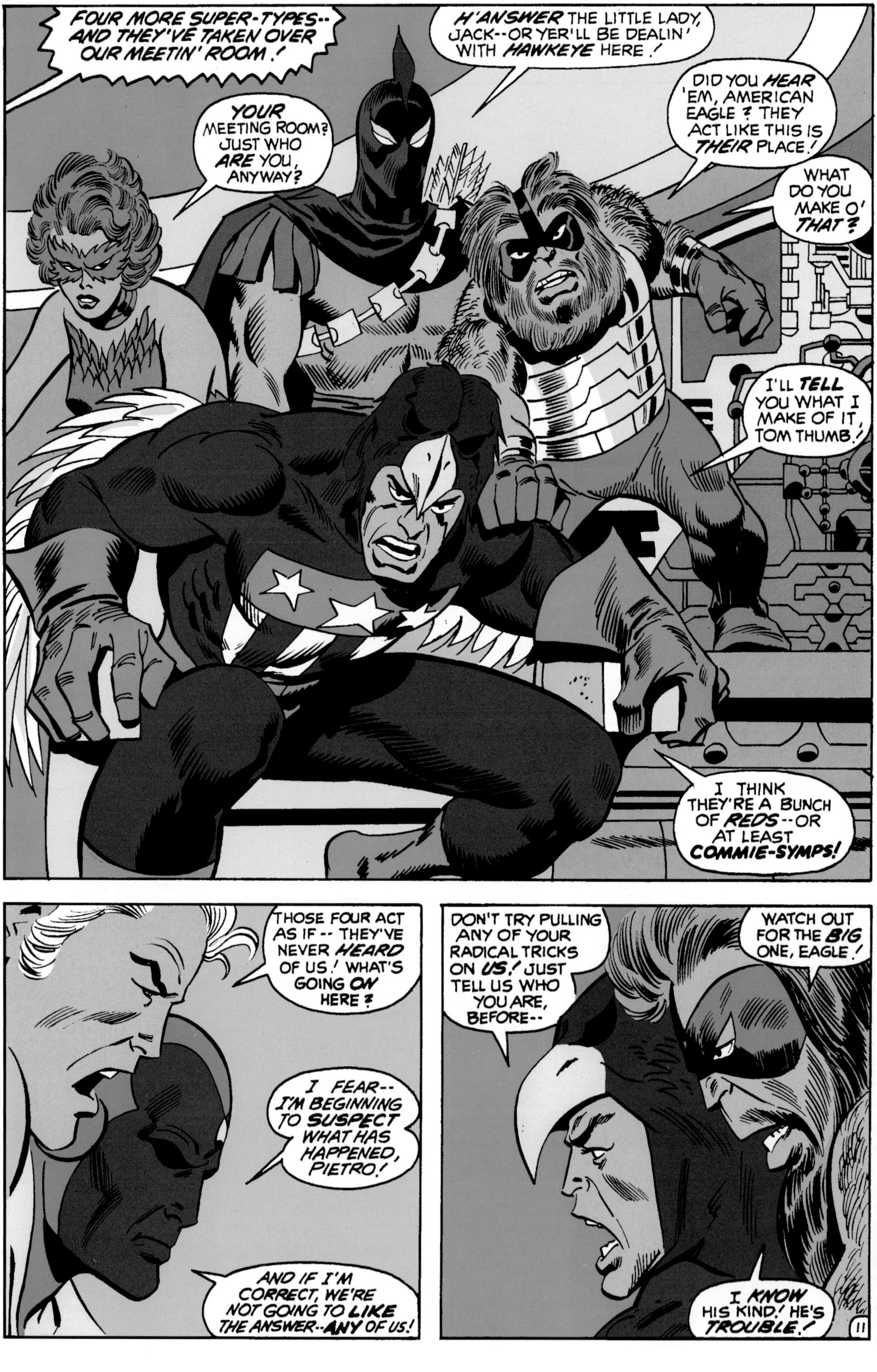

FOUR MORE SUPER-TYPES-- AND THEY'VE TAKEN OVER OUR MEETIN' ROOM!
H'ANSWER THE LITTLE LADY, JACK--OR YER'LL BE DEALIN' WITH HAWKEYE HERE!
YOUR MEETING ROOM? JUST WHO ARE YOU, ANYWAY?
DID YOU HEAR 'EM, AMERICAN EAGLE? THEY ACT LIKE THIS IS THEIR PLACE!
WHAT DO YOU MAKE O' THAT?
I'LL TELL YOU WHAT I MAKE OF IT, TOM THUMB!
I THINK THEY'RE A BUNCH OF REDS--OR AT LEAST COMMIE-SYMPS!
THOSE FOUR ACT AS IF -- THEY'VE NEVER HEARD OF US! WHAT'S GOING ON HERE?
I FEAR-- I'M BEGINNING TO SUSPECT WHAT HAS HAPPENED, PIETRO!
AND IF I'M CORRECT, WE'RE NOT GOING TO LIKE THE ANSWER--ANY OF US!
DON'T TRY PULLING ANY OF YOUR RADICAL TRICKS ON US! JUST TELL US WHO YOU ARE, BEFORE--
WATCH OUT FOR THE BIG ONE, EAGLE!
I KNOW HIS KIND! HE'S TROUBLE!
11

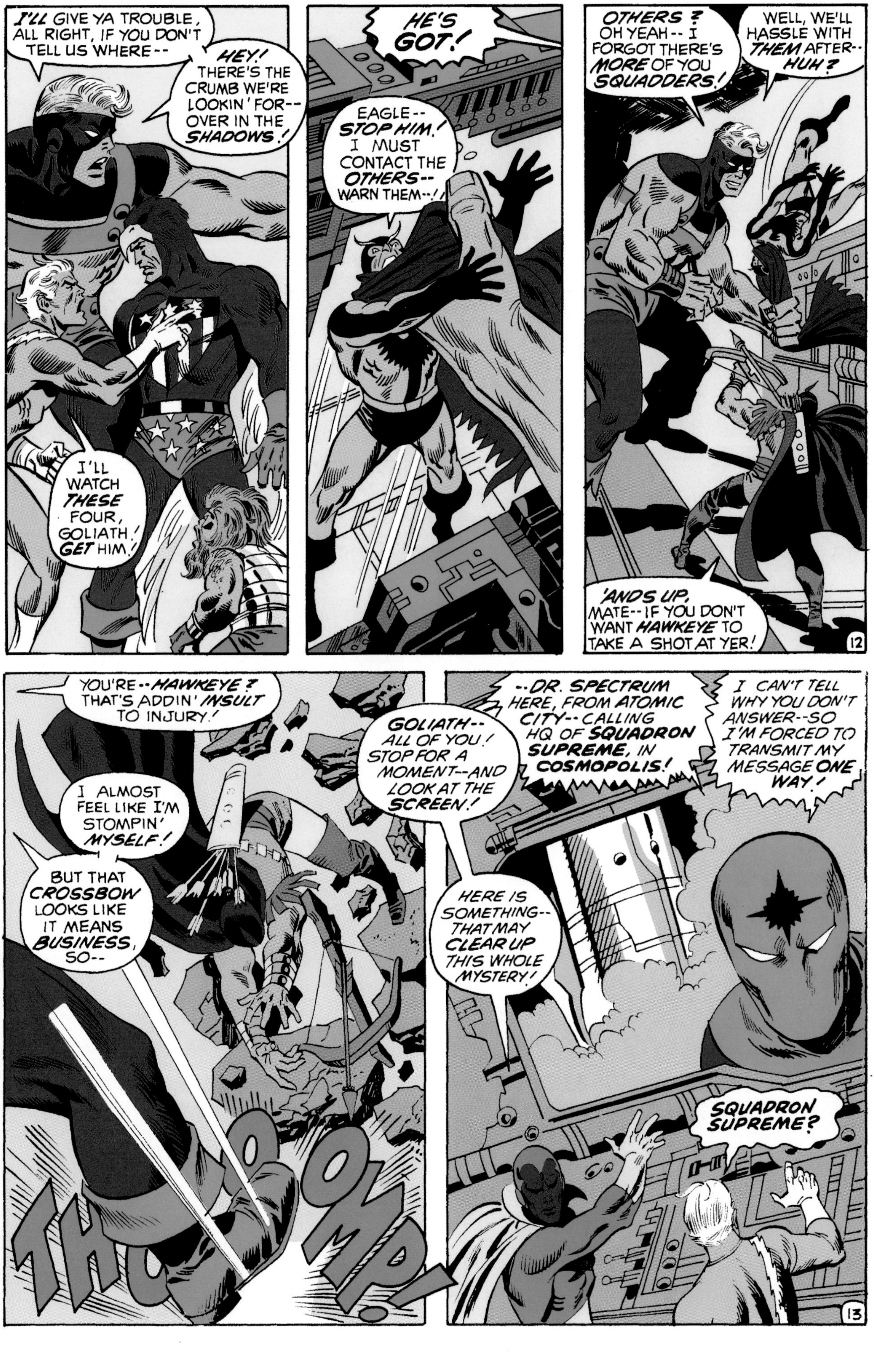
I'LL GIVE YA TROUBLE, ALL RIGHT, IF YOU DON'T TELL US WHERE--
HEY! THERE'S THE CRUMB WE'RE LOOKIN' FOR-- OVER IN THE SHADOWS!
I'LL WATCH THESE FOUR, GOLIATH! GET HIM!
HE'S GOT!
EAGLE-- STOP HIM! I MUST CONTACT THE OTHERS-- WARN THEM--!
OTHERS? OH YEAH-- I FORGOT THERE'S MORE OF YOU SQUADDERS!
WELL, WE'LL HASSLE WITH THEM AFTER-- HUH?
'ANDS UP, MATE-- IF YOU DON'T WANT HAWKEYE TO TAKE A SHOT AT YER!
12
YOU'RE--HAWKEYE? THAT'S ADDIN' INSULT TO INJURY!
I ALMOST FEEL LIKE I'M STOMPIN' MYSELF!
BUT THAT CROSSBOW LOOKS LIKE IT MEANS BUSINESS, SO--
THOOOMP!
GOLIATH-- ALL OF YOU! STOP FOR A MOMENT--AND LOOK AT THE SCREEN!
--DR. SPECTRUM HERE, FROM ATOMIC CITY-- CALLING HQ OF SQUADRON SUPREME, IN COSMOPOLIS!
I CAN'T TELL WHY YOU DON'T ANSWER--SO I'M FORCED TO TRANSMIT MY MESSAGE ONE WAY!
HERE IS SOMETHING-- THAT MAY CLEAR UP THIS WHOLE MYSTERY!
SQUADRON SUPREME?
13

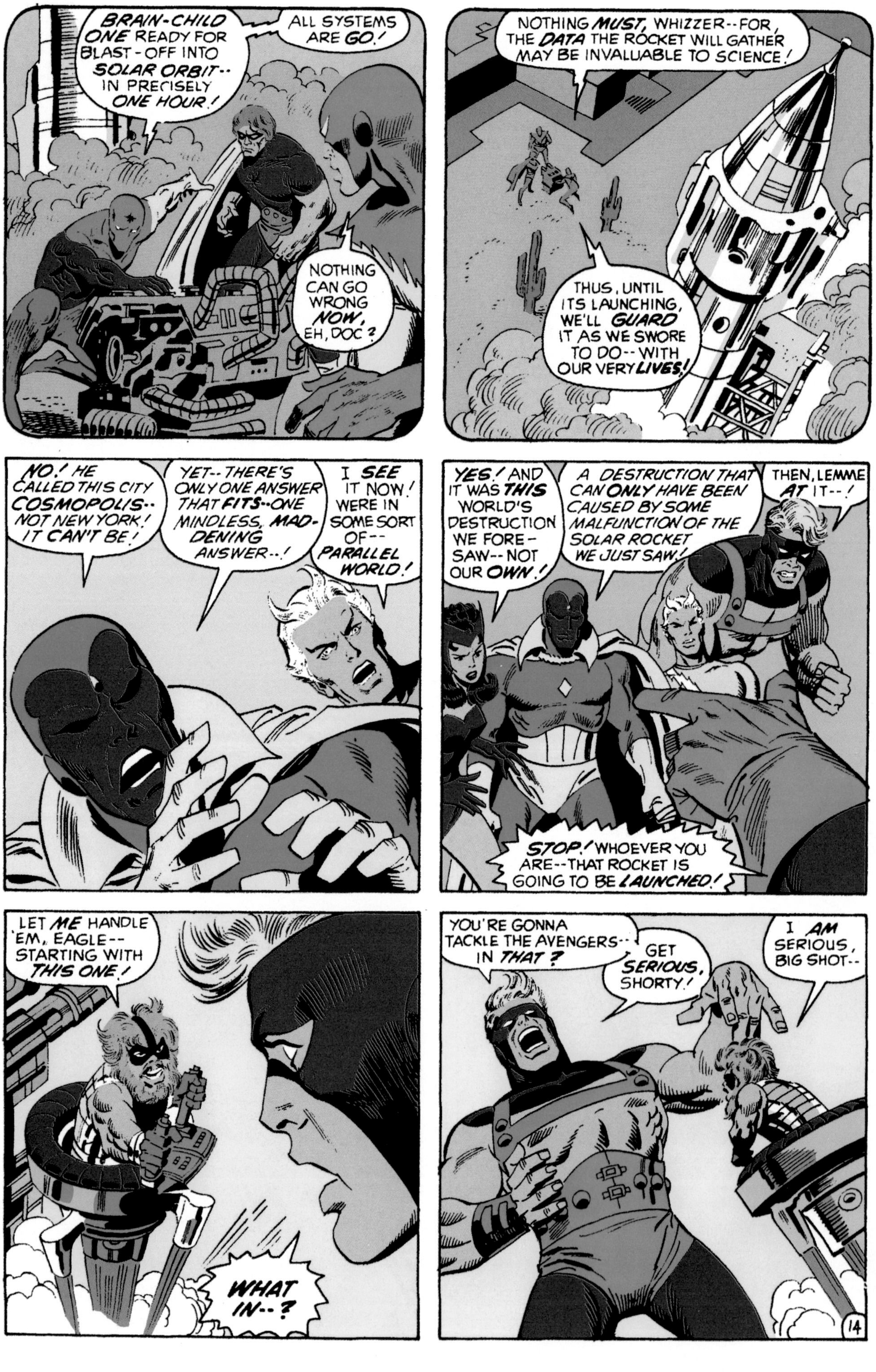

BRAIN-CHILD ONE READY FOR BLAST-OFF INTO SOLAR ORBIT-- IN PRECISELY ONE HOUR!
ALL SYSTEMS ARE GO!
NOTHING CAN GO WRONG NOW, EH, DOC?
NOTHING MUST, WHIZZER--FOR, THE DATA THE ROCKET WILL GATHER MAY BE INVALUABLE TO SCIENCE!
THUS, UNTIL ITS LAUNCHING, WE'LL GUARD IT AS WE SWORE TO DO--WITH OUR VERY LIVES!
NO! HE CALLED THIS CITY COSMOPOLIS-- NOT NEW YORK! IT CAN'T BE!
YET--THERE'S ONLY ONE ANSWER THAT FITS--ONE MINDLESS, MADDENING ANSWER--!
I SEE IT NOW! WERE IN SOME SORT OF-- PARALLEL WORLD!
YES! AND IT WAS THIS WORLD'S DESTRUCTION WE FORE-SAW--NOT OUR OWN!
A DESTRUCTION THAT CAN ONLY HAVE BEEN CAUSED BY SOME MALFUNCTION OF THE SOLAR ROCKET WE JUST SAW!
THEN, LEMME AT IT--!
STOP! WHOEVER YOU ARE--THAT ROCKET IS GOING TO BE LAUNCHED!
LET ME HANDLE 'EM, EAGLE-- STARTING WITH THIS ONE!
WHAT IN--?
YOU'RE GONNA TACKLE THE AVENGERS-- IN THAT?
GET SERIOUS, SHORTY!
I AM SERIOUS, BIG SHOT--
14

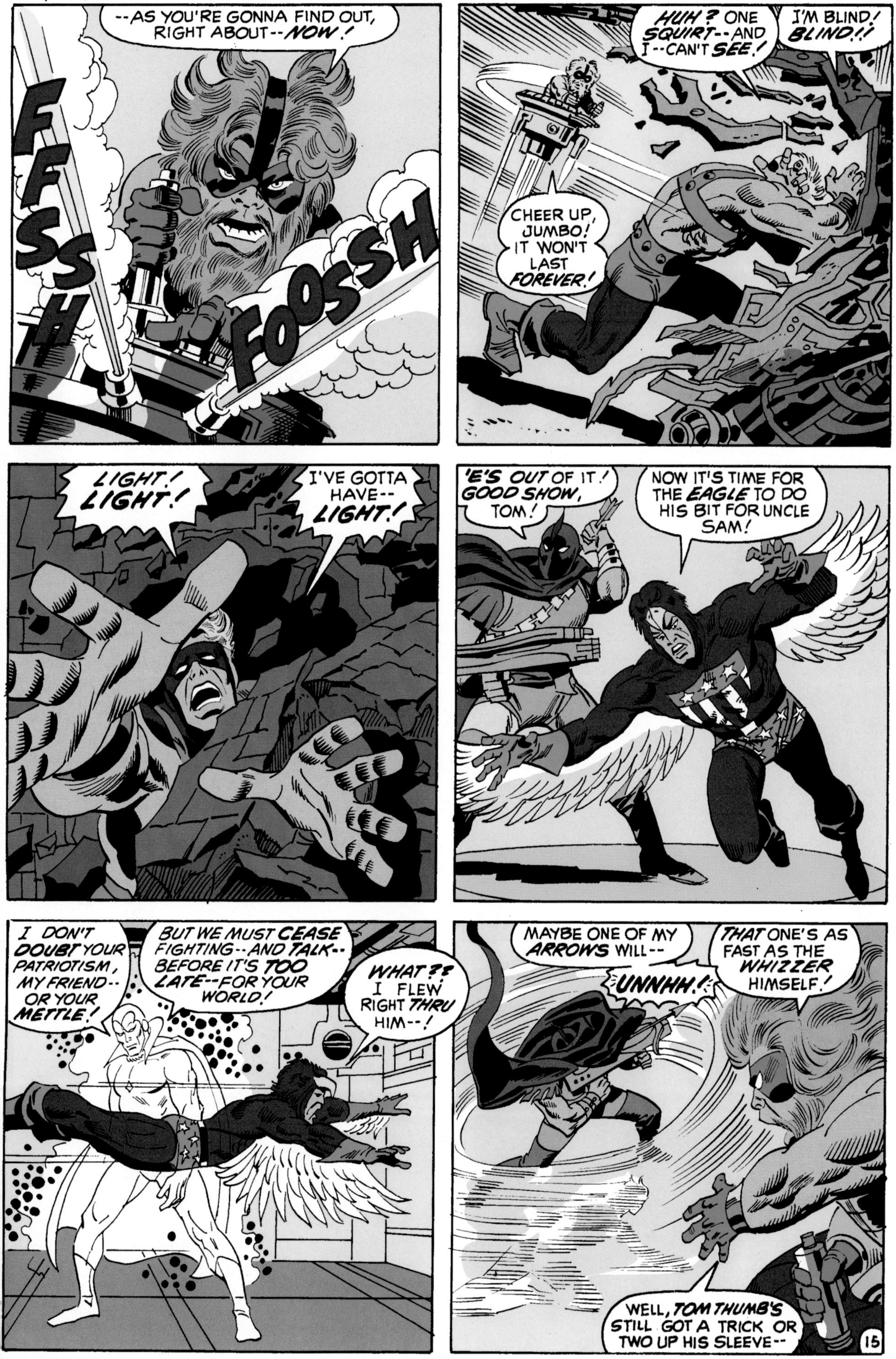
--AS YOU'RE GONNA FIND OUT, RIGHT ABOUT--NOW!
FFSSH
FOOSSH
HUH? ONE SQUIRT--AND I--CAN'T SEE!
I'M BLIND! BLIND!!
CHEER UP, JUMBO! IT WON'T LAST FOREVER!
LIGHT! LIGHT!
I'VE GOTTA HAVE--LIGHT!
'E'S OUT OF IT! GOOD SHOW, TOM!
NOW IT'S TIME FOR THE EAGLE TO DO HIS BIT FOR UNCLE SAM!
I DON'T DOUBT YOUR PATRIOTISM, MY FRIEND--OR YOUR METTLE!
BUT WE MUST CEASE FIGHTING--AND TALK--BEFORE IT'S TOO LATE--FOR YOUR WORLD!
WHAT?? I FLEW RIGHT THRU HIM--!
MAYBE ONE OF MY ARROWS WILL--
UNNHH!
THAT ONE'S AS FAST AS THE WHIZZER HIMSELF!
WELL, TOM THUMB'S STILL GOT A TRICK OR TWO UP HIS SLEEVE--
15

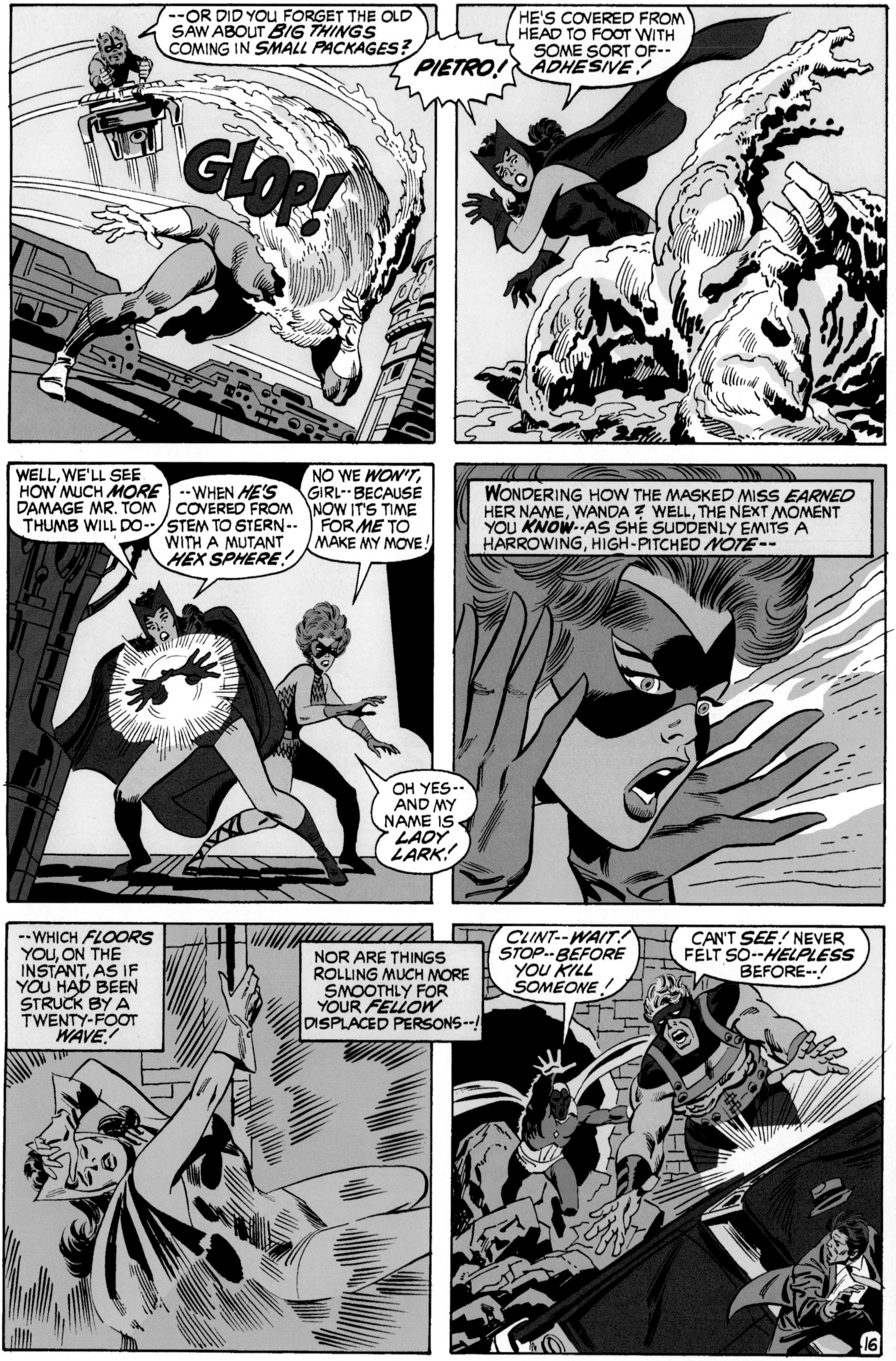
--OR DID YOU FORGET THE OLD SAW ABOUT BIG THINGS COMING IN SMALL PACKAGES?
GLOP!
PIETRO!
HE'S COVERED FROM HEAD TO FOOT WITH SOME SORT OF-- ADHESIVE!
WELL, WE'LL SEE HOW MUCH MORE DAMAGE MR. TOM THUMB WILL DO--
--WHEN HE'S COVERED FROM STEM TO STERN-- WITH A MUTANT HEX SPHERE!
NO WE WON'T, GIRL--BECAUSE NOW IT'S TIME FOR ME TO MAKE MY MOVE!
OH YES-- AND MY NAME IS LADY LARK!
WONDERING HOW THE MASKED MISS EARNED HER NAME, WANDA? WELL, THE NEXT MOMENT YOU KNOW--AS SHE SUDDENLY EMITS A HARROWING, HIGH-PITCHED NOTE--
--WHICH FLOORS YOU, ON THE INSTANT, AS IF YOU HAD BEEN STRUCK BY A TWENTY-FOOT WAVE!
NOR ARE THINGS ROLLING MUCH MORE SMOOTHLY FOR YOUR FELLOW DISPLACED PERSONS--!
CLINT--WAIT! STOP--BEFORE YOU KILL SOMEONE!
CAN'T SEE! NEVER FELT SO--HELPLESS BEFORE--!
16

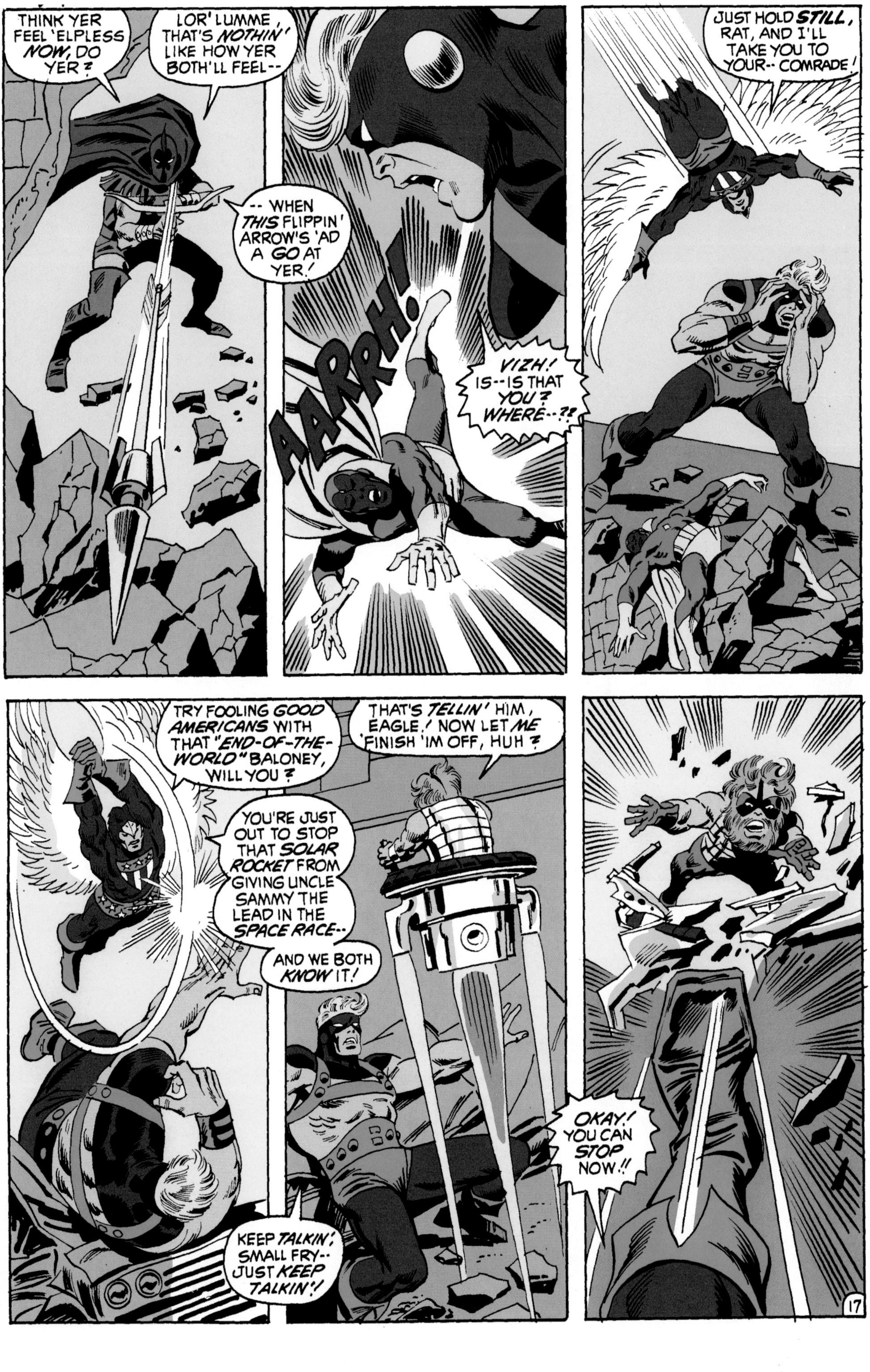

THINK YER FEEL 'ELPLESS NOW, DO YER?
LOR' LUMME, THAT'S NOTHIN' LIKE HOW YER BOTH'LL FEEL--
-- WHEN THIS FLIPPIN' ARROW'S 'AD A GO AT YER!
AARRH!
VIZH! IS--IS THAT YOU? WHERE--??
JUST HOLD STILL, RAT, AND I'LL TAKE YOU TO YOUR-- COMRADE!
TRY FOOLING GOOD AMERICANS WITH THAT "END-OF-THE-WORLD" BALONEY, WILL YOU?
YOU'RE JUST OUT TO STOP THAT SOLAR ROCKET FROM GIVING UNCLE SAMMY THE LEAD IN THE SPACE RACE--
AND WE BOTH KNOW IT!
KEEP TALKIN'! SMALL FRY-- JUST KEEP TALKIN'!
THAT'S TELLIN' HIM, EAGLE! NOW LET ME FINISH 'IM OFF, HUH?
OKAY! YOU CAN STOP NOW!!
17

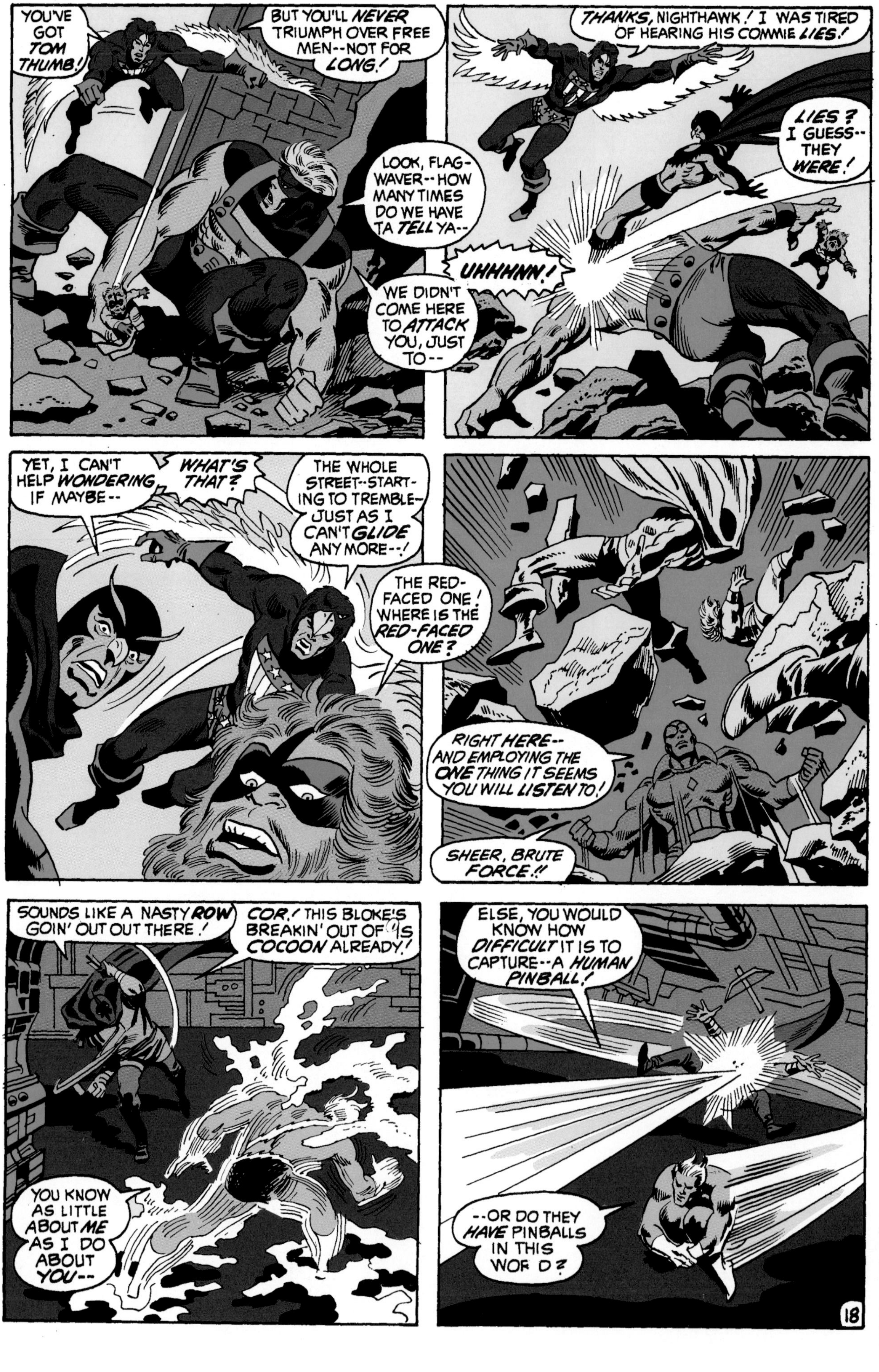

YOU'VE GOT TOM THUMB!
BUT YOU'LL NEVER TRIUMPH OVER FREE MEN--NOT FOR LONG!
LOOK, FLAG-WAVER--HOW MANY TIMES DO WE HAVE TA TELL YA--
WE DIDN'T COME HERE TO ATTACK YOU, JUST TO--
THANKS, NIGHTHAWK! I WAS TIRED OF HEARING HIS COMMIE LIES!
LIES? I GUESS--THEY WERE!
UHHHNN!
YET, I CAN'T HELP WONDERING IF MAYBE--
WHAT'S THAT?
THE WHOLE STREET--STARTING TO TREMBLE--JUST AS I CAN'T GLIDE ANY MORE--!
THE RED-FACED ONE! WHERE IS THE RED-FACED ONE?
RIGHT HERE--AND EMPLOYING THE ONE THING IT SEEMS YOU WILL LISTEN TO!
SHEER, BRUTE FORCE!!
SOUNDS LIKE A NASTY ROW GOIN' OUT OUT THERE!
COR! THIS BLOKE'S BREAKIN' OUT OF 'IS COCOON ALREADY!
YOU KNOW AS LITTLE ABOUT ME AS I DO ABOUT YOU--
ELSE, YOU WOULD KNOW HOW DIFFICULT IT IS TO CAPTURE--A HUMAN PINBALL!
--OR DO THEY HAVE PINBALLS IN THIS WOR D?
18

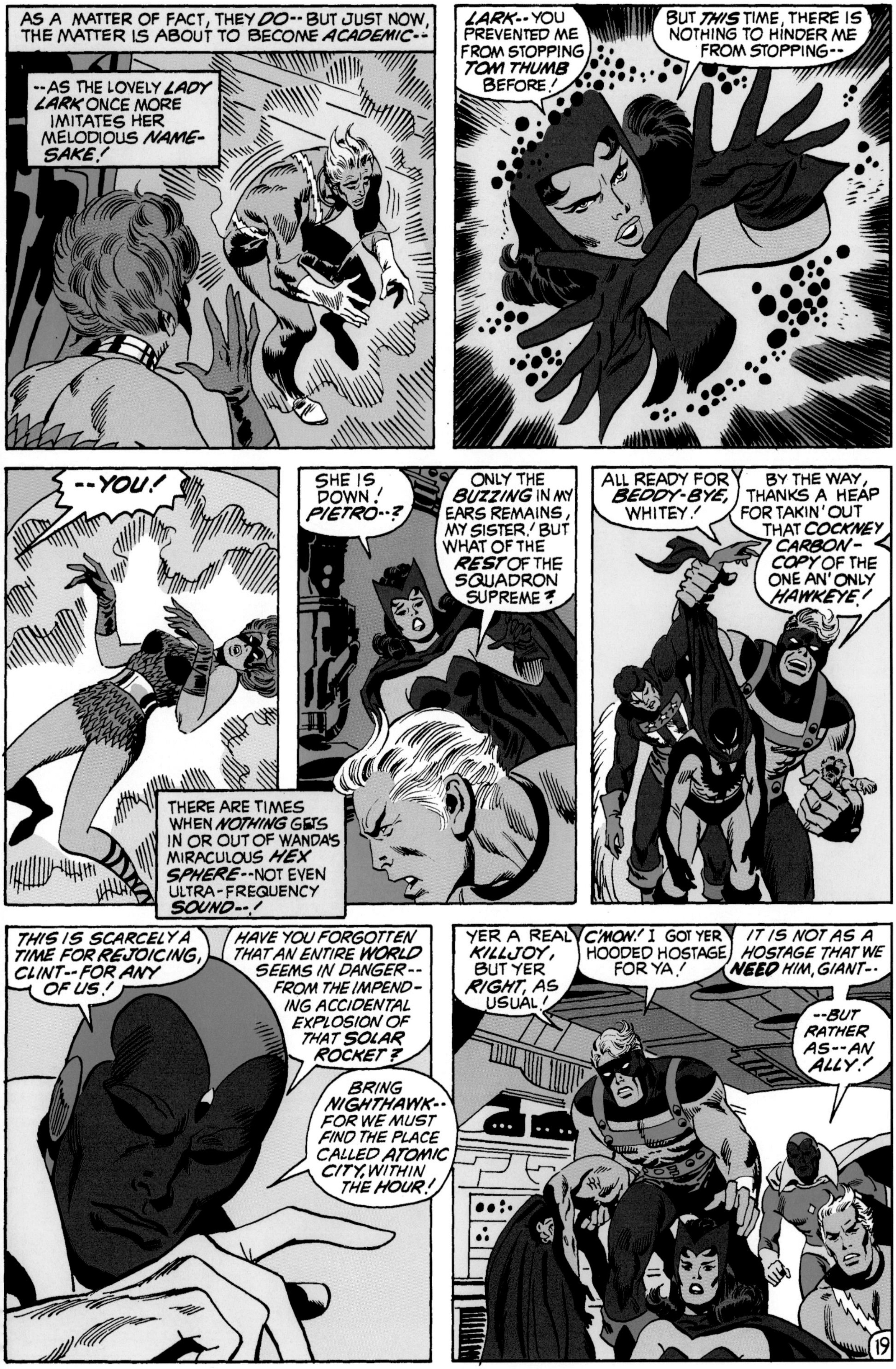

AS A MATTER OF FACT, THEY DO-- BUT JUST NOW, THE MATTER IS ABOUT TO BECOME ACADEMIC--
--AS THE LOVELY LADY LARK ONCE MORE IMITATES HER MELODIOUS NAME-SAKE!
LARK-- YOU PREVENTED ME FROM STOPPING TOM THUMB BEFORE!
BUT THIS TIME, THERE IS NOTHING TO HINDER ME FROM STOPPING--
--YOU!
SHE IS DOWN! PIETRO--?
ONLY THE BUZZING IN MY EARS REMAINS, MY SISTER! BUT WHAT OF THE REST OF THE SQUADRON SUPREME?
THERE ARE TIMES WHEN NOTHING GETS IN OR OUT OF WANDA'S MIRACULOUS HEX SPHERE--NOT EVEN ULTRA-FREQUENCY SOUND--!
ALL READY FOR BEDDY-BYE, WHITEY!
BY THE WAY, THANKS A HEAP FOR TAKIN' OUT THAT COCKNEY CARBON-COPY OF THE ONE AN' ONLY HAWKEYE!
THIS IS SCARCELY A TIME FOR REJOICING, CLINT--FOR ANY OF US!
HAVE YOU FORGOTTEN THAT AN ENTIRE WORLD SEEMS IN DANGER-- FROM THE IMPENDING ACCIDENTAL EXPLOSION OF THAT SOLAR ROCKET?
BRING NIGHTHAWK-- FOR WE MUST FIND THE PLACE CALLED ATOMIC CITY, WITHIN THE HOUR!
YER A REAL KILLJOY, BUT YER RIGHT, AS USUAL!
C'MON! I GOT YER HOODED HOSTAGE FOR YA!
IT IS NOT AS A HOSTAGE THAT WE NEED HIM, GIANT--
--BUT RATHER AS--AN ALLY!
19

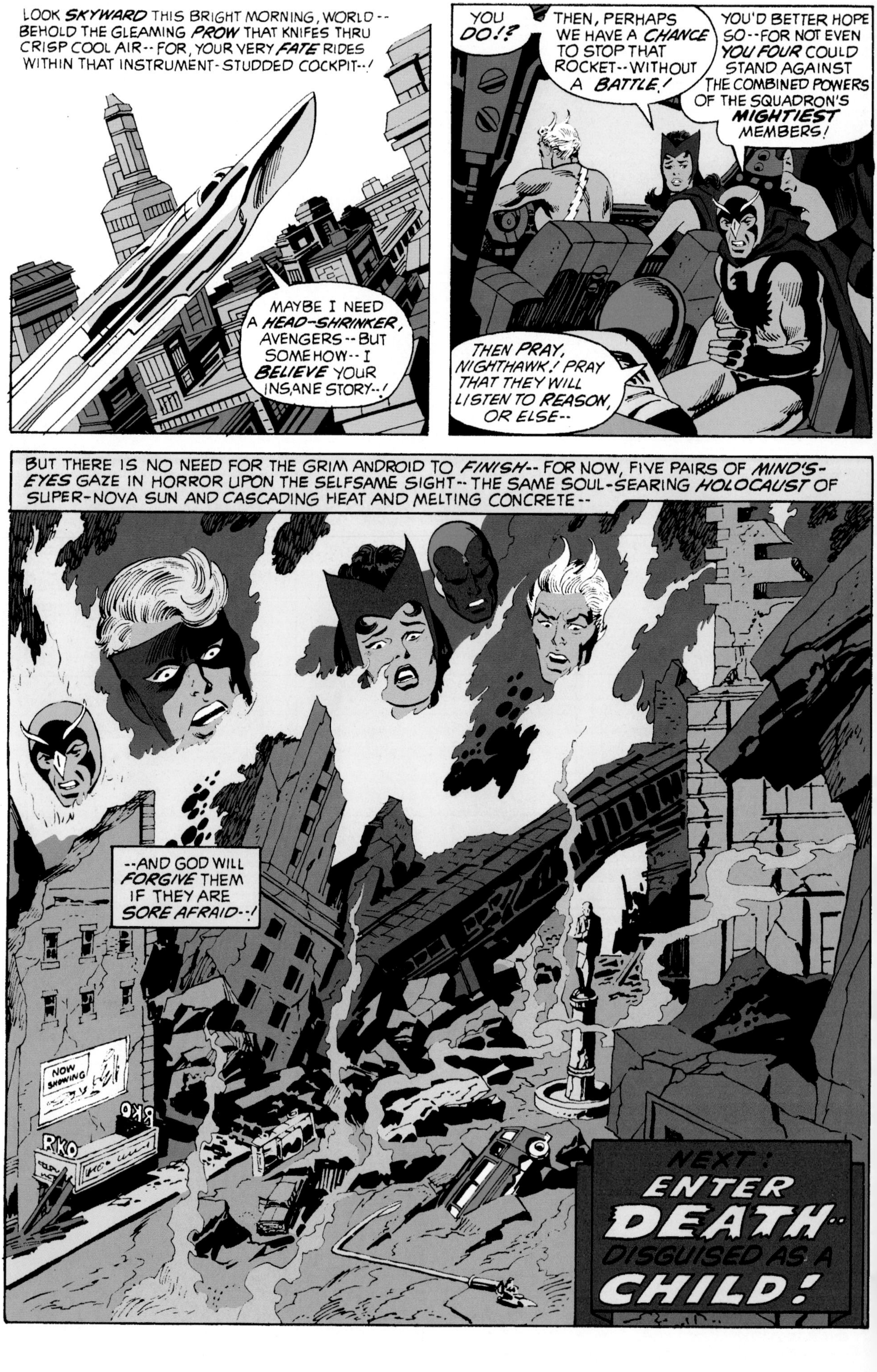
LOOK SKYWARD THIS BRIGHT MORNING, WORLD -- BEHOLD THE GLEAMING PROW THAT KNIFES THRU CRISP COOL AIR -- FOR, YOUR VERY FATE RIDES WITHIN THAT INSTRUMENT-STUDDED COCKPIT--!
MAYBE I NEED A HEAD-SHRINKER, AVENGERS -- BUT SOMEHOW -- I BELIEVE YOUR INSANE STORY--!
YOU DO!?
THEN, PERHAPS WE HAVE A CHANCE TO STOP THAT ROCKET -- WITHOUT A BATTLE!
YOU'D BETTER HOPE SO -- FOR NOT EVEN YOU FOUR COULD STAND AGAINST THE COMBINED POWERS OF THE SQUADRON'S MIGHTIEST MEMBERS!
THEN PRAY, NIGHTHAWK! PRAY THAT THEY WILL LISTEN TO REASON, OR ELSE--
BUT THERE IS NO NEED FOR THE GRIM ANDROID TO FINISH -- FOR NOW, FIVE PAIRS OF MIND'S-EYES GAZE IN HORROR UPON THE SELFSAME SIGHT -- THE SAME SOUL-SEARING HOLOCAUST OF SUPER-NOVA SUN AND CASCADING HEAT AND MELTING CONCRETE --
--AND GOD WILL FORGIVE THEM IF THEY ARE SORE AFRAID--!
NOW SHOWING
RKO
NEXT: ENTER DEATH -- DISGUISED AS A CHILD!

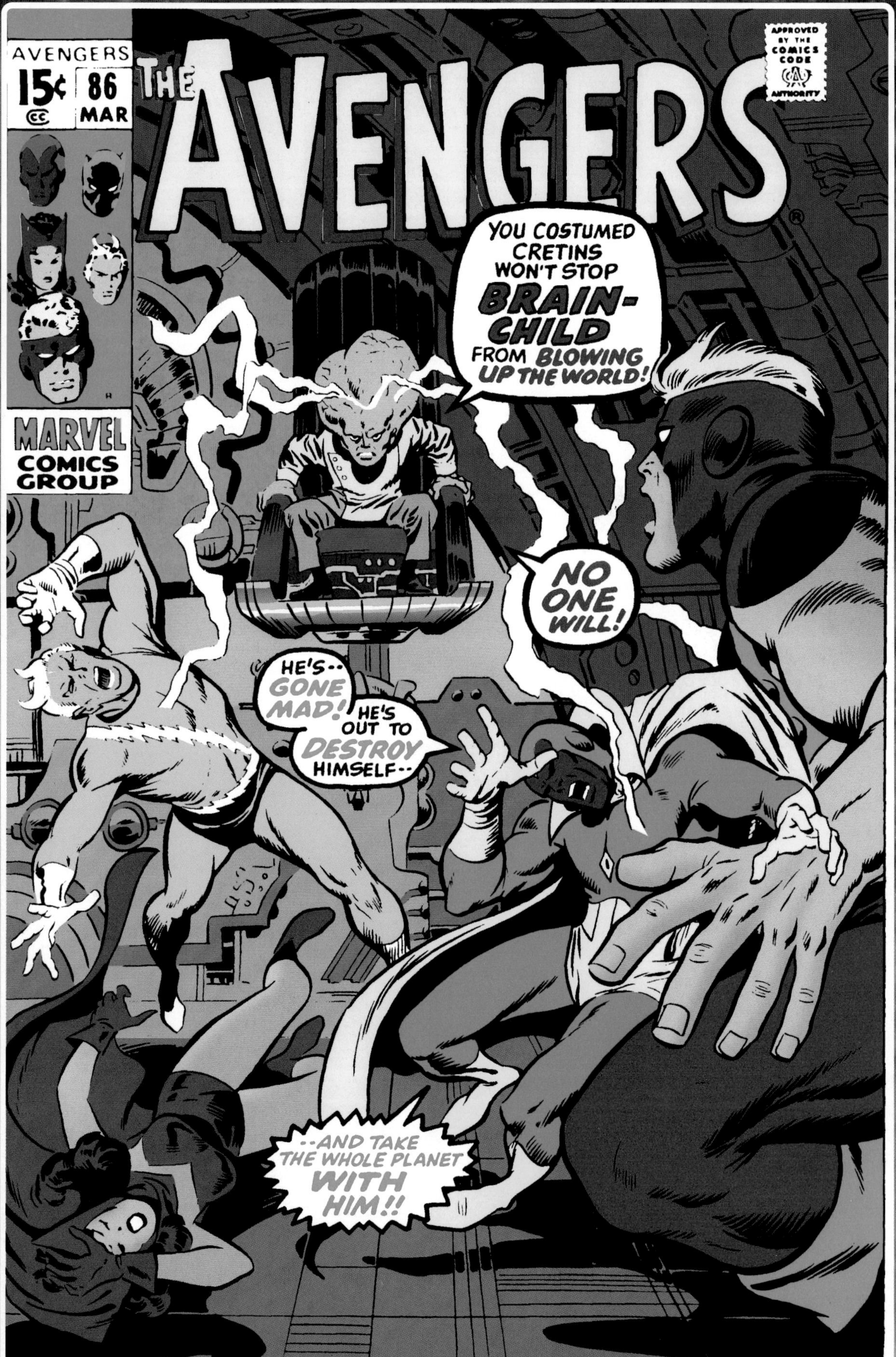
AVENGERS
15¢
86
MAR
THE AVENGERS
APPROVED BY THE COMICS CODE AUTHORITY
MARVEL COMICS GROUP
YOU COSTUMED CRETINS WON'T STOP BRAIN-CHILD FROM BLOWING UP THE WORLD!
NO ONE WILL!
HE'S-- GONE MAD!
HE'S OUT TO DESTROY HIMSELF--
--AND TAKE THE WHOLE PLANET WITH HIM!!

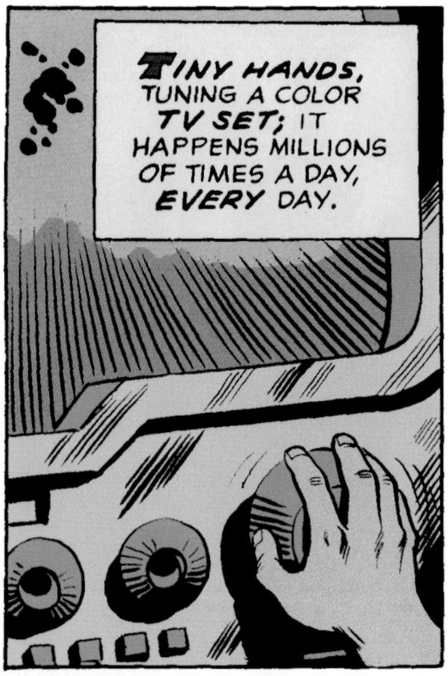
TINY HANDS, TUNING A COLOR TV SET; IT HAPPENS MILLIONS OF TIMES A DAY, EVERY DAY.

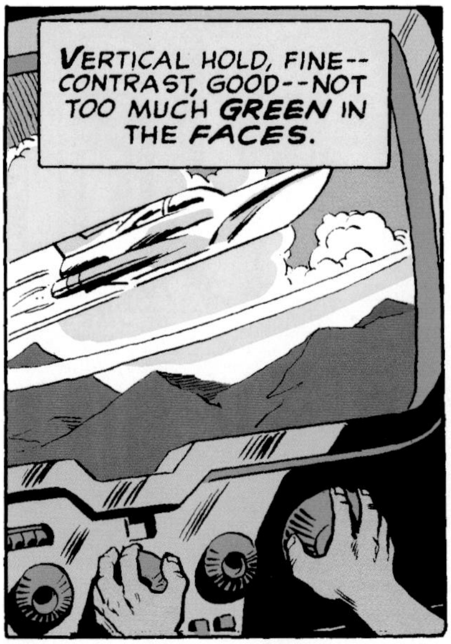
VERTICAL HOLD, FINE-- CONTRAST, GOOD--NOT TOO MUCH GREEN IN THE FACES.

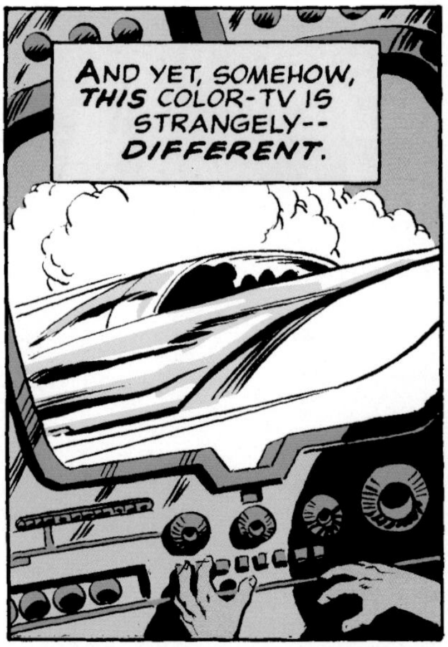
AND YET, SOMEHOW, THIS COLOR-TV IS STRANGELY-- DIFFERENT.

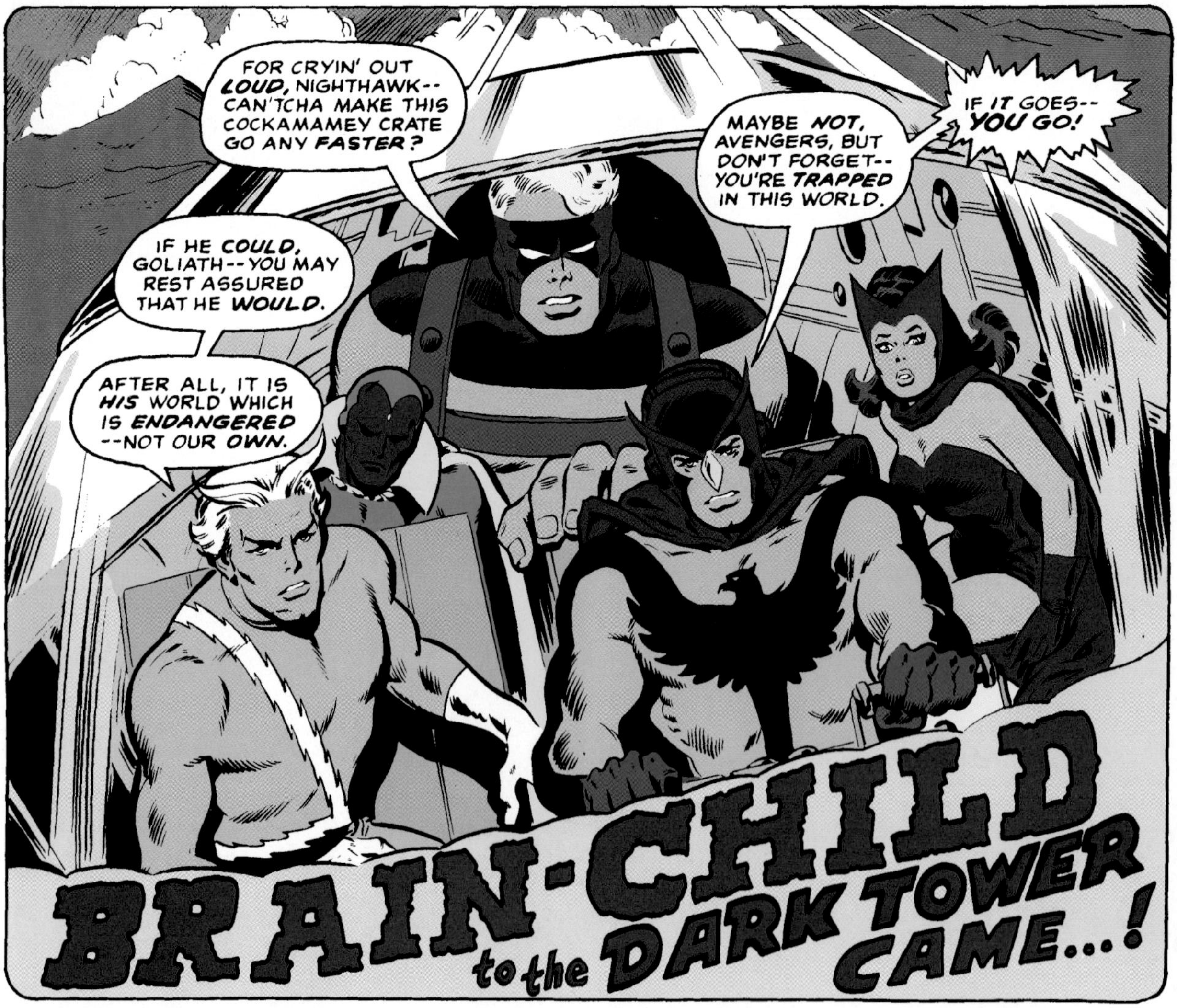
FOR CRYIN' OUT LOUD, NIGHTHAWK-- CAN'TCHA MAKE THIS COCKAMAMEY CRATE GO ANY FASTER?
IF HE COULD, GOLIATH--YOU MAY REST ASSURED THAT HE WOULD.
AFTER ALL, IT IS HIS WORLD WHICH IS ENDANGERED --NOT OUR OWN.
MAYBE NOT, AVENGERS, BUT DON'T FORGET-- YOU'RE TRAPPED IN THIS WORLD.
IF IT GOES-- YOU GO!
BRAIN-CHILD to the DARK TOWER CAME...!

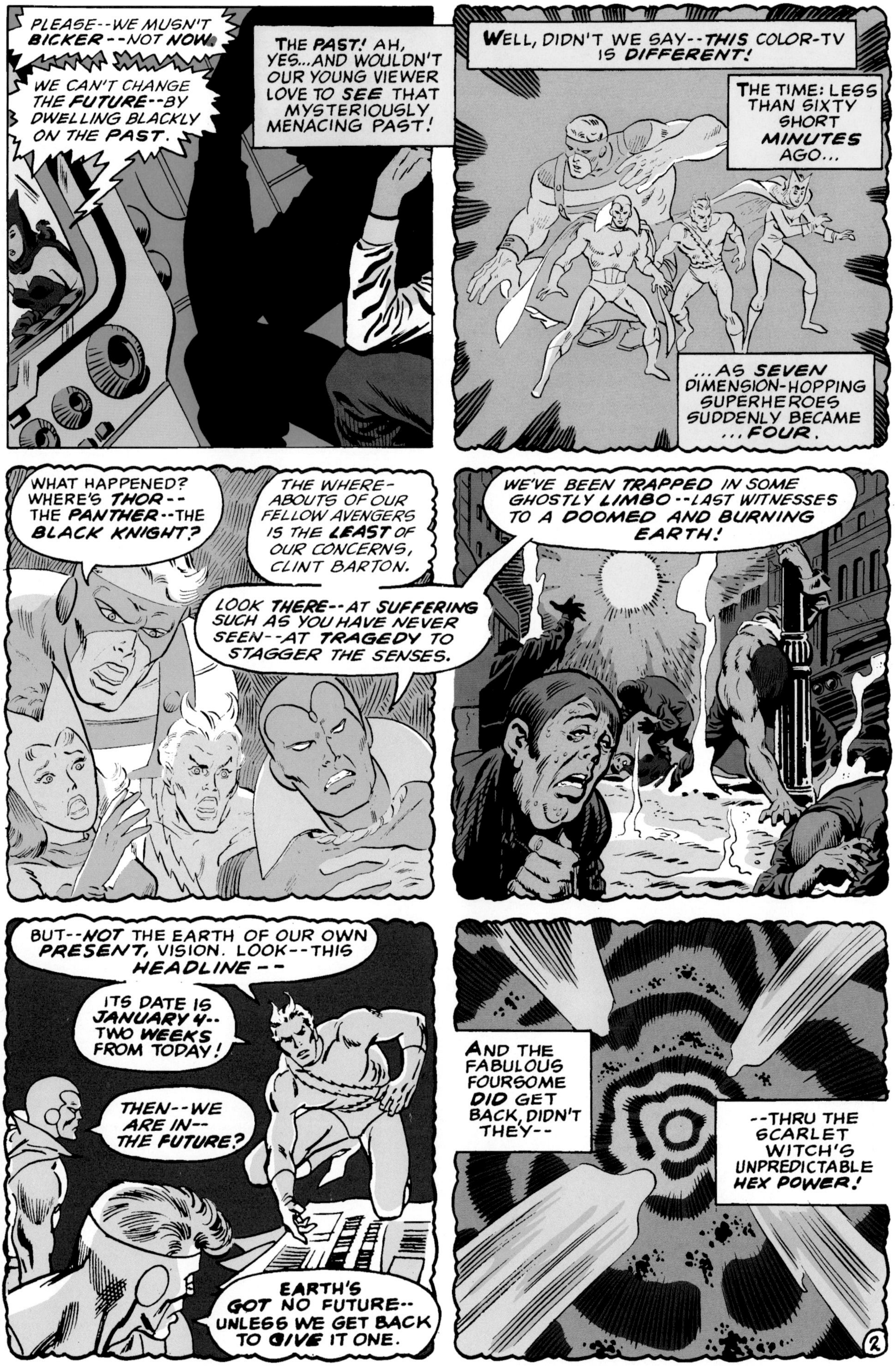
PLEASE--WE MUSN'T BICKER--NOT NOW.
WE CAN'T CHANGE THE FUTURE--BY DWELLING BLACKLY ON THE PAST.
THE PAST! AH, YES...AND WOULDN'T OUR YOUNG VIEWER LOVE TO SEE THAT MYSTERIOUSLY MENACING PAST!
WELL, DIDN'T WE SAY--THIS COLOR-TV IS DIFFERENT!
THE TIME: LESS THAN SIXTY SHORT MINUTES AGO...
...AS SEVEN DIMENSION-HOPPING SUPERHEROES SUDDENLY BECAME ...FOUR.
WHAT HAPPENED? WHERE'S THOR--THE PANTHER--THE BLACK KNIGHT?
THE WHEREABOUTS OF OUR FELLOW AVENGERS IS THE LEAST OF OUR CONCERNS, CLINT BARTON.
LOOK THERE--AT SUFFERING SUCH AS YOU HAVE NEVER SEEN--AT TRAGEDY TO STAGGER THE SENSES.
WE'VE BEEN TRAPPED IN SOME GHOSTLY LIMBO--LAST WITNESSES TO A DOOMED AND BURNING EARTH!
BUT--NOT THE EARTH OF OUR OWN PRESENT, VISION. LOOK--THIS HEADLINE--
ITS DATE IS JANUARY 4--TWO WEEKS FROM TODAY!
THEN--WE ARE IN--THE FUTURE?
EARTH'S GOT NO FUTURE--UNLESS WE GET BACK TO GIVE IT ONE.
AND THE FABULOUS FOURSOME DID GET BACK, DIDN'T THEY--
--THRU THE SCARLET WITCH'S UNPREDICTABLE HEX POWER!
2

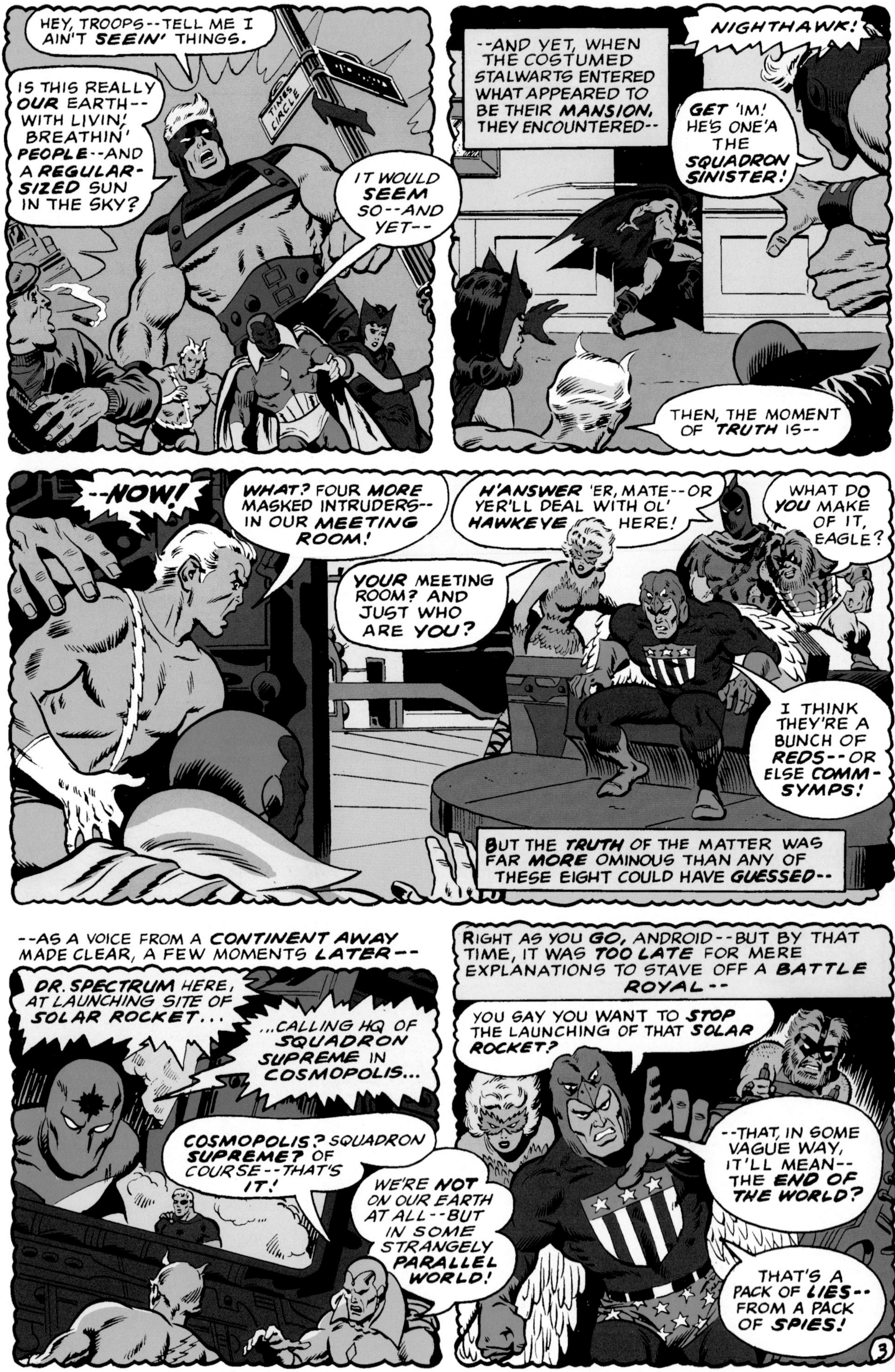
HEY, TROOPS--TELL ME I AIN'T SEEIN' THINGS.
IS THIS REALLY OUR EARTH--WITH LIVIN', BREATHIN' PEOPLE--AND A REGULAR-SIZED SUN IN THE SKY?
TIMES CIRCLE
IT WOULD SEEM SO--AND YET--
--AND YET, WHEN THE COSTUMED STALWARTS ENTERED WHAT APPEARED TO BE THEIR MANSION, THEY ENCOUNTERED--
NIGHTHAWK!
GET 'IM! HE'S ONE'A THE SQUADRON SINISTER!
THEN, THE MOMENT OF TRUTH IS--
--NOW!
WHAT? FOUR MORE MASKED INTRUDERS--IN OUR MEETING ROOM!
H'ANSWER 'ER, MATE--OR YER'LL DEAL WITH OL' HAWKEYE HERE!
WHAT DO YOU MAKE OF IT, EAGLE?
YOUR MEETING ROOM? AND JUST WHO ARE YOU?
I THINK THEY'RE A BUNCH OF REDS--OR ELSE COMM-SYMPS!
BUT THE TRUTH OF THE MATTER WAS FAR MORE OMINOUS THAN ANY OF THESE EIGHT COULD HAVE GUESSED--
--AS A VOICE FROM A CONTINENT AWAY MADE CLEAR, A FEW MOMENTS LATER--
DR. SPECTRUM HERE, AT LAUNCHING SITE OF SOLAR ROCKET...
...CALLING HQ OF SQUADRON SUPREME IN COSMOPOLIS...
COSMOPOLIS? SQUADRON SUPREME? OF COURSE--THAT'S IT!
WE'RE NOT ON OUR EARTH AT ALL--BUT IN SOME STRANGELY PARALLEL WORLD!
RIGHT AS YOU GO, ANDROID--BUT BY THAT TIME, IT WAS TOO LATE FOR MERE EXPLANATIONS TO STAVE OFF A BATTLE ROYAL--
YOU SAY YOU WANT TO STOP THE LAUNCHING OF THAT SOLAR ROCKET?
--THAT, IN SOME VAGUE WAY, IT'LL MEAN--THE END OF THE WORLD?
THAT'S A PACK OF LIES--FROM A PACK OF SPIES!
3

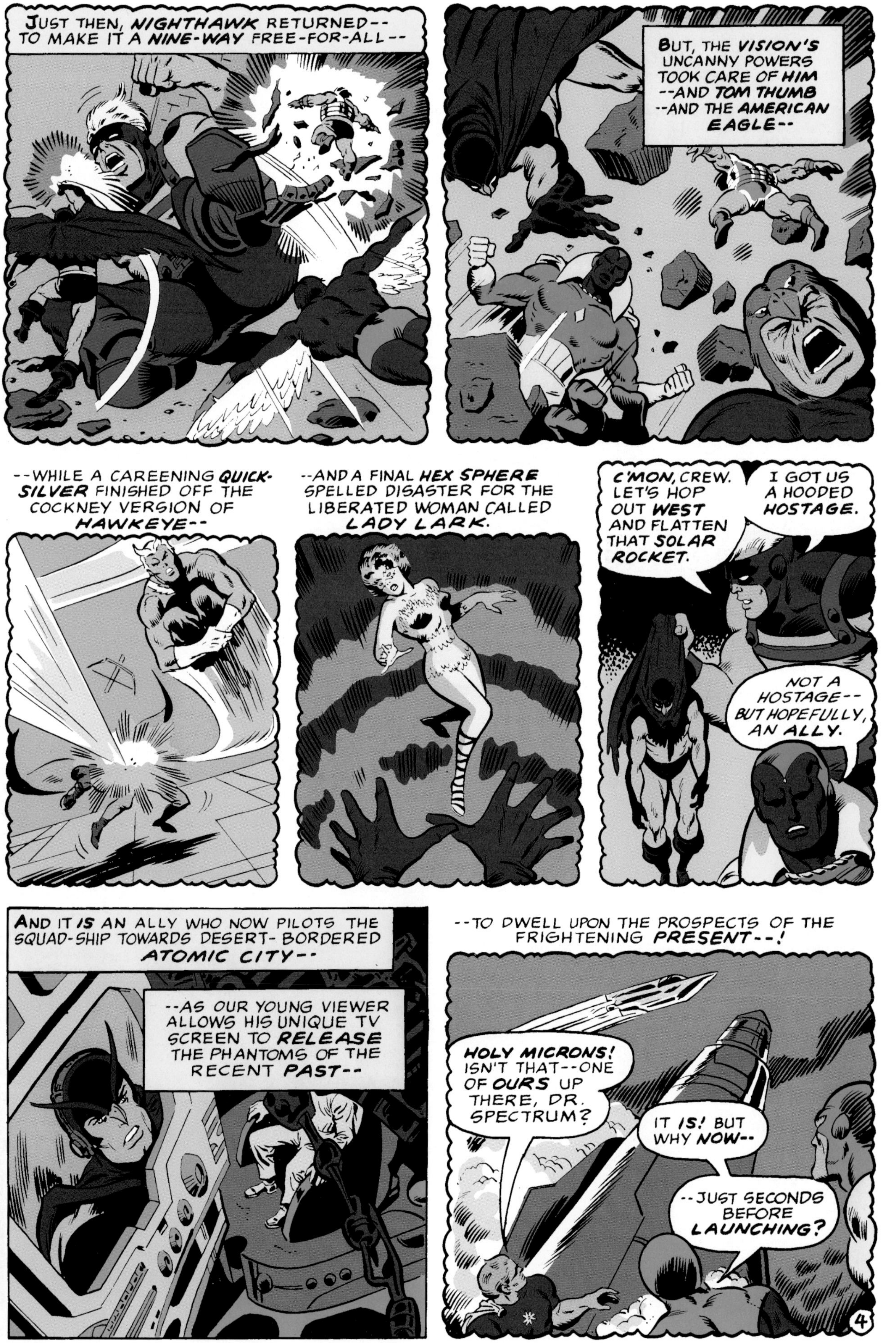

JUST THEN, NIGHTHAWK RETURNED-- TO MAKE IT A NINE-WAY FREE-FOR-ALL--
BUT, THE VISION'S UNCANNY POWERS TOOK CARE OF HIM --AND TOM THUMB --AND THE AMERICAN EAGLE--
--WHILE A CAREENING QUICK-SILVER FINISHED OFF THE COCKNEY VERSION OF HAWKEYE--
--AND A FINAL HEX SPHERE SPELLED DISASTER FOR THE LIBERATED WOMAN CALLED LADY LARK.
C'MON, CREW. LET'S HOP OUT WEST AND FLATTEN THAT SOLAR ROCKET.
I GOT US A HOODED HOSTAGE.
NOT A HOSTAGE-- BUT HOPEFULLY, AN ALLY.
AND IT IS AN ALLY WHO NOW PILOTS THE SQUAD-SHIP TOWARDS DESERT-BORDERED ATOMIC CITY--
--AS OUR YOUNG VIEWER ALLOWS HIS UNIQUE TV SCREEN TO RELEASE THE PHANTOMS OF THE RECENT PAST--
--TO DWELL UPON THE PROSPECTS OF THE FRIGHTENING PRESENT--!
HOLY MICRONS! ISN'T THAT--ONE OF OURS UP THERE, DR. SPECTRUM?
IT IS! BUT WHY NOW--
--JUST SECONDS BEFORE LAUNCHING?

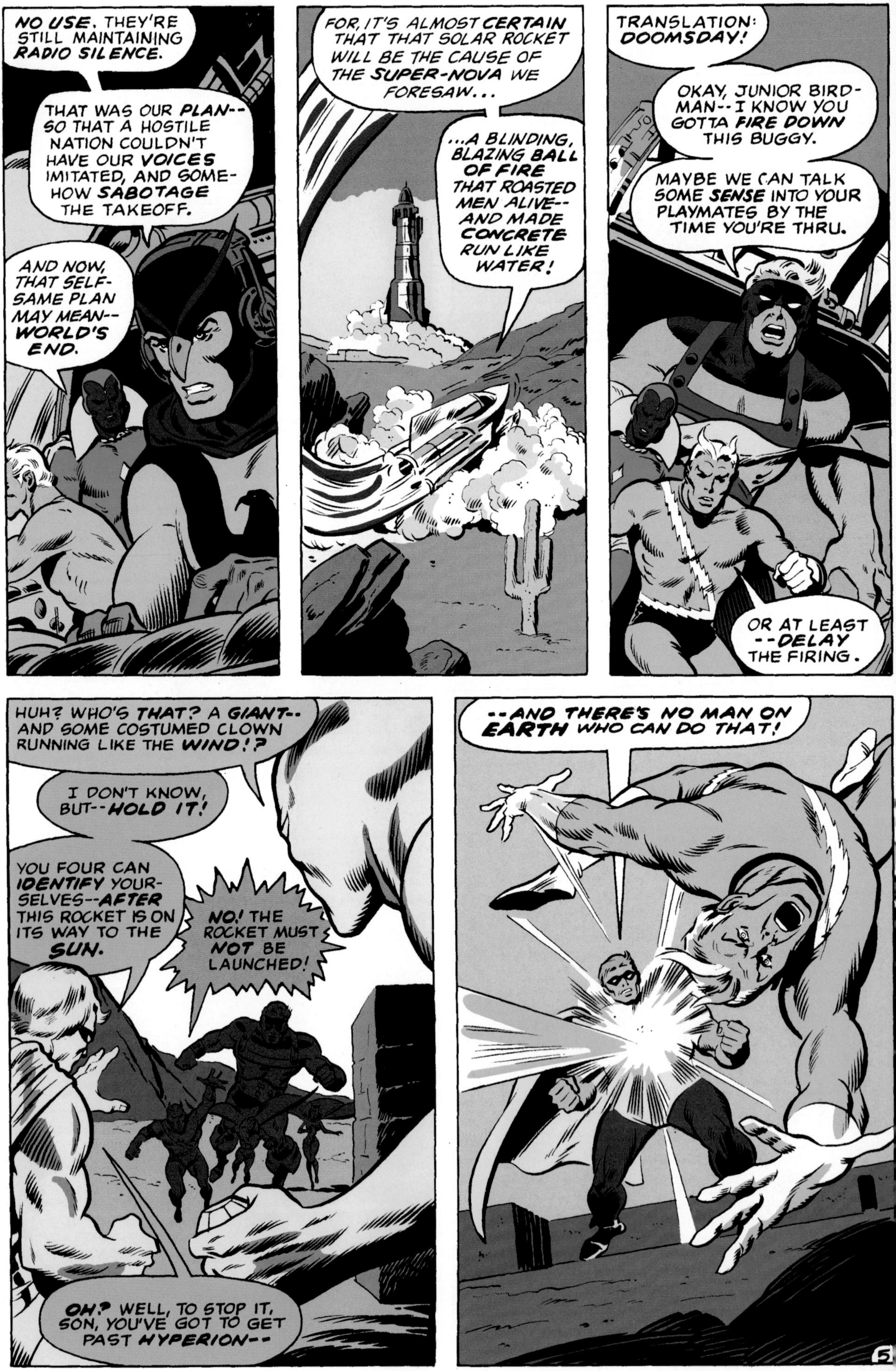

NO USE. THEY'RE STILL MAINTAINING RADIO SILENCE.
THAT WAS OUR PLAN-- SO THAT A HOSTILE NATION COULDN'T HAVE OUR VOICES IMITATED, AND SOMEHOW SABOTAGE THE TAKEOFF.
AND NOW, THAT SELF-SAME PLAN MAY MEAN-- WORLD'S END.
FOR, IT'S ALMOST CERTAIN THAT THAT SOLAR ROCKET WILL BE THE CAUSE OF THE SUPER-NOVA WE FORESAW...
...A BLINDING, BLAZING BALL OF FIRE THAT ROASTED MEN ALIVE-- AND MADE CONCRETE RUN LIKE WATER!
TRANSLATION: DOOMSDAY!
OKAY, JUNIOR BIRD-MAN-- I KNOW YOU GOTTA FIRE DOWN THIS BUGGY.
MAYBE WE CAN TALK SOME SENSE INTO YOUR PLAYMATES BY THE TIME YOU'RE THRU.
OR AT LEAST --DELAY THE FIRING.
HUH? WHO'S THAT? A GIANT-- AND SOME COSTUMED CLOWN RUNNING LIKE THE WIND!?
I DON'T KNOW, BUT--HOLD IT!
YOU FOUR CAN IDENTIFY YOURSELVES--AFTER THIS ROCKET IS ON ITS WAY TO THE SUN.
NO! THE ROCKET MUST NOT BE LAUNCHED!
OH? WELL, TO STOP IT, SON, YOU'VE GOT TO GET PAST HYPERION--
--AND THERE'S NO MAN ON EARTH WHO CAN DO THAT!

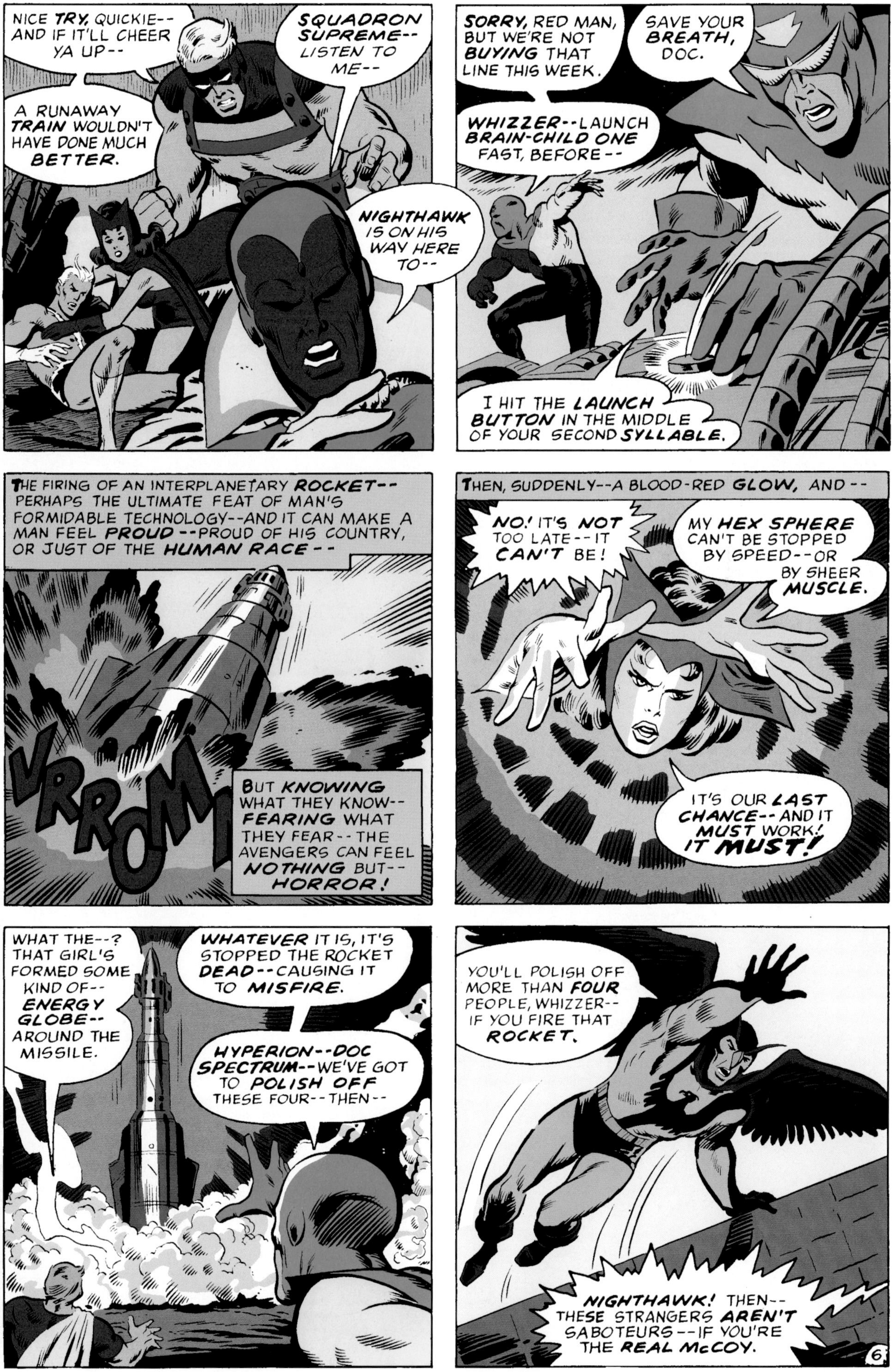

NICE TRY, QUICKIE-- AND IF IT'LL CHEER YA UP--
A RUNAWAY TRAIN WOULDN'T HAVE DONE MUCH BETTER.
SQUADRON SUPREME-- LISTEN TO ME--
NIGHTHAWK IS ON HIS WAY HERE TO--
SORRY, RED MAN, BUT WE'RE NOT BUYING THAT LINE THIS WEEK.
SAVE YOUR BREATH, DOC.
WHIZZER--LAUNCH BRAIN-CHILD ONE FAST, BEFORE--
I HIT THE LAUNCH BUTTON IN THE MIDDLE OF YOUR SECOND SYLLABLE.
THE FIRING OF AN INTERPLANETARY ROCKET-- PERHAPS THE ULTIMATE FEAT OF MAN'S FORMIDABLE TECHNOLOGY--AND IT CAN MAKE A MAN FEEL PROUD--PROUD OF HIS COUNTRY, OR JUST OF THE HUMAN RACE--
VRROOM
BUT KNOWING WHAT THEY KNOW-- FEARING WHAT THEY FEAR--THE AVENGERS CAN FEEL NOTHING BUT-- HORROR!
THEN, SUDDENLY--A BLOOD-RED GLOW, AND--
NO! IT'S NOT TOO LATE--IT CAN'T BE!
MY HEX SPHERE CAN'T BE STOPPED BY SPEED--OR BY SHEER MUSCLE.
IT'S OUR LAST CHANCE--AND IT MUST WORK! IT MUST!
WHAT THE--? THAT GIRL'S FORMED SOME KIND OF-- ENERGY GLOBE-- AROUND THE MISSILE.
WHATEVER IT IS, IT'S STOPPED THE ROCKET DEAD--CAUSING IT TO MISFIRE.
HYPERION--DOC SPECTRUM--WE'VE GOT TO POLISH OFF THESE FOUR--THEN--
YOU'LL POLISH OFF MORE THAN FOUR PEOPLE, WHIZZER-- IF YOU FIRE THAT ROCKET.
NIGHTHAWK! THEN-- THESE STRANGERS AREN'T SABOTEURS--IF YOU'RE THE REAL McCOY.

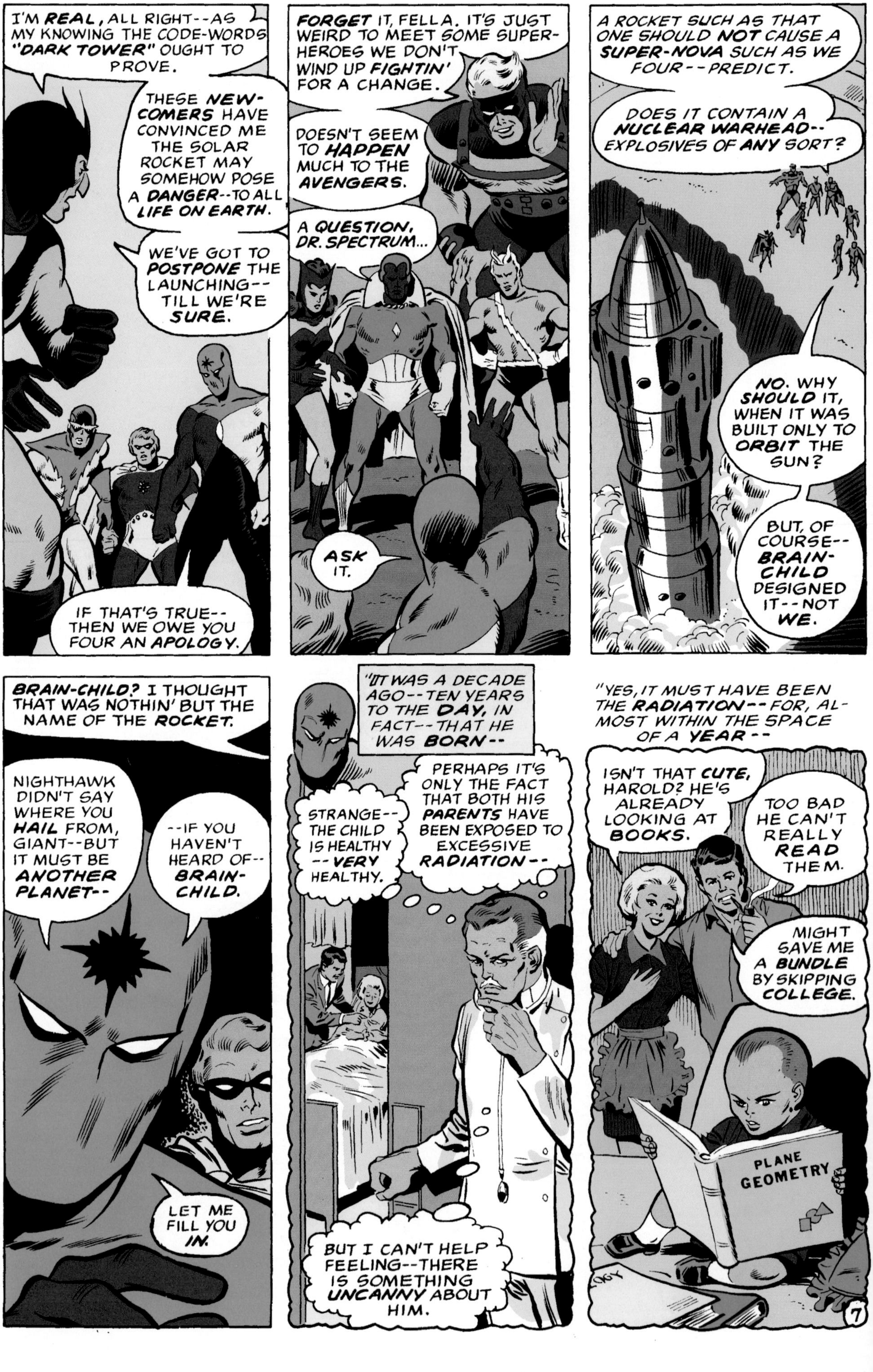
I'M REAL, ALL RIGHT--AS MY KNOWING THE CODE-WORDS "DARK TOWER" OUGHT TO PROVE.
THESE NEW-COMERS HAVE CONVINCED ME THE SOLAR ROCKET MAY SOMEHOW POSE A DANGER--TO ALL LIFE ON EARTH.
WE'VE GOT TO POSTPONE THE LAUNCHING--TILL WE'RE SURE.
IF THAT'S TRUE--THEN WE OWE YOU FOUR AN APOLOGY.
FORGET IT, FELLA. IT'S JUST WEIRD TO MEET SOME SUPER-HEROES WE DON'T WIND UP FIGHTIN' FOR A CHANGE.
DOESN'T SEEM TO HAPPEN MUCH TO THE AVENGERS.
A QUESTION, DR. SPECTRUM...
ASK IT.
A ROCKET SUCH AS THAT ONE SHOULD NOT CAUSE A SUPER-NOVA SUCH AS WE FOUR--PREDICT.
DOES IT CONTAIN A NUCLEAR WARHEAD--EXPLOSIVES OF ANY SORT?
NO. WHY SHOULD IT, WHEN IT WAS BUILT ONLY TO ORBIT THE SUN?
BUT, OF COURSE--BRAIN-CHILD DESIGNED IT--NOT WE.
BRAIN-CHILD? I THOUGHT THAT WAS NOTHIN' BUT THE NAME OF THE ROCKET.
NIGHTHAWK DIDN'T SAY WHERE YOU HAIL FROM, GIANT--BUT IT MUST BE ANOTHER PLANET--
--IF YOU HAVEN'T HEARD OF--BRAIN-CHILD.
LET ME FILL YOU IN.
"IT WAS A DECADE AGO--TEN YEARS TO THE DAY, IN FACT--THAT HE WAS BORN--
STRANGE--THE CHILD IS HEALTHY--VERY HEALTHY.
PERHAPS IT'S ONLY THE FACT THAT BOTH HIS PARENTS HAVE BEEN EXPOSED TO EXCESSIVE RADIATION--
BUT I CAN'T HELP FEELING--THERE IS SOMETHING UNCANNY ABOUT HIM.
"YES, IT MUST HAVE BEEN THE RADIATION--FOR, ALMOST WITHIN THE SPACE OF A YEAR--
ISN'T THAT CUTE, HAROLD? HE'S ALREADY LOOKING AT BOOKS.
TOO BAD HE CAN'T REALLY READ THEM.
MIGHT SAVE ME A BUNDLE BY SKIPPING COLLEGE.
PLANE GEOMETRY

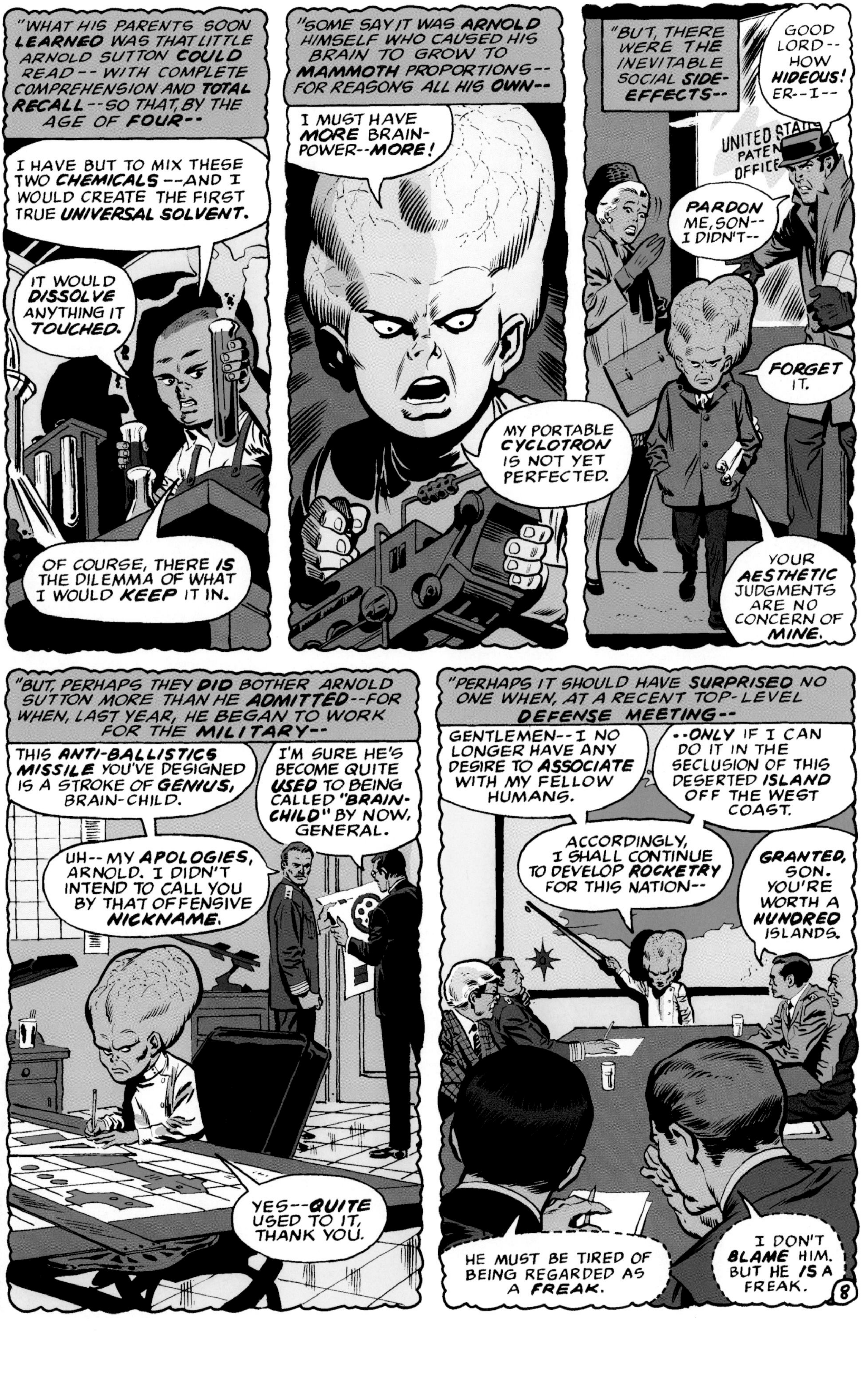
"WHAT HIS PARENTS SOON LEARNED WAS THAT LITTLE ARNOLD SUTTON COULD READ -- WITH COMPLETE COMPREHENSION AND TOTAL RECALL -- SO THAT, BY THE AGE OF FOUR--
I HAVE BUT TO MIX THESE TWO CHEMICALS -- AND I WOULD CREATE THE FIRST TRUE UNIVERSAL SOLVENT.
IT WOULD DISSOLVE ANYTHING IT TOUCHED.
OF COURSE, THERE IS THE DILEMMA OF WHAT I WOULD KEEP IT IN.
"SOME SAY IT WAS ARNOLD HIMSELF WHO CAUSED HIS BRAIN TO GROW TO MAMMOTH PROPORTIONS -- FOR REASONS ALL HIS OWN--
I MUST HAVE MORE BRAIN-POWER -- MORE!
MY PORTABLE CYCLOTRON IS NOT YET PERFECTED.
"BUT, THERE WERE THE INEVITABLE SOCIAL SIDE-EFFECTS--
GOOD LORD -- HOW HIDEOUS! ER -- I --
UNITED STATES PATENT OFFICE
PARDON ME, SON -- I DIDN'T--
FORGET IT.
YOUR AESTHETIC JUDGMENTS ARE NO CONCERN OF MINE.
"BUT, PERHAPS THEY DID BOTHER ARNOLD SUTTON MORE THAN HE ADMITTED -- FOR WHEN, LAST YEAR, HE BEGAN TO WORK FOR THE MILITARY--
THIS ANTI-BALLISTICS MISSILE YOU'VE DESIGNED IS A STROKE OF GENIUS, BRAIN-CHILD.
I'M SURE HE'S BECOME QUITE USED TO BEING CALLED "BRAIN-CHILD" BY NOW, GENERAL.
UH -- MY APOLOGIES, ARNOLD. I DIDN'T INTEND TO CALL YOU BY THAT OFFENSIVE NICKNAME.
YES -- QUITE USED TO IT, THANK YOU.
"PERHAPS IT SHOULD HAVE SURPRISED NO ONE WHEN, AT A RECENT TOP-LEVEL DEFENSE MEETING--
GENTLEMEN -- I NO LONGER HAVE ANY DESIRE TO ASSOCIATE WITH MY FELLOW HUMANS.
-- ONLY IF I CAN DO IT IN THE SECLUSION OF THIS DESERTED ISLAND OFF THE WEST COAST.
ACCORDINGLY, I SHALL CONTINUE TO DEVELOP ROCKETRY FOR THIS NATION--
GRANTED, SON. YOU'RE WORTH A HUNDRED ISLANDS.
HE MUST BE TIRED OF BEING REGARDED AS A FREAK.
I DON'T BLAME HIM. BUT HE IS A FREAK.
8

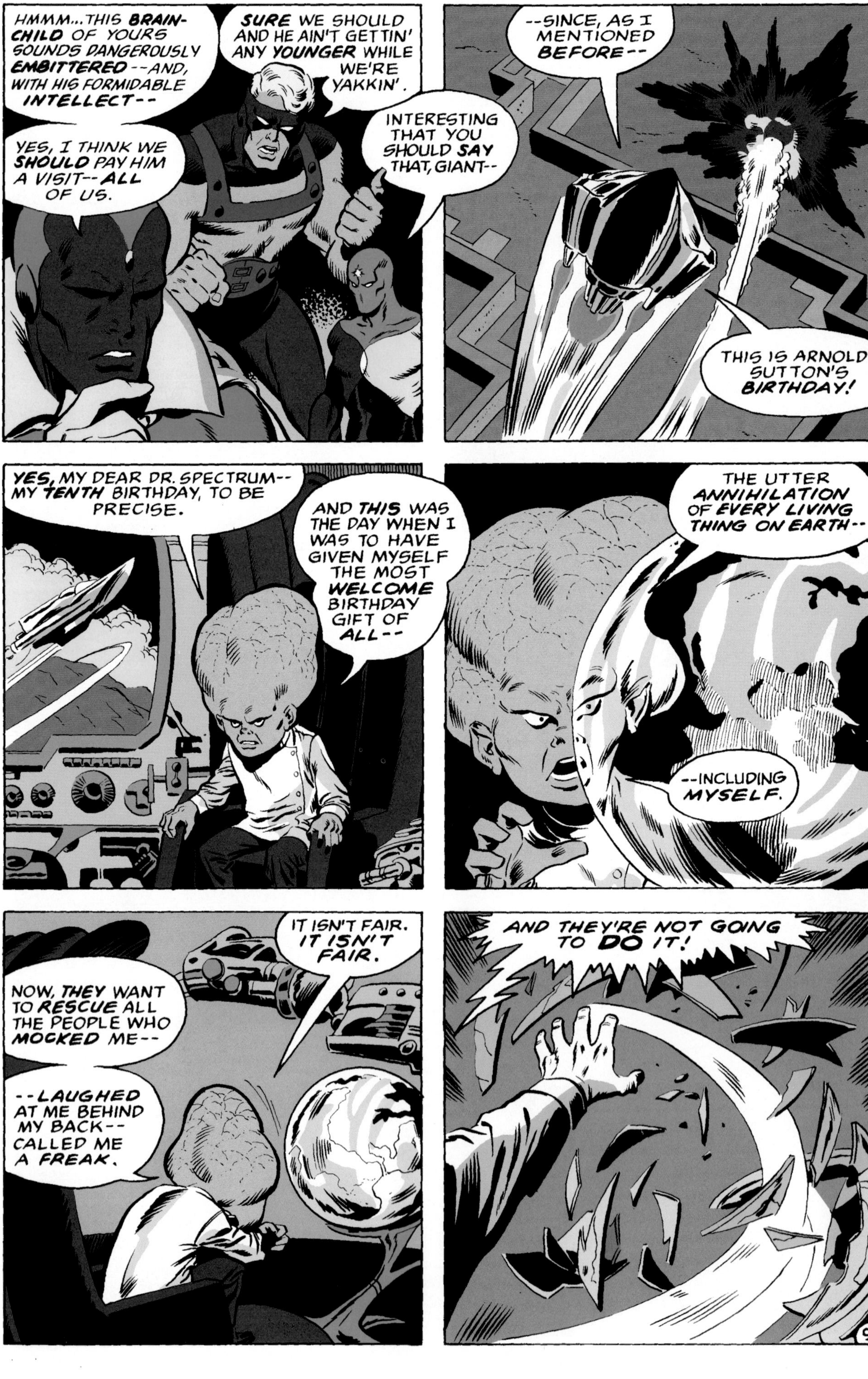
HMMM...THIS BRAIN-CHILD OF YOURS SOUNDS DANGEROUSLY EMBITTERED--AND, WITH HIS FORMIDABLE INTELLECT--
SURE WE SHOULD AND HE AIN'T GETTIN' ANY YOUNGER WHILE WE'RE YAKKIN'.
YES, I THINK WE SHOULD PAY HIM A VISIT--ALL OF US.
INTERESTING THAT YOU SHOULD SAY THAT, GIANT--
--SINCE, AS I MENTIONED BEFORE--
THIS IS ARNOLD SUTTON'S BIRTHDAY!
YES, MY DEAR DR. SPECTRUM--MY TENTH BIRTHDAY, TO BE PRECISE.
AND THIS WAS THE DAY WHEN I WAS TO HAVE GIVEN MYSELF THE MOST WELCOME BIRTHDAY GIFT OF ALL--
THE UTTER ANNIHILATION OF EVERY LIVING THING ON EARTH--
--INCLUDING MYSELF.
IT ISN'T FAIR. IT ISN'T FAIR.
NOW, THEY WANT TO RESCUE ALL THE PEOPLE WHO MOCKED ME--
--LAUGHED AT ME BEHIND MY BACK--CALLED ME A FREAK.
AND THEY'RE NOT GOING TO DO IT!

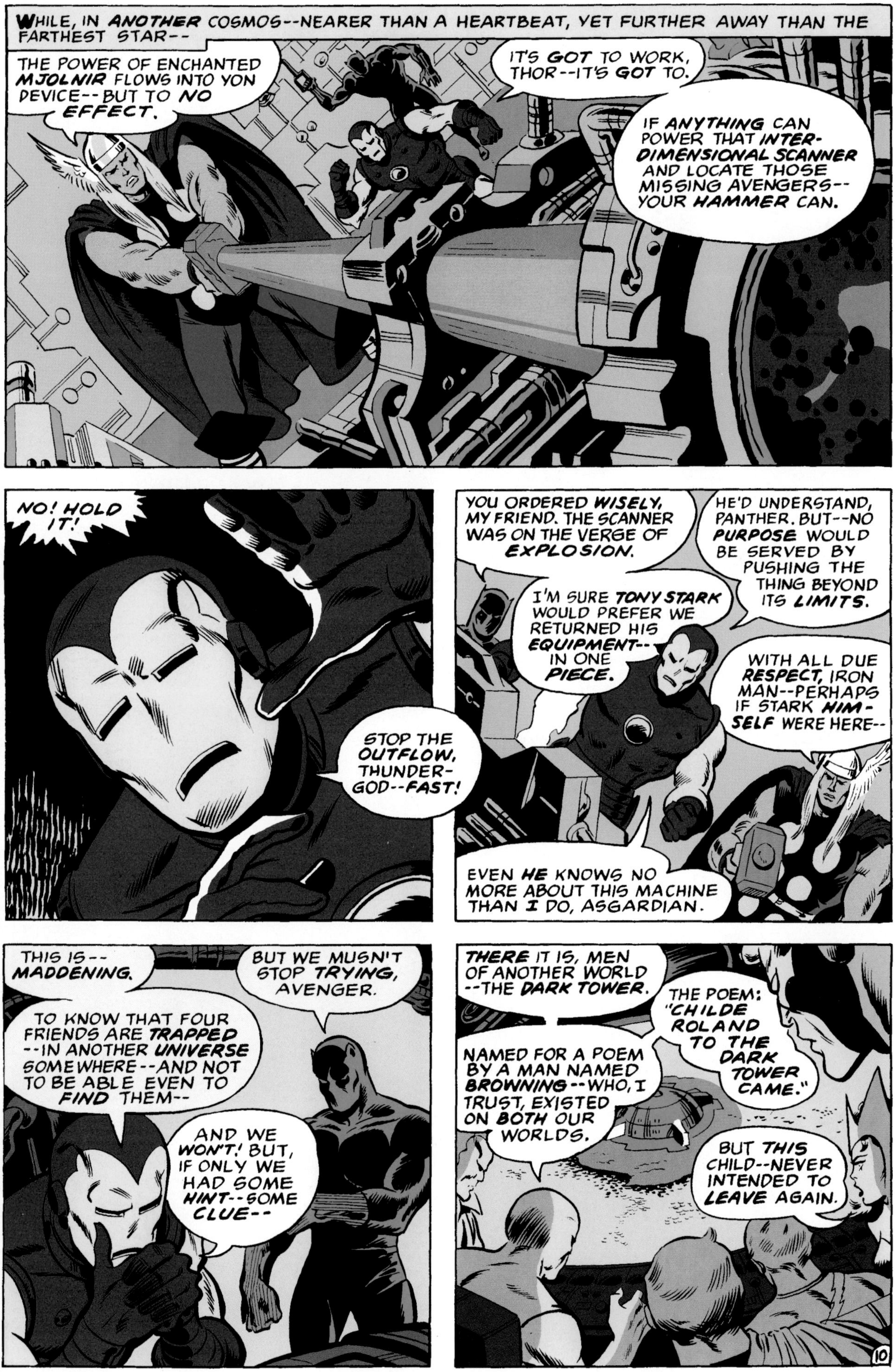
WHILE, IN ANOTHER COSMOS--NEARER THAN A HEARTBEAT, YET FURTHER AWAY THAN THE FARTHEST STAR--
THE POWER OF ENCHANTED MJOLNIR FLOWS INTO YON DEVICE--BUT TO NO EFFECT.
IT'S GOT TO WORK, THOR--IT'S GOT TO.
IF ANYTHING CAN POWER THAT INTER-DIMENSIONAL SCANNER AND LOCATE THOSE MISSING AVENGERS--YOUR HAMMER CAN.
NO! HOLD IT!
STOP THE OUTFLOW, THUNDER-GOD--FAST!
YOU ORDERED WISELY, MY FRIEND. THE SCANNER WAS ON THE VERGE OF EXPLOSION.
HE'D UNDERSTAND, PANTHER. BUT--NO PURPOSE WOULD BE SERVED BY PUSHING THE THING BEYOND ITS LIMITS.
I'M SURE TONY STARK WOULD PREFER WE RETURNED HIS EQUIPMENT--IN ONE PIECE.
WITH ALL DUE RESPECT, IRON MAN--PERHAPS IF STARK HIMSELF WERE HERE--
EVEN HE KNOWS NO MORE ABOUT THIS MACHINE THAN I DO, ASGARDIAN.
THIS IS--MADDENING.
BUT WE MUSN'T STOP TRYING, AVENGER.
TO KNOW THAT FOUR FRIENDS ARE TRAPPED--IN ANOTHER UNIVERSE SOMEWHERE--AND NOT TO BE ABLE EVEN TO FIND THEM--
AND WE WON'T! BUT, IF ONLY WE HAD SOME HINT--SOME CLUE--
THERE IT IS, MEN OF ANOTHER WORLD--THE DARK TOWER.
THE POEM: "CHILDE ROLAND TO THE DARK TOWER CAME."
NAMED FOR A POEM BY A MAN NAMED BROWNING--WHO, I TRUST, EXISTED ON BOTH OUR WORLDS.
BUT THIS CHILD--NEVER INTENDED TO LEAVE AGAIN.
10

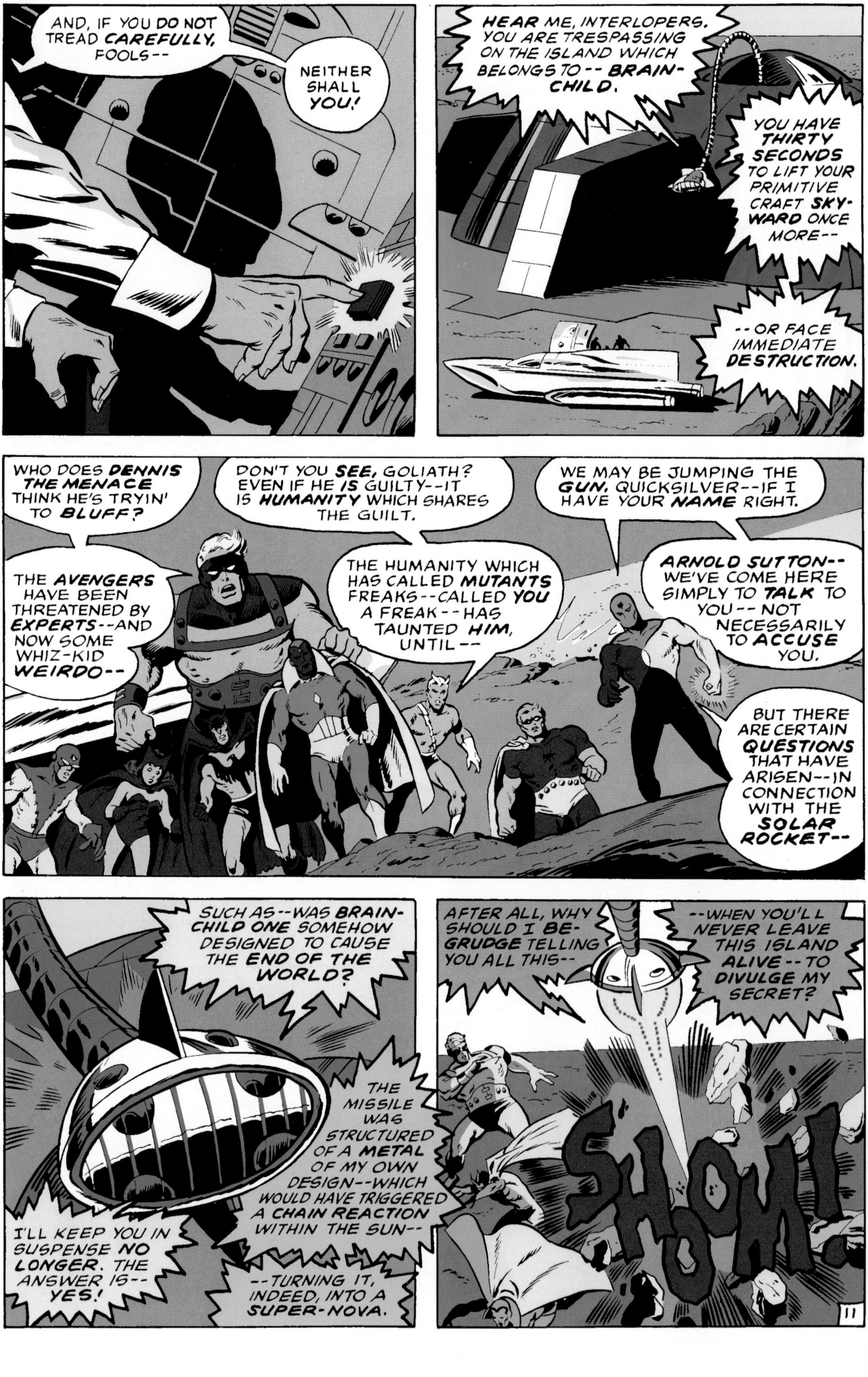
AND, IF YOU DO NOT TREAD CAREFULLY, FOOLS--
NEITHER SHALL YOU!
HEAR ME, INTERLOPERS. YOU ARE TRESPASSING ON THE ISLAND WHICH BELONGS TO -- BRAIN-CHILD.
YOU HAVE THIRTY SECONDS TO LIFT YOUR PRIMITIVE CRAFT SKYWARD ONCE MORE--
--OR FACE IMMEDIATE DESTRUCTION.
WHO DOES DENNIS THE MENACE THINK HE'S TRYIN' TO BLUFF?
THE AVENGERS HAVE BEEN THREATENED BY EXPERTS--AND NOW SOME WHIZ-KID WEIRDO--
DON'T YOU SEE, GOLIATH? EVEN IF HE IS GUILTY--IT IS HUMANITY WHICH SHARES THE GUILT.
THE HUMANITY WHICH HAS CALLED MUTANTS FREAKS--CALLED YOU A FREAK--HAS TAUNTED HIM, UNTIL--
WE MAY BE JUMPING THE GUN, QUICKSILVER--IF I HAVE YOUR NAME RIGHT.
ARNOLD SUTTON--WE'VE COME HERE SIMPLY TO TALK TO YOU--NOT NECESSARILY TO ACCUSE YOU.
BUT THERE ARE CERTAIN QUESTIONS THAT HAVE ARISEN--IN CONNECTION WITH THE SOLAR ROCKET--
SUCH AS--WAS BRAIN-CHILD ONE SOMEHOW DESIGNED TO CAUSE THE END OF THE WORLD?
I'LL KEEP YOU IN SUSPENSE NO LONGER. THE ANSWER IS--YES!
THE MISSILE WAS STRUCTURED OF A METAL OF MY OWN DESIGN--WHICH WOULD HAVE TRIGGERED A CHAIN REACTION WITHIN THE SUN--
--TURNING IT, INDEED, INTO A SUPER-NOVA.
AFTER ALL, WHY SHOULD I BEGRUDGE TELLING YOU ALL THIS--
--WHEN YOU'LL NEVER LEAVE THIS ISLAND ALIVE--TO DIVULGE MY SECRET?
SHOOM!

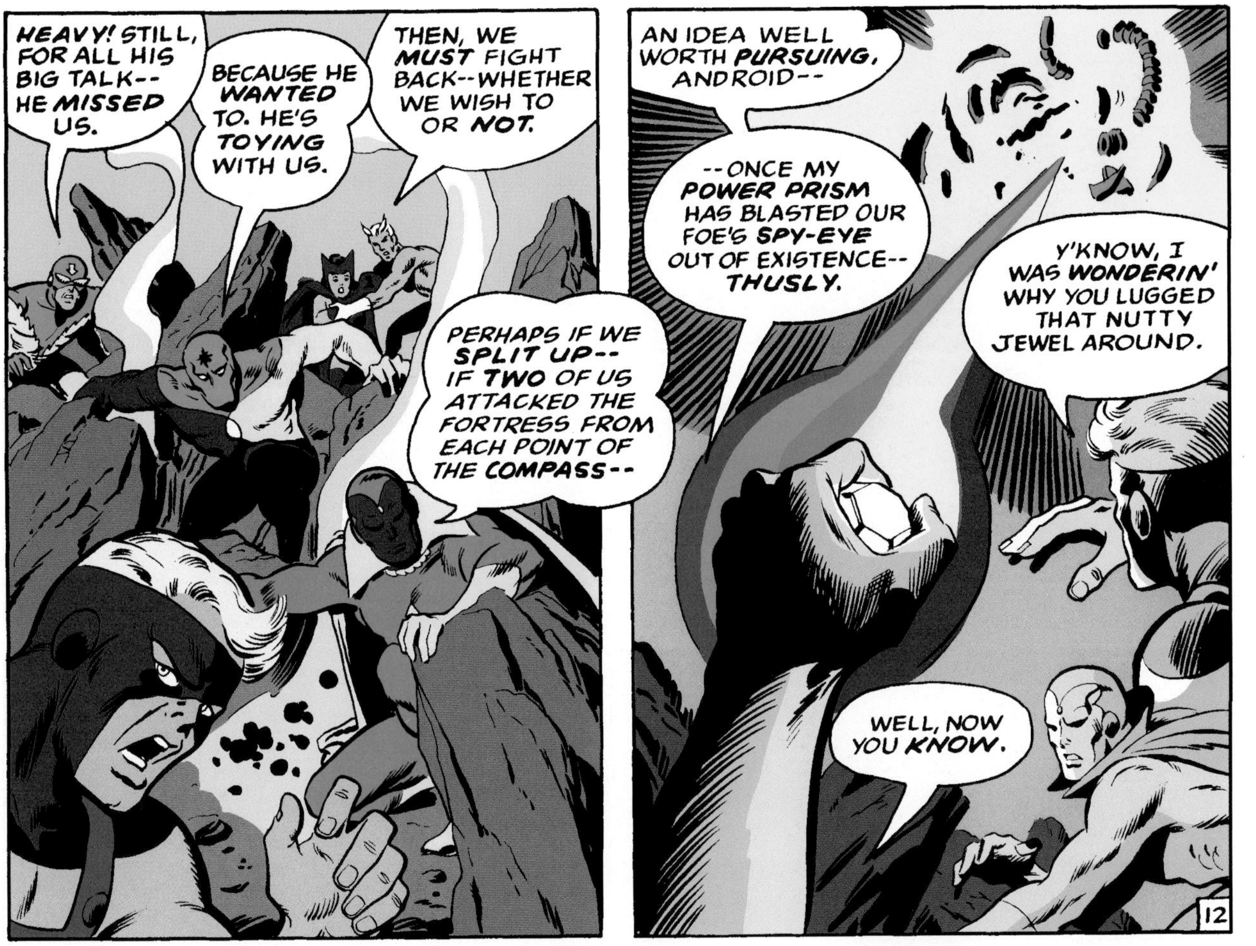
HEAVY! STILL, FOR ALL HIS BIG TALK-- HE MISSED US.
BECAUSE HE WANTED TO. HE'S TOYING WITH US.
THEN, WE MUST FIGHT BACK--WHETHER WE WISH TO OR NOT.
PERHAPS IF WE SPLIT UP-- IF TWO OF US ATTACKED THE FORTRESS FROM EACH POINT OF THE COMPASS--
AN IDEA WELL WORTH PURSUING, ANDROID--
--ONCE MY POWER PRISM HAS BLASTED OUR FOE'S SPY-EYE OUT OF EXISTENCE-- THUSLY.
Y'KNOW, I WAS WONDERIN' WHY YOU LUGGED THAT NUTTY JEWEL AROUND.
WELL, NOW YOU KNOW.
12

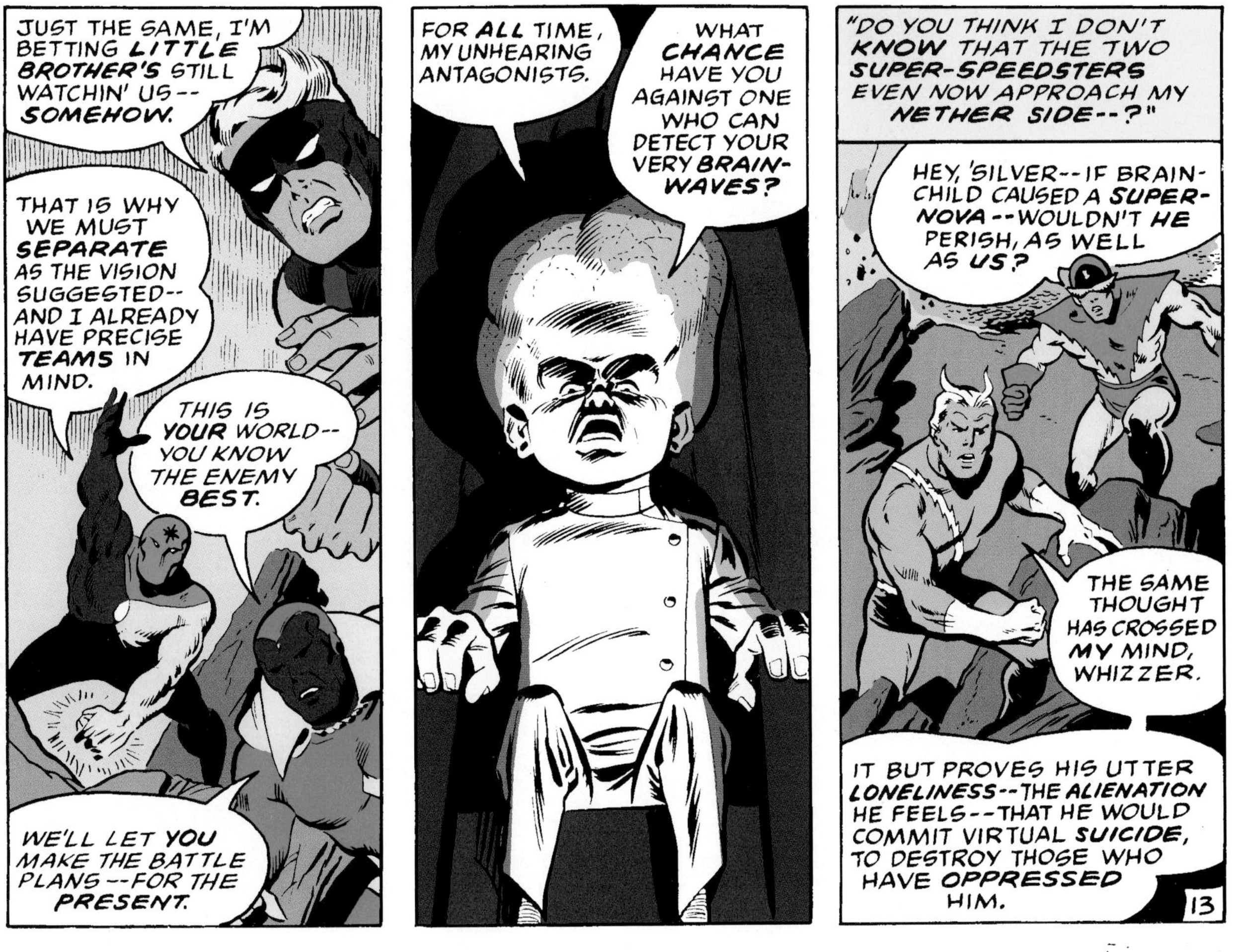
JUST THE SAME, I'M BETTING LITTLE BROTHER'S STILL WATCHIN' US-- SOMEHOW.
THAT IS WHY WE MUST SEPARATE AS THE VISION SUGGESTED-- AND I ALREADY HAVE PRECISE TEAMS IN MIND.
THIS IS YOUR WORLD-- YOU KNOW THE ENEMY BEST.
WE'LL LET YOU MAKE THE BATTLE PLANS --FOR THE PRESENT.
FOR ALL TIME, MY UNHEARING ANTAGONISTS.
WHAT CHANCE HAVE YOU AGAINST ONE WHO CAN DETECT YOUR VERY BRAIN-WAVES?
"DO YOU THINK I DON'T KNOW THAT THE TWO SUPER-SPEEDSTERS EVEN NOW APPROACH MY NETHER SIDE--?"
HEY, 'SILVER--IF BRAIN-CHILD CAUSED A SUPER-NOVA --WOULDN'T HE PERISH, AS WELL AS US?
THE SAME THOUGHT HAS CROSSED MY MIND, WHIZZER.
IT BUT PROVES HIS UTTER LONELINESS--THE ALIENATION HE FEELS--THAT HE WOULD COMMIT VIRTUAL SUICIDE, TO DESTROY THOSE WHO HAVE OPPRESSED HIM.
13

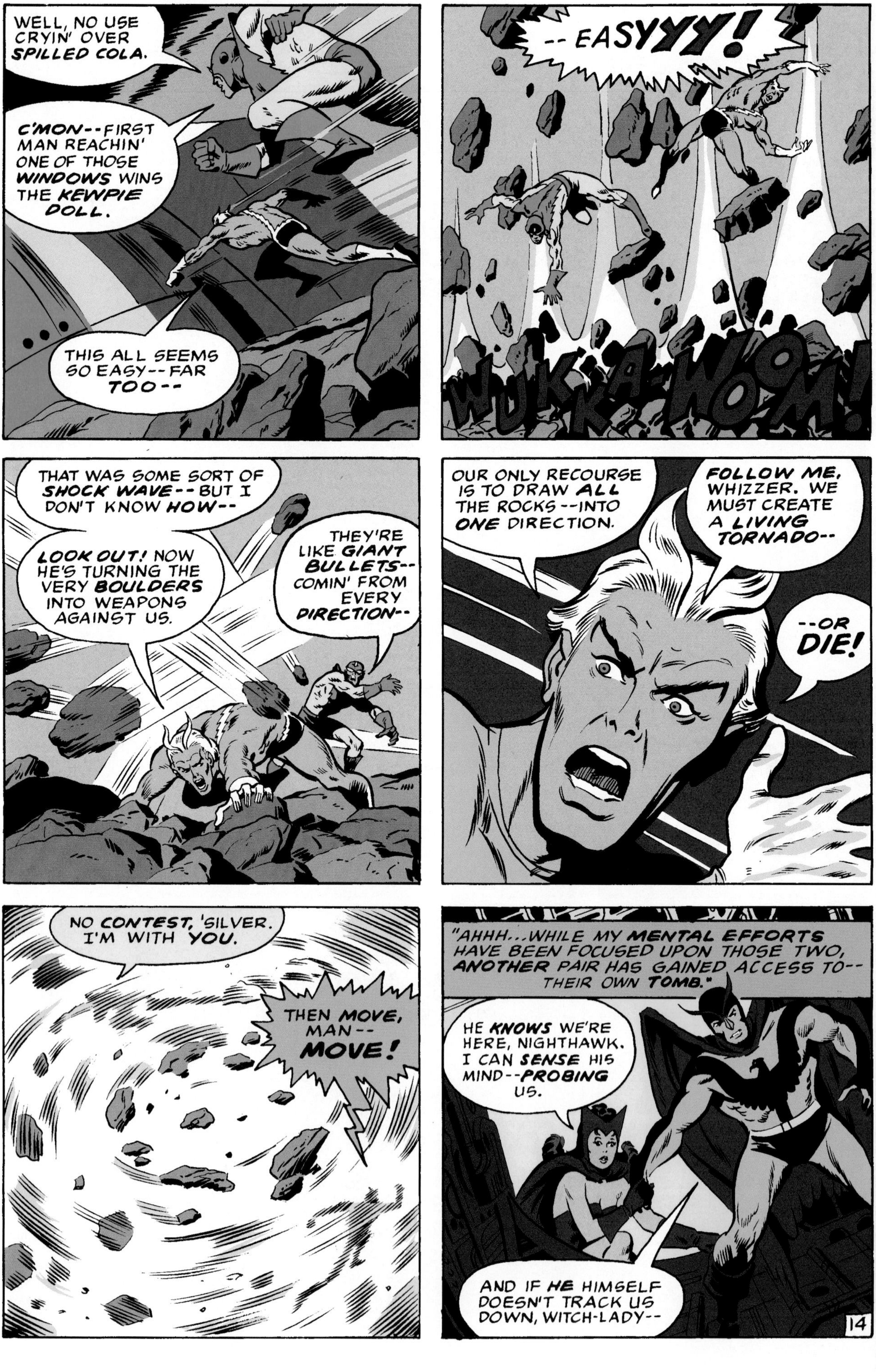

WELL, NO USE CRYIN' OVER SPILLED COLA.
C'MON--FIRST MAN REACHIN' ONE OF THOSE WINDOWS WINS THE KEWPIE DOLL.
THIS ALL SEEMS SO EASY--FAR TOO--
-- EASYYY!
WUKKA-WOOM!
THAT WAS SOME SORT OF SHOCK WAVE--BUT I DON'T KNOW HOW--
LOOK OUT! NOW HE'S TURNING THE VERY BOULDERS INTO WEAPONS AGAINST US.
THEY'RE LIKE GIANT BULLETS--COMIN' FROM EVERY DIRECTION--
OUR ONLY RECOURSE IS TO DRAW ALL THE ROCKS--INTO ONE DIRECTION.
FOLLOW ME, WHIZZER. WE MUST CREATE A LIVING TORNADO--
--OR DIE!
NO CONTEST, 'SILVER. I'M WITH YOU.
THEN MOVE, MAN--MOVE!
"AHHH...WHILE MY MENTAL EFFORTS HAVE BEEN FOCUSED UPON THOSE TWO, ANOTHER PAIR HAS GAINED ACCESS TO--THEIR OWN TOMB."
HE KNOWS WE'RE HERE, NIGHTHAWK. I CAN SENSE HIS MIND--PROBING US.
AND IF HE HIMSELF DOESN'T TRACK US DOWN, WITCH-LADY--
14

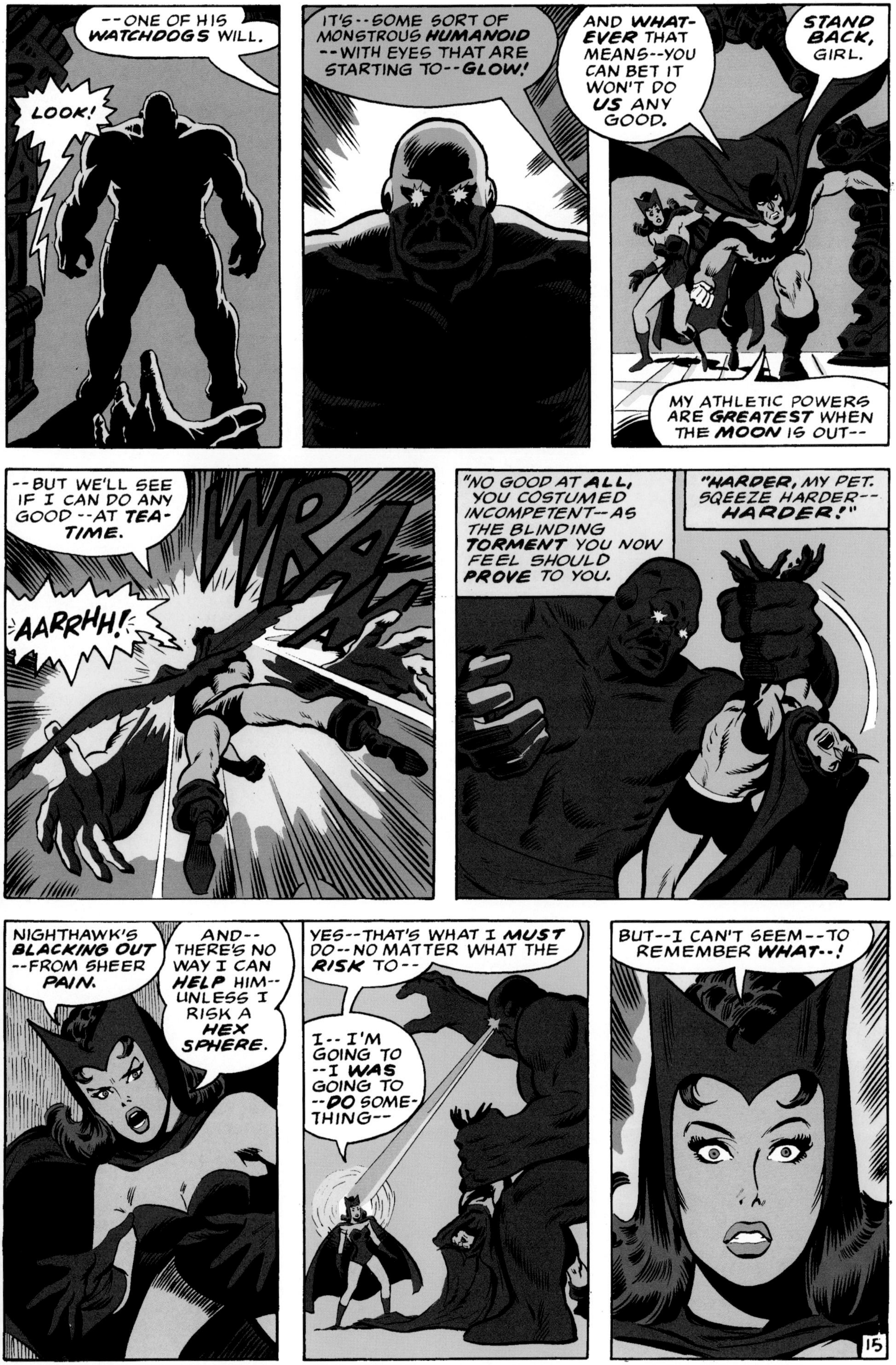
--ONE OF HIS WATCHDOGS WILL.
LOOK!
IT'S--SOME SORT OF MONSTROUS HUMANOID --WITH EYES THAT ARE STARTING TO--GLOW!
AND WHAT-EVER THAT MEANS--YOU CAN BET IT WON'T DO US ANY GOOD.
STAND BACK, GIRL.
MY ATHLETIC POWERS ARE GREATEST WHEN THE MOON IS OUT--
--BUT WE'LL SEE IF I CAN DO ANY GOOD--AT TEA-TIME.
WRAA
AARRHH!
"NO GOOD AT ALL, YOU COSTUMED INCOMPETENT--AS THE BLINDING TORMENT YOU NOW FEEL SHOULD PROVE TO YOU.
"HARDER, MY PET. SQEEZE HARDER-- HARDER!"
NIGHTHAWK'S BLACKING OUT --FROM SHEER PAIN.
AND-- THERE'S NO WAY I CAN HELP HIM-- UNLESS I RISK A HEX SPHERE.
YES--THAT'S WHAT I MUST DO--NO MATTER WHAT THE RISK TO--
I-- I'M GOING TO --I WAS GOING TO --DO SOME-THING--
BUT--I CAN'T SEEM--TO REMEMBER WHAT--!
15

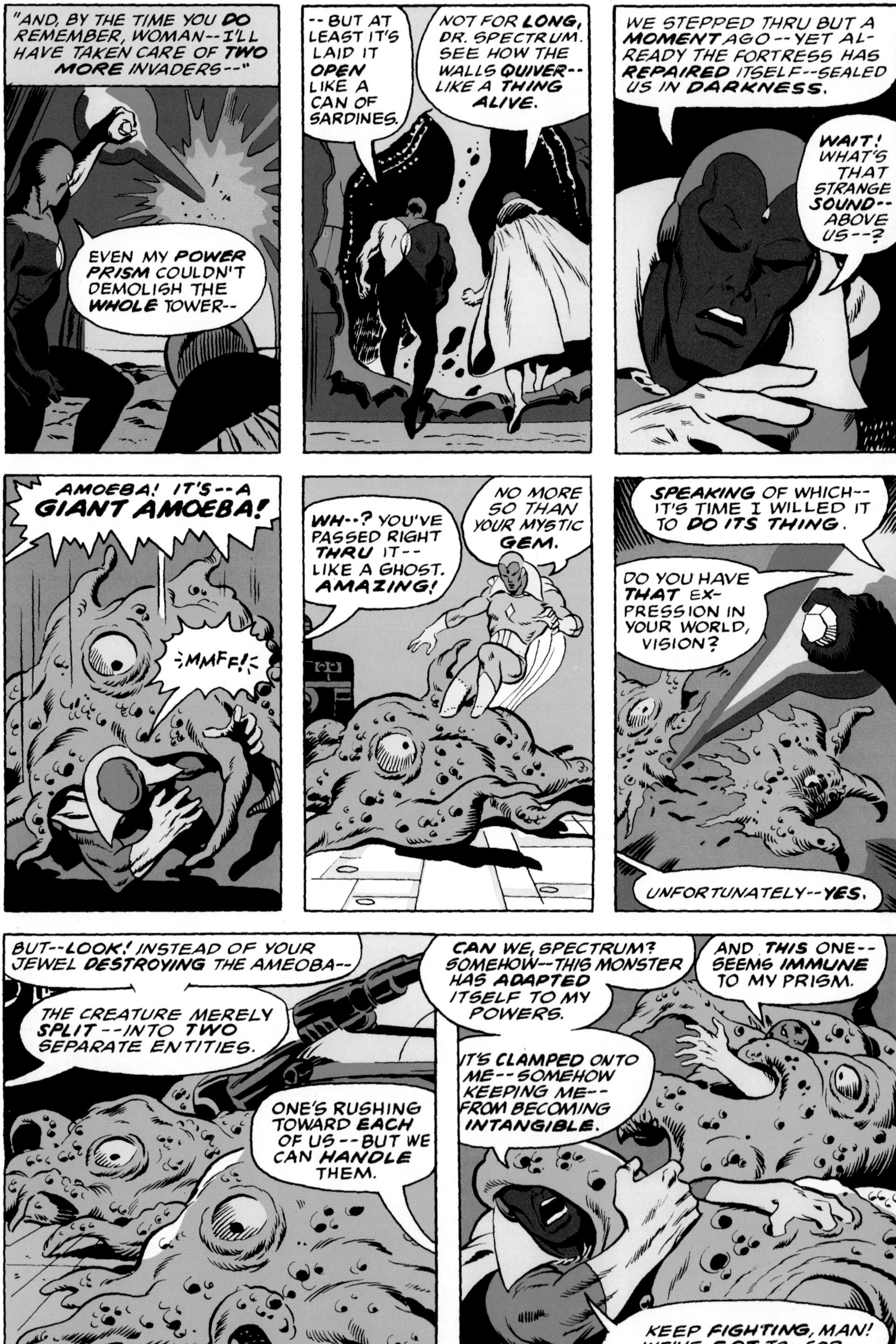
"AND, BY THE TIME YOU DO REMEMBER, WOMAN--I'LL HAVE TAKEN CARE OF TWO MORE INVADERS--"
EVEN MY POWER PRISM COULDN'T DEMOLISH THE WHOLE TOWER--
--BUT AT LEAST IT'S LAID IT OPEN LIKE A CAN OF SARDINES.
NOT FOR LONG, DR. SPECTRUM. SEE HOW THE WALLS QUIVER--LIKE A THING ALIVE.
WE STEPPED THRU BUT A MOMENT AGO--YET ALREADY THE FORTRESS HAS REPAIRED ITSELF--SEALED US IN DARKNESS.
WAIT! WHAT'S THAT STRANGE SOUND--ABOVE US--?
AMOEBA! IT'S--A GIANT AMOEBA!
MMFF!
WH--? YOU'VE PASSED RIGHT THRU IT--LIKE A GHOST. AMAZING!
NO MORE SO THAN YOUR MYSTIC GEM.
SPEAKING OF WHICH--IT'S TIME I WILLED IT TO DO ITS THING.
DO YOU HAVE THAT EXPRESSION IN YOUR WORLD, VISION?
UNFORTUNATELY--YES.
BUT--LOOK! INSTEAD OF YOUR JEWEL DESTROYING THE AMEOBA--
THE CREATURE MERELY SPLIT--INTO TWO SEPARATE ENTITIES.
ONE'S RUSHING TOWARD EACH OF US--BUT WE CAN HANDLE THEM.
CAN WE, SPECTRUM? SOMEHOW--THIS MONSTER HAS ADAPTED ITSELF TO MY POWERS.
IT'S CLAMPED ONTO ME--SOMEHOW KEEPING ME--FROM BECOMING INTANGIBLE.
AND THIS ONE--SEEMS IMMUNE TO MY PRISM.
KEEP FIGHTING, MAN! WE'VE GOT TO--FOR THE SAKE OF THE WORLD!
16

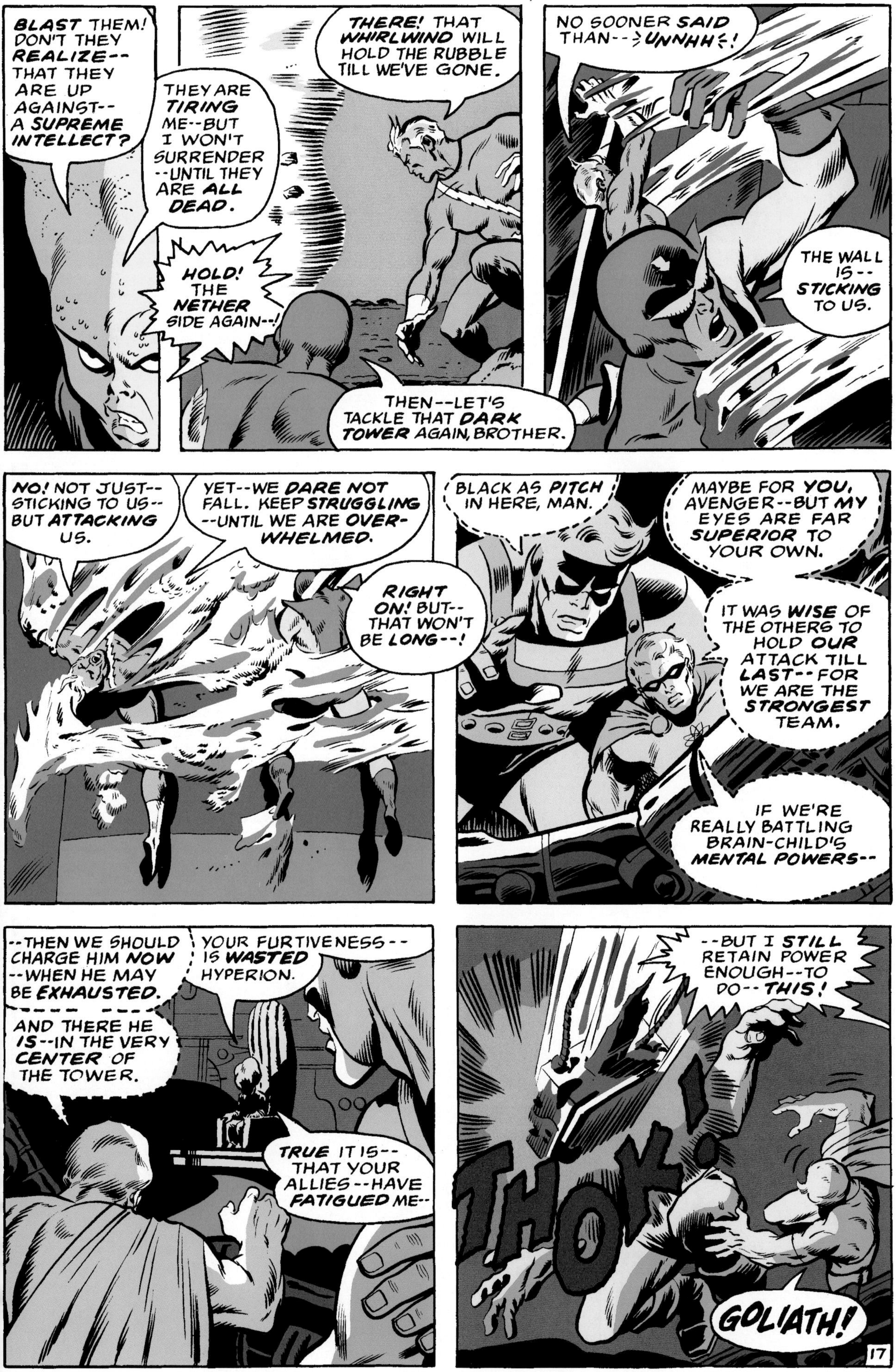
BLAST THEM! DON'T THEY REALIZE-- THAT THEY ARE UP AGAINST-- A SUPREME INTELLECT?
THEY ARE TIRING ME--BUT I WON'T SURRENDER --UNTIL THEY ARE ALL DEAD.
HOLD! THE NETHER SIDE AGAIN--!
THERE! THAT WHIRLWIND WILL HOLD THE RUBBLE TILL WE'VE GONE.
THEN--LET'S TACKLE THAT DARK TOWER AGAIN, BROTHER.
NO SOONER SAID THAN-- UNNHH--!
THE WALL IS-- STICKING TO US.
NO! NOT JUST-- STICKING TO US-- BUT ATTACKING US.
YET--WE DARE NOT FALL. KEEP STRUGGLING --UNTIL WE ARE OVER-WHELMED.
RIGHT ON! BUT-- THAT WON'T BE LONG--!
BLACK AS PITCH IN HERE, MAN.
MAYBE FOR YOU, AVENGER--BUT MY EYES ARE FAR SUPERIOR TO YOUR OWN.
IT WAS WISE OF THE OTHERS TO HOLD OUR ATTACK TILL LAST--FOR WE ARE THE STRONGEST TEAM.
IF WE'RE REALLY BATTLING BRAIN-CHILD'S MENTAL POWERS--
--THEN WE SHOULD CHARGE HIM NOW --WHEN HE MAY BE EXHAUSTED.
AND THERE HE IS--IN THE VERY CENTER OF THE TOWER.
YOUR FURTIVENESS-- IS WASTED HYPERION.
TRUE IT IS-- THAT YOUR ALLIES--HAVE FATIGUED ME--
--BUT I STILL RETAIN POWER ENOUGH--TO DO--THIS!
THOK!
GOLIATH!

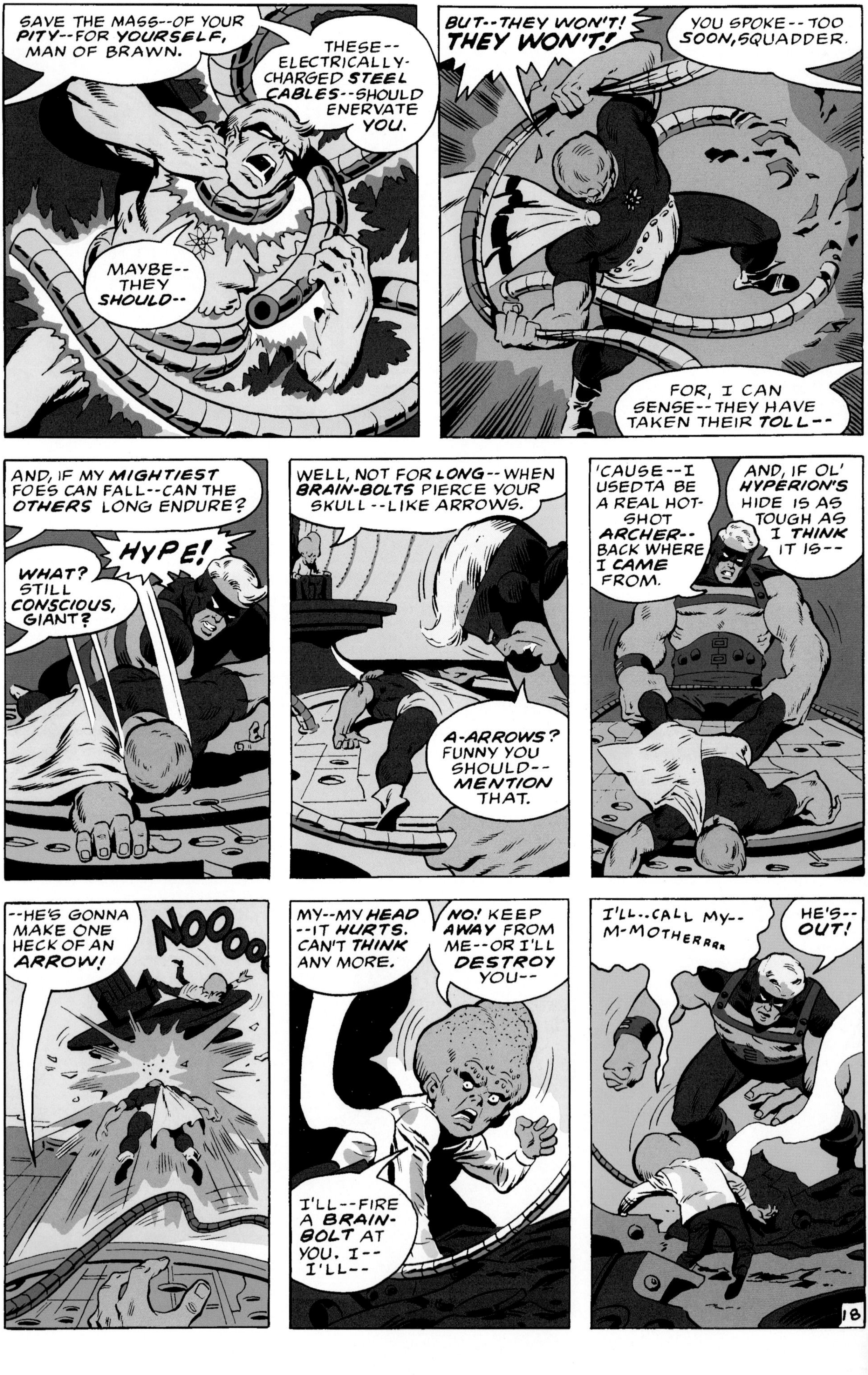
SAVE THE MASS--OF YOUR PITY--FOR YOURSELF, MAN OF BRAWN.
THESE--ELECTRICALLY-CHARGED STEEL CABLES--SHOULD ENERVATE YOU.
MAYBE--THEY SHOULD--
BUT--THEY WON'T! THEY WON'T!
YOU SPOKE--TOO SOON, SQUADDER.
FOR, I CAN SENSE--THEY HAVE TAKEN THEIR TOLL--
AND, IF MY MIGHTIEST FOES CAN FALL--CAN THE OTHERS LONG ENDURE?
HYPE!
WHAT? STILL CONSCIOUS, GIANT?
WELL, NOT FOR LONG--WHEN BRAIN-BOLTS PIERCE YOUR SKULL--LIKE ARROWS.
A-ARROWS? FUNNY YOU SHOULD--MENTION THAT.
'CAUSE--I USEDTA BE A REAL HOT-SHOT ARCHER--BACK WHERE I CAME FROM.
AND, IF OL' HYPERION'S HIDE IS AS TOUGH AS I THINK IT IS--
--HE'S GONNA MAKE ONE HECK OF AN ARROW!
NOOOO
MY--MY HEAD--IT HURTS. CAN'T THINK ANY MORE.
NO! KEEP AWAY FROM ME--OR I'LL DESTROY YOU--
I'LL--FIRE A BRAIN-BOLT AT YOU. I--I'LL--
I'LL--CALL MY--M-MOTHERRRR
HE'S--OUT!
18

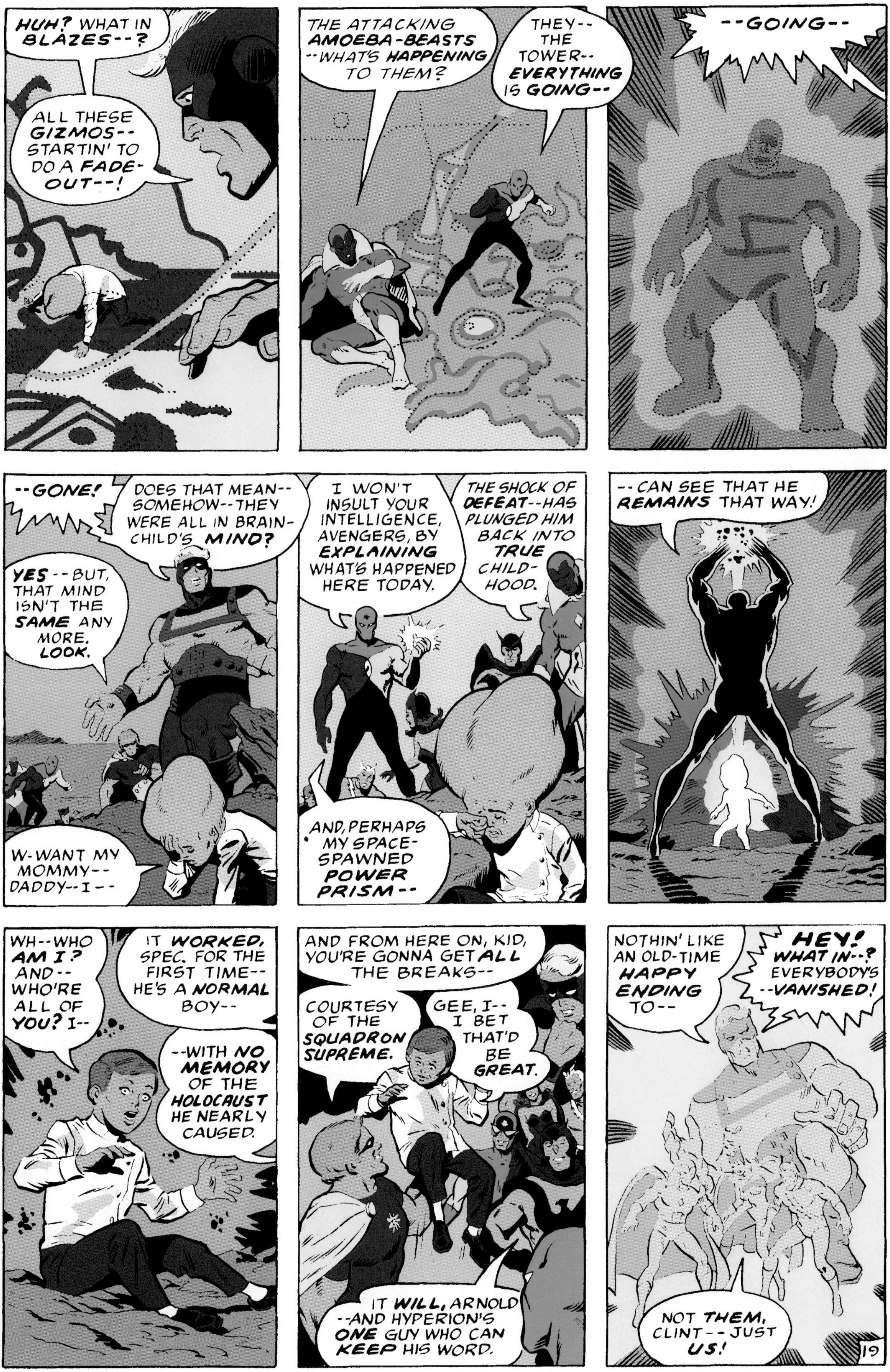
HUH? WHAT IN BLAZES--?
ALL THESE GIZMOS--STARTIN' TO DO A FADE-OUT--!
THE ATTACKING AMOEBA-BEASTS--WHAT'S HAPPENING TO THEM?
THEY--THE TOWER--EVERYTHING IS GOING--
--GOING--
--GONE!
DOES THAT MEAN--SOMEHOW--THEY WERE ALL IN BRAIN-CHILD'S MIND?
YES--BUT, THAT MIND ISN'T THE SAME ANY MORE. LOOK.
W-WANT MY MOMMY--DADDY--I--
I WON'T INSULT YOUR INTELLIGENCE, AVENGERS, BY EXPLAINING WHAT'S HAPPENED HERE TODAY.
THE SHOCK OF DEFEAT--HAS PLUNGED HIM BACK INTO TRUE CHILD-HOOD.
AND, PERHAPS MY SPACE-SPAWNED POWER PRISM--
--CAN SEE THAT HE REMAINS THAT WAY!
WH--WHO AM I? AND--WHO'RE ALL OF YOU? I--
IT WORKED, SPEC. FOR THE FIRST TIME--HE'S A NORMAL BOY--
--WITH NO MEMORY OF THE HOLOCAUST HE NEARLY CAUSED.
AND FROM HERE ON, KID, YOU'RE GONNA GET ALL THE BREAKS--
COURTESY OF THE SQUADRON SUPREME.
GEE, I--I BET THAT'D BE GREAT.
IT WILL, ARNOLD--AND HYPERION'S ONE GUY WHO CAN KEEP HIS WORD.
NOTHIN' LIKE AN OLD-TIME HAPPY ENDING TO--
HEY! WHAT IN--? EVERYBODY'S--VANISHED!
NOT THEM, CLINT--JUST US!
19

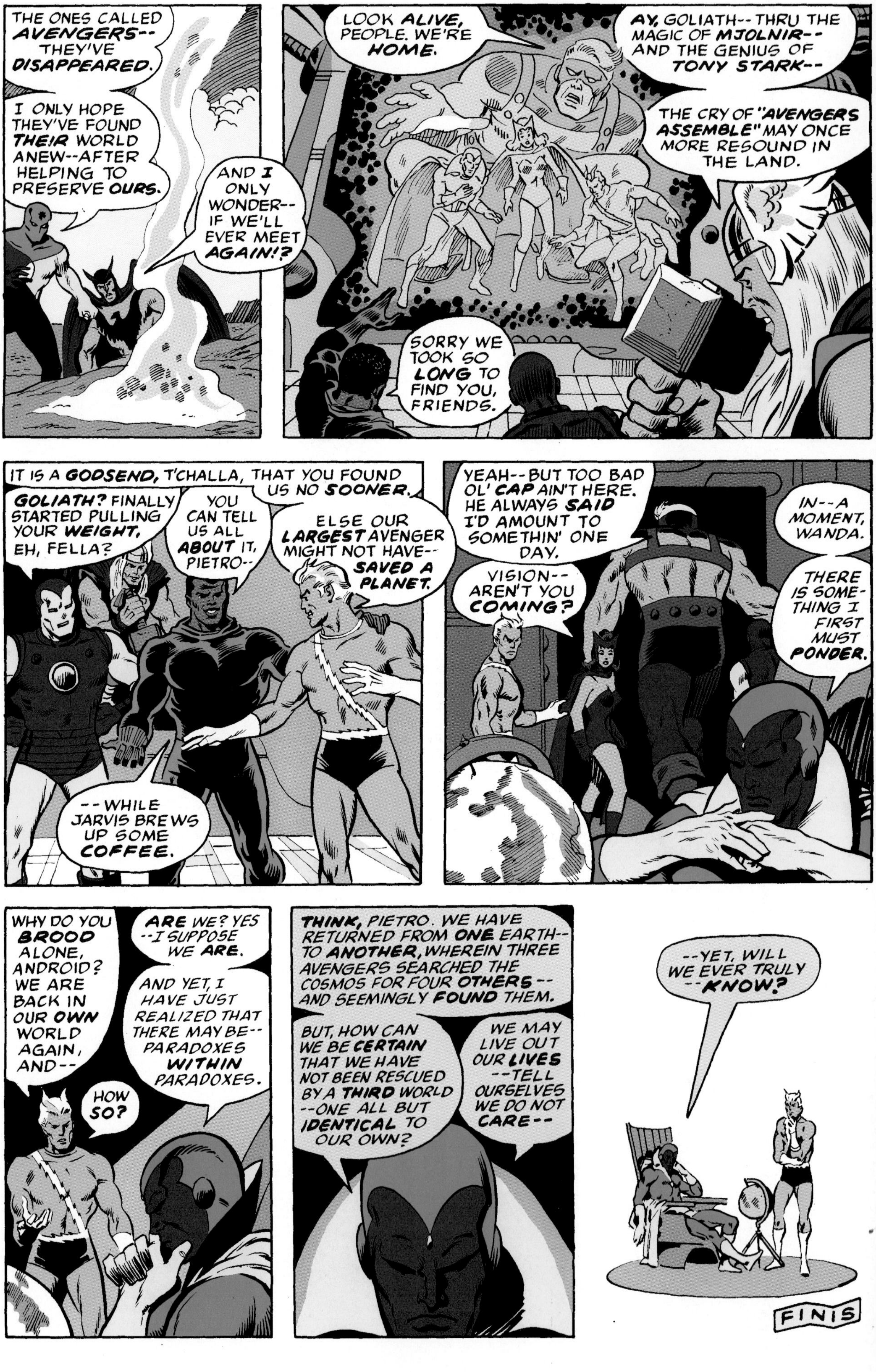
THE ONES CALLED AVENGERS-- THEY'VE DISAPPEARED.
I ONLY HOPE THEY'VE FOUND THEIR WORLD ANEW--AFTER HELPING TO PRESERVE OURS.
AND I ONLY WONDER-- IF WE'LL EVER MEET AGAIN!?
LOOK ALIVE, PEOPLE. WE'RE HOME.
AY, GOLIATH-- THRU THE MAGIC OF MJOLNIR-- AND THE GENIUS OF TONY STARK--
THE CRY OF "AVENGERS ASSEMBLE" MAY ONCE MORE RESOUND IN THE LAND.
SORRY WE TOOK SO LONG TO FIND YOU, FRIENDS.
IT IS A GODSEND, T'CHALLA, THAT YOU FOUND US NO SOONER.
GOLIATH? FINALLY STARTED PULLING YOUR WEIGHT, EH, FELLA?
YOU CAN TELL US ALL ABOUT IT, PIETRO--
ELSE OUR LARGEST AVENGER MIGHT NOT HAVE-- SAVED A PLANET.
--WHILE JARVIS BREWS UP SOME COFFEE.
YEAH--BUT TOO BAD OL' CAP AIN'T HERE. HE ALWAYS SAID I'D AMOUNT TO SOMETHIN' ONE DAY.
VISION-- AREN'T YOU COMING?
IN--A MOMENT, WANDA.
THERE IS SOMETHING I FIRST MUST PONDER.
WHY DO YOU BROOD ALONE, ANDROID? WE ARE BACK IN OUR OWN WORLD AGAIN, AND--
ARE WE? YES --I SUPPOSE WE ARE.
AND YET, I HAVE JUST REALIZED THAT THERE MAY BE-- PARADOXES WITHIN PARADOXES.
HOW SO?
THINK, PIETRO. WE HAVE RETURNED FROM ONE EARTH-- TO ANOTHER, WHEREIN THREE AVENGERS SEARCHED THE COSMOS FOR FOUR OTHERS-- AND SEEMINGLY FOUND THEM.
BUT, HOW CAN WE BE CERTAIN THAT WE HAVE NOT BEEN RESCUED BY A THIRD WORLD --ONE ALL BUT IDENTICAL TO OUR OWN?
WE MAY LIVE OUT OUR LIVES --TELL OURSELVES WE DO NOT CARE--
--YET, WILL WE EVER TRULY --KNOW?
FINIS